# A+

## Certification

### Third Edition

## Training Kit

PUBLISHED BY
Microsoft Press
A Division of Microsoft Corporation
One Microsoft Way
Redmond, Washington 98052-6399

Library of Congress Cataloging-in-Publication Data
A+ Certification Training Kit / Microsoft Corporation.--3rd Ed.
      p. cm.
   ISBN 0-7356-1265-X
   1. Electronic data processing personnel--Certification.   2. Computer
technicians--Certification--Study guides.     I. Microsoft Corporation.

QA76.3 .A1755   2001
004.16--dc21                            00-069440

Printed and bound in the United States of America.

1 2 3 4 5 6 7 8 9   QWT   6 5 4 3 2 1

Distributed in Canada by Penguin Books Canada Limited.

A CIP catalogue record for this book is available from the British Library.

Microsoft Press books are available through booksellers and distributors worldwide. For further information about international editions, contact your local Microsoft Corporation office or contact Microsoft Press International directly at fax (425) 936-7329. Visit our Web site at mspress.microsoft.com. Send comments to *tkinput@microsoft.com*.

**For Microsoft Press**
**Acquisitions Editor:** Thomas Pohlmann
**Project Editor:** Melissa von Tschudi-Sutton

**Author:** James Karney

**For nSight, Inc.**
**Project Manager:** Sarah Kimnach Hains
**Technical Editor:** Ronald Miller
**Copy Editor:** Teresa Horton
**Desktop Specialists:** Patty Fagan, Joanna Zito,
   Mary Beth McDaniels
**Proofreaders:** Shimona Katz, Rebecca Merz,
   Katie Pickett, Darla Bruno
**Indexer:** Jack Lewis

# Contents

**About This Book** . . . . . . . . . . . . . . . . . . . . . . . . . . . . . . . . . . . . . . . . . . . . . **xix**

Intended Audience . . . . . . . . . . . . . . . . . . . . . . . . . . . . . . . . . . . . . . xix

Prerequisites . . . . . . . . . . . . . . . . . . . . . . . . . . . . . . . . . . . . . . . . . . . xx

About the CD-ROM . . . . . . . . . . . . . . . . . . . . . . . . . . . . . . . . . . . . . xx

Features of This Book . . . . . . . . . . . . . . . . . . . . . . . . . . . . . . . . . . . xx

Chapter and Appendix Overview . . . . . . . . . . . . . . . . . . . . . . . . . . xxi

Finding the Best Starting Point for You . . . . . . . . . . . . . . . . . . . . xxiii

Where to Find Specific Skill Areas in This Book . . . . . . . . . . . . . . xxiv

A+ Core Hardware Examination . . . . . . . . . . . . . . . . . . . . . . . xxiv

A+ Operating System Technologies Exam . . . . . . . . . . . . . . . . xxiv

Getting Started . . . . . . . . . . . . . . . . . . . . . . . . . . . . . . . . . . . . . . . . . xxv

Hardware Requirements . . . . . . . . . . . . . . . . . . . . . . . . . . . . . . xxv

Software Requirements . . . . . . . . . . . . . . . . . . . . . . . . . . . . . . . xxv

About the Electronic Book . . . . . . . . . . . . . . . . . . . . . . . . . . . . . . . xxvi

The A+ Certification Program . . . . . . . . . . . . . . . . . . . . . . . . . . . . . xxvi

Benefits of Certification . . . . . . . . . . . . . . . . . . . . . . . . . . . . . . xxvi

The A+ Exam Modules and Domains . . . . . . . . . . . . . . . . . . . . xxvii

Registering for the A+ Exams . . . . . . . . . . . . . . . . . . . . . . . . . . . . . xxxi

**Chapter 1    Introduction to Computers** . . . . . . . . . . . . . . . . . . . . . . . . . . . . . **1**

About This Chapter . . . . . . . . . . . . . . . . . . . . . . . . . . . . . . . . . . . . . . 1

Before You Begin . . . . . . . . . . . . . . . . . . . . . . . . . . . . . . . . . . . . . . . 1

Lesson 1: The Development of the Computer . . . . . . . . . . . . . . . . . . 2

The Abacus . . . . . . . . . . . . . . . . . . . . . . . . . . . . . . . . . . . . . . . . . 2

The Analytical Engine (A Pre-Electronic Computer) . . . . . . . . . . 3

The First Electrically Driven Computer . . . . . . . . . . . . . . . . . . . 3

The Digital Electronic Computer . . . . . . . . . . . . . . . . . . . . . . . . 4

Lesson Summary . . . . . . . . . . . . . . . . . . . . . . . . . . . . . . . . . . . . 7

Lesson 2: The Role of a Computer Service Professional . . . . . . . . . 8

Lesson Summary . . . . . . . . . . . . . . . . . . . . . . . . . . . . . . . . . . . . 8

Chapter Summary . . . . . . . . . . . . . . . . . . . . . . . . . . . . . . . . . . . . . . . 9

Review . . . . . . . . . . . . . . . . . . . . . . . . . . . . . . . . . . . . . . . . . . . . . . . 10

**Chapter 2    Understanding Electronic Communication** . . . . . . . . . . . . . . . . **11**

About This Chapter . . . . . . . . . . . . . . . . . . . . . . . . . . . . . . . . . . . . . 11

Before You Begin . . . . . . . . . . . . . . . . . . . . . . . . . . . . . . . . . . . . . . . . . . . . . .11
Lesson 1: Computer Communication . . . . . . . . . . . . . . . . . . . . . . . . . . . . . . . .12
   Early Forms of Communication . . . . . . . . . . . . . . . . . . . . . . . . . . . . . . . .12
   The Binary Language of Computers . . . . . . . . . . . . . . . . . . . . . . . . . . . . .13
   ASCII Code . . . . . . . . . . . . . . . . . . . . . . . . . . . . . . . . . . . . . . . . . . . . . . . .17
   Lesson Summary . . . . . . . . . . . . . . . . . . . . . . . . . . . . . . . . . . . . . . . . . . . .19
Lesson 2: The Computer Bus . . . . . . . . . . . . . . . . . . . . . . . . . . . . . . . . . . . . .20
   Lesson Summary . . . . . . . . . . . . . . . . . . . . . . . . . . . . . . . . . . . . . . . . . . . .21
Chapter Summary . . . . . . . . . . . . . . . . . . . . . . . . . . . . . . . . . . . . . . . . . . . . . .22
Review . . . . . . . . . . . . . . . . . . . . . . . . . . . . . . . . . . . . . . . . . . . . . . . . . . . . . . .23

**Chapter 3   An Overview of the Personal Computer** . . . . . . . . . . . . . . . . . . . . . . . **25**
   About This Chapter . . . . . . . . . . . . . . . . . . . . . . . . . . . . . . . . . . . . . . . . . .25
   Before You Begin . . . . . . . . . . . . . . . . . . . . . . . . . . . . . . . . . . . . . . . . . . .25
   Lesson 1: The Three Stages of Computing . . . . . . . . . . . . . . . . . . . . . . . . .26
      Input . . . . . . . . . . . . . . . . . . . . . . . . . . . . . . . . . . . . . . . . . . . . . . . . . . .27
      Processing . . . . . . . . . . . . . . . . . . . . . . . . . . . . . . . . . . . . . . . . . . . . . .27
      Output . . . . . . . . . . . . . . . . . . . . . . . . . . . . . . . . . . . . . . . . . . . . . . . . . .27
      Input, Processing, and Output . . . . . . . . . . . . . . . . . . . . . . . . . . . . . . .27
      Lesson Summary . . . . . . . . . . . . . . . . . . . . . . . . . . . . . . . . . . . . . . . . .28
   Lesson 2: Components of a Computer . . . . . . . . . . . . . . . . . . . . . . . . . . . . .29
      Input . . . . . . . . . . . . . . . . . . . . . . . . . . . . . . . . . . . . . . . . . . . . . . . . . . .29
      Processing . . . . . . . . . . . . . . . . . . . . . . . . . . . . . . . . . . . . . . . . . . . . . .30
      Output . . . . . . . . . . . . . . . . . . . . . . . . . . . . . . . . . . . . . . . . . . . . . . . . . .32
      Input and Output . . . . . . . . . . . . . . . . . . . . . . . . . . . . . . . . . . . . . . . . .33
      Lesson Summary . . . . . . . . . . . . . . . . . . . . . . . . . . . . . . . . . . . . . . . . .34
   Lesson 3: Support Hardware . . . . . . . . . . . . . . . . . . . . . . . . . . . . . . . . . . .35
      Lesson Summary . . . . . . . . . . . . . . . . . . . . . . . . . . . . . . . . . . . . . . . . .36
   Chapter Summary . . . . . . . . . . . . . . . . . . . . . . . . . . . . . . . . . . . . . . . . . . .37
   Review . . . . . . . . . . . . . . . . . . . . . . . . . . . . . . . . . . . . . . . . . . . . . . . . . . . .38

**Chapter 4   The Central Processing Unit** . . . . . . . . . . . . . . . . . . . . . . . . . . . . . . . **39**
   About This Chapter . . . . . . . . . . . . . . . . . . . . . . . . . . . . . . . . . . . . . . . . . .39
   Before You Begin . . . . . . . . . . . . . . . . . . . . . . . . . . . . . . . . . . . . . . . . . . .39
   Lesson 1: Microprocessors . . . . . . . . . . . . . . . . . . . . . . . . . . . . . . . . . . . . .40
      The External Data Bus . . . . . . . . . . . . . . . . . . . . . . . . . . . . . . . . . . . . .40
      The CPU . . . . . . . . . . . . . . . . . . . . . . . . . . . . . . . . . . . . . . . . . . . . . . . .42
      Memory . . . . . . . . . . . . . . . . . . . . . . . . . . . . . . . . . . . . . . . . . . . . . . . . .47
      How Microprocessors Work . . . . . . . . . . . . . . . . . . . . . . . . . . . . . . . . .49

PC Microprocessor Developments and Features . . . . . . . . . . . . . . . . . . .50

The First Pentiums . . . . . . . . . . . . . . . . . . . . . . . . . . . . . . . . . . . . . . . . .59

Lesson Summary . . . . . . . . . . . . . . . . . . . . . . . . . . . . . . . . . . . . . . . . . .67

Lesson 2: Replacing and Upgrading a CPU . . . . . . . . . . . . . . . . . . . . . . . .68

Possible Upgrade Scenarios . . . . . . . . . . . . . . . . . . . . . . . . . . . . . . . . . .68

Inserting a CPU . . . . . . . . . . . . . . . . . . . . . . . . . . . . . . . . . . . . . . . . . . .69

Lesson Summary . . . . . . . . . . . . . . . . . . . . . . . . . . . . . . . . . . . . . . . . . .72

Chapter Summary . . . . . . . . . . . . . . . . . . . . . . . . . . . . . . . . . . . . . . . . . . .73

Review . . . . . . . . . . . . . . . . . . . . . . . . . . . . . . . . . . . . . . . . . . . . . . . . . . .74

**Chapter 5    Power Supplies** . . . . . . . . . . . . . . . . . . . . . . . . . . . . . . . . . . . . **77**

About This Chapter . . . . . . . . . . . . . . . . . . . . . . . . . . . . . . . . . . . . . . . . . .77

Before You Begin . . . . . . . . . . . . . . . . . . . . . . . . . . . . . . . . . . . . . . . . . . .77

Lesson 1: Power Supplies . . . . . . . . . . . . . . . . . . . . . . . . . . . . . . . . . . . . .78

Overview of Power Supplies . . . . . . . . . . . . . . . . . . . . . . . . . . . . . . . . . .78

Power Supply Sizes . . . . . . . . . . . . . . . . . . . . . . . . . . . . . . . . . . . . . . . .79

Power Supply Wattage . . . . . . . . . . . . . . . . . . . . . . . . . . . . . . . . . . . . . .80

Power Supply Connectors . . . . . . . . . . . . . . . . . . . . . . . . . . . . . . . . . . .80

Lesson Summary . . . . . . . . . . . . . . . . . . . . . . . . . . . . . . . . . . . . . . . . . .85

Lesson 2: Power Supply Problems . . . . . . . . . . . . . . . . . . . . . . . . . . . . . .86

Power Failures . . . . . . . . . . . . . . . . . . . . . . . . . . . . . . . . . . . . . . . . . . .86

Power Protection Devices . . . . . . . . . . . . . . . . . . . . . . . . . . . . . . . . . . .87

Power Supply Problems . . . . . . . . . . . . . . . . . . . . . . . . . . . . . . . . . . . . .88

Lesson Summary . . . . . . . . . . . . . . . . . . . . . . . . . . . . . . . . . . . . . . . . . .88

Chapter Summary . . . . . . . . . . . . . . . . . . . . . . . . . . . . . . . . . . . . . . . . . . .89

Review . . . . . . . . . . . . . . . . . . . . . . . . . . . . . . . . . . . . . . . . . . . . . . . . . . .90

**Chapter 6    Motherboard and ROM BIOS** . . . . . . . . . . . . . . . . . . . . . . . . . **93**

About This Chapter . . . . . . . . . . . . . . . . . . . . . . . . . . . . . . . . . . . . . . . . . .93

Before You Begin . . . . . . . . . . . . . . . . . . . . . . . . . . . . . . . . . . . . . . . . . . .93

Lesson 1: Computer Cases . . . . . . . . . . . . . . . . . . . . . . . . . . . . . . . . . . . .94

The Computer Case . . . . . . . . . . . . . . . . . . . . . . . . . . . . . . . . . . . . . . . .94

Working with Cases . . . . . . . . . . . . . . . . . . . . . . . . . . . . . . . . . . . . . . . .95

Lesson Summary . . . . . . . . . . . . . . . . . . . . . . . . . . . . . . . . . . . . . . . . . .96

Lesson 2: Motherboards . . . . . . . . . . . . . . . . . . . . . . . . . . . . . . . . . . . . . .97

The Motherboard . . . . . . . . . . . . . . . . . . . . . . . . . . . . . . . . . . . . . . . . . .97

Chip Sets . . . . . . . . . . . . . . . . . . . . . . . . . . . . . . . . . . . . . . . . . . . . . . . .99

Lesson Summary . . . . . . . . . . . . . . . . . . . . . . . . . . . . . . . . . . . . . . . . . 100

Lesson 3: ROM BIOS . . . . . . . . . . . . . . . . . . . . . . . . . . . . . . . . . . . . . . . 101

ROM BIOS . . . . . . . . . . . . . . . . . . . . . . . . . . . . . . . . . . . . . . . . . . . . . . 101
Updating CMOS . . . . . . . . . . . . . . . . . . . . . . . . . . . . . . . . . . . . . . . . . 103
The CMOS Battery . . . . . . . . . . . . . . . . . . . . . . . . . . . . . . . . . . . . . . . 109
All Other Chips . . . . . . . . . . . . . . . . . . . . . . . . . . . . . . . . . . . . . . . . . . 111
Power-On Self Test . . . . . . . . . . . . . . . . . . . . . . . . . . . . . . . . . . . . . . . 112
Lesson Summary . . . . . . . . . . . . . . . . . . . . . . . . . . . . . . . . . . . . . . . . . 115
Chapter Summary . . . . . . . . . . . . . . . . . . . . . . . . . . . . . . . . . . . . . . . . . . . 116
Review . . . . . . . . . . . . . . . . . . . . . . . . . . . . . . . . . . . . . . . . . . . . . . . . . . . . 117

**Chapter 7    Memory** . . . . . . . . . . . . . . . . . . . . . . . . . . . . . . . . . . . . . . . **119**
About This Chapter . . . . . . . . . . . . . . . . . . . . . . . . . . . . . . . . . . . . . . . 119
Before You Begin . . . . . . . . . . . . . . . . . . . . . . . . . . . . . . . . . . . . . . . . . 119
Lesson 1: ROM and RAM . . . . . . . . . . . . . . . . . . . . . . . . . . . . . . . . . . 120
Defining Memory . . . . . . . . . . . . . . . . . . . . . . . . . . . . . . . . . . . . . . . . . 120
Nonvolatile and Volatile Memory . . . . . . . . . . . . . . . . . . . . . . . . . . . . 120
ROM . . . . . . . . . . . . . . . . . . . . . . . . . . . . . . . . . . . . . . . . . . . . . . . . . . . . 121
RAM . . . . . . . . . . . . . . . . . . . . . . . . . . . . . . . . . . . . . . . . . . . . . . . . . . . . 121
RAM Packaging . . . . . . . . . . . . . . . . . . . . . . . . . . . . . . . . . . . . . . . . . . 123
SIPPs . . . . . . . . . . . . . . . . . . . . . . . . . . . . . . . . . . . . . . . . . . . . . . . . . . . 124
SIMMs (30-Pin) . . . . . . . . . . . . . . . . . . . . . . . . . . . . . . . . . . . . . . . . . . 124
Memory Configuration . . . . . . . . . . . . . . . . . . . . . . . . . . . . . . . . . . . . 125
Specifying SIPPs and SIMMs . . . . . . . . . . . . . . . . . . . . . . . . . . . . . . 127
The 72-Pin SIMM . . . . . . . . . . . . . . . . . . . . . . . . . . . . . . . . . . . . . . . . 127
Voltage . . . . . . . . . . . . . . . . . . . . . . . . . . . . . . . . . . . . . . . . . . . . . . . . . . 128
Installing SIMMs . . . . . . . . . . . . . . . . . . . . . . . . . . . . . . . . . . . . . . . . . 128
Dual Inline Memory Modules . . . . . . . . . . . . . . . . . . . . . . . . . . . . . . . 130
Cache Memory . . . . . . . . . . . . . . . . . . . . . . . . . . . . . . . . . . . . . . . . . . . 130
Lesson Summary . . . . . . . . . . . . . . . . . . . . . . . . . . . . . . . . . . . . . . . . . 133
Lesson 2: Memory Mapping . . . . . . . . . . . . . . . . . . . . . . . . . . . . . . . . . 134
The Workings of Hexadecimal Code . . . . . . . . . . . . . . . . . . . . . . . . . 134
Memory Allocation . . . . . . . . . . . . . . . . . . . . . . . . . . . . . . . . . . . . . . . . 136
Determining Usable Memory . . . . . . . . . . . . . . . . . . . . . . . . . . . . . . . 140
Lesson Summary . . . . . . . . . . . . . . . . . . . . . . . . . . . . . . . . . . . . . . . . . 142
Chapter Summary . . . . . . . . . . . . . . . . . . . . . . . . . . . . . . . . . . . . . . . . . . . 143
Review . . . . . . . . . . . . . . . . . . . . . . . . . . . . . . . . . . . . . . . . . . . . . . . . . . . . 144

**Chapter 8    Expansion Buses, Cables, and Connectors** . . . . . . . . . . . . . . . . . **147**
About This Chapter . . . . . . . . . . . . . . . . . . . . . . . . . . . . . . . . . . . . . . . 147
Before You Begin . . . . . . . . . . . . . . . . . . . . . . . . . . . . . . . . . . . . . . . . . 147

Lesson 1: Understanding Expansion Buses .......................... 148
   Development of the Expansion Bus ............................ 148
   Industry Standard Architecture ................................ 149
   Micro Channel Architecture .................................. 150
   Extended ISA ............................................... 151
   VESA Local Bus ............................................ 152
   Peripheral Component Interconnect ........................... 153
   Accelerated Graphics Port .................................... 154
   IEEE 1394 FireWire High-Performance Serial Interface ............. 156
   Universal Serial Bus ......................................... 156
   Lesson Summary ........................................... 157
Lesson 2: Configuring Expansion Cards ........................... 159
   I/O Addresses .............................................. 159
   Interrupt Request ........................................... 162
   Direct Memory Access ....................................... 166
   COM and Ports ............................................. 167
   Installing Expansion Cards ................................... 169
   Lesson Summary ........................................... 169
Lesson 3: Cables and Connectors ................................ 170
   Parallel Printer Cables ....................................... 170
   Serial Port Cables ........................................... 172
   Null Modem Cables ......................................... 173
   SCSI Cables ................................................ 173
   Keyboard Cables ........................................... 173
   Identifying Cables and Connectors ........................... 174
   Troubleshooting Cables ...................................... 174
   Summary of Connectors ..................................... 175
   Lesson Summary ........................................... 175
Chapter Summary .............................................. 176
Review ....................................................... 177

Chapter 9    Basic Disk Drives ................................... 181
   About This Chapter .......................................... 181
   Before You Begin ........................................... 181
Lesson 1: Floppy Disk Drives .................................... 182
   The Basics of Floppy Disk Drives ............................. 182
   Keeping a Floppy Disk Drive Running ......................... 185
   Errors Caused by the Floppy Disk ............................ 186
   Lesson Summary ........................................... 189

Lesson 2: Hard Disk Drives . . . . . . . . . . . . . . . . . . . . . . . . . . . . . . . . . . 190
   Physical Characteristics . . . . . . . . . . . . . . . . . . . . . . . . . . . . . . . . . . 190
   Storing Data . . . . . . . . . . . . . . . . . . . . . . . . . . . . . . . . . . . . . . . . . 191
   Actuator Arms . . . . . . . . . . . . . . . . . . . . . . . . . . . . . . . . . . . . . . . . 192
   Geometry . . . . . . . . . . . . . . . . . . . . . . . . . . . . . . . . . . . . . . . . . . . 193
   Hard Disk Drive Types . . . . . . . . . . . . . . . . . . . . . . . . . . . . . . . . . 196
   Installation and Setup . . . . . . . . . . . . . . . . . . . . . . . . . . . . . . . . . . 198
   Maintaining a Disk Drive . . . . . . . . . . . . . . . . . . . . . . . . . . . . . . . 212
   Lesson Summary . . . . . . . . . . . . . . . . . . . . . . . . . . . . . . . . . . . . . 215
Chapter Summary . . . . . . . . . . . . . . . . . . . . . . . . . . . . . . . . . . . . . . . 216
Review . . . . . . . . . . . . . . . . . . . . . . . . . . . . . . . . . . . . . . . . . . . . . . . . 217

**Chapter 10   Advanced Disk Drive Technology** . . . . . . . . . . . . . . . . . . . . . . . . **221**
   About This Chapter . . . . . . . . . . . . . . . . . . . . . . . . . . . . . . . . . . . . . 221
   Before You Begin . . . . . . . . . . . . . . . . . . . . . . . . . . . . . . . . . . . . . . 221
Lesson 1: CD-ROM and DVD Drives . . . . . . . . . . . . . . . . . . . . . . . . . . 222
   Advantages of CD-ROM and DVD Drives . . . . . . . . . . . . . . . . . . . 222
   Development of the CD . . . . . . . . . . . . . . . . . . . . . . . . . . . . . . . . . 223
   About CD-ROM Standards . . . . . . . . . . . . . . . . . . . . . . . . . . . . . . 223
   CD-ROM Technology . . . . . . . . . . . . . . . . . . . . . . . . . . . . . . . . . . 224
   DVD: A Super CD-ROM Alternative . . . . . . . . . . . . . . . . . . . . . . . 224
   DVD Formats . . . . . . . . . . . . . . . . . . . . . . . . . . . . . . . . . . . . . . . . 225
   Connecting CD-ROM and DVD Drives . . . . . . . . . . . . . . . . . . . . . 225
   Audio Capability . . . . . . . . . . . . . . . . . . . . . . . . . . . . . . . . . . . . . 226
   Access Time . . . . . . . . . . . . . . . . . . . . . . . . . . . . . . . . . . . . . . . . . 227
   Installing CD-ROM and DVD Drives . . . . . . . . . . . . . . . . . . . . . . 227
   Multimedia . . . . . . . . . . . . . . . . . . . . . . . . . . . . . . . . . . . . . . . . . 231
   Lesson Summary . . . . . . . . . . . . . . . . . . . . . . . . . . . . . . . . . . . . . 232
Lesson 2: Advanced Hard Disk Drives . . . . . . . . . . . . . . . . . . . . . . . . . . 233
   Limitations of Early Hard Disk Drives . . . . . . . . . . . . . . . . . . . . . . 233
   EIDE . . . . . . . . . . . . . . . . . . . . . . . . . . . . . . . . . . . . . . . . . . . . . . . 235
   Overcoming the 528-MB Barrier . . . . . . . . . . . . . . . . . . . . . . . . . 235
   Breaking the 8.4-GB Barrier . . . . . . . . . . . . . . . . . . . . . . . . . . . . . 237
   Ultra DMA . . . . . . . . . . . . . . . . . . . . . . . . . . . . . . . . . . . . . . . . . . 238
   Installing EIDE Drives . . . . . . . . . . . . . . . . . . . . . . . . . . . . . . . . . 238
   Other Settings . . . . . . . . . . . . . . . . . . . . . . . . . . . . . . . . . . . . . . . 241
   Lesson Summary . . . . . . . . . . . . . . . . . . . . . . . . . . . . . . . . . . . . . 242
Lesson 3: SCSI Drives . . . . . . . . . . . . . . . . . . . . . . . . . . . . . . . . . . . . . . 243
   SCSI-1 . . . . . . . . . . . . . . . . . . . . . . . . . . . . . . . . . . . . . . . . . . . . . 243

SCSI-2 . . . . . . . . . . . . . . . . . . . . . . . . . . . . . . . . . . . . . . . . 244
SCSI-3 . . . . . . . . . . . . . . . . . . . . . . . . . . . . . . . . . . . . . . . . 245
Noise and SCSI . . . . . . . . . . . . . . . . . . . . . . . . . . . . . . . . . . 247
Memory Management . . . . . . . . . . . . . . . . . . . . . . . . . . . . . 248
Costs and Benefits of SCSI . . . . . . . . . . . . . . . . . . . . . . . . . . 248
The Future of SCSI . . . . . . . . . . . . . . . . . . . . . . . . . . . . . . . 248
Setting SCSI IDs . . . . . . . . . . . . . . . . . . . . . . . . . . . . . . . . . 250
Logical Unit Numbers . . . . . . . . . . . . . . . . . . . . . . . . . . . . . 251
Termination . . . . . . . . . . . . . . . . . . . . . . . . . . . . . . . . . . . . 251
Lesson Summary . . . . . . . . . . . . . . . . . . . . . . . . . . . . . . . . 252
Chapter Summary . . . . . . . . . . . . . . . . . . . . . . . . . . . . . . . . . . 253
Review . . . . . . . . . . . . . . . . . . . . . . . . . . . . . . . . . . . . . . . . . . 254

Chapter 11    The Display System . . . . . . . . . . . . . . . . . . . . . . . . . . . 257
About This Chapter . . . . . . . . . . . . . . . . . . . . . . . . . . . . . . . 257
Before You Begin . . . . . . . . . . . . . . . . . . . . . . . . . . . . . . . . . 257
Lesson 1: Monitors . . . . . . . . . . . . . . . . . . . . . . . . . . . . . . . . . 258
Basic Monitor Operation . . . . . . . . . . . . . . . . . . . . . . . . . . . 258
Other Considerations in Choosing Monitors . . . . . . . . . . . . . 261
Power-Saving Features . . . . . . . . . . . . . . . . . . . . . . . . . . . . . 262
Tuning the Monitor's Display . . . . . . . . . . . . . . . . . . . . . . . . 262
Lesson Summary . . . . . . . . . . . . . . . . . . . . . . . . . . . . . . . . 265
Lesson 2: Flat-Panel Displays . . . . . . . . . . . . . . . . . . . . . . . . . 266
Flat-Panel and CRT Displays Compared . . . . . . . . . . . . . . . . 266
How Flat Panels Work . . . . . . . . . . . . . . . . . . . . . . . . . . . . . 267
Emerging Flat-Panel Technologies . . . . . . . . . . . . . . . . . . . . 268
Installing and Maintaining FPDs . . . . . . . . . . . . . . . . . . . . . . 268
Lesson Summary . . . . . . . . . . . . . . . . . . . . . . . . . . . . . . . . 269
Lesson 3: Display Adapters . . . . . . . . . . . . . . . . . . . . . . . . . . . 270
Evolution of the Display Adapter . . . . . . . . . . . . . . . . . . . . . 270
The Advent of Advanced Display Systems . . . . . . . . . . . . . . . 272
High Color, True Color, Photo-Realism, and Multimedia Displays . . . . . 272
Video Memory . . . . . . . . . . . . . . . . . . . . . . . . . . . . . . . . . . 274
Display Drivers . . . . . . . . . . . . . . . . . . . . . . . . . . . . . . . . . . 275
Lesson Summary . . . . . . . . . . . . . . . . . . . . . . . . . . . . . . . . 276
Lesson 4: Choosing and Troubleshooting Display Systems . . . . . . . . . . 277
Choosing a Display System . . . . . . . . . . . . . . . . . . . . . . . . . 277
Troubleshooting Display Systems . . . . . . . . . . . . . . . . . . . . . 278
Lesson Summary . . . . . . . . . . . . . . . . . . . . . . . . . . . . . . . . 279

Chapter Summary . . . . . . . . . . . . . . . . . . . . . . . . . . . . . . . . . . . . . . . . . . . . . . 280
Review . . . . . . . . . . . . . . . . . . . . . . . . . . . . . . . . . . . . . . . . . . . . . . . . . . . . . . 281

**Chapter 12    Printers** . . . . . . . . . . . . . . . . . . . . . . . . . . . . . . . . . . . . . . . . . **283**
About This Chapter . . . . . . . . . . . . . . . . . . . . . . . . . . . . . . . . . . . . . . . . . . . 283
Before You Begin . . . . . . . . . . . . . . . . . . . . . . . . . . . . . . . . . . . . . . . . . . . . . 283
Lesson 1: Printers . . . . . . . . . . . . . . . . . . . . . . . . . . . . . . . . . . . . . . . . . . . . . 284
Printer Basics . . . . . . . . . . . . . . . . . . . . . . . . . . . . . . . . . . . . . . . . . . . . . 284
Printer Ports . . . . . . . . . . . . . . . . . . . . . . . . . . . . . . . . . . . . . . . . . . . . . 286
Impact Printers . . . . . . . . . . . . . . . . . . . . . . . . . . . . . . . . . . . . . . . . . . . 286
Ink-Jet Printers . . . . . . . . . . . . . . . . . . . . . . . . . . . . . . . . . . . . . . . . . . . 288
Laser Printers . . . . . . . . . . . . . . . . . . . . . . . . . . . . . . . . . . . . . . . . . . . . 290
Primary Components of a Laser Printer . . . . . . . . . . . . . . . . . . . . . . . . . 290
The Mechanics of Laser Printing . . . . . . . . . . . . . . . . . . . . . . . . . . . . . 292
Lesson Summary . . . . . . . . . . . . . . . . . . . . . . . . . . . . . . . . . . . . . . . . . . 296
Chapter Summary . . . . . . . . . . . . . . . . . . . . . . . . . . . . . . . . . . . . . . . . . . . . 297
Review . . . . . . . . . . . . . . . . . . . . . . . . . . . . . . . . . . . . . . . . . . . . . . . . . . . . . . 298

**Chapter 13    Portable Computers** . . . . . . . . . . . . . . . . . . . . . . . . . . . . . . . . **299**
About This Chapter . . . . . . . . . . . . . . . . . . . . . . . . . . . . . . . . . . . . . . . . . . . 299
Before You Begin . . . . . . . . . . . . . . . . . . . . . . . . . . . . . . . . . . . . . . . . . . . . . 299
Lesson 1: Portable Computers . . . . . . . . . . . . . . . . . . . . . . . . . . . . . . . . . . 300
Types of Portables . . . . . . . . . . . . . . . . . . . . . . . . . . . . . . . . . . . . . . . . . 300
Computer Cards . . . . . . . . . . . . . . . . . . . . . . . . . . . . . . . . . . . . . . . . . . 302
Portable Computer Hardware . . . . . . . . . . . . . . . . . . . . . . . . . . . . . . . . 302
USB Ports . . . . . . . . . . . . . . . . . . . . . . . . . . . . . . . . . . . . . . . . . . . . . . . 307
Batteries . . . . . . . . . . . . . . . . . . . . . . . . . . . . . . . . . . . . . . . . . . . . . . . . 308
Power Management . . . . . . . . . . . . . . . . . . . . . . . . . . . . . . . . . . . . . . . 309
Lesson Summary . . . . . . . . . . . . . . . . . . . . . . . . . . . . . . . . . . . . . . . . . . 310
Chapter Summary . . . . . . . . . . . . . . . . . . . . . . . . . . . . . . . . . . . . . . . . . . . . 311
Review . . . . . . . . . . . . . . . . . . . . . . . . . . . . . . . . . . . . . . . . . . . . . . . . . . . . . . 312

**Chapter 14    Connectivity and Networking** . . . . . . . . . . . . . . . . . . . . . . . . **313**
About This Chapter . . . . . . . . . . . . . . . . . . . . . . . . . . . . . . . . . . . . . . . . . . . 313
Before You Begin . . . . . . . . . . . . . . . . . . . . . . . . . . . . . . . . . . . . . . . . . . . . . 313
Lesson 1: Networks . . . . . . . . . . . . . . . . . . . . . . . . . . . . . . . . . . . . . . . . . . . . 314
Basic Requirements of a Network . . . . . . . . . . . . . . . . . . . . . . . . . . . . . 314
Networking . . . . . . . . . . . . . . . . . . . . . . . . . . . . . . . . . . . . . . . . . . . . . . 315
Local Area Networks . . . . . . . . . . . . . . . . . . . . . . . . . . . . . . . . . . . . . . . 315

Wide Area Networks . . . . . . . . . . . . . . . . . . . . . . . . . . . . . . . . 316
Types of Networks . . . . . . . . . . . . . . . . . . . . . . . . . . . . . . . . . . 316
Network Topology . . . . . . . . . . . . . . . . . . . . . . . . . . . . . . . . . . 317
Network Operating System . . . . . . . . . . . . . . . . . . . . . . . . . . . 319
Network Interface Cards . . . . . . . . . . . . . . . . . . . . . . . . . . . . . 320
Network Cabling . . . . . . . . . . . . . . . . . . . . . . . . . . . . . . . . . . . 322
LAN Communication . . . . . . . . . . . . . . . . . . . . . . . . . . . . . . . 325
Network Protocols . . . . . . . . . . . . . . . . . . . . . . . . . . . . . . . . . 326
Extending a LAN . . . . . . . . . . . . . . . . . . . . . . . . . . . . . . . . . . 327
Maintaining and Troubleshooting Networks . . . . . . . . . . . . . . 328
Network Certification . . . . . . . . . . . . . . . . . . . . . . . . . . . . . . 329
Lesson Summary . . . . . . . . . . . . . . . . . . . . . . . . . . . . . . . . . . 330
Chapter Summary . . . . . . . . . . . . . . . . . . . . . . . . . . . . . . . . . . . . 331
Review . . . . . . . . . . . . . . . . . . . . . . . . . . . . . . . . . . . . . . . . . . . . 332

**Chapter 15   Telecommunications: Modems and the Internet** . . . . . . . . . . . . . . . . . **335**
About This Chapter . . . . . . . . . . . . . . . . . . . . . . . . . . . . . . . . . 335
Before You Begin . . . . . . . . . . . . . . . . . . . . . . . . . . . . . . . . . . . 335
Lesson 1: Modems . . . . . . . . . . . . . . . . . . . . . . . . . . . . . . . . . . . 336
Modem Basics . . . . . . . . . . . . . . . . . . . . . . . . . . . . . . . . . . . . 336
Modem Installation . . . . . . . . . . . . . . . . . . . . . . . . . . . . . . . . 346
Modem Speeds . . . . . . . . . . . . . . . . . . . . . . . . . . . . . . . . . . . 347
Fax Speeds . . . . . . . . . . . . . . . . . . . . . . . . . . . . . . . . . . . . . . 349
Information Transfer Protocols . . . . . . . . . . . . . . . . . . . . . . . . 350
Handshaking . . . . . . . . . . . . . . . . . . . . . . . . . . . . . . . . . . . . . 351
Modem Standards . . . . . . . . . . . . . . . . . . . . . . . . . . . . . . . . . 352
Modem Commands . . . . . . . . . . . . . . . . . . . . . . . . . . . . . . . . 354
Troubleshooting . . . . . . . . . . . . . . . . . . . . . . . . . . . . . . . . . . 355
Lesson Summary . . . . . . . . . . . . . . . . . . . . . . . . . . . . . . . . . . 355
Lesson 2: The Internet and Web Browsers . . . . . . . . . . . . . . . . . 356
The Internet . . . . . . . . . . . . . . . . . . . . . . . . . . . . . . . . . . . . . 356
Lesson Summary . . . . . . . . . . . . . . . . . . . . . . . . . . . . . . . . . . 362
Chapter Summary . . . . . . . . . . . . . . . . . . . . . . . . . . . . . . . . . . . . 363
Review . . . . . . . . . . . . . . . . . . . . . . . . . . . . . . . . . . . . . . . . . . . . 364

**Chapter 16   Operating System Fundamentals** . . . . . . . . . . . . . . . . . . . . . . . . . . . . **367**
About This Chapter . . . . . . . . . . . . . . . . . . . . . . . . . . . . . . . . . 367
Before You Begin . . . . . . . . . . . . . . . . . . . . . . . . . . . . . . . . . . . 368
Lesson 1: Operating System Basics . . . . . . . . . . . . . . . . . . . . . . . 369

The Software Core . . . . . . . . . . . . . . . . . . . . . . . . . . . . . . . . . . . . . . . . . 369
A Short History of MS-DOS . . . . . . . . . . . . . . . . . . . . . . . . . . . . . . . . 371
Understanding DOS . . . . . . . . . . . . . . . . . . . . . . . . . . . . . . . . . . . . . . 372
The Evolution of Microsoft Windows . . . . . . . . . . . . . . . . . . . . . . . . . 375
Windows for Workgroups 3.11 . . . . . . . . . . . . . . . . . . . . . . . . . . . . . . 379
Windows 95, Windows 98, and Windows Me . . . . . . . . . . . . . . . . . . 379
Windows NT . . . . . . . . . . . . . . . . . . . . . . . . . . . . . . . . . . . . . . . . . . . 379
Windows 2000 . . . . . . . . . . . . . . . . . . . . . . . . . . . . . . . . . . . . . . . . . 380
Lesson Summary . . . . . . . . . . . . . . . . . . . . . . . . . . . . . . . . . . . . . . . 380
Lesson 2: The Command Prompt and DOS Mode Operations . . . . . . . . . . . 381
The COMMAND Command . . . . . . . . . . . . . . . . . . . . . . . . . . . . . . 381
DOS Mode Navigation and File Management . . . . . . . . . . . . . . . . . . . 386
The PATH Command . . . . . . . . . . . . . . . . . . . . . . . . . . . . . . . . . . . 388
Using Edit . . . . . . . . . . . . . . . . . . . . . . . . . . . . . . . . . . . . . . . . . . . 391
Working with CONFIG.SYS and AUTOEXEC.BAT . . . . . . . . . . . . . . 393
Lesson Summary . . . . . . . . . . . . . . . . . . . . . . . . . . . . . . . . . . . . . . . 396
Lesson 3: File Systems . . . . . . . . . . . . . . . . . . . . . . . . . . . . . . . . . . . . . . 397
File System Basics . . . . . . . . . . . . . . . . . . . . . . . . . . . . . . . . . . . . . 397
Comparing and Choosing File Systems . . . . . . . . . . . . . . . . . . . . . . . 399
FAT-Based File Systems . . . . . . . . . . . . . . . . . . . . . . . . . . . . . . . . . 400
The NTFS File System . . . . . . . . . . . . . . . . . . . . . . . . . . . . . . . . . . 401
File System Size Limitations . . . . . . . . . . . . . . . . . . . . . . . . . . . . . . 402
File System Security . . . . . . . . . . . . . . . . . . . . . . . . . . . . . . . . . . . . 403
Lesson Summary . . . . . . . . . . . . . . . . . . . . . . . . . . . . . . . . . . . . . . . 405
Chapter Summary . . . . . . . . . . . . . . . . . . . . . . . . . . . . . . . . . . . . . . . . . 406
Review . . . . . . . . . . . . . . . . . . . . . . . . . . . . . . . . . . . . . . . . . . . . . . . . 407

Chapter 17    Introducing and Installing Microsoft Windows . . . . . . . . . . . . . . . . . . . . 409
About This Chapter . . . . . . . . . . . . . . . . . . . . . . . . . . . . . . . . . . . . . . . 409
Before You Begin . . . . . . . . . . . . . . . . . . . . . . . . . . . . . . . . . . . . . . . . . 410
Lesson 1: The Windows Family . . . . . . . . . . . . . . . . . . . . . . . . . . . . . . . . 411
The Expanding Windows Family . . . . . . . . . . . . . . . . . . . . . . . . . . . . 411
System Requirements Compared . . . . . . . . . . . . . . . . . . . . . . . . . . . . 414
Some System Configuration Considerations . . . . . . . . . . . . . . . . . . . . 416
Key Points to Remember . . . . . . . . . . . . . . . . . . . . . . . . . . . . . . . . . 417
Lesson Summary . . . . . . . . . . . . . . . . . . . . . . . . . . . . . . . . . . . . . . . 417
Lesson 2: Preparing for Windows Installation . . . . . . . . . . . . . . . . . . . . . . 418
Planning the Installation . . . . . . . . . . . . . . . . . . . . . . . . . . . . . . . . . 418
Decide on the Boot Method(s) . . . . . . . . . . . . . . . . . . . . . . . . . . . . . 419

Confirm Hardware Requirements and Compatibility . . . . . . . . . . . . . . . . 420
Obtain and Perform Updates to Firmware or Components . . . . . . . . . . . 420
Choose Between an Upgrade or a Clean Install . . . . . . . . . . . . . . . . . . . . 420
Record and Obtain Information . . . . . . . . . . . . . . . . . . . . . . . . . . . . . . . 421
Back Up Data and Key Files . . . . . . . . . . . . . . . . . . . . . . . . . . . . . . . . . 421
Remove or Disable Possible Conflicts and Verify Existing Settings . . . . . 421
Prepare the Hard Drive and File System . . . . . . . . . . . . . . . . . . . . . . . . 422
Lesson Summary . . . . . . . . . . . . . . . . . . . . . . . . . . . . . . . . . . . . . . . . . 424
Lesson 3: Installing Windows . . . . . . . . . . . . . . . . . . . . . . . . . . . . . . . . . 425
Performing a Windows 98 Setup . . . . . . . . . . . . . . . . . . . . . . . . . . . . . . 425
Making Use of Windows 98 Setup's Command-Line Switches . . . . . . . . 426
The Actual Windows 98 Installation Process . . . . . . . . . . . . . . . . . . . . . 428
Troubleshooting a Windows 98 Installation . . . . . . . . . . . . . . . . . . . . . 432
Beyond Safe Recovery . . . . . . . . . . . . . . . . . . . . . . . . . . . . . . . . . . . . . 433
The Setup Log Files . . . . . . . . . . . . . . . . . . . . . . . . . . . . . . . . . . . . . . . 434
Performing a Windows 2000 Installation . . . . . . . . . . . . . . . . . . . . . . . 436
Starting Setup . . . . . . . . . . . . . . . . . . . . . . . . . . . . . . . . . . . . . . . . . . . 439
The Step-by-Step Installation Process . . . . . . . . . . . . . . . . . . . . . . . . . . 442
Postinstallation Tasks . . . . . . . . . . . . . . . . . . . . . . . . . . . . . . . . . . . . . . 443
Troubleshooting . . . . . . . . . . . . . . . . . . . . . . . . . . . . . . . . . . . . . . . . . . 444
Lesson Summary . . . . . . . . . . . . . . . . . . . . . . . . . . . . . . . . . . . . . . . . . 445
Chapter Summary . . . . . . . . . . . . . . . . . . . . . . . . . . . . . . . . . . . . . . . . . . 446
Review . . . . . . . . . . . . . . . . . . . . . . . . . . . . . . . . . . . . . . . . . . . . . . . . . . 447

Chapter 18    Running Microsoft Windows . . . . . . . . . . . . . . . . . . . . . . . . . . . . . 449
About This Chapter . . . . . . . . . . . . . . . . . . . . . . . . . . . . . . . . . . . . . . . . 449
Before You Begin . . . . . . . . . . . . . . . . . . . . . . . . . . . . . . . . . . . . . . . . . 449
Lesson 1: How Windows 98 Works . . . . . . . . . . . . . . . . . . . . . . . . . . . . . 450
The Windows 98 System Architecture . . . . . . . . . . . . . . . . . . . . . . . . . . 450
The Windows 98 Virtual Memory Model . . . . . . . . . . . . . . . . . . . . . . . 452
The Windows 98 Boot Process . . . . . . . . . . . . . . . . . . . . . . . . . . . . . . . 456
The BIOS Initialization Phase . . . . . . . . . . . . . . . . . . . . . . . . . . . . . . . . 456
Hardware Profile and Real-Mode Driver Loading Phase . . . . . . . . . . . . 456
Protected Mode Initialization Phase . . . . . . . . . . . . . . . . . . . . . . . . . . . 461
Alternate Startup Methods and Resources . . . . . . . . . . . . . . . . . . . . . . 462
Lesson Summary . . . . . . . . . . . . . . . . . . . . . . . . . . . . . . . . . . . . . . . . . 464
Lesson 2: How Windows 2000 Works . . . . . . . . . . . . . . . . . . . . . . . . . . . 466
The Windows 2000 System Design . . . . . . . . . . . . . . . . . . . . . . . . . . . . 466
Two Modes, Several Subsystems . . . . . . . . . . . . . . . . . . . . . . . . . . . . . . 467

The Windows 2000 Boot Process ................................ 470
Lesson Summary ............................................. 473
Lesson 3: Managing Windows ................................... 474
Introducing the Windows Registry ............................ 474
A Major Change in Approach .................................. 475
A Critical Central Repository ............................... 475
Windows Configuration and Management Tools .................. 476
The Windows 2000 Administrative Tools ....................... 482
Working Directly with the System Registry ................... 486
Accessing and Managing the Registry ......................... 488
Using REGEDIT with Windows 9*x* ............................. 489
Editing the Registry with REGEDT32 in Windows 2000 .......... 491
Using REGEDT32 to Examine the Registry Contents ............. 492
Lesson Summary ............................................. 494
Chapter Summary ............................................. 495
Review ...................................................... 496

**Chapter 19    Maintaining the Modern Computer** ......................... **499**
About This Chapter ......................................... 499
Before You Begin ........................................... 500
Lesson 1: The Right Tools for the Job ...................... 501
Assembling a Complete Toolkit .............................. 501
Tools of the Trade ......................................... 501
Recommended Tools and Resources ............................ 502
Recommended Software ....................................... 503
Outside Resources .......................................... 505
Technical Support .......................................... 508
Working Safely ............................................. 509
Power and Safety ........................................... 510
Fire ....................................................... 512
Environmental Issues ....................................... 513
Lesson Summary ............................................. 514
Lesson 2: Planning and Performing Regular Maintenance ...... 515
Developing a Set of Maintenance Plans and Procedures ....... 515
Basic Hardware Maintenance ................................. 517
General Preventive Maintenance ............................. 518
Preventive Maintenance Schedule ............................ 521
Lesson Summary ............................................. 523

Lesson 3: Maintaining the Windows System Environment . . . . . . . . . . . . . . 524

    Virus Protection . . . . . . . . . . . . . . . . . . . . . . . . . . . . . . . . . . . . . . . . . 525

    Disk Cleanup . . . . . . . . . . . . . . . . . . . . . . . . . . . . . . . . . . . . . . . . . . . 527

    Checking Drive Integrity with ScanDisk . . . . . . . . . . . . . . . . . . . . . . 527

    Keeping Files Orderly with Disk Defragmenter . . . . . . . . . . . . . . . . . 528

    File Backups . . . . . . . . . . . . . . . . . . . . . . . . . . . . . . . . . . . . . . . . . . . 530

    Backing Up the Registry and Core System Files . . . . . . . . . . . . . . . . 533

    Verifying and Backing Up the Windows 98 Registry . . . . . . . . . . . . . 534

    Checking Critical Files with the Windows System File Checker . . . . . . 535

    Creating Emergency Recovery and Startup Disks . . . . . . . . . . . . . . . . 536

    Lesson Summary . . . . . . . . . . . . . . . . . . . . . . . . . . . . . . . . . . . . . . . . 537

Chapter Summary . . . . . . . . . . . . . . . . . . . . . . . . . . . . . . . . . . . . . . . . . . 538

Review . . . . . . . . . . . . . . . . . . . . . . . . . . . . . . . . . . . . . . . . . . . . . . . . . . 539

**Chapter 20     Upgrading a Computer** . . . . . . . . . . . . . . . . . . . . . . . . . . . . . . **541**

    About This Chapter . . . . . . . . . . . . . . . . . . . . . . . . . . . . . . . . . . . . . . 541

    Before You Begin . . . . . . . . . . . . . . . . . . . . . . . . . . . . . . . . . . . . . . . 541

Lesson 1: Computer Disassembly and Reassembly . . . . . . . . . . . . . . . . . . 542

    Preparation . . . . . . . . . . . . . . . . . . . . . . . . . . . . . . . . . . . . . . . . . . . . 542

    Tools and Components . . . . . . . . . . . . . . . . . . . . . . . . . . . . . . . . . . . . 543

    Disassembly . . . . . . . . . . . . . . . . . . . . . . . . . . . . . . . . . . . . . . . . . . . 544

    Reassembly . . . . . . . . . . . . . . . . . . . . . . . . . . . . . . . . . . . . . . . . . . . . 545

    Lesson Summary . . . . . . . . . . . . . . . . . . . . . . . . . . . . . . . . . . . . . . . . 545

Lesson 2: Upgrading a Computer . . . . . . . . . . . . . . . . . . . . . . . . . . . . . . . 546

    Memory, Memory, Memory . . . . . . . . . . . . . . . . . . . . . . . . . . . . . . . . 548

    CPU Upgrades . . . . . . . . . . . . . . . . . . . . . . . . . . . . . . . . . . . . . . . . . 552

    Expansion Cards . . . . . . . . . . . . . . . . . . . . . . . . . . . . . . . . . . . . . . . . 553

    Drives . . . . . . . . . . . . . . . . . . . . . . . . . . . . . . . . . . . . . . . . . . . . . . . . 557

    Operating System Driver Installation . . . . . . . . . . . . . . . . . . . . . . . . . 559

    Motherboards . . . . . . . . . . . . . . . . . . . . . . . . . . . . . . . . . . . . . . . . . . 560

    Lesson Summary . . . . . . . . . . . . . . . . . . . . . . . . . . . . . . . . . . . . . . . . 562

Chapter Summary . . . . . . . . . . . . . . . . . . . . . . . . . . . . . . . . . . . . . . . . . . 563

Review . . . . . . . . . . . . . . . . . . . . . . . . . . . . . . . . . . . . . . . . . . . . . . . . . . 564

**Chapter 21     Troubleshooting Techniques and Client Relations** . . . . . . . . . . . . . . . . **565**

    About This Chapter . . . . . . . . . . . . . . . . . . . . . . . . . . . . . . . . . . . . . . 565

    Before You Begin . . . . . . . . . . . . . . . . . . . . . . . . . . . . . . . . . . . . . . . 566

Lesson 1: Basic Troubleshooting Techniques . . . . . . . . . . . . . . . . . . . . . . 567

    Troubleshooting . . . . . . . . . . . . . . . . . . . . . . . . . . . . . . . . . . . . . . . . 567

Lesson Summary . . . . . . . . . . . . . . . . . . . . . . . . . . . . . . . . . . . . . . . . 572
Lesson 2: Windows Troubleshooting Tools . . . . . . . . . . . . . . . . . . . . . . . 573
  Basic Windows Troubleshooting Approach . . . . . . . . . . . . . . . . . . . . . 573
  Performing a Differential Diagnosis . . . . . . . . . . . . . . . . . . . . . . . . . 575
  Working Through the Phases . . . . . . . . . . . . . . . . . . . . . . . . . . . . . . 577
  Working with the Operating System Management Tools . . . . . . . . . . . . 578
  Using the Windows Troubleshooting Tools . . . . . . . . . . . . . . . . . . . . 581
  Shutdown and Related Problems . . . . . . . . . . . . . . . . . . . . . . . . . . . 585
  Resource Loss and System Monitoring . . . . . . . . . . . . . . . . . . . . . . 587
  The Windows 98 System and Resource Monitor . . . . . . . . . . . . . . . . 587
  Resource Meter . . . . . . . . . . . . . . . . . . . . . . . . . . . . . . . . . . . . . . . 588
  Registry Recovery . . . . . . . . . . . . . . . . . . . . . . . . . . . . . . . . . . . . . 589
  MS-DOS Application Incompatibilities . . . . . . . . . . . . . . . . . . . . . . . 591
  Printing Problems . . . . . . . . . . . . . . . . . . . . . . . . . . . . . . . . . . . . . 593
  Lesson Summary . . . . . . . . . . . . . . . . . . . . . . . . . . . . . . . . . . . . . . 595
Lesson 3: Client Relations . . . . . . . . . . . . . . . . . . . . . . . . . . . . . . . . . 596
  Getting Organized and Keeping Records . . . . . . . . . . . . . . . . . . . . . 596
  Levels of Support . . . . . . . . . . . . . . . . . . . . . . . . . . . . . . . . . . . . . 597
  Spare Parts . . . . . . . . . . . . . . . . . . . . . . . . . . . . . . . . . . . . . . . . . . 598
  Standardization . . . . . . . . . . . . . . . . . . . . . . . . . . . . . . . . . . . . . . . 598
  Customer Service . . . . . . . . . . . . . . . . . . . . . . . . . . . . . . . . . . . . . 599
  Lesson Summary . . . . . . . . . . . . . . . . . . . . . . . . . . . . . . . . . . . . . . 602
Chapter Summary . . . . . . . . . . . . . . . . . . . . . . . . . . . . . . . . . . . . . . . 603
Review . . . . . . . . . . . . . . . . . . . . . . . . . . . . . . . . . . . . . . . . . . . . . . . 604

**Chapter 22    The Basics of Electrical Energy** . . . . . . . . . . . . . . . . . . . . . . . . **607**
About This Chapter . . . . . . . . . . . . . . . . . . . . . . . . . . . . . . . . . . . . . . 607
Before You Begin . . . . . . . . . . . . . . . . . . . . . . . . . . . . . . . . . . . . . . . 607
Lesson 1: Power . . . . . . . . . . . . . . . . . . . . . . . . . . . . . . . . . . . . . . . . 608
  Understanding Electricity and Electrical Energy . . . . . . . . . . . . . . . . 608
  Personal Computers and Electrical Power . . . . . . . . . . . . . . . . . . . . 610
  Measuring Electricity . . . . . . . . . . . . . . . . . . . . . . . . . . . . . . . . . . . 613
  Testing a Power Supply . . . . . . . . . . . . . . . . . . . . . . . . . . . . . . . . . 615
  Electronic Components . . . . . . . . . . . . . . . . . . . . . . . . . . . . . . . . . 619
  Lesson Summary . . . . . . . . . . . . . . . . . . . . . . . . . . . . . . . . . . . . . . 623
Lesson 2: Electrostatic Discharge . . . . . . . . . . . . . . . . . . . . . . . . . . . . 624
  Causes of ESD . . . . . . . . . . . . . . . . . . . . . . . . . . . . . . . . . . . . . . . 624
  Preventing ESD . . . . . . . . . . . . . . . . . . . . . . . . . . . . . . . . . . . . . . . 625
  Lesson Summary . . . . . . . . . . . . . . . . . . . . . . . . . . . . . . . . . . . . . . 626

Lesson 3: Safety and Electrical Power ............................... 627
    Electrical Safety Is Your Responsibility ........................... 627
    Lesson Summary ......................................... 628
  Chapter Summary ......................................... 629
  Review ................................................. 630

**Appendix A   Questions and Answers** ....................................... **631**

**Appendix B   Table of Acronyms** ............................................. **669**

**Glossary** ............................................................. **673**

**Index** ................................................................ **687**

# About This Book

Welcome to the *A+ Certification Training Kit*. This technology-based training kit is intended to provide the user with the skills necessary for A+ Certification. It is a study of the computer—its hardware and software—from its earliest beginnings, through the advent of mainframe and personal computers, up to present-day Pentium processor-driven machines.

The computer industry has evolved and grown phenomenally since its commercial inception in the 1960s. This industry is so vast and complex that no one can claim to understand all its aspects. However, to participate in this ever-changing and growing industry, the computer technician must be able to demonstrate a level of proficiency with computers and technology. Certification is a first step in establishing your presence as a computer professional. It provides you with the opportunity to gain the skills you need, it helps you establish your knowledge base, and it gives you the confidence to get started.

**Note** For more information on becoming A+ Certified, refer to the section titled "The A+ Certification Program," later in this introduction.

Each chapter in this book is divided into lessons. Each lesson ends with a brief summary, and each chapter concludes with a chapter summary and a set of review questions to test your knowledge of the chapter material.

The "Getting Started" section of this introduction provides important instructions that describe the hardware and software recommendations presented in this course. Read through the section thoroughly before you start the lessons.

## Intended Audience

This book was developed for the entry-level computer technician, as well as the experienced technician who is seeking certification. For the entry-level student, it starts by explaining the basics and moves on to more complex topics. It introduces the simple concepts that underlie today's computers. Once this foundation is established, it brings you up to date with the latest technology covered by the A+ Exam. For the more experienced user, it provides a fresh review and focus on what is required to meet the objectives of the A+ Exam.

# Prerequisites

There are no formal prerequisites such as coursework or a specific knowledge base. This is an entry-level course, and everything you need to know is provided in the text. It is assumed that you are comfortable with computers, can use simple hand tools (like a screwdriver), and are familiar with the Microsoft Windows user interface.

To better understand the concepts presented and to complete any exercises or practices, it would be useful to have a computer with an Intel Pentium processor and, at the very least, a Microsoft Windows 98-based computer. Both the Windows 98 and Microsoft Windows 2000 operating systems are covered in the A+ Certification Program and this book. Please check the Microsoft Web site at *www.microsoft.com* for possible trial versions of the latest operating system.

# About the CD-ROM

The companion compact disc contains informational aids that can be used to supplement this book. These include demonstration videos and an electronic version of the book.

The electronic version of the book requires an HTML (Hypertext Markup Language) browser. If Microsoft Internet Explorer is installed on your system, click Install E-Book. If AutoRun is disabled on your machine, refer to the README.TXT file on the CD. The demonstrations are stored as HTML files with embedded Microsoft Windows Media Player files. If your machine has standard multimedia support and an HTML browser, you can view these demonstrations by double-clicking them.

For specific information about what is included on the companion CD and how to access this information, see the README.TXT file on the CD.

# Features of This Book

Each chapter opens with a "Before You Begin" section, which prepares you for completing the chapter.

The body of each chapter provides detailed coverage of the subjects you will need to study to prepare for the test. The "Review" sections at the end of each chapter allow you to test what you have learned in the chapter lessons. They are designed to familiarize you with the types of questions you might encounter on the exam.

# Chapter and Appendix Overview

This self-paced training course combines instruction, procedures, multimedia presentations, and review questions to teach you what you need to know for A+ Certification. It is designed to be completed from beginning to end, but you can choose a customized track and complete only the sections that interest you. (See the next section, "Finding the Best Starting Point for You.") If you choose the customized track option, be sure to check the "Before You Begin" section in each chapter. Any concepts or procedures that require preliminary work from preceding chapters will steer you to the appropriate chapters.

This self-paced book is divided into the following chapters:

- This "About This Book" section contains a self-paced training overview and introduces the components of this training. Read this section thoroughly to draw the greatest educational value from the self-paced training and to plan which lessons you will complete.

- Chapter 1, "Introduction to Computers," sets the background for the rest of the lessons. It provides a historic view of computers from their humble beginnings to today's high-speed marvels. This section also explores the role of today's computer technician.

- Chapter 2, "Understanding Electronic Communication," discusses how computers communicate. It explains the differences between the language we use and the language of machines.

- Chapter 3, "An Overview of the Personal Computer," defines the basic elements of a computer's hardware and how they interact.

- Chapter 4, "The Central Processing Unit," explains the development of the microprocessor, focusing on what differentiates each type of processor and how to identify each.

- Chapter 5, "Power Supplies," covers power supplies, including how they work and how to troubleshoot problems.

- Chapter 6, "Motherboard and ROM BIOS," discusses the design and function of primary foundation components: the motherboard and the BIOS (basic input/output system).

- Chapter 7, "Memory," covers the various types of memory found in a computer, what memory is used for, and how to upgrade or replace it.

- Chapter 8, "Expansion Buses, Cables, and Connectors," covers the computer's I/O (input/output) components and expansion buses that allow the PC to adapt and support new technology.

- Chapter 9, "Basic Disk Drives," discusses floppy disk drives and hard disk drives. It explores mass-storage devices, how they work, and their limitations.

- Chapter 10, "Advanced Disk Drive Technology," covers CD-ROM, digital video disc (DVD), and SCSI (Small Computer System Interface) drives and related technologies.

- Chapter 11, "The Display System," covers monitors, flat screen panels, display adapters, how they work, and how to troubleshoot them.

- Chapter 12, "Printers," covers the different types of printers, how they interact with the PC, and how to install and care for them.

- Chapter 13, "Portable Computers," explores the features of portable (laptop and notebook) computers.

- Chapter 14, "Connectivity and Networking," discusses the basics of how a computer network functions and technology that links a PC to the network.

- Chapter 15, "Telecommunications and the Internet," covers the installation and use of modems and other telecommunications devices, as well as the growing importance of the Internet to both technicians and their clients.

- Chapter 16, "Operating System Fundamentals," is an introduction to operating systems and applications software. It focuses on the early operating system MS-DOS and how to use the DOS-mode command prompt and programs that are still critical to performing many upgrade and maintenance functions.

- Chapter 17, "Introducing and Installing Microsoft Windows," discusses the development of this now dominant operating system from Microsoft. It presents the differences between the different versions and gives you a foundation for the advanced skills presented in the following chapters. Both Windows 9x and Windows 2000 installations are covered.

- Chapter 18, "Running Microsoft Windows," covers the various tools provided by the Windows 9x and Windows 2000 Professional operating systems that a computer technician uses to manage and maintain both the operating system and the hardware components of the computer.

- Chapter 19, "Maintaining the Modern Computer," focuses on the tools and techniques used to keep a computer operating properly, the use of system software, and how to safeguard critical system files and user data.

- Chapter 20, "Upgrading a Computer," covers the basic tools and techniques used to perform common upgrades to a computer, including upgrading memory, expansion card operations, and computer disassembly and reassembly.

- Chapter 21, "Troubleshooting Techniques and Client Relations," covers the techniques and procedures used to resolve problems related to both hardware and software. It also discusses how to recover from a complete hard drive failure and corruption of core system files and how to deal with clients.

- Chapter 22, "The Basics of Electrical Energy," covers electricity and how it relates to the computer. A computer technician does not need to be an electrical engineer but does need to be able to perform basic tests and to work safely. This chapter provides the reader with background in these issues.

- Appendix A, "Questions and Answers," lists all the review questions from each chapter of the book, including the page number where the question appears, and provides suggested answers.

- Appendix B, "Table of Acronyms," lists a number of acronyms relevant to the A+ Certification Exam.

- The Glossary provides concise definitions of terms used throughout this book that are relevant to the A+ Certification Exam.

## Finding the Best Starting Point for You

Because this book is self-paced, you can skip some lessons and visit them later. Note, however, that some sections require an understanding of the concepts presented in previous sections (prerequisites are noted at the beginning of each chapter).

| If... | Follow This Learning Path |
| --- | --- |
| You are preparing to take the A+ Certification Exam and have no experience | Read the "Getting Started" section. Then work through Chapters 1 through 22 in order. |
| You are preparing to take the A+ Certification Exam and are experienced with computer repair | Read the "Getting Started" section. Be sure to focus on the exam objectives as presented in the "The A+ Certification Program" section of this introduction. Then work through the remaining chapters in any order you wish. Be sure, however, to cover all the chapters. |
| You'd like to review information about specific topics for the exam | Use the "Where to Find Specific Skill Areas in This Book" section that immediately follows this table. |

# Where to Find Specific Skill Areas in This Book

The following tables provide a list of the skill areas measured on the A+ Certification Exam. The tables list the skill and where in this book you will find the lessons related to that skill.

## A+ Core Hardware Examination

The objectives for the core exam focus on computer hardware. Information relevant to the core exam objectives can be found in every chapter in this training kit, except in those that specifically cover operating system material.

| Skill Area Measured | Location in Book |
|---|---|
| Installation, Configuration, and Upgrading | Any chapter containing information specific to devices (printers, monitors, drives, and so on). Focus on Chapters 7–12 and 14, 15, and 20. |
| Diagnosing and Troubleshooting | Chapter 21 and any chapter containing information specific to devices (printers, monitors, drives, and so on). Focus on Chapters 8–13. |
| Safety and Preventive Maintenance | Focus on Chapters 18 and 19. Other safety and preventive maintenance tips are found in sections that cover a specific device. |
| Motherboard/Processor/Memory | Chapters 4, 6, and 7. |
| Printers | Chapter 12. |
| Portable Systems | Chapter 13. |
| Basic Networking | Chapter 14. |
| Customer Satisfaction | Chapter 21. |

## A+ Operating System Technologies Exam

The majority of information for this exam is found in Chapters 16 through 21. Specific information regarding a device will be found in the chapter that covers that device.

| Skill Area Measured | Location in Book |
|---|---|
| Function, Structure, Operation, and File Management | Chapters 16, 17, and 18. |
| Memory Management | Chapters 16 and 17. Also see Chapter 7. |
| Installation, Configuration, and Upgrading | Chapters 16, 17, and 18. |
| Troubleshooting | Chapter 21. |
| Networks | Chapters 14, 15, 16, and 17. |

# Getting Started

This self-paced training course contains hands-on procedures to help you learn about computer hardware and software. Although it is not a requirement to have a computer and software to complete the course, you will need one available for practice. It is recommended that you not use a computer that contains any important data that needs to be saved. Some of the concepts in this book require complete reformatting of the hard drive or major modifications of the operating system, during which all data will be lost.

## Hardware Requirements

This course builds knowledge that begins with early technology. Therefore, almost any computer will provide some level of skill building. In fact, a new computer with a Pentium III processor and full Plug and Play capability will be something of a detriment because it is overly capable for our purposes and does not require the interaction necessary for building these basic skills. However, to get the most out of this course, your computer should have the following minimum configuration (all hardware should be on the Microsoft Windows 98 or Windows 2000 Hardware Compatibility List):

- Pentium II processor and motherboard
- 32 MB of RAM (64 MB or more recommended)
- 2-GB hard disk drive
- 3.5-inch floppy disk drive
- CD-ROM drive (20x minimum recommended)
- A mouse or other pointing device
- Display system capable of 800 × 600 resolution or better (1024 × 768 recommended for best viewing of demonstration videos)
- A printer
- A modem with Internet connection

## Software Requirements

The following software is required to complete the procedures in this course:

- Microsoft Windows 98 (minimum)
- Microsoft Windows 2000 (recommended)
- Access to earlier operating systems (Microsoft Windows 95 and MS-DOS) is a plus

To view the electronic version of the book, you will need Microsoft Internet Explorer 4.01 or later. A version of Microsoft Internet Explorer 5.5 is supplied on the companion CD. For more information, see the README.TXT file on the companion CD. To view the demonstration videos on the companion CD, you will need a machine with standard multimedia support and an HTML browser. A version of Microsoft Windows Media Player 7 is supplied on the companion CD.

# About the Electronic Book

The companion CD also includes an electronic version of the book that you can use to search and view on-screen as you work through the exercises. See the README.TXT file on the companion CD for instructions on how to install and use the electronic version of this book.

# The A+ Certification Program

A+ Certification is a testing program sponsored by the Computing Technology Industry Association (CompTIA) that certifies the competency of service technicians in the computer industry. Many computer hardware and software manufacturers, vendors, distributors, resellers, and publications back the program.

Earning A+ Certification means that you possess the knowledge, skills, and customer-relations expertise that are essential for a successful computer service technician. The exams cover a broad range of hardware and software technologies but are not related to any vendor-specific products, including Microsoft Windows.

## Benefits of Certification

For most individuals entering the computer industry, A+ Certification is only the first step. If your goal is to enter the profession of computer service and repair, this might be all the certification you need. However, if you are interested in becoming a Microsoft Certified Systems Engineer (MCSE), this course provides just the foundation you need to get on your way with confidence.

As an A+ Certified Technician, you will receive many benefits, including:

- **Recognized proof of professional achievement.** The A+ credential asserts that the holder has reached a level of competence commonly accepted and valued by the industry.
- **Enhanced job opportunities.** Many employers give hiring preference to applicants with A+ Certification. Some employers require A+ as a condition of employment.
- **Opportunity for advancement.** The A+ credential can be a plus when an employer awards job promotions.

- **Training requirement.** A+ Certification is being adopted as a prerequisite to enrollment in certain vendors' training courses. Vendors find they can cut their training programs by as much as 50 percent when they require that all attendees are A+ Certified.

- **Customer confidence.** As the general public learns about A+ Certification, customers will request that only certified technicians be assigned to their accounts.

- **Companies benefit from improved productivity.** Certified employees perform work faster and more accurately. Statistics show that certified employees can work up to 75 percent faster than noncertified employees.

- **Customer satisfaction.** When employees have credentials that prove their competency, customer expectations are more likely to be met. More business can be generated for the employer through repeat sales to satisfied customers.

## The A+ Exam Modules and Domains

To become certified, you must pass two test modules: the Hardware Core and the Operating System Technologies Core. For the most current rules concerning taking the test, locations, fees, how the tests are administered, and the requirements for passing, check the CompTIA Web site at *www.comptia.com*.

This text prepares you to master the A+ Exams. By completing all course work, you will be able to complete the A+ Certification Exams with the confidence you need to ensure success. More important, you will be able to conduct your business with the knowledge that you are among the best and that you really "know your stuff."

### Hardware Core Exam

This examination measures essential competencies for a microcomputer hardware service technician with six months of on-the-job experience. It is broken down into six sections (called domains). The following table lists the domains and the extent to which they are represented.

| Domain | Percent of Examination |
| --- | --- |
| 1.0—Installation, Configuration, and Upgrading | 30 |
| 2.0—Diagnosing and Troubleshooting | 30 |
| 3.0—Preventive Maintenance | 5 |
| 4.0—Motherboard/Processors/Memory | 15 |
| 5.0—Printers | 10 |
| 6.0—Basic Networking | 10 |

## 1.0 Installation, Configuration, and Upgrading

This domain tests the knowledge and skills needed to identify, install, configure, and upgrade microcomputer modules and peripherals, following established basic procedures for system assembly and the assembly of field-replaceable modules. You will be expected to know how to

- Identify basic terms, concepts, and functions of system modules, including how each module should work during normal operation and during the boot process.

- Identify basic procedures for adding and removing field-replaceable modules for both desktop and portable systems.

- Identify common peripheral ports, associated cabling, and their connectors.

- Identify proper procedures for installing and configuring IDE/EIDE devices.

- Identify proper procedures for installing and configuring SCSI devices.

- Identify proper procedures for installing and configuring peripheral devices.

- Identify hardware methods of upgrading system performance, procedures for replacing basic subsystem components, unique components, and learn when to use them.

- Identify available IRQs (interrupt requests), DMA (direct memory access), and I/O addresses and procedures for configuring them for device installation.

## 2.0 Diagnosing and Troubleshooting

This domain tests the candidate's knowledge and skills in diagnosing and troubleshooting common problems and system malfunctions and requires knowledge of the symptoms relating to common problems. You will be expected to know how to

- Identify common symptoms and problems associated with each module and how to troubleshoot and isolate the problems.

- Identify basic troubleshooting procedures and good practices for eliciting problem symptoms from customers.

## 3.0 Preventive Maintenance

This domain requires the knowledge of safety and preventive maintenance. With regard to safety, it includes potential hazards to personnel and equipment when working with lasers, high-voltage equipment, electrostatic discharge (ESD), and items that require special disposal procedures that comply with environmental guidelines. With regard to preventive maintenance, this includes knowledge of preventive maintenance products, procedures, environmental hazards, and precautions when working on microcomputer systems. You will be expected to know how to

- Identify the purposes of various types of preventive maintenance products and procedures and when to perform them.
- Identify issues, procedures, and devices for protection within the computing environment, including people, hardware, and the surrounding workspace.

### 4.0 Motherboard/Processors/Memory

This domain requires knowledge of specific terminology, facts, ways and means of dealing with classifications, and categories and principles of motherboards, processors, and memory in microcomputer systems. You will be expected to know how to

- Distinguish between the popular CPU (central processing unit) chips in terms of their basic characteristics.
- Identify the categories of RAM (random access memory) terminology and their locations and physical characteristics.
- Identify the most popular types of motherboards, their components, and their architecture (for example, bus structure and power supplies).
- Identify the purpose of the CMOS (complementary metal-oxide semiconductor) chip, what it contains, and how to change its basic parameters.

### 5.0 Printers

This domain requires knowledge of basic types of printers, basic concepts, and printer components; how they work, how they print onto a page; paper path, care and service techniques, and common problems. You will be expected to know how to

- Identify the basic concepts, printer operations, and printer components.
- Identify care and service techniques and common problems with primary printer types.

### 6.0 Basic Networking

This domain tests skills and knowledge of basic network concepts and terminology, ability to determine whether a computer is networked, knowledge of procedures for swapping and configuring network interface cards, and knowledge of the ramifications of repairs when a computer is on the network. You will be expected to know how to

- Identify basic networking concepts, including how a network works and the ramifications of repairs on the network.

## A+ Operating System Technologies Examination

For A+ Certification, the examinee must pass both this examination and the A+ Core Hardware (formerly the A+ Core) Examination. This examination measures essential operating system competencies for entry-level PC hardware service technicians with six months of on-the-job experience. The examinee must demonstrate basic knowledge of the command-line prompt, Windows 9*x,* and Windows 2000 for installing, configuring, upgrading, troubleshooting, and repairing microcomputer systems. This examination is broken down into four domains.

| Domain | Percent of Examination |
| --- | --- |
| 1.0—Operating System Fundamentals | 30 |
| 2.0—Installation, Configuration, and Upgrading | 15 |
| 3.0—Diagnosing and Troubleshooting | 40 |
| 4.0—Networks | 15 |

## 1.0 Operating System Fundamentals

This domain tests required knowledge of underlying DOS (command prompt functions), Windows 9*x,* and Windows 2000 operating systems in terms of their function and structure, for managing files and directories, and reading programs. It also includes navigating through the operating system from command-line prompts and Windows procedures for accessing and retrieving information. You will be expected to know how to

- Identify the operating system's functions, structure, and major system files to navigate the operating system and obtain needed technical information.

- Identify basic concepts and procedures for creating, viewing, and managing files, directories, and disks. This includes procedures for changing file attributes and the ramifications of those changes (for example, security issues).

## 2.0 Installation, Configuration, and Upgrading

This domain requires knowledge of installing, configuring, and upgrading Windows 9*x* and Windows 2000. This includes knowledge of system boot sequences and minimum hardware requirements. You will be expected to know how to

- Identify the procedures for installing Windows 9*x* and Windows 2000 and bringing the software to a basic operational level.

- Identify steps to perform an operating system upgrade.

- Identify the boot sequences and boot methods, including the steps to create an emergency boot disk with utilities installed, for Windows 9*x,* Microsoft Windows NT, and Windows 2000.

- Identify procedures for loading or adding and configuring device drivers, applications, and the necessary software for certain devices.

### 3.0 Diagnosing and Troubleshooting

This domain requires the ability to apply knowledge to diagnose and trouble-shoot common problems relating to Windows 9x and Windows 2000. This includes understanding normal operation and symptoms related to common problems.

- Recognize and interpret the meanings of common error codes and startup messages from the boot sequence, and identify steps to correct the problems.
- Recognize common problems and determine how to resolve them.

### 4.0 Networks

This domain requires knowledge of the network capabilities of Windows and how to connect to networks on the client side, including what the Internet is about, its capabilities, basic concepts relating to Internet access, and generic procedures for system setup. You will be expected to know how to

- Identify the networking capabilities of Windows, including procedures for connecting to the network.
- Identify concepts and capabilities relating to the Internet and basic procedures for setting up a system for Internet access.

# Registering for the A+ Exams

The A+ Certification Exams are administered by Sylvan Prometric. They have hundreds of authorized testing centers in all 50 states in the United States and in more than 150 other countries worldwide. To register for the test, call 1-800-77-MICRO (1-800-776-4276).

When you call, please have the following information available:

- Social Security number or Sylvan Prometric ID number (provided by Sylvan Prometric)
- Mailing address and telephone number
- Employer or organization
- Date on which you wish to take the test
- Method of payment (credit card or check)

The test is available to anyone who wants to take it. Payment is made at the time of registration, either by credit card or by requesting that an invoice be sent to you or your employer. Vouchers and coupons are also redeemed at that time.

C H A P T E R   1

# Introduction to Computers

**Lesson 1: The Development of the Computer** ..................... 2

**Lesson 2: The Role of a Computer Service Professional** ........... 8

**Chapter Summary** ......................................... 9

**Review** ................................................. 10

## About This Chapter

We begin our introduction to computers with a brief history of how they evolved. Although this course and the A+ exam focus on the modern electronic computer, many principles used in early computational machines still apply to their modern successors. With a summary of computer development and discussion of the role of today's computer professional, this chapter lays the foundation for the chapters that follow.

## Before You Begin

There are no prerequisites for this chapter.

# Lesson 1: The Development of the Computer

In this lesson, we take a brief look at the development of the computer. By understanding its origins, you'll gain an appreciation for both the complexity and simplicity of today's computers.

### After this lesson, you will be able to

- Describe the major milestones in the development of the modern computer

### Estimated lesson time: 15 minutes

Many of us think only in terms of electronic computers, powered by electricity. (If you can't plug it in, is it a computer?) But as the definition in *Funk & Wagnalls Standard College Dictionary* makes clear, to "compute" is to "ascertain (an amount or number) by calculation or reckoning." In fact, the first computers were invented by the Chinese about 2500 years ago. They are called *abacuses* and are still used throughout Asia today.

## The Abacus

The abacus, shown in Figure 1.1, is a calculator; its first recorded use was circa 500 B.C. The Chinese used it to add, subtract, multiply, and divide. However, the abacus was not unique to the continent of Asia; archeological excavations have revealed an Aztec abacus in use around 900 or 1000 A.D.

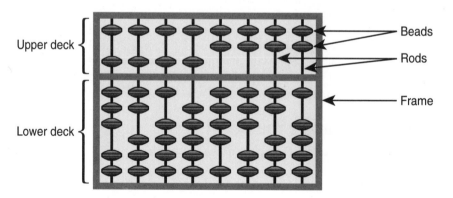

**Figure 1.1**   The first computer

## The Analytical Engine (A Pre-Electronic Computer)

The first mechanical computer was the analytical engine, conceived and partially constructed by Charles Babbage in London, England, between 1822 and 1871. It was designed to receive instructions from punched cards, make calculations with the aid of a memory bank, and print out solutions to math problems. Although Babbage lavished the equivalent of $6,000 of his own money—and $17,000 of the British government's money—on this extraordinarily advanced machine, the precise work needed to engineer its thousands of moving parts was beyond the ability of the technology of the day to produce in large volume. It is doubtful whether Babbage's brilliant concept could have been realized using the available resources of his own century. If it had been, however, it seems likely that the analytical engine could have performed the same functions as many early electronic computers.

## The First Electrically Driven Computer

The first computer designed expressly for data processing was patented on January 8, 1889, by Dr. Herman Hollerith of New York. The prototype model of this electrically operated tabulator was built for the U.S. Census Bureau to compute results of the 1890 census.

Using punched cards containing information submitted by respondents to the census questionnaire, the Hollerith machine made instant tabulations from electrical impulses actuated by each hole. It then printed out the processed data on tape. Dr. Hollerith left the Census Bureau in 1896 to establish the Tabulating Machine Company to manufacture and sell his equipment. The company eventually became IBM, and the 80-column punched card used by the company, shown in Figure 1.2, is still known as the Hollerith card.

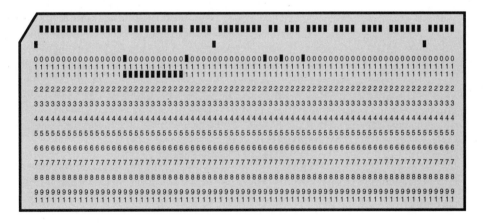

**Figure 1.2**   Typical 80-column punched card

## The Digital Electronic Computer

The first modern digital computer, the ABC (Atanasoff–Berry Computer), was built in a basement on the Iowa State University campus in Ames, Iowa, between 1939 and 1942. The development team was led by John Atanasoff, a professor of physics and mathematics, and Clifford Berry, a graduate student. This machine utilized concepts still in use today: binary arithmetic, parallel processing, regenerative memory, separate memory, and computer functions. When completed, it weighed 750 pounds and could store 3000 bits (.4 KB) of data.

The technology developed for the ABC machine was passed from Atanasoff to John W. Mauchly, who, together with engineer John Presper Eckert, developed the first large-scale digital computer, ENIAC (Electronic Numerical Integrator and Computer). It was built at the University of Pennsylvania's Moore School of Electrical Engineering. Begun as a classified military project, ENIAC was designed to prepare firing and bombing tables for the U.S. Army and Navy. When finally assembled in 1945, ENIAC consisted of 30 separate units, plus a power supply and forced-air cooling. It weighed 30 tons, and used 19,000 vacuum tubes, 1500 relays, and hundreds of thousands of resistors, capacitors, and inductors. It required 200 kilowatts of electrical power to operate.

Although programming ENIAC was a mammoth task requiring manual switches and cable connections, it became the workhorse for the solution of scientific problems from 1949 to 1952. ENIAC is considered the prototype for most of today's computers.

Another computer history milestone is the Colossus I, an early digital computer built at a secret British government research establishment at Bletchley Park, Buckinghamshire, England, under the direction of Professor Max Newman. Colossus I was designed for a single purpose: cryptanalysis, or code breaking. Using punched paper tape input, it scanned and analyzed 5000 characters per second. Colossus became operational in December 1943 and proved to be an important technological aid to the Allied victory in World War II. It enabled the British to break the otherwise impenetrable German "Enigma" codes.

The 1960s and 1970s marked the golden era of the mainframe computer. Using the technology pioneered with ABC, ENIAC, and Colossus, large computers that served many users (with accompanying large-scale support) came to dominate the industry.

As these highlights show, the concept of the computer has indeed been with us for quite a while. The following table provides an overview of the evolution of modern computers—it is a timeline of important events.

**Note**    Don't worry if you are not familiar with some terms in this timeline; they are explained in the chapters that follow, as well as in the Glossary.

| Year | Events |
|------|--------|
| 1971 | The 4004—the first 4-bit microprocessor—is introduced by Intel. It boasts 2000 transistors with a clock speed of up to 1 megahertz (MHz). |
| 1972 | The first 8-bit microprocessor—the 8008—is released. |
| 1974 | The 8080 microprocessor is developed. This improved version of the 8008 becomes the standard from which future processors will be designed. |
| 1975 | Digital Research introduces CP/M—an operating system for the 8080. The combination of software and hardware becomes the basis for the standard computer. |
| 1976 | Zilog introduces the Z80—a low-cost microprocessor (equivalent to the 8080). The Apple I comes into existence, although it is not yet in widespread use. |
| 1977 | The Apple II and the Commodore PET computers, both of which use a 6502 processor, are introduced. These two products become the basis for the home computer. Apple's popularity begins to grow. |
| 1978 | Intel introduces a 16-bit processor, the 8086, and a companion math coprocessor, the 8087. Intel also introduces the 8088. It is similar to the 8086, but it transmits 8 bits at a time. |
| 1980 | Motorola introduces the 68000—a 16-bit processor important to the development of Apple and Atari computers. Motorola's 68000 becomes the processor of choice for Apple. |
| 1981 | The IBM personal computer (PC) is born; it contains a 4.7-MHz 8088 processor and 64 kilobytes (KB) of RAM (random access memory), and is equipped with a version of MS-DOS 1.0 (three files and some utilities). Available mass-storage devices include a 5.25-inch floppy drive and a cassette tape drive. |
| 1982 | Intel completes development of the 80286—a 16-bit processor with 150,000 transistors. MS-DOS 1.1 now supports double-sided floppy disks that hold 360 KB of data. |
| 1983 | IBM introduces the XT computer with a 10-MB hard disk drive. MS-DOS 2.0 arrives; it features a tree-like structure and native support for hard disk drive operations. |
| 1984 | The first computer with an 80286 chip—the IBM AT—enters the market. It is a 6-MHz machine with a 20-MB hard disk drive and a high-density, 1.2-MB 5.25-inch floppy disk drive. Apple introduces the Macintosh computer, marking the first widespread use of the graphical user interface and mouse. |
| 1985 | MS-DOS 3.2, which supports networks, is released. |

*(continued)*

*(continued)*

| Year | Events |
|------|--------|
| 1986 | The first Intel 80386-based computer is introduced by Compaq; it features a 32-bit processor with expanded multitasking capability (even though no PC operating system yet fully supports the feature). |
| 1987 | MS-DOS 3.3 arrives, allowing use of 1.44-MB 3.5-inch floppy disk drives and hard disk drives larger than 32 MB. |
| 1988 | IBM introduces the PS/2 computer series. A complete departure from previous machines, its proprietary design does not support the hardware and software available on IBM PCs or clones. <br> Microsoft (with the help of IBM) develops OS/2 (Operating System 2), which allows 32-bit operations, genuine multitasking, and full MS-DOS compatibility. <br> Microsoft releases MS-DOS 4.0. |
| 1989 | Intel introduces the 80486 processor; it contains an on-board math coprocessor and an internal cache controller (offering 2.5 times the performance of a 386 processor with a supporting coprocessor). |
| 1991 | MS-DOS 5.0 offers a significantly improved DOS shell. |
| 1992 | The Intel i586 processor, the first Pentium, is introduced, offering 2.5 times the performance of a 486. <br> Microsoft introduces Windows 3.1, vastly expanding the use of a graphical user interface in the mass market. IBM expands OS/2. |
| 1993 | MS-DOS 6.0 arrives. The term "multimedia" (the inclusion of CD-ROM drives, sound cards, speakers, and so forth, as standard equipment on new personal computers) comes into use. |
| 1994 | Intel delivers the first 100-MHz processor. Compaq Computer Corporation becomes the largest producer of computers. |
| 1995 | Windows 95, code-named Chicago, is introduced by Microsoft. It features 32-bit architecture. <br> The Internet, having expanded far beyond its beginnings as a network serving government and university institutions, is now in everyday use by the rapidly growing proportion of the population with access to a modem. Computer prices drop as performance increases. IBM purchases Lotus (maker of the popular Lotus1-2-3 spreadsheet). |
| 1995–1996 | Software manufacturers scramble to make their products compatible with Windows 95. |
| 1997 | Microprocessor speeds exceed the 200-MHz mark. Hard disk drive and memory prices fall as basic system configuration sizes continue to increase. CD-ROM drives and Internet connections have become standard equipment for computers. |

*(continued)*

| Year | Events |
|------|--------|
| 1998 | PC performance continues to soar and prices continue to fall. Central processing unit (CPU) speeds exceed 450 MHz, and motherboard bus speeds reach 100 MHz. |
| | Entry-level machines are priced near the $500 mark. |
| | Universal serial bus (USB) is introduced. |
| | Windows 98 becomes the standard operating system for most new personal computers. Computer prices drop well under $1,000, increasing computer sales to the home market. |
| 1999 | Processor speeds exceed 1 gigahertz (GHz). E-commerce grows dramatically as the Internet expands. |
| 2000 | Microsoft releases Windows 2000 and the basic PC becomes a commodity item in discount stores. |
| | Broadband connections such as DSL and cable begin to take hold, making Internet access easier and faster than over the telephone line. |

## Lesson Summary

The following points summarize the main elements of this lesson:

- The concepts that form the basis of computer technology have a long history that stretches back 2500 years.

- Rudimentary, electrically powered computers were first developed in the 1950s and 1960s.

- The "standard" PC has undergone several stages of evolution, characterized by improvements to the processor, internal architecture, and types of storage devices.

# Lesson 2: The Role of a Computer Service Professional

As computers have evolved, so has the role of the computer technician. This lesson takes a look at the contemporary technician's role in maintaining and servicing computers.

### After this lesson, you will be able to

- Define your role as a modern computer technician

### Estimated lesson time: 5 minutes

Matching the rapid pace of change in the industry, the role of the computer professional is constantly changing, too. Not too many years ago, the only tools needed to repair a computer were a screwdriver, needle-nose pliers, the documentation for the computer, a boot disk with a few utilities, and a good MS-DOS reference manual. The screwdriver is still the standard repair tool, but the technician is confronted with a wider array of case types, motherboard designs, processor types, and operating systems—and a wider array of customer needs. Today's computer professional needs to be a technician, scholar, and diplomat rolled into one, as you can see by the table that follows.

| Title | Skills |
| --- | --- |
| Technician | You are able to troubleshoot and repair hardware and software efficiently and quickly. |
| Scholar | You have the wisdom and perseverance to seek answers to what you don't know and build your base of knowledge. Learning never stops. |
| Diplomat | You are able to instill in the user (your customer) the confidence that you are in control and can fix things, even when you are encountering problems for the first time. You are able to resolve the problem, even if your customer's (lack of) understanding of the computer might be part of that problem. |

## Lesson Summary

The following points summarize the main elements of this lesson:

- To be competent, the computer technician of today must master a variety of skills.

- Understanding how a computer functions and how the owner plans to use it are just as important to a technician as familiarity with parts and workbench tools.

# Chapter Summary

The following points summarize the key concepts in this chapter:

## The Development of the Computer

- The concepts that form the basis of computer technology have a long history that stretches back 2500 years.

- Modern computers have followed the growth and technology of the electronics industry.

## The Role of a Computer Service Professional

- The role of the computer technician has paralleled the evolution of the computer.

- A computer technician must combine troubleshooting and repair skills with on-the-job learning and customer support.

# Review

The following questions are intended to reinforce key information presented in this chapter. If you are unable to answer a question, review the appropriate lesson and then try the question again. Answers to the questions can be found in Appendix A, "Questions and Answers."

1. Give an example of an early electronic computer.

2. What are the three roles that today's computer service professional needs to assume?

C H A P T E R   2

# Understanding Electronic Communication

**Lesson 1:  Computer Communication** .......................... **12**

**Lesson 2:  The Computer Bus** ................................. **20**

**Chapter Summary** ........................................... **22**

**Review** ................................................... **23**

## About This Chapter

We normally think of communication as an act that involves people and activities like talking, writing, and reading. In this book, though, we are interested also with communication between computers and between people and computers. Communicating is the act of giving, transmitting, or exchanging information. In this chapter, we discuss how a computer processes data and communicates (transmits information) with its user. Understanding this process is fundamental to understanding how computers work.

## Before You Begin

There are no prerequisites for this chapter.

# Lesson 1:  Computer Communication

In this lesson, we examine the fundamentals of electronic communication and explore how computer communication differs from human communication.

## After this lesson, you will be able to

- Understand how a computer transmits and receives information
- Explain the principles of computer language

## Estimated lesson time: 20 minutes

## Early Forms of Communication

Humans communicate primarily through words, both spoken and written. From ancient times until about 150 years ago, messages were either verbal or written in form. Getting a message to a distant recipient was often slow, and sometimes the message (or the messenger) got lost in the process.

As time and technology progressed, people developed devices to help them communicate faster over greater distances. Items such as lanterns, mirrors, and flags were used to send messages quickly over an extended visual range.

All "out of earshot" communications have one thing in common: They require some type of "code" to convert human language to a form of information that can be packaged and sent to the remote location. It might be a set of letters in an alphabet, a series of analog pulses over a telephone line, or a sequence of binary numbers in a computer. On the receiving end, this code needs to be converted back to language that people can understand.

Obstacles to effective communications include differences in languages and in how the speaker and listener give meaning to words. Language between people is made up of more than words. Gestures, emphasis, body language, and social concepts have an impact on how we interpret interpersonal communications. Most of these elements have no bearing on human–machine interactions. There are other issues we must understand to be able deal and interact with computers.

### Dots and Dashes, Bits and Bytes

Telegraphs and early radio communication used codes for transmissions. The most common, Morse code (named after its creator, Samuel F. B. Morse), is based on assigning a series of pulses to represent each letter of the alphabet. These pulses are sent over a wire in a series. The operator on the receiving end converts the code back into letters and words. Morse code remained in official use for messages at sea almost until the end of the twentieth century—it was officially retired in late 1999.

Morse used a code in which any single transmitted value had two possible states: a dot or a dash. By combining the dots and dashes into groups, an operator was able to represent letters and, by stringing them together, words. That form of on–off notation can also be used to provide two numbers, 0 and 1. The value 0 represents no signal, or off, and the value 1 represents a signal, or on, state.

This type of number language is called *binary notation* because it uses only two digits, usually 0 and 1. It was first used by the ancient Chinese, who used the terms *yin* (empty) and *yang* (full) to build complex philosophical models of how the universe works.

Our computers are complex switch boxes that have two states and use a binary scheme. The value of a given switch's state—on or off—represents a value that can be used as a code. Modern computer technology uses terms other than yin and yang, but the same binary mathematics creates virtual worlds inside our modern machines.

# The Binary Language of Computers

The binary math terms that follow are fundamental to understanding PC technology.

## Bits

A *bit* is the smallest unit of information that is recognized by a computer: a single on or off event.

## Bytes

A *byte* is a group of 8 bits. A byte is required to represent one character of information. Pressing one key on a keyboard is equivalent to sending 1 byte of information to the computer's central processing unit (CPU). A byte is the standard unit by which memory is measured in a computer—values are expressed in terms of kilobytes (KB) or megabytes (MB). The table that follows lists units of computer memory and their values.

| Memory Unit | Value |
| --- | --- |
| Bit | Smallest unit of information; shorthand term for binary digit |
| Nibble | 4 bits (half of a byte) |
| Byte | 8 bits (equal to one character) |
| Word | 16 bits on most personal computers (longer words possible on larger computers) |
| Kilobyte (KB) | 1024 bytes |
| Megabyte (MB) | 1,048,576 bytes (approximately 1 million bytes or 1024 KB) |
| Gigabyte (GB) | 1,073,741,824 bytes (approximately 1 billion bytes or 1024 MB) |

## The Binary System

The binary system of numbers uses the base of 2 (0 and 1). As described earlier, a bit can exist in only two states, on or off. When bits are represented visually:

- 0 equals off.
- 1 equals on.

The following is 1 *byte* of information in which all 8 *bits* are set to 0. In the binary system, this sequence of eight 0s represents a single character—the number 0.

```
0     0     0     0     0     0     0     0
```

The binary system is one of several numerical systems that can be used for counting. It is similar to the decimal system, which we use to calculate everyday numbers and values. The prefix *dec* in the term *decimal system* comes from the Latin word for 10 and denotes a base of 10, which means the decimal system is based on the 10 numbers 0 through 9. The binary system has a base of 2, the numbers 0 and 1.

## Counting in Binary Notation

There are some similarities in counting with binary notation and the decimal system we all learned in grade school. In the decimal system, the rightmost whole number (the number to the left of the decimal point) is the "digits" column. Numbers written there have a value of 0 to 9. The number to the left of the digits column (if present) is valued from 10 to 90—the "10s" column. The factor of each additional row is 10 in the decimal system of notation. To get the total value of a number, we add together all columns in both systems: 111 is the sum of 100 + 10 + 1.

---

**Note**   A *factor* is an item that is multiplied in a multiplication problem. For example, 2 and 3 are factors in the problem 2 × 3.

---

Binary notation uses the same system of right-to-left columns of ascending values, but each row has only two (0 or 1) instead of 10 (0–9) possible values. Thus, in the binary system, the first row to the right can be only 0 or 1; the next row to the left can be 2 or 3 (if a number exists in that position). The columns that follow have values of 4, then 8, then 16, and so on, each column doubling the possible value of the one to its right. The factor used in the binary system is 2, and—just as in the decimal system—0 is a number counted in that tally. Examples of bytes of information (eight rows) follow.

## Byte—Example A

The value of this byte is 0 because all bits are off (0 = off).

```
0     0     0     0     0     0     0     0     8     bits
128   64    32    16    8     4     2     1     #     values
```

## Byte—Example B

In this example, two of the bits are turned on (1 = on). The total value of this byte is determined by adding the values associated with the bit positions that are on. This byte represents the number 5 (4 + 1).

```
0       0       0       0       0       1       0       1       8   bits
128     64      32      16      8       4       2       1       #   values
```

## Byte—Example C

In this example, two different bits are turned on to represent the number 9 (8 + 1).

```
0       0       0       0       1       0       0       1       8   bits
128     64      32      16      8       4       2       1       #   values
```

The mathematically inclined will quickly realize that 255 is the largest value that can be represented by a single byte. (Keep in mind that we start with 0 and go to 255, which corresponds to a possible 256 places on a number line.)

Because computers use binary numbers and humans use decimal numbers, A+ technicians must be able to perform simple conversions. The following table shows decimal numbers and their binary equivalents (0–9). You will need to know this information. The best way to prepare is to learn how to add in binary numbers rather than merely memorizing the values.

| Decimal Number | Binary Equivalent |
|---|---|
| 0 | 0000 |
| 1 | 0001 |
| 2 | 0010 |
| 3 | 0011 |
| 4 | 0100 |
| 5 | 0101 |
| 6 | 0110 |
| 7 | 0111 |
| 8 | 1000 |
| 9 | 1001 |

Numbers are fine for calculating, but today's computers must handle text, sound, streaming video, images, and animation as well. To handle all of that, standard codes are used to translate between binary machine language and the type of data being represented and presented to the human user. The binary system is still used to transfer values, but those values have a secondary meaning that is handled by the code. The first common, code-based language was developed to handle text characters and serves as a good example that lets us examine some other core concepts as well.

## Parallel and Serial Devices

The telegraph and the individual wires in our PCs are serial devices. This means that only one element of code can be sent at a time. Like a one-lane tunnel, there is only room for one person to pass through at one time. All electronic communications are—at some level—serial, because a single wire can have only two states: on or off.

To speed things up, we can add more wires. This allows simultaneous transmission of signals. Or, to continue our analogy, it's like adding another set of tunnels next to the first one: We still have only one person per tunnel, but we can get more people through because they are traveling in parallel. That is the difference between parallel and serial data transmission. In PC technology, we often string eight wires in a parallel set, allowing 8 bits to be sent at once. Figure 2.1 illustrates serial and parallel communication.

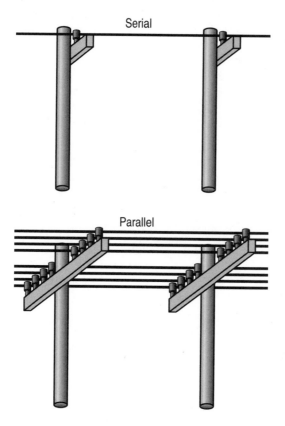

**Figure 2.1**   Serial and parallel communication

## ASCII Code

The standard code for handling text characters on most modern computers is
called *ASCII* (American Standard Code for Information Interchange). The basic
ASCII standard consists of 128 codes representing the English alphabet, punctuation, and certain control characters. Most systems today recognize 256 codes:
the original 128 and an additional 128 codes called the *extended character set.*

Remember that a byte represents one character of information; 4 bytes are
needed to represent a string of four characters. The following 4 bytes represent
the text string 12AB (using ASCII code):

```
00110001    00110010      01000001      01000010
1           2             A             B
```

The following illustrates how the binary language spells the word *binary*:

```
B           I           N           A           R           Y
01000010    01001001    01001110    01000001    01010010    01011001
```

---

**Note**   It is very important to understand that in computer processing, the "space"
is a significant character. All items in a code must be set out for the machine to
process. Like any other character, the space has a binary value that must be included in the data stream. In computing, the absence or presence of a space is
critical and sometimes causes confusion or frustration among new users. Uppercase and lowercase letters also have different values. Some operating systems
(for example, UNIX) distinguish between them for commands, whereas others
(for example, MS-DOS) translate the uppercase and lowercase into the same
word no matter how it is cased.

---

The following table is a partial representation of the ASCII character set. Even in
present-day computing, laden with multimedia and sophisticated programming,
ASCII retains an honored and important position.

| Symbol | Binary 1 Byte | Decimal | Symbol | Binary 1 Byte | Decimal |
|--------|---------------|---------|--------|---------------|---------|
| 0 | 00110000 | 48 | V | 01010110 | 86 |
| 1 | 00110001 | 49 | W | 01010111 | 87 |
| 2 | 00110010 | 50 | X | 01011000 | 88 |
| 3 | 00110011 | 51 | Y | 01011001 | 89 |
| 4 | 00110100 | 52 | Z | 01011010 | 90 |
| 5 | 00110101 | 53 | a | 01100001 | 97 |
| 6 | 00110110 | 54 | b | 01100010 | 98 |
| 7 | 00110111 | 55 | c | 01100011 | 99 |
| 8 | 00111000 | 56 | d | 01100100 | 100 |
| 9 | 00111001 | 57 | e | 01100101 | 101 |
| A | 01000001 | 65 | f | 01100110 | 102 |
| B | 01000010 | 66 | g | 01100111 | 103 |
| C | 01000011 | 67 | h | 01101000 | 104 |
| D | 01000100 | 68 | i | 01101001 | 105 |
| E | 01000101 | 69 | j | 01101010 | 106 |
| F | 01000110 | 70 | k | 01101011 | 107 |
| G | 01000111 | 71 | l | 01101100 | 108 |
| H | 01001000 | 72 | m | 01101101 | 109 |
| I | 01001001 | 73 | n | 01101110 | 110 |
| J | 01001010 | 74 | o | 01101111 | 111 |
| K | 01001011 | 75 | p | 01110000 | 112 |
| L | 01001100 | 76 | q | 01110001 | 113 |
| M | 01001101 | 77 | r | 01110010 | 114 |
| N | 01001110 | 78 | s | 01110011 | 115 |
| O | 01001111 | 79 | t | 01110100 | 116 |
| P | 01010000 | 80 | u | 01110101 | 117 |
| Q | 01010001 | 81 | v | 01110110 | 118 |
| R | 01010010 | 82 | w | 01110111 | 119 |
| S | 01010011 | 83 | x | 01111000 | 120 |
| T | 01010100 | 84 | y | 01111001 | 121 |
| U | 01010101 | 85 | z | 01111010 | 122 |

**Note** All letters have a separate ASCII value for uppercase and lowercase. The capital letter "A" is 65, and the lowercase "a" is 97.

Keep in mind that computers are machines, and they do not really "perceive" numbers as anything other than electrical charges setting a switch on or off. Like binary numbers, electrical charges can exist in only two states—positive or negative. Computers interpret the presence of a charge as 1 and the absence of a charge as 0. This technology allows a computer to process information.

## Lesson Summary

The following points summarize the main elements of this lesson:

- Computers communicate using binary language.

- A bit is the smallest unit of information that is recognized by a computer.

- ASCII is the standard code that handles text characters for computers.

# Lesson 2:  The Computer Bus

This lesson discusses the set of hardware lines, or conductors, by which data is transferred internally in the components of a computer system.

### After this lesson, you will be able to

- Understand the concept of an electronic bus

### Estimated lesson time: 5 minutes

For efficient use of system resources, most communications within a computer need to occur at a much quicker rate than processing signals one at a time would allow. Therefore, the computer moves information through a *bus*. Several types of buses are used within a computer, and they are discussed more fully in later chapters. For now, let's simply look at what a bus is and how it works.

A bus is a group of electrical conductors—usually wires—running parallel to one another that can carry a charge from one point to another. These conductors can be copper traces on a circuit board or wires in a cable. Usually, they are found in multiples of eight (8, 16, 32, 64, and so on). Early computers used eight conductors for the main system bus, thereby allowing the transmission of 8 bits, or 1 byte, of information at a time. Figure 2.2 illustrates an 8-bit and a 16-bit bus.

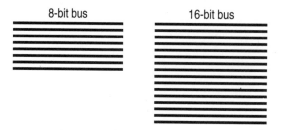

**Figure 2.2**   Computer bus

The physical configuration of a bus isn't as important as its function. A bus provides a common path along which to transmit information in the form of code. It allows any device to receive information from or send information to any other device on the same bus. This is not unlike the telegraph system, in which a single wire was strung from one end of the country to the other. Any town that tapped into the wire could exchange information with any other town also connected to the wire.

Another familiar example of a bus system is the electrical wiring in a home or office. The 110-volt AC outlets are wired with three wires—hot, neutral, and ground—that run in parallel from one outlet to another. Each time a device is plugged in, it is connected to the bus, in parallel (see Figure 2.3).

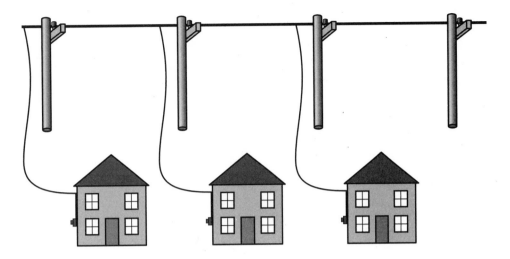

**Figure 2.3**  Connecting to a bus

Remember, in a computer, a bus is a set of parallel wires or lines to which the CPU, the memory, and all input/output devices are connected. Everything in a computer is connected to a bus. The actual number of wires, or lines, in a bus can vary from one computer to another or even from one part of a computer to another. The bus contains one line for each bit needed to give the address of a device or a location in memory. It also contains one line for each bit of data being transmitted from device to device.

A manufacturer might also use additional lines for power or other communication within the computer. When we speak of buses within a computer (data bus, expansion bus, or address bus), we are speaking of a specific number of wires dedicated to a specific purpose—connecting parts of the computer to each other for the exchange of data between components.

## Lesson Summary

The following points summarize the main elements of this lesson:

- A bus is the physical means by which data is made to move inside a computer.

- A bus can take on many different shapes (wires, flat cables, circuit traces), but it is basically a group of parallel wires.

# Chapter Summary

The following points summarize the key concepts in this chapter:

## Computer Communication

- Computers communicate using binary language.
- An A+ technician must be able to convert decimal numbers to binary and binary numbers to decimal.
- ASCII is the standard code that handles text characters for computers.

## The Computer Bus

- A computer uses a bus to move data from one device to another.

# Review

The following questions are intended to reinforce key information presented in this chapter. If you are unable to answer a question, review the appropriate lesson and then try the question again. Answers to the questions can be found in Appendix A, "Questions and Answers."

1. What is the definition of a bus in a computer?

2. What is the purpose of the computer bus?

3. Define the term *decimal*.

4. Describe the difference between serial and parallel communication.

5. What is binary code language?

6. How does ASCII use binary code to represent numbers or characters?

7. Define a bit.

8. Define a byte.

9. Which decimal number does the following binary number represent: 00001001?

10. What do 1s and 0s represent in computer operation?

11. Computer buses are usually made of multiples of _____ wires or traces.

C H A P T E R   3

# An Overview of the Personal Computer

**Lesson 1:  The Three Stages of Computing** . . . . . . . . . . . . . . . . . . . . . . 26

**Lesson 2:  Components of a Computer** . . . . . . . . . . . . . . . . . . . . . . . . 29

**Lesson 3:  Support Hardware** . . . . . . . . . . . . . . . . . . . . . . . . . . . . . 35

**Chapter Summary** . . . . . . . . . . . . . . . . . . . . . . . . . . . . . . . . . . . 37

**Review** . . . . . . . . . . . . . . . . . . . . . . . . . . . . . . . . . . . . . . . . . . 38

## About This Chapter

In this chapter, we expand on the material in the preceding chapters with an explanation of the Input/Process/Output (I/P/O) model and see how it can be used to help us understand the functional design of the personal computer (PC). We go on to define the hardware components that a computer professional can expect to encounter every day—the computer parts that you actually touch.

## Before You Begin

If possible, while you work through this chapter, have a PC at hand with its case open. Take a look at each piece of hardware and try to identify its function as you go over this material.

# Lesson 1:  The Three Stages of Computing

In this lesson, we discuss the three stages of computing and how they relate to the constituent parts that make up the modern PC.

---

### After this lesson, you will be able to

- Describe the three stages of computing

### Estimated lesson time: 5 minutes

---

A modern computer looks like a complicated device. On one level this is true, and it is the beneficiary of much development in electronics technology. It is constructed of many hardware components connected with what seem to be miles of interwoven wires. Despite this apparent complexity, however, a computer, just like a calculator, handles information in three stages: *input*, *processing*, and *output* (see Figure 3.1). Each piece of hardware can be classified as working in one (and sometimes two) of these three stages. We can also use these three stages to classify any aspect of a computer's operation or the function of any of its components. During the troubleshooting phase of a repair job, it is often useful to categorize a problem according to which of the three stages it occurs in.

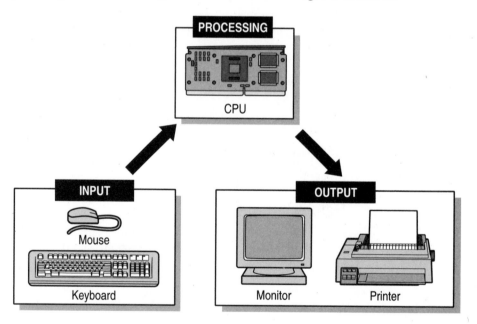

**Figure 3.1**  Three stages of computing

# Input

*Input* is the first stage of computing, referring to any means that moves data (information) from the outside world into the processor—or from one component of the computer to another. Today's PC can support a wide variety of input devices. Keyboards, mouse devices, voice recognition devices, sound cards, modems, scanners, tape drives, CD/DVD drives, and digital cameras are some of the most common.

# Processing

*Processing* is the second stage of computing. This is the actual manipulation of data by the computer. Processing on early computers involved the tedious task of "number crunching" and then, later, storing large amounts of often-redundant data. Today, computers process an ever-expanding list of activities, including scientific and business tasks, as well as processing information for education, entertainment, organization, and much more. Computer processing technology also hides in many everyday appliances. Microprocessors run most of our mechanical and electronic devices including cars, cameras, VCRs, microwave ovens, telephones, and even supermarket checkout systems.

# Output

*Output* is the third stage of computing. All the input and processing in the world won't do us any good unless we can get the information back from the computer in a comprehensible and usable form. Output devices today come in many forms: monitors, printers, fax machines, modems, plotters, CD-Rs, sound cards, and more.

# Input, Processing, and Output

Whenever you sit down at a computer and run an application—whether it is a game, spreadsheet, database, or word processor—you are an active part of the input, processing, and output operation of that computer. The following table provides some examples.

| Application | Function |
|---|---|
| Word processor | Input: Typing your words<br>Processing: Formatting the text (such as word wrap and fonts)<br>Output: Storing the text and allowing you to retrieve or print it |
| Spreadsheet | Input: Typing or providing numbers (such as sales figures)<br>Processing: Applying one or more formulas to the data<br>Output: Displaying the results of the calculation in numeric or graphical form |
| Database | Input: Typing information into a data form<br>Processing: Indexing and storing the data records<br>Output: Producing reports showing selected data records |
| Game | Input: Moving your chess piece<br>Processing: Computer calculating how to respond to your move<br>Output: Computer making a move |

Keep in mind that this is a short list focusing on human interaction with the machine. The PC often takes information for its own components and processes that data for internal use, as when a drive is accessed or a display adapter sends signals to the monitor.

## Lesson Summary

The following points summarize the main elements of this lesson:

- All computer hardware can be classified according to its primary function: input, processing, or output.

- Any time you sit down at a computer and run an application, you are using the input, processing, and output stages of computing.

# Lesson 2:  Components of a Computer

In this lesson, we take a look at the different components of a computer system.

## After this lesson, you will be able to

- Define the primary components that make up a computer

## Estimated lesson time: 10 minutes

As you might expect, the components of a computer reflect the function of the machine—specifically, the three stages of computing, as outlined in Lesson 1. Let's examine the components.

## Input

The following table lists some examples of devices that are used to put information into a computer.

| | Device | Description |
|---|---|---|
| | Keyboard | The primary input device for a computer, allowing users to type information just as they once did on a typewriter. |
| | Mouse | Used with graphical interface environments to point to and select objects on the system's monitor. Can be purchased in a variety of sizes, shapes, and configurations. |
| | Scanner | Converts printed or photographic information to digital information that can be used by the computer. Works similar to the scanning process of a photocopy machine. |

*(continued)*

*(continued)*

| | Device | Description |
|---|---|---|
| | Microphone | Works like the microphone on a tape recorder. Allows input of voice or music to be converted to digital information and saved to a file. |
| | CD-ROM /DVD drive | Compact disc–read only memory: stores large amounts of data on a CD that can be read by a computer. |

## Processing

The central processing unit (CPU) is the heart and brain of the computer. This one component, or "chip," is responsible for all primary number crunching and data management. It is truly the centerpiece of any computer. It is so important that whole generations of computer technology are based and measured on each "new and improved" version of the CPU.

When we refer to the CPU, we are usually speaking of the processor. However, the CPU requires several other components that support it with the management of data to operate. These components, when working in harmony, make up the primary elements of the PC we know today. The following table lists these fundamental support components.

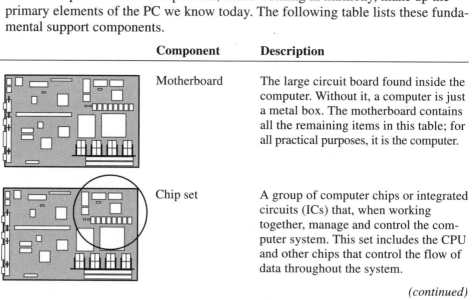

| | Component | Description |
|---|---|---|
| | Motherboard | The large circuit board found inside the computer. Without it, a computer is just a metal box. The motherboard contains all the remaining items in this table; for all practical purposes, it is the computer. |
| | Chip set | A group of computer chips or integrated circuits (ICs) that, when working together, manage and control the computer system. This set includes the CPU and other chips that control the flow of data throughout the system. |

*(continued)*

*(continued)*

| | Component | Description |
|---|---|---|
| 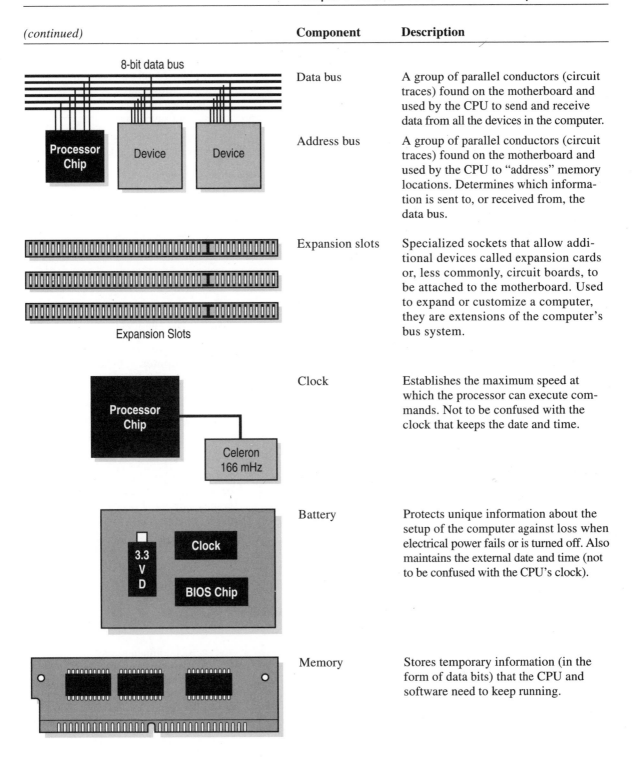 | Data bus | A group of parallel conductors (circuit traces) found on the motherboard and used by the CPU to send and receive data from all the devices in the computer. |
| | Address bus | A group of parallel conductors (circuit traces) found on the motherboard and used by the CPU to "address" memory locations. Determines which information is sent to, or received from, the data bus. |
| | Expansion slots | Specialized sockets that allow additional devices called expansion cards or, less commonly, circuit boards, to be attached to the motherboard. Used to expand or customize a computer, they are extensions of the computer's bus system. |
| | Clock | Establishes the maximum speed at which the processor can execute commands. Not to be confused with the clock that keeps the date and time. |
| | Battery | Protects unique information about the setup of the computer against loss when electrical power fails or is turned off. Also maintains the external date and time (not to be confused with the CPU's clock). |
| | Memory | Stores temporary information (in the form of data bits) that the CPU and software need to keep running. |

8-bit data bus

Processor Chip    Device    Device

Expansion Slots

Processor Chip

Celeron 166 mHz

3.3 V D    Clock    BIOS Chip

## Output

The following table lists some common devices, known as *peripherals*, used exclusively for output.

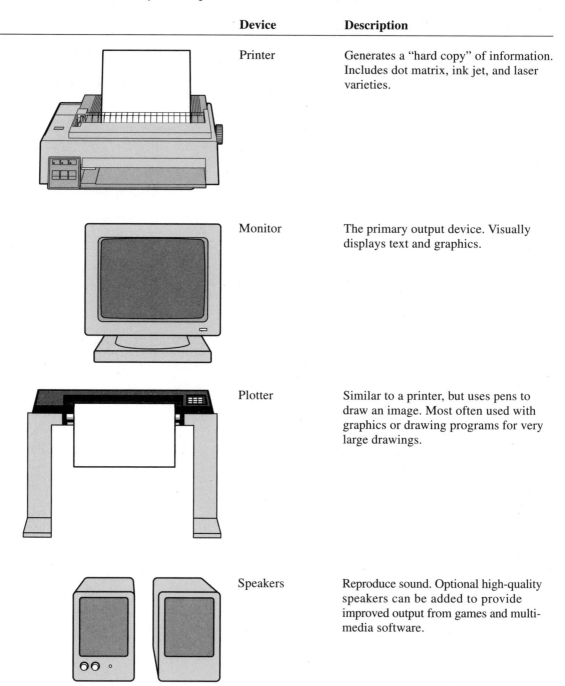

| | Device | Description |
|---|---|---|
| | Printer | Generates a "hard copy" of information. Includes dot matrix, ink jet, and laser varieties. |
| | Monitor | The primary output device. Visually displays text and graphics. |
| | Plotter | Similar to a printer, but uses pens to draw an image. Most often used with graphics or drawing programs for very large drawings. |
| | Speakers | Reproduce sound. Optional high-quality speakers can be added to provide improved output from games and multi-media software. |

## Input and Output

Some devices handle both input and output functions. These devices are called *input/output (I/O)* devices, a term you will encounter quite often.

| Device | Description |
| --- | --- |
| Floppy disk drive | Mechanism for reading and writing to low-capacity, removable, magnetic disks. Used to store and easily transport information. |
| Hard disk drive | High-capacity internal (and sometimes external) magnetic disks for storing data and program files. Also called fixed disks. |
| Modem | Converts computer data to information that can be transmitted over telephone wires and cable lines. Allows communication between computers over long and short distances. |
| Network card | An expansion card that allows several computers to connect to each other and share information and programs. Also called network interface card (NIC). |

*(continued)*

| (*continued*) | Component | Description |
|---|---|---|
| | CD recorder | Also called CD-R. You can copy data to a CD with this device, but you can only write to a section of the disc once. Variations on this type of device include compact disc–rewritable (CD-RW) drives. These drives allow you to read, write, and overwrite a special CD-ROM-type disc. |
| | Tape drive | Large-capacity, magnetic, data storage devices. Ideal for backup and retrieval of large amounts of data. Works like a tape recorder and saves information in a linear format. |

Other external storage devices include Iomega Zip drives, which allow users to store 100 MB or 250 MB of data on a single Zip disk.

## Lesson Summary

The following points summarize the main elements of this lesson:

- All computer hardware can be classified by primary function (input, processing, or output).

- Some hardware devices combine multiple functions (input and output).

# Lesson 3:  Support Hardware

Lesson 2 covered the basic hardware that makes up a computer. There are, however, additional components needed to support safe computer operation. In this lesson, we look at several devices that protect and enhance the value of a computer.

## After this lesson, you will be able to

- Identify additional support hardware for a computer
- Understand the functions of some of the add-on hardware

## Estimated lesson time: 5 minutes

In addition to the devices that support a computer's data-processing functions, there are others that enhance its operation and performance. The following table lists some of these devices.

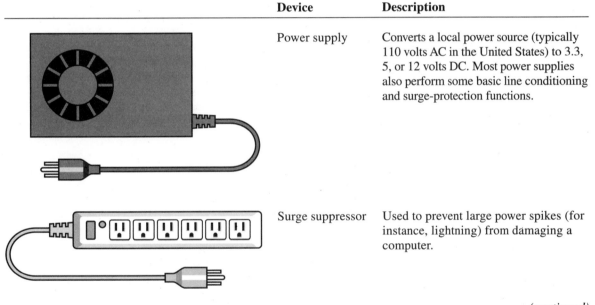

| Device | Description |
| --- | --- |
| Power supply | Converts a local power source (typically 110 volts AC in the United States) to 3.3, 5, or 12 volts DC. Most power supplies also perform some basic line conditioning and surge-protection functions. |
| Surge suppressor | Used to prevent large power spikes (for instance, lightning) from damaging a computer. |

*(continued)*

| (continued) | Device | Description |
|---|---|---|
| | UPS | Uninterruptible power supply. Acts as both a surge suppresser (to prevent high-power spikes) and a power leveler to provide the computer with a constant source of power. Can even provide power during a power failure or inter-ruption (although the duration depends on the UPS and the computer's power consumption) so that the user can safely save data before shutting down. |
| | Case | The box that houses most of the system must provide an environment that mini-mizes electrical interference to other electronic devices in the area. It should provide a proper heat level for safe operation and bays and connections for drives, circuit boards, and I/O devices. |

Don't let the term *support hardware* lead you to underestimate the importance of these components. How important are roads to commerce, or water to a city? Without a reliable power source, modern PCs would not exist. The internal power supply keeps a clean current running to the system.

## Lesson Summary

The following points summarize the main elements of this lesson:

- Support equipment protects a computer or makes it easier to operate.
- Support equipment, such as the power supply, is critical to the operation of the computer.

# Chapter Summary

The following points summarize the key concepts in this chapter:

### The Three Stages of Computing

- Computing occurs in three stages: input, processing, and output.
- All computer hardware can be classified in one or more of these stages.

### Components of a Computer

- An input device retrieves data from an outside source and brings it into the computer for processing.
- A processing device takes information and alters it in some useful manner.
- An output device takes the altered information and stores or displays it.

### Support Hardware

- Computers require additional components to protect operations and ensure optimal performance.
- Use of surge suppressors and UPSs can protect computers from damage caused by power spikes and surges.

# Review

The following questions are intended to reinforce key information presented in this chapter. If you are unable to answer a question, review the appropriate lesson and then try the question again. Answers to the questions can be found in Appendix A, "Questions and Answers."

1. Describe the three stages of computing and the role of each.

2. What is the purpose of the central processing unit (CPU)?

3. Describe two devices that process information inside a computer.

4. What is a chip set?

5. Name and describe three input devices.

6. What type of device is a scanner?

7. Describe three output devices.

8. What is I/O?

9. Name three I/O devices.

CHAPTER 4

# The Central Processing Unit

**Lesson 1: Microprocessors** ................................... **40**

**Lesson 2: Replacing and Upgrading a CPU** ...................... **68**

**Chapter Summary** ........................................... **73**

**Review** ................................................... **74**

## About This Chapter

This chapter presents an overview of the CPU (central processing unit), which functions as the "brain" of the personal computer. Like the human brain, a CPU is a complicated, highly integrated component performing many simultaneous functions. Understanding the principles that underlie the workings of the microprocessor is critical to understanding the computer and its operation.

## Before You Begin

You should be familiar with the terms and concepts introduced in Chapter 1, "Introduction to Computers," and Chapter 2, "Understanding Electronic Communication."

# Lesson 1: Microprocessors

A *microprocessor* is an integrated circuit (IC) that contains a complete CPU on a single chip. In this lesson, we examine the microprocessor from its inception to the current state-of-the-art chip. It is important for a computer technician to understand the development of the processor and what makes each version different from its predecessors. This knowledge gives us an understanding of the enhancements each new design offers over earlier ones and how the system components can take advantage of the new features.

---

### After this lesson, you will be able to

- Describe how a microprocessor works
- Define different types of processors and describe their advantages and limitations

### Estimated lesson time: 40 minutes

---

Fortunately, computer technicians aren't required to design microprocessors, only to understand how they work. Microprocessors can be viewed as little black boxes that provide answers or perform a variety of chores on command. We also need to understand the external data bus because it is the means by which the CPU accesses system resources.

## The External Data Bus

In previous lessons, you learned that information is transmitted throughout a computer using binary code traveling through a bus. The *external data bus* (also known as the external bus or simply data bus) is the primary route for data in a PC (personal computer). All data-handling components or optional data devices are connected to it; therefore, any information (code) placed on that bus is available to all devices connected to the computer.

As mentioned in Chapter 1, "Introduction to Computers," early computers used eight conductors (an 8-bit data bus), which allowed for the transfer of 1 byte of information at a time. As computers evolved, the width of the external data bus increased to 16, 32, and the current width of 64 conductors. The wider bus lets more data flow at the same time, just as adding more lanes to a highway allows more cars to move through a point in a given amount of time.

Figure 4.1 shows a Pentium II CPU attached to its motherboard. The motherboard is the main circuit board, which contains the external data bus and connection for expansion devices that are not part of the board's basic design. Expansion slots act as "on ramps" to the external bus. Expansion cards, once commonly known as daughter cards, are placed in slots on the motherboard. Other forms of on ramps are the slots that hold memory or the sets of pins used to attach drive cables. Connectors on the motherboard grant access to the data bus for keyboards, mouse devices, and peripheral devices like modems and printers through the use of COM and LPT ports.

**Figure 4.1**    Motherboard

To understand how a computer moves data between components, visualize each device on the data bus (including the CPU) connected to the bus by means of a collection of on–off switches. By assessing which conductors have power and which ones do not, the device can read the data as it is sent by another device. The on–off state of a line gives the value of 0 (off) or 1 (on). The wires spell out a code of binary numbers that the computer interprets and then routes to another system component or to the user by means of an output device such as a monitor or printer. Communication occurs when voltage is properly applied to or read from any of the conductors by the system. Figure 4.2 illustrates a data bus connected to a CPU and a device.

Coded messages can be sent into or out of any device connected to the external data bus. Think of the data bus as a large highway with parallel lanes. Extending that analogy, bits are like cars traveling side by side—each carries part of a coded

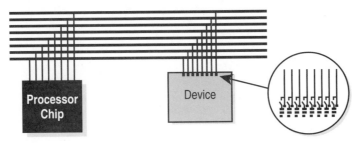

**Figure 4.2**    External data bus

message. Microprocessors are used to turn the coded messages into data that performs a meaningful task for the computer's user.

---

**Note**    All hardware that uses data is connected in some way to the data bus or to another device that is connected to the data bus.

---

## The CPU

The CPU is the part of a computer in which arithmetic and logical operations are performed and instructions are decoded and executed. The CPU controls the operation of the computer. Early PCs used several chips to handle the task. Some functions are still handled by support chips, which are often referred to collectively as *chip set.* Figure 4.3 shows a close-up of the working portion of a CPU.

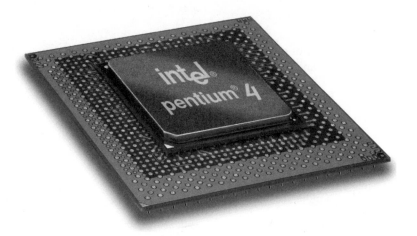

**Figure 4.3**   Close up of a CPU

Although it is not necessary to know exactly what goes on inside the processor, learning a few terms that you will encounter as a computer professional will help you in the discussion that follows.

### Transistors

*Transistors,* the main components of microprocessors, are small, electronic switches. The on–off positions of the transistors form the binary codes discussed earlier in this lesson. Although transistors might seem simple, their development required many years of painstaking research. Before transistors were available, computers relied on slow, inefficient vacuum tubes and mechanical switches to process information. The first large-scale computers took up a huge amount of space, and technicians actually went inside them to "program" by turning on and off specific tubes!

Many materials, including most metals, allow electrical current to flow through them; these are known as electrical conductors. Materials that don't pass electrical current are called insulators. Pure silicon, which is used to make most transistors, is a *semiconductor*; its degree of conductivity can be adjusted, or modulated, by adding impurities during production.

Transistor switches have three terminals: the source, the gate, and the drain. When positive voltage is applied to the gate, electrons are attracted, forming an electron channel between the source and the drain. Positive voltage applied to the drain pulls electrons from the source to the drain, turning the transistor on. Removing the voltage turns it off by breaking the pathway.

In the late 1950s, a major development in transistor technology took place. A team of engineers put two transistors on a silicon wafer, creating the world's first IC and paving the way for the development of compact computers.

## Integrated Circuits

An IC is an electronic device consisting of a number of miniature transistors and other circuit elements (resistors and capacitors, for instance). An IC functions just as a large collection of these parts would, but it is a fraction of the size and uses a fraction of the power. ICs make today's microelectronics possible. The original transistors were small plastic boxes about the size of a peanut that could handle only one function. The word *integrated* denotes that IC devices combine many circuits—and some of their functions—into one package. A prime example of this technology is the microprocessor.

## Microprocessors

On November 15, 1971, Intel shipped the commercial microprocessor Model 4004. It ran a product called the Busicom calculator. The 108-KHz 4004 had 2300 transistors and a 4-bit data bus and could address 640 bytes of RAM. Computer engineers quickly took advantage of the potential this new type of chip offered, leading the way to the first personal computers.

A year later, the Intel 8008 appeared. *Radio Electronics Magazine* reported that hobbyist Don Lancaster used an 8008 to build what was considered the first personal computer. The article called it a "TV typewriter."

The Intel 8080 appeared in 1974. It sold then for $400 and now sells for about $1. It powered traffic lights, but of more interest to our discussion, it formed the core of the Altair computer of 1975. It was sold in kit form for $395 and was named for a world in the *Star Trek* TV series. Figure 4.4 shows a picture of the 8080 die. By today's standards, it was very weak: 6000 transistors, an 8-bit bus, and a 2-MHz clock speed. It could address 64 K of RAM (random access memory), and users programmed the Altair by throwing manual switches located on the case.

**Figure 4.4**   The Intel 8080 microprocessor

## Microprocessor Design

Before going further into the history of microprocessor development, it is important to discuss in general terms how microprocessors operate. Microprocessors are usually divided into three subsystems: the control unit (CU), the arithmetic logic unit (ALU), and the input/output (I/O) unit. The term *CPU* is used to denote a combined CU and ALU, contained in a single package.

The advent of the CU marked a radical improvement in processor design, allowing CPU operations to be based in part on code provided by an external program like a BIOS (basic input/output system). This extended the ability of a PC to use new hardware components that were not part of the original design.

The ALU is just what its name implies—the part of the IC that handles the basic math functions of computation. The I/O unit fetches data from the outside and passes data back to the external bus.

## Registers

*Registers* are temporary memory storage areas used during data manipulation. Physically, registers are rows of microscopic switches that are set on or off. Each row forms a binary number: off = 0 and on = 1. Hence (reading from right to left) off.off.on equals the number 1. Off.on.on equals the number three (0 + 2 + 1). The CPU uses registers, like scratch pads, to hold data while it works on a task. Changes in data during an operation are also stored in a register, then sent out to other components as the job is finished. The number and width of a register vary from one type of machine to another. The wider the register, the more bits the machine can handle at one time—just as with the width of the external bus. As register width moved from 4 to 8 to 16 to 32 to 64 to 128 bits, PCs increased in performance.

## Codes

Computers use various binary-based codes to represent information. In Chapter 2, "Understanding Electronic Communication," we saw how ASCII (American Standard Code for Information Interchange) code is a binary representation of characters on a keyboard. These codes are sent on the external data bus by a system component to be read by other devices. When you press a key on a PC keyboard, an ASCII code is generated and sent over the data bus. Transferring information to and from the CPU (and other hardware) is only the first step in manipulating data.

Other codes tell the PC how to display data on the monitor, talk to devices such as printers, and take in data streams from scanners. Each of those operations requires system resources and the manipulation of binary numbers.

In addition to the code that requires data, special *machine code* is required for the CPU to turn the string of numbers into something useful to an application. As with the data code, this machine code is sent in the form of binary numbers on the data bus. The CPUs in turn are different enough that a code system must be written specifically for each of them.

## The Clock

Timing is essential in PC operations. Without some means of synchronization, chaos would ensue. Timing allows the electronic devices in the computer to coordinate and execute all internal commands in the proper order.

Placing a special conductor in the CPU and pulsing it with voltage creates timing. Each pulse of voltage received by this conductor is called a *clock cycle*. All the switching activity in the computer occurs while the clock is sending a pulse. This process somewhat resembles several musicians using a metronome to synchronize their playing, with all the violinists moving their bows at the same time. Thanks to this synchronization, you get musical phrasing instead of a jumble of notes.

Virtually every computer command needs at least two clock cycles. Some commands might require hundreds of clock cycles to process. Figure 4.5 shows an external data bus with a CPU and two devices. Notice that the crystal or clock is attached to the CPU to generate the timing.

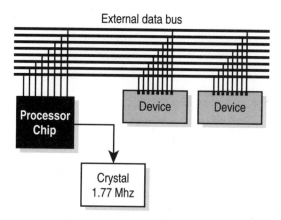

**Figure 4.5**  CPU with clock

## Clock Speed

It is common for computers to be marketed to consumers based on features that show off their best points. One main selling point is the system clock rate, which is measured in megahertz (MHz), or millions of cycles per second. The clock rate suggests how many commands can be completed in two cycles (the minimum time required to execute a command). The process of adding two numbers together would take about four commands (eight clock cycles). A computer running at 450 MHz can do about 44 million simple calculations per second.

Clock speed is determined by the CPU manufacturer and represents the fastest speed at which the CPU can be reliably operated. The Intel 8088 processor, as used in the original IBM PC, had a clock speed of 4.77 MHz. Today's processors have clock speeds that run up to and, in some cases, exceed 750 MHz.

**Note**   Remember that this speed is the CPU's maximum speed. If you place too many clock cycles on a CPU, it can fail or overheat and stop working.

The system crystal determines the speed at which a CPU operates. The system crystal is usually a quartz oscillator, very similar to the one in a wristwatch. You can find the system crystal soldered to the motherboard. Look for a silver part, usually with a label that indicates the crystal speed.

**Important**   A computer has two clocks: one to set the speed and timing and a second clock to keep time for date and time calculations. They are two entirely different devices.

# Memory

The CPU can only hold a limited amount of information. To compensate, additional chips are installed in the computer for the sole purpose of temporarily storing information that the CPU needs. These chips are called *RAM* (random access memory). The term *random access* is used because the CPU can place or retrieve bytes of information in or from any RAM *location* at any time. RAM is explored in greater detail in Chapter 7, "Memory."

## Address Bus

The word *location* is italicized in the last paragraph to underscore the importance of location in PC memory operations. The content of RAM is constantly changing as programs and the computer itself use portions of it to note, calculate, and hold results of actions. It is essential for the system to know what memory is assigned to which task and when that memory is free for a new use. To do so, the system has to have a way to address segments of memory and to quickly change the holdings in that position. The portion of the PC assigned this task is the *address bus*.

Think of the address bus as a large virtual table in which the columns are individual bits (like letters) and each row contains a string of bits (making up a word). The actual lengths of these words will vary depending on the number of bits the address bus can handle in a single pass. Figure 4.6 shows a table containing 1s and 0s. Each segment is given an address, just like the one that identifies a home or post office box. The system uses this address to send data to or retrieve data from memory.

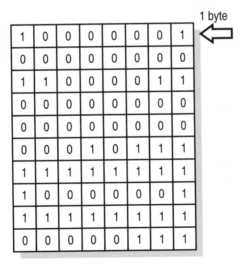

**Figure 4.6**    Memory spreadsheet

Like all the other buses in a PC, the address bus is a collection of conductors. It links the physical memory to the system and moves signals as memory is used. The number of conductors in the address bus determines the maximum amount of memory that can be used (memory that is *addressable*) by the CPU. Remember that computers count in binary notation. Each binary digit—in this case, a conductor—that is added to the left will double the number of possible combinations.

Early data buses used eight conductors and, therefore, 256 ($2^8$) combinations of code, where possible. The maximum number of patterns a system can generate determines how much RAM the data bus can address. The 8088 used 20 address conductors and could address up to 1,048,576 bytes of memory locations, or $2^{20}$. Today's PCs can address a lot more than that, and, in many cases, the actual limiting factor is not the number of patterns, but the capacity of the motherboard to socket memory chips. In all cases, the total amount of memory is the factor of $2^X$, where $X$ = the number of connectors.

The CPU does not directly connect to the memory bus, but sends requests and obtains results using the system's memory controller. This circuitry acts as both postmaster and translator, providing the proper strings of data in the right order, at the right time, and in a form the CPU can use. As mentioned before, any write or read action will require at least two clock cycles to execute. (It can require more clock cycles on systems that do not have memory tuned to the maximum system clock speed. In that case, the PC will have to use additional clock cycles while it waits for the memory to be ready for the next part of the operation.)

Figure 4.7 shows a diagram of the process with the CPU and RAM stack on the external data bus. The address bus is connected to the memory controller. It fetches and places data in memory.

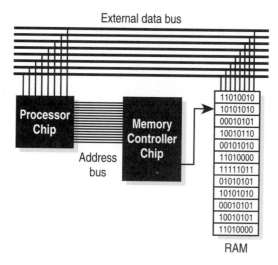

**Figure 4.7** CPU and RAM

## How Microprocessors Work

Current CPUs, such as the Intel Pentium III, are collections of millions of switches and bus pathways. They operate all kinds of machines, in addition to PCs, and are found in cameras, cars, microwave ovens, and TVs, among other things. Here, however, we are interested only in how they work inside a PC. Let's look at a simple task: adding two numbers such as 2 and 2 together and obtaining their sum (2 + 2 = 4). The CPU can do math problems very quickly, but it requires several very quick steps to do it. Knowing how a CPU performs a simple task will help you understand how developments in PC design have improved PC performance.

When the user pushes a number key (in a program like Calculator, which can add numbers), the keystroke causes the microprocessor's prefetch unit to ask for instructions on what to do with the new data. The data is sent through the address bus to the PC's RAM and is placed in the instruction cache, with a reference code (let's call it 2 = a).

The prefetch unit obtains a copy of the code and sends it to the decode unit, where it is translated into a string of binary code and routed to the CU and the data cache to tell them what to do with the instruction. The CU sends it to an address called X in the data cache to await the next part of the process.

When the plus (+) key is pressed, the prefetch unit again asks the instruction cache for instructions about what to do with the new data. The prefetch unit translates the code and passes it to the CU and data cache, which alerts the ALU that an ADD function will be carried out. The process is repeated when the user presses the 2 key.

Next (yes, there's still more to do), the CU takes the code and sends the actual ADD command to the ALU. The ALU sums a and b are added together after they have been sent up from the data cache. The ALU sends the code for 4 to be stored in an address register.

Pressing the equal sign (=) key is the last act the user must execute before getting the answer, but the computer still has a good bit of work ahead of it. The prefetch unit checks the instruction cache for help in dealing with the new keystroke. The resulting instruction is stored, and a copy of the code is sent to the decode unit for processing. There, the instruction is translated into binary code and routed to the CU. Now that the sum has been computed, a print command retrieves the proper address, registers the contents, and displays them. (That involves a separate flurry of activity in the display system, which we won't worry about.)

As you can see, a microprocessor must go through many more steps than human beings do merely to arrive at the conclusion that 2 + 2 = 4. The computer must execute a complicated sequence to manage the code, place it, and fetch it from memory; then it has to be told what to do with it. Yet the result usually appears as fast as you can type the request. You can see that clock cycles and, hence, processor speed, have a significant effect on performance. Other issues that affect performance include memory access and speed, as well as the response time of components such as the display system.

# PC Microprocessor Developments and Features

PC microprocessor design grows more complex with each generation, and CPU packaging keeps changing to provide room for additional features and operating requirements. Microprocessors have evolved from the 4004 described earlier into today's high-speed Pentiums. Each new processor has brought higher performance and spawned new technology. Six basic elements are customarily used to gauge the performance and capability of a CPU design.

- **Speed.** The maximum number of clock cycles measured in MHz. The higher the speed, the quicker a command will be executed.

- **Number of transistors.** More switches means more computing power.

- **Registers.** The size (in bits) of the internal registers. The larger the registers, the more complicated the commands that can be processed in one step.

- **External data bus.** As data bus size increases, so does the amount and complexity of code (information) that can be transferred among all devices in the computer.

- **Address bus.** The size of the address bus determines the maximum amount of memory that can be addressed by the CPU.

- **Internal cache.** The internal cache is high-speed memory built into the processor. This is a place to store frequently used data instead of sending it to slower devices (speed is relative in computers) such as RAM and hard disk drives. It is built into the processor and has a dramatic effect on speed. We cover cache in more detail later in this lesson.

Intel has held most of the PC CPU market share since the original IBM PC was introduced. Closely following each new Intel launch, rivals such as Advanced Micro Devices (AMD) and Cyrix have offered alternative chips that are generally compatible with the Intel models. This development, in turn, drives prices down and spurs a new round of CPU design. Another player is Motorola, a firm that manufactures the microprocessors used in the Apple family of computers, among others.

## Intel's 8086 and 8088: The Birth of the PC

We have already introduced the "pre-PC" CPUs. Now we take a look at the models that have powered one of the most dramatic developments of the modern world: the inexpensive, general-purpose computer.

On June 6, 1978, Intel introduced its first 16-bit microprocessor, known as the 8086. It had 29,000 transistors, 16-bit registers, a 16-bit external data bus, and a 20-bit address bus to allow it to access 1 MB of memory. When IBM entered the computer business, the 8086 was too powerful (and expensive) to meet its requirements.

Intel then released the 8088 processor, which was identical to the 8086 except for an 8-bit external data bus and a slower top clock rate. This meant that 8-bit components (more common at the time) could be used for the construction of PCs, and 8-bit applications written for earlier machines could be converted for PC use. The following table compares the 8088 and 8086 chips.

| Chip | Number of Transistors | CPU Speed (MHz) | Register Width | External Data Bus | Address Bus | Internal Cache |
|------|------------------------|------------------|-----------------|--------------------|--------------|-----------------|
| Intel 8088 | 29,000 | 4.77–8 | 16-bit | 8-bit | 20-bit | None |
| Intel 8086 | 29,000 | 4.77–10 | 16-bit | 16-bit | 20-bit | None |

The early 8088 processors ran at 4.77 MHz, whereas later versions ran at 8 MHz. The 8086 and 8088 processors came as a 40-pin DIP (dual inline package) containing approximately 29,000 transistors. The DIP is so named because of the two rows of pins on either side of the processor, as shown in Figure 4.8. These fit into a set of slots on a raised socket on the motherboard. The small u-shaped notch at one end of a DIP-style CPU denotes the end that has pin 1. During installation, you need to be sure to line it up correctly or you might have to repeat the process. While this operation is now pretty rare, it does need to be done once in a while.

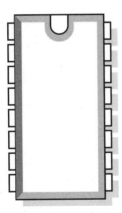

**Figure 4.8**   DIP processor used for 8086, 8088, and 80286 CPUs

**Note**   The 8088 and 8086 are software-compatible—they can run exactly the same programs (assuming the PCs that use them don't have other complicating factors). The benefit of using an 8086 is its 16-bit external data bus. This allows an 8086-based computer to execute the same software faster than an 8088 computer with the same clock speed.

The early IBM personal computers based on the 8086 and 8088 chips featured

- 16 KB of memory
- A cassette tape recorder or a floppy disk drive for program and data storage
- A nongraphics monochrome monitor and Monochrome Display Adapter (MDA)

Soon, a new industry was born as third-party vendors started manufacturing add-ons and improved models of the basic design. Graphics cards with color and better resolution, clocks, additional memory, and peripherals, such as printers, extended the features of the new appliance. "Clones" offered some of these extras at very competitive prices, as a way to attract buyers who wanted a lower price and did not need the comfort of purchasing from a large company like IBM.

**Note**   *Clone* is a computer term that was used in the heyday of the early IBM PCs through the 386. It denoted a computer that contained the same microprocessor and ran the same programs as a better known, more prestigious, and often more expensive machine.

Most of the 8088- and 8086-based PCs used some variation of MS-DOS. The variations limited the growth of the software market because of the compatibility issues they presented among versions of MS-DOS. Buyers had to be sure that a program would run on their specific version of MS-DOS.

As users found more ways to take advantage of the PC's power, developers and owners alike soon felt the limitations of the original IBM PC design. The engineers who created it never envisioned the need for more than 16 K of RAM. "Who would ever need more than that?" one was quoted as saying. The cassette drive was never a big seller; most buyers opted for one or two 5.25-inch floppy disk drives, and many soon craved color graphics and the space of the seemingly massive 5- and 10-MB hard disk drives.

To meet that growing demand, IBM introduced a more robust PC, the XT (eXtended Technology), which could take advantage of a hard disk drive. It came with either a monochrome or four-color display and more RAM. Clone makers soon followed suit.

## The 80286 and the IBM PC AT

In February 1982, Intel introduced the 80286 6-MHz microprocessor (later pushing clock speeds to 10 and 12.5 MHz), commonly called the 286, with a 24-bit address path. In 1983, IBM unveiled its PC AT (Advanced Technology) computer, based on the 286. It had a larger, boxier design and it came with a standard hard drive and a new expansion slot format, rendering older add-on cards obsolete.

The AT could run the same applications as the PC XT (8088), but run them faster. The use of a 24-bit address path allowed the 286 to access up to 16 MB of memory. The clone makers soon followed suit, taking advantage of third-party versions of the 286. Chip makers Harris and AMD produced versions of the 286 that could run at up to 20 MHz.

Computers based on the 80286 chip featured

- Two memory modes (real and protected)
- 16 MB of addressable memory
- Clock speeds of up to 20 MHz
- A reduced command set (fewer program commands to do more work)
- Multitasking abilities
- Virtual memory support

### Virtual Memory

Virtual memory is the art of using hard disk space to hold data not immediately required by the processor; it is placed in and out of RAM as needed. Although using virtual memory slowed the system down (electronic RAM is much faster than a mechanical hard drive), it allowed the 286 to address up to 1 gigabyte (1 GB = 1000 MB) of memory (16 MB of actual memory and 984 MB of virtual memory). Virtual memory required the use of operating systems more advanced than MS-DOS, leading to the development of products such as Microsoft Windows, IBM OS/2, and SCO's (Santa Cruz Operation) PC version of UNIX.

### Real Mode vs. Protected Mode

The 286 might have outdated older hardware, but Intel had no desire to invoke industry ire and slow the adoption of the new chip by requiring all-new software applications. The result was a CPU with two operating modes: real and protected.

In *real mode,* sometimes called compatibility mode, a 286 emulates the 8086 processor and addresses only the first 1 MB of memory. This mode is used to run older software. *Protected mode* allows access to all memory on the system, physical and virtual. In protected mode, a program can write only to the memory allocated to it, with specific memory blocks allocated to different programs. This mode can go well beyond the 16 MB of "true" memory, opening up the possibility of multitasking—running more than one program at a time.

This development required new, more powerful operating systems and applications, but they were slow in coming. By the time they arrived on the market, the 286 was functionally obsolete, but it paved the way for today's powerful multitasking environments such as Microsoft Windows 95, Windows 98, Windows NT, and Windows 2000. Another major drawback to the 286's memory management scheme was its need to reboot the system when changing between real and protected modes.

The original 286 processor came packaged in DIP (already shown), pin grid array (PGA), and PLCC (plastic leadless chip carrier) designs. The PLCC can be recognized by the arrangement of thin legs around its perimeter. The PLCC's major advantage is its stronger leads (pins), which make it more difficult to damage during removal or installation. PLCCs became popular because they made it easier to upgrade a PC with a faster CPU (see Figure 4.9).

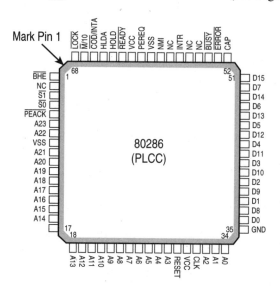

**Figure 4.9**   PLCC CPU package

## The 80386 Arrives

On June 16, 1985, Intel introduced the original 80386 (commonly known as the 386). This true 32-bit processor was equipped with a 32-bit external data bus, 32-bit registers, and a 32-bit address bus. The first models shipped with a clock speed of 16 MHz, and the CPU contained 275,000 transistors. It could directly address 4 GB of RAM and 64 terabytes (TB = approximately 1 trillion bytes) of virtual memory. According to Intel, the 386 could hold an eight-page history of every person on earth in that address space. The 386 was a true generational leap in PC computing, with true multitasking capability—it really could run more than one program at a time. That was due to a third memory mode, called *virtual real mode,* which allowed independent MS-DOS sessions (called *virtual machines*) to coexist on the same system at once. It spawned a host of programs called *memory managers* designed to optimize (and troubleshoot) the more complex world of virtual memory.

The original 80386 chips shipped with speeds of 12 or 16 MHz. Intel produced faster versions—25 and 33 MHz—and AMD manufactured a 40-MHz variant. The 386 provided both the real and protected mode available in the 286.

By April 1989, the 386 was running at clock speeds of 33 MHz, and Intel was calling it the 80386DX to distinguish it from a lower-cost model, the 386SX.

### The 386SX: A Scaled-Down Version

The 386SX came on the scene in June 1988. Intel wanted to increase the sales of 386-based machines without dramatically dropping the price of its flagship CPU. The result was the introduction of a scaled-down model for "entry-level" computers. It had a 16-bit external data bus and a 24-bit address bus (it could address only 16 MB of memory). The 16-bit configuration allowed the 386SX to be used as an upgrade chip for existing 16-bit motherboards, thereby providing an easy transition to the next generation of computers.

The following table compares members of the 80386 chip family from Intel and rival AMD. The AMD 80386DXLV is notable as the first PC CPU with an internal cache.

| Chip | Number of Transistors | CPU Speed (MHz) | Register Width | External Data Bus | Address Bus | Internal Cache |
|------|----------------------|-----------------|----------------|-------------------|-------------|----------------|
| Intel 80386SX | 275,000 | 16–25 | 32-bit | 16-bit | 24-bit | None |
| Intel 80386DX | 275,000 | 16–33 | 32-bit | 32-bit | 32-bit | None |
| AMD 80386DX | 275,000 | 20–40 | 32-bit | 32-bit | 32-bit | None |
| AMD 80386DXL | 275,000 | 20–33 | 32-bit | 32-bit | 32-bit | None |
| AMD 80386DXLV | 275,000 | 20–33 | 32-bit | 32-bit | 32-bit | 8 KB |

**Note**    The terms *SX* and *DX* are not acronyms, which means that they do not stand for longer terms.

### 386 Packaging

The 386 was usually placed in either a PLCC package or a PGA package. This type of mount can be found with the 80386, 486, and some older Pentiums up to the 166-MHz models. The pins are evenly distributed in concentric rows along the bottom of the chip (see Figure 4.10).

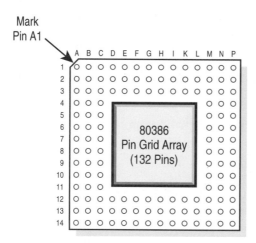

**Figure 4.10**    PGA

PGA chips go into regular PGA or the popular ZIF (zero-insertion-force) sockets. You will probably never have to contend with either mount today, but if you do, keep the following in mind. Care must be used when inserting or removing CPUs from a PGA mount—it is very easy to bend the pins if you do not pull perfectly straight up from the socket or have a slight uneven push downward. ZIF mounts are a bit better, but much technician time has been wasted straightening pins, and it is possible to ruin a CPU. PGA mounts are often "hidden" under a CPU fan, which presents another hurdle during repair or upgrade.

A variation of the PGA is the staggered pin grid array (SPGA). It looks almost the same, but with staggered rows of pins. This allows engineers to place more connectors in a smaller area. It also adds emphasis to the caution given earlier about not bending pins through careless removal or insertion.

Both the PGA and SPGA have three pointed corners and a "snipped corner" on one side. Use that corner to align the chip with the socket. If it does not go in smoothly, double-check before trying to force it!

## Laptop Designs and the Plastic Quad Flat Pack

Some forms of portable PC have existed from the days of the 8088. The early models, such as the Osborne and the original Compaq, were known as "luggables"—tipping the scales at close to 30 pounds. Their cases looked more suited for holding sewing machines than computers. Modern laptop computers started to gain popularity with the advent of the 386 chip and the use of flat-screen monitors incorporated in the design, rather than conventional video tubes (see Chapter 11, "The Display System," for more information).

To seat 80286, 80386, and 80486 CPUs (the latter are covered in the section that follows) on the more compact laptop motherboards, many vendors use plastic quad flat pack (PQFP) mounts, which are also more secure than traditional socket types designed for systems that will not be moved as much. PQFPs require a submount called a *carrier ring* (see Figure 4.11). PQFPs require a special tool for placing or removing a CPU. Be sure to get the tool before attempting repairs on PQFP-mounted CPUs.

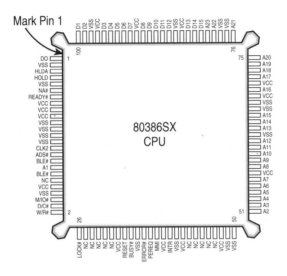

**Figure 4.11**    PQFP

## 80486

On April 10, 1989, Intel introduced the 80486 line of processors. Once again, the rallying cry was "better and faster." By this time, applications like CorelDRAW and Adobe PhotoShop, and desktop publishing tools like Aldus PageMaker and Ventura Publisher were generating more interest in faster systems. Microsoft Windows was gaining popularity on its way to becoming the standard desktop environment.

The 486 processor started life at 25 MHz and could address 4 GB of RAM and 64 TB of virtual memory. It is the first PC CPU to break the 1-million transistor mark with 1.2 million. It provided a built-in math coprocessor (older PC CPUs offered separate math coprocessors as an option, usually with a similar number ending in a 7 rather than a 6. The combination speeded up graphics programs that used floating-point math).

## The 486SX and Beyond

Once again, Intel sought a way to increase sales without weakening the price of the flagship version of its 486DX CPU, so it added an SX version in April 1991. This time, the company achieved its goal by removing the math coprocessor, reducing the number of transistors to 1,185,000. Users could upgrade the SX to a 486DX by adding an optional OverDrive processor to restore the missing component.

The 486 label was attached to other chip designs during its active development phase, both by Intel and third-party chip makers. The 486SL, a variant with a 20- to 33-MHz clock and 1.4 million transistors, debuted in 1992. It was very popular in high-performance laptop computers, running at lower voltage (3.3 volts instead of 5 volts) than the usual 486. The small and (for that time) powerful machines also included System Memory Management (SMM) mode, which could dim the liquid crystal display (LCD) screen and power down the hard disk drive, extending the life of the battery.

## System Memory Management

SMM is a hardware-based function that allows the microprocessor to selectively shut down the monitor, hard drives, and any other peripherals not in use. SMM works at the chip level; the microprocessor can be operating in real, protected, or virtual 8086 mode. SMM is transparent to all software running on the system, which decreases the likelihood of lockups.

## Clock-Doubling Debuts

The need for speed spurred the introduction of new models of the 486 family through the spring of 1994, the last variations being the DX2 and DX4. These chips were models with faster clock speeds of up to 100 MHz. The processors were either 25- or 33-MHz versions that had been altered to run internally at double or triple their external speed. For example, the DX4 version of the 486 33-MHz processor ran at 33 MHz externally, but at 100 MHz internally (3 × 33.3 MHz). This meant that internal operations, such as numeric calculations or moving data from one register to another, occurred at 100 MHz, whereas external operations, like loading data from memory, took place at 33 MHz.

Slower external clock speeds allowed existing motherboard and memory designs to be used. Upgrades were less expensive, and new machines based on the DX technology could quote faster benchmarks at lower costs. The DX4 offered 16 KB of on-board cache, further boosting performance. The DX2 50-MHz-based machines should not be confused with machines designed around the 50-MHz 486DX processor—the latter performed much better.

Vendors such as AMD rode the wave with their own editions of the 486 for users with a need for greater speed. The following table lists the most popular 486 chips and third-party work-alikes.

| Chip | CPU Speed (MHz) | Register Width | External Data Bus | Address Bus | Internal Cache |
|------|-----------------|----------------|-------------------|-------------|----------------|
| Intel 80486DX | 25, 33, 50 | 32-bit | 32-bit | 32-bit | 8 KB |
| Intel 80486DX/2 | 50, 66 | 32-bit | 32-bit | 32-bit | 8 KB |
| Intel 80486DX/4 | 75, 100 | 32-bit | 32-bit | 32-bit | 16 KB |
| Intel 80486SX | 16, 20, 25 | 32-bit | 32-bit | 32-bit | 8 KB |
| Intel 80486SL | 16, 20, 25 | 32-bit | 32-bit | 32-bit | 8 KB |
| AMD AM486DX | 33, 40 | 32-bit | 32-bit | 32-bit | 8 KB |
| AMD AM486DXLV | 33 | 32-bit | 32-bit | 32-bit | 8 KB |
| AMD AM486DX2 | 50, 80 | 32-bit | 32-bit | 32-bit | 8 KB |
| AMD AM486DX4 | 100, 120 | 32-bit | 32-bit | 32-bit | 8 KB |
| AMD AM486DX "Enhanced" | 120, 133 | 32-bit | 32-bit | 32-bit | 16 KB write-back |
| AMD AM486DXL2 | 50, 80 | 32-bit | 32-bit | 32-bit | 8 KB |
| AMD AM486SX | 33, 40 | 32-bit | 32-bit | 32-bit | 8 KB |
| AMD AM486SXLV | 33 | 32-bit | 32-bit | 32-bit | 8 KB |
| AMD AM486SX2 | 33 | 32-bit | 32-bit | 32-bit | 8 KB |
| CYRX CX486DX | 33 | 32-bit | 32-bit | 32-bit | 8 KB write-back |
| CYRX CX486DX2 | 50–80 | 32-bit | 32-bit | 32-bit | 8 KB write-back |
| CYRX CX486DLC | 33–40 | 32-bit | 32-bit | 32-bit | 1 KB write-back |
| CYRX CX486SLC | 20–33 | 32-bit | 32-bit | 32-bit | 1 KB write-back |
| CYRX CX486SLC2 | 50 | 32-bit | 32-bit | 32-bit | 1 KB write-back |

**Note**  Write-through and write-back caches are explained in Chapter 7, "Memory."

### Heat Sinks and Fans

The 486 is notable for one other reason: the addition of a standard heat sink and, usually, a fan mounted on the CPU and powered by the PC. To maintain stable operation, the PC must provide proper cooling for the 486 and newer CPUs. Failure of the cooling apparatus can lead to erratic behavior and, if left uncorrected, can damage the chip. If a customer complains of strange noises inside the PC, the CPU fan is a good place to check. As their bearings age, CPU fans may start to whine.

## The First Pentiums

By 1993, Windows was standard, and users expected a lot more from PCs in performance and features. Increasing software sophistication led to increasing memory usage and hard disk drive requirements. The market was ready for a major upgrade in CPUs, and Intel once again addressed that need. The new Pentium processor signaled a radical redesign of both the CPU and naming conventions.

With its CPUs identified by numbers, Intel faced a business problem: Numbers cannot be trademarked. The company's strategy was to substitute a name that could be trademarked, Pentium, for its upcoming chips that would otherwise have been named 586. The word is based on the Latin word for the number five, and this chip would have been the 80586. The original design has been revamped several times since 1993 with the introduction of the Pentium II in 1997, the Pentium III in 1999, and the Pentium 4 in 2000. Like the older PC CPUs, the Pentium has spawned its share of clones, leading to entry-level PCs priced under $400.

The Pentium (Series I) offered the following features:

- Speeds of 60 MHz to greater than 200 MHz.
- 32-bit address bus and 32-bit registers.
- 64-bit data path to improve the speed of data transfers.
- Dual pipeline, 32-bit data bus that allows the chip to process two separate lines of code simultaneously.
- At least an 8-KB write-back cache for data and an 8-KB write-through cache for programs. (Types of caches are explained in more detail in Chapter 7, "Memory.")
- *Branch prediction,* in which the program cache attempts to anticipate branching within the code. The CPU stores a few lines of code from each branch so that when the program reaches the branch, the Pentium already has the code stored within the cache.

The following table lists the first generation of Pentium and Pentium-compatible chips.

| Chip | Speed (MHz) | Register Width | External Data Bus | Address Bus | Internal Cache |
|---|---|---|---|---|---|
| Intel Pentium | 60, 66 | 32-bit | 64-bit | 32-bit | 8 KB write-back and 8KB write-through |
| Intel Pentium | 75 | 32-bit | 64-bit | 32-bit | 8 KB write-back and 8KB write-through |
| Intel Pentium | 90, 100 | 32-bit | 64-bit | 32-bit | 8 KB write-back and 8KB write-through |
| Intel Pentium | 120, 130 | 32-bit | 64-bit | 32-bit | 8 KB write-back and 8KB write-through |
| Intel Pentium | 150, 166 | 32-bit | 64-bit | 32-bit | 8 KB write-back and 8KB write-through |
| Intel Pentium | 180, 200 | 32-bit | 64-bit | 32-bit | 8 KB write-back and 8KB write-through |
| Cyrix 6x86 (P-rating) | 100, 120, 133, 200 | 32-bit | 64-bit | 32-bit | 8 KB write-back and 8 KB write-through |
| AMD K5 (P-rating) | 75, 90 | 32-bit | 64-bit | 32-bit | 8 KB write-back and 8 KB write-through |

**Note**  Write-through and write-back caches are explained in Chapter 7, "Memory." P-rating is a standard method of rating chips by their equivalency to a Pentium chip. It avoids direct comparison of clock speeds. Each processor is tested on an identical system and measured accordingly. If a chip performs 1.5 percent slower than a Pentium chip, it gets the same rating as the next lower chip.

Mass-producing reliable Pentium 66 (P66) chips proved difficult, and many were rejected during quality control. The faulty chips were stable at clock speeds of 60 MHz, so Intel sold them as the P60. Some users change their P60 processor clock speed to 66 MHz by changing a jumper on the motherboard. Although this might have worked, it made computer performance and longevity unpredictable.

Intel continued to use the 0.8-micron manufacturing process (the ability to draw lines as fine as 1/1000 of a millimeter on the die, about 16,000 lines per inch), begun with the 486, to fit 3.1 million transistors on the Pentium chip. The P66 used considerable power and consequently generated a large amount of heat. Operating a reliable heat sink and fan became critical with the advent of the Pentium.

The Pentium 75 was released in 1994. These chips were made using a 0.6-micron manufacturing process (approximately 21,000 lines and spaces per inch) and, as a result, they required considerably less power, despite an additional 200,000 transistors. Intel was able to change the power supply from 5 volts to 3.3 volts (the DX4 also had a reduced power supply), which reduced by nearly one-half the amount of heat produced. The P90 and P100 processors were also released at this time. These processors ran internally at 1.5 times the external speed (60 or 66 MHz, which was the fastest system board). A P75 processor was also released for use in lower specification machines and laptop computers.

## Superscalar Technology

The main components of a processor—registers, decoders, and ALUs—are collectively known as the *instruction pipeline*. To carry out a single instruction, a processor must

- Read the instruction
- Decode the instruction
- Fetch operands (for math functions)
- Execute the instruction
- Write back the results

Early processors carried out these steps one at a time. Combining these steps into a single clock cycle, a process known as *pipelining*, thereby increases the speed of processing. *Superscalar technology* allows the Pentium to have two instruction pipelines—called U and V. The U pipeline can execute the full range of Pentium instructions, whereas the V pipeline can execute a limited number. When possible, the Pentium processor breaks up a program into discrete tasks that are then shared between the pipelines, allowing the Pentium to execute two simple instructions simultaneously. Software must be specifically written to take advantage of this innovative feature, which is known as *multithreading*.

## Pentium On-Board Cache

The original Pentium series came with two 8-KB caches—one for data and one for program code—compared with the single 8-KB cache on the 486 (16 KB on the DX4). As described with the 486 chip, the cache uses a technique called branch prediction to improve its ability to guess what data or program code will be required next by the processor.

## Intel's Competitors

Competitors have moved away from simply making clones of the Intel processors. They are currently designing their own processors with unique features. AMD and Cyrix are among the best known. Until recently, all the Intel processors had been based on a CISC (complex instruction set computing) architecture. Processors based on RISC (Reduced Instruction Set Computing) have been used in high-powered machines since the mid-1980s. Intel has produced its own version of a RISC-based processor that uses a much smaller and simpler set of instructions, greatly enhancing the speed of the processor.

## Pentium Pro

Intel made CPU selection even more complex with the introduction of the Pentium Pro in 1995, offering varied features, in different models, of the Pentium design. This processor was aimed at a 32-bit server and workstation-level applications such as CAD (computer-aided design), mechanical engineering, and advanced scientific computation. The Pentium Pro was packaged with a second speed-enhancing cache memory chip, and it boasted 5.5 million transistors. Introduced in November 1995, it incorporated an internal RISC architecture with a CISC–RISC translator, three-way superscalar execution, and dynamic execution. While compatible with all the previous software for the Intel line, the Pentium Pro is optimized to run 32-bit software. Its pin structure and mount differ from the basic Pentium, requiring a special ZIF socket. Some motherboards have sockets for both Pentium and Pentium Pro chips, but most machines use motherboards designed for one or the other. The package, a 2.46-inch by 2.66-inch 387-pin PGA configuration, houses a Pentium Pro processor core and an on-board L2 cache. Although mounted on one PGA device, they are two ICs. A single, gold-plated copper and tungsten heat spreader gives them the appearance of a single chip.

The main CPU and 16-KB first-level (L1) cache consist of 5.5 million transistors; the second chip is a 256- or 512-KB second-level (L2) cache with 15 million transistors. A 133-MHz Pentium Pro processes data about twice as fast as a 100-MHz Pentium.

One reason for the better performance is a technology called *dynamic execution.* Before processing, the data flow is analyzed and sequenced for optimal execution. Then the system looks ahead in the program process and predicts where the next branch or group of instructions can be found in memory, processing up to five instructions before they are needed. By using a technique known as *data-flow analysis*, the Pentium Pro can determine dependencies among data items so they can be processed as soon as their inputs are available, regardless of the program's order.

## Pentium MMX

Soon, more choices were on the way. About the time the 166-MHz Pentiums shipped, Intel introduced MMX (Multimedia Extension) technology, designed to enhance performance of data-hungry applications like graphics and games. With larger data and code caches, Pentiums with MMX technology can run non-MMX-enhanced software approximately 10 to 20 percent faster than a non-MMX CPU with the same clock speed.

To reap the full benefits of the new processor, MMX-enhanced software makes use of 57 special multimedia instructions. These new MMX operators use a technology called *SIMD* (single-instruction multiple-data) stream processing. SIMD allows different processing elements to perform the same operations on different data—a central controller broadcasts the instruction to all processing elements in the same way that a drill sergeant would tell a whole platoon to "about face," rather than instruct each soldier individually.

The MMX chips also take advantage of dynamic branch prediction using the *branch target buffer* (BTB) to predict the most likely set of instructions to be executed.

The MMX Pentium processor is also more compatible with older 16-bit software than is the Pentium Pro; consequently, it soon doomed the Pro to the backwaters of PC computing. All later versions of the Pentium have incorporated some variation of MMX and improved on it. The original Pentium desktop line ended with the release of the 233-MHz MMX in June 1997.

## Pentium II

By 1997, multimedia was becoming mainstream, and high performance in a graphical user environment was critical to CPU market success. Intel upped the ante for its competitors in 1997 with a radical redesign. The first 233-MHz, 7.5-million-transistor, Pentium II processor incorporated MMX technology and was packaged with a high-speed cache memory chip (see Figure 4.12). Intel released Pentium II versions operating at speeds of up to 450 MHz. This period also marked the introduction of the 100-MHz system bus.

The Pentium II incorporated the features of its older designs and added a number of enhancements, including:

- **Multiple branch prediction.** Predicts program execution through several branches, accelerating the flow of work to the processor.

- **Data-flow analysis.** Creates an optimized, reordered schedule of instructions by analyzing data dependencies among instructions.

- **Speculative execution.** Carries out instructions speculatively and, based on this optimized schedule, ensures that the processor's superscalar execution units remain busy, boosting overall performance.

- **Single-edge connector (SEC) cartridge packaging.** Developed by Intel, this enables high-volume availability and offers improved handling protection and a common form factor for future high-performance processors. This development eliminated problems caused by pins accidentally bent during installation or removal of CPUs.

- **High-performance Dual Independent Bus (DIB) architecture.** System bus and cache bus.

- **System bus that supports multiple outstanding transactions to increase bandwidth availability.** It also provides "glueless" support for up to two processors. This enables low-cost, two-way symmetric multiprocessing, providing a significant performance boost for multitasking operating systems and multithreaded applications. Many inexpensive motherboards offer two Slot 1 sockets, making it easy to build a dual processor system for use with operating systems like Windows NT or Windows 2000.

- **512-KB unified, nonblocking, L2 cache.** Improves performance by reducing average memory access time and providing fast access to recently used instructions and data. Performance is enhanced through a dedicated 64-bit cache bus. The speed of the L2 cache scales with the processor core frequency. This processor also incorporates separate 16-KB, L1 caches, one for instructions and one for data.

- **Models available in 450, 400, and 350 MHz.** Support memory caches for up to 4 GB of addressable memory space.

- **Error-correction coding (ECC) functionality on the L2 cache bus.** For applications in which data intensity and reliability are essential.

- **Pipelined FPU (floating-point unit).** Supports the 32-bit and 64-bit formats specified in IEEE (Institute of Electrical and Electronics Engineers) standard 754, as well as an 80-bit format.

- **Parity-protected address/request and response system bus signals.** Includes a retry mechanism for high data integrity and reliability.

## Variations on a Theme: The Intel Celeron CPUs

As it had in the past, Intel faced competitors who sold CPUs with similar performance at lower prices. Most high-priced desktop computers and servers were sold with a Pentium of one sort or another, but home and entry-level PCs were another matter. Enter a variation of the SX concept—the Celeron.

Celeron models available in 500, 466, 433, 400, 366, and 333 MHz have expanded Intel processing into the market for computers selling for less than $1,200.

All the Intel Celeron processors are available in PGA packages. The versions operating at 433, 400, 366, 333, and 300 MHz are also available in single-edge processor packages (see Figure 4.12).

Key features include the following

- MMX media enhancement technology.
- Dynamic Execution Technology.
- A 32-KB (16-KB/16-KB) nonblocking, L1 cache for fast access to heavily used data.
- Celerons operating at 500, 466, 433, 400, 366, and 333 MHz include integrated 128-KB L2 cache.
- All Celeron processors use the Intel P6 microarchitecture's multitransaction system bus at 66 MHz. Processors at 766, 733, 700, 667, 633, 600, 566, 533, 500, 466, 433, 400, 366, and 333 MHz use the Intel P6 microarchitecture's multitransaction system bus with the addition of the L2 cache interface.
- Like the Pentium family, the Celerons offer multiple branch prediction, data-flow analysis, and speculative execution.

**Figure 4.12**    Intel Pentium II in a SEC package

### Xeon: The Premium Pentium

Intel has labeled a new CPU brand to denote high-end server and high-performance desktop use. First introduced in June 1998, the Xeon line commands a premium price and offers extra performance-enhancing technology. The Pentium II models incorporate 7.5 million transistors, clock speeds to 450 MHz, bus speeds of 100 MHz, full-speed L2 caches in varying sizes up to 2 MB, new multiprocessing capabilities, and compatibility with previous Intel microprocessor generations. All models use the SEC package.

### Pentium III Processor

The Intel Pentium III processor is the newest member of the P6 family. With 28 million transistors, speeds from 450 MHz to 1 GHz, and system bus speeds of 100 to 133 MHz, they mark a significant jump in PC CPU technology. They employ the same dynamic execution microarchitecture as the Pentium II—a combination of multiple branch prediction, data-flow analysis, and speculative execution. This provides improved performance over older Pentium designs, while maintaining binary compatibility with all previous Intel processors. The Pentium III processor, shown in Figure 4.13, also incorporates MMX technology, plus streaming SIMD extensions for enhanced floating-point and 3-D application performance. It also utilizes multiple low-power states, such as AutoHALT, Stop-Grant, Sleep, and Deep Sleep to conserve power during idle times.

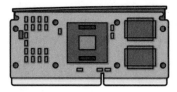

**Figure 4.13**    The Intel Pentium III processor

Intel offers a Xeon version of the Pentium III processor at speeds up to 1 GHz, aimed at high-performance workstations and servers.

### Motorola

Motorola has been the mainstay CPU for Apple computers. The 68000 processor was introduced in 1979 as a 32-bit chip with a 16-bit data path. At that time, the 68000 outperformed the Intel 8086. In 1982, the 68010 arrived, adding virtual memory support and a cache capable of holding three instructions.

1984 saw the advent of the Macintosh II-series computer, which used the 68020 processor. It was the first full 32-bit chip, with a 32-bit data path, math coprocessor, and the ability to access up to 4 GB of RAM. Introduced in the same year as Intel's 80286 processor, the Motorola ran faster. However, it lacked the market share and third-party support to gain real marketplace momentum. PC clones offered more programs at a lower cost than the Apple offerings.

The 68030 chip, introduced in 1987, provided increased data and instruction speed. This was comparable to the 80386 chip. The 68040 processor was introduced (in the Macintosh Quadra) as a competitor to the 80486. It has internal caches for data and program code.

The PowerPC processor was developed jointly by IBM, Motorola, and Apple. The name stands for performance optimization with enhanced RISC. The chips in this family of processors are suitable for machines ranging from laptop computers to high-powered network servers. It can run MS-DOS software without using emulation.

## Lesson Summary

The following points summarize the main elements of this lesson:

- The microprocessor is the centerpiece of today's computers.

- Understanding the development and progression of the processor is essential in understanding how to mix older technology with new technology.

- The three key elements that go into measuring a CPU's performance are its speed, address bus, and external data bus.

- The development of the 80286 processor introduced the concepts of real and protected modes and allowed the use of up to 16 MB of memory.

- The development of the 80386 processor brought about 32-bit processing and allowed up to 4 GB of memory.

- The 80486 processor is a "souped-up" version of the 80386 that introduced the use of cache memory.

- The Pentium chip began a new line of processors and technology, incorporating RISC and true multithreading capabilities in an Intel microprocessor for the first time.

- Pentium MMX technology was developed to meet the needs of today's multimedia world.

- The Intel Pentium III further extended PC performance with advanced cache technology and streamlined code handling.

- Several players are currently competing with Intel for the processor market (NextGen, AMD, Cyrix, IBM), but Intel has the largest market share by far.

- Today's standard processor is the Pentium III, with processor speeds of 500 MHz and faster.

# Lesson 2:  Replacing and Upgrading a CPU

A computer technician is commonly expected to upgrade computers. Because the CPU is the "brain" of a computer, replacing this single component can bring new life to an aging system. Replacing the chip is easy, but understanding the possible scenarios for a successful upgrade can be more challenging.

### After this lesson, you will be able to

- Decide whether a CPU is worth upgrading
- Find the type of CPU required for upgrade
- Install a new CPU

### Estimated lesson time: 15 minutes

Replacing a CPU can be very simple, but it is important to first carefully consider whether to do so. If you do decide to replace it, you will need to take care to avoid damaging the chip during installation. Before undertaking this process, always ask yourself, "What CPUs can be put on this motherboard?" The best source for an answer is the documentation packaged with the computer or motherboard. If the motherboard manual is not available and you do not have a reference, the document should be available on the manufacturer's Web site.

## Possible Upgrade Scenarios

There are a number of issues to think about when deciding whether to upgrade a CPU or replace a machine altogether. Perhaps the most important issue is the value of the upgrade. Will the suggested upgrade meet the operational requirements for that computer? There are limits to what can be upgraded and the results that can be expected from the upgrade. A poor upgrade can lead to total failure and could ultimately require replacement of the motherboard. Again, the best source of information regarding CPU upgrades is the documentation that comes with the motherboard. The following table lists several possible scenarios for upgrading a CPU.

| Existing CPU | Recommendation |
| --- | --- |
| 8086/8088 | Cannot be upgraded. |
| 80286 through 486 | Replace the system. It may be possible to use isolated components, but not worth the effort. |
| 80386SX | Same as for 80286. Replace the motherboard. |
| Pentium I | Replace a Pentium I motherboard, display adapter, and sound card with newer components. Depending on the customer's needs and budget, you may save floppy drives, mouse, and other minor components. |

*(continued)*

| Existing CPU | Recommendation |
|---|---|
| Pentium II | May upgrade either just the CPU or CPU and motherboard, depending on the system, the case, and the BIOS. In the case of AT-style PCs, you may need to change the case to an ATX form factor, and upgrade the motherboard, keyboard, and mouse to newer designs. |
| Pentium III | Possible to just upgrade CPU; it may require a new motherboard if the CPU is not supported by the chip set. |

On average, it is more cost-effective to replace an entire motherboard than it is to upgrade a CPU. However, you have to judge for yourself. Make sure that the new motherboard will fit into the computer case (check size and alignment of expansion buses) before starting the installation. Be sure that the power supply of the old case and new motherboard are of the same type with the proper connectors (such as AT, ATX). Always make sure that you can return a CPU and motherboard to the vendor if they won't fit. Be sure to determine this before you open the packaging or attempt to install the components. Keep in mind that many suppliers charge a restocking fee of 15 to 20 percent for returns.

## Inserting a CPU

There are several types of CPU sockets available. Today virtually all desktop PCs come with some variation of the SEC packaging. Other CPUs are generally not worth upgrading and may be one of two common types of package:

- Low-insertion-force (LIF)
- Zero-insertion-force (ZIF)

**Note**   You may encounter a situation where a person wants to hand off an older computer to a relative or friend who does not have a computer. For completeness, we have included information on these older form factors. You will rarely encounter machines older than a 486, and most of your experience will be with Pentium-class machines.

### LIF Socket

Removing an old CPU from an LIF socket is a muscular business! Luckily, there are special tools designed for this. However, a flat-head screwdriver or a plate cover for an expansion card slot will also work—just be sure to pry evenly around the CPU or you will risk damaging the CPU, the socket, or both.

**Note** There is a notch in one corner of an LIF socket. The CPU will also have a notch and a dot in one corner, designed to help align the CPU correctly. The index corner of the CPU must line up with the notch on the socket. Firmly press the CPU into the PGA socket, making sure all the pins are lined up.

## ZIF Socket

The ZIF socket, shown in Figure 4.14, was the most popular mount for desktop and tower PCs with 486 and early Pentium CPUs.

**Figure 4.14**   ZIF socket with CPU inverted showing matching pins

A ZIF socket has a lever arm that allows for simple removal and installation of CPUs. ZIF sockets were introduced during the early 1990s as a safe means of providing a user-friendly CPU upgrade. The first ZIF socket had 169 pins and was used on 486SX systems. These systems were sold with a 486SX chip already installed in a PGA socket and provided a ZIF socket for a 486 OverDrive chip, a special processor designed to increase the speed of 486 computers. (It works much like the standard clock-doubling processors—DX2 and DX4—used on 486 motherboards.) Often, this is a good method of increasing the speed of a computer without replacing the motherboard.

The following table describes the types of ZIF sockets.

| CPU Type | Number of Pins | Pin Layout | Voltage |
|---|---|---|---|
| 486SX/SX2, DXUDX2, DX4ODPR | 169 | 17 × 17 PGA | 5v |

*(continued)*

| CPU Type | Number of Pins | Pin Layout | Voltage |
|---|---|---|---|
| SX/SX2, DX/DX2, DX4ODPR, Pentium OverDrive | 238 | 19 × 19 PGA | 5v |
| SX/SX2, DX/DX2, DX4ODP, Pentium OverDrive | 237 | 19 × 19 PGA | 5v/3.3v |
| Pentium 60/66 | 273 | 21 × 21 PGA | 5v |
| Pentium 75/90/100/120 | 320 | 37 × 37 SPGA | 3.3v |
| 486 DX4, Pentium OverDrive | 235 | 19 × 19 PGA | 3.3v |
| Pentium 75–200 | 321 | 21 × 21 SPGA | VRM |

**Note**  ODPR stands for overdrive processor replacement. PGA is a pin grid array. SPGA is a staggered pin grid array, and VRM is a voltage regulator module.

## Care When Handling a CPU

Be very careful when handling a CPU or any exposed IC. Static discharge can damage or ruin the chip. Be sure to use a wrist-grounding strap or other approved antistatic device. Take great care to not bend any pins, and make sure the CPU is properly lined up to seat Pin 1 by using the code notch.

**Caution**  If you encounter any resistance, stop at once and determine what is wrong.

Check the memory and bus speed required for the new CPU before attempting to boot the PC after the procedure. It might require new RAM and will most often demand that a jumper be set on the motherboard before operating at the new speed.

## SEC Package/Slot 1 Upgrades

The Pentium II and III series are most commonly packaged in an SEC. This package, shown in Figure 4.15, is very simple to work with. You will need a motherboard mount and might have to purchase a fan and heat sink before installing the CPU. Check the manual for jumper-setting adjustments and follow the simple directions that come with the CPU.

**Figure 4.15**    Pentium processor in an SEC package and Slot 1

The actual task involves seating two plastic pins, sliding two guides over the sides of the CPU, and then pushing the frame and CPU into the slot on the board. With dual CPU boards, you need to know which slot to use, and you might have to place a special card (which comes with the motherboard) in the second CPU position if it is to remain empty.

---

**Caution**    Be sure to properly mount the cooling system, and make sure the fan works before running the new CPU for any amount of time or closing the case. Failure to ensure proper heat removal will destroy the CPU very quickly!

---

## Lesson Summary

The following points summarize the main elements of this lesson:

- Replacing a CPU is usually a simple task.

- It is important to consider the limitations and potential of an upgrade before deciding to replace a CPU.

- Be very careful of electrostatic discharge (ESD) and potential pin damage when handling a CPU.

# Chapter Summary

The following points summarize the key concepts in this chapter.

## Microprocessors

- The CPU—a microprocessor—is the centerpiece of today's computers.
- Clock speed is only one determining factor in identifying overall performance of a processor.
- Processors are generally defined by their speed, the size of the external data bus, and the size of the address bus.
- The development of the 80286 processor introduced the concepts of real and protected modes and allowed the use of up to 16 MB of memory.
- The development of the 80386 processor brought about 32-bit processing and allowed up to 4 GB of memory.
- The 80486 processor is a "souped-up" version of the 80386 and it introduced the use of cache memory.
- The Pentium chip began a new line of processors and technology, incorporating RISC and true multithreading capabilities in an Intel microprocessor for the first time.
- The Pentium II chip further extended the power of the PC and introduced a new packaging method that made handling the CPU and performing upgrades much simpler.
- The Intel Pentium III further extended PC performance with advanced cache technology and streamlined code handling.
- Today's standard processor is the Pentium III, with processor speeds of 500 MHz and faster.

## Replacing and Upgrading Chips

- It is important for a computer technician to know the technological advances made by each successive generation of computers.
- Simply upgrading the CPU can often lengthen the life span of a computer.

# Review

The following questions are intended to reinforce key information presented in this chapter. If you are unable to answer a question, review the appropriate lesson and then try the question again. Answers to the questions can be found in Appendix A, "Questions and Answers."

1. What is the language of the computer?

2. What is an external data bus?

3. Describe an integrated circuit (IC).

4. Define a clock cycle.

5. What are the advantages of a Pentium processor over a 486?

6. What is the difference between SX and DX in a 386 chip?

7. Which computers use the Motorola 68040 chip?

8. Define microprocessor.

9. In computer code language _____ means on and _____ means off.

10. Define clock speed.

11. What is the function of the address bus?

12. Microprocessor chips (CPUs) are manufactured in a variety of sizes and shapes. Name as many different kinds as possible.

13. Name the basic types of CPU sockets.

14. If a customer brought you an old Pentium 60-based computer and asked you to install a new processor, what would your advice be?

C H A P T E R   5

# Power Supplies

Lesson 1: Power Supplies . . . . . . . . . . . . . . . . . . . . . . . . . . . . . . . . . . . . . . 78

Lesson 2: Power Supply Problems . . . . . . . . . . . . . . . . . . . . . . . . . . . . 86

Chapter Summary . . . . . . . . . . . . . . . . . . . . . . . . . . . . . . . . . . . . . . . . 89

Review . . . . . . . . . . . . . . . . . . . . . . . . . . . . . . . . . . . . . . . . . . . . . . . . . 90

## About This Chapter

The power supply is an often-underrated part of a computer. Many transient problems can be related to a faulty power supply or to poor electrical supply from the local provider. Electronic components require a steady electrical current, free of surges or drops. The power supply is responsible for providing clean, constant current.

## Before You Begin

No specialized knowledge is required; however, a fundamental understanding of terms related to power and electricity such as voltage and wattage is helpful when learning about power supplies.

# Lesson 1:  Power Supplies

This lesson presents basic information about power supplies for computer systems. We take a look at the different variations of power supplies, how to identify the proper type, and how to connect it to the computer (both motherboard and related devices). We also examine the safety considerations related to working with power supplies. As a certified computer technician, you will often be called on to troubleshoot, identify, and replace power supplies.

## After this lesson, you will be able to

- Define the current and voltage requirements for a computer power supply
- Identify when you need to replace a power supply ·
- Specify the correct surge suppressors for a computer system
- Select a backup power supply for a computer system

## Estimated lesson time: 15 minutes

## Overview of Power Supplies

A standard power supply draws power from a local, alternating current (AC) source (usually a wall outlet) and converts it to either 3.3 or 5 volts direct current (DC) for on-board electronics, and 12 volts DC for motors and hard drives. In all cases, it delivers both positive and negative DC to the computer. Power supplies must "condition" the power, smoothing out any radical changes in its quality. Many homes and offices have power that fluctuates far more than the delicate parts of a PC can tolerate and survive under. Most PC power supplies also provide electricity to the system's cooling and processor fans that keep the machine from overheating.

If the computer's power supply is providing reliable, clean power and its own cooling fan works, all is well. If the power supply or its fan should fail or cause erratic behavior by the PC, the power supply must be replaced. (Although it is possible to remove and replace a power supply fan, the low cost of a power supply makes it more practical to replace the power supply itself.)

Most supplies have a universal input that will accept either 110 volts alternating current (VAC), 60 hertz (Hz) (U.S. standard power), or 220 VAC, 50 Hz (European and Asian standard). When replacing a power supply, there are three things to consider: physical size, wattage, and connectors. The remainder of this chapter covers the basics of power supplies.

**Note**   A hertz is a measure of unit frequency: 1 cycle per second equals 1 hertz. A kilohertz (kHz) is 1,000 cycles per second; a megahertz (MHz) is 1 million cycles per second.

# Power Supply Sizes

Power supplies are available in a few standard sizes and shapes. However, the names for power supplies are anything but standard. They are based on the type of case in which they are installed and the types of motherboard connections they will support. This is because different styles of cases place items such as plug fittings, mounting screws, and fans in different places, and motherboard styles offer different connections and placement of plugs. These cables and fittings must be compatible to work together.

The very first PCs all used the same type of power supply with a large, red switch on the side. Variations were manufactured for early portables and tower cases, with longer or shorter cables and different types of switches. They all shared a common pair of motherboard connectors. Collectively they are known as *AT-style*. When replacing an AT-style power supply, you generally only need to be concerned about the type of case that it will go in. The exceptions are some high-end network servers, which sometimes allow for an extra power lead to the motherboard. All newer desktop PCs (Pentium II and later) and servers use *ATX-style* power supplies. The ATX design simplifies motherboard connection by combining the two power leads in the AT-style power supply into one. The main issues to be aware of are how much wattage the PC needs to power its parts and how many peripheral connectors are required. Generally speaking, older Pentium-based computers and all 486-based and earlier PCs used AT-style supplies; almost all Pentium II and later-based systems use ATX-style supplies. The ATX design is preferable for two reasons:

- The on–off power control circuit (not the button) on ATX boards is built into the motherboard. On AT-style PCs, it comes from the power supply.

- AT-style power supplies connect to the motherboard through a pair of six-wire connectors. ATX-style power supplies connect through a single 20-pin connector.

A few motherboards and power supplies provide both AT and ATX fittings and switch support. These are rare, but provide more options should you have to repair such a system. Generally, you should use ATX-style power supplies for all replacements, if possible.

When replacing a power supply, it's a good idea to compare the existing power supply to the new one. Make sure that they are physically the same size, have the same connectors, and that the new one has at least the same power rating. Some high-quality power supplies offer "silencer" fans that are much quieter than most models.

## Power Supply Wattage

Power supplies are rated according to the maximum sustained power (measured in watts) that they can produce. A *watt* is a unit of electrical power equivalent to one volt-ampere. It is important to keep in mind that the power supply must produce at least enough energy to operate all the components of the system at the same time.

You can determine a computer's power consumption by adding the power requirements, measured in watts, for all the devices in the unit. When evaluating a power supply, however, don't rely on the computer's operating consumption alone. Remember that a much larger drain occurs as the machine powers up, when hard drives and other heavy feeders simultaneously compete for the available startup power. Most general-use computers require 130 watts while running and about 200–205 watts when booting (at startup). Sound cards, modems, and (worst of all) monitors attached with an accessory plug in the case can push a weak power supply to its limit and beyond.

Servers and high-performance workstations often have an abundance of random access memory (RAM), multiple drives, SCSI (Small Computer System Interface) adapters, and power-hungry video cards, along with one or more network cards. They often demand power supplies of 350–500 watts.

**Caution**   The label on a power supply that says "Don't Open" means just that! Opening a power supply is dangerous. It is better to completely remove and replace a defective power supply as needed.

## Power Supply Connectors

Power supplies employ several types of connectors, all of which are easy to identify and use. On the outside of the computer enclosure, a standard male AC plug and three-conductor wire (two power wires and a ground) draws current from a wall outlet, with a female connection entering the receptacle in the back of the power supply. There are three types of connectors on the inside: the power main to the motherboard (which differs, as mentioned, in AT and ATX models) and two types of four-pin fittings to supply 5 volts and 3.3 volts of power to peripherals such as the floppy disk and hard disk drives. Let's take a close look at each in turn.

### AT-Style Connections to the Motherboard

A pair of almost identical connectors, designated P8 and P9, links the power supply to the motherboard (see Figure 5.1). These connectors are seated into a row of six pins and matching plastic guides, or *teeth,* on the motherboard. The P8 and P9 connectors *must* be placed in the proper orientation. The motherboard manual will show which fittings are for P8 and P9. If the connectors are not marked,

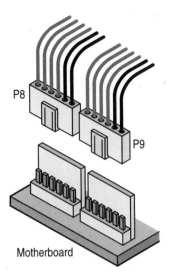

P8

P9

Motherboard

**Figure 5.1**   P8 and P9 connectors and motherboard fitting

make sure that the two black wires on each plug are side by side and that the orange wire (on P8) and the two red wires (on P9) are on the outside as you push them into place.

The following table of power cables shows voltage values for each of the color-coded wires on P8 and P9. The ground wires are considered 0 volts; all voltage measurements (see Chapter 22, "The Basics of Electrical Energy") are taken between the black wires and one of the colored wires.

| Cable Color | Supply In | Tolerance |
|---|---|---|
| Yellow | +12 | ±10% |
| Blue | −12 | ±10% |
| Red | +5 | ±5% |
| White | −5 | ±5% |
| Black | Ground | N/A |

**Note**   Some computer makers employ proprietary power connections that require a special power supply. To install a new part in these types of computers, you will need to follow the instructions that come with the computer.

Remember to install the P8 and P9 plugs so that the black wires are side by side. Installing them on the wrong receptacle can damage both the motherboard and the power supply. Figure 5.2 shows the P8 and P9 connectors and a motherboard.

---

**Note**   Some power supplies have a third P-style connector. This is used only on very few motherboards and it can be ignored on those on which it is found. If you come across one, refer to the manual that came with the part for instructions on its requirements and installation.

---

**Figure 5.2**   Connecting P8 and P9

## ATX-Style Motherboard Connections

The newer ATX main power connection, found on Pentium II computers and later, is much easier to install. A single 20-pin plug is set into a fitted receptacle and secured with a catch on the side of the plug that snaps over the fitting. Figure 5.3 shows how to properly seat the connection. A small, flat-tip screwdriver is a handy tool for easing the pressure on the catch to remove the plug. In some cases, you can use a screwdriver to ease installation as well.

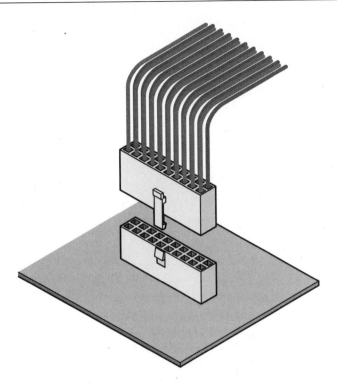

**Figure 5.3**   Placing an ATX plug in its motherboard receptacle

## Connections to Peripheral Hardware

Two standard types of connectors are used to connect the power supply to peripheral hardware:

- **Molex connector.**   This is the most commonly used power connector. It provides both 12-volt and 5-volt power. Hard disk drives, internal tape drives, CD-ROM drives, DVD (digital video disc) drives, and older 5.25-inch floppy disk drives all use this fitting. The Molex connector has two rounded corners and two sharp corners to ensure that it installs properly (see Figure 5.4).

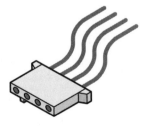

**Figure 5.4**   Molex connector (not to scale)

■ **Mini connector.**    Most power supplies provide one or more mini connectors (see Figure 5.5). The mini is used primarily for 3.5-inch floppy disk drives. It has four pin-outs and, usually, four wires. Most are fitted with keys that make it difficult, but not impossible, to install upside down. Be sure to orient the connector correctly; applying power with the connector reversed can damage or destroy the drive.

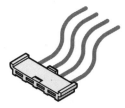

**Figure 5.5**    Mini connector (not to scale)

## Two- and Three-Pin Mini Plugs

A less common type of power connector is used to connect the fan of a Pentium II or III processor to the motherboard for power, to connect a CD-ROM drive to a sound card, and to provide power for 3.5-inch floppy disk drives. These connectors have two or three wires that are usually red and black or red, yellow, and black.

**Caution**    Do not connect power-carrying mini plugs to audio or data devices such as a CD drive or a sound card, because you could damage or destroy those devices.

## Extenders and Splitters

PCs can run out of power connections, and large cases can have drives beyond the reach of any plug on the supply. A good technician has a quick solution on hand to both of these common problems: extenders and splitters.

*Extenders* are wire sets that have a Molex connector on each end; they are used to extend a power connection to a device beyond the reach of the power supply's own wiring. *Splitters* are similar to extenders, with the exception that they provide two power connections from a single power supply connector.

## Lesson Summary

The following points summarize the main elements of this lesson:

- Power supplies come in a variety of sizes and shapes.
- There are two types of main power connectors: AT and ATX.
- A power supply must be capable of handling the requirements of the computer and all internal devices.
- Be careful when attaching some connectors; if connected incorrectly, they can damage the computer.
- Do not open the power supply housing!
- Keeping a few splitters and extenders in the repair kit can help the technician easily solve some common problems.

# Lesson 2: Power Supply Problems

Power supply problems can come from both internal and external sources. Component failure within a computer can cause a power supply to fail, but the most common failures come externally from the power source itself. In this lesson, we look at common problems associated with power supplies and what you, as a technician, can do about them.

### After this lesson, you will be able to

- Determine the types of problems that can be caused by power supplies
- Know when to check and when to replace a power supply
- Plan how to protect your system from external power supply problems

### Estimated lesson time: 10 minutes

## Power Failures

Power supplies are affected by the quality of the local power source. Common power delivery problems such as spikes, surges, sags, brownouts, and blackouts affect the stability and operation of the main power supply and are passed on to the computer. Although most users don't notice sudden changes in the quality of electrical power, computers and other sensitive electronics are affected. Although we can't fully control these problems, there are a few things we can do, noted in the following table, to protect our equipment and data and ensure a reasonably clean electrical supply.

| Problem | Description |
| --- | --- |
| Surges | These are brief (and sometimes catastrophic) increases in the voltage source (very high voltage for a very short time). They can originate with the power source (the local power company) but most often are due to lightning strikes. |
| Spikes | Spikes are very short overvoltage conditions. Spikes are measured in nanoseconds, whereas a surge is measured in milliseconds. |
| Sags | These are brief decreases of voltage at the power source. |
| Brownouts | If a sag lasts longer than 1 second, it is called a brownout. The overloading of a primary power source can cause brownouts. Some brownouts are "scheduled" by power companies to prevent overloading of circuits and potential catastrophic failure of the system. |
| Blackouts | A blackout is a complete power failure, which can be caused by equipment failure (local or regional) or accidental cutting of power cables. When the power returns after a blackout, there is a power spike and the danger of a power surge. |

## Power Protection Devices

*Surge suppressors* are devices used to filter out the effects of voltage spikes and surges that are present in commercial power sources and smooth out power variations. They are available from local computer dealers and superstores. A good surge suppressor will protect your system from most problems, but if you purchase an economy model, it might not work when you need it most. Keep in mind that almost nothing will shield your hardware from a very close lightning strike.

---

**Note**  Most power strips with surge protection have a red indicator light. If the light goes out, this means that the unit is not providing protection. These types of surge suppressors need to be replaced every year or so. If the indicator light starts flashing before then, it means the power strip is failing and should be replaced immediately.

---

When evaluating the quality of surge suppressors, look for performance certification. At a minimum, it should have an Underwriters Laboratory (UL) listing and power ratings. A high-quality unit will also provide protection for phone/fax/modem and network connections. These units protect up to a point; however, for complete protection from power fluctuations and outages, an uninterruptible power supply (UPS) is recommended.

A *UPS* is an inline battery backup. When properly installed between a computer and the wall outlet, a UPS protects the computer from surges and acts as a battery when the power dips or fails. It also provides a warning that the power is out of specification (above or below acceptable levels). Many models can also interact with the computer and initiate a safe shutdown in the event of a complete power failure using software that runs in the background and sends a signal through one of the computer's COM ports when the power goes down.

The amount of time that a UPS device can keep a system running is determined by battery capacity and the power demands of the equipment connected to it. A more powerful UPS device will need its own line and circuit breaker. One of the principal power drains is the monitor. To keep a system online as long as possible during a power failure, turn off the monitor immediately after the failure commences.

When considering a UPS, take into account how much protection is needed, as well as the importance of peace of mind to the user. The VA rating (voltage × amps = watts) must be sufficient to supply the computer and all its peripherals with power for enough time to safely shut down the system. The easiest way to calculate this number is to add the power rating (watts) for *all* pieces of equipment that are to be connected to the UPS, as shown in the following table.

| Device | Power Rating (Watts) | Connected to UPS | Power Required |
|---|---|---|---|
| Computer | 200–350 | Yes | 250 |
| Monitor | 80–100 | Yes | 80 |
| External modem | 5.5 | No | 0 |
| External backup drive | 50 | Yes | 50 |
| Total | 335.5–505.5 | — | 380 |

**Caution**   Never plug a laser printer into a UPS unless the UPS is specifically rated to support that type of device. Laser printers often require more power than a UPS is able to provide, potentially placing the printer, the UPS, and the computer at risk.

## Power Supply Problems

The most easily recognized problem is a complete failure of the power supply. This is easy to detect because, in the event of a failure, the computer will not boot up (no lights, no sound). If there is apparently no power, be sure to check the power source and the plug at both ends: the outlet and the computer.

If you are experiencing intermittent failures such as memory loss, memory corruption, or unexplained system crashes, don't rule out the power supply—it is often the culprit. Fortunately, it is easy to check and replace.

Good power supplies have line-conditioning circuits, but these might not be sufficient in locations where the power source has substantial quality flaws. If you have problems with several systems, or if a second power supply still does not fix a related complaint, add a UPS with good line-conditioning features.

Most power grids in the United States provide current that is far from ideal for sensitive electronic components. Line-conditioning hardware added in the chain just before the current reaches the machine adds a much needed level of protection from spikes (very fast jumps in power levels), surges (longer ones), and drops. All can cause transient problems with operations. These are often erroneously blamed on the operating system or software.

## Lesson Summary

The following points summarize the main elements of this lesson:

- Power supply problems can be caused by component failures within the power supply or from the power source.

- Two devices protect against external power problems: surge suppressors and UPSs.

# Chapter Summary

The following points summarize the key concepts in this chapter:

## Power Supplies

- The key to specifying the proper size of a power supply for a computer is to add together the power requirements for all the components. It is important to be sure to add extra power to allow for boot up.

- Electrical power is measured in watts.

- Proper installation of the P8 and P9 connectors is important to prevent damage to the motherboard. The black (ground) wires must be installed side by side.

- Molex and mini connectors are used to connect power to devices such as floppy disk and hard disk drives.

## Power Supply Problems

- The flow of power into a computer must be managed to prevent damage and/ or loss of data.

- Surge suppressors will protect against higher-than-normal voltage problems.

- High-quality UPS devices will protect a computer from most power fluctuations.

- Check power supplies when there are unusual problems with memory and PC operations that do not have a reasonable cause.

# Review

The following questions are intended to reinforce key information presented in this chapter. If you are unable to answer a question, review the appropriate lesson and then try the question again. Answers to the questions can be found in Appendix A, "Questions and Answers."

1. Explain the differences among spikes, surges, and sags.

2. What are the two types of power supply connectors to the motherboard?

3. What are the two types of power supply connectors for devices such as drives?

4. Name two benefits of having a UPS on a system.

5. Describe the difference between a brownout and a blackout.

6. When you purchase a UPS, what is the most important thing to consider?

7. Will any surge suppressor provide protection against lightning strikes?

8. What is the best defense against spikes caused by lightning?

9. What is the most important thing to remember when connecting a P8 and P9 connector to a motherboard?

10. Explain the difference between the mini connector and the Molex connector.

11. Describe the best way to make sure a new power supply matches the one you are replacing.

12. What is the primary use of mini connectors?

13. A computer power supply has both 5-volt and 12-volt outputs. The 5-volt output is used to power _____, and the 12-volt output is used to power _____.

C H A P T E R    6

# Motherboard and ROM BIOS

Lesson 1: Computer Cases . . . . . . . . . . . . . . . . . . . . . . . . . . . . . . . . . 94

Lesson 2: Motherboards . . . . . . . . . . . . . . . . . . . . . . . . . . . . . . . . . . . 97

Lesson 3: ROM BIOS . . . . . . . . . . . . . . . . . . . . . . . . . . . . . . . . . . . . . 101

Chapter Summary . . . . . . . . . . . . . . . . . . . . . . . . . . . . . . . . . . . . . . . 116

Review . . . . . . . . . . . . . . . . . . . . . . . . . . . . . . . . . . . . . . . . . . . . . . . 117

## About This Chapter

In earlier lessons, we provided an overview of the computer. In this chapter, we focus on the computer's infrastructure. We begin with the centerpiece of the computer, the *motherboard,* also called the *mainboard.* The motherboard is the key part of the hardware infrastructure. It is a large circuit board that serves as a home for the central processing unit (CPU) and all its associated chips, including the chip set and RAM (random access memory), and connects them to the rest of the physical elements and components of the computer.

## Before You Begin

Although this chapter can be studied independently, it is suggested that you review the preceding chapters, which discuss microprocessors, basic input/output, and how power gets to the system, before reading this material.

# Lesson 1:  Computer Cases

The case, or chassis, which usually is made of metal, holds all the primary electronics of the personal computer (PC) and often all the drives as well.

## After this lesson, you will be able to

- Identify the primary types of PC cases
- Explain how the case helps to protect the PC and surrounding devices from electromagnetic interference

## Estimated lesson time: 5 minutes

## The Computer Case

To casual users, the PC is a metal container, attached by a few cables to a keyboard, mouse, and monitor. In fact, the case is more than just a box to house a computer.

The real value of a case does not lie in the label, color, or how pretty it looks. Instead, the case houses all the internal components, offers access to the outside world via ports and connectors, and protects the PC's delicate circuits from damage and electromagnetic interference (EMI). It also protects surrounding devices, such as TVs, from the PC's EMI.

**Note**   *Electromagnetic interference (EMI)* is a newer term for *radio frequency interference (RFI)*. EMI is any radio frequency that is emitted from an electrical or electronic device that is harmful to the surrounding equipment or that interferes with the operation of another electrical or electronic device. A computer interferes with radio, telephone, or TV reception when it generates EMI. Any high-quality computer will contain special circuits and grounding to prevent emissions from escaping into the surrounding area. Running a computer without its cover is a sure way to generate EMI.

The case design is also often used to underscore the identity of a specific brand of computer, and can often be part of the reason we purchase a particular computer. Some people will also choose a case design for its appearance. We do, after all, want something that looks good, especially if we are spending a lot of money on it. With some cases, however, there may be a more technical reason for the case choice, such as the number of drive bays available.

Early computer cases were little more than boxes that sat on the desk and served as monitor stands. Today, some manufacturers build "designer" computers that come in fancy colors and command premium prices.

As computer technicians, we don't usually concern ourselves with the computer case; we simply deal with whatever our customer uses. However, when it comes to recommending a computer for purchase, the size and configuration of the case should be considered. Depending on the business application, the difference between a tower and a desktop design can be important.

When considering the case, there are four general rules to keep in mind:

- The bigger the box, the more components it can hold (providing greater expansion potential) and, often, the better the air flow (essential for cooling). Large cases are also easier to work with.

- The more compact the box, the less expansion potential it has; working on it is often much more difficult, and usually air flow is more restricted.

- Smaller cases that come with a power supply usually have lower wattage, reducing the number of internal devices that can be installed.

- The more features in a case design, like the power wattage or the number of bays, the higher the cost.

---

**Important**   It is *not* a good idea to run a computer for extended periods of time with the case open or removed entirely. This not only produces EMI, but also results in improper air flow and reduced cooling of the system components. If you must do so, consider placing a small fan so that it blows an air stream over the CPU and chip set.

---

## Working with Cases

In any repair job that involves inspecting or replacing internal components, the technician has to open the case. That used to be very simple; the technician would remove four screws in the back of the computer with a Phillips screwdriver, then pull the case's cover forward to reveal the contents. Today, however, cases come in a variety of forms, with screws in the front or back, fancy plastic bevels in front, and featuring one of several types of metal wraps—some in several parts, some in a single piece.

The majority of cases still open the old-fashioned way. However, if you find yourself with one of the exceptions and can't locate screws in the back, check to see if the plastic cover in the front can be pulled off. If so, that should reveal three or four screws. Then see if the main cover can be pulled forward. If not, look for screws that secure one or more of the side panels. Some side panel designs are great for granting easy access to our next topic, motherboards. This style of case allows one to inspect or remove the motherboard without having to remove the entire outer covering.

Another trend is a case design using fittings that can be opened without any tools.  Some computers now provide easy opening with a thumb screw that doesn't even require a screw driver. If you are working with one of these computers, simply turn the thumb screw and slide the case back.

## Lesson Summary

The following points summarize the main elements of this lesson:

- The case of the PC defines the size, shape, and configuration of the motherboard, the amount of expansion possible, and the space into which hard drives and other internal accessories can be fitted.

- To prevent EMI and ensure system components are properly cooled, you should avoid running a computer without its cover.

# Lesson 2:  Motherboards

The motherboard is the PC's center of activity. All devices in a computer are in some way connected to the motherboard. It hosts the largest single collection of chips of any PC component and serves as the "street system" for the grid of wires that link all the components, making it possible for them to communicate.

## After this lesson, you will be able to

- Identify a motherboard and its functions
- Locate and define the components of a motherboard
- Safely remove and replace a motherboard

## Estimated lesson time: 15 minutes

## The Motherboard

The motherboard (one is shown in Figure 6.1) defines the computer's limits of speed, memory, and expandability. A computer needs more than just a CPU and memory. To accept input from the user, it needs devices, such as a keyboard and a mouse. It also needs output devices, such as monitors and sound cards, to cope with the powerful graphics and sound capabilities of the programs available today. A computer also needs "permanent" storage devices, such as floppy disk drives and hard disk drives, to store data when it is turned off. It is the function of the motherboard to provide the connectivity for all these devices, as well as for the CPU, RAM, and support integrated circuits (ICs).

**Figure 6.1**   Motherboard with CPU

The motherboard is usually the largest circuit board found inside the computer case. Motherboards come in a variety of shapes. One size does not fit all, and careful attention to size and location of mounting holes is required before installing a new motherboard in an older computer. A motherboard needs to fit in the space allotted for it, be secure in its mounts, be properly grounded, receive sufficient ventilation (for cooling of the CPU and other heat-sensitive components), and must not conflict with other hardware. When considering the purchase of a new motherboard (see Lesson 2 of Chapter 4, "The Central Processing Unit"), keep these things in mind:

- Most "generic" motherboards will fit into "generic" computers. One reason some people consider purchasing a PC clone is that it is easier to upgrade. Keep in mind that a hybrid PC (assembled by a small vendor, made from untested components) may be constructed of parts that may or may not be totally compatible. There may also be questions about EMI due to interaction between components or the way the parts set in the case.

- There are two major categories of motherboards: AT and ATX. The main difference between them is the type of power supply and main power switch each requires. When you order a new motherboard, be sure to first verify that it is compatible with the case and power supply to be used.

- If you are working on a brand-name computer, you might be required to purchase a new motherboard or other custom components from the same manufacturer.

- Before buying a motherboard, check its technical references to be sure that the new board will fit and will be compatible with any of the RAM and expansion cards the owner intends to use. Often, this information can be found in the owner's manual. If not, check the manufacturer's Web site, if one is available, or check other online resources such as technical libraries. A Web search using the keyword "motherboard" will yield sites dedicated to computer hardware.

- For all practical purposes, you cannot repair motherboards. They should be replaced if physically or electrically damaged. Your customer will get new technology, usually for a price lower than the cost of the repair.

- Because it is often the most difficult part of a system to replace (you have to remove all the equipment that is connected to it), check all other internal and external components before removing or replacing the motherboard.

- When obtaining a replacement, be sure to factor in the cost of all critical options found on the existing motherboard. Some have a built-in SCSI (Small Computer System Interface) Host Adapter or display adapters that might not be common. In that case, either make sure the new board offers the same level of support or install the appropriate add-on card(s) to bring the system up to the existing level of operation.

## Chip Sets

A motherboard comes with a variety of support chips soldered in place. The primary elements constitute the *chip set* and are designed to work with the CPU. These chips are highly complex and coordinated ICs that help the CPU manage and control the computer's system. When replacing a CPU, you must make sure that it is compatible with the chip set and supported by the motherboard. If not, the computer won't work. A basic chip set (see Figure 6.2) consists of a

- Bus controller
- Memory controller
- Data and address buffer
- Peripheral controller

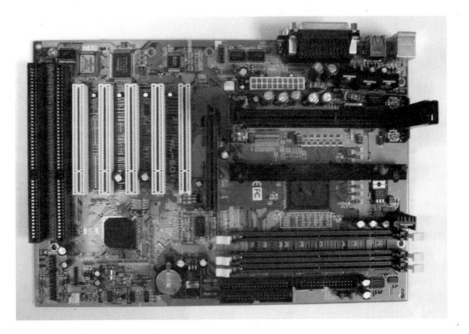

**Figure 6.2**  Motherboard with chip set

On modern motherboards, you will find specialized chips to control things such as cache memory and high-speed buses. You will also find boards with fewer individual chips because the manufacturer has incorporated several functions into one chip.

Keep in mind that there is a wide range of features (with attendant cost increases for extras) available when selecting a motherboard. You will need to keep up to date on the types of processors, memory design, CPUs, and expansion slots available to recommend and obtain the right product for your customers.

Be careful in choosing motherboards with components like display adapters and sound cards on board. These are components that may not have all the features of their expansion card versions, and customers may decide to upgrade, leaving them with motherboard-based elements that could cause conflicts.

## Lesson Summary

The following points summarize the main elements of this lesson:

- Motherboards come in many sizes and shapes, but generic boards are available that fit most clone computers.
- The motherboard determines the limits of the computer's capabilities.
- Chip sets are unique to each motherboard design and work with the CPU to manage and control the computer's system.
- You should make sure any new motherboard is compatible with the CPU, RAM, and any other critical hardware and features that are already installed on the computer.

# Lesson 3:  ROM BIOS

In addition to the chip set, you will find other chips called *ROM BIOS*. A ROM BIOS chip contains data that specifies the characteristics of hardware devices, such as memory and hard disk and floppy disk drives, so the system can properly access them. This lesson explores ROM BIOS and what it does.

### After this lesson, you will be able to

- Identify the different types of ROM

- Modify the CMOS settings in a computer

- Identify POST codes and take appropriate corrective action when a problem is identified

### Estimated lesson time: 30 minutes

## ROM BIOS

*ROM (read-only memory)* is a type of memory that stores data even when the main computer power is off. This is necessary so that the system can access the data it needs to start up. When stored in ROM, information that is required to start and run the computer cannot be lost or changed. The *BIOS (basic input/ output system)* is software in the form of programs stored on ROM chips. The *system BIOS* is a ROM chip on the motherboard used by the computer during the startup routine (boot process) to check out the system and prepare to run the hardware. The BIOS is stored on a ROM chip because ROM retains information even when no power is being supplied to the computer. The downside of storing data in an older computer's ROM is that a chip may have to be changed to update information.

More recent systems use a technology called *flash ROM* or *flash BIOS* that allows code in the core chips to be updated by software available through the BIOS or motherboard supplier. Check the Internet site of the supplier if you suspect your ROM chip has flash ROM technology; the software and instructions are generally downloadable.

**Caution**   Upgrade a BIOS only when necessary! Be sure to follow all precautions included with the motherboard manual and instructions for the upgrade. Improper installation can render the motherboard useless.

BIOS (also referred to as *firmware*) can be subdivided into three classes, depending on the type of hardware it controls.

- The first class, called *core chips,* includes support for hardware that is common to all computers, is necessary, and never changes.

- The second class, called *updateable chips,* encompasses hardware that is also common and necessary, but that might change from time to time.

- The third class of chips includes anything that is not included in one of the first two classes.

## Core Chips

Look on any motherboard: ROM chips for the core chips are found everywhere. They are often distinctive because they are in DIP (dual in-line package) form and are almost always labeled. These chips are commonly used for the keyboard, parallel ports, serial ports, speakers, and other support devices. Each ROM chip contains between 16 and 64 KB of programming. If the functions have been combined, it may be harder to determine the chip's purpose by appearance.

## Updateable Chips

Several devices on a computer often contain their own flash BIOS or updateable ROMs including SCSI controllers and video cards. Because this information is subject to change (for instance, you can upgrade a hard disk drive or change a video card), it is stored on a special chip called the *complementary metal-oxide semiconductor* (CMOS). This chip gets its name from the way it is manufactured and what it is made from, not from the information it holds.

Unlike other ROM chips, CMOS chips do not store programs, but instead store data that actually configures the features of the motherboard. For example, it notes the number of floppy drives, the type(s) of hard drives, and if power-saving options or administrator passwords are active. The CMOS chip also maintains date and time information when power to the computer is off.

CMOS chips can store about 64 KB of data. However, storage of the data needed to boot a computer requires only a very small amount of memory (about 128 bytes).

If the data stored on the CMOS is different from the hardware it keeps track of, the computer, or part of it, will probably not work. For example, if the hard disk drive information is incorrect, the computer can be booted from a floppy disk, but the hard disk drive might not be accessible. The technician or owner will have to reset the CMOS values before the computer can use the device if it is not properly defined in the CMOS registry.

The information contained in a CMOS chip will depend on the manufacturer. Typically, the CMOS contains at least the following information:

- Floppy disk and hard disk drive types
- CPU
- RAM size
- Date and time

- Serial and parallel port information
- Plug and Play information
- Power-saving settings

---

**Important**   It is critical that the core information on a CMOS chip be correct. If you change any of the related hardware, the CMOS must be updated to reflect those changes. If the CMOS loses power from its battery, it will lose its data. The next time the system is started, the setup program will revert to its default settings. It is a good idea to write down the primary system settings (like hard drive parameters) and tape them inside the case for reference.

---

## Updating CMOS

To make changes to a CMOS chip, you need to run a CMOS setup program. This application is independent of the operating system, because it must work even if an operating system is not loaded, or even if there is no form of disk drive. The way to start this program depends on the manufacturer of the BIOS, not the manufacturer of the computer. Manufacturers of motherboards purchase the BIOS from other companies, most of which specialize in making these chips. Many different computer suppliers use the same BIOS. The BIOS manufacturer and version number are the first things you see displayed when you boot up your computer. Figure 6.3 shows examples of startup information for three different types of BIOS chips.

```
AMIBOS (C) 1996 American Megatrends Inc.,

PRESS <DEL>, IF YOU WANT TO RUN SETUP

                OR

(C) American Megatrends Inc.,
40-0100-006259-00101111-060692-SYMP-F

                OR

Phoenix BIOS TM A486 Version 1 03 (225B)
Copyright © 1985-1996 Phoenix
Technologies Ltd.
All Rights Reserved
```

**Figure 6.3**   BIOS information

Although several companies write BIOS code and sell it to computer makers, three companies—American Megatrends (AMI), Phoenix, and Award—dominate the BIOS market. Motherboard vendors might use one supplier for a series of products; however, it is not uncommon for a manufacturer to change sources within a series due to design or cost considerations. A good technician should be familiar with the basic CMOS setup procedures for BIOS manufactured by all three.

Because of its flexibility, the Hi-Flex BIOS, manufactured by AMI, has taken a large share of the computer market. Motherboard manufacturers can purchase a basic BIOS from AMI and then add setup parameters to meet the needs of their products. For this reason, the number of setup parameters available on one computer can differ from those on another computer, even though they use the same motherboard. Award competes directly with AMI, providing very flexible BIOS chips. Award was the first BIOS to heavily support Peripheral Component Interconnect (PCI) motherboards.

Phoenix is considered a manufacturer of high-end BIOS. Phoenix creates individual BIOS chips for specific machines. As a result, Phoenix BIOS chips have fewer setup parameters available. These chips are commonly used in machines with proprietary motherboards, such as laptops. Vendors can tune the BIOS for performance, basing new code on the Phoenix core. Keep in mind that Phoenix also makes parts that are sold and employed without custom code.

There are several ways to determine who the BIOS manufacturer is:

- Watch the monitor when the computer boots. A BIOS screen will usually be displayed, indicating the manufacturer and version number. (This screen might not be visible if the computer is warm booted. In that case, power off the unit and restart.)
- Check the computer or motherboard manual. Most include a section on entering the setup program and setting options.
- Remove the cover of the computer and look at the chip. Most BIOS chips have a manufacturer's label.
- Try a good third-party utility program. These products are available at almost any software store. A Web search for a key phrase such as "BIOS diagnostic" will yield the names of a number of them.
- Reboot the computer and hold down several keys at once or unplug a drive. This will often cause an error and prompt you to get into the setup program. Unplugging the keyboard will accomplish the same goal with less work; however, you won't be able to make adjustments on most systems with the keyboard inoperative.

## A Typical CMOS Setup

Every CMOS setup program looks slightly different. Do not be too concerned about the differences—all BIOS routines contain basically the same information.

Take your time and get comfortable navigating in the setup programs. Most of the CMOS setup programs are text-based, so you will have to use keystrokes to navigate through the information. However, some newer machines use a Windows-like CMOS setup (they have the look of a Windows environment and will let you use a mouse to select changes).

## The Most Common Ways to Access BIOS Setup Programs

- For AMI, press DELETE when the machine first begins to boot.
- For Phoenix, press CTRL+ALT+ESC, DEL, or F2 when requested.
- For Award, you can usually follow either of the other two procedures.

Motherboard makers can change the key combinations to access the CMOS setup. This can be especially true for brand-name computers, and manufacturers are not likely to publish the information on the startup screen.

---

**Tip**  If all else fails, try any of these key combinations: CTRL+ALT+INSERT, CTRL+A, CTRL+S, CTRL+F1, F2, and F10.

---

Let's look at some typical screens from a Phoenix BIOS setup program. They are good examples of how typical CMOS settings are presented and adjusted.

Figure 6.4 shows the first screen of this CMOS setup. From this point, you can select alternate tabs (Advanced, Security, Power) or adjust any of these individual items: floppy disk drive, hard disk drive, date and time, or RAM settings.

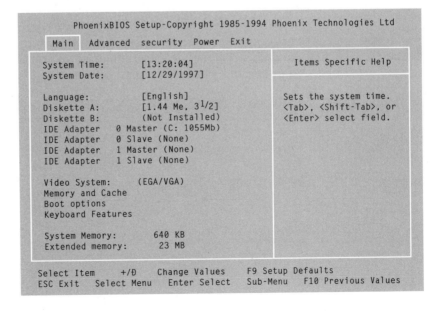

**Figure 6.4**  Main screen

The hard disk drive setup screen (Figure 6.5) is where individual hard drive parameters are set. Today, most hard drives based on IDE (Integrated Device Electronics) can be automatically detected by the BIOS. The CMOS settings are then made by the BIOS automatically. However, you should still know how to do this manually, both to be able to work with an older machine and in case the setup program fails to recognize the drive.

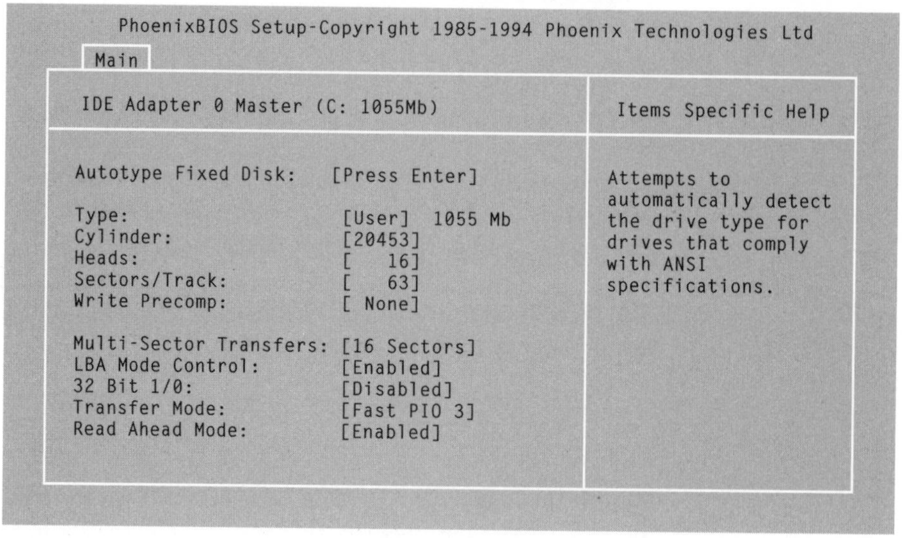

```
PhoenixBIOS Setup-Copyright 1985-1994 Phoenix Technologies Ltd
  Main

  IDE Adapter 0 Master (C: 1055Mb)              Items Specific Help

  Autotype Fixed Disk:    [Press Enter]
                                             Attempts to
  Type:                   [User]  1055 Mb     automatically detect
  Cylinder:               [20453]             the drive type for
  Heads:                  [   16]             drives that comply
  Sectors/Track:          [   63]             with ANSI
  Write Precomp:          [ None]             specifications.

  Multi-Sector Transfers: [16 Sectors]
  LBA Mode Control:       [Enabled]
  32 Bit 1/0:             [Disabled]
  Transfer Mode:          [Fast PIO 3]
  Read Ahead Mode:        [Enabled]
```

**Figure 6.5**   Hard disk drive setup screen

The Advanced tab (Figure 6.6) leads to more advanced setup parameters. A great deal of customization can be achieved using these settings. Pay careful attention to any warnings that come up before you make any changes to device settings. If you don't understand a setting, it is best to leave the default option.

The Security tab allows you to set security parameters. Be careful: Once you set a password, you have to remember that password to change the security parameters. If you encounter a situation in which an owner has set and forgotten a password, you will have to flush and reset the CMOS to the factory default settings. Check the motherboard manual for information on how to do this. It usually involves changing jumper settings twice.

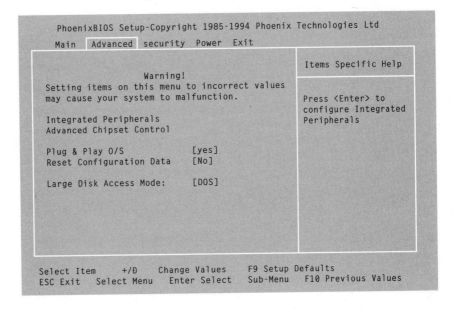

```
    PhoenixBIOS Setup-Copyright 1985-1994 Phoenix Technologies Ltd
    Main   Advanced  security  Power  Exit
  ┌──────────────────────────────────────────┬─────────────────────┐
  │                                           │ Items Specific Help │
  │                   Warning!                ├─────────────────────┤
  │  Setting items on this menu to incorrect values                 │
  │  may cause your system to malfunction.    │ Press <Enter> to    │
  │                                           │ configure Integrated│
  │  Integrated Peripherals                   │ Peripherals         │
  │  Advanced Chipset Control                 │                     │
  │                                           │                     │
  │  Plug & Play O/S            [yes]         │                     │
  │  Reset Configuration Data   [No]          │                     │
  │                                           │                     │
  │  Large Disk Access Mode:    [DOS]         │                     │
  │                                           │                     │
  │                                           │                     │
  │                                           │                     │
  │                                           │                     │
  └──────────────────────────────────────────┴─────────────────────┘
    Select Item    +/Ð     Change Values    F9 Setup Defaults
    ESC Exit   Select Menu   Enter Select   Sub-Menu   F10 Previous Values
```

**Figure 6.6**  Advanced tab

Notice in Figure 6.7 that the virus check reminder option is disabled. If you find a CMOS virus checker enabled, turn it off. This is especially important during operating system and program installation. If you are certain that no virus software is on the computer, yet you continue to get error messages warning you to turn off all anti-virus software, the CMOS virus checker is the most likely source of these erroneous messages. If you find this happening, disable the CMOS virus checker. Of course, if you still get the message, you should check for a real virus. Figure 6.7 shows the Security tab.

---

**Tip**   These built-in CMOS virus checkers actually do very little to protect your system. For the best possible protection against viruses, be sure to install a good anti-virus program designed for the operating system on the computer and suggest that the customer run and update it regularly.

---

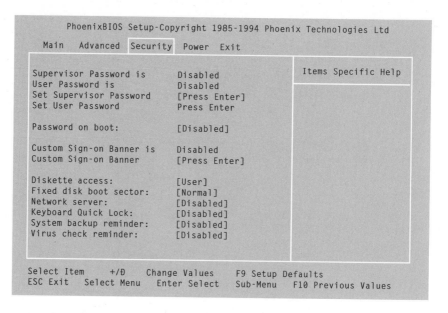

**Figure 6.7**   Security tab

The Power tab, shown in Figure 6.8, allows the user to set up any power conservation options provided by the manufacturer. These features typically include setting a time limit for reducing power to the monitor and hard disk drive.

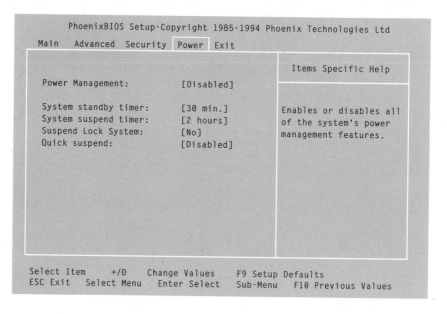

**Figure 6.8**   Power tab

### Maintaining CMOS

Losing CMOS information is, unfortunately, a common problem. If the information on the CMOS chips is erased or corrupted, the computer will not be able to boot or you will get nasty-looking errors. Some of the more common reasons that CMOS data is lost include the following:

- The on-board battery has run out.
- Cards have been removed or inserted in a way that releases electrostatic discharge (ESD).
- Improper handling of the motherboard has caused electrical short circuits or failure due to ESD.
- Something has been dropped on the motherboard.
- There is dirt on the motherboard.
- The power supply is faulty.
- There have been electrical surges.

The following types of errors indicate lost or corrupt CMOS data:

- CMOS configuration mismatch
- CMOS date/time not set
- No boot device available
- CMOS battery state low
- Cannot locate hard disk drive or floppy disk drive

It is wise to back up the CMOS setup just as you back up important data. One way to do this is to write down the information (especially before making hardware changes). There are many third-party CMOS save-and-restore utility programs available.

---

**Note**   Many newer machines that run versions of Windows 95 and later and that offer Plug and Play place less emphasis on the CMOS. The BIOS information is stored with the device and is automatically detected at boot.

---

## The CMOS Battery

The CMOS chip requires a small trickle voltage from a battery to keep its memory alive. When the battery gets low or dies, the computer will experience a sudden memory loss and thus lose settings. It might not be able to find the floppy disk or first hard disk drive and therefore display an error indicating that it cannot find the system or nonsystem disk.

The voltage of CMOS batteries ranges from 3 to 6 volts. Check the motherboard or the motherboard documentation to determine the actual battery requirements. Batteries come as either on-board (NiCad batteries, soldered in place or in a fixture, that last from five to seven years) or external (nonrechargeable AA alkaline batteries that last from two to four years). The 3-volt lithium watch battery is becoming very popular with motherboard suppliers. Many of these are mounted in a special holder so that the battery can be easily changed; however, some manufacturers solder them in place.

The first clue that the battery is weakening is that the CMOS clock begins to slow down. Exit to DOS and, when you see the C prompt (C:), type **time**. If you notice the clock is slow, it's probably time to change the battery.

---

**Note**    Remember that an MS-DOS machine (as well as those running Windows 95 and later) uses the CMOS clock to get the date and time at startup. After the computer is running, MS-DOS uses the memory refresh timer on the memory controller to keep time. This works well, but because the refresh timer is not very accurate about seconds, you will lose one or two seconds per day. If you never turn off a computer, it could lose time. Do not confuse this with a bad battery. When you reboot, the computer will update itself to the correct time from the CMOS. If the CMOS battery is low, it will still show the incorrect time.

---

When the CMOS battery dies completely, you will get lost CMOS errors, as previously described. If you reload the CMOS data and the errors return, it's time to change the battery. Although the computer will hold CMOS information during the week, sometimes, over the weekend—when the computer is turned off for two days—the CMOS data will be lost. Do not let these seemingly "intermittent" problems fool you. Sometimes, before a battery dies, but after it has started to fail, it will still be able to hold CMOS settings for a short time after the computer is off. Any time a computer loses the CMOS information more than once in a week, it's a sure sign that you need to replace the battery immediately—if only to eliminate the battery as the source of the problem. After replacing the battery, you must run the setup utility and restore any CMOS settings.

---

**Note**    The CMOS chip contains a capacitor that allows replacement of the battery without losing data. For motherboards with soldered on-board batteries, there is usually a connection that allows you to add an external battery to replace a worn-out internal one. Be sure that the external battery has the same voltage as the on-board battery you are replacing. Some older PCs use a battery pack with four AA cells or a single 9-volt battery. These should be replaced with a special PC battery pack to provide longer life.

---

The best source of information about replacing a CMOS battery is the documentation that comes with the motherboard.

Today's computers are becoming less reliant on battery backup for CMOS. With Windows Plug and Play technology, devices come with their own BIOS, which the system reads each time the computer is booted. This does not eliminate the need for CMOS or batteries, but it minimizes the impact of a battery failure. At the very least, you will still need to retain the date and time information.

# All Other Chips

It would be impossible to put all the necessary BIOS information for every conceivable piece of hardware on one chip. It would also be impractical, as new devices are released almost monthly. Upgrading a machine would require a new BIOS chip (or a new version of the flash BIOS) every time. Fortunately, there are other ways to handle this challenge.

## ROM Chips with BIOS

BIOS can be put on the hardware device itself. Many new add-on boards, such as display adapters, network interface cards, and sound cards, have their own onboard ROM chip. Because the system BIOS doesn't have a clue about how to communicate with the new device, this card includes its own BIOS.

## Loading Device Drivers

Using device drivers is the most popular way to provide BIOS support for hardware. A device driver is a program that acts as an interface between the operating system and the control circuits that operate the device. For example, Windows has "generic" code that opens a file, but the driver for the disk drive takes care of low-level tasks like positioning the read head, reading or writing blocks of data, and so on. Thus, applications programmers don't usually have to worry about these details and can assume that any hardware supported by a device driver will work.

Just how a device driver is invoked depends on the operating system, the hardware, and the software design. Although few devices still use the CONFIG.SYS file to load drivers, it provides an easy way to see how they work.

Every time the computer is booted up, the CONFIG.SYS file is read and the device drivers are loaded from the hard disk drive into RAM.

Some examples of device drivers in CONFIG.SYS are:

```
DEVICE=C:\DOS\HIMEM.SYS
DEVICE=C:\DOS\EMM386.EXE NOEMS
DEVICEHIGH =C:\SCSI\ASPIPP3.SYS /D /Z
DEVICEHIGH =C:\DOS\DRVSPACE.SYS
DEVICEHIGH =C:\CDROM\MTMCDAI.SYS /L=001
```

Loading device drivers in CONFIG.SYS is a requirement for machines running MS-DOS. The Windows 95, Windows 98, Windows Me, and Windows 2000 operating systems have their own drivers that are loaded as part of startup. (Drivers are covered in more detail in the appropriate operating system chapters later in this book.) Occasionally, drivers become outdated or have problems. You can obtain new drivers directly from the device manufacturers (often directly from their Web sites).

---

**Note**   Even hardware that installs without a setup disk can be changing the registry if it is a Plug and Play device that is recognized by the operating system. Erratic problems can occur if a device is improperly identified. Under Windows 95, Windows 98, Windows Me, or Windows 2000, check the System section of the Control Panel to identify possible conflicts.

---

## Power-On Self Test

Every time a PC is turned on or reset using the Reset button or Windows Restart command, the computer is rebooted and reset to its basic operating condition. The system BIOS program starts by invoking a special program (stored on a ROM chip) called the *power-on self test* (POST). The POST sends out standardized commands that check every primary device (in more technical terms, it runs an internal self-diagnostic routine).

The POST has two stages:

- Test 1 occurs before and during the test of the video.
- Test 2 occurs after the video has been tested.

This division determines whether the computer will display errors by beeping or showing them on the screen. The POST does not assume the video works until it has been tested. The POST does assume that the speaker always works, but to let you know that the speaker is working, all computers beep on startup. Depending on the BIOS type, the POST might also sound a single beep when it's done to let you know the boot process was successful. If something goes wrong, the POST sends a series of beep codes to let you know what the problem is or where to start looking for it.

### Beep Codes Before and During the Video Test

The purpose of the first POST test is to check the most basic components. The exact order, number of tests, and error states will vary from product to product. In a healthy system, the POST reports by using a series of beep codes and screen messages to convey that all components are working. Then it transfers control to the boot drive, which loads the operating system. The POST is a good indication that the hardware is in working order.

If a problem occurs, the POST routine attempts to report the problem. This is also done using beep codes and (if possible) screen prompts. Some error codes are specific to chip sets or custom products, and the exact message and meaning can vary from system to system. (See the POST code references in the system manual that shipped with the PC or the motherboard to obtain references for detailed error messages and beeps.) The following table lists the basic beep codes for AMI and Phoenix BIOSs.

| Number of Beeps | Possible Problem |
| --- | --- |
| 1 | DRAM refresh failure |
| 2 | Parity circuit failure |
| 3 | Base 64 KB or CMOS RAM failure |
| 4 | System timer |
| 5 | Processor failure |
| 6 | Keyboard controller or Gate A20 error |
| 7 | Virtual mode exception error |
| 8 | Display monitor write/read test failure |
| 9 | ROM BIOS checksum error |
| 10 | CMOS RAM shutdown register failure |
| 1 long, 3 short | Conventional/extended memory test failure |
| 1 long, 8 short | Display test and display vertical and horizontal retrace test failure |

## Troubleshooting After a Beep

After a beep code has been recognized, there are a few things you can do to troubleshoot the error. The following table suggests some solutions. Keep in mind that, in many cases, it can be less expensive to replace the motherboard than to replace a chip.

| Problem | Solution |
| --- | --- |
| RAM refresh failure | Reseat and clean the RAM chips. |
| Parity error RAM bit error Base 64-KB error | Replace individual memory chips until the problem is corrected. |
| 8042 error (keyboard chip) | Reseat and clean keyboard chip. |
| Gate A20 error | Check operating system. Replace keyboard. Replace motherboard. |
| BIOS checksum error | Reseat ROM chip. Replace BIOS chip. |
| Video errors | Reseat video card. Replace video card. |
| Cache memory error | Reseat and clean cache chips. Verify cache jumper settings are correct. Replace cache chips. |
| Any other problems | Reseat expansion cards. Clean motherboard. Replace motherboard. |

**Note**  Many computers will generate beep codes when the only problem is a bad power supply! Turn the computer off and on three or four times to see if the same beep code is generated every time. If so, it's probably a legitimate beep code that concerns the hardware and not the power supply.

Since early 1996, some BIOS programs have eliminated many beep codes. However, identifying beep codes can still be part of the A+ Certification exam.

## Error Messages—After the Video Test

After successfully testing the video, the POST will display any error messages on the screen. These errors are displayed in one of two ways: numeric error codes or text error messages.

## Numeric Error Codes

When a computer generates a numeric error code, the machine locks up and the error code appears in the upper-left corner of the screen. The following table lists some common numeric error codes, but it is a good idea to check the manual before beginning repairs based on a beep code or error message.

| Error Code | Problem |
|---|---|
| 301 | The keyboard is broken or not plugged in. |
| 1701 | The hard disk drive controller is bad. |
| 7301 | The floppy disk drive controller is bad. |
| 161 | The battery is dead. |
| 1101 | The serial card is bad. |

## Text Error Codes

BIOS manufacturers have stopped using numeric error codes and have replaced them with about 30 text messages. Instead of numbers, you get text that is usually, but not always, self-explanatory.

## How Bad Is It?

There are two levels of error codes during POST: fatal and nonfatal. As the name implies, fatal errors will halt the system without attempting to load the operating system. Memory problems or a faulty disk or display adapter are examples of fatal errors. Nonfatal errors like a "missing" floppy disk drive will still result in the system attempting to load the operating system (and often succeeding).

In most cases, the POST procedure does a good job of testing components. If it gives a clean bill of health to the hardware, failure to boot will often lie in the operating system. You can use a bootable floppy disk in most cases to access the hard disk drive, or boot Windows using the Safe Start approach (press the F8 key just after the POST completes) and check for conflicting settings.

## POST Cards

More difficult to resolve is a hardware problem that keeps the POST from issuing any report at all. When you face this type of situation, you will find that this is where a POST card earns its keep. These special diagnostic expansion cards monitor the POST process and display all codes (usually in two-digit hexadecimal format) as the system runs the POST. The technician can then decode this information using the manufacturer's manual. More advanced models can also run advanced series of tests to isolate erratic problems.

When choosing a POST card, be sure that it will work with the types of machines you plan to test. Most are based on the Industry Standard Architecture (ISA) slot and work with most Intel CPUs. That means they should help with AT (80286 processors) and later-based PCs that use x86 processors. Basic models give only POST codes. More advanced models also can check direct memory access (DMA), IRQ (interrupt request), and port functions. Some come with fancy diagnostic software. The more features, the higher the price tag. However, a POST card will save a lot of time and frustration, making it a worthwhile addition to any PC toolkit.

# Lesson Summary

The following points summarize the main elements of this lesson:

- Understanding ROM BIOS is key to keeping a computer up and running.
- CMOS setup defines the data a computer needs to communicate with its hardware (such as its drives).
- The CMOS battery maintains BIOS data when computer power is turned off.
- A POST card can quickly pay for itself by helping to isolate problems when the POST routine fails to provide a report.

# Chapter Summary

The following points summarize the key concepts in this chapter:

## Computer Cases

- The functions of the case are to house the computer's internal components, connect the computer to the outside world via ports and connectors, and protect the computer from damage.
- To prevent EMI, avoid running a computer without the cover on.

## Motherboards

- The motherboard components define the capabilities of a computer.
- Not all motherboards are the same. Some manufacturers have proprietary motherboards that can be used only in their own computers. They will also require proprietary parts for expansion. Generally, these motherboards are of higher quality (and price).

## ROM BIOS

- BIOS chips are used to provide data to the CPU; this data tells the CPU how to operate specific devices.
- CMOS is a BIOS chip that can have its data updated. The CMOS setup program is used to make changes.
- CMOS chips require a battery to save the data when power to the computer is off.
- Some of the newer BIOS chips are updatable. These are called flash BIOS.
- A device driver is a program that acts as an interface between the operating system and the control circuits that operate the device.
- On machines running MS-DOS, device drivers are loaded by the CONFIG.SYS file.
- Computers running Windows 95, Windows 98, Windows Me, or Windows 2000 load their own device drivers and do not require a CONFIG.SYS file.
- POST is used to check a computer before it boots.
- POST errors are indicated by beeps before the video is checked, and by text after the video check.

# Review

The following questions are intended to reinforce key information presented in this chapter. If you are unable to answer a question, review the appropriate lesson and then try the question again. Answers to the questions can be found in Appendix A, "Questions and Answers."

1.  What is the main function of the motherboard?

2.  Name the typical chips found in a chip set.

3.  What is EMI?

4.  What are ROM chips used for?

5.  Name the three types of ROM chips.

6.  Describe what makes the CMOS special.

7.  How can a technician use the POST beep codes?

8.  What is a device driver?

9.  What information is contained in the CMOS?

10. Define the POST and describe its function.

C H A P T E R   7

# Memory

**Lesson 1: ROM and RAM** ..................................... **120**

**Lesson 2: Memory Mapping** .................................. **134**

**Chapter Summary** ........................................... **143**

**Review** ...................................................... **144**

## About This Chapter

In earlier chapters, we learned that the CPU (central processing unit) and motherboard (bus and controllers) are critical components that help determine the overall speed with which a computer can process data. This chapter looks at another important system component and performance factor: memory.

Technicians are often asked to upgrade PCs by adding more memory, and memory conflicts or errors commonly prompt calls for assistance by users. Understanding how memory works, how to choose the right memory for a given system, and how to troubleshoot memory problems is critical to being successful as a computer technician.

## Before You Begin

A clear understanding of microprocessors, motherboards, and computer buses, covered in earlier chapters, is required before beginning this chapter.

# Lesson 1:  ROM and RAM

As a computer technician, you will encounter various types of memory. This lesson defines the different types of memory, shows you how to locate memory in a computer, and discusses how to expand or add new memory.

---

### After this lesson, you will be able to

- Identify basic concepts related to computer memory
- Define the types of memory and describe their advantages and disadvantages
- Explain memory upgrade options and issues

### Estimated lesson time: 45 minutes

---

## Defining Memory

A host of terms and acronyms relate to the memory technology used in personal computers. A technician must understand the key concepts involved. You must be able to identify the distinctions among the major memory components and to distinguish between memory and storage.

All computer memory is used to hold binary strings of data to be manipulated by the CPU. Think of memory as a vast bank of switches with two positions: on or off. Off is given the value of 0; on is given the value of 1. This allows the switches to hold binary data based on whether they are open or closed. By stringing a series of switches together, larger numbers and code values can be represented.

## Nonvolatile and Volatile Memory

There are two major classes of computer memory: nonvolatile and volatile. *Nonvolatile memory* is retained even if the power to the computer is shut off. The setup data held in CMOS (complementary metal-oxide semiconductor), discussed in the preceding lessons, is a good example of nonvolatile memory. If the data is lost when the computer loses power, the memory is said to be *volatile*.

Active memory is a state in which a block of code or data is directly accessible to the CPU for reference or manipulation. When data is located outside the system's active memory, it is said to be in storage. Storage devices include floppy disk and hard disk drives, optical media, and tape units.

Active memory is faster than storage because the information is already on the system, there are fewer physical (and no mechanical) operations involved in obtaining the data, and the CPU has direct control over the memory.

# ROM

ROM (read-only memory) is nonvolatile memory, generally installed by the vendor of the computer during the process of manufacturing the motherboard or secondary components that need to retain code when the machine is turned off. With the use of ROM, information that is required to start and run the computer cannot be lost or changed.

ROM is used extensively to program operation of computers, as well as in devices like cameras and controls for the fuel injectors in modern cars. However, ROM plays a limited role in the PC (personal computer). Here, it holds the instructions for performing the power-on self test (POST) routine and the BIOS (basic input/output system) information used to describe the system configuration. For more detailed information, refer to Chapter 6, "Motherboard and ROM BIOS."

In most cases, a technician will be concerned with ROM only if it has failed and requires replacement, needs to be upgraded, or conflicts with other memory installed in the system. A repairperson or technician does not usually directly control the actual code in ROM.

# RAM

RAM (random access memory) is what is most often referred to when PC memory is discussed. RAM is the form of volatile memory used to hold temporary instructions and data for manipulation while the system is running. The term *random* is applied because the CPU can access or place data to and from any addressable RAM on the system. If power to the system is lost, all RAM is lost as well.

Usually, when referring to RAM, we are speaking of some variation of DRAM (dynamic RAM) or the newer SDRAM (synchronous DRAM). These are the most common forms of RAM used in the modern PC.

DRAM works by using a microscopic capacitor and a microscopic transistor to store each data bit. A charged capacitor represents a value of 1, and a discharged capacitor represents a value of 0. A capacitor works like a battery—it holds a charge and then releases it. Unlike a battery, which holds a charge for months, the tiny capacitors in DRAM hold their charges for only fractions of a second. Therefore, DRAM needs an entire set of circuitry just to keep the capacitors charged. The process of recharging these capacitors is called *refreshing*. Without refreshing, the data would be lost. This is another reason DRAM is called volatile memory.

All PC CPUs handle data in 8-bit blocks. Each block, known as a byte, denotes how many bits the CPU can move in and out of memory at one time. The number is an indication of how rapidly data can be manipulated and arranged in system memory. Don't confuse this byte with the amount of system memory, which is usually expressed in megabytes (MB). System memory is the total amount of active memory that is available to the CPU as a temporary work area.

Each transaction between the CPU and memory is called a *bus cycle*. The amount of memory that a CPU can address in a single bus cycle has a major effect on overall system performance and determines the design of memory that the system can use. The width of the system's memory bus must match the number of data bits per cycle of the CPU.

All computers have some form of memory controller, which handles the movement of data to and from the CPU and the system memory banks. The memory controller is also responsible for the integrity of the data as it is swapped in and out. There are two primary methods of ensuring that the data received is the same as the data sent: parity and error-correction coding (ECC).

## Parity

*Parity* is a method of ensuring data integrity that adds an extra bit (the parity bit) along with each 8-bit bus cycle. There are two kinds of parity: even and odd. Both use a three-step process to validate a bus transaction; however, they do it in opposite ways.

- In Step 1, both methods set the value of the parity bit based on the even or odd number that represents the sum of the data bits as the first step.

- In Step 2, the string goes into DRAM.

- In Step 3, the parity circuit checks the math. If the parity bit matches the parity bit of the number that represents the sum of the binary string sent, the data is passed on. If it fails the test, an error is reported. Just how that error is handled and reported to the user varies with each operating system.

## ECC

A more robust technology, *ECC* can detect errors beyond the limits of the simpler parity method. It adds extra information about the bits, which is then evaluated to determine if there are problems with individual bits in the data string.

## Access Speed

Access speed, denoted in nanoseconds (ns), is the amount of time it takes for the RAM to provide requested data to the memory controller. Here, smaller is better. Be sure to buy RAM that is at least as fast as that listed as standard for the computer in question.

A typical total response time for a 70-ns DRAM chip is between 90 and 120 ns. This includes the time required to access the address bus and data bus. Most 486- and Pentium-based machines use either 70-ns or 60-ns DRAM chips, although 50-ns chips are now available. The access speed of a chip is usually printed on the chip (often as part of the identification number).

Here are a few important things to remember about access speed when adding memory:

- Any add-on memory should be the same speed as or faster (lower number) than any existing memory.
- You cannot mix memory modules with different speeds in the same bank (a bank is a set of several memory modules).
- You should check the motherboard specifications for the recommended memory chip speed.

## RAM Packaging

Over the years, the way memory has been packaged and placed on the motherboard has changed several times. As faster processors developed and system requirements for applications increased, so did the need for more and faster memory. The new memory designs often required new packaging and connection technology. That trend will continue, and technicians must stay current on the different memory types and their appropriate applications.

Early versions of RAM were installed as single chips, usually 1-bit-wide DIP (dual inline package), as shown in Figure 7.1. In some cases, this was soldered right onto the motherboard, but most often it was seated in a socket, offering a simpler method of removal and replacement. Some older machines have special memory expansion cards that contain several rows of sockets. These cards are placed in a slot on the motherboard.

To upgrade or add memory, new chips had to be individually installed on the motherboard (eight or nine chips per row—nine chips if using parity). This could be challenging, because each chip had 16 wires that needed to be perfectly aligned before insertion into the base. The notch in one end denoted the side that had pin 1.

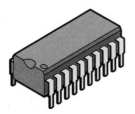

**Figure 7.1**  A DIP DRAM chip

As the amount of memory and the need for speed increased, manufacturers started to market modules containing several chips that allowed for easier installation and larger capacity. These modules come in a variety of physical configurations. Technicians must be able to identify both the type and amount of memory a computer requires for optimum performance.

---

**Tip**   Identifying the amount of memory actually working on a PC is easy if the PC is operational: Simply boot the system and view the memory values given during the POST. In some cases, this is also a useful way to determine if a memory block is improperly installed. If that is the case, the computer might fail to boot or the POST might report a lower figure than the actual amount of RAM present.

---

## SIPPs

One of the first module forms of DRAM, the SIPP (single inline pinned package) is a printed circuit board with individual DRAM chips mounted on it, as shown in Figure 7.2. Physically, a SIPP module looks like a rectangular card with a single row of pins along one edge. The SIPP had a very short time in the sun due to the fragile nature of these pins.

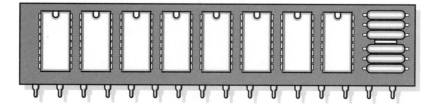

**Figure 7.2**   SIPP

---

**Caution**   You won't likely see any SIPPs, but if you do, take special care when replacing them in the motherboard. SIPPs have a row of pins along one side. These pins are easily broken, and care should be taken to avoid damaging them during installation.

---

## SIMMs (30-Pin)

SIMMs (single inline memory modules) quickly replaced SIPPs because they are easier to install. They are similar to SIPPs with one exception—they require no pins; 30-pin SIMMs have 30 contacts in a single row along the lower edge (see Figure 7.3). A 30-pin SIMM can have as few as two or as many as nine individual DRAM chips. Although SIMM modules can have pin counts as high as 200, in PCs, 30- and 72-pin versions are the most common.

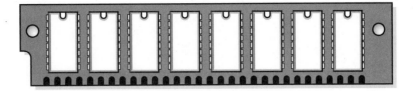

**Figure 7.3**    30-pin SIMM

**Caution**    Avoid touching the contacts on SIMMs, and use proper handling to reduce the risk of damage from electrostatic discharge (ESD).

## Memory Configuration

The capability of the computer's CPU, its memory configuration, and its operating system all play roles in how the computer's memory is allocated. Technicians should understand the terms and processes involved, both for their own benefit and to explain the details to a customer if the question arises.

The power of a processor is often expressed by how many such pieces it can handle at a time. For example, the original Intel Pentium is a 64-bit CPU, meaning that it can handle 64 bits at once. That amounts to 8 bytes ($8 \times 8$). These terms always refer to byte-wide memory (8 bits).

When the bus cycle demand is greater than the number of bits a memory module provides, more modules must be added to be able to meet the demand. The most common approach is to employ a bank of modules, matched to the bit width equal to the data demands of the CPU, and the entire data bus. When most new CPUs are introduced, the width of the design is the same as the old memory types, and modules must be used in banks until a new memory design is available. For example, an 8-bit data bus (8086 or 8088) needs 8-bit-wide memory to fill one bank. A 16-bit data bus requires 16-bit-wide memory to fill one bank, and so on. If you install 30-pin SIMMs (each is 8 bits wide) on a 16-bit machine, you will need two rows of chips to completely fill the data bus.

**Note**    Each of the rows that make a bank must be filled with identical chips (size and speed). See Figure 7.4.

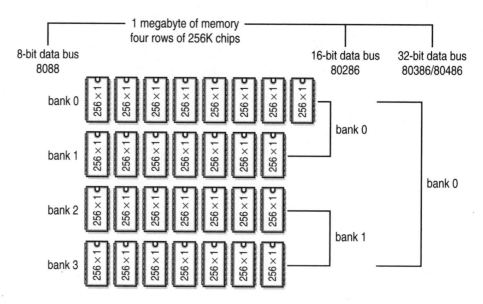

**Figure 7.4**  Banking

Most motherboards provide several rows of slots for adding memory, often referred to as banks. Be careful with the word *bank*. It is used to describe the necessary rows of chips, as well as the slots into which they are inserted.

SIMMs usually require matched pairs to form a bank of memory, whereas DIMMS (dual inline memory modules) require only one card (we will examine different types of modules later in this chapter). To calculate the number of SIMMs needed to make one bank, use the following formula: Divide the number of data bits per CPU cycle by the bit width of the module. (For 30-pin SIMMs, that is always 8 bits.) A 32-bit external data bus with 30-pin SIMMs requires 32 (the width of the data bus) divided by 8 (the number of bits per SIMM module), or 4 modules per bank.

There are some rules to follow when banking:

- All rows in a bank must be either completely filled or completely empty.
- Each bank is numbered, starting with bank 0.
- In most systems, DRAM should be installed in bank 0 before any other bank is used.
- Refer to the motherboard documentation for bank numbering and installation directions.

## Specifying SIPPs and SIMMs

When speaking of DRAM SIPPs and SIMMs, we use two values to determine how much memory a unit can hold:

- **Width.** 1 bit, 4 bits (a nibble), 8 bits (a byte), or 16 bits (a word), and so on.
- **Depth.** How deep the chip is: 256 KB, 1 MB, 4 MB, 8 MB, 16 MB, 32 MB, and so on.

You can determine the size of the DRAM chip by combining the depth and width of the chip.

Here are a few points to remember when specifying DRAM:

- When upgrading memory, you add megabytes.
- When purchasing DRAM, you buy bits, usually in the form of MB.
- Calculate chip size by multiplying depth by width; the result is measured in bits.
- One KB of memory is equal to 8192 bits ($1024 \times 8$).
- One MB is equal to 8,388,608 bits ($1024 \times 1024 \times 8$).

The following table lists common DRAM module sizes.

| Chip (Depth × Width) | Number of Chips per Module | Memory per Module |
|---|---|---|
| 1 MB × 1 | 8 | 1 MB |
| 1 MB × 4 | 2 | 1 MB |
| 1 MB × 16 | 1 | 2 MB |
| 2 MB × 8 | 1 | 2 MB |
| 4 MB × 1 | 8 | 4 MB |
| 4 MB × 4 | 2 | 4 MB |

## The 72-Pin SIMM

With the advent of 32- and 64-bit CPUs, the bank began to take up too much space on the motherboard and added to the cost of memory. (The board that houses the chips often costs more than the DRAM chips.) Enter 72-pin SIMMs, with 72 pins on each card. One of these is four times wider than a 30-pin SIMM, which is 8 bits wide (see Figures 7.5 and 7.6). Therefore, a motherboard requiring four rows of 30-pin SIMMs to fill one bank needs only one 72-pin SIMM. Virtually all Pentium and Pentium Pro systems use 72-pin SIMMs.

Because 72-pin SIMMs are 32 bits wide, the term *x 32* is used to describe them. A 1 MB × 32 SIMM contains 4 MB of RAM because it is 4 bytes wide (1 MB of

RAM is 1,048,576 × 32, which equals 4 MB). Remember, memory is measured in bytes, and chips are measured in bits.

**Figure 7.5**   A 72-pin SIMM

There are many varieties of SIMMs on the market. The following table lists some common 72-pin SIMMs.

| Configuration | Memory |
| --- | --- |
| 4 MB × 36 | 16 MB, parity |
| 8 MB × 32 | 32 MB, no parity |
| 8 MB × 36 | 32 MB, parity |
| 16 MB × 32 | 64 MB, no parity |
| 16 MB × 36 | 64 MB, parity |

## Voltage

All early PCs used 5-volt circuits to power components, including memory. Today, the trend is to use 3.3-volt power unless 5 volts are required for a specific part of the system (such as a hard disk drive). Be sure to check the voltage of the memory before installing a module.

## Installing SIMMs

When installing SIMMs:

- Always use precautions to avoid ESD. Refer to Chapter 22, "The Basics of Electrical Energy," for details.

- Always handle SIMMs carefully—keep your fingers on the plastic edges. There is little worse than destroying a 16-MB SIMM because of static discharge.

- All SIMMs have a notch on one side that prevents them from being installed improperly. If you cannot insert the SIMM easily, it's probably backward.

- SIMMs are inserted into the slot at a 45-degree angle along the wide side (see Figure 7.6).

- After the SIMM is securely seated in the slot, push it upright until the holding clamps on either side are secured.

**Important**   SIMMs are extremely sensitive to static. Be sure to handle them carefully.

**Figure 7.6**   Installing SIMMs

After the chip is physically installed:

- Turn on the computer. If the DRAM is installed correctly, the RAM count on the computer will reflect the new value.

- If the RAM value has not changed, it is likely that either a bank is disabled or the SIMMs are installed incorrectly. Check the motherboard documentation to determine if a jumper needs to be changed to turn on the SIMM.

- If the computer does not boot and the screen is blank, the RAM was not installed correctly.

> **Note** When a computer is booting, the RAM count is based on units of 1024 bytes. One MB of RAM should show as 1024, 2 MB as 2048, 4 MB as 4096, and so on. Most RAM counts appear to stop before they get to the value expected (less than 1 MB). In reality, the computer is finished and moving on to the next task so fast that the result does not display on the screen. If the POST reports the full number, the memory is all there. If the POST does not report the full number, you should make sure that all modules are properly seated, of the right type, and working.

- After the RAM is installed, and the RAM count correctly reflects the new value, the CMOS needs to be updated. On most machines, this is done automatically and no intervention is required.

If you get an error similar to "CMOS Memory Mismatch—Press Fl to continue," access the CMOS with the CMOS setup program, then save and exit (changes will be automatically recorded). The CMOS will be reset.

If the system fails to boot or reports less than the amount of memory actually installed, recheck the modules to make sure they are seated properly according to the motherboard manual and that the right type and amount are present.

## Dual Inline Memory Modules

These newer modules look much like SIMMs, but come in a package with 168 pins and have a different wiring structure, so that one card can form a complete bank. These are the memory packages used on virtually all new motherboards.

DIMMS are a real improvement over older memory modules. They provide larger amounts of RAM on a single module and are easy to install. They slide straight down into a slot and are secured by a pair of locks that swing into place above the card as it seats fully in the slot. Check the motherboard manual or the vendor's Web site for the approved list of DIMM modules. There are many variations in electronic design (parity, non-parity, etc.), and you must make sure that the DIMM will actually work with the combination of motherboard and CPU you are working on. Just because the card fits does not mean it will work.

## Cache Memory

To *cache* is to set something aside, or to store for anticipated use. Early explorers would arrange to have a cache of food or other supplies positioned along their route of travel. This made their travel easier since they didn't have to carry anything other than essentials needed for each portion of the trip. The same concept can be applied to CPU operations and computer system design. Caching, in PC terms, is the holding of a recently or frequently used code or data in a special memory location for rapid retrieval. Speed is everything when it comes to computers. Mass storage is much slower than RAM, and RAM is much slower than the CPU. The high-speed memory chip generally used for caching is called *static RAM* (SRAM).

## SRAM

SRAM does not use capacitors to store 1s and 0s. Instead, SRAM uses a special circuit called a *flip-flop*. The advantages of SRAM are that it is fast and it does not have to be refreshed because it uses the flip-flop circuit to store each bit. A flip-flop circuit will toggle on or off and retain its position, whereas a standard memory circuit requires constant refreshing to maintain an on state. The main disadvantage of SRAM is that it is more expensive than DRAM.

### Caching: The Layered Look

Caching is a very common technology in PC operations and can be found on individual computers, peripheral devices like graphics cards, and on and around the CPU. While working, the CPU is constantly requesting and using information and executing code. The closer the necessary data is to the CPU, the faster the system can locate it and execute the operation. Of course, it would be impossible to keep all necessary information in active memory; cost and logistics make it necessary to prioritize how large the cache is on a system, and how it is organized.

Caches are organized into layers. The highest layer is closest to the device (such as the CPU) using it. On early PCs, caches were usually separate chips. Today, it is not uncommon to have two levels of cache built right into the CPU, but a cache is not limited to dynamic memory. Mass storage devices like hard drives can also be used to store less commonly used code or data.

### Internal Cache (L1)

Starting with the 486 chips, a cache has been included on every CPU. This original on-board cache is known as the *L1* (level 1) or *internal cache*. All commands for the processor go through the cache. The cache stores a backlog of commands so that if a wait state is encountered, the CPU can continue to process using commands from the cache. Caching will store any code that has been read and keep it available for the CPU to use. This eliminates the need to wait for fetching of the data from DRAM.

## External Cache (L2)

Additional cache can be added to most computers, depending on the motherboard. This cache is mounted directly on the motherboard, outside the CPU. The external cache is also called *L2* (level 2) and is the same as L1, but larger. L2 can also (on some motherboards) be added or expanded. When installing any L2 cache, be sure to check the CMOS setup and enable the cache. Some computer systems are now also employing a Level 3 cache.

## Write-Back vs. Write-Through

As mentioned, the primary use of a cache is to increase the speed of data from RAM to the CPU. Some caches immediately send all data directly to RAM, even if it means hitting a wait state. This is called *write-through cache,* shown in Figure 7.7.

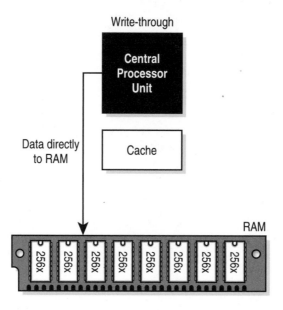

**Figure 7.7**   Write-through cache

Some caches store the data for a time and send it to RAM later. This is called *write-back cache,* shown in Figure 7.8.

Write-back caches are harder to implement but are much more powerful than write-through caches, because the CPU does not have to stop for the wait state of the RAM. However, write-through caches are less expensive.

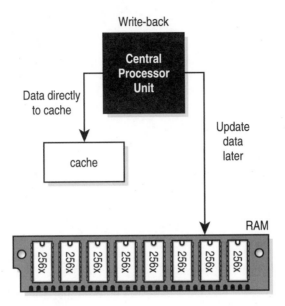

**Figure 7.8**    Write-back cache

## Lesson Summary

The following points summarize the main elements of this lesson:

- There are two basic kinds of memory in a computer: ROM and RAM.

- Memory chips come in many sizes and shapes: DIPPs, SIPPs, DRAM, SRAM.

- Installing memory (RAM) is easy; however, you must be able to match the size and configuration of the memory chips to the motherboard.

- The number of memory modules needed to fill one memory bank equals the width of the external data bus (in bits) divided by the width of the SIMM (in bits).

- Cache memory is used to increase the performance of a computer.

- Cache memory (SRAM) is faster, but more expensive, than the standard DRAM; therefore, it is used in small quantities and for special purposes.

- There are two types of cache memory: L1 and L2.

# Lesson 2: Memory Mapping

Computer memory has many functions. Some memory is reserved for particular uses by the processor and, if improperly allocated, will cause problems. Understanding how to identify and manage memory is key to optimizing a computer. In this lesson, you learn how memory is allocated.

## After this lesson, you will be able to

- Use hexadecimal numbers
- Define the different types of memory access
- Optimize memory allocation

## Estimated lesson time: 20 minutes

## The Workings of Hexadecimal Code

Chapter 2, "Understanding Electronic Communication," introduced the concept of binary notation. This is how computers count—by setting the value of a two-position switch to either 0 (off) or 1 (on). Ones and zeroes work well when machines are conversing, but that language can be somewhat confusing for computer designers and programmers. To simplify the representation of numbers and notations, designers and programmers use a numbering system called *hexadecimal notation* (also known simply as *hex*). This is a numbering system based on 16 instead of 10. Fortunately, computer technicians do not have to be experts in hexadecimal notation. You do, however, need to know how to use the numbering system as it relates to computer memory.

Hexadecimal notation is used to simplify notation of binary code in much the same way that we sometimes count in fives or tens when it is more convenient than working our way through a problem by ones. You might ask how anyone would find it simpler to count in hex. Well, in dealing with a system that uses 8 bits, addressing counting locations in hex (a system based on eight positions) makes perfect sense.

All address buses and wires within a computer come in some multiple of 4 (8, 16, 20, 24, 32). Because there are 16 different combinations, the 16 unique characters of the base-16 numbering system are a natural choice for computer shorthand when referring to memory locations or a bus address. The following table contrasts binary notation with hex shorthand.

| Binary Number | Hex Shorthand | Binary Number | Hex Shorthand |
|---|---|---|---|
| 0000 | 0 | 1010 | A |
| 0001 | 1 | 1011 | B |
| 0010 | 2 | 1100 | C |
| 0011 | 3 | 1101 | D |
| 0100 | 4 | 1110 | E |
| 0101 | 5 | 1111 | F |
| 0110 | 6 | | |
| 0111 | 7 | | |
| 1000 | 8 | | |
| 1001 | 9 | | |

## Hexadecimal Shorthand

There is no need to say:

```
10110110011000101101
```

To use hex shorthand:

- Break the 20 digits into 5 sets:

```
1011    0110    0110    0010    1101
```

- Give each 4-character set its hex shorthand:

```
1011    0110    0110    0010    1101
B       6       6       2       D
```

```
Hex shorthand = B662D
```

To represent all the possible addresses for the 20-bit address bus, we use 5 hex values (0 to F) that map to their binary equivalents, from all 0s:

```
0000    0000    0000    0000    0000
0       0       0       0       0
```

to all 1s:

```
1111    1111    1111    1111    1111
F       F       F       F       F
```

Each of the possible memory locations for the Intel 8088 can be represented by 5-digit hexadecimal values, starting at 00000 and ending at FFFFF.

## Memory Allocation

Previously in this chapter, we discussed memory in terms of the chips themselves. In this section, we look at how that memory is allocated for use by the CPU. This is called *memory mapping* and it uses hexadecimal addresses to define ranges of memory.

The original processors developed by Intel were unable to use more than 1 MB of RAM, and the original IBM PC allowed only the first 640 KB of memory for direct use. MS-DOS applications were written to conform to this limitation. As application requirements grew, programmers needed to optimize the use of memory to make the most of the available space. This 1 MB of memory was divided into two sections. The first 640 KB was reserved for the operating system and applications (designated as conventional memory). The remaining 384 KB of RAM (designated as upper memory) was earmarked for running the computer's own housekeeping needs (BIOS, video RAM, ROM, and so on). Although some early PC clones had firmware that could make direct use of the upper memory block available to programmers, actually doing so would result in hardware and software incompatibility issues (see Figure 7.9).

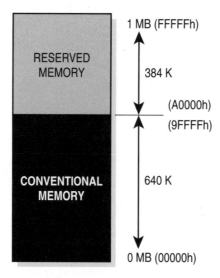

**Figure 7.9**   IBM PC/MS-DOS memory map

Under MS-DOS and Microsoft Windows 3.*x*, the 640-KB area needed to be kept as free as possible for program use. MS-DOS memory optimization ensures that MS-DOS applications have as much of this memory as possible. The MS-DOS limitations no longer apply to Windows versions operating in 32-bit mode (Microsoft Windows 95 and later) and most newer operating systems. However, the old memory problems still are a factor when running MS-DOS, Windows 3.x-based programs on older machines, or MS-DOS compatibility mode with the more advanced operating systems. While you may never run into this problem, you should be aware of it as it can cause very erratic—and often severe—problems.

## Types of Memory Access

When we speak of memory in a computer, we are generally speaking of RAM, because ROM cannot be written to by either the system or applications. Although we have only one single supply of RAM, under MS-DOS-based operating systems, it is usually segmented into smaller blocks for actual use.

## Extended Memory Specification (XMS)

RAM above the 1-MB address is called *extended memory*. With the introduction of the 80286 processor, memory was addressable up to 16 MB. Starting with the 80386DX processor, memory was addressable up to 4 GB. Extended memory is accessed through an extended memory manager (HIMEM.SYS).

## Conventional Memory

Conventional memory is the amount of RAM, typically 640 KB, addressable by an IBM PC or compatible machine operating in real mode. (Real mode is the only operating mode supported by MS-DOS.) Conventional memory is located in the area between 0 and 640 KB. Without the use of special techniques, conventional memory is the only kind of RAM accessible in DOS mode and DOS mode programs.

## MS-DOS Protected Mode Interface

MS-DOS Protected Mode Interface (DPMI) is a specification that allows multiple applications to access extended memory at the same time. Most memory-manager producers and applications developers have endorsed this specification, and Windows uses the DPMI specification.

## Expanded Memory Specification

EMS (Expanded Memory Specification), developed by Lotus/Intel/Microsoft, uses a 64-KB section of memory (usually in upper memory) to provide a "window" in which data can be written. Once in this area, the data can be transferred to the expanded memory. The memory chips are located on an expansion card installed inside the computer. The data is paged or swapped to and from the CPU through this window (see Figure 7.10).

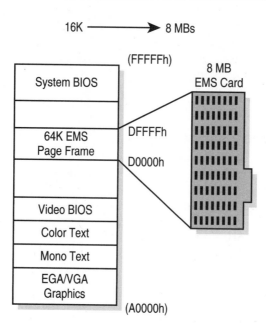

**Figure 7.10**  Expanded memory

Expanded memory can provide up to 32 MB of additional memory, and because it is loaded from a 64-KB section, it is below the 1-MB limit and therefore recognizable by MS-DOS.

MS-DOS applications must be specifically written to take advantage of expanded memory. Windows applications do not use expanded memory; 80386 and newer processors can emulate expanded memory by using memory managers such as EMM386.EXE and HIMEM.SYS.

## High Memory Area

An irregularity was found in the Intel chip architecture that allowed MS-DOS to address the first 64 KB of extended memory on machines with 80286 or faster processors. This special area is called the *high memory area* (HMA). A software driver called an A20 handler must be run to allow the processor to access the HMA. Some versions of Windows use HIMEM.SYS for this purpose. The only limitation is that HIMEM.SYS can load only a single program into this area (see Figure 7.11).

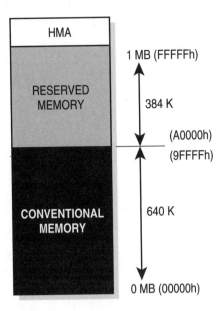

**Figure 7.11**    High memory area

## Protected Mode

Beginning with 80286 processors using an operating system such as OS/2 or Windows, a computer can create "virtual machines," providing all the functionality of a standard computer in real mode but allowing multiple tasks to take place at the same time. This is called *protected mode* because the processor, memory, and other hardware are protected from the software application taking direct control of the system by the operating system, which allocates memory and processor time.

## Real Mode

In *real mode* (MS-DOS), a computer can perform only one operation at a time and an application expects full control of the system. Real mode operates within the MS-DOS 1-MB limitation.

## Shadow RAM

Many high-speed expansion boards use shadow RAM to improve the performance of a computer. *Shadow RAM* rewrites (or shadows) the contents of the ROM BIOS and/or video BIOS into extended RAM (between the 640-KB boundary and 1 MB). This allows systems to operate faster when application software calls any BIOS routines. In some cases, system speed can be increased up to 400 percent (see Figure 7.12).

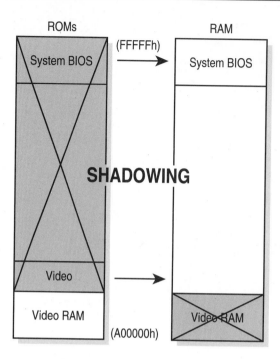

**Figure 7.12**    Shadow RAM

## Upper Memory Area

The *upper memory area* (UMA), the memory block from 640 KB to 1024 KB, is designated for hardware use, such as video RAM, BIOS, and memory-mapped hardware drivers that are loaded into high memory.

# Determining Usable Memory

The MS-DOS command MEM (MEM.COM; still available in newer versions of Windows, type **mem** in a command window) provides information about the amount and type of memory available (see Figure 7.13). It provides a quick way to determine how all of the different areas in physical memory are being used and the total amount of RAM actually active on the system.

Most MS-DOS and many early Windows systems load numerous device drivers and TSR (terminate-and-stay-resident) programs using the CONFIG.SYS and AUTOEXEC.BAT routines during the boot cycle.

```
Memory Type                    Total    =   Used   +   Free
Conventional                   640 KB       122K       518K
Upper                          155K         41K        144K
Reserved                       128K         128K       0K
Extended (XMS)                 7,269K       2,486K     4,783K
Total Memory                   81,259K      21,777K    5,415K
Total under 1 MB               795K         163K       632K
Largest executable program size        518K (530,096 bytes)
Largest free upper memory block        114K (116,352 bytes)
```

**Figure 7.13**   MEM.COM

---

**Note**   Avoid using any DOS or 16-bit TSRs in Windows 95, Windows 98, Windows NT, Windows 2000, or Windows Me, if at all possible. Their presence degrades system performance and can disable some of the more advanced memory-handling features of Windows. Properly configured, newer versions of Windows 98 and beyond will not need either CONFIG.SYS or AUTOEXEC.BAT, and some versions don't support them.

---

TSRs are usually loaded into conventional memory by the operating system, taking up valuable space. Memory-management techniques are used to load these device drivers and TSRs into the upper memory, allowing more lower memory to be made available to applications.

To determine which device drivers and TSRs are loaded, use the command

```
MEM /C
```

The /c is a classify switch. This determines how much conventional memory a certain real-mode program is using (see Figure 7.14).

We will cover troubleshooting and applications such as Windows System Information in Chapter 18, "Running Microsoft Windows."

```
Name                Total  =  Conventional  +  Upper Memory

MSDOS      21,581  (21K)    21,581  (21K)        0  (0K)
HIMEM       1,168   (1K)     1,168   (1K)        0  (0K)
EMM386      3,120   (3K)     3,120   (3K)        0  (0K)
IFSHLP      3,872   (4K)     3,872   (4K)        0  (0K)
NECIDE     20,544  (20K)    20,544  (20K)        0  (0K)
ANSI        4,208   (4K)     4,208   (4K)        0  (0K)
COMMAND     2,928   (3K)     2,928   (3K)        0  (0K)
GUARD       9,360   (9K)     9,360   (9K)        0  (0K)
MSCDEX     36,244  (36K)    36,244  (35K)        0  (0K)
SHARE      17,904  (17K)    17,904  (17K)        0  (0K)
DOSKEY      4,144   (4K)     4,144   (4K)             0(0K)
SETSERV       512   (1K)         0   (0K)      512   (1K)
VSDINIT     4,192   (4K)         0   (0K)    4,192   (4K)
SMARTDRV   30,368  (30K)         0   (0K)   30,368  (30K)
KEYB        6,944   (7K)         0   (0K)    6,944   (7K)
Free      646,768 (632K)   530,208 (518K)  116,560 (114K)
```

**Figure 7.14**   MEM /C

## Lesson Summary

The following points summarize the main elements of this lesson:

- Hexadecimal notation is used as shorthand for writing binary numbers.

- Memory is defined in terms of the physical characteristics of the chips and how the memory is allocated for use.

- The MS-DOS operating system can address only the first 1 MB of memory.

- Expanded memory was an early method of adding memory to an MS-DOS-based system. It paged, or swapped, 64-KB chunks of data through a window (a 64-KB block of memory in the UMA) to an expansion card.

- Extended memory, used by Windows 3.x and newer systems, allows the addressing of memory above the MS-DOS limit and has virtually replaced expanded memory.

- Understanding memory allocation and the different memory locations is key to optimizing a computer's memory.

- The MS-DOS command MEM.COM is a utility that provides information about memory allocation.

# Chapter Summary

The following points summarize the key concepts in this chapter:

## ROM and RAM

- ROM is a form of nonvolatile memory that is used in PCs to hold POST commands.

- RAM is the memory that is used by the CPU to temporarily hold data that is currently used by the system. It is cleared any time the system is powered down or rebooted.

- RAM chips come in many sizes and shapes. It is important for the computer technician to be able to identify the different types and calculate how many chips, banks, or rows of memory modules are needed to upgrade a computer.

- The number of SIMMs required is based on the width of the data bus.

## Memory Mapping

- Memory (RAM) is allocated to different parts of the CPU. A computer technician uses a memory map to describe how memory is allocated.

- Hexadecimal numbers are used to identify the location of memory on a memory map.

- MS-DOS can access only the first 1 MB of memory.

- Several commands, such as MEM.COM, are used to identify memory allocation in a computer.

- A computer technician must know the difference between conventional and high memory.

# Review

The following questions are intended to reinforce key information presented in this chapter. If you are unable to answer a question, review the appropriate lesson and then try the question again. Answers to the questions can be found in Appendix A, "Questions and Answers."

1. What is hexadecimal shorthand used for?

2. Define the following terms: conventional memory, expanded memory, extended memory, HMA, shadow RAM.

3. Describe the difference between ROM and RAM.

4. How many 30-pin SIMM boards are required for one bank of memory on a computer with a 486 processor?

5. What is the difference between write-through and write-back cache?

6. What is DRAM?

7. Define access speed.

8. Describe the major difference between SIPPs and SIMMs.

9. Define cache memory.

10. One of the differences between DRAM and SRAM is that SRAM does not have to be refreshed. What does this mean, and how does it affect the cost of each type of chip?

C H A P T E R  8

# Expansion Buses, Cables, and Connectors

**Lesson 1: Understanding Expansion Buses** .................... **148**

**Lesson 2: Configuring Expansion Cards** ...................... **159**

**Lesson 3: Cables and Connectors** ........................... **170**

**Chapter Summary** ......................................... **176**

**Review** .................................................. **177**

## About This Chapter

The success of the personal computer is due largely to its ability to expand to meet the changing needs and economic requirements of the user. In this chapter, we describe the array of expansion buses that help to expand the system and work with an ever-growing number of enhancements, including modems, video cards, and portable drives. We also discuss conflicts within the computer—how they are created and reconciled.

A competent technician has to know how to attach new devices to a computer. Knowledge of the different methods of doing so and the various cables used to link devices is critical in day-to-day operations. This chapter explores the various options and how to employ them properly and safely.

## Before You Begin

This chapter requires knowledge of processors, motherboards, and the binary and hexadecimal number systems. If you are not familiar with these concepts, take some time to review earlier chapters.

# Lesson 1:  Understanding Expansion Buses

Expansion buses connect devices to the motherboard using the motherboard's data bus. They allow the flow of data between internal and external devices that make up the computer system. Early computers moved data between devices and the processor at about the same rate as the processor. As processor speeds increased, the movement of data through the bus became a bottleneck. Therefore, the design capability of the buses needed to evolve, too. This lesson discusses that evolution.

## After this lesson, you will be able to
- Identify the different types of expansion buses in a computer
- Understand the difference between the system bus and the expansion bus

## Estimated lesson time: 30 minutes

## Development of the Expansion Bus

As discussed earlier in Chapter 4, "The Central Processing Unit," every device in the computer—random access memory (RAM), the keyboard, network interface card (NIC), sound card, and so forth—is connected to the external data bus. Expansion slots on the motherboard are standardized connections that allow the installation of devices not soldered to the motherboard. The function of an expansion slot is to provide configuration flexibility when devices are added to a computer.

Whether a device is soldered to the motherboard or connected through an expansion slot, all integrated circuits (ICs) are regulated by a quartz crystal. The crystal sets the timing for the system, giving all parts access to a common reference point for performing actions. Most central processing units (CPUs) divide the crystal speed by two. (If the CPU has a 33-MHz speed, a 66-MHz crystal is required.) Every device soldered to the motherboard—keyboard chip, memory controller chip, and so on—is designed to run at the speed (or at half the speed) of the system crystal.

Although CPU speeds have continually increased as technology has improved, the speeds of expansion cards has remained relatively constant. It was not practical to redesign and replace every expansion card each time a new processor was released—this would have been complicated and expensive for manufacturers. (And, of course, the additional expense would have been passed along to the consumer.) The commitment of the industry to maintain backward compatibility further complicated design tasks because any new technology would have to be compatible with the older, slower devices.

To resolve this dilemma, designers divided the external data bus into two parts:

- **System bus.** This supports the CPU, RAM, and other motherboard components and runs at speeds that support the CPU.

- **Expansion bus.** This supports any add-on devices by means of the expansion slots and runs at a steady rate, based on the specific bus design.

Dividing the bus enhances overall system efficiency. Because the CPU runs off the system clock, upgrading a CPU requires changing only the timing of the system bus, and the existing expansion cards continue to run as before. There is usually a jumper setting that changes the system clock speed to match the CPU. The ability of the motherboard to make this change sets the limit for the processor speed. Next, we take a look at the evolving types of expansion buses.

## Industry Standard Architecture

The first-generation IBM XT (with the 8088 processor) had an 8-bit external data bus and ran at a speed of 4.77 MHz. These machines were sold with an 8-bit expansion bus (PC bus) that ran at 8.33 MHz (see Figure 8.1).

**Figure 8.1**    8-bit PC bus slot

When IBM designed the first PC back in 1981, it took steps that fueled the rapid development of the PC market. IBM's engineers designed the PC as an open system, capable of using standard, off-the-shelf components. This allowed third-party developers to manufacture cards that could snap into the PC bus. IBM also allowed competitors to copy the PC bus.

With this decision, IBM established the *Industry Standard Architecture* (ISA) interface, thus generating the market for "clones." A host of third-party companies developed products that enhanced the basic PC design and kept prices much lower for add-ons than those for competing proprietary systems such as the Apple II. Without this push, the PC market would not have developed as rapidly as it did.

In 1984, when IBM released the AT (Advanced Technology) PC, featuring Intel's 80286 16-bit processor, it wanted to include a new expansion bus—one that would be compatible with previously released devices. To accomplish this, the designers added a bus that allowed insertion of either an 8-bit card or a 16-bit card. This change resulted in the standard 16-bit ISA slot. This new 16-bit bus officially ran at a top speed of 8.33 MHz, but on some Peripheral Component Interconnect (PCI)-based systems, the actual rate for ISA slots proved to be as high as about 10 MHz. (PCI is discussed later in this lesson.)

**Note**   The term "ISA" did not become official until 1990. Therefore, the 8-bit slot is called the XT, and the 16-bit slot is called the AT. When we refer to an ISA slot or an ISA card, we generally mean the 16-bit AT-style interface. The speed of the slots remained at about 7 MHz.

### Problems with the ISA Design

The ISA design is one of the most enduring elements of the PC. It can be found on virtually all systems, from the second-generation IBM PC to machines built today. However, it suffers from two major shortcomings: lack of speed and compatibility problems stemming from card design.

As CPU performance increased and applications became more powerful, card designers sought an interface that would allow add-on cards to keep up with the need for improved hard drives, display adapters, and similar products.

Expansion cards must make use of system resources in an orderly way, so that they do not conflict with other devices. When demands for these system resources are not coordinated, the system could behave erratically or even fail to boot up. Formerly, ISA cards often used a bewildering array of jumpers and switches to set addresses for memory use or the IRQ (interrupt request) locations they would use.

The need to overcome the expansion card's lack of speed and compatibility problems led to a search for a new, standard expansion card interface—one that everyone could agree on and that would gain user acceptance.

## Micro Channel Architecture

In 1986 the market came to be dominated by the new 386 machines with their 32-bit architecture. Most PC manufacturers stuck to the same basic ISA design and MS-DOS. Expansion devices based on ISA technology for the 286 AT class machines could be placed in a new 386 clone without problems.

IBM, however, was feeling the pinch of competition from cheaper clones, and sought to retain its dominance in the PC market. IBM designers produced a new version of the PC, the PS/2 (Personal System/2), and created a proprietary expansion bus called *Micro Channel Architecture* (MCA) as part of the design. Running at 10 MHz, it offered more performance and provided a 32-bit data path, but was also totally incompatible with older ISA cards.

A feature of MCA was its ability to "self-configure" devices. Unlike devices that use technology in which the PC configures itself automatically to work with peripherals such as monitors, modems, and printers, an MCA device always came with a configuration disk. When installing a new device in an MCA computer, the technician inserted the configuration disk (when prompted), and the IRQs, input/output (I/O) addresses, and direct memory access (DMA) channels were configured automatically. (IRQs, I/O addresses, and DMA channels are discussed in detail in the next lesson.) An MCA bus is shown in Figure 8.2.

The PS/2 and its Micro Channel Architecture expansion bus never gained enough market share to compete with the 386. MCA cards were few and far between, and more expensive than competing interface designs.

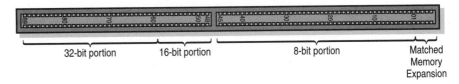

32-bit portion     16-bit portion          8-bit portion          Matched
                                                                   Memory
                                                                   Expansion

**Figure 8.2**    MCA bus

MCA is now a lost technology. As a computer technician, you will not encounter MCA on new computers. However, it is still found in some older machines, and you will need to know how to identify it. If (by some rare chance) a customer brings in a PS/2 machine for service, be sure to obtain the configuration disks for the computer as well as any MCA cards that go with it.

## Extended ISA

In 1988 an industry group answered the challenge of MCA and released a new 32-bit, 8-MHz open standard called *Extended ISA* (EISA—pronounced *ee-suh*).

EISA is an improved variation of the ISA slot that accepts older ISA cards, with a two-step design that uses a shallow set of pins to attach to ISA cards and a deeper connection for attaching to EISA cards. In other words, ISA cards slip partway down into the socket; EISA cards seat farther down.

**Caution**    Be very careful to line up cards being placed in an EISA slot precisely and push straight down! If you try to angle the card in, it can be very difficult to seat and you might damage either the connector or the slot.

Although EISA is faster and cheaper than MCA, it never gained much more acceptance than MCA.

Confusion between MCA and EISA technology—along with a limited need for cards that ran at the faster rate and the fact that only a few display, drive controller, and network cards were made available—led to the early demise of both bus technologies. Figures 8.3 and 8.4 show how the slot design of the two technologies differs.

**Figure 8.3**   Top view of ISA and EISA bus

**Figure 8.4**   Cross-section of ISA and EISA bus

# VESA Local Bus

The problems posed by MCA and EISA designs meant that developers needed an improved bus architecture to speed up graphics adapter performance and keep up with the evolving operating system technologies, such as Microsoft Windows. The Windows graphical user interface (GUI) required a much faster display adapter, because every pixel (not just lines of character data) had to be represented and refreshed. About the same time, laser printers and graphics programs like PageMaker and CorelDRAW entered the mainstream market, extending the desktop publishing revolution. The hardware industry developed the *VESA local bus* (VLB) to meet the need for a faster expansion interface. (VESA, the Video Electronics Standards Association, was the driving force behind the new bus technology.) Found only in 386 and 486 machines, the VLB had a short life span. The cards based on this design are connected directly to the system-bus side of the PC's external data bus (see Figure 8.5).

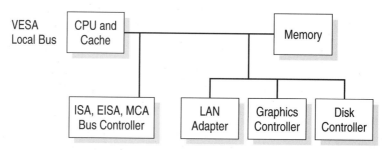

**Figure 8.5**   VESA local bus design

The speed of the system data bus is based on the clock rate of the motherboard's crystal. During the heyday of the VLB, this was usually 33 MHz, and VLB cards usually ran at half that rate, far outpacing the ISA bus. Some cards ran as fast as 50 MHz, using the full speed of the souped-up system bus. That often caused system crashes, because 50 MHz was outside the VLB specification.

The chip design for the VLB controller was relatively simple because many of the core instructions were hosted by the ISA circuits already on the motherboard, but the actual data passes were on the same local bus as the one used by the CPU.

The design specification provides two other performance-boosting features: *burst mode* and *bus mastering*. In burst mode, VLB devices gain complete control of the external data bus for up to four bus cycles, passing up to 16 bytes (128 bits) of data in a single burst. Bus mastering allows the VLB controller to arbitrate data transfers between the external data bus and up to three VLB devices without assistance from the CPU. This limit of three devices also limited the maximum number of VLB slots to three and called for the use of a coprocessor. Display-system design is covered in more detail in Chapter 11, "The Display System."

The actual connectors on the motherboard resemble an ISA slot with an additional short slot aligned with it. On systems that support this interface, one to three slots are located on the side of the motherboard closest to the keyboard connection.

## Peripheral Component Interconnect

PCI allows developers to design cards that will work in any PCI-compatible machine. It overcomes the limitations of ISA, EISA, MCA, and VLB, and it offers the performance needed for today's fast systems.

At first glance, there are many similarities between PCI and the older VLB specifications. Both are local bus systems with 32-bit data paths and burst modes. Also, the original PCI design operates at 33 MHz—roughly the same speed as the VLB. However, the important differences between them allowed PCI to dominate in expansion bus technology. These differences stem from the following features:

- The PCI design's special bus and chip set are designed for advanced bus-mastering techniques and full arbitration of the PCI local bus. This allows support of more than three slots.

- The PCI bus has its own set of four interrupts, which are mapped to regular IRQs on the system. If a PC has more than four PCI slots, some will be sharing interrupts and IRQs.

**Note** Under Windows 95 or with poorly designed PCI cards (both are becoming rarities), the shared addresses could lead to system conflicts and resource problems. Installing PCI cards one at a time minimizes these problems. Also, be aware that on many systems not all PCI slots offer full bus mastering. Check the owner's manual for details, especially on machines with more than four slots. In general, the PCI slots closest to the keyboard connector are the best choices for full bus mastering.

- The PCI bus allows multiple bus-mastering devices. Advanced controllers such as SCSI (Small Computer System Interface) cards can incorporate their own internal bus mastering and directly control attached devices, then arbitrate with the PCI bus for data transfers across the system bus.

- Autoconfiguration lets the PC's BIOS assign the IRQ linking the card to the system bus. Most PCI cards have no switches or jumpers to set, speeding installation and preventing many hardware conflicts.

Most PCs on the market today have one or more ISA slots for backward compatibility; however, most expansion cards are now built using the PCI interface. Although Intel was the original driving force behind PCI development, a PCI standards committee maintains the specification, and it is an open design—meaning that anyone can design hardware using PCI without being required to pay royalties.

### Variations on a Theme: Differences in PCI Versions

The earlier discussion makes PCI sound like a technician's dream interface: fast, reliable, and doing most of the work itself. In most cases, that's true; still, there is always a "but." PCI has gone through many changes, and there are some features to be aware of when you work with a PCI card:

- The early PCI motherboards often have jumpers and BIOS settings that must be set to enable proper PCI operation. These are most often found on Pentium 60-MHz and 66-MHz machines.

- The PCI bus speed is not fixed. Newer chip sets can drive it—and the cards on it—at 66 MHz. At full performance, the PCI bus can deliver data transfers at up to 132 MB per second.

- PCI is not used only by PCs. Macintosh and some other non-PC-style computers incorporate PCI. Manufacturers appreciate this feature because it allows them to design core technology and port it to different models using the same production line. You still need to be certain, however, that a particular card is actually designed for the machine you are working on, even if it fits.

Keep in mind that PCI is evolving. That will help to keep it a viable interface for the foreseeable future, but it might also lead to incompatibilities between new cards and older machines.

## Accelerated Graphics Port

In the early days of PCI, the major market for that technology was the high-performance display adapter. The popularity of PCI led to its dominance of the expansion bus market. Today, the PCI market includes NICs, sound cards, SCSI adapters, Ultra Direct Memory Access (UDMA) controllers, and DVD (digital video disc) interfaces. The variety of devices posed a problem for display-card designers: Having more cards on a single bus slowed down the performance, just when the increasing popularity of 24-bit graphics and 3D rendering called for greater demands on the display system. The search was on for yet another interface; this time, the solution was a single slot—tuned for the display adapter. Once again, Intel led the way and developed the *Accelerated Graphics Port* (AGP).

The AGP removes all the display data traffic from the PCI bus and gives that traffic its own 525-MB-per-second pipe into the system's chip set and, from there, straight to the CPU. It also provides a direct path to the system memory for handling graphics. This procedure is referred to as Direct Memory Execute (DIME). The AGP data path is shown in Figure 8.6.

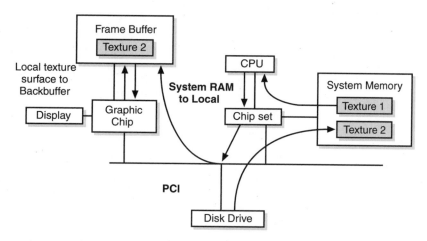

**Figure 8.6**    AGP Direct Memory Execute offers priority access to display data

The AGP slot, if present, is the only one of its kind on the motherboard and is usually the slot closest to the keyboard connector (see Figure 8.7). It is set farther from the back of the PC's case than the PCI slots. AGP connectors are found only on Pentium II-based and later computers or on similar CPUs from non-Intel vendors.

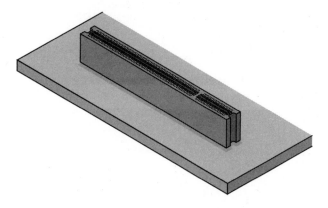

**Figure 8.7**    An AGP slot on the motherboard

## IEEE 1394 FireWire High-Performance Serial Interface

One contender that has been touted as a possible replacement for SCSI (see Chapter 9, "Basic Disk Drives," for details on the SCSI interface) in connecting external peripherals is IEEE 1394, known also by its Apple trade name of FireWire. We'll use the short form and call it 1394. This high-speed serial interface allows up to 62 devices on a chain, at data transfer rates of up to 50 MB per second.

This new interface offers several advantages: a hot swap capability (the ability to add and remove components while the machine is running), small and inexpensive connectors, and a simple cable design. Right now, few devices support 1394, but it is seen as a viable method for connecting multimedia devices like camcorders and other consumer electronic devices to PCs. Its isochronous transfer method (sending data at a constant rate) makes it a natural for video products. Currently, many 1394 PC products are expensive and there is no provision for connecting internal devices. Both 1394 and SCSI will coexist much like SCSI and universal serial bus (USB) for the foreseeable future. (USB is discussed in the next section.)

Although there are some standards defining how connections are made with 1394, several vendors are offering custom ways of linking products.

## Universal Serial Bus

The newest addition to the general PC bus collection, the USB connects external peripherals such as mouse devices, printers, modems, keyboards, joysticks, scanners, and digital cameras to the computer. The USB port is a thin slot; most new motherboards offer two, located near the keyboard. They can also be provided through an expansion card.

USB supports isochronous (time-dependent) and asynchronous (intermittent) data transfers. Isochronous connections transfer data at a guaranteed fixed rate of delivery. This is required for more demanding multimedia applications and devices. Asynchronous data can be transferred whenever there is no isochronous traffic on the bus. USB supports the following data transfer rates, depending on the amount of bus bandwidth a peripheral device requires:

- 1.5 megabits per second (Mbps) asynchronous transfer rate for devices, such as a mouse or keyboard, that do not require a large amount of bandwidth.

- 12 Mbps isochronous transfer rate for high-bandwidth devices such as modems, speakers, scanners, and monitors. The guaranteed data-delivery rate provided by isochronous data transfer is required to support the demand of multimedia applications and devices.

USB devices can be attached with the computer running. A new device will usually be recognized by the operating system (assuming the operating system has Plug and Play capability), and the user will be prompted for drivers, if required. Bear in mind that USB is a new standard, and some early USB ports and chip sets do not properly support some newer devices. Problems with embedded USB ports are not generally worth repairing. It is usually better to install a new USB interface card.

Attaching a new USB device is usually little more complicated than hooking up the appropriate cables and loading a driver disk if requested (see Figure 8.8). Keep in mind that older products may not be adequately supported, and that some devices will require an external power supply.

**Figure 8.8**   USB connectors

## Lesson Summary

The following points summarize the main elements of this lesson:

- Expansion buses provide a way of connecting devices to the motherboard.
- ISA could accommodate both 8-bit and 16-bit expansion cards.
- MCA was a proprietary architecture for IBM's PS/2 computers.
- EISA 32-bit architecture could accommodate older ISA expansion cards.
- VLB architecture employed burst mode and bus mastering to boost performance.

- PCI architecture makes use of autoconfiguration to let the PC's BIOS assign the IRQ linking the card to the system bus.
- AGP architecture removes display data traffic from the PCI bus.
- USB architecture supports both isochronous (time-dependent) and asynchronous (intermittent) data transfers.
- IEEE 1394 is mostly used for multimedia applications on desktop computers.
- Expansion buses have changed to keep up with increases in processor speed.
- A computer technician must know how to identify the various expansion buses (ISA, MCA, EISA, PCI, AGP, and USB) to ensure compatibility and know how to maximize performance when upgrading a computer.

# Lesson 2: Configuring Expansion Cards

In the previous lesson, we discussed the different kinds of expansion buses. The purpose of these buses is to accept expansion cards. Internal and external computer hardware, such as disk drives and monitors, can be connected to the computer's motherboard by means of these expansion cards. As we learned in earlier lessons, the expansion buses connect to an external data bus. All devices are connected to the same communication bus. In this lesson, we look at how the computer keeps track of each device and controls the flow of data.

## After this lesson, you will be able to

- Define addresses
- Describe the attributes and limitations of an IRQ
- Identify the causes of conflicts within a computer
- Locate and resolve hardware conflicts

## Estimated lesson time: 30 minutes

## I/O Addresses

The bus system establishes a connection between the CPU and expansion devices and provides a path for the flow of data. The computer needs a way to track and control which device is sending data and which device is receiving; without such a means—the bus system—there would be complete chaos. The first step to establishing orderly communication is to assign a unique I/O address to each device.

**Note**  Everything in a computer, hardware or software, requires a unique name and address for the CPU to be able to identify what is going on. Bus-mastering devices might seem to get around this requirement, but they have their own controllers that track local traffic and "talk" to the CPU as needed.

I/O addresses are patterns of 1s and 0s transmitted across the address bus by the CPU. The CPU must identify the device before any data is placed on the bus. The CPU uses two bus wires—the Input/Output Read (IOR) wire and the Input/Output Write (IOW) wire—to notify the devices that the address bus is not being used to specify an address in memory, but rather to read to or write from a particular device. The address bus has at least 20 wires. However, when the IOW or IOR wire has voltage, only the first 16 wires are monitored.

To allow communication directly between the CPU and a device, each device responds to unique, built-in patterns or code. If the CPU needs to check the error status of a hard disk drive controller, for instance, it activates the IOW wire and puts the correct pattern of 1s and 0s onto the address bus. The controller then sends back a message describing its error status.

All I/O addresses define the range of patterns assigned to each device's command set. The device ignores all commands outside its range. All devices must have an I/O address, and no two devices can have overlapping ranges. Basic devices on the address list have preset I/O addresses that cannot be changed. Other devices must be assigned to the open addresses, and they must be configured at installation. The following table lists standard PC I/O port address assignments.

| PC/XT Port | Used By | PC/XT Port | Used By |
|---|---|---|---|
| 000h–00Fh | DMA chip 8237A | 2F0h–2F7h | Reserved |
| 020h–021h | PIC 8259A | 2F8h–2FFh | COM2 |
| 040h–043h | PIT 8253 | 300h–31Fh | Prototype adapter |
| 060h–063h | PPI 8255 | 320h–32Fh | Hard disk controller |
| 080h–083h | DMA page register | 378h–37Fh | Parallel interface |
| 0A0h–0AFh | NMI mask register | 380h–38Fh | SDLC adapter |
| 0C0h–0CFh | Reserved | 3A0h–3AFh | Reserved |
| 0E0h–0EFh | Reserved | 3B0h–3BFh | Monochrome adapter /parallel interface |
| 100h–1FFh | Unused | 3C0h–3CFh | EGA |
| 200h–20Fh | Game adapter | 3D0h–3DFh | CGA |
| 210h–217h | Extension unit | 3E0h–3E7h | Reserved |
| 220h–24Fh | Reserved | 3F0h–3F7h | Floppy disk controller |
| 278h–27Fh | Parallel printer | 3F8h–3FFh | COM1 |

| AT Port | Used By | AT Port | Used By |
|---|---|---|---|
| 000h–00Fh | First DMA chip 8237A | 278h–27Fh | Second parallel interface |
| 020h–021h | First PIC 8259A | 2B0h–2DFh | EGA |
| 040h–043h | PIT 8253 | 2F8h–2FFh | COM2 |
| 060h–063h | Keyboard controller 8042 | 300h–31Fh | Prototype adapter |
| 070h–071h | Real-time clock | 320h–32Fh | Available |
| 080h–083h | DMA page register | 378h–37Fh | First parallel interface |
| 0A0h–0AFh | Second PIC 8259A | 380h–38Fh | SDLC adapter |
| 0C0h–0CFh | Second DMA chip 8237A | 3A0h–3AFh | Reserved |
| 0E0h–0EFh | Reserved | 3B0h–3BFh | Monochrome adapter /parallel interface |
| 0F0h–0FFh | Reserved for coprocessor 80287 | 3c0h–3CFh | EGA |
| 100h–1FFh | Available | 3D0h–3DFh | CGA |
| 200h–20Fh | Game adapter | 3E0h–3E7h | Reserved |
| 210h–217h | Reserved | 3F0h–3F7h | Floppy disk controller |
| 220h–26Fh | Available | 3F8h–3FFh | COM1 |

I/O addresses have several important characteristics to remember:

- I/O addresses have 16 bits; they are displayed with a hexadecimal number.
- By convention, the lead 0 is dropped (because all I/O addresses have it).
- Hexadecimal I/O addresses must use capital letters; they are case-sensitive.

## Setting I/O Addresses

Run the Jumpers video located in the Demos folder on the CD accompanying this book to view a presentation of how jumpers are used to configure expansion cards.

As mentioned, each device in a computer must have an I/O address. If a device qualifies as a basic device, it will have a standard, preset I/O address. The default setting for the I/O address will work and no changes are required.

If a device is not a basic device, and does not conform to the PCI Plug and Play specification on a Plug and Play–compatible system, read the manual that came with it. The manual will explain how to set the I/O address and define the limits for that device.

On non-Plug and Play devices, I/O addresses are often set by changing jumpers, changing DIP switches, or through use of software drivers. DIP switches are like mini-rocker panel switches. Jumpers are small caps that are used to link pairs of pins to close a circuit. Devices using these techniques should have instructions on how to configure the settings and locate the switch block or jumpers.

On Plug and Play systems, PCI cards are self-configuring, and usually no intervention is needed to set I/O addresses for those cards. It is possible for Plug and Play cards to conflict with older ISA cards that don't recognize the Plug and Play devices. If you are confronted with this problem, refer to the cards and the motherboard manual for possible resolution.

## Managing I/O Addresses

Devices assigned overlapping I/O addresses usually do not respond to commands and stop functioning. In such a scenario, a modem will dial but not connect; a sound card will start to play but will stop; a mouse pointer will appear but the mouse will not move. I/O overlaps can also sometimes cause the machine to lock up intermittently.

I/O overlaps never happen independently. They usually appear immediately after a new device is installed. The best way to prevent I/O address overlaps is to document all I/O addresses. There are many commercially available programs that will check the I/O addresses for every device on your computer. You can also use Microsoft Diagnostics, a program provided with MS-DOS.

**Note**   If you are running Windows 95 or Windows 98, Windows Me, Windows NT, or Windows 2000, you can use the Device Manager or System Information to locate and resolve IRQ and address conflicts. (See Chapter 16, "Operating System Fundamentals," for more information on the Device Manager.)

## Interrupt Request

The I/O address and the address bus establish a method of communication. The next step is to prevent multiple devices from "talking" at the same time. If the CPU needs to communicate with a device, BIOS routines or device drivers can use I/O addresses to initiate conversations over the external data bus.

Controlling the flow of communication is called *interruption*. Every CPU has a wire called the interrupt (INT) wire. If voltage is applied to the wire, the CPU interrupts what it is doing and attends to the device. For example, when a mouse button is pressed, the CPU attends to the interrupt request, invoking the necessary BIOS routine to query the mouse.

Because the CPU has only one INT wire and must handle many peripheral devices, a specific type of chip, called the 8259 chip, is present on the system to help the CPU detect which device is asking for attention. Every device that needs to interrupt the CPU is provided with a wire called an IRQ. If a device needs to interrupt the CPU, it goes through the following steps:

1. The device applies voltage to the 8259 chip through its IRQ wire.
2. The 8259 chip informs the CPU, by means of the INT wire, that an interrupt is pending.
3. The CPU uses a wire called an INTA (interrupt acknowledge) to signal the 8259 chip to send a pattern of 1s and 0s on the external data bus. This information conveys to the CPU which device is interrupting.
4. The CPU knows which BIOS to run.

The 8088 computers used only one 8259 chip (see Figure 8.9), which limited these computers to using only eight available IRQs. Because a keyboard and system timer were fixtures on all computers, these IRQs were permanently wired into the motherboard. The remaining six wires were then made part of the expansion bus and were available for use by other devices.

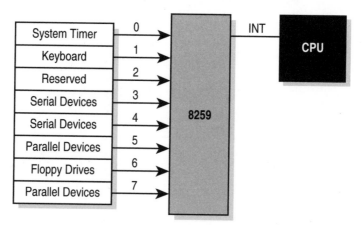

**Figure 8.9**   8259 chip with IRQ assignments

Starting with the generation of computers based on the 80286 chip, two 8259 chips were used to add 8 more available IRQs (see Figure 8.10). These new wires were run to the extension on the 16-bit ISA expansion slot (the 8-bit XT slot was extended to a 16-bit XT slot). Because the CPU has only one IRQ wire, one of the IRQs is used to cascade the two 8259 chips together. This gives a total of 15 available IRQs.

**Note**   When a device is *cascaded*, this means that data is passed through a common path between two devices, usually on to another destination. The term denotes a situation much like water cascading over a waterfall on its journey to the sea.

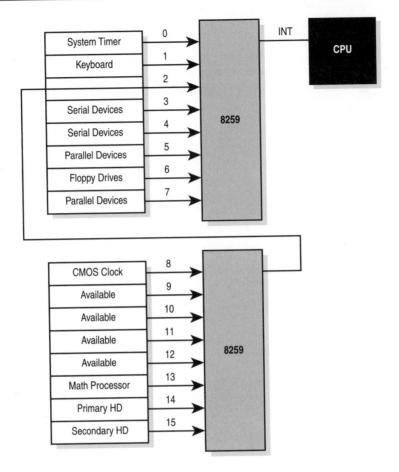

**Figure 8.10**   Cascading 8259 chips

Notice that the cascade removes IRQ 2. IRQ 9 is directed to the old IRQ 2 wire. Any older device designed to run on IRQ 2 will now run on IRQ 9. Some important facts to remember about IRQs include the following:

- IRQ 2 and IRQ 9 are the same IRQ.

- Three IRQs are hardwired (0—system timer, 1—keyboard controller, and 8—real-time clock).

- Four IRQ assignments are so common that no computer or device manufacturer dares to change them for fear their devices will cause conflicts (6—floppy disk controller, 13—math coprocessor, 14—primary IDE [Integrated Device Electronics] controller, and 15—secondary IDE controller).

- Four IRQs default to specific types of devices but can be changed: IRQ 3—COM2 and COM4, 4—COM1 and COM3, 5—LPT2, and 7—LPT1 (see table that follows).

- The rest (IRQs 2/9, 10, 11, and 12) are not specific and are available for use.

**Note**  The 8259 chips no longer exist on a motherboard. Their functions have become part of the multifunction chips called chip sets that perform all the functions of the 8259 chips and more. However, the information provided in the preceding section is still useful for understanding how this portion of the chip set operates. Also, the IRQ assignments generally are the same.

The following table provides typical IRQ assignments.

| IRQ | Function | Available for Change |
|-----|----------|----------------------|
| IRQ 0 | System timer | No |
| IRQ 1 | Keyboard controller | No |
| IRQ 2/9 | Available | Yes |
| IRQ 3 | COM2, COM4 | Usually |
| IRQ 4 | COM1, COM3 | Usually |
| IRQ 5 | LPT2 | Usually |
| IRQ 6 | Floppy disk controller | No |
| IRQ 7 | LPT1 | Usually |
| IRQ 8 | Real-time clock | No |
| IRQ 10 | Available | Yes |
| IRQ 11 | SCSI/available | Yes |
| IRQ 12 | Available | Yes |
| IRQ 13 | Math coprocessor | If there is no math coprocessor |
| IRQ 14 | Primary IDE controller | No |
| IRQ 15 | Secondary IDE controller | Usually |

## Setting IRQs

Devices lacking a fixed or standard IRQ (except for newer PCI cards in compatible PCs) must have their IRQs set during installation. Read the accompanying manuals to learn about these devices. Setting IRQs is one of the first topics discussed in any device's installation instructions. The manual will tell you not only how to set the IRQ, but also the limits, if any, of the device.

Just like I/O addresses, IRQs can be set using hardware, software, or a combination of both. The best way to ensure that no two devices share the same IRQ is to document the IRQs for each device you install in a computer and file that documentation in a location where you can find it easily if needed. As an example, suppose one of your customers has recently installed a sound card that now locks up when a parallel-port tape backup unit is used on the system. This strongly indicates an IRQ conflict. You need merely to check the sound card and the tape backup IRQ settings you have on file and change one if necessary.

**Important**  Some devices have a limited number of IRQ settings; you might need to change the IRQs of other devices to free one of these IRQs.

# Direct Memory Access

The CPU runs the BIOS, operating system, and applications, and it also handles interrupts and accesses I/O addresses. This requires the CPU to move a lot of data, using considerable CPU power and time for what is essentially a simple task. Therefore, moving data is a waste of the CPU's resources.

To reduce this waste, another chip is installed to work with the system CPU called a DMA chip. The only function of the DMA chip (the 8237 chip) is to move data. It handles all the data passing from peripherals to RAM and vice versa.

DMA transfers are not automatic. Hardware and device drivers must be designed to take advantage of this chip. Originally, DMA was used only to transfer data between floppy disk drives and RAM; early computers had only four wires and one DMA chip. Any device requiring DMA had to send a request, just like an IRQ.

DMA channels use the same rules as IRQs. Just as with the 8259 chip, DMA availability soon became a problem because an insufficient number of channels was available. A second DMA chip was added for 80286-based computers. Just like the second IRQ chip, these two are cascaded, allowing a total of eight DMA channel assignments (usually referred to simply as DMA channels). Every computer uses DMA 2 for the floppy disk drive.

## Setting DMA Channels

Fortunately, not many devices use DMA, but sound cards, a few SCSI controllers, and some CD-ROM drives and network cards do require DMA. Just as with IRQs and I/O addresses, DMA can be set by means of either hardware or software. However, manufacturers started using DMA for devices other than the floppy disk drive only recently. As a result, almost all devices set DMA through software (although some still use jumpers). If two devices share the same DMA channel and "talk" at the same time, the computer will lock up. The following table provides DMA channel assignments.

| DMA Channel | Function |
| --- | --- |
| 0 | Available |
| 1 | Available |
| 2 | Floppy disk controller |
| 3 | ECP (Enhanced Capabilities Port) parallel/available |
| 4 | First DMA controller |
| 5 | Second sound card |
| 6 | SCSI/available |
| 7 | Available |

## Managing DMA

DMA and IRQ work in the same way; therefore, DMA conflicts look and act exactly like IRQ conflicts. Always check for IRQ conflicts first (although it is possible for a computer professional to spend hours trying to solve IRQ problems when the source of the problem is actually the DMA). If you are sure all IRQs are correct, yet the computer continues to experience a problem, check the DMA. There is very little diagnostic software for resolving DMA problems, so it is important to maintain careful documentation.

# COM and Ports

IBM created preset combinations of IRQs and I/O addresses for serial and parallel devices. These preset combinations are called *ports*. The word *port* simply means a portal or two-way access. The preset combinations are called COM ports for serial devices and LPT (line printer) ports for parallel devices.

The purpose of a port is to make installation easier. Modems and printers, therefore, do not require IRQ or I/O settings. When assigned to an active port (as long as no other device is using that port), they will work. The following table lists standard ports.

| Port | I/O Address | IRQ |
|------|-------------|-----|
| COM1 | 3F8 | 4 |
| COM2 | 2F8 | 3 |
| COM3 | 3E8 | 4 |
| COM4 | 2E8 | 3 |
| LPT1 | 378 | 7 |
| LPT2 | 278 | 5 |

Most computers are manufactured to offer built-in physical ports with cable connections available either directly to the motherboard or in an expansion slot. In this case, the standard port addresses and IRQs are assigned to them. This makes it possible to install an external device simply by plugging in the port and assigning addresses to the device. If necessary, these ports can be disabled (by using CMOS setup), freeing their I/O addresses and IRQs for another device.

For example, suppose you want to install a new internal modem on a machine that has two external serial ports on the motherboard. By disabling one of these ports, you have made its address and IRQ available for use by the internal device. Simply assign the device to the port that is now free.

## Installation Problems with COM Ports

Assume you have a modem set to COM1. You buy a network card that comes out of the box with a default setting of IRQ4. You realize the network card and the modem will conflict, and the computer will lock up. What should you do?

You should change the IRQ on one of the devices. The network card is probably the best choice, because the modem is installed and already working.

## COM Ports

The original 8088-based IBM PCs were equipped with two serial ports: COM1, set to IRQ4, and COM2, set to IRQ3. Although those two IRQs are still the standard for COM ports 1 and 2, many BIOS routines will allow different IRQ assignments or even allow an unused port to be disabled. Because of the limited number of IRQ addresses available, any additional COM ports would have to share IRQs with existing ports. COM3 shared the interrupt of COM1 (IRQ4), and COM4 shared the interrupt of COM2 (IRQ3). To enable use of these additional ports, COM3 was assigned I/O address 3E8-3EF, and COM4 was assigned I/O address 2E8-2EF. This sharing was possible because the IRQ-sharing devices would be unlikely to use them at the same time.

Today we have many other ways of adding printers and other peripherals to PCs, but such conflicts can still be a problem with modems and UPS (uninterruptible power supply) devices that might need simultaneous access.

**Note**   The first rule for setting IRQs is to ensure that two devices never share the same IRQ. The only exception is that two (or more) devices can share an IRQ if they never "talk" at the same time. Common IRQ conflicts occur among a serial mouse, sound card, modem, and/or serial printer. (Remember that PCI devices can share an IRQ if the IRQ is managed by the same PCI controller.)

## LPT Ports

LPT ports are for parallel data connections. The name is derived from their original use with printers. The original IBM standard LPT port did not provide bidirectional communications (talkback) and was designed solely for one-way data streams to a printer. The standard addresses are IRQ7 for LPT1 and IRQ5 for LPT2, if it is present. IRQ5 quickly became the favorite for devices like sound cards and other add-ons. Today, many devices are made that can use the parallel plug in the back of a computer, thus reducing costs. These devices (tape backups, SCSI drives, or modems) use bidirectional communication and, therefore, need an interrupt. This situation is easing as USB connections replace many of the parallel designs.

## Installing Expansion Cards

The rules for installing expansion cards are simple:

- First read the manual.
- Document addresses and DMA and IRQ settings for any non-Plug and Play device.
- Keep the IRQs, DMAs, and I/O addresses unique.

Windows 95, Windows 98, Windows Me, and Windows 2000 support Plug and Play. In most cases, you can insert a Plug and Play card into the proper type of expansion slot and turn on the computer. Windows will find the card and guide you through the setup. The savvy computer professional documents and keeps track of the IRQ, DMA, and I/O addresses, in case a conflict arises with a Plug and Play device on the system.

Windows 95, Windows 98, and Windows Me use Hardware Properties, under the System option in the Control Panel, which does a good job of identifying (and allowing) changes to these settings. To view assignments, from Control Panel, select System, select the Device Manager tab, and then click Properties.

---

**Tip**  A good way to document a computer is to print a complete list of the computer's hardware settings, listed in the Computer Properties dialog box.

---

**Note**  For Plug and Play to work, the computer must have a Plug and Play BIOS, and the operating system and the device card must be Plug and Play–compliant.

---

## Lesson Summary

The following points summarize the main elements of this lesson:

- Every device in a computer needs a unique name and address.
- In order for the CPU to identify which devices need to use the data bus, it monitors the IRQs.
- Generally, no two devices can use the same IRQ or DMA channel.
- Most conflicts during installation of a new device are caused by IRQ conflicts.
- BIOS routines or device drivers can use I/O addresses to initiate "conversations" over the external data bus by means of an IRQ.
- DMA handles all the data passing from assigned peripherals to RAM and vice versa.
- COM ports are for serial devices; LPT ports are for parallel devices.
- The computer technician should document addresses and DMA and IRQ settings for any non-Plug and Play device installed in a computer.

# Lesson 3: Cables and Connectors

Cables and connectors are critical to the operation of any computer peripherals. A computer professional must be able to identify and understand the various types of cables and connectors. This lesson discusses common connectors and their functions.

---

### After this lesson, you will be able to

- Identify cables and connectors by their names and functions

### Estimated lesson time: 20 minutes

---

### Parallel Printer Cables

Parallel printer ports and cables are used to connect printers and other add-on items such as CD-ROM drives, tape drives, and scanners. Centronics Corporation invented the most common type. It is an 8-bit parallel connection with handshaking signals between the printer and the computer—these tell the computer when to start or stop sending data. A standard printer cable is configured with a 36-pin Centronics connector on the printer end and a standard 25-pin "D" (male) on the computer end. A standard 25-pin "D" (female) connector found on the back of the computer designates it as a parallel port (see Figure 8.11).

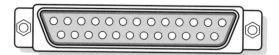

**Figure 8.11**   Standard 25-pin D connector

The original parallel port was designed only to send information to printers and was unidirectional. However, some bidirectional communication was possible by manipulating the handshaking lines. Today, computer manufacturers have developed updated versions that allow better bidirectional communication while maintaining the original Centronics specification. The Institute of Electrical and Electronic Engineers (IEEE) developed a standard—IEEE 1284—to oversee the standardization of these ports.

There are three bidirectional standards used today:

- **Bi-Tronics.** This modified Centronics connection was created by Hewlett-Packard. It utilizes bidirectional communication, allowing the printer to send messages to the computer (out of paper, paper jam, and so forth).

- **EPP (Enhanced Parallel Port).** This features 2-MB-per-second data-transfer rates, bidirectional 8-bit operation, and addressing to support multiple (daisy-chained) peripherals on a single computer.

- **ECP (Extended Capabilities Port).** This was developed by Hewlett-Packard and Microsoft. It features 2-MB-per-second data transfer and bidirectional 8-bit operation. ECP will specify whether transmitted information consists of data or commands for the peripheral. ECP supports CD-ROM drive and scanner connections, run length encoded (RLE) data compression, and DMA support to increase transfer speed and reduce processor overhead.

**Note** The EPP and ECP standards often have to be enabled in the CMOS setup before the specified port can use them.

### IEEE 1284 Printer Modes

A vast array of printers is available, and to ensure that you are obtaining optimum performance, the printer, the printer driver, and the software using the printer must be configured for the same mode. The following table describes various printing modes and their capabilities.

| Mode | Capabilities | Speed | Notes |
|------|-------------|-------|-------|
| Compatibility | 8-bit output; hardware handshaking; no DMA | 100–200 KB per second out | Original parallel port |
| 4-bit | 4-bit input using some of the printer's handshaking lines | 100–200 KB per second out; 40–60 KB per second in | Hewlett-Packard Bi-Tronics mode |
| 8-bit | 8-bit I/O bidirectional | 80–300 KB per second | Original bidirectional port |
| ECP | 8-bit I/O; can use DMA | >2 MB per second | Scanners and high-speed printers |
| EPP | 8-bit I/O | Up to 2 MB per second | Very flexible modes of operation |

### Parallel Pin Assignments

Just like modem cables, it is important for printer cables to have the correct pin connections. The following table describes the standard parallel pin assignments for the computer-end (25-pin) and the printer-end (Centronics) connectors.

| Computer | Direction of Data Flow | Printer | Name | ID | Function |
|---|---|---|---|---|---|
| 1 | → | 1 | Strobe | STROBE | Sends data to printer |
| 2 | → | 2 | Data bit 0 | DB0 | |
| 3 | → | 3 | Data bit 1 | DB1 | |
| 4 | → | 4 | Data bit 2 | DB2 | |
| 5 | → | 5 | Data bit 3 | DB3 | |
| 6 | → | 6 | Data bit 4 | DB4 | |
| 7 | → | 7 | Data bit 5 | DB5 | |
| 8 | → | 8 | Data bit 6 | DB6 | |
| 9 | → | 9 | Data bit 7 | DB7 | |
| 10 | ← | 10 | Acknowledge | ACK | Printer acknowledges receipt of data |
| 11 | ← | 11 | Printer busy | BUSY | |
| 12 | ← | 12 | Paper error | PE | |
| 13 | ← | 13 | Select | SLCT | Indicates printer is online |
| 14 | ← | 14 | Autofeed | AUTOFD | |
| 15 | ← | 32 | Error | ERROR | |
| 16 | → | 31 | Initialize printer | INIT | |
| 17 | ← | 36 | Select input | SLECT IN | |
| — | ← | 18 | 5v | | 5 volts available from some printers |
| 18–25 | ← | 16, 19–30, 33 | Ground | | Sometimes to pin 17 |

# Serial Port Cables

A serial port allows a computer to send data over long distances by converting parallel data to serial data. Typical computers will have one or two serial ports, usually designated as COM1 and COM2. The "standard" port is a 9-pin male connector on the computer, shown in Figure 8.12. (There are also 25-pin cables available.)

**Figure 8.12**   Standard 9-pin D connector

The following table describes the pin connection for the 9-pin and 25-pin serial cable connectors.

| 9-Pin | 25-Pin | Name | ID | Function |
|---|---|---|---|---|
| | 1 | Shield | | |
| 3 | 2 | Transmit data | TD | Data sent from computer |
| 2 | 3 | Receive data | RD | Data sent to computer |
| 7 | 4 | Request to send | RTS | Computer is ready to send |
| 8 | 5 | Clear to send | CTS | "Other end" is ready to receive |
| 6 | 6 | Data set ready | DSR | "Other end" is ready to receive |
| 5 | 7 | Signal ground | SG | GND |
| 1 | 8 | Data carrier detect | DCD | Modem detects a signal from another modem |
| 4 | 20 | Data terminal ready | DTR | Computer is ready to send |
| 9 | 22 | Ring indicator | RI | Modem detects line ringing |

## Null Modem Cables

Null modem cables are used to directly connect two computers together without the need for a modem. The transmit and receive wires in the cable (wires 2 and 3) are switched to make the computers "think" they are using modems.

## SCSI Cables

SCSI cables come in a variety of sizes depending on the type of SCSI used and the manufacturer of the device. Typically, internal cables are flat ribbon types and external cables are shielded bundles.

## Keyboard Cables

Another peripheral device with a cable that we encounter and yet never think about is the keyboard. Because there are different types of keyboard cables (and connectors) and because, on occasion, the technician might encounter a problem with a keyboard connector, they are worthy of mention.

Keyboards are manufactured in two different styles with different cables and connectors. Earlier versions used a 5-pin DIN connector (DIN stands for

Deutsch Industrie Norm, the German national standards organization), and most new keyboards use a 6-pin DIN connector, the same used on a PS/2 mouse. Connectors are available to convert the 5-pin DIN to a 6-pin mini-DIN. Although they have a different number of pins, they use the same wires and pinouts. Data is sent serially to the keyboard using the keyboard interface. Data is written to the controller's input buffer to accomplish this. Keyboard data passes through pin 2 of the connector, and clocking signals move through pin 1. A keyboard reset, which can be connected to the system's reset line, is included at pin 3. Ground and +5-volt DC connections are applied to the keyboard through pins 4 and 5.

## Identifying Cables and Connectors

Because printers and modems can both use 9-pin and 25-pin connectors and cables, a computer technician must be able to identify the function of the cables by their connectors. Other devices, such as monitors and game ports, use 15-pin connectors. Cable identification can be confusing, but it is important. The following table summarizes how to identify common cables and connectors.

| Function | Computer Connector | Cable Connector |
|---|---|---|
| Communication (serial) | 9-pin or 25-pin male | 9-pin or 25-pin female |
| Printer (parallel) | 25-pin female | Centronics 36-pin female |
| Monitor (VGA and SVGA) | 15-pin female (three rows of pins) | 15-pin male (three rows of pins) |
| Monitor (MGA and CGA) | 9-pin female | 9-pin male |
| Game port (joystick) | 15-pin female (two rows of pins) | 15-pin male (two rows of pins) |
| Keyboard | 5-pin DIN female or 6-pin DIN female (PS/2) | 5-pin DIN male or 6-pin DIN male (PS/2) |

## Troubleshooting Cables

Cables and connectors are a very common source of problems. Here are a few suggestions for troubleshooting:

- If a peripheral device doesn't work, always check the cables, especially if the device has been working recently.

- Always check for loose connections.

- Check for bent or broken pins on the connector. Bent pins can sometimes be repaired; however, they will always be susceptible to damage later, because the pin has been weakened. It is a good idea to mark these connectors and use them with care. A better idea is to replace them.

- If a connector or cable doesn't fit or if you have to push hard to make the connection, something is wrong. Either a connector has been damaged or it is not the right match.

- Check for worn or frayed cables. Replace if necessary.

- Make sure you have the right cable. Some, such as null modem cables, look just like standard communication cables, but will not work with a modem.

- Always be wary of "homemade" cables.

## Summary of Connectors

Computers use a large variety of connectors for various peripherals. The following table offers a summary of the most common connectors and their uses.

| Name | Uses |
| --- | --- |
| DB-9 | Serial ports—external modem, mouse, printer. |
| DB-25 | Parallel port—printer, scanner, removable drive. |
| RJ-11 | Standard telephone connector—2 wires. |
| RJ-12 | Standard telephone connector—4 wires—used with dual phone connections. |
| RJ-45 | Network connector. |
| PS/2 (mini-DIN) | Mouse, scanners, and some keyboards. |
| Centronics | Printers. |
| USB | Technology that allows multiple peripherals to be attached to one cable. Popular devices are keyboards, mouse devices, modems, video cameras, and external Zip drives. |

## Lesson Summary

The following points summarize the main elements of this lesson:

- There are many different types of computer cables and connectors. It is important for the computer technician to be able to identify each of them.

- The evolution of a technology often brings modification to cables, the way they are wired, and their lengths.

- Distinguishing between a male and a female connector is often the key to identifying the connector's function.

- Loose or poorly connected cables are often the cause of computer problems.

# Chapter Summary

The following points summarize the key concepts in this chapter:

### Understanding Expansion Buses

- Expansion slots are standardized connections that provide a common access point for installing devices.

- The different types of expansion bus architecture are ISA, MCA, EISA, VESA VLB, and PCI.

- USB architecture supports both isochronous (time-dependent) and asynchronous (intermittent) data transfers.

- PCI architecture makes use of autoconfiguration to let the PC's BIOS assign the IRQ linking the card to the system bus.

- AGP architecture removes display data traffic from the PCI bus.

### Configuring Expansion Cards

- For a CPU to keep track of its devices and communicate with them, a unique I/O address must be assigned to each device.

- To prevent devices from "talking" to the CPU at the same time, an IRQ number is assigned to the devices to inform the CPU which device is requesting its attention. It is recommended that you memorize as many of the typical IRQ assignments as possible.

- The DMA chip moves data, handling all the data passing from peripherals to RAM and vice versa.

- To avoid problems similar to IRQ conflicts, no two devices should have the same DMA channel assignment. COM ports are used for serial devices (such as modems) and LPT ports are used for parallel devices (such as printers). COM ports put these devices in direct communication with the CPU and make installation easier.

### Cables and Connectors

- There are many different types of computer cables and connectors. It is important for the computer technician to be able to identify each of them.

- Distinguishing between a male and a female connector is often the key to identifying the connector's function.

- Loose or poorly connected cables are often the cause of computer problems.

# Review

The following questions are intended to reinforce key information presented in this chapter. If you are unable to answer a question, review the appropriate lesson and then try the question again. Answers to the questions can be found in Appendix A, "Questions and Answers."

1. Why does a computer need an expansion bus?

2. Name the available expansion buses.

3. What happens if two non-PCI devices use the same I/O address?

4. How many IRQs are available on most PCs?

5. Under what conditions would a second modem—installed and assigned to COM3—not work?

6. Identify the two divisions of the external data bus and describe the purpose of each.

7. What is the standard that governs computer buses?

8. What is the difference between ISA and EISA cards?

9. Why was VESA created?

10. What is bus mastering?

11. Describe ways in which the PCI bus is better than previous technologies.

12. How does the CPU use I/O addresses?

13. What is the I/O port address of COM2?

14. What are the functions of IRQs?

15. List as many of the standard IRQ assignments as you can.

16. What is the function of the DMA chip?

17. Why is it important not to assign an IRQ to more than one device?

18. What is the difference between COM ports and LPT ports?

19. Why is it important to document IRQs, DMAs, and I/O addresses?

20. Identify as many cables and connectors as you can.

21. What type of connector is used for a parallel port on the computer?

22. Describe a null modem cable.

23. What type of connector is used for a parallel port on the printer?

24. Describe a USB connector.

C H A P T E R   9

# Basic Disk Drives

**Lesson 1: Floppy Disk Drives** ................................. 182

**Lesson 2: Hard Disk Drives** ................................... 190

**Chapter Summary** .......................................... 216

**Review** .................................................. 217

## About This Chapter

This chapter is all about drives—disk drives—that come in assorted sizes and shapes. The first disk drives were physically large, small in capacity (limited in the amount of data they could store), and very expensive. Today, disk drives are physically small, large in capacity, and (compared to early drives) very inexpensive.

The history of disk drives is long and complex. In this chapter, we begin our exploration by first looking briefly at the history and development of disk drives. We start with the most basic of drives (the floppy disk drive), and continue through the early hard disk drives, examining their complexities and limitations along the way.

## Before You Begin

Before starting this chapter, you should review the discussions of memory, hexadecimal notation, and basic input/output system (BIOS) operations in Chapter 6, "Motherboard and ROM BIOS," and Chapter 7, "Memory."

# Lesson 1:  Floppy Disk Drives

The most basic input device is the floppy disk drive. It is perhaps the only computer component that has retained its original technology. Other than increased storage capacity and the adoption of a hard plastic shell, the floppy disk drive still works essentially the same way (in terms of cabling and BIOS configuration) it did 15 years ago. In this lesson, we explore this venerable standard.

---

### After this lesson, you will be able to

- Describe floppy disk drive technology
- Troubleshoot a floppy disk drive problem

### Estimated lesson time: 20 minutes

---

## The Basics of Floppy Disk Drives

In 1972, IBM developed the first floppy disk drives for its System 370 machines. These drives used 8-inch floppy disks. Other companies, such as Wang, adapted the same basic design for its dedicated word processing machines used in the 1970s and 1980s. The actual disks came pre-formatted, and only worked on a given operating system or computer. This resulted in high-cost drives and reduced the ability to use floppies as a quick means of transporting files from one system to another.

When IBM introduced the personal computer (PC) in 1981, it came standard with a 5.25-inch floppy disk drive. Floppy disks were included in PCs before hard disk drives, mostly out of economic considerations. The cost of an early PC hard disk drive was more than the total cost of a system today and took half of a day to prepare and install. Some very old PCs may have a 5.25-inch drive installed. The only reason a newer machine might need one is to maintain compatibility with an old program or data stored on such disks.

Today's 3.5-inch floppy disks (see Figure 9.1) are made of flexible plastic and coated with a magnetic material. To protect the disk from dust and physical damage, it is packaged in a plastic or coated paper case. The main reason for the popularity of floppy disk drives and disks is that they provide inexpensive read/write (R/W) removable media. The data stored on a floppy disk can be moved from one computer to another, provided both have the same type of drive. In general, it is a good idea to protect your data by always keeping two copies of any data file that you create (the original and a backup), and the floppy disk is an excellent medium for backing up, storing, or distributing copies of relatively small files, such as word processing documents.

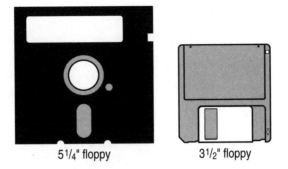

5¼" floppy          3½" floppy

**Figure 9.1**   Floppy disks

The following table describes various floppy disks and their capacities.

| Disk Size | Capacity | Description |
|-----------|----------|-------------|
| 5.25 inch | 160 KB | Single-sided, single-density—the first model. |
| 5.25 inch | 360 KB | Double-sided, single-density. |
| 5.25 inch | 720 KB | Double-sided, double-density. |
| 5.25 inch | 1.2 MB | Double-sided, high-density. |
| 3.5 inch | 720 KB | Double-sided, double-density. |
| 3.5 inch | 1.44 MB | Double-sided, high-density—today's standard. |
| 3.5 inch | 2.88 MB | Double-sided, quad-density. This format has never really gained in market share and is not common on today's PCs. |

The only major differences between the 5.25-inch and the 3.5-inch disk drives (other than physical size) are that the 5.25-inch drive has a slot connector and the 3.5-inch drive has a pin connector for engaging and spinning the disk, and they use different power plugs and voltages.

All floppy disk drives are connected to the motherboard's external data bus by a 34-lead ribbon cable, shown in Figure 9.2. This cable has a seven-wire twist in lines 10 through 16. This ensures that when two floppy disk drives are attached, the drive-select and motor-enable signals on those wires can be inverted to "select" which drive becomes the active target. The remaining wires carry data and ground signals. The connector end of the cable with the twist always goes toward the drives.

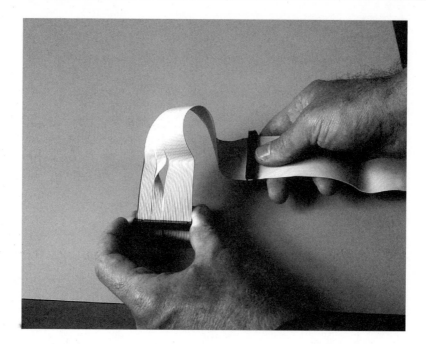

**Figure 9.2**    Floppy disk drive cable with a twist

Early PC BIOS logic was developed to recognize one or two floppy disk drives. In such systems, no more than one 34-pin cable for floppy disk drives can be installed in the computer without resorting to special hardware. When a floppy disk drive is installed on the end connector (near the twist), the drive is logically designated as the first or primary or *A drive* by the BIOS. The drive attached in the middle of the cable is always the secondary or *B drive*. The BIOS will not recognize a B drive unless an A drive is physically installed.

The number 1 red wire must be connected to the number 1 pin on the drive. If this is not correctly installed, the drive will not work (although no permanent damage can be done by installing the connector backward).

---

**Tip**    If you install a new drive and notice that the indicator light comes on and stays on, the cable is most likely backward.

---

The power connection for a floppy disk drive, shown in Figure 9.3, is either the large, Molex-type connector on the 5.25-inch drive (see Lesson 1 of Chapter 5, "Power Supplies," for details) or the smaller mini connector on the 3.5-inch drive. Older power supplies may only have the Molex connections, and you will need an adapter to attach a 3.5-inch drive. Newer power supplies, and all power supplies for the ATX-style cases, should have both Molex and the two-strand connection for providing a 5-volt power connection to the 3.5-inch drive.

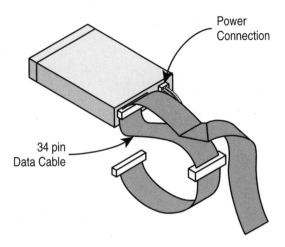

**Figure 9.3**   Floppy disk drive cable connections

After you physically install a floppy disk drive, you need only use the BIOS Setup program to adjust the proper CMOS (complementary metal-oxide semi-conductor) settings for the type and position (first or second), and the installation will be complete. In CMOS setup, select the drive (A or B) and enter the correct capacity.

**Note**   Very old CMOS chips won't have settings for 1.44-MB or 2.88-MB 3.5-inch floppy disk drives because they were developed before these drives were introduced. Today the 5.25-inch drives are obsolete, and the CMOS of the future might not have settings for them. Several third-party utilities will allow the CMOS to accept the necessary values to support these drives.

## Keeping a Floppy Disk Drive Running

Although floppy disk drives are usually rugged and dependable, they do take a lot of abuse and sometimes they fail. Some failures are simply caused by improper use, some by overuse combined with a lack of cleaning, and some-times the mechanism just stops working.

Floppy disk drives are one of the most fragile parts of a computer system. They are highly susceptible to failure because their internal components are directly exposed to the outside world. Often, there is only a small door or slot that sepa-rates the R/W heads from dust, grime, and cigarette smoke. Floppy disk drives are often the victims of inverted disks, paper clips, and other foreign objects that can cause mechanical damage.

The good news is that floppy disk drives are inexpensive and easy to replace. The only preventive maintenance required is to keep the floppy disk drive clean! Excellent cleaning kits are available in most computer and discount stores. To achieve the best performance from a floppy disk drive in a high-use or industrial environment, schedule monthly cleaning.

### Always an Exception

One unusual floppy disk drive solution that appeared during the time that the 3.5-inch models gained dominance was the hybrid 3.5/5.25 drive. This married the slots for both formats in a single housing. These installed just like a single drive, but the chances of coming across such a drive today are pretty rare.

## Errors Caused by the Floppy Disk

If a floppy disk drive doesn't work, the first thing you should suspect is the floppy disk. To check a floppy disk, use the following procedure:

1. First, make sure the disk is not write protected. The hole on the right top corner of a 3.5-inch disk (viewed from the front) should be closed. On a 5.25-inch disk, the notch on one side should be visible (not covered).

2. Try another disk.

3. Try a new (formatted) disk.

4. Try someone else's disk—one that is known to work on another computer (first make sure there is no critical data on the disk).

5. If two or more disks are unreadable, the drive is suspect; try going to MS-DOS and reading a directory using the DIR command.

**Caution**   Never test a drive by using a disk that contains important data! If the drive is bad, it may destroy any disks placed into it.

### Detecting Data Errors on a Disk

If you can read data from one disk, but not another, or if a disk is very slow reading or writing data, the problem is the floppy disk. Throw the offending disk away. Data errors on floppy disks generally result in an error message that ends with the words "Abort, Retry, Fail." The system will make 10 attempts to read data from a drive before reporting an error. If you get an error, it indicates that the disk is in pretty bad shape. Transfer the data as best you can to another drive, and discard the old disk.

The process for repairing floppy disks is identical to the process for repairing hard disk drives, should there be data on the disk that must be recovered (see "ScanDisk" in Lesson 2, later in this chapter).

## Check the CMOS Setting

Occasionally, the CMOS settings for floppy disks cause problems with drive operations. Any of the following errors indicates a possible CMOS setup problem:

- General failure reading drive A: (or B:)
- Not ready error reading drive A: (or B:)
- Insert disk for drive A: (or B:) and press any key when ready

BIOS makers often use the 3.5-inch high-density disk drive as the default CMOS setting for the A drive. With this BIOS, failure of the CMOS battery, or even accidental erasure of the CMOS, will still allow most floppy disks to work. Always double-check the CMOS if you are experiencing a recurrent floppy disk drive failure. It is quick, easy, and might save you time.

**Tip**   It is possible for the CMOS to be corrupted by a software or hardware conflict and yet appear to be fine. If all else fails, reset the CMOS and reinstall the CMOS setup (check the motherboard manual for the jumper or disconnect the battery).

## Check or Change the Floppy Disk Drive Cable

Cables wear out, work themselves loose, and are sometimes improperly installed. Check out both the data cable and the power jack as possible causes of the errant floppy disk drive before moving on to the controller.

## Change the Floppy Disk Drive Controller

Today, most floppy drive controllers are built onto the motherboard. These are quite reliable. In the event one does fail, however, you will usually have to disable the on-board controller and add a separate controller on an expansion card or replace the motherboard. It's actually less expensive to replace the entire motherboard than to repair the floppy-related components.

Separate floppy disk drive controller cards are durable and highly resistant to failure. Left alone, they generally cause no problems. However, cards that have recently been handled, such as during a move or repairs to the computer, can be suspect. They are extremely sensitive to shock and static discharge.

In the event of a loose data cable or power plug, the power-on self test (POST) will return "FDD Controller Failure" or "Drive Not Ready" errors. (For more information about POST, refer to Chapter 6, "Motherboard and ROM BIOS.") Verify all the connections and try again. If the connections are sound, try removing and reseating the controller (being careful of electrostatic discharge). If the same errors continue, replace the controller. Floppy disk drives and controllers are inexpensive.

When replacing a floppy disk drive controller (see Figure 9.4), keep in mind that most of these controllers on pre-Pentium machines (486 and older) are bundled as part of a combination input/output (I/O) card. These cards include some (often all) of the following: hard disk drive controllers, serial ports, parallel ports, and joystick ports. If the new card contains any duplicate ports (they already exist elsewhere on the computer), a potential for conflict exists.

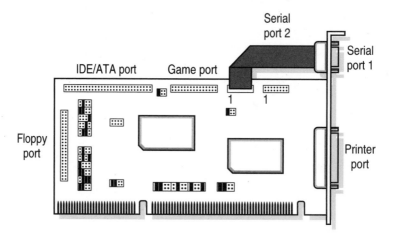

**Figure 9.4**   I/O card with floppy disk controller

---

**Tip**   If you are installing a card that includes devices already installed on the computer, be sure to disable duplicate devices on the card before adding an I/O card. If not disabled, the duplicate components will cause conflicts, and may keep the machine from booting successfully, or force Microsoft Windows into safe mode. If you have a new card with improved devices, disable or remove the older items.

---

## Replace the Floppy Disk Drive

When replacing floppy disk drives, be sure to throw away the old drive. Floppy disk drives are inexpensive compared to other components in the computer. Consider purchasing them in quantity to save money. It is a good idea to have a spare floppy disk drive and I/O card available for testing purposes.

## Lesson Summary

The following points summarize the main elements of this lesson:

- The 3.5-inch floppy disk drive has become an industry standard.

- Floppy disk drive technology has not changed much over the years.

- Floppy disk drives fail more than any other part of a computer system.

- Floppy drive parameters must be properly set in the system CMOS.

- When a drive fails to read or write, check the drive (or, in the case of floppies, the individual disk) for errors first, then the CMOS settings, and, finally, the cable. If all of these fail, replace the drive.

# Lesson 2: Hard Disk Drives

Hard disk drives are mass storage devices. Virtually all of today's PCs have at least one hard disk drive. The first hard disk drives were small in capacity, physically large, and expensive when compared to the cost of drives today. They were about 4 inches tall, 5.25 inches wide, and 8 inches long, and they weighed almost 10 pounds. In 1981, IBM introduced the XT computer with a 10-MB hard drive, and new owners wondered what they would do with all that space. Today, a new hard disk drive can fit in your pocket and hold over 17 GB of data. In this lesson, we examine hard disk drives, from the early versions to today's minimonsters.

### After this lesson, you will be able to

- Explain the operation of a hard disk drive
- Define the different types of hard disk drives, including their advantages and disadvantages
- Partition a hard disk drive
- Troubleshoot hard disk drives

### Estimated lesson time: 45 minutes

## Physical Characteristics

The first form of PC mass storage was the magnetic tape drive, basically the same as a music cassette recorder. Although tape proved a good medium for storing large amounts of data, it had some significant limitations. The typical cassette drive cartridge was easily damaged. Further, gaining access to the data was slow due to the way data is organized on tape, as a long stream of 1s and 0s, an arrangement known as "sequential." Tapes were hundreds of feet long, and users often had to run the entire length of the tape to find the data they were seeking. By providing random access (the ability to go directly to any point on the data surface), floppy disks are a major improvement, but they are too slow and too limited in capacity for modern applications.

The original concept behind the hard disk drive was to provide a storage medium that held large amounts of data and allowed fast (random) access to that data. Data on a hard drive can be accessed directly, without requiring the user to start at the beginning and read everything until finding the data sought.

The first IBM hard disk drives came out in the late 1970s and early 1980s and were code-named "Winchester." The original design concept included two 30-MB units in one enclosure: 30-30 (hence Winchester, after the well-known rifle cartridge popular in western movies). The PC-XT was the first personal computer to include a hard disk. They were called *fixed disks* because they were not removable by the end user, like a floppy. (Old mainframe computers had hard platters that were removable by a trained technician.) The Winchester technology is the forerunner of all PC fixed disks.

Hard disk drives are composed of several platters, matched to a collection of R/W heads and an actuator. Unlike floppy disk drives, a hard disk drive assembly is housed in a sealed case, which prevents contamination from the surrounding environment. Each case has a tiny aperture with an air filter. This allows the air pressure to be equalized between the interior and the exterior of the drive.

The platters are often made of an aluminum alloy and have a thin magnetic-media coating on both sides. After coating, the platters are polished and given another thin coating of graphite for protection against mechanical damage caused by physical contact between the data heads and the platter surface.

The R/W heads "float on a cushion of air" above the platters, which spin at 3500 to 12,000 revolutions per minute (rpm). The distance (flying height) between the heads and the disk surface is less than the thickness of a fingerprint.

## Storing Data

As noted in previous chapters, data is stored using binary code. Within the computer's memory, 1s and 0s are stored as electrical impulses. On magnetic media, the 1s and 0s can be stored as either magnetic or nonmagnetic areas on the drive surface. Although there are magnetized and nonmagnetized positions on the hard disk drive, the 1s and 0s of the binary code are stored in terms of *flux reversals*. These flux reversals are actually the transitions between magnetized and nonmagnetized positions on the hard drive surface.

Early hard disk drives used a method of encoding called *frequency modulation* (FM). FM technology is based on timing. To differentiate a 1 from a 0, it measures the time the drive head spends in a magnetized state. For FM to work, it requires every 1 or 0 to be preceded by a *timing bit*. The early FM drives worked well, but all the extra bits added to the work and slowed the process of data transfer. To improve efficiency and speed of the data transfer, FM was replaced by an improved version that reduced the number of timing bits required. This new technology was called *modified frequency modulation* (MFM). MFM uses the preceding data bit to indicate whether the current bit is a 1 or a 0, thus reducing the number of timing bits by more than 50 percent.

Another method used to place data on hard disk drives is *run-length limited* (RLL) encoding. RLL replaces the timing bits with patterns of 1s and 0s that represent longer patterns of 1s and 0s. Although this looks inefficient, the elimination of the timing bits speeds overall performance.

**Tip**   Unless you're working with hard disk drives manufactured before 1989, it is not necessary to know which type of data encoding is used.

## Actuator Arms

The goal of a hard disk drive is to quickly and directly access data stored on a flat surface. To do this, two different motions are required. As the disk spins, the R/W heads move across the platter perpendicular to the motion of the disk. The R/W heads are mounted on the ends of the actuator arms (much like the arm of an old record player). A critical element in hard disk drive design is the speed and accuracy of these actuator arms.

Early hard disk drives used a *stepper motor* to move the actuator arms in fixed increments or steps. This early technology had several limitations:

- The interface between the stepper motor and actuator arm required that slippage be kept to a minimum. The greater the slippage, the greater the error.

- Time and physical deterioration of the components caused the positioning of the arms to become less precise. This deterioration eventually caused data transfer errors.

- Heat affected the operation of the stepper motor negatively. The contraction and expansion of the components caused positioning accuracy errors. (Components expand as they get warmer and contract as they cool. Even though these changes are very small, they make it difficult to access data, written while the hard drive is cold, after the disk has warmed up.)

- The R/W heads need to be "parked" when not in use. Parking moves the heads to an area of the disk that does not contain data. Leaving the heads on an area with data can cause that data to be corrupted. Old hard disk drives had to be parked with a command. Most drives today automatically park the heads during spin-down.

**Note**   Older hard disk drives (pre-EIDE or SCSI-2) require that the heads be parked before moving the computer. With these units it is recommended that you use the appropriate command to park the heads. The actual command can vary depending on the drive manufacturer, but you can try typing **park** at an MS-DOS prompt. Newer computers, including laptops, do not require that the drives be parked.

Hard disk drives with stepping motor actuator arms have been replaced by drives that employ a linear motor to move the actuator arms. These linear *voice coil motors* use the same type of voice coil found in an audio loudspeaker, hence the name. This principle uses a permanent magnet and a coil on the actuator arm. By passing electrical current through the coil, it generates a magnetic field that moves the actuator arm into the proper position.

Voice coil hard disk drives offer several advantages:

- The lack of mechanical interface between the motor and the actuator arm provides consistent positioning accuracy.

- When the drive is shut down (the power is removed from the coil), the actuator arm, which is spring-loaded, moves back to its initial position, thus eliminating the need to park the head. In a sense, these drives are self-parking.

There is a drawback to this design: Because a voice coil motor can't accurately predict the movement of the heads across the disk, one side of one platter is used for navigational purposes, and so is unavailable for data storage. The voice coil moves the R/W head into an approximate position. Then the R/W heads on the reserved platter use the "map" to determine the head's true position and make any necessary adjustments. This is why hard drive specifications list an odd number of heads.

### Head-to-Disk Interference

Head-to-disk interference (HDI) is a fancy term for *head crash*. These terms describe the contact that sometimes occurs between the fragile surface of the disk and the R/W head. This contact can cause considerable damage to both the R/W head and the disk. Never move—or even pick up—a hard disk drive until it is completely stopped; the momentum of the drive can cause a crash if it is moved or dropped during operation.

Picking up a disconnected hard disk drive that is still spinning is not a good idea either. The rotation force of the platters can wrench it out of your hands, and the drive is not likely to survive the trip to the floor.

## Geometry

Hard disk drives are composed of one or more disks or platters on which data is stored. The *geometry* of a hard drive is the organization of data on these platters. Geometry determines how and where data is stored on the surface of each platter, and thus the maximum storage capacity of the drive. There are five numerical values that describe geometry:

- Heads
- Cylinders
- Sectors per track
- Write precompensation
- Landing zone

Write precompensation and landing zone are obsolete, but often seen on older drives. Let's take a look at each of these components.

---

**Tip**   All hard disk drives have geometry factors that must be known by the BIOS to read and write to the drive. Knowledge of the geometry is required to install or reinstall a hard drive. New PCs and drives often have technology that lets the BIOS get the information directly from the drive. You still need to know the figures, however, in case this technology fails.

---

## Heads

The number of heads is relative to the total number of *sides* of all the platters used to store data (see Figure 9.5). If a hard disk drive has four platters, it can have up to eight heads. The maximum number of heads is limited by BIOS to 16.

4 Platters
8 Heads

**Figure 9.5**   Drive heads

Hard disk drives that control the actuator arms using voice coil motors reserve a head or two for accuracy of the arm position. Therefore, it is not uncommon for a hard disk drive to have an odd number of heads.

Some hard disk drive manufacturers use a technology called *sector translation*. This allows some hard drives to have more than two heads per platter. It is possible for a drive to have up to 12 heads but only one platter. Regardless of the methods used to manufacture a hard drive, the maximum number of heads a hard drive can contain is 16.

## Cylinders

Data is stored in circular paths on the surface of each platter. Each path is called a *track*. There are hundreds of tracks on the surface of each platter. A set of tracks (all of the same diameter) through each platter is called a *cylinder* (see Figure 9.6). The number of cylinders is a measurement of drive geometry; the number of tracks is not a measurement of drive geometry. BIOS limitations set the maximum number of cylinders at 1024.

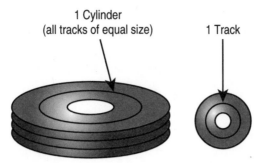

**Figure 9.6**   Cylinders

## Sectors per Track

A hard disk drive is cut (figuratively) into tens of thousands of small arcs, like a pie. Each arc is called a sector and holds 512 bytes of data. A sector is shown in Figure 9.7. The number of sectors is not important and is not part of the geometry; the important value is the number of sectors per track. BIOS limitations set the number of sectors per track at 63.

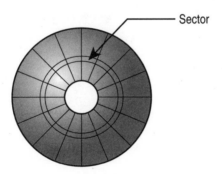

**Figure 9.7**   Sector

## Write Precompensation

All sectors store the same number of bytes—512; however, the sectors toward the outside of the platter are physically longer than those closer to the center. Early drives experienced difficulty with the varying physical sizes of the sectors. Therefore, a method of compensation was needed. The *write precompensation value* defines the cylinder where write precompensation begins.

---

**Note**   The write precompensation value is now obsolete, but is often seen on older drives.

---

### Landing Zone

A landing zone defines an unused cylinder as a "parking place" for the R/W heads. This is found in older hard disk drives that use stepper motors. It is important to park the heads on these drives to avoid accidental damage when moving hard disk drives.

### CHS Values

Cylinders, heads, and sectors per track (see Figure 9.8) are known collectively as the CHS values. The capacity of any hard disk drive can be determined from these three values.

**Figure 9.8**   Cylinders, heads, and sectors per track

The maximum CHS values are:

- 1024 cylinders
- 16 heads
- 63 sectors per track
- 512 bytes per sector

Therefore, the largest hard disk drive size recognized directly by the BIOS is 504 MB. Larger drive sizes can be attained by using either hardware or software translation that manages access to the expanded capacity without direct control by the system BIOS:

$1024 \times 16 \times 63 \times 512$ bytes/sector = 528,482,304 bytes (528 million bytes or 504 MB)

There are many hard disk drives that are larger than 504 MB. These drives manage to exceed this limitation in one of two ways: Either they bypass the system BIOS (by using one of their own) or they change the way the system BIOS routines are read. (For a fuller discussion of this, refer to Chapter 10, "Advanced Disk Drive Technology.")

## Hard Disk Drive Types

The original PC design did not include hard disk drives. Hard disk drives were reserved for large mainframe computers and remained highly proprietary in design. Today, there are four types of hard drives, each with its own method of installation.

## ST506

The very first hard disk drives for personal computers used the ST-506/412 interface. It was developed by Seagate Technologies in 1980 and originally appeared with the 5-MB ST-506 drive. The ST-506 was priced at $3,000 and had a capacity of 5 MB. The ST-506/412 was the only hard drive available for the IBM computer and was the first to be supported by the ROM BIOS chip on the motherboard.

## ESDI

The ESDI (Enhanced Small Device Interface) was introduced in 1983 by the Maxtor Corporation. This technology moved many of the controller functions directly onto the hard disk drive itself. This greatly improved data transfer speeds. Some ESDI controllers even offered enhanced command sets, which supported automatic sensing of the drive's geometry by the motherboard's ROM BIOS. The installation of ESDI drives was almost identical to the installation of ST-506 drives. Their high performance made them the darlings in their day for power users and network servers, but the high cost of ESDI drives and advances in other drive technologies spelled their doom. Today they are obsolete.

## IDE/EIDE

The IDE (Integrated Device Electronics) drive arrived on the scene in the early 1990s and incorporated the benefits of both its predecessors. IDE quickly became the standard for computers. It supports the ST-506 standard command set, and its limited controller functions build directly on the drive's logic board. This results in a much less expensive design. Most new motherboards have the IDE connections built in; thus, the chips are part of the board design.

Western Digital and Compaq developed the 40-pin IDE ISA (Industry Standard Architecture) pinout specification. ANSI (American National Standards Institute) standards committees accepted the standard as the Common Access Method (CAM) Advanced Technology (AT). The official name for these drives is now ATA/CAM (Advanced Technology Attachment/Common Access Method). The terms IDE and ATA/CAM are interchangeable.

Enhanced IDE (EIDE) adds a number of improvements to the standard IDE drives, including:

- Increased data throughput.
- Support of storage devices other than hard disk drives.
- Up to four IDE devices instead of just two. This actually allows the BIOS to support two controllers (each with two drives).
- Support for hard disk drives larger than 528 MB.

**Note**    EIDE is the standard for most hard disks in today's PCs. A new type of EIDE, Ultra DMA/66, doubles the base speed of existing EIDE drives on motherboards that have a 66-MHz bus (hence the name).

## SCSI

SCSI (Small Computer System Interface, pronounced *scuzzy*) has been around since the mid-1970s in one or more forms. It is the most robust of the hard disk drive interfaces, and it is popular on network servers and high-performance workstations. Apple adopted SCSI as its expansion bus standard. The original SCSI standard allowed up to seven peripheral devices to be daisy chained (connected in a series) to one common bus through a single host adapter connected to the computer bus. SCSI-2 upped that to 15, and some adapters allow multiple chains for even more devices. (See Chapter 10, "Advanced Disk Drive Technology," for more information on SCSI technology.)

The SCSI bus functions as a communications pathway between the computer system bus and the SCSI device controller. That improves performance, because the card takes over the low-level commands and frees the system bus during operations that do not involve RAM. A SCSI adapter uses its own BIOS and firmware to talk to its devices, then uses a software interface layer and drivers to communicate with the operating system. There are two software interface layers: ASPI (Advanced SCSI Programming Interface) and CAM. CAM is now obsolete, and ASPI drivers come with Windows and other operating systems. In most cases, you won't have to worry about loading the drivers unless you are updating them or installing a new card that does not have native drivers available to the operating system.

**Note**    Most SCSI cards can be configured to mimic the ST-506 hard disk drive and talk directly to the PC BIOS. This lets you install a SCSI hard drive without additional drivers. You will need the ASPI or CAM software to get full use of advanced SCSI performance features or to attach non-hard disk drive SCSI peripherals to the system.

SCSI usually costs more than other hard disk drive interfaces, but is the only one that allows both internal and external connections on the same adapter. It also allows you to attach more types of devices than any other interface. A single chain can include hard drives, CD-ROM and other optical drives, scanners, and tape drives.

## Installation and Setup

All boot devices must be configured outside the operating system (MS-DOS or Windows 95, Windows 98, Windows Me, Windows NT, or Windows 2000) regardless of the level of Plug and Play compatibility. (Devices such as disk drives and CD-ROM drives that are used to boot must be configured at the BIOS and hardware levels because they typically contain the operating system and must run properly before the operating system can be started.)

Installation of a hard disk drive consists of five simple steps:

1. Physical installation and cabling
2. CMOS setup
3. Low-level formatting (if required)
4. Partitioning
5. Formatting

## Cabling

Just as there are different types of drives, there are different cabling requirements for each. Let's look at the three most common types.

## ST-506

The ST-506 uses a 34-connector control cable (daisy chained for dual drives) and a 20-connector data cable for each drive. The 34-wire control cable has a twist in it for line 25 through 29 configuration (similar to the floppy disk drive cable); this twist determines which hard disk drive is hard drive 0 and which is hard drive 1. The drive at the end is drive 0.

---

**Caution**   Do not confuse or use a floppy drive cable to attach a hard drive to a computer or vice versa; they are not interchangeable.

---

## IDE/EIDE

IDE uses a simple 40-pin cable that plugs into the controller and into the drive (see Figure 9.9). There are no twists. IDE controllers identify the two drives as either master or slave. Drive makers use different methods to set up their drives. The most common system uses jumpers. Setting these jumpers serves the same function as the twist used with other drive cables: It identifies whether the drive is a master or slave. Other drives use switches, and some new drives use software to determine which is the dominant drive. Be sure to check the manufacturers' specifications to properly set up the drive.

## Ultra DMA/66

A special version of the 40-pin IDE cables is used for Ultra DMA/66. Be sure to obtain and install it if you are working with one of these newer drives. It is also 40-pin, but it has a blue connector on one end and a black one on the other. All the other installation and cabling procedures are the same as for traditional IDE devices.

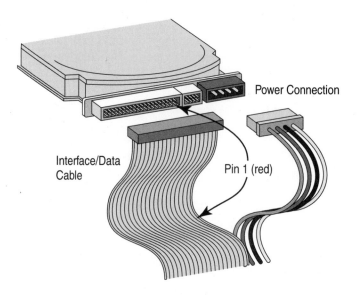

Power Connection

Interface/Data
Cable

Pin 1 (red)

**Figure 9.9**    IDE connections

**Tip**    When installing a new secondary IDE hard disk drive in a system, be sure to set the new drive as slave and verify that the first drive is set to master. The documentation supplied with the drive should provide the necessary information. Often, this information is printed on the label of the drive. Both drives must be properly configured before the system is started. If the drives are not properly jumpered, they won't work.

If you don't know the settings for the drive's jumpers (see Figure 9.10), try calling the hard disk drive manufacturer (or look for its Web site on the Internet).

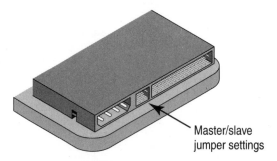

Master/slave
jumper settings

**Figure 9.10**    Master and slave jumper settings

## Setting the System CMOS for the Hard Drive

After a hard disk drive has been installed physically, the geometry of the drive must be entered into the CMOS through the CMOS setup program before the PC will recognize the new device. This information must be entered exactly as specified by the manufacturer. Figure 9.11 shows hard disk drive configuration information in a typical CMOS. Figure 9.12 shows a subscreen of the main hard drive setup screen.

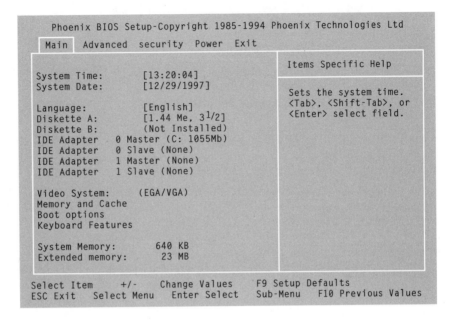

**Figure 9.11**   CMOS main screen

Originally, CMOS would allow for only two drives. Later versions allow up to four drives, because most new PCs have two IDE channels, but you still have to contend with IDE's limit of two devices per channel. Another thing to be aware of is the number of non-hard drive devices (tape, CD-ROM, CD-R, and so on) that may also be attached to a PC. When configuring a new system, it's a good idea to ask customers if they plan on upgrading before making a final decision on how to attach the drives. In most cases, the primary hard disk can take the master position on the primary IDE channel, and the CD drive the primary position on the second channel. For best performance, only hard drives should be placed on the primary IDE channel, if possible.

The CHS, along with write precompensation and landing zone, determine how the hard disk drive controller accesses the physical hard drive. The creators of the first CMOS routines for the 286 AT believed that the five different geometry numbers would be too complicated for the average user to configure, so they established 15 preset combinations of hard drive geometries. These preset combinations are called *types*. With types, the user simply enters a hard drive type number into the CMOS.

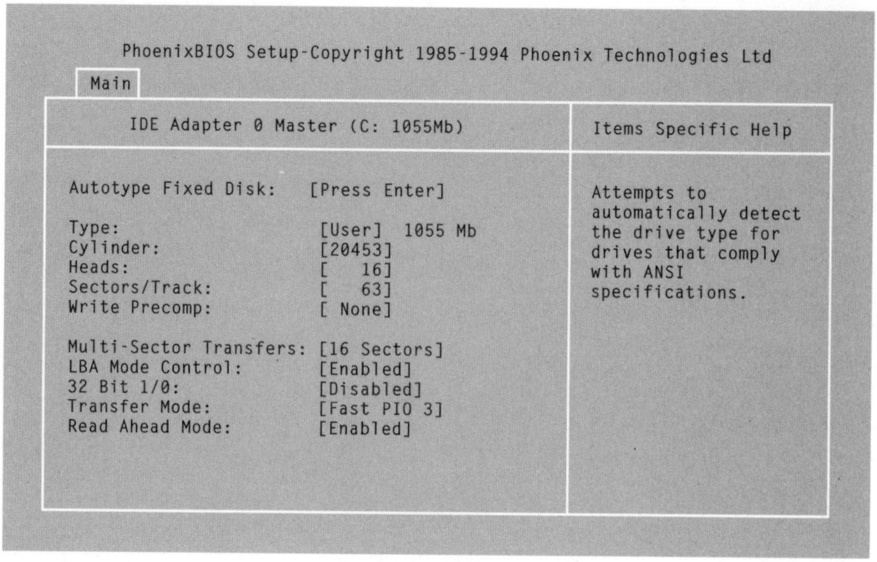

```
PhoenixBIOS Setup-Copyright 1985-1994 Phoenix Technologies Ltd
  Main

      IDE Adapter 0 Master (C: 1055Mb)              Items Specific Help

    Autotype Fixed Disk:    [Press Enter]         Attempts to
                                                  automatically detect
    Type:                   [User]   1055 Mb      the drive type for
    Cylinder:               [20453]               drives that comply
    Heads:                  [   16]               with ANSI
    Sectors/Track:          [   63]               specifications.
    Write Precomp:          [ None]

    Multi-Sector Transfers: [16 Sectors]
    LBA Mode Control:       [Enabled]
    32 Bit 1/0:             [Disabled]
    Transfer Mode:          [Fast PIO 3]
    Read Ahead Mode:        [Enabled]
```

**Figure 9.12**   Hard disk drive setup screen

This system worked well for a period of time, but with each new hard disk drive that manufacturers designed, a new type also had to be created and added to the list. BIOS makers continued to add new types until there were more than 45 variations. To deal with this issue, setup routines now include a *user* type. This allows manual entry of the geometry values, increasing both the flexibility and complexity of hard drive installation.

CMOS setup is easy with IDE drives. Most CMOS chips today have a setting known as IDE *autodetection,* which runs the IDENTIFY DRIVE command, gathering and setting the proper geometry values. To use it, simply connect the drive to the computer, turn it on, and run the CMOS. The IDENTIFY DRIVE command instructs the drive to transmit a 512-byte block of data containing the following information:

- Manufacturer
- Model and serial numbers
- Firmware revision number
- Buffer type indicating sector buffering or caching capabilities
- Number of cylinders in the default translation mode
- Number of heads in the default translation mode
- Number of sectors per track in the default translation mode
- Number of cylinders in the current translation mode

- Number of heads in the current translation mode
- Number of sectors per track in the current translation mode

---

**Important**  Be sure to save your settings before you exit the setup program.

---

What happens if wrong data is entered into the CMOS? For example, what if a 1.2-GB hard disk drive is installed and the CMOS is set up to make it a 504-MB hard drive? When you boot the computer, you will see a perfect 504-MB hard drive. You will need to correct the entry to obtain proper use of the drive. It should always make sure you go back and enter the correct information or it could render the drive inaccessible by the system.

If the computer you are working on does not support autodetection, you must be able to determine the geometry of a drive before you can install it.

There are many ways to determine the geometry of a hard disk drive:

- Check the label. The geometry or type appears on the label of many hard drives.
- Check the documentation that came with the hard drive. All drives have a model number that can be used to obtain the geometry parameters either from the manufacturer or a third party. The hard drive manufacturers usually reserve a section of their Web sites for providing configuration data and the setup utilities available for download.
- Contact the manufacturer. Many manufacturers have toll-free phone numbers.

After a drive is installed, it must be assigned a drive name or letter that is unique. There are several drive-naming conventions that help identify this unique name. If only one hard disk drive is installed, it must be configured as drive 0, or master. If a second drive is installed, it is recognized as hard drive 1, or slave. Many CMOS configurations use the terms C and D. Under all versions of MS-DOS and Windows, hard drive 0 is recognized as C and hard drive 1 is recognized as D.

As more drives are added to a system (including tape, CD-ROM, and network drives), the names of existing drives might change. For example, installing a portable drive such as an Iomega Zip drive can change a CD-ROM drive from the D drive to the E drive. When the portable drive is removed, the CD-ROM drive will once again be the D drive. Keep in mind the difference between *logical* and *physical* drives. A physical drive is the hardware—it can be divided into two or more logical drives. (See the "Partitioning" section later in this lesson.) Drives on a network server are also logical drives. Write down the configuration and keep track as changes in the system are made. The only drive letters that are fixed are the A and B drives, which are always the floppy disk drives, and the C drive, the boot drive where the operating system resides.

**Note**  Confusion in drive letters can also confuse the operating system, making it hard or impossible for it to locate drivers. In such cases, you might need to reinstall the drivers before the system can make use of the affected hardware, and a Windows 95, Windows 98, Windows Me, or Windows 2000 machine might automatically start in safe mode. Check the Device manager by double-clicking the System icon in the Control Panel after the PC is operational, and look for duplicate hardware items or items denoted by flags noting missing or inoperable conditions.

## Low-Level Formatting

Low-level formatting means creating all the sectors, tracks, cylinders, and head information on the drive, and this is the third step in installing hard disk drives; generally, it applies only to older drives. Low-level formatting by the end user has virtually been eliminated with today's drives (it's done at the factory).

A low-level format performs three simultaneous functions:

- It creates and organizes the sectors, making them ready to accept data.
- It sets the proper interleave (records the sector header, trailer information, and intersector and intertrack gaps).
- It establishes the boot sector.

Every hard disk drive arrives from the factory with bad spots on the platters. Data cannot be written to these areas. As the sectors are being created, the low-level format attempts to skip over these bad spots. Sometimes, it is impossible to skip over a spot, so the sector is marked as "bad" in the ID field.

**Caution**  Low-level formatting is not required on IDE and Ultra DMA drives. Performing a low-level format on these devices might render the drives unusable. SCSI drives are low-level formatted using a utility that is built into the SCSI adapter card's firmware. Format a low-level drive only if it is absolutely necessary (for example, if a virus has contaminated the boot sector and that is the only remedy) and if you are sure you know and can follow the proper procedure. Remember, as soon as you issue the FORMAT command, all data on the drive will be lost.

IDE drives use a special type of low-level formatting called *embedded servo*. This type of low-level formatting can be done by the manufacturer only, or with a special utility provided by the manufacturer. When installing an IDE drive, go straight to the partitioning step after the CMOS is set up. To continue with hard disk drive installation for MS-DOS and Windows 3.x, Windows 95, Windows 98, and Windows Me versions, you will need a bootable floppy disk containing several programs that are required to prepare the new drive. (For Windows NT and 2000, there are options that will allow you to prepare a drive from the bootable CD-ROM.)

To create a bootable floppy disk, a computer is required that has an installed working hard disk drive, or floppy disk drive, and a compatible operating system. Be sure to use the same operating system on the floppy disk as the one you'll use for the new drive.

Insert a floppy disk into the A drive and type:

```
format a: /s to
```

This will copy system files to the disk, making it a bootable disk.

The next step is to copy the necessary files from the MS-DOS directory to the floppy disk. The default location for these files is the C:\DOS directory for MS-DOS and the C:\Windows\Command directory for Windows 95, Windows 98, and Windows Me. Copy these files:

```
FORMAT.COM (or FORMAT.EXE)
```

```
FDISK.COM
```

This bootable disk can be used for partitioning and high-level formatting as discussed in the following sections.

## Partitioning

Partitions are *logical* divisions of a hard drive. A computer might have only one physical hard drive (called hard drive 0), but it can have anywhere from 1 to 24 logical drives, identified as C to Z.

Partitions exist for two reasons:

- To divide the disk into several drive letters to make it easier to organize data files. Some users separate data, programs, and operating system files onto different drives.
- To accommodate more than one operating system.

When MS-DOS was first designed to use hard disk drives, the largest hard drive that could be used was 32 MB (because of the way MS-DOS stored files on the hard drive). Partitioning was included in MS-DOS 3.3. This allowed for the development of larger physical hard drives by creating multiple logical drives of up to 32 MB each. Starting with MS-DOS 4.0, the partition size was increased to 512 MB. Beginning with MS-DOS 5.0, the partitions could be as large as 2 GB. Windows 98, Windows Me, and Windows 2000 support much larger drive sizes, and many new disks exceed 20 GB.

**Note**   Some hard disk drives that exceed 4 GB might not work with an older computer, BIOS, or operating system. They will physically function, but the whole drive cannot be accessed—disk access will be limited to the largest size that can be recognized by that system.

## Primary and Extended Partitions

There are two types of partitions: primary and extended. The *primary* partition is the location where the boot information for the operating system is stored. To boot from a hard disk drive, the drive must have a primary partition. Primary partitions are for storage of the *boot sector,* which tells the computer where to find the operating system. The primary partition is always identified as drive C.

The *extended* partition is for a hard disk drive, or part of a hard disk drive, that does not have an operating system. The extended partition is not associated with a physical drive letter. Instead, the extended partition is further divided into logical drives starting with D and progressing until drive letter Z is created. (Remember: A and B are reserved for floppy disk drives.)

Newer operating systems can use all of the drive as a single primary partition. The logical drive concept was invented to allow older versions of MS-DOS and Windows to make use of drives that exceeded their maximum drive size.

## How to Partition

The fdisk utility is used to partition a drive under DOS, Windows 3.*x*, Windows 9*x*, and Windows Me. After the drive is installed and the CMOS is updated, run fdisk to partition the drive(s). Figure 9.13 shows the fdisk startup screen. Windows NT and 2000 have options during setup that are offered to partition a drive during installation of a new operating system. Follow the prompts for these environments as they appear.

You also have the option of using a third-party utility to partition the hard drive, which often provides more sophisticated and graphical methods for partitioning a drive, thereby simplifying the partition process.

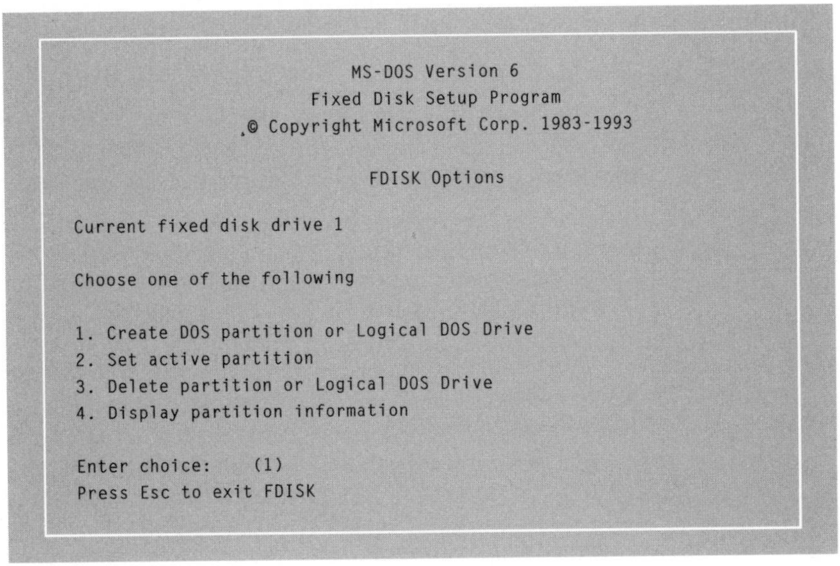

```
                        MS-DOS Version 6
                     Fixed Disk Setup Program
                  .© Copyright Microsoft Corp. 1983-1993

                           FDISK Options

Current fixed disk drive 1


Choose one of the following

1. Create DOS partition or Logical DOS Drive
2. Set active partition
3. Delete partition or Logical DOS Drive
4. Display partition information

Enter choice:    (1)
Press Esc to exit FDISK
```

**Figure 9.13**   The fdisk startup screen

The function of lines 1, 3, and 4 is clear. Line 2 sets the active partition. The active partition is the partition where the BIOS will look for an operating system when the computer is booted.

Don't confuse the primary partition with the active partition. On a computer with a single operating system, the primary and active partitions are usually the same. A computer with dual-boot capability might have separate partitions for each operating system. In that case, the active and primary partitions might not be the same.

The primary partition is where MS-DOS (or the Windows boot information) is stored on the hard disk drive, and the active partition is where the operating system is stored on the hard drive. (If MS-DOS is the only operating system, the primary partition and active partition are the same.) Other operating systems—Windows NT, Windows 2000, and LINUX, for instance—can exist on an extended partition.

Advanced operating systems can create a special partition called a *boot partition*. When the computer boots, a menu prompts the user to pick which operating system to use. The boot manager then sets the chosen partition as *active*, which starts the operating system located in that partition. As with partitioning software, you can also purchase third-party boot managers for systems that do not provide an option for booting to multiple operating systems.

---

**Note**    MS-DOS has a limitation not shared by any other operating system: it must be placed on the primary partition, and that partition must always be named C. LINUX, UNIX, and Windows NT and 2000 can boot from another drive letter, as well as from the C drive.

---

## High-Level Formatting

The high-level format is simply called "format" (the program used to perform a high-level format is called FORMAT.COM). This is the same format command used to prepare floppy disk drives. The high-level format performs two major functions:

- It creates and configures the file allocation tables (FATs).
- It creates the root directory, which is the foundation on which files and subdirectories are built.

## File Allocation Tables

The base storage unit for drives is a sector. Each sector can store between 1 byte and 512 bytes of data. Any file less than 512 bytes is stored in a single sector, and only one file can be assigned a sector. Therefore, any part of a sector left unfilled is wasted. When files are stored in more than one sector (if they are greater than 512 bytes), MS-DOS needs a way to keep track of each location and the order in which data is stored. MS-DOS also needs to know which sectors are full and which sectors are available for data, so it uses the FAT to keep track of this information.

There are several versions of FAT, as well as other disk allocation schemes used by operating systems like Windows NT, 2000, and various versions of LINUX and UNIX. We will consider these versions in later chapters as we examine operating system issues. For our current discussion we will focus on the basics of FAT to show how data is stored on a disk drive. All operating systems must use some well-defined method of writing, addressing, and reading data in a way that is compatible with the drive technology being used. In some cases, as with SCSI drives (see Chapter 10, "Advanced Disk Drive Technology"), the hardware may actually "pretend" to use a system like FAT but translate its own addressing scheme into FAT when it communicates with the operating system.

The FAT is simply an index that keeps track of which part of the file is stored in which sector. Each partition (or floppy disk) has two FATs stored near the beginning of the partition. These FATs are called FAT #1 and FAT #2. They are identical. Each FAT can be looked at as a two-column spreadsheet.

| **Left Column** | **Right Column** |
|---|---|
| Gives each sector a number (in hex) from 0000 to FFFF (65,536 sectors). The left side contains 16 bits (4 hex characters = 16 bits). This FAT is called a 16-bit FAT. Floppy disk drives use 12-bit FATs because they store substantially less data. | Contains information on the status of the sector. During formatting, any bad sectors are marked with a status code of FFF7 and good sectors are marked 0000. |

## Sectors and Clusters

As mentioned, the CHS values limit the maximum size of a hard disk drive to 504 MB under the older PC operating systems. The 16-bit FAT can address 64,000 ($2^{16}$) locations. Therefore, the size of a hard drive partition should be limited to 64,000 × 512 bytes per sector or 32 MB. With this limitation, you might ask, how are larger hard drives possible?

There are two solutions to this problem. The first method, used with earlier drives (under 100 MB), was to use fdisk to break the drive up into multiple partitions, each less than 32 MB.

The second method is called *clustering*. Clustering means combining a set of contiguous sectors and treating them as a single unit in the FAT. The number of sectors in each cluster is determined by the size of the partition. There can never be more than 64,000 clusters. To determine the number of sectors in a partition, divide the number of bytes in the partition by 512 (bytes per sector). Then divide the number of sectors by 64,000 (maximum allowable clusters). The following table provides an estimate of sectors per cluster.

| Partition (in MB) | Total Bytes | Total Sectors | Sectors per Cluster | Bytes per Cluster |
|---|---|---|---|---|
| 32 | 33,554,432 | 65,536 | 1 | 524 |
| 64 | 67,108,864 | 131,072 | 2 | 1,049 |
| 128 | 134,217,728 | 262,144 | 4 | 2,097 |
| 256 | 268,435,456 | 524,288 | 8 | 4,194 |
| 512 | 536,870,912 | 1,048,576 | 16 | 8,389 |
| 1,000 | 1,048,576,000 | 2,048,000 | 32 | 16,384 |
| 2,000 | 2,097,152,000 | 4,096,000 | 64 | 32,768 |
| 4,000 | 4,194,304,000 | 8,192,000 | 128 | 65,536 |

---

**Note**  Remember, for this table, a sector is not the basic unit of storage—it is now the cluster.

---

## How the File Allocation Table Works

When a file is saved:

1. MS-DOS starts at the beginning of the FAT and looks for the first space marked "open for use" (0000). It begins to write to that cluster.
2. If the entire file can be saved within that one cluster, the code FFFF (last cluster) is placed in the cluster's status field and the filename is added to the directory.
3. The cluster number is placed with the filename.
4. If the file takes more than one cluster, MS-DOS searches for the next open cluster and places the number of the next cluster in the status field. MS-DOS continues filling and adding clusters until the entire file is saved.
5. The last cluster then receives the end-of-file code (FFFF).

## FAT32

Windows 95 (OSR2—the final version of Windows 95, available only on new machines, also called version C), Windows 98, and Windows Me support the new FAT32 file system. FAT32 can create partitions of up to 2 terabytes (TB; equivalent to 2 trillion bytes) in size (much larger than the 2-GB limit of FAT16) and uses smaller clusters than FAT16. This results in a more efficient use of space on a large hard disk.

When deciding whether to use FAT32, take the following into consideration:

- Don't use advanced file allocations systems (FAT32, NTFS) on any partition shared by other operating systems unless they can specifically support it.
- MS-DOS, Windows 3.x, the original release of Windows 95, and Windows NT clients can read FAT32 partitions shared across a network.
- If you dual boot between Windows 98 and another operating system (such as Windows NT 4.x), the drive C partition cannot be FAT32.
- You cannot compress FAT32 partitions.
- Windows 98 MS-DOS mode fully supports FAT32, so you can run most MS-DOS-mode games and applications from FAT32 partitions.
- Some older applications written to FAT16 specification might not display disk space larger than 2 GB.
- Do not use any utilities that do not support FAT32. This could result in data loss and might corrupt the file system on the hard drive.

## Fragmentation

*Fragmentation* is the scattering of parts of the same disk file over different areas of the disk. During PC use, files are opened and then saved back to disk. As mentioned earlier, the file is often stored in several small sections. Fragmentation is caused by the following:

1. As a file is written to sectors (clusters), it is placed in the first available location.
2. The continual addition and deletion of files begins to leave open clusters.
3. These open clusters are filled by the first part of the next file to be saved.
4. Soon, files become fragmented, or scattered, all over the drive.

This is an acceptable way to operate and causes no problems for the computer itself. However, excessive fragmentation slows down the hard disk drive because it has to access two or more areas to retrieve a file. It is possible for a single file to be fragmented into hundreds of pieces, forcing the R/W heads to travel all over the hard disk drive.

Most operating systems have either native or third-party applications that will *defragment* a drive. These should be used on a regular basis to improve performance and save wear and tear on the drive.

The elimination of fragmentation improves the speed of the hard disk drive dramatically. Running a program to eliminate fragmentation is called defragmenting a drive. The slang term "defrag" is often used. MS-DOS installations include a defragmentation program called DEFRAG. Windows 95, Windows 98, and Windows Me include a defragmentation program, which can be accessed by clicking Start, selecting Programs, then Accessories, then System Tools, and then Disk Defragmenter.

**Note** DEFRAG cannot rewrite or move systems and hidden files. These files might be program files that are copy protected and must not be moved after the program is installed. System files such as the MS-DOS core program must occupy a particular position on the disk.

**Caution** Never run a defragmentation program designed for MS-DOS or Windows 3.*x* on a Windows 95 or 98 system. The program might not understand the Windows 95 and 98 long filenames, and data might be lost.

## Disk Compression

Disk compression is offered as part of the Microsoft Plus add-on product for Windows 95, but is included in Windows 98 as the DriveSpace 3 program (Windows Me includes DriveSpace 3, but does not support compression). It works by creating a single large file (called a compressed volume file, or CVF) that acts like a virtual disk drive (with its own drive letter). Files you write to the CVF will become records within the one large file. This process is normally transparent to the user.

---

**Note**   Keep in mind that you cannot use DriveSpace 3 with partitions that use the FAT32 file system. If you wish to compress a drive under Windows 98, use the FAT16 file system when installing the drive.

---

Compression saves space in two ways:

- It eliminates the wasted cluster space used by separate disk files.
- It replaces sequences of identical values or characters in the file data with a special reference that represents the actual data, but occupies less disk space than the data itself would.

  When the data is retrieved from the file, the real values are extracted from the special references. The result can be a dramatic reduction in the disk space occupied by files, especially with uncompressed graphics files and word processing documents.

Using compression introduces some risk because an error in the CVF can make data inaccessible. It is safest not to use a compressed file for critical data, and some older programs (particularly games) might not work with compression. With DriveSpace 3 you can use the Troubleshooter to identify and fix problems.

Compression is less necessary today because of the advent of large hard disk drives and the availability of the FAT32 file system with its smaller cluster sizes.

## Maintaining a Disk Drive

Being prepared for a potential failure before a hard disk drive fails to work properly can save lost data and time. How fully you should prepare depends on the answers to two questions:

- Can you afford to lose the data in question?
- How much time do you have to start over?

With this in mind, to minimize the impact of a hard disk drive failure:

- Perform comprehensive, regularly scheduled backups.
- Save a copy of the boot sector and partition table information.

You should have the following tools on hand to perform hard disk repairs:

- A list of the hard disk drive's parameters and the correct CMOS settings required.
- A bootable floppy disk with the fdisk, format, chkdsk, and mscdex (if using a CD-ROM) command files. Adding EDIT or another text editor is handy for tweaking the CONFIG.SYS and AUTOEXEC.BAT files. Windows users can

create a startup disk with these files by clicking Start, selecting Settings, then Control Panel, double-clicking Add/Remove Programs, and clicking the Startup Disk tab. Third-party utilities also provide the ability to create these "emergency" disks.

- Drivers needed to get the operating system running with any primary expansion cards (drive controllers, SCSI card, display adapter, and so on).

- Good cables for the kinds of drives you might have to repair.

- Chkdsk or other hard disk inspection programs that are part of the operating system on the drive in question. Be sure to use the right version.

A number of third-party programs are also available for use with older hardware and operating systems. These programs are available at most computer software stores.

---

**Caution**    When using any third-party programs to troubleshoot or repair a drive, be sure they are certified for the hard disk drive and operating system in question. Use uncertified third-party programs only when such a step is the last resort before discarding the drive. Even then, be aware that the program may cause problems of its own. Keep the software up to date; changes in the operating system or bugs found in the utility can render the product more of a problem than a cure. If possible, back up any critical data before using the software.

---

## Abort, Retry, Fail or Abort, Retry, Fail, Ignore Errors

The most common drive errors begin with "Abort, Retry, Fail," or "Abort, Retry, Fail, Ignore." When you see any of the following errors, you have a drive problem:

```
Sector not found reading drive C:
Abort, Retry, Fail?

Data error reading drive C:
Abort, Retry, Fail, Ignore?

Read fault reading drive C:
Abort, Retry, Fail, Ignore?

Invalid media type reading drive C:
Abort, Retry, Fail?
```

These errors are the easiest to fix and can usually be attributed to a bad sector on the drive. When this happens, try the following.

## ScanDisk

MS-DOS, Windows 3.*x*, Windows 95, Windows 98, and Windows Me contain versions of the ScanDisk program. ScanDisk performs a battery of tests on a hard disk, including searching for invalid filenames, invalid file dates and times, bad sectors, and invalid compression structures. In the file system, ScanDisk looks for lost clusters, invalid clusters, and cross-linked clusters. Regular use of ScanDisk can help prevent problems as well as fix them. Windows 95-, Windows 98-, and Windows Me-based computers will automatically run ScanDisk any time the operating system is improperly shut down—that is, when the power is turned off before the system is allowed to complete its shutdown procedures.

### Verify the Media

Most SCSI drives have a program built into the controller that will verify the hard disk drive and make repairs if a sector has become unusable or unstable. Boot the PC and watch for a prompt to enter the SCSI BIOS setup (usually CTRL+A). Then choose Disk Utilities and the option to verify or inspect the drive. Do not select the low-level format option. After the program is finished, reboot the computer and see if the problem is resolved. If the disk fails verification, it might need to undergo low-level formatting or be replaced.

### CMOS Errors

At times, the system CMOS becomes unstable. This can result in the following error messages:

```
CMOS configuration mismatch
```

```
No boot device available
```

```
Drive not found
```

```
Missing operating system
```

Checking the CMOS is quick and easy. It is a good idea to always have a backup of the CMOS data on paper.

---

**Note**   After booting up, if you receive the message "Strike F1 key to continue," this indicates that your system configuration is invalid and you will need to check the CMOS settings.

---

### Connectivity Errors

Connectivity problems (when something is not connected or plugged in) usually appear when you boot up a computer. Look for the following messages:

```
HDD Controller failure
```

```
No boot device available
```

```
Drive not found
```

Connectivity errors are overcome by inspecting the entire connection system (including power). You might want to try removing and reseating the controller if you get an HDD controller failure.

---

**Tip**  As a computer technician, you should keep an extra controller and cables around. Often, substituting a good cable or controller is the quickest way to solve a hard disk drive problem.

---

### Lost Boot and Partition Information

It is possible for a drive to lose partition information. Look for these errors:

```
Invalid partition table
```

```
Corrupt boot sector
```

```
Non-system disk or disk error
```

Boot and partition information is stored on sectors and can fail. If the partition table or boot sector is corrupted, the best solution is to restore the data on the drive from a backup copy after repartitioning the drive and reloading the operating system.

## Lesson Summary

The following points summarize the main elements of this lesson:

- The maximum storage capacity of a hard disk drive is determined by its geometry.
- CHS values define the geometry of a hard disk drive.
- The largest hard disk drive recognized by the BIOS will vary with the age of the system.
- Proper CMOS settings are required for hard disk drives.
- There are two types of partitions: primary and extended.
- A cluster is the basic unit of storage.
- The fdisk program is used to partition drives under MS-DOS.
- Microsoft ScanDisk is a useful tool for diagnosing and repairing many disk problems.
- The proper drive information must be held in CMOS for proper drive operation.

# Chapter Summary

The following points summarize the key concepts in this chapter:

## Floppy Disk Drives

- The first disk drives were floppy disk drives. The technology of floppy disks has changed little in the past decade.

- Floppy disk drives are designated as A or B. The drive letter designation is determined by the location of the drive on the cable.

- Floppy disk drives fail more than any other part of a computer system.

## Hard Disk Drives

- The three major steps in installing a hard disk drive are to partition the drive, set the CMOS settings, and format the drive.

- Fdisk is used to partition hard disk drives. A computer technician should be familiar with the use of fdisk and partitioning.

- The geometry of a hard disk drive (CHS values) determines its storage capacity.

- There are two types of partitions: primary and extended. The operating system must be on the primary partition.

- The active partition is where the operating system is stored. The active partition is usually (but not always) the primary partition.

# Review

The following questions are intended to reinforce key information presented in this chapter. If you are unable to answer a question, review the appropriate lesson and then try the question again. Answers to the questions can be found in Appendix A, "Questions and Answers."

1. What is the purpose of an IDE drive?

2. How many drives can be connected to a single IDE connector?

3. What is the best method of determining the number of drives available on a computer?

4. What three things should be checked when a floppy disk drive fails?

5. What is the best way to ensure long life from a floppy disk drive?

6. When you purchase a new floppy disk drive controller, what can you expect to receive with it?

7. Other than physical size, what are the only differences between a 5.25-inch floppy disk drive and a 3.5-inch floppy disk drive?

8. What type of cable is used to connect a floppy disk drive to the external data bus?

9. What is the proper way to install a floppy disk drive cable?

10. To which pin must the number 1 wire of the floppy disk drive cable be connected?

11. You've received the following error message: "General failure reading Drive A:". What is the most likely problem?

12. Are floppy disk controllers sensitive to ESD?

13. You receive an error message that ends with "Abort, Retry, Fail?". What is the most likely cause of the error?

14. Why is a voice coil actuator arm better than a stepper motor actuator arm?

15. Define hard disk drive geometry.

16. What is the best way to determine the geometry of an unknown drive?

17. Describe HDI.

18. BIOS limits the number of heads to _____.

19. BIOS limits the number of cylinders to _____.

20. How many bytes of data does a sector hold?

21.  What is the maximum number of sectors per track?

22.  What does CHS stand for?

23.  What type of drive is standard on today's personal computer?

24.  Name the characteristics of the three different hard disk drive types.

25.  What is a partition? What are the two types of partitions?

26.  Define a cluster.

27.  What is the FAT and how does it work?

28.  What is fragmentation?

29.  How can you minimize the impact of a hard disk drive failure?

30.  What is the function of ScanDisk?

C H A P T E R    1 0

# Advanced Disk Drive Technology

**Lesson 1: CD-ROM and DVD Drives** ........................... **222**

**Lesson 2: Advanced Hard Disk Drives** ........................ **233**

**Lesson 3: SCSI Drives** ..................................... **243**

**Chapter Summary** .......................................... **253**

**Review** ................................................... **254**

## About This Chapter

This chapter picks up where the previous chapter left off; we continue our look at disk drives, moving on to more advanced technologies. The lessons in this chapter cover CD-ROM/DVD drives, newer and larger hard disk drives, and Small Computer System Interface (SCSI) drives. In the final lesson, we also explain the basics of the SCSI interface.

## Before You Begin

Before starting this chapter, you should review Chapter 9, "Basic Disk Drives."

# Lesson 1: CD-ROM and DVD Drives

Both CD-ROM (compact disc read-only memory) and DVD (digital video disc) drives are based on technology taken directly from the multimedia world, and both have become standard equipment for computers. This lesson covers the basics of installing and using CD-ROM drives.

---

### After this lesson, you will be able to

- Define the advantages of using CD-ROMs
- Explain the differences between CD-ROMs and DVDs
- Install and operate both CD-ROM and DVD drives

### Estimated lesson time: 30 minutes

---

## Advantages of CD-ROM and DVD Drives

If a hard disk drive holds more information than a floppy disk drive, accesses the information faster, and reads and writes information, then why do we need CD-ROM drives? The answer is simple: A compact disc (CD) can hold large amounts (650 MB) of removable data and can be mass-produced at a very low cost.

Both CD-ROM and DVD technologies make use of high-capacity optic media in the form of a silvery platter that holds digital data that is decoded by striking it with a laser beam. To the casual observer, the discs used by both are the same. In fact, most new DVD technology employs a shorter wavelength laser to read the data than the type found in CD-ROM drives. That lets manufacturers cram more data (like an entire movie, including the soundtrack) on a single platter.

Many new PCs come with a DVD drive that can also read CD-ROMs. To play movies effectively, they must also have decoding hardware, either on the drive or on a companion card (sometimes part of the display adapter). Without the performance boost the additional hardware provides, the playback will be choppy with lost frames and erratic sound.

The CD has become the medium of choice for software distribution by manufacturers. Because there are many PCs with only CD-ROM capability, and several lingering questions about standards for DVD formats, it is expected that CD-ROM will be a standard distribution method for the foreseeable future.

One CD can store an entire software package. While early versions of the Microsoft Office Suite were supplied on 32 floppy disks, today the entire program suite and its manuals are stored on a single CD. It is also much faster to install a CD. The user simply starts it up, enters any required information, and comes back later; it is no longer necessary to feed disk after disk into the computer. When they were introduced, CDs held large databases such as ency-clopedias. Today, they are used for every possible type of data, from national phone directories and software libraries to collections of clip art, music, and games. The following table lists the advantages of storing data on a CD.

| Advantage | Description |
|---|---|
| Large storage capacity compared to floppy-type media | Up to 650 MB of data fit on a single 5-inch disc. (Smaller than the original 5.25-inch floppy disk, a CD holds almost 2000 times as much information.) |
| Portability | The CD is a portable medium. |
| Data cannot be changed | A CD is read-only, which prevents accidental erasure of programs or files. |
| Sturdiness | More durable than the standard 5.25-inch or 3.5-inch disks, CDs are not magnetic media and thus are not subject to the same dangers posed by proximity to electrical sources or magnets (although you need to handle them carefully to avoid finger prints and scratches). |
| Special capabilities | CD-ROMs are audio-capable, allowing special compression of audio, image, and video data. They can be used to play standard audio CDs and have the capacity to store and record video data. |

## Development of the CD

The development of the computer CD roughly paralleled the audio (music) CD:

- In 1979, the CD, as a storage medium, was introduced in the audio industry.
- In 1985, the CD came to the computer industry. Development was slow because the hardware was too expensive for most manufacturers and users.
- In 1991, the CD-ROM/XA standard was enhanced, and multimedia require-ments for hardware were specified.
- In 1993, high-quality video playback came to the computer.
- Today, the price of CD-ROM drives continues to drop, while their speed climbs. Almost all new computers include an internal CD-ROM drive as stan-dard equipment. Most software packages are shipped in CD-ROM versions (3.5-inch floppy disk versions are available but usually only by special order, and often they do not contain all the extras of the CD version).

## About CD-ROM Standards

The CD-ROM world makes use of several standards. These are usually referred to by the color of the cover of the volume issued by the ISO (International Orga-nization for Standardization) committee—for example, the White Book, Yellow Book, and so on. We discuss ISO formats in more detail later in this lesson.

# CD-ROM Technology

CD-ROMs store data as a series of 1s and 0s, just like a floppy disk or a hard disk drive. However, instead of using magnetic energy to read and write data, CD readers and writers use laser energy. There are two major advantages to using lasers:

- There is no physical contact between the surface of the CD and the reading device.

- The diameter of the laser beam is so small that storage tracks can be written very close together, allowing more data to be stored in a smaller space.

## Hard Disk Drives vs. CD-ROMs

With the cost of hard disk drives falling and the amount of available data storage rising, the hard drive is still king of the storage media. Optical data storage devices hold their place as removable media and as the media of choice for archival data storage.

A CD platter is composed of a reflective layer of aluminum applied to a synthetic base that is composed of polymers. A layer of transparent polycarbonate covers the aluminum. A protective coating of lacquer is applied to the surface to protect it from dust, dirt, and scratches.

---

**Note**    CD-recordable (CD-R) discs use materials other than aluminum. They often have a yellow or green cast on the data side. Not all CD-ROM readers are able to read these discs—some older readers based on Integrated Device Electronics (IDE) are incompatible with CD-R technology.

---

Data is written by creating pits and lands on the CD's surface. A *pit* is a depression on the surface, and a *land* is the height of the original surface. The transition from a land to a pit or a pit to a land represents a binary character of 1. Lands and pits represent binary 0. The reading of data is based on timing—the speed at which the CD is rotating—and the reflection of light. If no data is on the disk, the reflectivity will not change and the CD will read a series of binary 0s. There are approximately 4 to 5 million pits per CD, arranged in a single outward-running spiral (track) approximately 3.75 miles (6 kilometers) long. The distance between each element is 1.6 thousandths of a millimeter.

# DVD: A Super CD-ROM Alternative

As already noted, DVD drives are becoming more popular and are usually backward compatible with CD-ROMs. They come in several varieties, both internal and external. The most popular in the PC market is the Enhanced IDE (EIDE) internal style. While this product looks much like a CD-ROM drive, and installs virtually the same way, you need to be at least somewhat familiar with the different standards that exist in the DVD arena.

# DVD Formats

## DVD-ROM

This a data read-only format, much like a CD-ROM disc, that can be engineered to hold up to 17 GB of digital information by encoding data on both sides of the disc.

## DVD Video

A 4.7-GB disc format designed to distribute movies, these platters hold up to 135 minutes of high-quality video. In addition, this format can store eight digital soundtracks (AC3 and/or Digital Dolby) and subtitles. Many movies on DVD also come with commentary, interviews with the artists, theatrical trailers, and even alternate versions of endings or scenes deleted from the version shown in theaters.

## DVD-R

The R stands for recordable. This type of DVD media is similar in use to the single record type of CD-R platter and contains up to 3.95 GB of data per side. Like CD-R, you can only record to the disc once.

## DVD RAM/RW

There are several Read/Write (RW) DVD drives on the market. Because of the incompatibilities among vendors, this DVD technology has been very slow in gaining acceptance. Keep in mind that the "Write" aspect is not unlimited and that the actual number of changes varies based on the technology.

# Connecting CD-ROM and DVD Drives

In most cases, there is no difference in attaching a CD-ROM or DVD drive. The speed rates described later (like 4X) are based on the speed of the original CD-ROM drives and are used to gauge the relative speed of both CD-ROM and DVD products. Depending on the features and design, you may have to install an add-on decoder card with a DVD product to improve performance when playing movies. Both types of drives are peripheral devices and must be connected to the bus of the computer through a controller. There are several ways to install them.

## Adapter Boards

Some manufacturers provide a proprietary adapter board made specifically for their product. These boards are supplied with the drive and are not usually inter-changeable. Early CD-ROM drives used either SCSI or a special version of a parallel port. Most modern CD-ROM devices are either EIDE or SCSI. Many DVD drives come with a decoder board to improve movie and audio playback. When installing a drive with such a card, check if the system's display adapter can handle the decoding. If so, you may be able to streamline the process by using the existing card.

### Sound Cards with CD-ROM Interface

Many add-on sound cards have built-in CD-ROM controllers. Most sound cards come with a 15-pin female connector known as the MIDI (Musical Instrument Digital Interface) connector. Some of the newer cards come with a SCSI interface. Sound cards with the built-in controller interface were very useful for earlier computers that did not have a controller available on the motherboard. Because today's motherboards have the ability to connect four IDE devices, a sound card with a controller is generally not required.

---

**Tip**   If you purchase a sound card with a controller and you already have a CD-ROM drive installed, be sure to disable the controller on the sound card. This will prevent IRQ (interrupt request) and other potential conflicts.

---

### SCSI Host Adapter

The SCSI interface, the most advanced CD-ROM interface, often operates at higher data transfer rates than other interfaces. A single card can handle both internal and external drives, including CD-ROM and other optical devices. You can find a more detailed discussion of SCSI drives in Lesson 3, "SCSI Drives." A SCSI CD-ROM drive can be installed in any SCSI chain. You can purchase SCSI adapters that connect directly to a parallel port on the computer.

### EIDE

Most computers have primary and secondary EIDE connectors as part of the motherboard and BIOS (basic input/output system) setup. It is becoming commonplace to install CD-ROM drives on the secondary controller.

## Audio Capability

Any CD-ROM drive that meets the Yellow Book standards (created by the audio industry for sound and adopted by the computer industry) has the ability to play back audio. Most CD-ROM drives contain the circuitry and chips to convert digital audio data into sound data. Most drives and sound cards also have a headphone jack, as well as audio jacks to connect to a stereo system. The only requirement is that the drive support the ISO 9660 standard, also known as the High Sierra specification, for the file system. The ISO 9660 format is a standard for writing data to a CD-ROM for use in a cross-platform environment. This standard is compatible with MS-DOS, Microsoft Windows, UNIX, Macintosh, and other operating systems.

## Access Time

When purchasing or recommending a CD-ROM drive, you need to consider two values. The first is data transfer rate. The longtime standard for transfer rate has been 150 KB per second, and this is the basis for measuring CD-ROM drives today. A 2X CD-ROM drive operates at 300 KB per second, a 4X at 600 KB per second, and so on. A typical CD-ROM drive today will operate at 24X, 32X (4.8 MB per second), or faster. A hard disk drive typically operates between 800 KB and 1.8 MB per second.

The second value you should look at is the drive's mean access time, the time it takes the head to move over half the tracks. Typical access time is 200 to 400 milliseconds (ms). Today's CD-ROM drives can have faster data transfer speeds than many hard drives, but their mean access time is 20 or so times slower. This means that, although a CD-ROM drive will outperform the hard disk drive for copying or loading a large chunk of contiguous data, the hard drive will perform better on random access tasks.

Although the transfer rate increases in multiples, the mean access time does not. The following table lists transfer rates and access speeds for some common CD-ROM drives.

| CD-ROM Speed | Transfer Rate | Access Speed |
| --- | --- | --- |
| 4X | 600 KB per second | 220 ms |
| 6X | 900 KB per second | 145 ms |
| 8X | 1200 KB per second | 100 ms |
| 12X | 1800 KB per second | 125 ms |
| 16X | 2.4 MB per second | 100 ms |
| 24X | 3.6 MB per second | 95 ms |

## Installing CD-ROM and DVD Drives

Installing an internal drive is a four-step process.

1. Install the drive controller or decoder card, if needed, following the instructions that come with the card.
2. Install the drive in the computer case.
3. Attach the data and power cables.
4. Install the necessary operating system drivers and set up the drive.

## Controller Cards

The most difficult part of installing a CD-ROM or DVD drive is determining which controller card is best for the system.

A quick review of how the computer is currently equipped will guide you in the selection of the proper card. In most cases, there will be a SCSI or IDE interface available. Whatever card arrangement you choose, be sure to disable any other possibly conflicting cards. Confirming the extent of the computer's resources before purchasing a new CD-ROM drive can save you the time and frustration of having to return or exchange it.

You should select the controller card before buying the CD-ROM drive because it must be compatible with both the CD-ROM drive and the motherboard's expansion slot. There are several ways to ensure a proper connection:

- Use the secondary IDE controller on the motherboard.
- Install a new controller card (this might be supplied with the CD-ROM drive).
- Install the CD-ROM drive in an existing SCSI chain.
- Install a new SCSI host adapter and create a new SCSI chain.
- Use an existing sound card with a CD-ROM connection.

## Installing an Internal Drive

You can mount both CD-ROM and DVD drives easily in any computer that has an open bay for a 5.25-inch disk drive. Physical installation is as simple as installing a floppy disk drive. Most new drives come with a hardware kit that includes a combination of screws and brackets.

Make sure you have all the tools and parts before beginning. These include:

- The drive
- The correct cables
- The appropriate hardware (including special mounting rails for the PC's case)
- A flat-head screwdriver
- A Phillips screwdriver
- Needle-nose pliers or tweezers (for jumper settings)

Connecting the cables for a CD-ROM drive is as simple as installing a floppy disk drive. There are two cables—a flat ribbon cable (for data) and a power cable. Be sure to connect the flat ribbon cable to the correct location on both the controller and the CD-ROM drive (with the red wire going to pin 1). If there are no available power cables, use a Y power splitter cable (this will split a single

Molex connector into two connectors; these are discussed earlier in Lesson 1 of Chapter 5, "Power Supplies"). There might also be an audio out cable (two to four wires) that connects to a sound card (see Figure 10.1). This connection will allow you to take full advantage of the audio capabilities of the CD-ROM drive.

The cabling for a DVD drive can be a little more complex. Check the documentation to see how the sound and video are cabled. In some cases you will have to link the decoder to the video display adapter and link another loopback to bring the sound through the sound card to the speakers.

If you are adding an IDE-style drive, be sure to set the master/slave jumper as required (see Lesson 2 of Chapter 9, "Basic Disk Drives"). For SCSI drives, you must set the proper SCSI ID using either a jumper or switch and make sure the chain is properly terminated.

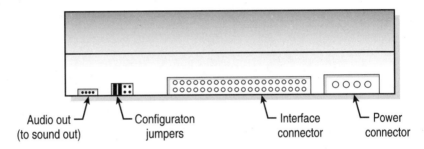

Audio out &#8212; (to sound out)     &#8212; Configuraton jumpers     &#8212; Interface connector     &#8212; Power connector

**Figure 10.1**   Cable connections to a typical CD-ROM drive

## Software Setup

The file structure for a CD-ROM or DVD drive is different from the directory used by the MS-DOS file allocation table (FAT). Therefore, you will need a special driver for MS-DOS to be able to recognize this device as a drive. A standard device driver supplied by the manufacturer (for BIOS) might also be required.

## Windows 3.*x*

Microsoft's MSCDEX.EXE, an MS-DOS resident application, provides the required translation and also specifies the device driver required by the device. The following changes in CONFIG.SYS and AUTOEXEC.BAT will do the job.

- Changes to CONFIG.SYS

    To load the device driver, type the following line and include the directory and driver for the CD to be installed. (The exact name and location of your driver file might be different from what is shown in this example.)

    ```
    device=C:\CDROM\MTMCDAI.SYS /D:MSCD001
    ```

To ensure drive number assignment space, type the following line. (Note that the last drive letter assignment and, therefore, the number of drives, can be limited by assigning a lower value letter.)

```
lastdrive=z
```

- Add the following line to AUTOEXEC.BAT:

```
c:\dos\mscdex.exe /d:mscd001 /1:e /m:10
```

This instruction provides the location of the driver and should include any switches required to set up the driver. You might have to consult the documentation for the CD-ROM drive to determine exactly which, if any, switches are required.

Many CD-ROM drive installation disks will make these changes automatically. (You can find additional information for configuring CONFIG.SYS and AUTOEXEC.BAT in Chapter 16, "Operating System Fundamentals.")

## Windows 95, Windows 98, and Windows Me

Windows 95, Windows 98, and Windows Me use a 32-bit protected-mode driver called VCDFSD.VXD. This driver replaced MSCDEX.EXE, the MS-DOS real-mode driver. When adding a new CD-ROM drive after Windows 95 has been installed, be sure to use the Add New Hardware Wizard. This wizard will properly identify and set up the CD-ROM drive. With later versions of Windows that support the Plug and Play feature, installing a new CD-ROM drive is simple—the operating system will recognize the new drive and run the install wizard automatically.

---

**Note**   If you intend to use a CD-ROM drive in the MS-DOS mode (from a bootable disk), you will have to install the real-mode drivers and add them to the CONFIG.SYS and AUTOEXEC.BAT files of the boot disk.

---

**Tip**   You can use a Windows 98 Startup disk to obtain the files required to recognize a CD-ROM drive. Be sure that the PC has the proper software licenses to use those files.

---

## Windows NT and Windows 2000

The Windows 2000 operating system offers native Plug and Play support for most CD-ROM drives. Many can also be configured as bootable devices, allowing you to install the operating system directly from the installation CD-ROM. If not, you will have to use the startup floppy disk, along with driver disks from the vendor to complete an initial installation. For adding a new drive to an existing system, most new products should have the needed drivers, and many older products will have drivers as part of the operating system release. Keep in mind that Windows NT was not as widely supported for multimedia products, so older DVD drives may not have drivers available, or some of the features (such as playing movies) may not be supported.

## Multimedia

The term *multimedia* embraces a number of computer technologies, but refers primarily to video, sound, and the storage required by these large files. Basically, multimedia is a combination of graphics, data, and sound on a computer. In all practicality, the concept of adding multimedia simply means adding and configuring a sound card, a video card, and a CD-ROM or DVD drive to a system.

Microsoft formed an organization called the Multimedia PC Marketing Council in 1991 to generate standards for multimedia computers. The council created several Multimedia PC (MPC) standards and licensed its logo and trademark to manufacturers whose hardware and software conform to these guidelines.

The Multimedia PC Marketing Council formally transferred responsibility for its standards to the Multimedia PC Working Group of the Software Publishers Association (SPA). This group includes many of the same members as the original Multimedia PC Marketing Council. The group's first creation was a new MPC standard.

The Multimedia PC Marketing Council originally developed two primary standards for multimedia: MPC Level 1 and MPC Level 2. Under the direction of the SPA, the first two standards have been replaced by a third, called MPC Level 3 (MPC 3), which was introduced in June 1995. There are currently no plans for the publication of any additional MPC standards. New PCs all well exceed the limits of the MPC requirements, and all new Windows machines generally will support a wide range of multimedia applications and hardware. To run the latest multimedia applications requires at least a Pentium II machine with a 64-bit sound card, 24-bit display adapter, 20X CD-ROM or DVD drive, and 64 MB of random access memory (RAM). Speakers able to handle the features of the sound card are also needed for full use of the system.

### Video-Capture Software

With the advent of multimedia computers and software, manipulating full-motion video was the next logical step. Modern high-speed multimedia computers have become standard equipment in the moviemaking industry. Today, even amateur filmmakers can use their computers to give home movies a touch of professionalism.

Video-capture software provides an interface that allows users to import and export video formats to edit them with their computers. With this software, users can view audio waveforms and video images, create files, capture single-frame or full-motion video, and edit video clips and still frames for content and effects.

File editing functions such as zoom, undo, cut, paste, crop, and clear can be used to edit audio and visual files. Users can also set the compression controls to the type of format desired and determine the capture rates. The capture rate for full-motion video (equivalent to what you would find on TV or on the big screen) is 30 frames per second (fps), but some systems might not be able to reach this potential. Professional systems include very large, fast hard disk drives for data buffering. A typical user of video-capture software might realize a frame-capture rate of only up to 15 fps without adding an arsenal of hardware to enhance the system.

## Lesson Summary

The following points summarize the main elements of this lesson:

- A CD-ROM or DVD drive is now a standard component of a computer system.

- CD-ROM and DVD data transfer rates are based on a factor of 150 KB per second (1X).

- Installing a CD-ROM or DVD drive is little more complicated than installing a floppy disk drive.

- The proper drivers must be loaded before a CD-ROM or DVD drive can be accessed by the operating system. To run a CD-ROM drive from MS-DOS, the real-mode drivers must be loaded.

# Lesson 2:  Advanced Hard Disk Drives

Chapter 9, "Basic Disk Drives," covered the basics of hard disk drives. In this lesson, we broaden our discussion of hard disk drives to include the newer large-capacity drives and several of the newest methods.

## After this lesson, you will be able to

- Configure the newer large-capacity hard disk drives
- Define the limitations of hard disk drives
- Identify the advantages and disadvantages of SCSI connections

## Estimated lesson time: 45 minutes

## Limitations of Early Hard Disk Drives

The original basic hard disk drives—specifically the ST-506—were relatively simple to install because the primary input/output (I/O) commands were handled by the PC AT system BIOS. They used the routines built into the original IBM AT and the same interface command set as the original ST-506 hard drive. As drive capacities grew, they required many changes in setup to get around the limitations imposed by earlier models. Often, these changes added to the workload of the processor, which had a net effect of slowing down the processing of data. This resulted in research for new methods to overcome those bottlenecks, which in turn led to other design considerations that had to be addressed. The end result is that storage technology is still evolving. Drives increase in capacity and speed, causing changes in PC design and operating system support to take advantage of the larger capacity, faster drives.

### IDE and EIDE Drives

IDE drives have been in use since the late 1980s. The purpose of the IDE was to integrate the drive controller with the drive itself rather than use a separate controller card. The Advanced Technology Attachment (ATA)—the official name for IDE drives—standard is based on the original IBM AT standard for hard disk drives. ATA drives use the same interface command set as the original ST-506 drives and are handled by the system BIOS built into the original IBM AT. ATA was, and is, a good command set, but its limitations led to its decline as a viable hard drive interface. These limitations set the stage for the development of EIDE. The EIDE drive system was developed with two essential objectives: increasing the size of available disk drives and increasing the speed of data transfer between the host and the disk drive.

The EIDE specification

- Increased the numbers of drives available to the average computer
- Increased the data transfer rate

- Allowed for non-hard disk drives such as CD-ROM, Zip, and tape drives to be configured to EIDE standards and be connected to an EIDE controller
- Broke the 528-MB storage capacity limit of the ATA standard

**Note**   These remarks apply only to IDE-style drives. SCSI drives and how they deal with the size and number of drive issues are covered later in this chapter.

Let's examine these improvements in detail.

### Number of Drives

The ATA standard allows two hard disk drives to connect to one common controller. IBM set aside (reserved) I/O address 1FOh and IRQ 14 for the use of hard disk drive controllers. IBM also reserved I/O address 170h and IRQ 15 for a second controller (two more hard drives). Early computers had no BIOS support for this second controller. The BIOS installed on newer computers takes full advantage of both controllers, allowing up to four EIDE devices. (You'll find a fuller discussion of addresses and IRQs in Chapter 8, "Expansion Buses, Cables, and Connectors.")

Most SCSI controllers offer the ability to use IRQ 13 for hard disk drive support without the use of special drivers. To do so, set the SCSI card with boot BIOS enabled and make sure the hard disk drive is properly formatted for the operating system in question.

### Data Transfer Rate

ATA drives transfer data to and from the hard disk drive and memory using standardized protocols called *PIO (Programmed Input/Output)* modes. With PIO, data is exchanged between the main memory and a peripheral device, not by means of direct memory access (DMA), but with in-and-out instructions through the central processing unit (CPU). The Small Forms Factor (SFF) standards committee defined these data transfer rates as PIO mode 0, PIO mode 1, and PIO mode 2. ATA drives can use PIO mode 0, 1, or 2. With each improved PIO standard, the efficiency and speed of data transfer increased. The original ATA drives could transfer data from the hard disk drive to RAM at a maximum rate of roughly 3.3 MB per second. Speed increases to 5.2 MB per second, and then 8.3 MB per second and beyond, followed shortly thereafter.

### Non-Hard Disk Drives

The original controllers allowed only for hard disk drives—and just two of them. An independent industry group developed the AT Attachment Packet Interface (ATAPI) to allow non-hard disk drives (CD-ROM drives and high-speed streaming tape units) access to the ATA interface.

### The 528-MB Limit

Early BIOSs had a limitation on the maximum cylinder, head, and sector (CHS) values allowed, and the ATA standard added to that. As a result, for several years the maximum hard disk drive size was restricted to 528 MB. The following table shows how CHS limits are determined.

|  | BIOS Limit | IDE (ATA) Limit | Maximum Usable Limit |
|---|---|---|---|
| Cylinders | 1024 | 65,536 | 1024 |
| Heads | 255 | 16 | 16 |
| Sector/track | 63 | 255 | 63 |
| Maximum capacity | 8.4 billion bytes | 136.9 billion bytes | 528 million bytes |

**Important**   There are two ways to look at 528,000,000 bytes: the marketers' way (528 MB means 528 million bytes) or the literal way, which takes into account that there are 1,048,576 bytes per megabyte (1024 bytes × 1024 bytes). The second way, which is more accurate, yields a value of 528,000,000 divided by 1,048,576—a total of 504 MB. Also be aware that an operating system will have to use part of the space for its housekeeping functions, as well as command and system files. The actual usable space for application and data files could be considerably smaller.

## EIDE

EIDE specifies the incorporation of four major upgrades to the ATA/IDE specification:

- Logical Block Addressing (LBA) translation standards for BIOSs to support IDE drives larger than the old limit of 528 MB.

- Industry standards for improved data throughput to and from IDE drives— PIO modes 3 and 4.

- Industry standard instruction sets that allow CD-ROM drives and tape backups to connect to the same controller using the ATAPI standards.

- Use of the old, mostly unused IBM standard for a secondary controller calling IRQ 15 and I/O address 170h.

## Overcoming the 528-MB Barrier

There are several methods used to overcome the 528-MB hard disk barrier. When developing these methods, the difficult task was to create novel ways to access more data while maintaining backward compatibility. In most cases, designers found ways to address larger drives while "fooling" the operating system into functioning as if the drive were still within the proper limits.

When working with high-capacity drives, the computer professional must understand these different methods and apply the best method for a given situation. This is especially true if you encounter a situation in which different oversized drives are installed in an older system; these older systems often require special drivers or partitioning software. Using multiple hard disk drive drivers can confuse older operating systems due to incompatibilities. Never use drive data compression software in such cases without being sure that all the code involved is compatible.

---

**Important**  The new, super-large hard disk drives might not work with some older machines. They will run, but will not take advantage of the extra high capacity.

---

## Logical Block Addressing

LBA is a means of addressing the physical sectors on a hard disk drive in a linear fashion. A translating BIOS detects the capacity of the drive and manipulates the CHS values so that the cylinder value is always less than 1024. Here's how it works:

- Before LBA (limit 528 MB):
  capacity = cylinders × heads × sectors per track
  528,482,304 = 1024 × 16 × 63 × 512
- With LBA:
  cylinders = capacity divided by (heads × sectors per track)

When the computer boots up, an enhanced drive parameter table is loaded into memory. When data is transferred, this table intercepts the request and converts the system's CHS values to LBA values that the computer's BIOS can handle.

## Enhanced CHS Translation

Enhanced CHS is a standard that competes with LBA. This standard allows drives to be manufactured a little faster and more easily than LBA. IBM and other manufacturers support this standard.

## Fast ATA

Fast ATA uses PIO mode 3, while Fast ATA-2 uses PIO mode 4. It is a technique used by Seagate Technologies (and others) to compete with EIDE. Fast ATA drives will support either LBA or CHS drive translation to break the 528-MB barrier.

## Logical CHS and Physical CHS

Logical cylinders, heads, and sectors (LCHS) is a value used by the operating system (MS-DOS, Windows 95, Windows 98, OS/2, and so forth) to determine the size of the hard disk drive. Physical cylinders, heads, and sectors (PCHS) is a value used within the device to determine its size. A translating BIOS and the operating system use different algorithms to determine the address of the data.

## DMA Transfer

DMA is a transfer method that, although not a PIO mode, also works to overcome the size limitations of hard disks. DMA bypasses the CPU to transfer data directly into memory. This is the preferred way to move large chunks of data in a multitasking environment. UNIX and Windows NT take advantage of DMA transfers. These transfers can function by using either the DMA controller on the Industry Standard Architecture (ISA) bus or a bus-mastering controller that takes over the expansion bus and bypasses the built-in DMA controller.

DMA data transfers can be either 16 bits (single word) or 32 bits (double word) wide. The transfer width depends on the data bus used—ISA, EISA, or VLB (see Chapter 8, "Expansion Buses, Cables, and Connectors" for details). DMA data transfer for ATA hard disk drives is extremely rare.

Be warned, however, that using DMA data transfer can lead to data loss, although this should be a concern only when transferring partitioned and formatted hard disk drives between computers that use different BIOSs to make the translation. The following table shows the various DMA modes.

| DMA Modes | PCHS | LCHS |
|---|---|---|
| Cylinders | 2304 | 576 |
| Heads | 8 | 32 |
| Sectors/track | 63 | 63 |
| Capacity | 594.5 million bytes | 594.5 million bytes |

# Breaking the 8.4-GB Barrier

Hard disk drives larger than 8.4 GB require a BIOS that supports enhanced interrupt 13h extensions for very large drives. Which method is used will depend on the system's age, operating system, and the drive in question. Newer machines come with built-in support in the system BIOS. There are three methods you can use to enable this function on older PCs that do not come with native support:

- Upgrade the system BIOS
- Install a hard disk drive adapter with interrupt 13h support
- Use a software program from the drive maker to allow the system to access the drive

Depending on the system BIOS, you might not be able to display the entire size of the drive while in BIOS/CMOS Setup. Check the manual for the BIOS and operating environment for more details.

The procedures just described will let the system recognize the drive, but the maximum partition size will still be determined by the operating system in question. Be sure to check the procedures for the version you will be using with any third-party software. Newer versions of Windows (98, Me, NT, and 2000) allow very large partitions.

If you use an older version of the MS-DOS FDISK utility to prepare the drive, you will not be able to use the entire contents as a single volume. If you use Microsoft's FAT12- or FAT16-based FDISK, the largest single partition will still be 2.1 GB unless a third-party partitioning program is used. Newer versions of Windows can access partitions greater than 2.1 GB, but if you plan to use a dual-boot configuration, be sure that any partition is compatible with the operating system you want to use to view the files it contains. NTFS and FAT32 partitions are not visible to older versions of Windows, MS-DOS, or UNIX.

## Ultra DMA

Although questions about the latest incarnation of ATA/DMA drives are not likely to appear on the current A+ Exam, a good computer technician should be conversant with them and expect to see them as part of the certification renewal process. Ultra DMA/33 is a faster drive technology that can be used on virtually any Pentium motherboard. Ultra DMA/66 offers raw data transfers at twice the speed of its older DMA/33 sibling. It requires a compatible system bus on the motherboard (or a special controller card), BIOS, and special IDE cable certified for that speed. They are easy to identify. One 40-pin connector is blue, and the other is black. Most are also labeled for Ultra DMA/66.

## Installing EIDE Drives

Installing an EIDE drive is similar to installing an ATA drive, but in your presetup examination, you should consider secondary controllers, proper translations, and verifying PIO modes on older systems. Before undertaking an installation, you should collect all the information from the new drive as well as from the existing drive. Consider all the options on paper before removing any screws. If you don't have enough information on hand, consult the drive manufacturer or resources on the Internet. If you are installing a very new EIDE or Ultra DMA drive on an old system, make sure the motherboard, Peripheral Component Interconnect (PCI) bus, cables, and IDE interface are compatible with the drive specification.

### Secondary Controllers

Many EIDE I/O cards support secondary controllers, allowing for up to four ATA devices, as mentioned earlier. Before installing a card, be sure that jumper settings are set properly (see Figure 10.2). Secondary controllers are always set at I/O address 170h and IRQ 15.

Many cards come preset with the secondary controller disabled. Also check the advanced CMOS settings to make sure that any secondary controller enable/disable options are set to enabled.

**Note**   Some EIDE controller cards require that the CMOS options for secondary port hard disk drives be left as "Not Installed." Be sure to read all documentation that comes with these cards.

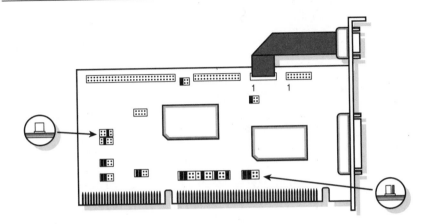

**Figure 10.2**   Controller card with jumpers

Secondary IDE interface and on-board channels are best suited for use with CD-ROM, DVD, or tape drives. Many secondary controllers on older machines run at a lower PIO mode (0 or 1) than the primary controller (3 or 4). It is always best to check the documentation before installing.

## LBA or CHS?

Most BIOSs can support both LBA and CHS. Enhanced BIOS allows the system to get around the MS-DOS limitation of 528 MB per hard disk and is the easiest way to install an EIDE drive. An enhanced BIOS will support either the Western Digital LBA mode or the Seagate Extended CHS mode.

**Note**   The two translation options are not interchangeable. You cannot partition a drive in one computer using one option and move it to a system that uses the other option. Also, see the earlier information about drives of over 8.4-GB capacity. CHS settings are not "real" for drives larger than that size, and they must use some form of controller, system, or third-party software translation to work.

What if a computer does not support either CHS or LBA? Most newer, large-capacity drives will provide a disk manager disk, or the ability to make one from the drive itself. (If the information is on the disk, you will be able to access a small MS-DOS partition with the data. The instructions for accessing this data are very specific and must be followed according to the manufacturer's requirements.) This software, when installed properly, performs the same task as CHS or LBA. When using this method, you need to first answer this question: Is the drive in the master or slave position?

- If it is in the slave drive, install the appropriate driver in the CONFIG.SYS file, if required by the operating system.

- If it is in the master drive, the driver must be loaded *before* anything else, including the CONFIG.SYS file. You can accomplish this by changing the Dynamic Drive Overlay (DDO) in the master boot record. The software provided by the drive manufacturer should make these changes for you.

There are some drawbacks to using this method rather than LBA or CHS:

- Microsoft no longer supports the use of DDO software.

- When booting up from a floppy disk, for the hard disk drive to be accessible, the device must be loaded from the floppy disk's CONFIG.SYS file.

- A virus might attack the master boot record, where this file resides. This can cause serious problems and at the very least will require reinstallation of the DDO file. Always keep a bootable, virus-free floppy disk on hand.

- The driver that allows use of a large hard disk drive might also use a large chunk of conventional memory. The trade-off might not be worth it.

- Many hard disk drive repair programs cannot be used with DDO.

- The software might cause conflicts with the operating system or other drivers.

### Setting PIO Mode

There are five PIO modes. A drive must be set properly to achieve the best performance. The following table shows the parameters of PIO modes.

| PIO Mode | Cycle Time in Nanoseconds (ns) | Transfer Rate (MB per second) |
| --- | --- | --- |
| 0 | 600 | 3.3 |
| 1 | 383 | 5.2 |
| 2 | 240 | 8.3 |
| 3 | 180 | 11.1 |
| 4 | 120 | 16.6 |

Answer the following questions before setting the mode:

- What is the fastest mode supported by the hard disk drive?

- What is the fastest mode supported by the controller?

- What is the fastest mode supported by the BIOS or device driver?

**Caution**   The maximum achievable PIO will be limited by the slowest component. Setting a mode that is too fast will not damage the driver, but it might damage your data.

To set up the PIO mode:

- Determine the PIO of the drive. This is preset by the manufacturer and cannot be changed. See the documentation that comes with the product or visit the vendor's Web site for details if it is not on the drive or handled by the system BIOS.

- Determine the fastest speed your controller can handle. Most hard disk drives can support PIO mode 2. If you're using an ISA card, PIO mode 2 is the highest PIO available. The two fastest PIO modes, 3 and 4, must be run from either a VESA local bus (VLB) or a PCI controller. Be careful with on-board controllers! On PCI systems, almost all on-board controllers are PCI; on VESA machines, they are VLB.

- Use the BIOS Setup program to adjust the CMOS settings. If auto setup (where the firmware can auto-detect the drive parameters and set the BIOS) is available, use it.

  PIO modes 3 and 4 use a hardware flow control called IORDY (I/O ReaDY), also known as IOCHRDY. This setting allows the drive to slow down the data transfer as the head moves across the disk.

## Other Settings

There are several other drive settings that are not necessarily limited to EIDE but are generally associated with these larger hard disk drives.

### Multiple Block Reads

The ATA standard requires each drive to activate its IRQ (see Chapter 8, "Expansion Buses, Cables, and Connectors" for details of IRQ) every time it sends one sector of data. This process helps to verify good data transmission, but it slows down the computer. Multiple block reads speed up the process by reading several sectors of data at a time.

Many BIOS chips have multiple block read as an advanced feature. Enabling multiple block read can be done with third-party utilities as well. Multiple block read can also be installed using a device driver that comes with a hard disk drive controller. Always use multiple block read, if possible.

### 32-Bit Access

Providing 32-bit disk access is a major speed improvement over MS-DOS for the Windows 3.x and Windows for Workgroups 3.11 environments. Every time an operation is performed under Windows, Windows must use the BIOS routines to access the hard disk drive. To do this, it creates a virtual MS-DOS world, a "bubble" of conventional memory that looks and runs just as if the machine were running MS-DOS.

Enabling 32-bit file access allows later versions of Windows 3.x to talk directly to the ROM BIOS, using a protected-mode driver called VFAT.386 (found in the Windows\System directory). VFAT.386 is loaded using the [386Enh] section of the SYSTEM.INI file. With the 32-bit file loaded, Windows does not have to create an MS-DOS "bubble" to talk to the hard disk drive.

For 32-bit file access to work in older versions of Windows:

1. Enter the line

   ```
   device=c:\windows\ifshlp.sys
   ```

   into your CONFIG.SYS file. This loads the 32-bit file access driver.

2. In the SYSTEM.INI file, add two lines to the [386enh] section:

   ```
   device=vfat.386
   device=vcache.386
   ```

   (These protected-mode drivers replace MS-DOS FAT functions and SMARTDRV.EXE functions.)

---

**Note**   Windows 95 and later versions of that operating system automatically install a 32-bit file access driver. 32-bit file access is transparent to EIDE and requires no special settings.

---

There are some other potential problems with Windows 3.x and large drives. Windows 3.x uses a file called *WDCTRL for 32-bit disk access. This file is enabled from the SYSTEM.INI [386enh] section. This driver predates LBA and will generate the error: "32 file access validation failed." If this happens, *WDCTRL needs to be updated. Most EIDE controllers and all drives now come from the factory with a software disk that should include the latest drivers. If it is not available on your disk, look up the Web site of the hard disk drive manufacturer and download the driver.

Whenever possible, check the CMOS, look for a 32-bit disk access option, and enable it.

## Lesson Summary

The following points summarize the main elements of this lesson:

- Originally, hard disk drives were limited to storage capacity that did not exceed 528 MB.
- Using new technology, the old hard disk drive limit has been exceeded.
- Modern computers allow up to four IDE drives to be installed on built-in controllers.
- Properly setting PIO will enhance the performance of a drive.
- 32-bit disk access provides a major speed improvement for disk drives.

# Lesson 3:  SCSI Drives

SCSI has become the mass-storage device of choice for large network installations. SCSI, first introduced in Lesson 2 of Chapter 9, "Basic Disk Drives," has many advantages over standard IDE and EIDE drives. SCSI is the favored drive for high-end workstations, network and Internet servers, and the Macintosh line of personal computers. In many installations, the advantages far outweigh the slight extra effort in configuration. In this lesson, we explore the advantages and uses of a SCSI system.

### After this lesson, you will be able to

- Define the advantages and disadvantages of a SCSI system
- Determine whether a SCSI system is best for your client
- Set up a SCSI system

### Estimated lesson time: 30 minutes

SCSI was introduced in 1979 as a high-performance interface, allowing connection of both internal and external devices. Because it runs on virtually any operating system, it was adopted by the American National Standards Institute (ANSI) Standards Committee and is now an open standard in its third generation.

At its core, SCSI is a simple design. A single card, the host adapter (or a chip set on the motherboard) connects up to 15 devices. These devices can be attached inside or outside the PC using standard cables and connectors. SCSI is the only interface that can connect such a wide variety of devices. Communication between the devices and the host adapter is done without involving the CPU or the system bus until data must be passed to one or the other.

This design frees expansion slots and reduces the number of interrupts and memory addresses needed, while cutting down the number of drivers required. Less robust solutions, such as IDE and EIDE, are little more than switching stations, relying on the PC's CPU to manage the data bus. SCSI host adapters are true subsystems with advanced commands that can order and route data to improve performance.

## SCSI-1

In the late 1970s, Shugart Associates developed an interface to handle data transfers between devices, regardless of the type of device. The interface operated at the logical—or operating system—level instead of at the device level. This new interface was called the Shugart Associates System Interface (SASI)—the precursor to SCSI.

In June 1986, the ANSI X3.131-1986 standard, known as SCSI-1, was formally published. This was a very loose definition, with few mandates. As a result, manufacturers of SCSI products developed a variety of competing designs.

SCSI-1 supported up to seven devices on a chain (plus the host adapter), each of which transferred data through an 8-bit parallel path. Compatibility of SCSI drives was nearly impossible because many SCSI devices had their own custom commands on top of the limited SCSI standard.

You might encounter older SCSI adapters, drives, and peripherals that are based on the original SCSI-1 standard. In reality, this standard amounts to little more than a few agreed-on commands. The wide range of proprietary drivers, operating system interfaces, setup options, and custom commands made true compatibility a real problem and gained SCSI a bad reputation on the PC platform. It was, however, popular with Apple and UNIX developers, who could work with a limited range of devices.

In most cases, it is best to upgrade any SCSI-1 devices to SCSI-2. If circumstances require you to work on an early SCSI product, you will have to contend with both hardware and driver issues. Check the Web site of your SCSI device's manufacturer for possible new drivers.

## SCSI-2

The limited acceptance, but great potential, of SCSI-1 led to a more robust standard with a range of commands and a layered set of drivers. The result was a high-performance interface that began to take over the high-end market. It was the interface of choice for fast hard disk drives, optical drives, scanners, and fast tape technology.

One of the most important parts of the SCSI-2 specification is a larger (and mandatory) standard command set. Recognition of this command set (18 commands) is required for a device to be SCSI-2 compliant. The Common Command Set (CCS) made compatibility of multivendor devices possible. The CCS also introduced additional commands to more easily address devices such as optical drives, tape drives, and scanners.

SCSI-2 also supports:

- Wide (16-bit) SCSI
- Fast SCSI
- Fast/Wide (combines fast and wide features)
- Ultra (32-bit) SCSI SI-2
- Backward compatibility with SCSI-1

## Fast SCSI-2

This standard uses a fast synchronous mode to transfer data, doubling the data transfer speed from 5 MB/s to 10 MB/s. Wide SCSI doubles that again.

Plug and Play SCSI adapters first arrived with the advent of the SCSI-2 standard. Today, all new SCSI host adapters are Plug and Play. The SCSI-2 standard took a long time to gain final approval, requiring agreement by many vendors. As a result, you might run into products labeled "Draft SCSI-2." In almost all cases, you can get these products running on any SCSI-2 or later system if you get the appropriate drivers from the vendor or the maker of the host adapter or operating system.

# SCSI-3

To speed the pace of development, the SCSI Committee approved a "fast-track" system for the SCSI-3 standard. A subcommittee handled most of the work, and new subsections were adopted without waiting for the publication of the entire SCSI definition.

That bright idea, plus the advent of the PCI bus and mature Plug and Play operating systems, has made it easy to install components and has given users excellent control and flexibility. All SCSI-3 cards have ways to support existing SCSI-2 devices. Some of the highlights of current state-of-the-art SCSI technology on the desktop include the following seven features.

### High-Performance Products

The success and stability of the SCSI standard makes it an ideal platform for developing high-performance products. SCSI's robust, reliable interface and advanced commands allow manufacturers to build "best-of-breed" products to take advantage of its power. The fastest hard disk drives and CD-ROM devices traditionally show up first, sporting a SCSI interface. The most advanced scanners are SCSI-based, and many optical products come only in SCSI versions. Even when non-SCSI versions reach the market, they generally underperform their SCSI siblings.

### Plug and Play Installation

Well-designed SCSI cards are recognized and drivers are installed automatically with Plug and Play operating systems such as Windows 98, Windows Me, Windows NT, Windows 2000, and the Macintosh OS. Most SCSI-based peripherals provide Plug and Play setup. The first time the system is booted up after a peripheral is added to a SCSI chain, the system notices the new device and asks for the product's setup disk.

### Simple Expansion

Adding external devices is as simple as connecting an industry standard cable and power cord. If users decide to add additional host adapters, they can share the same drivers, reducing system overhead.

## Advanced Management

SCSI products generally offer a range of tools to tune the bus and devices attached to it. For example, many host adapters have firmware that provides the ability to format and inspect hard disk drive reliability and define custom settings for each device on the chain. Operating system utilities are provided to check the status of a device and enable advanced features.

## SCAM Support

SCAM stands for "SCSI configured auto-magically." Most new SCSI products are SCAM-enabled, meaning that the user does not have to worry about setting the ID numbers for them because they will configure themselves using an open ID position on the SCSI chain.

**Note**   Even if a hard disk drive is SCAM-enabled, you might have to set an ID on multidrive PCs because the host adapter will need it to determine which drive is the normal boot device.

## Connect/Disconnect

This command allows a SCSI device handling a large amount of data or performing complex operations to disengage from the host adapter's bus while performing the task, allowing other devices free access until it is finished.

## Tag Command Queuing

SCSI devices with this feature can reorder how blocks of data are moved on the bus to speed transfer. This function compares to letting a shopper with only a few items move to the head of the checkout line to reduce the average wait time per shopper.

The table below offers a quick guide to the basic differences between SCSI and IDE.

**SCSI and IDE Compared**

| Feature | SCSI | Ultra DMA/IDE |
|---|---|---|
| Devices per channel | 7/15 per chain | 2 per chain |
| Maximum potential throughput for major classes of SCSI and IDE | 160 MB per second (Ultra 160) 80 MB per second (Ultra2) 40 MB per second (Wide SCSI) | 66 MB per second (Ultra DMA) 33 MB per second (Ultra DMA) 16.7 MB per second (Fast ATA) |
| Connection types | Internal and external | Internal only |
| True bus mastering | Yes | No |
| Operate more than one I/O device at a time? | Yes | No |
| Advanced commands (such as tag command queuing, connect/ disconnect) | Yes | No |

# Noise and SCSI

Any electrical signal other than data is called *noise*. Due to the many signals and electrical devices present, the interior of a computer is a noisy place. Computer manufacturers do many things to contain the noise inside the case, including adding shielding and grounding. Anything inside, or directly connected to, a computer is either a contributor to or a victim of the noise.

Because of the high data transfer speed, products using the SCSI-2 and later standards can be very sensitive to noise. Cables tend to act as antennae for noise. For this reason, proper cabling and minimizing of cable length are needed to maintain low noise in a SCSI system. Any noise spread through either the electrical power cables or the data cable is called *common-mode noise.*

A single-ended device communicates through only one wire per bit of information. This one wire is measured, or referenced, against the common ground provided by the metal chassis. Single-ended devices are vulnerable to common-mode noise (they have no way of telling the difference between valid data and noise). SCSI-1 devices are all single-ended.

Some SCSI-2 and SCSI-3 devices are differential-ended. These products employ two wires per bit of data—one wire for the data and one for the inverse of the data. The inverse signal takes the place of the ground wire in the single-ended cable. By taking the difference of the two signals, the device is able to reject common-mode noise in the data stream.

**Caution**    Under no circumstances should you try to connect single-ended and differential-ended devices on the same SCSI chain. You might fry the single-ended device and, if the differential-ended device lacks a security circuit to detect your mistake, you will probably destroy it as well.

## Troubleshooting a Device Conflict

Determine which is the offending device by taking the following measures:

- Load only the device drivers for the SCSI devices.
- If the problem still occurs, use the F8 key to determine which driver conflicts. (Press F8 when starting MS-DOS, Windows 95, Windows 98, or Windows Me. This will allow step-by-step confirmation of the startup process.)
- If the device driver is an executable file, try running it with the /? option. This will usually show a variety of command-line switches for the device driver (for instance, MOUSE.EXE /?). For more details on MS-DOS command programs and switches, see Chapter 16, "Operating System Fundamentals."

Here are some ways to correct the problem after you've found it:

- Look in the manuals or Readme files of both devices. The problem might be a common one with a known solution.

- Try a variety of switches to see if any of them solves the problem.

- Attempt to find an updated driver for one or both of the devices (the Internet is a good place to look).

- If none of those solutions fixes the problem, you might be forced to choose between the devices or go to a multiple boot configuration.

## Memory Management

SCSI host adapters typically have their own ROM chips. For MS-DOS systems, put the appropriate "X=" statements in the EMM386.EXE line of the CONFIG.SYS and the appropriate EMMEXCLUDE= statement in the SYSTEM.INI file. (For more details about configuring these files, see Chapter 16, "Operating System Fundamentals.") A missing or erroneous "exclude" statement can cause intermittent lock-up problems.

## Costs and Benefits of SCSI

Initially, the cost of a SCSI system and SCSI devices is greater than the costs involved in IDE. However, there are several environments in which a SCSI system might justify the increased cost. Some ideal uses for SCSI include:

- File servers

- Workstations (both graphical and audio)

- Multitasking systems

- Systems moving large amounts of data among peripheral devices

- Systems with a large number of peripheral devices

- Systems requiring fault tolerance (mostly file servers)

## The Future of SCSI

SCSI continues to be the device of choice for systems in which speed and compatibility are important. The ability of the SCSI format to provide fast and efficient fault tolerance for network systems through the use of redundant array of independent disks (RAID) will keep it the drive of choice for networks. Although it is not required, the SCSI drive is generally preferred over IDE by Windows NT and 2000 system designers for its performance and flexibility. SCSI continues to be more expensive than IDE, but SCSI's ability for RAID, hot swapping (changing drives without shutting down a system), and machine independence will keep it popular for workstations and servers.

### Setting Up a SCSI Subsystem

There are several steps in setting up a SCSI-based system or adding a new SCSI peripheral to an existing system. Performing these steps in the proper order, without shortcuts, is the key to a fast, easy installation.

## Start with the Host Adapter

SCSI cards come in a wide variety of sizes, shapes, and configurations. Some offer one connection, whereas others have four. Options include secondary or even tertiary channels—RAID, cache RAM, and so forth. Be sure that the card will be able to service the devices planned for it. Begin by setting the jumpers, then install the SCSI adapter card in the appropriate expansion slot.

## Set the SCSI IDs, Termination, and Peripheral Cabling

Write down the ID for each device—including the host adapter—as it is assigned. After the IDs are set, verify termination for each end of the chain. Finally, attach the cables—first to the host adapter, then to the closest internal device—and move outward on the chain. Repeat the process for the external devices.

External devices usually use some form of switch to set the ID. Most allow setting IDs from 0 through 7 only. You might need to adjust that with internal devices that often allow a wider range of ID numbers. Cable types include 50-pin Centronics type, SCSI-2 D-Shell 50, and 68-pin type connectors. Make sure the last device in the chain is properly terminated.

Internal SCSI devices are installed inside the computer and are connected to the host adapter through an interior connector on the host adapter. Check the connection diagram to be sure the fitting is the right one for that type of device. The options are a 50-pin ribbon cable (similar to a 40-pin IDE cable) and two similar 68-pin cables. Be sure to use the right type of 68-pin cable: One is for ultra-low voltage differential and the other is for single-ended drives. They are not interchangeable.

**Important**   Connecting a SCSI device incorrectly (for instance, with the cable plugged backwards) can cause damage! Be sure the red or blue strip on the cable is facing toward pin 1. Some SCSI devices allow only a proper connection.

## Power Up One Device at a Time

It is good practice to connect the power to one device, power up, and check for problems. Power up additional devices one at a time and make sure everything is working and without conflict.

## Load Operating System Drivers and SCSI Software

Finally, load any software required to allow the operating system to recognize the new hardware and take full advantage of its features.

Using a cable with enough connectors enables you to easily link multiple internal devices. You can have up to eight (numbered 0–7) devices, or 16 (numbered 0–15, depending on the host adapter and the devices) on a single SCSI chain. Don't forget that the host adapter takes up one position in each SCSI chain. Figure 10.3 shows a SCSI chain.

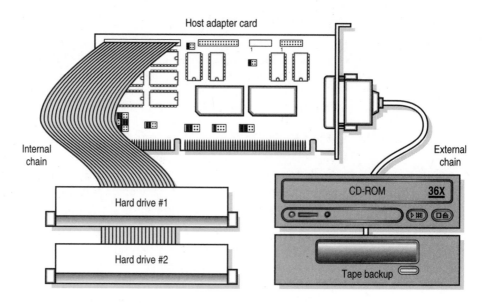

**Figure 10.3**   SCSI chain

The exact number of devices will vary depending on a number of conditions. The host adapter must support the number selected, the installer must be able to set proper IDs, and the cables and connectors must be compatible. Older adapters allow only seven total IDs, and the card will use one, leaving you with six devices. Some SCSI devices have limited ID options. Many older products have only seven possible settings; some scanners or optical products are factory-set to an ID. Given the range of cable options and performance considerations, you might have to limit the number of devices on a single chain to get maximum performance.

## Setting SCSI IDs

A simple SCSI chain works like a network, and, like a network, each device requires its own unique address. Unlike a network, however, setting an address on a SCSI chain is simple. A SCSI device can have any ID number in a range recognized by the host adapter, as long as no other device on the same chain has been set to the same number.

In SCSI numbering conventions:

- The host adapter is typically set to SCSI ID 7. (This is a de facto standard, not a requirement.)

- There is no mandated order for the use of SCSI IDs, but the SCAM feature will use a preestablished pattern of IDs if one is available.

- The host adapter manufacturer may preset the ID of a bootable hard disk drive. Most manufacturers use SCSI ID 0, although a few are configured to SCSI ID 6.

Setting a SCSI ID for a device is accomplished using jumpers or switches located on, or inside, the SCSI device. Typically, all internal SCSI hard disk drives use jumpers to set their IDs. External devices usually (but not always) have switches. Some SCSI devices have automatic ID and termination, using SCAM.

**Caution**    Some external devices will offer a limited number of choices. This lack of choices could cause problems when the chain is full. You might then have to adjust other drive IDs to find a unique ID for the new drive.

If you plan to utilize a SCSI drive as your C drive (this is required if you want to boot from this drive), it must be configured as a bootable drive. You can do this by either specifying the host adapter as the "bootable" SCSI ID or setting the host adapter to emulate a standard AT-style controller.

## Logical Unit Numbers

It is possible to have a single SCSI ID support more than one device. *Logical unit numbers* (LUNs) can be used to provide a unique identifier for up to seven sub-units per ID number. These are used primarily in hard disk drive arrays to create one large logical drive out of several smaller physical drives. LUNs require highly specialized software and are most often found in network servers running Novell NetWare, Windows NT, Windows 2000, or UNIX.

## Termination

Whenever you send a signal through a wire, some of that signal will reflect back up the wire, creating an echo. To *terminate* a device simply means to put a terminating resistor on the ends of the wire. The purpose of this terminator is to prevent the occurrence of this echo. Two kinds of termination are used in SCSI technology: active and passive. Most older (and all SCSI-1) devices use passive termination. Proper termination of a SCSI device requires special consideration. Older hardware can be damaged by improper termination but, more often, lack of proper termination will result in a boot failure or the failure of the system to recognize a device that has been connected to the SCSI chain.

On most devices within a computer, the appropriate termination is built–in. On other devices, including SCSI chains and some network cables, termination must be set during installation. The only absolute termination rule is that both ends of the chain must be terminated and that devices that are not on either end must not be terminated. Most SCSI devices come equipped with some form of termination. For most internal products, jumpers can be set to enable termination and connectors can be attached to cables that lead to one of the two SCSI connectors on an external device. Internal Ultra-SCSI 80 and Ultra-SCSI 160 drives do not have termination options on the actual devices. A termination block on the end of the cable handles their termination.

Most new SCSI host adapters are equipped with autotermination circuitry, which polls the chain and sets the proper termination at their ends (or middles). On older cards, you might have to set jumpers. Check the manual for any SCSI device you are installing for instructions on how to set termination and ID before powering it up.

## Lesson Summary

The following points summarize the main elements of this lesson:

- SCSI was introduced in 1979 as a system-independent means of mass storage.
- A SCSI chain is a series of devices that work through a host adapter.
- SCSI chains can have up to 8 devices, including the host adapter (or 16, depending on the configuration) connected together.
- SCSI chains must be terminated on both ends.
- SCSI is used with many different types of peripherals, including printers, scanners, hard disk drives, and tape units.
- Bus mastering is a method used by SCSI to transfer data independently of the CPU.
- RAID uses several SCSI hard disk drives to provide improved performance and fault tolerance for data storage.

# Chapter Summary

The following points summarize the key concepts in this chapter:

### CD-ROM and DVD Drives

- CD-ROM data transfer rates are based on a factor of 150 KB per second.
- Before a processor can access a CD-ROM drive, the proper drivers must be loaded.
- To run a CD-ROM drive from MS-DOS, the real-mode drivers must be loaded.
- CD recordable technology allows end users to create their own CD-ROM disks using a variation of write-once, read many.
- CD RW (read/write) takes CD recordable one step further with CD platters that can incorporate write-many, read-many.
- DVD is an extension of CD-ROM technology, allowing a much more densely packed disk.
- DVD can be used to store data, multi-media, and full-length motion pictures with multiple soundtracks.

### Advanced Hard Disk Drives

- For many years, hard disk drives were limited to 528 MB.
- There are four ways to overcome the 528-MB barrier: LBA, Enhanced CHS translation, Fast ATA, and DMA transfer.
- EIDE controllers and I/O cards support up to four EIDE drives including hard disk drives, tape drives, CD-ROM drives, and removable disk drives.

### SCSI Drives

- SCSI chains can have up to 8 devices, including the host adapter (or 16, depending on the configuration) connected together.
- SCSI chains must be terminated at both ends.
- Each device in a SCSI chain must have a unique ID.
- RAID uses SCSI drives to provide improved data storage and fault tolerance.

# Review

The following questions are intended to reinforce key information presented in this chapter. If you are unable to answer a question, review the appropriate lesson and then try the question again. Answers to the questions can be found in Appendix A, "Questions and Answers."

1. Name four methods of overcoming the 528-MB hard disk limitation.

2. How do multiple block reads speed up a computer?

3. How many devices can be installed on a SCSI chain?

4. What is the effect of improper termination on a SCSI chain or device?

5. Sometimes the SCSI device driver conflicts with other drivers. What steps need to be taken to resolve the problem?

6. Describe three advantages of using a CD-ROM drive.

7. What are the four steps required to install a CD-ROM drive?

8. Is a 16X CD-ROM drive 16 times faster than a 1X? Why?

9. How would you determine which type of CD-ROM drive to install in a computer?

10. Why would you use the MSCDEX.EXE real-mode driver with Windows 95?

11. Instead of using magnetic energy for storing data, a CD-ROM uses
    _____ technology.

12. Name some possible controller card combinations.

13. What software is required for a CD-ROM drive installation?

C H A P T E R   1 1

# The Display System

**Lesson 1: Monitors** ........................................... **258**

**Lesson 2: Flat-Panel Displays** ................................ **266**

**Lesson 3: Display Adapters** ................................... **270**

**Lesson 4: Choosing and Troubleshooting Display Systems** ....... **277**

**Chapter Summary** ............................................. **280**

**Review** ...................................................... **281**

## About This Chapter

Early personal computers employed text-based displays, offering green, white, or amber characters against a black background. Today the average PC monitor can provide life-like colors and reproduce images of near-photographic quality. In some cases, more compact flat-panel displays have replaced bulky monitors. This dramatic change is the result of radical improvements in monitors and the display-adapter technology that drives them. This chapter discusses how these devices work in unison to provide an acceptable display for applications ranging from simple desktop productivity tools like word processors to advanced graphics workstations that can create life-like animations for big-screen movies.

## Before You Begin

An understanding of the principles of memory, expansion bus types, and expansion cards is essential. If you need a refresher course on these subjects, review Chapter 7, "Memory," and Chapter 8, "Expansion Buses, Cables, and Connectors."

# Lesson 1:  Monitors

In this lesson, we discuss today's most obvious and necessary computer output device: the display screen. For most desktop users, this is a monitor. It is important for the computer technician to understand the basics of how monitors work and how they are adjusted. In many cases, a simple modification can correct a problem; in others, the intervention of a specially trained technician is required. This lesson focuses on traditional monitors, which still have the lion's share of the display device market.

### After this lesson, you will be able to

- Identify the various types of monitors
- Recognize the components of monitor resolution
- Determine the amount of video memory your system requires
- Troubleshoot common monitor problems

### Estimated lesson time: 20 minutes

## Basic Monitor Operation

A monitor operates fundamentally like a TV set, except that it is designed to receive signals from a card in the PC, rather than a broadcast signal. A variety of design factors and the features of a monitor's companion adapter card influence the quality of a monitor's display.

**Caution**    Repairing the inside of monitors is a job more in the realm of a TV repairman than a computer technician. Monitors generally carry warnings that they contain no user-serviceable parts for good reason. Although we discuss the inner workings of monitors in this chapter, do not take this as an invitation to probe inside them because of the high risk of serious electrical shock.

### The CRT

The CRT (cathode-ray tube) is the main component of a traditional monitor. The rear of the CRT holds a cylinder that contains one or more *electron guns*. Most color monitors have three guns in back—one for each of the colors red, green, and blue. This combination (usually referred to as RGB) allows the visual production of all colors.

The wide end of the CRT is the display screen, which has a *phosphor coating* (a substance that can emit light when hit with radiation). When active, the guns beam a stream of charged electrons onto the phosphorus coating. When the coating is hit with the right amount of energy, light is produced in a pattern of very small dots. This same technology is used in X-ray imaging, oscilloscopes, and other CRT devices. Similarly, monitors emit X-radiation. There is one dot for each primary color (RGB), and the dots are grouped in patterns close together. The name for a collection of all dots in a specific location is a *pixel* (which stands for picture element).

## Image Formation and Refresh Rates

The human eye perceives the collection of pixels painted at the front of a CRT as a compound image, in much the same way as it interprets the pattern of ink dots in a newspaper halftone as a photograph. The term *persistence* is used to define how long the phosphors on the screen remain excited and emit light.

The image on the screen is not painted all at once. The stream is directed in rows, usually starting in an upper left corner. A series of *raster lines* are drawn down the face of the screen until the beam reaches the lower right, whereupon the process starts over. The persistence rate (how long a given line is visible) must hold for long enough to allow formation of a complete image, but not so long that it blurs the dots painted in the next pass.

These raster passes take place very quickly. The time required to complete a vertical pass is called the *vertical refresh rate* (VRR); the time required to pass once from left to right is known as the *horizontal refresh rate* (HRR). Generally speaking, faster is better. If the vertical rate is too slow, it can cause flicker, which is not only annoying, but can lead to eye strain. The larger the CRT, the faster the refresh rate must be to cover the entire area within the amount of time needed to avoid flicker. At 640 × 480 resolution, the minimum refresh rate is 60 Hz; at 1600 × 1200, the minimum rate is 85 Hz. Both the monitor and the display adapter produce the refresh rate, shown in Figure 11.1.

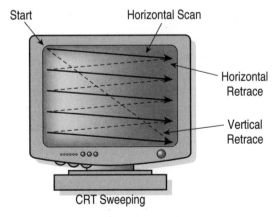

**Figure 11.1**  Horizontal and vertical refresh rates

Early monitors had fixed refresh rates. In 1986, NEC introduced the first *multifrequency* monitor that could automatically adjust the refresh rate to take advantage of the highest rate supported by the display adapter of that time. NEC used the term "MultiSync" to trademark name its line of multifrequency monitors. Today, this feature is standard on most monitors.

---

**Caution**   Do not exceed the approved refresh rate for a monitor, even if the adapter can produce a higher scan of the screen. The result will be an unstable or unreadable image, which can damage a monitor very quickly.

---

The direction and point of contact of the electron stream on the phosphor display are determined by deflection coils coupled with a series of magnetic fields generated by a ring of electromagnets placed around the narrow end of the tube. This collection is called the *yoke,* because it forms a yoke around the tube. Figure 11.2 shows a cathode-ray tube.

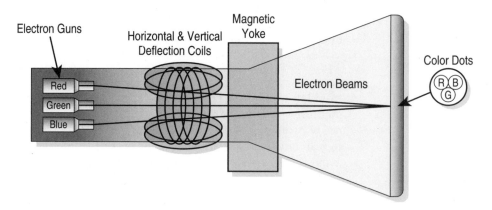

**Figure 11.2** Cathode-ray tube

---

**Note**   The CRT-based monitor has been around for a long time; recently, its successor, the liquid crystal display (LCD) monitor, commonly found on laptop computers, has started to show up on desktops (although its high price has limited its impact on the monitor market).

---

## Screen Resolution and Pitch

The term *resolution* refers to the degree of detail offered in the presentation of an image. The method of measurement varies, based on the medium—photographic lenses, films, and paper are measured using lines per inch, whereas computer monitor manufacturers express resolution in pixels per inch. The greater the number of pixels per inch, the smaller the detail that can be displayed and, consequently, the sharper the picture.

Monitor resolution is usually expressed as a × b where *a* is the number of horizontal pixels, and *b* is the number of vertical pixels. For example, 640 × 480 means that the monitor resolution is 640 pixels horizontally by 480 pixels vertically. Modern monitors usually offer a variety of resolutions with different refresh rates. Price and quality should be compared at the maximum for both, along with two other factors, dot pitch and color depth (the latter is covered in the next lesson).

*Dot pitch* is a term used to define the diagonal distance between the two closest dots of the same color, usually expressed in hundredths of millimeters (see Figure 11.3). For example, you might see .25 dot pitch. Generally speaking, the smaller the pitch, the greater the number of dots, and the sharper the resulting image. The values for dot pitch are generally reflected in the monitor's price, and they are getting smaller as manufacturing technology improves. You should match the monitor's dot pitch and maximum resolution numbers to the needs of the customer, and install a graphics display card that will meet or exceed them.

**Note**   Do not confuse pixels with dots. A pixel is the smallest image unit the computer is capable of printing or displaying. It is usually the first number given in screen resolution: horizontal pixels × vertical raster lines. For example, 640 × 480 is the standard VGA resolution of 640 pixels per line, 480 lines deep.

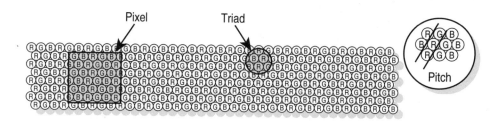

**Figure 11.3**  Color dots on a monitor

# Other Considerations in Choosing Monitors

## Cost and Picture Area

There is a direct link between the size of the picture tube and the cost of the monitor. The CRT is the most expensive part of the monitor. Graphical user interface (GUI) operating systems have increased the demand for bigger screens, to allow for more working area so that users can have more applications open at once or more working room for graphics.

## Bandwidth

When referring to computer monitors, the term *bandwidth* is used to denote the greatest number of times an electron gun can be turned on and off in 1 second. Bandwidth is a key design factor because it determines the maximum vertical refresh rate of a monitor, measured in megahertz (MHz). Higher numbers are better. The lower the resolution, the faster the bandwidth. When comparing products, remember to measure bandwidth at the same resolution for each product.

### Interlacing

Interlacing refreshes the monitor by painting alternate rows on the screen and then coming back and sweeping the sets of rows that were skipped the first time around. This increases the effective refresh rate but can lead to eye strain. Interlacing is found on less expensive monitors, and it should be avoided unless achieving the very lowest initial cost is the client's key concern.

## Power-Saving Features

Because they are the highest consumers of electrical current in the average PC, most new monitors provide some level of power-saving technology. Consequently, VESA (the Video Electronics Standards Association) has established a standard set of power economy controls to reduce power use when the monitor is idle. These are collectively referred to as *DPMS* (Display Power Management Signaling) *modes*.

DPMS technology uses monitors to gauge activity levels of the display. If there is no change in the data stream from the adapter, as set in either the BIOS (basic input/output system) or operating system controls, the monitor is switched to inactive status. The goal is to reduce power consumption while minimizing the amount of time required to restore the display to full intensity when needed. The following table lists DPMS stages, arranged in order from most to least power used.

| Monitor Status | Video Signal Sent | Monitor Activity Level | Amount of Power Saved | Recovery Time to Normal Display |
| --- | --- | --- | --- | --- |
| On | Yes | Active | None | N/A |
| Standby | No | Inactive | Fair | Minimal |
| Suspend | Yes | Inactive | Good | Long |
| Off | No | Inactive | Excellent | Longest (virtually the same as full power) |

Frequently turning a monitor on and off places stress on the components. DPMS reduces the need to use the mechanical switch to turn the device on or off. You should advise clients without power-saving systems in place to turn on the display only when it is first needed and to turn it off at the end of each workday.

DPMS can be configured in one of three ways: using hardware, software, or a combination of both. When configuring a system for a new monitor, check the manufacturers' manuals for recommendations on appropriate settings and setup instructions.

## Tuning the Monitor's Display

In most cases, the monitor must be adjusted for a proper picture when the screen resolution or refresh rate is changed or a new display card is added to the system. The following table lists typical monitor adjustments.

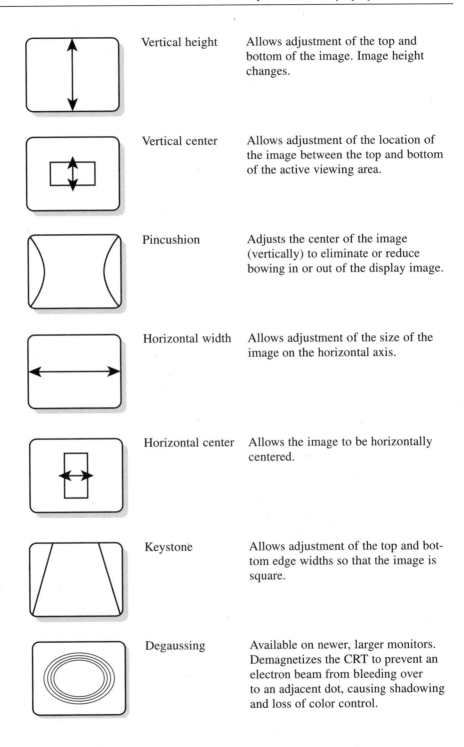

Vertical height — Allows adjustment of the top and bottom of the image. Image height changes.

Vertical center — Allows adjustment of the location of the image between the top and bottom of the active viewing area.

Pincushion — Adjusts the center of the image (vertically) to eliminate or reduce bowing in or out of the display image.

Horizontal width — Allows adjustment of the size of the image on the horizontal axis.

Horizontal center — Allows the image to be horizontally centered.

Keystone — Allows adjustment of the top and bottom edge widths so that the image is square.

Degaussing — Available on newer, larger monitors. Demagnetizes the CRT to prevent an electron beam from bleeding over to an adjacent dot, causing shadowing and loss of color control.

> **Caution**   When using the degaussing button, hold it down for only one or two seconds; longer use could harm the monitor.

Some monitors offer advanced adjustment screws that allow the user, without opening the monitor shell, to tune the settings that are usually available only with interior controls. Adjust these tools only if you understand the process and after you have reviewed the instructions in the product's manual. Any internal repairs or adjustments to the monitor that require opening the shell should be left to technicians with the appropriate tools and training.

> **Caution**   Working inside a monitor is dangerous. The high voltages inside a monitor can cause *sudden death or serious injury*. It's important to realize that monitors contain their high-voltage charge even when they're not operating or even plugged in. A monitor can hold its charge for days. Before you can work safely inside the monitor, such energy must be discharged. Remember that this is often best left to someone who specializes in repairing monitors.

## Monitor Maintenance

Monitor care and troubleshooting are usually simple tasks. Here are some general guidelines to follow:

- Make sure the enclosure is properly ventilated. Covering the opening on the case can lead to overheating. Dust the unit at regular intervals.

- Clean the face of the CRT gently: Follow the instructions in the product manual. In most cases, this means dusting the glass with a clean, soft cloth. Do not use window cleaners that contain solvents on the unit.

- Make sure that all driver settings are kept within the operating guidelines of the product. Never operate at higher resolutions or refresh rates than those specified by the vendor, and stay within the limits of the display adapter.

- Use any automatic energy-conservation features supported by the hardware and operating system. Employ a screen saver on older models that lack energy-saving features. If possible, do not turn the monitor on and off more than twice a day.

- When a monitor fails to operate or produces an improper image, do the following:

  1. Check all cables, including power and display.

  2. Check the front panel controls. Make any appropriate minor adjustments that are needed.

  3. Check and, if needed, reinstall the display drivers. Make sure all settings are within the required limits. Reinstall by returning to a plain 16-color, VGA display mode and adding resolution; then increase the refresh rate.

4. Try another display adapter. If the problem is still unresolved, try another computer.

5. If the monitor still shows problems, refer to a specialist for further tests.

## Lesson Summary

The following points summarize the main elements of this lesson:

- The CRT is the main component of a traditional monitor.

- Price, screen size, resolution, and refresh rate are primary considerations when purchasing a monitor.

- Resolution is a combination of horizontal pixels, vertical lines, and the refresh rate.

- Color depth indicates the maximum number of colors that can be shown.

- The higher the refresh rate, the more subtle the display will appear to the viewer, and the less flicker will be present.

- A CRT has very high voltage and should be serviced only by trained personnel.

# Lesson 2:  Flat-Panel Displays

Flat-panel displays do the same job as CRT monitors but have some fundamental differences that make them more suitable for some environments than others. This lesson shows how they work, their advantages and disadvantages, and the issues involved in adding them to a PC system and maintaining them.

### After this lesson, you will be able to

- Understand how flat-panel displays differ from CRT systems
- Know what is required to install a flat-panel display

### Estimated lesson time: 20 minutes

## Flat-Panel and CRT Displays Compared

Flat-panel displays (FPDs) are thin, bright display outputs that are gaining a foothold on desktops as a replacement for traditional CRT monitors. The most obvious benefit is the much smaller amount of desk space required, because there is no big case housing the electron gun, nor a heavy glass front. Because they don't rely on transitory phosphors to create an image, they are free from flicker (and produce no radiation). FPDs are also two to three times brighter than CRT screens. Since the screen is flat, this means that there is no distorted image at the edge of the viewing area, as there is with curved CRT monitors. FPDs are generally easier on the eyes and don't require a "warm-up" period to reach full color saturation.

With all those advantages, it would seem that only cost (they are much more expensive than CRT solutions) keeps them from sweeping the market. Not so. All technology has its pluses and minuses, and FPDs are no exception.

Take viewing angle, for example. If several people look at a CRT screen at angles up to 50 degrees off the center, they will all experience the same image—unless glare from a bright light source is reflected in someone's eyes. FPDs have limited optimal viewing angles, usually much narrower than CRTs.

Most FPDs also lack the range of resolutions of their CRT-based kin. To drive them, you will need a digital graphics adapter that is tuned to that FPD. The limited choice means an upgrade will usually require the purchase of a new card, and the cost will often be greater than a similar card for a comparable CRT monitor. The following table highlights the differences between FPD and CRT technology.

| Type of Display | FPD | CRT |
| --- | --- | --- |
| Cost | More expensive, few manufacturers; less expensive to operate due to lower power consumption | Wider range of vendors, lower initial cost; high cost to operate due to higher electrical power demands |
| Compatibility | Limited selection of display adapters, fewer supported resolutions | Wide range of display adapters and drivers for most popular resolutions |
| Ergonomics | Flicker-free operation at all resolutions; better brightness and contrast at optimal viewing angles; no noticeable distortion at edges | No fall-off of image quality at reasonable viewing angles; wider range of resolutions to meet user's needs and working conditions |
| Size | Smaller "footprint" on desk, lighter weight | Larger for given screen size, much heaver construction |
| Emissions | Lower radio and virtually no magnetic emissions | Electron gun and phosphors create both RFI (radio frequency interference) and radiation |

# How Flat Panels Work

FPDs create an image made of pixels, just like their CRT counterparts, but they use different technology to accomplish that task. Several different types of FPDs are available today, varying in cost, image quality, and several other factors that affect both suitability to different computing applications and user acceptance.

## Liquid Crystal Displays

Even the most computer-illiterate individuals probably have experience with LCD technology. It is used for a wide variety of inexpensive applications, from digital watches to children's toys, from pagers and cell phones to ATMs. LCDs form an image by using transparent organic polymers sandwiched between a pair of polarizing filters, with some form of back-lighting.

The filters are set at a 90-degree angle to each other. In an uncharged state (no current applied), the crystals are aligned so that light can pass through the top filter. When a current is added, the crystals align to the electric field, blocking the transmission of light. Not all LCD panels are created equal. The greater the twist angle, the higher the contrast and the more responsive the display is to changes in current.

Color light-emitting diode (LED) displays have three adjoining cells, each equipped with a different color filter: one red, one blue, and one green. This allows a display that makes use of the RGB color system.

There are several different types of LCD displays, varying in quality of output and cost. *Passive-matrix displays* (PMDs) are the simplest, and they have been used in calculators and watches since 1970. PMDs are too slow for today's demanding multimedia PCs.

*Active-matrix displays* use TFTs (thin film transitors; TFT also describes this type of display) at each pixel to control each pixel's on–off state. TFT makes up the majority of both laptop and desktop FPDs today. The image is formed by an array of LCDs on a wire grid. The result is a faster response than the passive array.

# Emerging Flat-Panel Technologies

## Electroluminescent Displays

Electroluminescent displays (ELDs) actually emit light, rather than simply controlling the transmission of a back-light source. The light generation comes from phosphors layered between front and back electrodes. There are both passive- and active-matrix variations of ELDs, much like those in LED technology. Right now most ELD products are found in technical applications (medical and defense) as well as ATM machines. Vendors will have to overcome problems in the quality of color and the higher power usage of ELDs compared to existing PC screens for these displays to gain acceptance as an alternative to CRT or TFT products.

## Plasma Display Panels

Plasma display panels (PDPs) work much like the fluorescent lights found in most offices by energizing an inert gas. Phosphor films are used to produce a color image. This technology is used to manufacture very large FPDs. Like fluorescent lights, PDPs are relatively inexpensive to produce, but lower contrast and brightness, as well as higher relative power consumption, have thus far limited their use for PC applications.

# Installing and Maintaining FPDs

In most respects there are few differences between adding and using an FPD and adding and using a traditional CRT monitor. Add the display card to the computer if the existing one is not compatible. Attach the cables, load the proper driver, then make any resolution and color adjustments needed for a proper display. Finally, adjust the brightness and contrast to comfortable levels.

You will need a compatible display card, the appropriate cables (power and display, usually supplied with the product), and drivers for the operating system involved. Be sure the drivers are available for the operating system before promising to add an FPD for a customer. Older operating systems may never have drivers, and some versions of new operating systems may not have enough sales in the right market segments to warrant the added cost to the vendor.

**Note**   Due to the need for special cables, multisystem switches that allow one display to be used with several computers may not be compatible. You will need to take extra care to ensure that the placement of the case and the display are within reach of the cables. Some FPDs are designed to sit next to the computer, and a tower case on the other side of a desk may be too far away.

There is little involved in maintaining an FPD. Wipe the screen with a dry, soft cloth (per vendor recommendations) if the unit becomes dusty. Never use any commercial cleansers or fluids on or near the screen. The unit should be plugged into a properly selected and maintained UPS (uninterruptible power supply) or surge protector to ensure a clean and safe electrical current.

## Lesson Summary

The following points summarize the main elements of this lesson:

- There are several types of flat-panel displays.
- Price, image quality, and compatibility are all factors when considering an FPD for a system as opposed to a CRT monitor.
- Resolution ranges are not as great for FPDs compared to CRTs.
- Most FPD products will require a special digital graphics adapter.
- Passive FPDs are too slow for today's multimedia PC environment.

# Lesson 3: Display Adapters

A monitor or FPD device is only half of a computer's display system; it must be matched to a display adapter (also commonly referred to as a graphics adapter, video card, or video controller). This lesson discusses the different types of display adapters and design issues that affect quality and performance.

## After this lesson, you will be able to
- Identify the different types of display adapters
- Understand display memory and how it affects quality and performance
- Select the right card for a monitor

## Estimated lesson time: 25 minutes

## Evolution of the Display Adapter

The display adapter has gone through several major evolutions as the nature of PC computing has changed from simple word processing and number crunching to the graphics-intensive world of Microsoft Windows and multimedia.

### The First PC Display Cards

The two "official" video cards for the early 8088-based IBM personal computers (the PC and XT) were matched to the limited capabilities of the early monitors. The MDA (Monochrome Display Adapter) offered a simple text-based monochrome display. This adapter produced an 80-character-wide row of text at a resolution of 720 × 350 pixels. Shortly after that, the CGA (Color/Graphics Adapter) card appeared, providing up to four "colors" (actually, just different intensities of the monitor's active color: amber, green, or white). In four-color mode, CGA provided a resolution of 320 × 200 pixels. Using just two colors allowed a resolution of 640 × 200 pixels.

With the release of the EGA (Enhanced Graphics Adapter) card, the IBM PC AT became the first PC with the actual capability to use color. This adapter was an improved version of CGA, offering a top resolution of 640 × 350 with 16 colors in text-only mode, and 640 × 200 with two colors in graphics mode. The EGA also ushered in the era of video conflicts. It was not fully backward-compatible with CGA and MDA, and some programs would display improperly or even lock up the system. The MDA, CGA, and EGA cards all shared the same connection, a 9-pin d-shell, male fitting.

The human eye can distinguish 256 shades of gray and about 17 million variations of color in a scene, the minimum required to produce true photographic realism on a screen. EGA did not even come close. Its aim was to offer the ability to incorporate color in pie charts and other forms of business graphics.

Although the first graphics programs came about to make use of the EGA's graphics capability, serious computer graphics had to wait for better hardware.

## Memory and the Arrival of the Display Coprocessor

A brief digression to explain pixel depth and video memory demands will help you understand what follows. Both the MDA and CGA adapters were equipped with 256 KB of dynamic RAM (DRAM). The amount of memory on a display card determines the amount of color and resolution that it can image and send to the monitor. As the desire for better graphics and color displays increased, so did the complexity of graphics cards, and with them, memory requirements and cost.

Remember that the image on the monitor is a collection of dots called pixels. Each image placed on the screen requires that code be placed in the adapter's memory to describe how to draw it using those dots and their position in the grid. The MDA cards featured a *lookup table* for each character. For MDA adapters, a code number for that symbol and each position on the grid was stored in memory, and the card had a chip set that told it how to construct each of those items in pixels. The MDA and CGA cards each had 256 KB of memory, just enough to map the screen at their maximum resolution. That's why the CGA card had two different modes: the more colors were used, the more memory was required. When it displayed four colors instead of two, the resolution had to drop.

The MDA card was a 1-bit device. In other words, each pixel used 1 bit, valued either 0 or 1 to represent whether a given position on the screen (a pixel) was on or off. To represent colors or shades of gray, a card must use memory to describe color and intensity. This attribute of the display, measured in bits, is known as *color depth*. Color depth multiplied by resolution (the number of horizontal pixels multiplied by the number of vertical rows on the screen) determines the amount of memory needed on a given display adapter.

The adapters that followed the EGA cards to market all offered more colors and, very quickly thereafter, higher resolution. That, in turn, required more processing. The MDA, CGA, and EGA cards all relied on the host computer's CPU (central processing unit). Although that was sufficient in the days before widespread use of graphical interfaces and lots of color, with the advent of the GUI, all that changed.

The new generation of display cards started the practice of including their own display coprocessors. Coprocessors, which have their own memory, are tuned to handle tasks that would usually slow down the PC, and many display cards use bus mastering to reduce the amount of traffic on the system bus and to speed display performance. Video coprocessing is also called *hardware acceleration*. This process uses one or more techniques to speed up the drawing of the monitor image. For example, one or more screen elements can be described without using calculations that have to determine the placement of every pixel on the screen.

These new graphics chips were designed to do one thing: push pixels to the screen as efficiently as possible. At first, the cards that used them were expensive and often prone to memory conflicts with the host CPU. Their growing popularity led to rapid advances in design. In the mid-1990s, a new graphics card was introduced on the market almost every day, and a new processor almost every ten days.

Today, high-performance graphics adapters are the norm. Although there is no longer a mad rush to market, the graphics coprocessor is a key element of fast Windows performance. Next, we return to our review of standards and see how the industry progressed to today's world of high-speed, full-color computing.

## The Advent of Advanced Display Systems

Graphic artists, engineering designers, and users who work with photo-realistic images needed more than a coarse, 16-color display. To tap into this market, which was employing $40,000 workstations, PC vendors needed more powerful display systems. IBM offered a short-lived and very complicated engineering display adapter, the *Professional Graphics Adapter* (PGA). It required three ISA (Industry Standard Architecture) slots, and provided limited three-dimensional manipulation and 60-frames-per-second animation of a series of images. It was also very expensive and a dismal failure in the marketplace.

One reason for the demise of the PGA was the advent of the VGA (Video Graphics Adapter) standard. All the preceding cards were digital devices, but the VGA produced an analog signal. That required new cards, new monitors, and a 15-pin female connector. Developers were then able to produce cards that provided the user with up to 262,144 colors and resolutions up to 640 × 480.

The VGA card quickly became commonplace for a PC display system, and the race was on to produce cards with more colors, more resolution, and additional features. VESA agreed on a standard list of display modes that extended VGA into the high-resolution world of color and photographic quality we know today, known as SVGA (Super Video Graphics Array). The SVGA set specifications for resolution, refresh rates, and color depth for compatible adapters. On Pentium and later PCs, an SVGA adapter is the minimum standard for display systems. The lowest resolution needed for SVGA compatibility is 640 × 480 with 256 colors, and most modern adapters usually go far beyond that. The other standard SVGA resolutions are 800 × 600 and 1024 × 768. High-end systems with large monitors are sold at 1600 × 1200 resolution at high refresh rates.

## High Color, True Color, Photo-Realism, and Multimedia Displays

The SVGA specification for 256 shades of gray is one of the basic SVGA specifications for true photographic reproduction of monochrome images; it's the number of shades that the human eye expects in a grayscale photo. Color requires the same number of shades for each color in the image to achieve the same level of visual realism. To get 256 shades requires an 8-bit memory address system inside the card ($2^8 = 256$). In the early days of SVGA, vendors worked to increase color quality without significantly increasing cost.

In color mode, an 8-bit card can't display all the colors in a full-color picture, so a lookup table is used to figure the closest match to a hue that can't be represented directly. Although this method isn't ideal, it was, for several years, state of the art on desktop PCs. Then, early in the era of the 80486 processor, came the 16-bit SVGA card, which allowed approximately 64,000 colors. More bits require more memory, more processing requirements, a larger lookup table, and a higher cost. These cards were designed to be used with larger monitors, 15 to 17 inches at 800 × 600 or 1024 × 768 resolution. The new systems were too expensive for average users, but graphics professionals and power users generated a large enough market to fuel development.

## Short-Lived Standards

During the early days of VGA and SVGA, three other graphics-card standards were introduced by IBM for the PS/2. Although they never gained significant market share or full support among adapter developers, they did increase the demand for higher resolution and faster performance. The following list highlights these three standards and their role in the evolution of PC graphics standards:

- 8514/A, a 256-color competitor to VGA, with some hardware acceleration capability, offered 640 × 480 resolution in noninterlaced mode, and 1024 × 768 resolution at 43.3 Hz in interlaced mode.

- The eXtended Graphics Array (XGA) offered a resolution of 1024 × 768 in 8-bit (256-color) mode, and 640 × 480 in 16-bit mode (high color). It came with 1 MB of memory and limited bus mastering.

- XGA/2 boosted the high-color mode to 1024 × 768 and increased the available refresh rates.

## True Color Arrives

The SVGA adapters were a stepping stone; the growing popularity of Microsoft Windows and scanners pushed the demand for cards that could deliver photographic-quality color. In the early 1990s, several manufacturers introduced add-on cards that could be attached to SVGA cards to deliver 16.7 million colors. Soon after, stand-alone products that offered both SVGA resolution and true-color operation arrived. These adapters, known as true-color or 24-bit displays, come with coprocessors and large amounts of memory. In true-color mode, they have 256 shades (8-bit) available for each of three colors: red, green, and blue. By mixing them, the system can display $2^{24}$ colors. Eight bits are used in each of the three color channels. Some monitors use traditional 15-pin cables, and some use BNC (bayonet-Neill-Concelman) cables, with a separate cable for each RGB color, and one each for vertical and horizontal synchronization. The latter are found on many high-performance systems.

True-color cards originally sold for $3,000 or so, but within two years, prices dropped under $800. These cards are now available for $150 or less. To add value, the better cards now have TV output ports that send an NTSC (National Television Standards Committee) signal that can be used to record images from the monitor onto a VCR or TV set. Multimedia cards are equipped with a TV tuner, letting the owner view TV programs on the monitor or watch DVD (digital video disc) movies on a PC. The dramatic cost reduction and added features result from the mass production of the coprocessors—which reduced their cost to the manufacturer—along with the decreasing cost of video memory.

## Video Memory

As mentioned earlier, the amount of memory on a display adapter is a major factor in determining the screen resolution and color depth that the card can manage. Just as with system RAM (random access memory), the video memory must be able to operate at a speed that can keep up with the processor and the demands of the system clock. If the display adapter is too slow at updating the image on the monitor, the user is left waiting or is presented with jerky mouse movements and keystrokes that appear in delayed bursts rather than as typed.

### Fast Page DRAM

Early video cards used *fast page-mode RAM* (FPM RAM), a series of chips that were basically the same as the RAM used on the early PC's motherboard. This memory form was fine for MDA and CGA cards, and even the 8514/A, but with the higher resolution, increasing pixel depth, and faster refresh rates of VGA displays and beyond, vendors sought improved memory models to get maximum performance out of their video coprocessors.

### Video RAM

Enter dual-ported memory in the form of *video RAM* (VRAM). It can read and write to both of its input/output (I/O) ports at the same time. It allows the processor to talk to the system bus and the monitor simultaneously: fast, but very expensive. VRAM showed up in the best cards, but vendors wanted a low-cost option as well. Some vendors just used FPM RAM, leaving the user to discover that, at high resolution, the display was too slow for efficient operation. These cards did sell well in the low-end market, as they allowed the budget-minded user to operate in low-color modes for most tasks, switching only to higher color depth for projects that required high-color or true-color mode. Users who regularly worked in high-color or true-color mode often quickly considered an upgrade.

### EDO DRAM

An alternate is EDO DRAM (extended data out DRAM), which can begin reading a new set of instructions before the preceding set of instructions has been completed. This is a common form of system DRAM that boosts performance to about 15 percent above conventional DRAM.

## WRAM

*WRAM* (window random access memory, unrelated to the Microsoft operating system) is a high-speed variant of VRAM that costs less to produce and boosts performance by about 20 percent beyond regular VRAM. VRAM and WRAM have become the standard memory types for high-end display adapters.

### Synchronous Graphics RAM

The midrange display market makes use of *synchronous graphics RAM* (SGRAM). As the name implies, it is tuned to the graphics-card market, offering faster transfers than DRAM, but not as fast as VRAM and WRAM.

### MDRAM

*Multibank DRAM (MDRAM)* is the final stop on our tour of memory acronyms. It uses interleaving (the dividing of video memory into 32-KB parts that can be accessed concurrently) to allow faster memory I/O to the system without expensive dual porting. It is also a more efficient type of chip that is practical to produce in sizes smaller than a full megabyte. A vendor can save money by just buying the amount needed to actually draw the screen. This saves about 1.75 MB per card for a resolution of 1024 × 768.

The following table lists the standard memory requirements for the most common resolutions and pixel depths used today. As stated previously, keep in mind that the minimum amount of memory for MDRAM is usually less than for other types of RAM. Some graphics cards offer additional memory and even incorporate different types of RAM on the same card. In such cases, some of the memory might be used for features other than merely imaging the picture to be sent to the CRT in pixels.

| Screen Resolution | 8-Bit (256-Color) | 16-Bit (65-KB Color) | 24-Bit (16.7-Million Color) |
|---|---|---|---|
| 640 × 480 | 512 KB | 1 MB | 1 MB |
| 800 × 600 | 512 KB | 1 MB | 2 MB |
| 1024 × 768 | 1 MB | 2 MB | 4 MB |
| 1280 × 1024 | 2 MB | 4 MB | 4 MB |
| 1600 × 1200 | 2 MB | 4 MB | 6 MB |

# Display Drivers

Text-based adapters under MS-DOS didn't need software drivers to interface between the operating system and the image on the screen. Windows, OS/2, and other graphics-rich environments do need drivers. In addition, controls are needed to adjust the refresh rate, resolution, and any special features the card offers. Display drivers, a software layer that marries the card and monitor to the operating environment, handle these needs.

When installing a new card or operating system for a client, be sure to check the manufacturer's Web site for the latest display drivers. You will reduce the likelihood of problems in using the new addition, and you will find that most new cards incorporate setup routines that can make quick work of getting a new display running.

## Lesson Summary

The following points summarize the main elements of this lesson:

- Display adapters have gone through significant changes since the first PCs entered the marketplace.
- SVGA is considered the standard for applications today. The increasing use of graphical operating systems fueled the need for bigger monitors, higher resolutions, and more colors.
- The coprocessor is a key factor in graphics-adapter performance.
- 24-bit cards are required to offer photo-realistic color displays.
- Memory is a limiting factor in resolution and color depth.
- Drivers are the link between the display hardware and the operating system.
- The type and amount of memory have a direct impact on video performance. Less memory means fewer colors, and slower memory types mean poorer performance.

# Lesson 4: Choosing and Troubleshooting Display Systems

Matching the components of the display system to the needs of the computer owner is critical to user satisfaction when upgrading or purchasing a system. Knowledge of the basic steps in troubleshooting a display is the key to making a quick repair when a component fails to operate properly. In this lesson, we set out the basic steps to follow in selecting the right class of display hardware for a client, proper care, and troubleshooting common problems.

### After this lesson, you will be able to

- Understand the basic criteria used to advise a customer about display-system options
- Troubleshoot common display problems

### Estimated lesson time: 10 minutes

## Choosing a Display System

Helping a user choose the right display is relatively simple, despite the variety of monitors and adapters on the market. The display is the part of the system the user interacts with and "sees" the most, and it is a major factor in overall performance. Within limits, the buyer needs to get the best display possible.

One major consideration is the maximum viewable area. For users who will work in only one program at a time, or who don't need high resolution, a basic monitor should suffice. Graphics-intensive applications and multitasking call for larger monitors with faster refresh rates, and display cards to match.

Users who will be using graphics-intensive applications designed for drawing and painting or for CAD (computer-aided design) and games will prefer a fast graphics adapter, usually with VRAM or WRAM and high resolution and refresh rates.

Multimedia systems can benefit from cards that offer TV out (usually in the form of an RCA jack that lets the signal be displayed on a regular TV set using the NTSC format), TV tuner, and hardware DVD acceleration.

The usual trade-offs between cost and performance apply, but less so now than in the days of $3,000 high-end cards. Today, a user can purchase a fast, high-quality adapter for $250 to $300, and an adapter of acceptable speed with true-color display for $150 without the extras and expensive memory types.

Consider offering an FPD, especially if the customer has limited desktop space. Remember that the FPD may require the purchase of a special display adapter.

In recommending a display system, start with your customers' needs, followed by their preferences, and match the two as closely as possible to the available budget. Keep in mind that the display adapter is only part of the equation. Cost can be contained by using a smaller monitor or by accepting slower refresh rates. Cutting the cost excessively can leave clients with a display that does not support the tasks they perform or that might lead to user eye strain from the flicker that occurs at slower-than-acceptable refresh rates for the selected resolution.

## Troubleshooting Display Systems

When MDA cards were standard, technicians had few problems with display systems. If the cable was properly attached and the monitor was working, the user got a picture. Today, the wide range of card options and the mix of resolutions, refresh rates, and operating systems mean that users require help with displays more often.

In spite of the increasing complexity of display systems, most problems can be traced to a few common sources: cables improperly connected or damaged, lack of power, improper monitor adjustment, corrupt or incorrect drivers, and memory conflicts with other components. The following checklist can help you troubleshoot the common display problems you are likely to encounter:

- Verify that both the power and monitor-display adapter cables are properly attached. Failure to attach them properly can lead to no picture at all or to an erratic image with incorrect colors. If the monitor cable has been removed and reseated, bent pins could be the problem. Make sure power is reaching both the PC and the monitor and that they are turned on.

- Make sure that the adapter is properly seated in the expansion slot.

- Boot the system. If you get an image during the power-on self test (POST) but the computer does not load the operating system, suspect memory or driver problems. The same is true if the system repeatedly hangs during Windows operation. Try working in safe mode. If that succeeds, reinstall the drivers and use Device Manager in the Control Panel System utility to resolve any hardware or memory conflicts. (From Start, select Settings, click Control Panel, double-click System, and then select the Device Manager tab.)

- Reset the card to the 640 × 480 resolution in 16-color VGA mode at the 60-Hz refresh rate. If the card works in normal mode, in Windows, at these settings, but fails at higher resolution, color depth, or refresh rates, check the drivers and the capabilities of the display components.

**Caution**    Do not exceed the approved refresh rate for a monitor, even if the adapter can produce a higher scan of the screen. The result will be an unstable or unreadable image, which can damage a monitor very quickly.

If all these enumerated attempts fail, try a different display adapter or monitor or test the hardware set on a different PC to see if one of the components has failed and requires repair or replacement. In most cases, an out-of-warranty card is not worth repairing; a specialist should examine a monitor that has failed.

## Lesson Summary

The following points summarize the main elements of this lesson:

- Choosing a new display system or upgrading components is a matter of matching the user's needs to the available hardware within the budget allowed.

- Price is not the sole issue when buying a display system. The quality of a display is a major factor in the performance and usability of the computer.

- PC display problems can cause a variety of symptoms on a system, from screen distortion to failure of the machine to boot.

- Using a step-by-step approach and walking through possible problem–solution combinations offers a quick way to resolve many display-related difficulties.

# Chapter Summary

The following points summarize the key concepts in this chapter:

## Displays

- The CRT is the main component of most monitors. The slender end of the cylinder contains an electron gun, and the larger end is the display screen.

- Resolution is a measurement of the detail of images produced by the monitor. It is measured in dots or pixels per inch.

- Flat-panel displays are becoming a viable alternative to CRT monitors. Although they offer real advantages in some applications, drawbacks include higher price and limited resolution options.

- The monitor is the primary power consumer in a computer system.

- A monitor can be dangerous and should never be worked on without being discharged first. In fact, in most cases, you should leave monitor repair to a trained professional.

## Video Cards

- The video card is the interface between the expansion bus and the monitor.

- The PGA, VGA, and SVGA monitors each use a 15-pin, three-row, female DB connector.

- Coprocessors are used to speed up graphics-intensive displays.

## Video Memory

- The amount of video memory on a display card determines the maximum resolution and color depth that the video card can provide.

- Several types of DRAM are used for video memory; VRAM and WRAM are used for high-performance displays.

# Review

The following questions are intended to reinforce key information presented in this chapter. If you are unable to answer a question, review the appropriate lesson and then try the question again. Answers to the questions can be found in Appendix A, "Questions and Answers."

1. Describe the three elements that make up one dot of color.

2. What is the advantage of interlacing? Is it worth doing?

3. Should a monitor be turned on and off or left on all day?

4. What is the "standard" type of video card used with today's computers?

5. What is the formula for calculating the required memory for a monitor–video card combination?

6. What does CRT stand for?

7. What are HRR and VRR?

8. Define resolution.

9. What is bandwidth?

10. Why is it dangerous to open the monitor's cover?

11. Name four common sources of video problems.

12. Explain one similarity and one difference between VRAM and WRAM.

13. What is a raster?

14. What type of connector is used for an SVGA monitor?

15. Explain the advantages of a TFT active-matrix display over a passive-matrix display.

C H A P T E R   1 2

# Printers

**Lesson 1:  Printers** .......................................... **284**

**Chapter Summary** ........................................... **297**

**Review** ..................................................... **298**

## About This Chapter

This chapter discusses one of the most important add-ons to the typical PC (personal computer). After monitors, printers are the second most common output devices.

## Before You Begin

It is a good idea to familiarize yourself with parallel ports, covered in Chapter 8, "Expansion Buses, Cables, and Connectors," before studying this lesson.

# Lesson 1: Printers

Printers are considered standard PC components; they are often bundled with computers and sold to consumers as part of a complete package. The most common add-ons, printers are manufactured in several popular forms. Like other devices, each type has unique advantages and disadvantages. This lesson covers all types and aspects of printers.

## After this lesson, you will be able to

- List the various types of printers and their advantages and disadvantages
- Possess a working knowledge of laser printers
- Troubleshoot printer problems
- Identify the differences between parallel and serial printers
- Understand expansion cards and how to use them

## Estimated lesson time: 45 minutes

## Printer Basics

Printers have virtually replaced the typewriter in the contemporary office. The simplest printers are designed for the bargain-seeking home user, and the most complex are designed for production use, producing over 80 pages per minute and offering features like collating, stapling, and duplexing (internal two-sided printing).

When evaluating printers, you should keep the following issues in mind:

- **Printer resolution.** Resolution is usually measured in dots per inch (dpi). This indicates the number of vertical and horizontal dots that can be printed. The higher the resolution, the better the print quality.
- **Speed.** This is usually given in pages printed per minute, where the page consists of plain text with 5 percent of the printable page covered in ink or toner.
- **Graphics and printer-language support.** If the device is used to print graphics, it should support one or more of the popular printer languages, such as Adobe PostScript and Hewlett Packard's LaserJet Printer Control Language (PCL).
- **Paper capacity.** The number and type of paper trays available, the number of pages that can be placed in them, and the size of pages that can be printed all vary widely among printers. Some smaller units hold as few as 10 sheets, whereas high-volume network printers hold several reams of different sizes. Some printers can also be set to automatically choose which tray to use based on the type of paper best suited for a job.

- **Duty cycle.** This is the number of sheets of paper the printer is rated to print per month. It is based on a plain-text page with 5 percent coverage and does not include graphics.

- **Printer memory.** Laser printers that will be used to print complex graphics and full-color images require larger amounts of memory than those that print simple text only. In many cases, this memory can be added as an option.

- **Cost of paper.** Will a printer require special paper? Some printers must use special paper to produce high-quality (photo-quality) images or even good text. Some paper stocks are too porous for ink-jet printers and will cause the ink to smear or distort, causing a blurred image or text.

- **Cost of consumables.** When comparing the cost of various printers, be sure to calculate and compare the total cost per page for printing, rather than just the cost of a replacement ink or toner cartridge.

## Common Printer Terms

You should familiarize yourself with these basic terms used with printer communication:

- **ASCII (American Standard Code for Information Interchange).** A standard code representing characters as numbers, used by most computers and printers.

- **Font.** A collection of characters and numbers in a given size, usually expressed in style name and size, and expressed in points (pts.)—for example, Times Roman 10-pt. bold (one point equals 1/72 inch). Although many people think that bold and italic are variations of the same font, technically they are different fonts. Some printers are sold with limited fonts, such as bold only or no-bold varieties of the typefaces.

- **LPT (line print terminal) port.** Term that describes parallel printer ports on a computer.

- **PCL.** Hewlett-Packard's printer control language for printers.

- **PostScript.** The most common page-description language (PDL). A method of describing the contents of a page as scalable elements, rather than bitmapped pixels on the page. The printer is sent a plain ASCII file containing the PostScript program; the PostScript interpreter in the printer makes the conversion from scale to bitmap at print time.

- **Resolution enhancement.** Technology that improves the appearance of images and other forms of graphics by using such techniques as modifying tonal ranges, improving halftone placement, and smoothing the jagged edges of curves.

- **Portrait.** The vertical orientation of printing on a piece of paper so that the text or image is printed across the 8.5-inch width of the paper.

- **Landscape.** The horizontal orientation of printing on a piece of paper so that the text or image is printed across the 11-inch width of the paper.

- **Duplexing.** The ability to print on both sides of a page. This cuts operating costs and allows users to create two-sided documents quickly.

## Printer Ports

Although some printers make use of serial, SCSI (Small Computer System Interface), and other interfaces to communicate with a PC, most today use the standard parallel printer port or one of its bidirectional variations. Two other common communication methods are the USB (universal serial bus), covered in Chapter 8, "Expansion Buses, Cables, and Connectors," and a network interface.

The standard parallel port uses cable with a 25-pin female connector on one end and a Centronics-compatible D-Shell fitting on the other. You simply connect the Centronics-compatible end of the printer cable to the printer and attach the 25-pin plug to an LPT port on the computer. Although parallel ports are relatively trouble-free, they have some disadvantages:

- The data transfer rate is 150 KB. This is slow compared to network cards and other high-speed interfaces.
- Parallel communication consumes system resources because it relies on the PC's system bus and CPU (central processing unit) for transport and management.
- There are no standards for parallel cables or ports. Although parallel port configurations follow a few common practices, this form of communication remains the source of compatibility problems.
- Parallel cables usually have a maximum effective length of 10 feet. This can be extended by using a booster device, but at an added cost.

## Impact Printers

In the early days of PC printing, the most commons forms of printers were dot-matrix and daisy-wheel designs. Both these designs create an impression by striking an inked ribbon with enough force to place ink on the page. In this, they function very much like typewriters. Except for a few special cases, impact printers (one is shown in Figure 12.1) have been replaced by ink and laser technology.

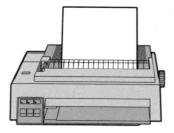

**Figure 12.1**   Impact printer

## Dot-Matrix Printers

A quick trip through a consumer electronics store might lead the average person to believe the age of the dot-matrix printer is over. The home and home office segments of the market are now the domain of the ink-jet and low-cost laser products. Still, in business locations, where the ability to print several copies at once is a driving factor, the loud and lowly dot-matrix still rules. As a result, you must understand how they work and how to maintain them.

Dot-matrix printers form characters as raster images on paper by pressing pins onto an inked ribbon, which then is pressed onto paper. Dot-matrix printers use an array of pins (commonly 9 or 24 pins) that are made of stiff wire. The higher the number of pins, the more dots per square inch and the higher the print quality. The pins are held in a print head that travels on a rail in front of a roller that transports the paper. The pins are controlled by electromagnets; dots are created when power is applied to selected electromagnets in the print head, forcing the desired pin away from a magnet in the print head. The pins strike an inked ribbon, which then strikes the paper. A character is formed as the individual dots are struck. Each character produced by the print head is made up of several rows and columns of dots (see Figure 12.2). High-resolution dot-matrix printers use more dots to form one character.

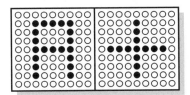

**Figure 12.2**   Dot-matrix letters formed from dots

Maintaining a dot-matrix printer is very simple.

- Change the ribbon.
- Keep the printer clean.
- Keep the print head clean.
- Replace the print head if it fails.

Troubleshooting a dot-matrix printer usually requires a reference manual. There are so many printers on the market that no single guide will suffice to help a computer technician troubleshoot all printer problems. If a manual for a particular printer is unavailable, check the printer itself for instructions (sometimes there are diagrams inside the printer). Usually, a thorough inspection of the mechanical parts will uncover the problem. The following table lists common problems encountered with dot-matrix printers and possible causes.

| Symptom | Possible Cause |
|---|---|
| Printer does not function at all. | No power is getting to printer. Fuse is blown. |
| Device does not print although power is on. | Printer is not online. Printer is out of paper. Printer cable is disconnected. |
| Printer won't go online. | Printer is out of paper. (Check connections.) |
| Paper slips around platen. | Paper is not being gripped properly. (Adjust paper-feed selector for size and type of paper.) |
| Head moves but does not print. | Ribbon is not installed properly or is out of ink. |
| Head tears paper as it moves. | Pins are not operating properly. (Check pins; if any are frozen, the head needs to be replaced.) |
| Paper bunches up around platen. | There is no reverse tension on paper. |
| Paper has "dimples." | Paper is misaligned or the tractor feed wheels are not locked in place. |
| Paper/Error indicator flashes continuously. | There is an overload condition. |
| Printout is double-spaced or there is no spacing between lines. | Printer configuration switch is improperly set. (Make sure it isn't set to output a carriage return or linefeed after each line.) |
| Printer cannot print ASCII characters above code 127. | Printer configuration switch is improperly set. |
| Print mode cannot be changed. | Printer configuration switch is improperly set. |

## Ink-Jet Printers

Run the Inkjet video located in the Demos folder on the CD accompanying this book to view a presentation of ink-jet printers.

Ink-jet printers have replaced dot-matrix printers in the low-end market and thermal wax printers (not covered in the exam) in the low-end color market. Many computer manufacturers and large computer stores offer an ink-jet printer as part of a computer system package deal.

Ink-jet printers spray ink onto paper to form images. They produce good-quality printing and—compared to dot-matrix and wax printers—they are relatively fast. They also require little maintenance beyond cleaning and ink cartridge replacement. Their ability to easily produce color as well as standard black-and-white images makes them attractive.

---

**Important**   When installing a new ink-jet cartridge or replacing the cartridge on an existing ink-jet printer, follow the instructions carefully! The cartridge is not just a simple ink container. It must be properly pressurized, and there are sensors on the unit (small metal plates) that must line up with contacts on the cartridge transport. Read the product manual for details.

---

When recommending an ink-jet printer, consider the cost of printing as well as the cost of the printer itself. Ink-jet cartridges are usually more expensive per page than those for a laser printer.

You might find it cost-effective to equip an office with more than one kind of printer. Many offices have a heavy-duty, high-speed, black-and-white laser printer for text printing, an aging dot-matrix printer for forms and labels, and a color ink-jet printer for graphics. It is also common to find several printers available on a local office network.

If a printer fails to operate, the first step in determining the source of the problem is to decide if the problem lies with the printer or with the computer. The best place to start is at the printer, with a visual inspection. Look for simple issues, like a tray out of paper or a paper jam. Most printers have either a light-emitting diode (LED) panel or lights that warn of common problems.

If visual inspection of the printer does not turn up an obvious fault, proceed to the printer's self-test program. In most cases, you can initiate this routine by holding down a specified combination of control keys on the printer (check the owner's manual for diagnostic procedures) while you turn it on. If a test page prints successfully, the problem is most likely associated with the computer, the cabling, or the network. The following table lists some typical problems encountered with ink-jet printers and possible causes.

| Symptom | Possible Cause |
| --- | --- |
| Power is on but device does not print. | Printer is not online. Printer is out of paper. |
| Printer won't go online after user has replaced ink cartridge. | Cartridge is installed incorrectly. Printer cable is disconnected. |
| Printer is plugged in, but all indicator lights are off and the printer appears to be dead. | Check the drive mechanisms and motors for signs of binding. They might need to be replaced. Fuse is blown. (Check the power supply's fuse and replace with one of the same type and rating, if necessary.) |
| Print head does not print. | Ink reservoirs are empty. (Check the ink supply and replace the ink cartridge, as necessary.) |

*(continued)*

*(continued)*

| Symptom | Possible Cause |
|---------|----------------|
| Paper does not advance. | Paper-handling hardware is jammed. (Check the Control Panel to confirm that the printer is online. If so, you will need to inspect the paper-handling motor and gear train. You can do this by setting the printer offline and pressing the form-feed button.) |

# Laser Printers

Run the Laser video located in the Demos folder on the CD accompanying this book to view a presentation of laser printers.

The laser printer has become the dominant form of computer output device, with models ranging from personal, low-volume, desktop printers to behemoths that fill half a room and serve hundreds of users, churning out reams of pages every day.

All laser printers follow one basic engine design, similar to the one used in most office copiers. They are nonimpact devices that precisely place a fine plastic powder (the toner) on paper. Although they cost more to purchase than most ink-jet printers, they are much cheaper to operate per page, and the "ink" is permanent. (Most ink-jet images are, at best, water-resistant.)

## Primary Components of a Laser Printer

A laser printer is a combination of mechanical and electronic components. Although the internal workings of the printer generally are not a concern for the average PC technician, you should be familiar with the parts and processes involved in their operation.

### Paper Transport

The paper path for laser printers ranges from a simple, straight path to complicated turns in devices with options such as duplexers, mailboxes, and finishing tools like collators and staplers. All these devices have the same goal: to move the paper from a supply bin to the engine where the image is laid on the paper and fixed to it, and then to a hopper for delivery to the user. Most printers handle a set range of paper stocks and sizes in the normal paper path, and a more extensive range (usually heavier paper or labels) that can be sent though a second manual feed, one sheet at a time. When users fail to follow the guidelines for the allowed stocks, paper jams often result.

### Logic Circuits

Laser printers usually have a motherboard much like that of a PC, complete with CPU, memory, BIOS (basic input/output system), and ROM (read-only memory) modules containing printer languages and fonts. Advanced models often employ a hard disk drive and its controller, a network adapter, a SCSI host adapter, and secondary cards for finishing options. When upgrading a printer, check for any updates to the BIOS, additional memory requirements for new options, and firmware revisions.

## User Interface

The basic laser printer often offers little more than a "power on" LED and a second light to indicate an error condition. Advanced models have LED panels with menus, control buttons, and an array of status LEDs.

## Toner and Toner Cartridges

To reduce maintenance costs, laser printers use disposable cartridges and other parts that need periodic replacement. The primary consumable is toner, a very fine plastic powder bonded to iron particles. The printer cartridge also holds the toner cylinder, and often the photosensitive drum. The cartridge requires replacement when the level of toner is too low to produce a uniform, dark print. Some "starter" cartridges shipped with a new printer print only 750 sheets or so, whereas high-capacity units can generate 12,000 or more pages. Keep in mind that what constitutes a "page" is based on a 5 percent coverage area, less than a standard letter and far below that of a page of graphics or images.

## Photosensitive Drum

The photosensitive drum is a key component that is usually part of the toner cartridge. The drum is an aluminum cylinder coated with a photosensitive compound and electrically charged. It captures the image to be printed on the page and also attracts the toner to be placed on the page.

---

**Important**   The drum should not be exposed to any more light than is absolutely necessary. Such exposure will shorten its useful life. Keep the surface free of fingerprints, dust, and scratches. If these are present, they will cause imperfections on any prints made with the drum. The best way to ensure a clean drum is to install it quickly and carefully and leave it in place until it must be replaced.

---

## The Laser

The laser beam paints the image of the printed page on the drum. Before the laser is fired, the entire surface of the photosensitive drum and the paper are given an electrical charge carried by a pair of fine wires.

## Primary Corona

The primary corona charges the photosensitive particles on the surface of the drum.

### Transfer Corona

The transfer corona charges the surface of the paper just before it reaches the toner area.

### Fuser Rollers

The toner must be permanently attached to the paper to make the image permanent. The fuser rollers—a heated roller and an opposing pressure roller—fuse toner onto the page. The heated roller employs a nonstick coating to keep the toner from sticking to it. The occasional cycling heard in many laser printers is generated when the fuser rollers are advanced a quarter turn or so to avoid becoming overheated.

### Erase Lamp

The erase lamp bathes the drum in light to neutralize the electrical charge on the drum, allowing any remaining particles to be removed before the next print is made.

### Power Supply

Laser printers use a great deal of power and so should not be connected to a UPS (uninterruptible power supply) device. The high voltage requirements of the imaging engine and heater will often trip a UPS. In addition to the motors and laser print heads, the printer also has a low direct current (DC) voltage converter as part of the power package for powering its motherboard, display panel, and other more traditional electronic components.

### Drivers and Software

Most laser printers ship with a variety of software that includes the basic drivers that communicate with the operating system, diagnostic programs, and advanced programs that allow full control of all options and real-time status reporting. New advances in network laser printing allow print-management tools and printing to work over the Internet. A user can send a print job to an Internet site or manage a remote print job using a Web browser.

## The Mechanics of Laser Printing

Now that you know the major parts of the printer, here's a quick survey of how the laser printer works and the components needed to handle each task. (Some of these tasks occur simultaneously in actual printing.)

### Communicating

The following sequence occurs as computer-to-printer communication is established:

1. The operating system sends a request to the printer and is informed that the printer is online and ready to accept data.
2. The PC starts sending data.

3. During the printing process, the printer—if it is able to handle bidirectional communications—informs the computer of any problems encountered while handling the print job so the user can address the complaint. These messages might include an out-of-paper condition, paper jam, or low toner.

4. After the entire job has been sent, the printer acknowledges the receipt of all data and waits for the next request.

Many printers can store more than one job, and network printers often have hard disk drives that can hold common jobs to allow the printer to print without being connected to a PC.

## Warming Up

The printer might delay accepting the job or printing the first page while it warms up its rollers and the imaging drum.

## Raster Image Processing

The image (text and graphics) to be made is converted into a series of raster lines that can be drawn much the same way as the image is formed on the PC's monitor. The data is stored in memory, waiting for the send command.

## Paper Feeding

The printer moves a sheet of paper from the proper tray onto a series of rollers, through the imaging and fixing areas, and to the output hopper.

## Drum Cleaning and Charging

Any residual toner from past jobs is scraped from the printer's photosensitive drum. A fine wire (the primary corona) produces a negative electrical charge across the entire face of the drum. The image is set in raster lines as a series of fine dots on the drum.

## Imaging the Drum

The information from the raster image processor is read from memory and sent to the print engine one line at a time. The laser sets a positive charge in the areas of the image to be filled with toner.

## Transferring Toner to the Drum

A film of fine plastic powder is placed on the toner transfer roller, which is turning close to the photosensitive drum. This toner is then attracted to the positively charged areas of the drum.

## Transferring Toner to the Paper

The corona wire places a positive electrical charge on the paper as it moves close to the drum. The toner is attracted to the page, forming an image.

## Fusing the Toner

The page passes through a pair of rollers. The roller on the side toward the toner that has been placed on the page is heated just enough to melt the plastic toner particles onto the page without smearing. The roller on the other side supplies the needed pressure.

## Finishing and Output

After the toner has been fused to the paper, the next step is usually to transport the page to the output tray. However, if other options—such as a duplexer or collator—are available, the page might be routed through a separate path, based on the options for the current print job, and then sent to the output tray. Figure 12.3 shows the process of laser printing.

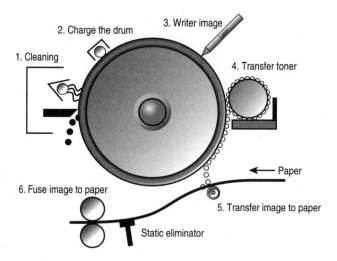

**Figure 12.3**   The laser printing process

## Laser Printer Resolution

The quality of a laser printer is directly related to its resolution, given in dpi. Horizontal resolution is determined by how fine a line can be focused on the drum by the laser (the number of dpi across the page); vertical resolution is based on the increment by which the photosensitive drum is turned for each pass of the raster line.

In most cases, resolution is given as a single number, indicating that both the horizontal and vertical increments are the same. The first laser printers provided 300 dpi resolution; printers today commonly provide 600 and 1200 dpi. The higher the number, the sharper the detail and the more memory required to image the page. In general, the human eye cannot distinguish between 600 dpi and 1200 dpi text on bond paper, but the higher resolution does benefit images and drawings by providing a smoother transition between tones and curved lines.

**Tip**  Many laser printers offer a "toner saver" setting that uses a lower-resolution draft mode, thereby extending the life of a toner cartridge by placing less toner on each page.

## Troubleshooting Laser Printer Problems

Properly installed laser printers are quite reliable when operated and maintained within the guidelines set by the manufacturer. Still, given the combination of mechanical parts, the variety of steps in printing, and the innovative ways some users use the printer, problems do occur. The following table lists a few problems that can be encountered with laser printing and their possible causes.

| Symptom | Possible Cause |
|---|---|
| Ghost images appear at regular intervals on the printed page. | Photosensitive drum is not fully discharged. Previous images used too much toner, and the supply of charged toner is either insufficient or not adequately charged to transfer to the drum. |
| Light ghosting appears on pages. | Previous page(s) used too much toner; therefore, the drum could not be properly charged for the image (called *developer starvation*). |
| Dark ghosting appears on pages. | Drum is damaged. |
| Page is completely black. | Primary corona, laser scanning module, or main central board has failed. |
| Random black spots or streaks appear on page. | Drum was improperly cleaned; residual particles remain on drum. |
| Marks appear on every page. | Drum is damaged and must be replaced. |
| Printing is too light (appears in a column-like streak). | Toner is low. |
| Memory overflow error. | Not enough RAM—printing resolution too high. |
| Characters are incomplete. | Print density is incorrect. (Adjust the darkness setting on the toner cartridge.) |
| Mass of melted plastic is spit out. | Wrong transparency material is used (see section on transparency, later in this lesson). |
| Pages are creased. | Paper type is incorrect. |
| Characters are warped, overprinted, or poorly formed. | There is a problem with the paper or other media or with the hardware. (For media, avoid paper that is too rough or too smooth. Paper that is too rough interferes with fusing of characters and their definition. If the paper is too smooth, it can feed improperly, causing distorted or overwritten characters. For hardware, run the self-test to check for connectivity and configuration problems.) |

*(continued)*

*(continued)*

| Symptom | Possible Cause |
|---|---|
| After clearing a paper jam from the tray, printer still indicates a paper jam. | Printer has not reset. (Open and close the cover.) |
| Paper continues to jam. | Problem with the pickup area, turning area, and registration (alignment) area. (Look for worn parts or debris.) |

## Ghosting

The term *ghosting* is used to describe unwanted images that are produced on the printed page at regular intervals. This usually occurs when the drum is not fully discharging or is being saturated with excess toner. One remedy is to print one or two totally black pages; this will pull the toner off the drum and onto the paper. If the problem persists, try using a new toner cartridge (if the toner is part of the cartridge assembly). If those steps fail, the printer will require servicing by a trained technician who is able to adjust the internal settings that regulate toner levels during printing.

## Printing on Transparencies

When printing on transparencies, use only materials approved for laser printers. Laser printers generate far more heat than other types of printers, and using the wrong material can cause serious damage.

**Caution**    Check the printer documentation before printing transparencies with a laser printer. Unauthorized materials could melt and damage a laser printer's internal components. Be sure that the media is placed in the proper tray, with the proper side facing up. A mistake here can ruin the printer!

## Hardware Problems

Most laser printers offer the ability to print a page or more of diagnostic and configuration information. If you suspect a hardware problem, print these sheets. Check for status lights, menu warnings, or error messages. The manual should list steps to be taken in troubleshooting common problems that are indicated by the printer's display. The variety of error codes that exist, the result of different options on printers, even from the same vendor, makes a detailed listing beyond the scope of this volume and beyond the skills required for the exam. Refer to the printer's manual for details concerning codes for a given printer.

# Lesson Summary

The following points summarize the main elements of this lesson:

- The three most common printers are dot-matrix, ink-jet, and laser printers.

- Computer technicians can expect to encounter printing problems regularly.

# Chapter Summary

The following points summarize the key concepts in this chapter:

## Printers

- Most printer problems can be resolved quickly by checking for paper jams, expended consumables, or improper use.

- The key components of a laser printer are the power supply, photosensitive drum, eraser lamp, primary corona, laser, transfer corona, and fuser.

# Review

The following questions are intended to reinforce key information presented in this chapter. If you are unable to answer a question, review the appropriate lesson and then try the question again. Answers to the questions can be found in Appendix A, "Questions and Answers."

1. Name the three most common types of printers and describe their advantages and disadvantages.

2. The dot-matrix printer is an _____ printer. Name at least one advantage of this type of printer. Name at least one disadvantage.

3. What are the six steps of laser printing?

4. Which components are usually included in a laser printer's replaceable toner cartridge? Why?

5. What causes black spots to appear on a document that has been printed on a laser printer? How can this problem be resolved?

6. In addition to the cost of the printer, what other costs should be considered when purchasing a printer?

C H A P T E R   1 3

# Portable Computers

**Lesson 1: Portable Computers** .................................. **300**

**Chapter Summary** ............................................ **311**

**Review** .................................................... **312**

## About This Chapter

Portable computers, once a novelty, are now a part of everyday business life. Portable computers work and act just like larger systems, except they are very compact. In this chapter, we look at those elements that make a portable computer unique.

## Before You Begin

Although there are no prerequisites for this chapter, you should be familiar with all aspects of the hardware presented in earlier chapters.

# Lesson 1:  Portable Computers

Portable computers are a growing part of everyday life, both for users and technicians. In general, the A+ technician has a very limited role in repairing these machines. Still, you must understand how to deal with minor problems and answer user questions about proper operation and care.

---

### After this lesson, you will be able to

- Distinguish among the different categories of portable computers
- Identify the unique components of portable systems
- Define the unique problems of portable systems
- Distinguish among the different types of computer cards designed for portable computers

### Estimated lesson time: 50 minutes

---

The category of portable computers includes laptop, notebook, and subnotebook (palmtop) computers, as well as the newest categories, PDA (personal digital assistant) and handheld computers.

## Types of Portables

Portable computers are classified according to size and function. Today there are three basic types of portable computers: laptops, notebooks, and subnotebooks.

The first "portable" computers were often called "luggables." The size of a portable sewing machine, they tipped the scales at 30 pounds. Equipped with a small CRT (cathode-ray tube) display, they were actually a traditional PC in a slightly smaller case.

The real change in portable computers came with the advent of the flat-panel display, allowing the portable to take on the now-familiar slim design. *Laptop* is the term used for the heavier version, usually offering most of the features of a full-fledged PC but with a folding flat-panel display and integrated keyboard. Notebooks are slender devices that often lack the full range of storage as part of the normal configuration. PDAs, a special group of products offering a subset of features including e-mail, schedule tracking, contact records, and limited note taking and Web browsing, are beyond the scope of this chapter.

### Laptop Computers

With advancements in battery technology and the advent of functional, large-screen, liquid crystal displays (LCDs), the first truly portable computers, referred to as *laptops*, were produced in the late 1980s. These units featured integrated AT-compatible computer boards, including I/O (input/output) and video controller functions. Laptops, as mentioned, usually feature a folding LCD display and a built-in keyboard and pointing device. They also use an external power supply and a removable, rechargeable battery. Today's laptops have fairly large (2 GB or more) hard drives, a CD-ROM drive (or DVD drive), and a floppy disk drive (often the latter two are interchangeable plug-ins).

When laptops originally appeared on the market, they were the smallest portable computers made. Today, they are high-end machines that offer features and performance comparable to a desktop system.

## Notebook Computers

Advances in integrated circuit (IC) technology allowed the size of computer components to be reduced even further, and, in the early to mid-1980s, the *notebook computer* was born. Notebooks are roughly 8.75 inches deep × 11 inches wide × 2.25 inches thick, and designers are working to decrease the size and power consumption of these units even further. The reduction in size comes at a cost, however, and notebooks typically have smaller and less capable displays and keyboards than laptops. A wide variety of specialty items have appeared on the market designed to overcome some of the notebook's shortcomings. Docking ports are one such item.

## Docking Ports

*Docking ports* (also known as docking stations) are specialized cases into which an entire notebook computer can be inserted. This allows the notebook to be connected to desktop I/O devices such as full-sized keyboards, CRT monitors, and network connections. At minimum, a docking station provides an alternating current (AC) power source for the notebook. Docking stations are highly proprietary items designed for use with specific computer models. They are handy for the user who wants to maintain only one computer system and avoid the necessity of transferring information between two systems. With a docking port and a well-equipped notebook computer, it is possible to have the best of both worlds.

It is not necessary to have a docking port to use a portable computer with a full-sized keyboard, pointing device, and monitor. Most portables have standard connectors for these peripherals. However, be aware that you might have to connect the devices before booting up the computer.

## Subnotebook (Palmtop) Computers

Even smaller than the notebook computers are *subnotebook* computers, also known as *palmtops* or *handhelds*. These tiny systems are 7 inches wide × 4 inches deep × 1 inch high. Due to their size, they are rather limited in function. Keyboards, for example, are too small to permit touch-typing. With notebooks decreasing in cost and weight, palmtops have been losing market share and popularity.

# Computer Cards

To provide laptop and notebook computers with the same expandability associated with desktop computers, the PCMCIA (Personal Computer Memory Card International Association) established several standards for credit-card-sized expansion boards that fit into small slots on these smaller machines. These expansion boards are now commonly referred to as PC Cards. The PCMCIA standards have revolutionized mobile personal computers, providing them with the ability to add memory expansion cards, network interface cards (NICs), SCSI (Small Computer System Interface) devices, communication hardware (for instance, modems and faxes), and many other devices that were previously unavailable to laptop and notebook computer users.

Compatibility problems surfaced along with the development of the PC Card for portable computers. To overcome these incompatibilities, PCMCIA standards were created. The following table outlines the four PCMCIA types and their guidelines.

| Type | Standard Description |
|------|----------------------|
| Type I | This original computer-card standard is now referred to as the Type I standard. These slots work only with memory expansion cards. Type I cards are 3.3 mm thick. |
| Type II | Type II cards support most types of expansion devices (like communication hardware) or network adapters. Type II can accommodate cards that are 5 mm thick. |
| Type III | Type III slots are primarily for computers with removable hard disk drives. This standard was introduced in 1992. They are 10.5 mm thick; however, they are compatible with Type I and Type II cards. |
| Type IV | Type IV slots are intended to be used with hard disk drives that are thicker than the 10.5 mm Type III slot. |

The PC Card itself is usually sealed in a thin metal case. One end contains the interface to the PC Card adapter (68 tiny pinholes); the other end might contain a connector for a telephone line, a network, or another external device.

PC Card is part of the Plug and Play standard, which means it allows you to add components without first shutting off or rebooting the computer. In short, PC Cards are not configured with jumper settings (because they don't have any) but with software.

# Portable Computer Hardware

Although many components in a portable computer are similar to those of a desktop system, some components are very different. The major difference between a portable system and desktop system is the display screen.

## Displays

Portable computers have a flat LCD screen that is about .5 inch thick. The display is typically the most expensive component in a portable system. Often it is more economical to replace the entire computer than to replace the screen. An LCD display is designed to operate at a specific resolution because the size of the pixels on an LCD panel cannot be changed. On a desktop system, by contrast, the signal output from the video adapter can change the resolution on the monitor, thereby changing the number of pixels on the screen. An LCD panel should be thought of as a grid ruled to a specific resolution. Transistors control the color that is displayed by each pixel. The two major types of LCD displays used in portable systems today (dual-scan and active-matrix) are defined by their arrangement of transistors.

## Dual-Scan Displays

The dual-scan display (also known as a passive-matrix display) consists of transistors running down the *x*- and *y*-axis of the screen. The number of transistors determines the screen's resolution. The two transistors that intersect on the *x*- and *y*-axis control each pixel on the screen.

If a transistor fails, the entire line of pixels is disabled, leaving a black line across the screen. There is no way to repair this problem except to replace the display. The term *dual-scan* is derived from the fact that the processor redraws half of the screen at a time, which speeds up the refresh rate a little.

Dual-scan displays are considered inferior to active-matrix screens because they tend to be dimmer. For this reason, portable computers with this technology are becoming rare. They work by modifying the properties of reflected light rather than generating their own light. They are also more prone to ghost images, and it is difficult for two people to see the screen at the same time, because these displays can't be viewed well from an angle. The standard size for this type of screen is 10.5 inches (measured diagonally) with a resolution of 640 × 480. New systems are available with 12.1-inch and larger displays that have a resolution of 800 × 600.

## Active-Matrix Displays

Active-matrix displays are also known as TFTs (thin film transistors). They differ from dual-scan screens because they have a transistor for every pixel on the screen rather than just at the edges. Electrodes apply voltages at the perimeter of the grid to address each pixel individually.

Because each pixel is powered individually, generating its own light and the appropriate color, a much brighter and more vivid picture results. Creating light instead of altering reflection provides a wider viewing angle, which allows more than one viewer to see the screen at a time. The refreshes are faster and the display lacks the fuzziness associated with the dual-scan systems.

Naturally, the cost of having 480,000 transistors instead of merely 1400 (on an 800 × 600 screen) makes the active-matrix screen more expensive. It also requires a lot more power and drains batteries faster. Failure of a transistor causes individual "dead pixels," but this is far less noticeable than the black line caused by a transistor failure of the dual-scan screen.

Larger screens and higher resolutions mimicking that of desktop models have become the standard on high-end laptops. Many portable systems today also include PCI (Peripheral Component Interconnect) bus video adapters. These screens come very close to the quality of a desktop display, but lack some of the fine controls available on fixed units.

## Screen Resolution

An LCD display's resolution is determined as much by the screen hardware as by the drivers and amount of installed video memory. Some machines with less robust screens achieve resolutions of 1024 × 600 (and even more) by using a virtual screen. This is a memory-swapping technique whereby a larger display is held in video memory while the actual screen displays the portion that fits into a 640 × 480 window. The cursor can be used to "pan" the image so that the viewable desktop is within the physical limits of the actual display.

As in regular desktop systems, color depth is affected by video memory. To operate any LCD display in 16-bit or 24-bit color mode, you must have sufficient video memory available. Portables usually have video adapter hardware permanently installed on the motherboard, which makes an upgrade of the display features virtually impossible. Most portables allow connection to an external monitor to increase video capabilities.

---

**Note**  LCD technology is not limited to portables. Large, flat-panel LCD-type displays are now available for desktop computers, although they are quite expensive. (See Chapter 11, "The Display System," for more information.)

---

## Processors

Computer CPU (central processing unit) manufacturers spend a great deal of time and effort on designing chips specifically for the portable market. In desktop systems, cooling fans housed inside the case dissipate CPU heat. There is no room for this solution in a portable system, so manufacturers have addressed this problem in the packaging of the chip itself.

Chip manufacturer Intel's solution to the size and heat problems is the *Tape Carrier Package*. This method of packaging reduces the size, power consumption, and heat generated by the chip. A Pentium mounted on a motherboard using Tape Carrier Packaging is much smaller and lighter than the pin grid array (PGA) used in desktop systems. The 49-mm square of the PGA is reduced to 29 mm, the thickness to approximately 1 mm, and the weight from 55 grams to less than 1 gram.

The Tape Carrier Packaging processor is bonded to a piece of polyamide film, which is like photographic film, using *tape automated bonding* (TAB). This is the same process used to attach electrical connections to LCD panels. The film (called *tape*) is laminated with copper foil etched to form the leads that connect the processor to the motherboard. When the leads are formed, they are gold-plated to protect them against corrosion, bonded to the processor chip itself, and then the entire assembly is coated with a protective resin.

After being tested, the tape is cut to the proper size and the ends are folded into a "gull wing" shape that allows the leads to be soldered to the motherboard while the processor is suspended slightly above it. A thermally conductive paste is inserted between the processor chip and the motherboard, allowing heat to be dissipated through a sink on the underside of the motherboard, keeping it away from the soldered connections. Of course, because Tape Carrier Packaging processors are soldered to the motherboard, they usually cannot be upgraded.

Some manufacturers use standard PGA processors, sometimes accompanied by fans. In addition to having a greatly reduced battery life, these systems can be too hot to touch comfortably. Always check the exact model of processor that is used in a system you intend to purchase, not just the processing speed. You might not want to purchase a non-Tape Carrier Packaging processor for the aforementioned reasons.

## Voltage Reduction

Mobile Pentiums have operated at 3.3 volts from the days of the original 75-MHz chip, but the newer and faster models have reduced the voltage to only 2.9 volts for internal operations, retaining the 3.3-volt interface with the motherboard. This translates into a processor that uses as little as 60 percent of the power of a desktop system.

## Memory

As with desktop systems, adding memory is one of the most common upgrades to portable computers. Unlike desktop computers, which offer only three basic types of slots for additional RAM (random access memory), there are dozens of different memory-chip configurations designed to squeeze memory upgrades into the small cases of portable systems.

Some portables use memory cartridges that look a lot like PC Cards, but they plug into a dedicated IC memory socket. Others use extender boards like SIMMs (single inline memory modules) and DIMMs (dual inline memory modules). In any case, it is strongly recommended that you only install memory modules that have been designed for your system, and only in the configurations recommended by the manufacturer. This does not necessarily limit you to products made by your system's manufacturer, however, because a number of companies manufacture upgrade modules for dozens of systems.

Portable computers use the same types of dynamic RAM (DRAM) and static RAM (SRAM) as desktops and, thanks to advances in thermal management, today's high-end portable systems usually include SRAM cache memory.

## Hard Disk Drives

Except for its size and packaging, portable hard disk drive technology is similar to desktops. EIDE (Enhanced Integrated Drive Electronics) drives are standard in portable computers with the exception of the Macintosh computer, which uses SCSI. Internal hard drives, depending on the size of the system, are typically 12.5 mm or 19 mm tall, and use 2.5-inch platters. As with memory modules, hard drives are also mounted in the system a little differently by manufacturers; this can cause upgrade compatibility problems.

Some manufacturers use a caddy to hold the drive and make connections to the system. This makes upgrading as simple as inserting a new hard disk drive into the caddy and then mounting it in the system. Other systems require purchase of a specifically designed drive, complete with the proper connections built into it. Replacing the hard drive can be much easier in many portable systems than in their desktop counterparts.

The result is that multiple users can share a single machine by simply snapping in their own hard drives. However, because laptops are specialized equipment, any servicing beyond batteries, hard drives, and memory is usually left to specialists or the manufacturer.

The support provided by the system's BIOS (basic input/output system) determines the upgradability of a system. Older systems, particularly those manufactured before 1995, might offer only limited drive-size options. BIOS chips made before EIDE hard disk drives became the standard can support a maximum hard drive size of 528 MB. A flash BIOS upgrade might be available for your system to provide additional drives. Another option for expanding hard drive space is the PC Card hard drive. This device fits into a Type III PC Card slot and can provide as much as 1-2 GB of additional space. External drives are also available and can be connected using a PC Card SCSI host or specialized parallel port drive interfaces—you can use any size SCSI drive you choose without being limited by your system's BIOS.

## Removable Media

Portable systems are now equipped with other types of storage media that can provide access to large amounts of data. CD-ROM and Zip drives are now available, as well as standard floppy disk drives. Just as in desktop counterparts, CD-ROM is becoming standard on portables.

The swappable drive bay is increasing in popularity. This product allows the user to switch one of several types of components in the unit. For example, you might not need a floppy disk drive when traveling, so you can insert an extra battery.

## Keyboards

Portable keyboards are integrated into the one-piece unit and are therefore very difficult to repair or replace. Unfortunately, the keypad is almost always the first component to fail in a portable. The functionality and durability of the keyboard should be an important concern when purchasing a portable system.

Today's portable keyboards are approaching the size and functionality of desktop systems, thanks to the larger screens found on most systems. This has created more space for manufacturers to utilize in the overall design.

## Pointing Devices

Today's portable computers come with built-in pointing devices. Most of these pointing devices are one of three types: trackball, trackpoint, or trackpad.

- **Trackball.** This small ball (approximately .5 inch in diameter) is partially embedded in the keyboard below the spacebar. The user's fingers manipulate the ball. These devices are accurate and serviceable, but they are unpopular because of their tendency to gather dirt and dust, which dramatically reduces performance.

- **Trackpoint.** IBM developed the trackpoint, which many manufacturers install in their systems. It is a small, rubberized button (approximately .25 inch in diameter) located above B and below G and H on the keyboard. The user nudges it in any direction (rather like a tiny version of a joystick) to move the cursor around the screen. It is convenient because the user's hands don't need to leave the keyboard to manipulate the trackpoint.

- **Trackpad.** The trackpad (also known as the *touchpad*) is the most recent development of the three. It is an electromagnetically sensitive pad measuring about 1 inch × 2 inches located in the keyboard below the spacebar. It responds to the movement of a finger across its surface to move the cursor. Tapping the pad simulates mouse clicks (although buttons are also provided). It is a truly innovative device, but does tend to be overly sensitive to accidental touches and taps. It is also sensitive to humidity, so moist fingers can cause unpredictable performance.

# USB Ports

The addition of USB (universal serial bus) technology to portables has made it much easier to add new devices or share them with other computers, like the owner's desktop machine. The hot-swap capability, coupled with the wide range of products (from printers and scanners to Zip drives and modems), makes this a must-have for any new portable. Keep in mind that there are PCMCIA USB cards on the market that can add the functionality to older machines as well. (See Chapter 8, "Expansion Buses, Cables, and Connectors," for more information.)

# Batteries

A great deal of technology has been developed to extend battery life and improve power management in portable systems. However, battery life is still one of the most significant complaints about portable systems. Even though power management and batteries themselves have improved dramatically over the last few years, the power needed to run faster processors and external devices has increased, leaving battery life about the same. Actual battery life depends as much on how the computer is used as it does on power-management technology. Simply put, the more you ask the computer to do, the shorter the battery life. Today, battery life is still an issue with portable system users. Most systems use one of three types of batteries.

## Nickel Cadmium Batteries

The oldest of the three technologies, nickel cadmium (NiCad) batteries are rarely used today. They have a short life and are sensitive to improper charging and discharging. After being charged, NiCad batteries hold a charge very well. However, their life can be severely shortened if they are not fully discharged before recharging or if they are overcharged.

## Nickel Metal Hydride Batteries

Nickel metal hydride (NiMH) batteries have a longer life than NiCad batteries (about 50 percent longer) and are less sensitive to improper charging and discharging. They are also more expensive than NiCad batteries and don't hold a charge as well when not used. They usually cannot be recharged as many times. They are, however, used in most portable systems, especially those at the lower end of the market.

## Lithium Ion Batteries

Lithium ion batteries cannot be overcharged, hold a charge well when not in use, and last longer than the other two types of batteries. They are also proficient at handling the heavy-duty power requirements of today's higher-end portables. Because they are the most expensive of the three battery technologies, lithium ion batteries are usually found only in high-end systems. Unfortunately, these batteries can be used only in systems specifically designed for them.

---

**Caution**    Never install a lithium ion battery in a system designed for a NiCad or NiMH battery. Doing so could result in a fire.

---

Buying a system with a lithium ion battery does not necessarily ensure a longer battery life. Some manufacturers take the opportunity to make the battery smaller because it is more powerful, thereby saving some space inside the computer while delivering the same performance as a NiCad or NiMH battery.

## New Technology

Battery technology has trailed behind nearly all the other advances of the portable system. A battery life of two hours is considered very good even when a system's power-saving features are utilized. Some manufacturers are designing systems that hold two batteries to try to overcome this limitation.

A fourth type of battery technology—the lithium polymer—has been in development for several years, but it has not yet appeared on the market. Lithium polymer batteries can be formed into thin, flat sheets and installed behind the LCD panel. They provide approximately 40 percent more battery life while adding far less weight to the system.

---

**Tip**   All battery types function best if they are completely discharged before recharging. Even lithium ion batteries perform better and last longer if they are discharged before being recharged. You can also store charged batteries in the refrigerator to help them maintain their charges longer.

---

## Proper Battery Disposal

Many people give no thought to discarding exhausted batteries in the nearest trash container, but you should take a more professional approach. Batteries contain hazardous and environmentally detrimental materials. Be sure and check your company policy and recommendations from the manufacturer before disposing of any battery. Failure to do so is both poor practice and an invitation for a fine.

# Power Management

Some components in a computer system do not need to run continuously. The purpose of power management is to conserve battery life by shutting down these components when they're not needed.

Most portable computers include power-saver modes that suspend system operations when the computers are not in use. Different manufacturers have different names for their power-saver modes such as *suspend*, *hibernate*, or *conserve*, but they all usually refer to two different states of power conservation: One state continues to power the system's RAM, and the other does not.

Generally, the suspend mode virtually shuts down the entire system after a certain period of inactivity. However, power continues to be supplied to RAM, and the system can be reawakened almost immediately.

The hibernate mode writes the entire contents of memory into a special swap file and then shuts down the system. When reactivated, the file is read back to memory. The hibernate mode takes a little longer to reactivate than the suspend mode, but it conserves more battery life. In some systems, the swap file used for the hibernate mode is located in a special partition of the hard drive. If it is inadvertently destroyed, it might require a special utility from the manufacturer to re-create it.

A document jointly developed by Intel and Microsoft, the Advanced Power Management (APM) standard, has been, for the most part, responsible for defining the interface (interaction) between the power-management policy driver and the operating system. This interface is usually implemented in the system BIOS.

Another standard currently under development by Intel, Microsoft, and Toshiba is called the Advanced Configuration and Power Interface (ACPI). This standard is designed to place the power-management functions under the control of the operating system. As power-management techniques develop, it becomes difficult for the BIOS to maintain the complex information states needed to run the more advanced functions. Placing power management under the control of the operating system allows applications to interact with the operating system to let it know which of its activities are crucial and which can wait until the next time the hard disk drive is activated.

## Lesson Summary

The following points summarize the main elements of this lesson:

- Portable computers are classified as laptops, notebooks, or palmtops.
- PC Cards provide expandability to portable computers.
- Type I PC Cards are used for memory; they are 3.3 mm thick.
- Type II PC Cards are used for expansion devices; they are 5.0 mm thick.
- Type III PC Cards are used for hard drives; they are 10.5 mm thick.
- Display screens for portable computers are either dual-scan or active-matrix.
- Tape Carrier Packaging is used to make processors consume less energy and put out less heat.
- Good power management is the key to long battery life in a portable computer.

# Chapter Summary

The following points summarize the key concepts in this chapter:

- Early "portable" computers were heavy and usually more worthy of the term "luggable."
- Today's laptops and notebooks have most of the features of a desktop machine in a very compact package—but at a much higher cost.
- A computer technician should know the four types of PC Cards and their uses.
- Batteries and power management are key factors to consider when maintaining portable computers.

# Review

The following questions are intended to reinforce key information presented in this chapter. If you are unable to answer a question, review the appropriate lesson and then try the question again. Answers to the questions can be found in Appendix A, "Questions and Answers."

1. Name the three main types of portable computers.

2. What is a docking station?

3. What is the purpose of PC Cards?

4. Describe the different PC Card types.

5. How do you configure a computer card?

6. What are the two kinds of displays found on laptop computers?

7. Why is heat dissipation a concern in computer-chip technologies for portable computers?

8. With the exception of Macintosh, what drives are standard in a portable computer?

C H A P T E R   1 4

# Connectivity and Networking

**Lesson 1: Networks** .......................................... **314**

**Chapter Summary** ............................................. **331**

**Review** ...................................................... **332**

## About This Chapter

The ability to expand beyond the limit of a single computer in a single office has extended the reach of the PC to global proportions. Two technologies have driven this expansion: computer networking and the global network known as the Internet. While we cover modems and simple Internet connections in Chapter 15, "Telecommunications and the Internet," some of the basic concepts of Internet addressing are covered in this chapter. (The Internet uses the same protocol as many PC LANs.)

## Before You Begin

Although there are no prerequisites for this chapter, you should be familiar with all aspects of the hardware presented in earlier chapters.

# Lesson 1: Networks

A *network* is defined as two or more computers linked together for the purpose of communicating and sharing information and other resources. Most networks are constructed around a cable connection that links the computers. This connection permits the computers to talk (and listen) through a wire. More recently, a number of wireless solutions have become available. Infrared ports, Bluetooth radio links, and other protocols allow a variety of new devices to link with PCs.

## After this lesson, you will be able to

- Define basic networking concepts and describe how a network functions
- Configure and change network interface cards
- Define basic Internet terms

## Estimated lesson time: 40 minutes

## Basic Requirements of a Network

In order for a network to function, three basic requirements must be met: The network must provide connections, communications, and services.

### Connections

Connections include the hardware (physical components) required to hook up a computer to the network. Two terms are important to network connections:

- **The network medium.** The network hardware that physically connects one computer to another. This is the cable between the computers or a wireless connection.

- **The network interface.** The hardware that attaches a computer to the network medium and acts as an interpreter between the computer and the network. Attaching a computer to a network requires an add-in board known as a network interface card (NIC).

### Communications

Communications establish the rules concerning how computers talk and understand each other. Because computers often run different software, to communicate with each other they must speak a shared language. Without shared communications, computers cannot exchange information, and they remain isolated.

### Services

A service defines those things a computer shares with the rest of the network. For example, a computer can share a printer or specific directories or files. Unless computers on the network are capable of sharing resources, they remain isolated, even though physically connected.

## Networking

Next we look at how the basic elements of connections, communications, and services work together to make networks function properly.

- The connections must operate so that any computer can send or receive electrical signals (data) across the physical media that link them.

- Communications must function so that when one computer sends a message, the receiving computer can listen and understand the message.

- Computers on a network must either provide a service to other computers or make use of a service provided by other computers.

## Local Area Networks

A LAN *(local area network)* is a network that covers a limited distance (usually a single site or facility) and allows sharing of information and resources. A LAN can be as simple as two connected computers or as complicated as a large site connecting many computers. This type of network is very popular because it allows individual computers to provide processing power and utilize their own memory, while programs and data can be stored on any computer in the network. Some older LANs also include configurations that rely totally on the power of a mini- or mainframe computer (a server) to do all the work. In this case, the workstations are no more than "dumb" terminals (a keyboard and a monitor). With the increased power of today's PC, these types of networks are rare.

The primary benefit of a LAN is its ability to share. The following table lists some of the benefits of sharing the most common resources on a LAN.

| Resource | Benefit |
|---|---|
| Data | The sharing of data files that reside in a common location makes multiple-user access easier. Also, it's much easier to maintain data integrity when there is a single, central database. Large customer databases and accounting data are ideal for a LAN system. |
| Peripherals | Sharing printers, for example, allows more than one user to send jobs to a single printer. This is useful when there is only one high-quality printer in an office and the entire office needs to use it. It also allows one user to access multiple printers, providing cost savings in hardware and redundant resources in case one device fails. Other low-usage peripherals, such as scanners and plotters, will be better utilized. |
| Software | Sharing a single copy of an application can be cost-effective (many software manufacturers provide site licenses—licenses for multiple users on a server). It also allows easier maintenance and upgrading. |
| Storage | Larger, faster disk systems can be used cost-effectively for easy backups. |

In addition to the ability to share resources, LANs offer many other benefits that include:

- **Resilience.** Regular backups of the entire system greatly reduce the risk of data loss. Copying data to backup servers allows network operations to continue in the event of a primary server failure.
- **Communication gateways.** Low-cost access to fax and Internet connections.
- **Electronic mail.** Cost-effective and convenient communication throughout the network.

## Wide Area Networks

A *wide area network* (WAN) spans relatively large geographical areas. Connections for these sites require the use of ordinary telephone lines, T1 lines, ISDN (Integrated Services Digital Network) lines, radio waves, cable, or satellite links. WANs can be accessed through dial-up connections, using a modem or leased-line direct connection. The leased-line method is more expensive but can be cost-effective for transmission of high volumes of data.

## Types of Networks

There are essentially two types of networks that differ in how information is stored, how security is handled, and how the computers on the network interact.

In a *peer-to-peer network*, each computer acts as either a server (sharing its data or services with other computers) or a client (using data or services on another computer), depending on the user's needs. Each user or workstation establishes its own security and determines which resources are available to other users. Typically these networks are limited in size (15–20 workstations). Microsoft Windows for Workgroups, Windows 95, Windows 98, Windows Me, Windows NT Workstation, Windows 2000, Novell's NetWare, UNIX, and Linux are some software packages available for peer-to-peer networking.

A *server network* requires a central server (dedicated computer) to manage access to all shared files and peripherals. This is a secure environment suitable for most organizations. In this case, the *server* computer that runs the network operating system (NOS) manages security and administers access to resources. The *client* computer connects to the network and uses the available resources. Among the most common server operating systems are Microsoft's Windows NT Server 4, Windows 2000 Server, and Novell's NetWare. Prior to the release of Windows NT, most dedicated servers worked only as hosts. Windows NT allows the server to operate as an individual workstation as well. More than one server can provide services on the network, but only one can be responsible for the security and overall operation of the network.

# Network Topology

LAN design is called *topology,* which describes the appearance or layout of a network and how data flows through the network. There are three basic types of topologies: star, bus, and ring. In the real world, you are likely to encounter some hybrid combinations of these topologies, but for the A+ exam, we focus only on these three.

---

**Note**   The illustrations that follow should not be used as exact wiring diagrams but as sample network designs.

---

## Star Topology

In a *star* network (see Figure 14.1), all devices are connected to a central point called a *hub.* These hubs collect and distribute the flow of data within the network. Signals from the sending computer go to the hub and are then transmitted to all computers on the network. Large networks can feature several hubs. A star network is easy to troubleshoot because all information goes through the hub, making it easier to isolate problems.

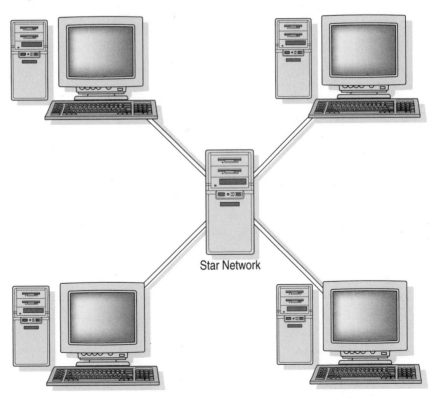

Star Network

**Figure 14.1**   Star topology

## Bus Topology

In a *bus* network (see Figure 14.2), all devices are connected to a single linear cable called a *trunk* (also known as a backbone or segment). Both ends of the cable must be terminated (like a SCSI [Small Computer System Interface] bus) to stop the signal from bouncing. Because a bus network does not have a central point, it is more difficult to troubleshoot than a star network. A break or problem at any point along the bus can cause the entire network to go down.

**Note**    A bus network is often referred to as an *Ethernet network*.

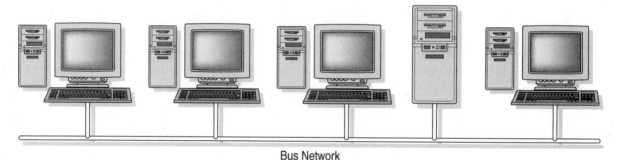

Bus Network

**Figure 14.2**    Bus topology

## Ring Topology

In a *ring* network (see Figure 14.3), all workstations and servers are connected in a closed loop. There are no terminating ends; therefore, if one computer fails, the entire network will go down. Each computer in the network acts like a repeater and boosts the signal before sending it to the next station. This type of network transmits data by passing a "token" around the network. If the token is free of data, a computer waiting to send data grabs it, attaches the data and the electronic address to the token, and sends it on its way. When the token reaches its destination computer, the data is removed and the token is sent on.

**Note**    This type of network is commonly called a *token ring network*.

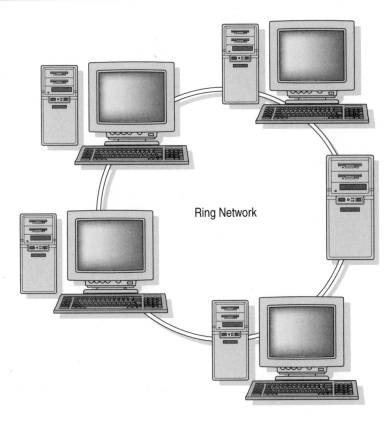

**Figure 14.3** Ring topology

## Network Operating System

The NOS consists of a family of programs that run in networked computers. Some programs provide the ability to share files, printers, and other devices across the network. As previously mentioned, computers that share their resources are called servers; computers that use the resources on other computers are called clients. It is common to run client and server software on the same computer. This enables you to access the resources on another computer while coworkers make use of resources on your computer.

Networking software can be a special program added on to the computer, such as Artisoft's LANtastic or Novell's NetWare, or it can be an integral part of an operating system such as Microsoft's Windows 95, Windows 98, Windows Me, Windows NT, or Windows 2000.

## Network Interface Cards

NICs link a computer to the network cable system. They provide the physical connection between the computer's expansion bus and the network cabling. The low-powered digital signals that transmit data inside a computer are not powerful enough to travel long distances. An NIC boosts these signals so they can cross a network cable. The interface card also must change the form of data from a wide parallel stream—coming in 8, 16, or 32 bits at a time—to a narrow stream, moving 1 bit at a time in and out of the network port (parallel to serial conversion; see Lesson 2 of Chapter 12, "Printers").

The NIC takes data from the computer, packages the data for transmission, and acts as a gatekeeper to control access to the shared network cable. Because the NIC functions as an interface between the computer and the network cabling, it must serve two masters. Inside the computer, it moves data to and from RAM (random access memory). Outside the computer, it controls the flow of data in and out of the network cable system. Because the computer is typically much faster than the network, the NIC must buffer the data between the computer and cable. This means it must temporarily store the data coming from the computer until it can place it on the network.

Installation of the NIC (see Figure 14.4) is the same as for any other expansion card. It requires setup of the system resources: IRQ (interrupt request), address, and software. Most cards today allow connection for either thin Ethernet or UTP (unshielded twisted-pair) cabling. Thin Ethernet uses a round BNC (bayonet-Neill-Concelman) connector, and UTP uses an RJ-45 connector (similar to a telephone jack).

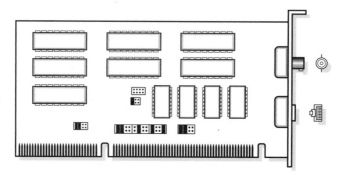

**Figure 14.4**   Network interface card

Installing an NIC is just like installing any other expansion card. If you are installing a Windows 95–compliant Plug and Play card in a Windows 95 or Windows 98 machine, you'll simply need to physically install the card and boot up the computer. The card will be detected and, more than likely, install itself. You might only need to answer a few questions along the way. It requires a little more work to install an NIC in an operating system that is not Plug and Play–compliant. Installing network cards includes the following steps.

1. Be sure to document any changes that you make to the existing computer. This will eliminate any confusion in the installation process and provide future reference in case of problems.

2. Determine whether the card needs IRQ, direct memory access (DMA), or address settings. Remember that you might have to configure these manually, so be sure to check the card's documentation for default settings and instructions for how to make any required changes.

3. Determine whether the necessary settings are available on the machine on which they will be installed. If proper documentation is not available, use diagnostic software such as Microsoft Diagnostics (MSD) to determine settings. Check your AUTOEXEC.BAT, CONFIG.SYS, and SYSTEM.INI files; they might give clues about which settings are already in use.

4. Turn off the machine and remove the cover. Be sure to take all appropriate measures for protection against electrostatic discharge (ESD).

5. Set the NIC's jumpers or DIP (dual inline package) switches as necessary and insert the card.

6. Turn on the machine and run the setup utility provided by the manufacturer. If you are using Windows 95, Windows 98, Windows Me, or Windows 2000, and the NIC is not Plug and Play, you can use the Add New Hardware Wizard in the Control Panel to install the drivers and set up the card. (Remember to document all settings.)

If you are replacing (upgrading) an existing NIC, follow the same steps as just described, with one addition. Before removing the card, document all its settings. Figure 14.5 shows an example of an NIC information card. You can use these cards to create a file documenting the specifics of the cards in your network.

```
Network Adapter Manufacturer: _____

Type of Adapter: (Ethernet, token ring or other) _____

    Model Number: _____

    IRQ setting: _____

    DMA setting: _____

    Speed setting: (if token ring) _____

    Base memory address: _____
```

**Figure 14.5** Information card

**Important** An improperly configured NIC could prohibit network access. Check your settings carefully.

## Network Cabling

Most networks need cables. The three main types are twisted-pair cable, coaxial cable, and fiberoptic cable (FDDI [Fiber Distributed Data Interface]).

### Twisted-Pair Cable

*Twisted-pair cable*, shown in Figure 14.6, consists of two insulated strands of copper wire twisted around each other to form a pair. One or more twisted pairs are used in a twisted-pair cable. The purpose of twisting the wires is to eliminate electrical interference from other wires and outside sources such as motors. Twisting the wires cancels any electrical noise from the adjacent pair. The more twists per linear foot, the greater the effect.

Twisted-pair wiring comes in two types: STP (shielded twisted pair) and UTP. STP has a foil or wire braid wrapped around the individual wires of the pairs; UTP does not. The STP cable uses a woven-copper braided jacket, which is a higher-quality, more protective jacket than UTP.

**Figure 14.6** Twisted-pair cable

Of the two types, UTP is more common. UTP cables can be divided further into five categories:

- **Category 1.** Traditional telephone cable. Carries voice but not data.
- **Category 2.** Certified UTP for data transmission of up to 4 megabits per second (Mbps). It has four twisted pairs.
- **Category 3.** Certified UTP for data transmission of up to 10 Mbps. It has four twisted pairs.
- **Category 4.** Certified UTP for data transmission of up to 16 Mbps. It has four twisted pairs.
- **Category 5.** Certified for data transmission of up to 100 Mbps. It has four twisted pairs of copper wire.
- **Category 6.** Offers transmission speeds up to 155 Mbps.

Twisted-pair cable has several advantages over other types of cable (coaxial and fiberoptic): It is readily available, easy to install, and inexpensive. Among its disadvantages are its sensitivity to electromagnetic interference (EMI), its susceptibility to eavesdropping, its lack of support for communication at distances of greater than 100 feet, and its requirement of a hub (multiple network connection point) if it is to be used with more than two computers.

## Coaxial Cable

*Coaxial cable* (see Figure 14.7) is made of two conductors that share the same axis; the center is a copper wire that is insulated by a plastic coating and then wrapped with an outer conductor (usually a wire braid). This outer conductor around the insulation serves as electrical shielding for the signal being carried by the inner conductor. A tough insulating plastic tube outside the outer conductor provides physical and electrical protection. At one time, coaxial cable was the most widely used network cabling. However, with improvements and the lower cost of twisted-pair cables, it has lost its popularity.

**Figure 14.7**   Coaxial cable

Coaxial cable is found in two types: thin (*ThinNet*) and thick (*ThickNet*). Of the two, ThinNet is the easiest to use. It is about .25 inches in diameter, making it flexible and easy to work with (it is similar to the material commonly used for cable TV). ThinNet can carry a signal about 605 feet (185 meters) before signal strength begins to suffer. ThickNet, on the other hand, is about .38 inches in diameter. This makes it a better conductor, and it can carry a signal about 1640 feet (500 meters) before signal strength begins to suffer. The disadvantage of ThickNet over ThinNet is that it is more difficult to work with. The ThickNet version is also known as standard Ethernet cable.

When compared to twisted-pair cable, coaxial cable is the better choice even though it costs more. It is a standard technology that resists rough treatment and EMI. Although more resistant, it is still susceptible to EMI and eavesdropping. Use coaxial cable if you need

- A medium that can transmit voice, video, and data
- To transmit data longer distances than less expensive cabling allows
- A familiar technology that offers reasonable data security

## A Mixed-Cable System

Many networks use both twisted-pair and coaxial cable. Twisted-pair cable is used on a per-floor basis to run wires to individual workstations. Coaxial cable is used to wire multiple floors together. You should also consider coaxial cable for a small network because you can purchase prefabricated cables (with end connectors installed) in various lengths.

## Fiberoptic Cable

Fiberoptic cable (see Figure 14.8) is made of light-conducting glass or plastic fibers. It can carry data signals in the form of modulated pulses of light. The plastic-core cables are easier to install but do not carry signals as far as glass-core cables. Multiple fiber cores can be bundled in the center of the protective tubing.

**Figure 14.8**  Fiberoptic cable

When both material and installation costs are taken into account, fiberoptic cable can prove to be no more expensive than twisted-pair or coaxial cable. Fiber has some advantages over copper wire: It is immune to EMI and detection outside the cable and provides a reliable and secure transmission media. It also supports very high bandwidths (the amount of information the cable can carry), so it can handle thousands of times more data than twisted-pair or coaxial cable.

Cable lengths can run from .25 to 2.0 kilometers depending on the fiberoptic cable and network. If you need to network multiple buildings, this should be the cable of choice. Fiberoptic cable systems require the use of fiber-compatible NICs.

## Specifying the Right Cable

To ensure trouble-free operation, network cabling must match the system requirements. Cable specifications are based on three factors: speed, bandwidth, and length. Cables are designated with names like 10Base5. Speed is the first number in the identification, representing the maximum transmission speed (bandwidth) in Mbps. This will be 1, 5, 10, or 100. The second part of the identification is bandwidth. It is either base or broad, depending on whether the cable is baseband or broadband. The last part of the identification refers to the cable length or cable type. If the unit is a number, it is the maximum length of the cable segments in hundreds of meters (1 meter is approximately 3.3 feet). In some cases, it can refer to 50-meter increments (1Base5 is five 50-meter increments, or 250 meters). In other cases, it represents cable type: T (twisted-pair) or F (fiberoptic). The following table shows the common types of cables and their specifications.

| Name | Description | Type | Segment | Speed |
|------|-------------|------|---------|-------|
| 10BaseT | Common; being phased out for 100BaseT | UTP | .5 to 100 meters | 10 Mbps |
| 10Base2 | Ethernet ThinNet | Coaxial | 185 meters | 10 Mbps |
| 10Base5 | Thick Ethernet | Coaxial | 500 meters | 10 Mbps |
| 100BaseT | Common | Twisted-pair | .5 to 100 meters | 100 Mbps |

The preceding table covers the basic cable requirements for the A+ networking objective; however, there are many other forms of network connections. For example, you'll find microwave links; forms of radio; and, for small offices and homes, power-line networks (whose NICs have connectors that plug into wall sockets, allowing regular wiring to carry the signal), and telephone-line networks that use standard phone jacks to plug into existing lines. These have relatively short ranges (generally limited to one office or one floor of a building).

# LAN Communication

A LAN is similar to a telephone system with one party line—not everyone can talk at the same time. The difference is that, with a LAN, the speed is so fast that it fosters the perception that many transactions are taking place at the same time. Just like a one-lane road, the heavier the traffic, the slower it moves.

## Ethernet

Ethernet uses a system known as CSMA/CD (Carrier Sense Multiple Access with Collision Detection). It also uses the bus topology discussed earlier in this lesson. The term *carrier sense* means that the network card listens to the cable for a quiet period during which it can send messages. *Multiple access* refers to the fact that more than one computer can be connected to the same cable. *Collision detection* is the ability to detect whether messages have collided in transit (in which case neither message will arrive at its destination and both will be retransmitted).

Fast Ethernet was developed to meet the increasing demands on networks. Fast Ethernet works on the same principles as the original Ethernet but operates at 10 times the speed. Ethernet transmits at 10 Mbps, and Fast Ethernet transmits at 100 Mbps.

### Token Ring

As described earlier, a token ring network uses a token as the basis for deciding who can communicate on the network. Token rings transmit at 4 or 16 Mbps.

## Network Protocols

A network protocol is a set of rules that govern the way computers communicate over a network. For computers using different software to communicate, they must follow the same set of networking rules and agreements, called *protocols*. A protocol is like a language; unless both computers are speaking and listening in the same language, no communication will take place.

Networking protocols are grouped according to their functions, such as sending and receiving messages from the NIC, or talking to the computer hardware and making it possible for applications to function in a network. Early computer networks had manufacturer-unique inflexible hardware and strict protocols. Today's protocols are designed to be open, which means they are not vendor-, hardware-, or software-specific. Protocols are generically referred to as protocol families or protocol suites because they tend to come in groups, usually originating from specific vendors.

The following is a list of standard network protocols:

- **IPX/SPX (Internetwork Packet Exchange/Sequenced Packet Exchange).** The NetWare core protocol developed by Novell in the early 1980s.

- **NetBIOS/NetBEUI (Networked Basic Input/Output System/NetBIOS Enhanced User Interface).** A local area protocol developed by IBM and refined by Microsoft; originally the native protocol for LAN Manager and Windows NT. IBM developed NetBIOS as a way to permit small groups of computers to share files and printers efficiently. NetBIOS is the original edition; NetBEUI is an enhanced version for more powerful networks based on 32-bit operating systems.

- **TCP/IP (Transmission Control Protocol/Internet Protocol).** A set of standard protocols and services. It was developed by the Department of Defense beginning in the early 1970s as part of an effort to link government computers. This project led to the development of the Internet. Because TCP/IP is the foundation of the Internet, as well as the most widely used networking protocol, it is a good choice for networks.

- **AppleTalk.** A networking protocol utilized by Macintosh computers.

- **DLC (Data Link Control) protocol.** The oldest protocol of this group. IBM developed DLC to connect token-ring-based workstations to IBM mainframe computers. Printer manufacturers have adopted the protocol to connect remote printers to network print servers.

Depending on the operating systems and the function of the network you work on, you will probably use more than one network protocol. It's important to get and install LAN drivers that can switch between protocols as needed. The aforementioned protocol information provides you with a rudimentary understanding of basic network techniques and terminology. However, networks are a very complicated subject, and you should obtain additional training resources before installing a network on your own.

## Extending a LAN

The previous section on network cables mentioned some limits to the length of cables. The requirements of today's LANs will often exceed the capability of these cables. The following table lists several devices that can be used to extend a LAN network beyond its normal limits.

| Devices | Description |
| --- | --- |
| Repeaters | The main purpose of a repeater is to extend the length of a network beyond its normal cable lengths. A repeater works like an amplifier to increase or boost the signal to allow transmissions over longer distances. Repeaters are used to connect network segments (groups of computers on the same network). They can also be used to connect segments composed of different media (for instance, a ThinNet segment to a fiberoptic segment). |
| Bridges | Bridges work like repeaters, but offer additional advantages. They can isolate network traffic or problems. Should any problems occur within one segment, the bridge will isolate that segment and not affect other segments on the network, thereby reducing the load on the network as a whole. Bridges can also link segments that are not alike (such as Ethernet and token ring). |
| Routers | Routers provide interconnectivity between like and unlike devices on the LAN and WAN. Routers work like bridges, but can connect networks using different protocols. They are able to select the best route from one network to another network based on traffic load. Routers determine the flow of data based on such factors as lowest cost, minimum delay, minimum distance, and least congestion. Routers are generally used to create a WAN and connect dissimilar networks. |
| Gateways | Gateways provide all the connectivity of, and even greater functionality than, routers and bridges. A gateway usually resides on a dedicated computer that acts as a translator between two completely dissimilar systems or applications. Because gateways are both translators and routers, they tend to be slower than bridges or routers. Gateways also provide access to special services such as e-mail or fax functions. |

# Maintaining and Troubleshooting Networks

Maintaining and troubleshooting networks differ according to the operating system. Therefore, you will need to refer to the operating systems' manuals for detailed troubleshooting procedures. A thorough understanding of network troubleshooting is not a requirement of the A+ Certification program. (The section that follows describes some advanced certification programs that focus on networks.) As an A+ technician, you should be familiar with some generic troubleshooting concepts as presented in the following table.

| Situation | Probable Cause |
|---|---|
| Reduced bandwidth | Called a *bottleneck,* this occurs when the network doesn't handle as much data as usual. A bottleneck is some constraint that limits the rate at which a task can be completed. If a task uses the processor, network, and disk resources, and spends more of its time transferring data to and from the disk, you could have a memory bottleneck. A memory bottleneck might require additional RAM. |
| Loss of data | If data transfers are incomplete or inaccurate, check to ensure that all network cabling and connectors are intact. |
| Slow loading of programs and files | Fragmentation (see Lesson 2 of Chapter 9, "Basic Disk Drives") occurs when the operating system saves, deletes, and moves information. You must defragment the drive. If slow loading persists even after defragmenting, check for memory bottlenecks. |
| Unauthorized software | You must manage software distribution to ensure that users are not loading unlicensed software and computer viruses on the network. One way is to load only software from a centralized location or server and then remotely copy it to local hard disk drives. Depending on the NOS, you can use built-in tools or third-party software to made this task easier than manual tracking. |
| Traffic overloads | A hardware or software failure can bring a LAN to a halt, or the failure can result in more data traffic than the network is designed to handle. You might receive an error message or you might not see any signs other than poor network performance. You must have a system in place that can monitor and manage network traffic. To resolve this problem, you will need to reduce the traffic on the LAN or expand its capabilities. |
| Common mode failures | Some LAN component failures affect other components. This is known as a *common mode failure.* For example, the on-board logic of an NIC might jumble the data format. The NIC will hand the result to the NOS, which might not detect the error. If the NOS puts that data into a file, the file will become corrupt. |
| Network security violations | Entire books address the subject of network security alone. Every operating system is different, and every customer requires a different level of security. First determine the customer's needs, and then find and read the appropriate documentation. |

# Network Certification

This chapter is designed to give you a foundation in networks and a general understanding of network design and applications. Technician certification is a growing trend in the computer industry. The A+ Certification exam touches on network terminology and design; however, some of the most popular networking certification programs are available through Microsoft and other NOS manufacturers. These companies offer many levels of certification; you should consult manufacturer Web sites and community colleges for detailed course contents. Let's take a look at some of the available programs.

## Microsoft Certified Product Specialist

Microsoft Certified Product Specialist (MCPS) certification is designed for advanced end users, computer service technicians, and network administrators who want to demonstrate expertise with a particular Microsoft product, such as Windows NT Server or Windows NT Workstation. It is also a first step toward becoming a Microsoft Certified Systems Engineer (MCSE).

## Microsoft Certified Systems Engineer

The MCSE certification is one of the most sought-after certifications in the computer industry. Qualified MCSEs plan, implement, maintain, and support information systems in a wide range of computing environments using the Microsoft Windows NT Server and the Microsoft BackOffice integrated family of server products. To become an MCSE, you must pass four core modules and two elective exams. For a detailed outline of the MCSE certification track, please visit *http://www.microsoft.com*.

## Certified Novell Administrator

The Certified Novell Administrator (CNA) certification is frequently the first credential earned by NetWare career professionals. CNA training provides you with the critical day-to-day maintenance and management skills you need to survive in the world of Novell NetWare and IntranetWare. The CNA certification is the first step to becoming a Certified Novell Engineer (CNE).

## Certified Novell Engineer

The CNE certification is currently one of the most popular credentials in the field of networking. It can give a tremendous boost to the career of any serious networking professional. Novell's certification curriculum is 50 percent industry-generic—as a CNE, you are qualified to support Novell-specific products as well as non-Novell products.

## Lesson Summary

The following points summarize the main elements of this lesson:

- The three benefits provided by a network are connections, communications, and services.
- The three primary network topologies are bus, ring, and star.
- NICs provide the connection between the computer and the network cabling.
- The three network cabling types are twisted-pair, coaxial, and fiberoptic.
- Network cabling is designated by transmission speed, length, or type.
- Network protocols provide the rules for network communications.
- Networks can be extended with repeaters, bridges, routers, and gateways.

# Chapter Summary

The following points summarize the key concepts in this chapter:

## Networks

- The benefits provided by a network are connections, communications, and services.

- There are two types of networks: server networks and peer-to-peer networks.

- A network topology describes the physical layout of the network. There are three basic topologies: bus, star, and ring.

- To function on a network, each computer must have an NIC and an NOS.

- The three types of network cabling are twisted-pair, coaxial, and fiberoptic.

# Review

The following questions are intended to reinforce key information presented in this chapter. If you are unable to answer a question, review the appropriate lesson and then try the question again. Answers to the questions can be found in Appendix A, "Questions and Answers."

1. Name the three basic elements required to create a network.

2. The primary benefit of a LAN is its ability to share resources. Name some of the other benefits of networking.

3. What is the difference between a peer-to-peer and a server-based network?

4. Name the three network topologies.

5. What type of cabling do thin Ethernet and UTP cabling use?

6. What is the function of a network interface card?

7. Name the three main types of network cabling. What are their advantages?

8. What is the purpose of network protocols?

9. Describe the functions of a router, a bridge, and a gateway.

10. What is the most widely used network protocol?

11. What is the difference between a LAN and a WAN?

12. Your network is showing signs of reduced bandwidth. What is causing this problem?

13. Besides A+ Certification, what are some of the other computer-related certifications available?

C H A P T E R   1 5

# Telecommunications: Modems and the Internet

Lesson 1:  Modems . . . . . . . . . . . . . . . . . . . . . . . . . . . . . . . . . . . . . . . . . . . 336

Lesson 2:  The Internet and Web Browsers . . . . . . . . . . . . . . . . . . . . . . 356

Chapter Summary . . . . . . . . . . . . . . . . . . . . . . . . . . . . . . . . . . . . . . . . . . 363

Review . . . . . . . . . . . . . . . . . . . . . . . . . . . . . . . . . . . . . . . . . . . . . . . . . . 364

## About This Chapter

The rapid advance of the Internet into modern life has made telecommunications activity a key function of the personal computer both at work and home. The laptop user relies on the modem to link the mobile machine to e-mail and the online world. This chapter covers the use of modems, the fundamentals of the Internet, and configuration of a PC for accessing the World Wide Web.

## Before You Begin

This chapter assumes basic familiarity with the Microsoft Windows user interface and PC serial ports. Some experience using the Internet and telecommunications is helpful, but not necessary.

# Lesson 1: Modems

Once an expensive and complicated option, the modem is now an integral part of the modern PC, thanks to the popularity of the Internet, faxes, and e-mail.

## After this lesson, you will be able to

- Define how modems transmit data
- Define the difference between serial and parallel data transfer
- Install a modem
- Troubleshoot basic modem and communication problems
- Set up and test a modem

## Estimated lesson time: 45 minutes

## Modem Basics

A modem is a peripheral device that enables computers to communicate with each other over conventional telephone lines or cable lines, or even without wires. The word *modem* comes from combining the words *modulator* and *demodulator*. In radio parlance, to *modulate* a signal is to change the frequency (FM) or amplitude (AM) of a carrier (fixed signal) by superimposing a code (voice or other information) on top of the signal. The reverse is to *demodulate*, to remove the fixed signal and have the superimposed code remain. For many years, this has been an effective way to communicate over long distances, using both wires and radio waves.

ISDN (Integrated Services Digital Network) devices offer a high-speed digital alternative to modems. Terminal adapters (TAs) link the computer digitally to the telephone line without the need for either complicated handshaking or modulation conversion. This makes ISDN connections even faster (under proper line conditions) than the simple bit transfer rating might imply. Most ISDN products can also use two 64 K bits per second (bps) lines at once, allowing transfers of up to 128 bps.

The following table defines some basic terms used with modem communication.

| Term | Definition |
| --- | --- |
| Baud rate | The number of events, or signal changes, that occur in one second. It was used as an early measurement of how fast a modem could send data, because, at that time, modems transmitted data at a speed equal to the baud rate (1 bit per cycle). Today's high-speed modems use complex signals to send more data; therefore, data transfer can exceed baud rate. The baud rate is limited by the capability of copper wires to transmit signals. |

*(continued)*

| Term | Definition |
| --- | --- |
| bps | Stands for bits per second—the speed at which a modem transmits data. Typical rates are 14,400, 28,800, 33,600, and 56,600 bps. These numbers represent the actual number of data bits that can be transmitted per second. |
| Browser | Software used to explore sites on the World Wide Web using HTTP (Hypertext Transfer Protocol). |
| Bulletin board system (BBS) | Interactive software that offers the user the ability to log on directly to a remote computer to post and retrieve messages and to upload and download files. Some BBSs offer the opportunity to chat live with other members who are online at the same time. The Internet has changed the very nature of BBS software, replacing it with discussion boards. |
| Download | The act of transferring a file from a remote computer (host) to a local computer (client). When downloading, you are receiving a file. |
| DTMF | Stands for Dual Tone Multiple Frequency, the technology behind the tones of a touch tone phone. |
| Internet | A worldwide, online network that links computers by means of the TCP/IP (Transmission Control Protocol/Internet Protocol) protocol. (See TCP/IP, later in this table.) |
| Internet server | A computer and software combination that provides a gateway and supporting services for linking other computers to the Internet. |
| IP | Internet Protocol; the network protocols used to define how data is transmitted on the Internet. |
| IP address | Internet Protocol address; a unique, 32-bit address that identifies every network and host on the Internet. (A host is the TCP/IP network interface within the computer, not the computer itself; a computer with more than one network interface card [NIC] can have more than one IP address, one for each card.) |
| ISDN | A digital telephone connection like a modem that uses digital links and offers speeds about five times that of an analog modem. The ISDN system is a packet system that can also handle voice communication. |
| ISP | Internet service provider; a company or server that provides the connection gateway to the Internet. |
| Logging on | The process of sending the appropriate signals and gaining access to a remote computer over a modem or other remote connection. |
| Modem | A device for converting a computer's digital data stream to and from an analog form so that it can be sent over a telephone line. |
| Offline | Status of a computer that is not connected to another device over a modem or other telecommunications device. |
| Offline reader | A program designed to display e-mail messages or other information that has been downloaded to one computer from another. |
| Online | An active connection between two computers, making possible the exchange of data. |

*(continued)*

*(continued)*

| Term | Definition |
|---|---|
| POTS | Plain Old Telephone Service; a common term that denotes the basic analog phone network as compared to newer digital networks used for packet transfer of data. |
| Protocol | A set of rules that govern the transfer and verification of data between two or more systems. |
| Proxy server | A computer/modem/software combination that manages Internet traffic to and from a LAN (local area network). A proxy server can provide other features, such as document caching and access control. |
| Settings (modem) | Configuration required by the telecommunications software for data to be transmitted. Usually 8 bits, no parity, 1 stop bit (8-N-1) will work. Some BBSs require special terminal emulation, a software configuration that mimics the operation of proprietary mainframe terminals like the VT100. |
| TCP/IP | Transmission Control Protocol/Internet Protocol; the name given to a collection of protocols that were designed for use on the large-scale, mixed-platform environment that became the Internet. |
| Telecommunications | The ability to transmit data over telephone lines to a remote computer. Often abbreviated as *telecom*. |
| Telecommunications software | An application that allows two computers to communicate with each other. Both computers must use compatible software for communication to take place. |
| Upload | The ability to transfer a file from a local computer to a remote computer. When uploading, you are sending a file to another computer. |
| Webmaster | A person who manages a Web site on the Internet's World Wide Web. The Webmaster's duties are analogous to those of a BBS sysop. |

## Communication

Two basic problems arise from using modems to transmit data. The first problem is that, as we saw in Chapter 4, "The Central Processing Unit," computers transfer data using 8, 16, or 32 parallel wires or buses, whereas telephone systems use only two wires (see Figure 15.1). The second problem is that telephone and radio systems use analog signals (based on waveforms), and computers use digital signals, either on or off, as shown in Figure 15.2.

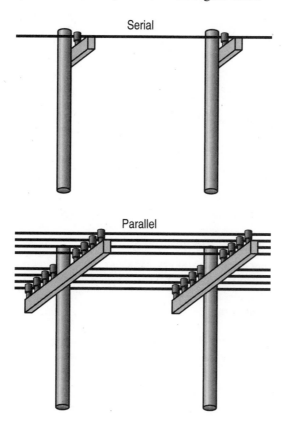

**Figure 15.1**   Serial and parallel communication

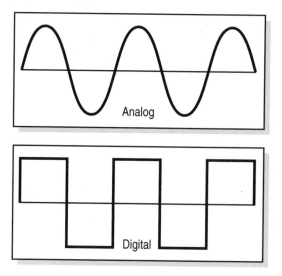

**Figure 15.2**    Analog and digital signals

A modem resolves both of these problems by acting as an analog-to-digital (A-D) converter as well as a modulator/demodulator.

## Serial/Parallel Conversion

Virtually all personal computers use a family of chips produced by National Semiconductor to run serial ports. Known as UARTs (universal asynchronous receiver-transmitters), these chips convert an 8-bit-wide parallel data path to a 1-bit-wide serial path.

The UART has gone through several major changes during the PC era, and there are many different types of UARTs with different functions. The following table lists several of the more common ones.

| Chip | Description |
| --- | --- |
| INS8250 | The original chip used in the IBM PC, the INS8250 operated at speeds up to 56 kilobits per second (Kbps). The 8250A and 8250B incorporated fixes for minor bugs in the original design, but the 8250 series was unreliable at speeds over 9600 bps. |
| 16450 | Designed for 286-based PCs, the 16450 was the first UART that reliably operated at 9600 bps and higher. |
| 16550 | The 16550 allowed use of more than one direct memory access (DMA) channel to achieve improved throughput over the 16450. |
| 16550A | An improved version of the 16550, the 16550A is the only UART installed on today's computers. It adds support for first in, first out (FIFO) communication. This is the only UART that should be installed in current PCs or add-on cards that are used to provide expansion-card-based COM ports. |

Today, virtually all systems are equipped with UART devices fast enough for the current range of modems and other telecommunications devices. That is not true of all older systems. The newer versions of Windows are all very adept at configuring modems for use with the Internet. DSL, ISDN, and cable connections may require custom setup and configuration.

You can easily determine settings and, often, which UART chip is installed in a computer by using the System Information utilities or Control Panel functions that come with the various versions of Windows or the MSDs (Microsoft Diagnostics) that are a part of DOS. Open the Communications Port (COM1) Properties dialog box to review settings (see Figure 15.3).

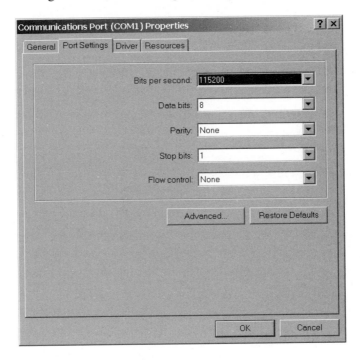

**Figure 15.3**   Communications Port (COM1) Properties dialog box

## Digital Communication

The movement of data from one computer to another over telephone lines is a multistep process. The first step is conversion of the data from parallel to serial form. The digital information must then be broken into uniquely marked packets (this allows the receiving computer to distinguish one byte from another).

## Asynchronous Communication

*Asynchronous communication* is any data transmission that does not link the two devices with a common data clock. This is useful because the length of time between sending a packet and its receipt on the other end can vary between the communicating devices. A signal called a *start bit* is sent at the beginning of each segment, and a signal called a *stop bit* is sent at the end. These let the receiving device note the boundaries (beginning and end) of a transmission packet. Early PC modems were almost always asynchronous devices operating at speeds of no more than 18,000 bps.

## Synchronous Communication

*Synchronous communication* sends data blocks at strictly timed intervals that are monitored at both ends. Modems operating at speeds up to 56 Kbps over standard telephone audio lines are usually synchronous devices.

Communications Protocols are standard "languages" used to transmit data between systems. They involve a wide range of methods for ensuring that the data sent at one end is accepted at the other. The following is a summary of how these protocols work.

1. Before a modem sends any data, a communication link must be established. To do this, the modem sends a series of standardized bytes—called *sync bytes*—to the device it is to communicate with.

2. The modem on the other end receives the sync bytes.

3. The receiving modem perceives that it is receiving sync byte data and synchronizes with the incoming data.

4. After sending the sync bytes, the sending modem adds a start-of-text (STX) character.

5. The data bytes are sent. The data in synchronous transmission is processed in packets or in blocks of fixed length, depending on the protocol used.

6. Each packet ends with an end-of-text (ETX) character and two error-checking characters called CRC (cyclical redundancy check) characters or BCCs (block check characters).

7. The receiver then responds with an ACK (acknowledgment character) if the data is good, or an NAK (negative acknowledgment) if transmission errors have occurred.

---

**Note**   In asynchronous communication, the receiving modem does not respond—it just reads the data and acts on it—unless a timing error is reported. In synchronous modes the receiving modem must respond.

---

## Parity

Asynchronous communication packets have an optional *parity* bit that is used for error detection. The receiving port uses the parity bit to verify whether the data is intact or has been corrupted. There are two types of parity:

- **Even parity.** The sending computer counts the 1s in the data part of the packet; if the number of 1s is even, the parity bit is 0—this makes the total number of bits even. If the number of 1s in the data part of the packet is odd, the parity bit is set to 1—again making the total number of bits even. The receiving port counts the data bits and compares its answer to the parity bit. If the two fail to match, an error is reported, and a request to retransmit the packet is passed to the sending computer.

- **Odd parity.** This works in exactly the same way as even parity, except that the total number of bits must be odd.

The use of parity bits is optional. The quality of data transmission and telephone lines has improved to the extent that parity bits are no longer required. However, if data accuracy is critical or telephone-line quality is questionable, use parity.

## Hardware

Now that we've seen how modems send and receive data, we'll examine the hardware involved.

### Internal Modems

The entire modem and even its serial port can be accommodated on a single expansion card. This configuration offers lower cost than that of an external modem, but it is more prone to compatibility problems with either the on-board UART or the COM port IRQs (interrupt requests).

### USB Modems

Most new PCs offer two universal serial bus (USB) ports, either of which can be used to attach a modem. USB is a hot swap (the device can be added or removed without powering down the PC), Plug and Play interface (see Chapter 8, "Expansion Buses, Cables, and Connectors") well suited to this task. To install a modem this way, usually all that is required is to attach a USB cable between the modem and PC, connect the phone-line cable between the modem and a wall jack, and load the modem-driver software from the manufacturer's configuration disk when prompted.

### External Analog Modems

The original modems used a pair of cups to cradle a telephone handset over a built-in speaker and microphone; in this way, the modem would send and receive tones acoustically, and the telephone handset would relay the tones. Today, the external modem is usually a rectangular box with a row of status lights on the front, a speaker to give audible feedback, and a number of ports on the back. Two of those ports are telephone jacks—one to connect to the wall line and the other to pass the telephone signal to a phone for regular voice conversations when the modem is not in data mode. A third port on the back of the modem is a serial port using a standard 25-pin RS-232 connector that passes data to and from a serial port on the PC.

## ISDN Terminal Adapters

Until about 30 years ago, the North American telephone network was an analog system connecting phones by means of a grid of copper wires. Today, the long line sections (intercity telecom lines) are part of a packet-based, digital switching system, but the final run from the local switch to most homes is the aged copper-wire POTS line.

ISDN is an all-digital phone connection that uses special high-quality phone lines to ensure clean, high-speed data transfers directly to the user's home or business. B channels (bearer channels) carry both voice and data with a maximum speed per channel of 64 Kbps. A companion D channel (data channel) handles signaling at 16 Kbps (or 64 Kbps, depending on service provided by the carrier).

---

**Note**   In the context of ISDN communications, K means 1000; in other computing contexts, K means 1024.

---

ISDN connections do not make use of a modem. Instead, a terminal adapter (TA) serves as the interface for both computers and analog phones served in a location. Most small business and residential customers make use of a TA that has a 25-pin serial connection to attach to a computer serial port. It also provides analog telephone connections for two lines.

ISDN is more complicated to install than a modem and should be set up using the help of a vendor or the local telephone company. After installation, ISDN functions like a high-speed modem, offering not only faster data transfers, but faster connections to remote ISDN providers such as ISPs. Because each TA unit is completely digital, there is no testing of the nature of the remote source by the hardware to establish the maximum connection rate (as with a modem), and links are typically established in less than 3 seconds.

## The RS-232 Port

External modems and TAs communicate with their host computers by means of an RS-232 communications port. The EIA (Electronic Industries Association) developed the RS-232 standard for low-speed data communication; the standard defines a series of signals that are sent between two telecommunications devices to indicate line and transmission status. The following table shows the most common signals.

| Signal | Definition |
| --- | --- |
| CTS | Clear To Send |
| DCD | Data Carrier Detected |
| DSR | Data Set Ready |
| DTR | Data Terminal Ready |
| RI | Ring Indicator |
| RTS | Request To Send |
| RTSRD | Request To Send/Receive Data |

## RS-232 Cables

RS-232 connections can make use of either 25-pin or 9-pin connectors. On many PCs, the end attaching to a modem or TA has a 25-pin connector, whereas the PC has a 9-pin connector. The following table presents the layout and signals for both.

| Description | Pin Outs on 9-Pin Cable | Signal 25-Pin Cable | Direction |
| --- | --- | --- | --- |
| Protective Ground | — | — | — |
| Transmitted Data | 3 | TD | DTE (Data Terminal Equipment) → DCE (Data Communications Equipment) |
| Received Data | 2 | RD | DCE→DTE |
| Request To Send | 7 | RTS | DTE→DCE |
| Clear To Send | 8 | CTS | DCE→DTE |
| Data Set Ready | 6 | DSR | DCE→DTE |
| Signal Ground (Common) | 5 | — | — |
| Data Carrier Detected | 1 | DCD | DCE→DTE |
| Data Terminal Ready | 4 | DTR | DTE→DCE |
| Ring Indicator | 9 | RI | DCE→DTE |
| Data Signal Rate Detector | — | DSRD | DCE↔DTE |

## Telephone-Line Basics for Modems

Modem connections to the telephone service are made using two wires (*ring* and *tip*) that are used in a standard telephone jack. The wires are named for the plug wires used in the original telephone lines by which telephone operators would manually connect two telephones at the phone company switchboard. There are two versions of the telephone jack:

- **Half-duplex.** The RJ-11 has only two wires, which make up one line. Therefore, only one signal can be sent or received at a time.
- **Full-duplex.** The RJ-12 uses four wires to make up two lines; it can be used to simultaneously send and receive.

### Multifunction Modems

Most modems offer some form of fax capability, along with software that adds functions beyond the average, small, stand-alone fax machine. Such a modem is usually labeled a *fax modem*. They can store faxes, both incoming and outgoing, for reference or online reading. Most allow direct faxing of a document from a word processor, generally by using the print command to send the pages to the modem, where they are converted on the fly to the bitmap form used to send and receive fax transmissions. Many programs let you automatically attach a predesigned cover sheet with each fax.

Another addition to the basic data out/data in modem is voice mail. Here, the PC and telephone work just like an answering machine. If the phone rings and the modem does not detect either a data or fax tone, it switches modes and streams a recorded message (the outgoing message). The caller can be prompted to record a message for the owner, and in some cases the modem will even forward a pager call or fax with the message contents.

## Modem Installation

With the advent of Plug and Play technology; Windows 98, Windows Me, and Windows 2000; and the growing popularity of the USB port, installing a modem has become a generally simple process. Summaries of the general installation process for both internal and external modems follow.

---

**Note**  A good technician always reviews the product documentation before setting up a modem to ensure proper operation and the inclusion of all desired features.

---

### Internal Modem Expansion Card

As with installing any card or internal board, remember to take the proper precautions against electrostatic discharge (ESD), and, of course, back up your data before you open the computer case. Follow these steps:

1. Check and document the current IRQ settings and I/O (input/output) addresses in the computer. Make a note of available IRQs and addresses.

2. Configure IRQ and I/O settings for non–Plug and Play–compliant systems: Set the modem to an unused COM port and IRQ.

3. Install the board. Physically install the board in an available expansion bus slot.

4. Install any software. Follow the software setup routine and, if needed, fill in the modem settings and any dial-up connections the user requests for Internet access or for logging on to a remote system. To avoid generating any security concerns, do not ask for or accept account passwords. Show the user how to set that part of the connection personally.

   For older machines running Windows 3.*x* or MS-DOS and non-Internet connections under Windows 95 and later versions, additional work might be required. Here is a sample of how this part of a typical Windows 3.*x* SYSTEM.INI file might look:

```
[386enh]
COM3Irq=5
COM3Base=03E8
```

5. Set up the command set. Any software that will access the modem must know the correct command set to use for that modem. This means identifying the type of modem so the software will use the correct AT commands. When all else fails, try using a Hayes-compatible modem setting.

6. Document your work. Write down all the new settings and changes.

### External Modem

External modems are easier to install than internal modems because they do not run the risk of conflicting COM ports.

1. Connect to a COM port. Choose either COM1 or COM2. Be sure to confirm that the COM port you are using is assigned to the connector on the computer. If the computer is using a serial mouse, that will be using one of the COM ports, too, and this sets up a potential conflict. You can also use COM3 or COM4 if they are properly installed and configured.

2. Plug in the cabling. Connect the modem to its power source and to the computer. You will also have to connect a telephone line (RJ-11) from the wall jack to the modem.

3. Configure the software to select the required COM port and the type of modem (command set) used by the specific modem installed if the operating system or installer does not identify the settings properly.

## Modem Speeds

When installing and using a modem, the primary factor you should consider is speed. The multimedia World Wide Web requires far more speed than the simple data transfers of just a few years ago. Modem speed is measured in baud and bps.

## Baud Rate

As mentioned earlier, baud rate refers to how fast a modem can transmit data. Technically, the baud is the number of voltage or frequency changes that can be made in one second. When a modem is working at 2400 baud, this means that the basic carrier frequency has 2400 cycles per second. Due to restrictions imposed by the physics of the wiring, a dial-up phone line can go up to 2400 cycles, a baud rate of 2400.

If each cycle is one bit, the fastest rate at which data can be transmitted is 2400 bps. However, by using different types of modulation, more than one bit can be transmitted per cycle. Earlier modems used the baud rate to measure their speed (see Figure 15.4).

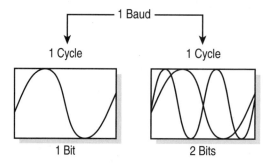

**Figure 15.4**    Baud

## Bits per Second

The actual modem speed, or rate, at which data is transmitted is measured in bps. If a modem modulates one bit for each baud cycle, then the modem speed is 2400 bps. If a 2400-baud modem modulates two bits for one cycle of time, the modem is said to have a speed of 4800 bps (not a baud rate of 4800). If four bits are modulated with one cycle of time, then a modem speed of 9600 bps is achieved.

**Note**    Do not confuse baud with bps.

Modem speed standards are designated by the CCITT (Comité Consultatif International Télégraphique et Téléphonique), an international body that develops fax and modem standards. The CCITT is now a branch of the International Telecommunication Union—Telecommunication Standardization Sector (ITU-T). The following table lists the standard rates designated by the CCITT.

| CCITT Term | Bps |
|---|---|
| V.21 | 300 |
| V.22 | 1200 |
| V.22bis | 2400 |
| V.23 | 1200 bps in one direction and 75 bps in the other |
| V.29 | 9600 |
| V.32 | 4800 and 9600 |
| V.32bis | 14,400 |
| V.32fast | 28,800 |
| V.34 | 28,800 |
| V.42bis | 38,400 |
| V.90 | 56,600 |

**Note**   The term *bis* refers to the second revision of the standard.

## Fax Speeds

Faxes are transmitted using one of several variations of an international standard. These standards are divided into four groups.

### Groups 1 and 2

Groups 1 and 2 are based on 300-baud communication rates. They pertain to analog devices and do not include a modem. Group 1 transmits one page in 6 minutes. Group 2 transmits one page in 3 minutes.

### Group 3

Group 3 is for digital equipment and can use the same modem for data and fax. Not all modems in this group are compatible. Group 3 is comprised of several subclasses, as shown in the following table.

| CCITT Term | Bps |
|---|---|
| V.21 Channel 2 | 300 |
| V.27 Turbo | 4800 |
| V.29 | 9600 |
| V.17 | 14,400 |

### Group 4

Group 4 allows the highest resolution of output to date (400 by 400, up to 1200 dots per inch [dpi]). These speeds are for use with digital telephone circuits, ISDN, or leased lines.

# Information Transfer Protocols

Communication relies on protocols. To ensure clear and clean communication without any errors, the device on each end must follow a very strict set of rules. If either device violates any of the rules, the communication will fail. This set of rules is called the *FTP* (File Transfer Protocol).

All the necessary protocols should be included with the software that came with the modem. After communication is established with the host (usually the computer that receives the call), it can be asked what type of protocol to use. The call initiator can then select the matching protocol before starting a file transfer. Both computers must use the same protocol. There are five basic protocols used by modems.

## ASCII

This protocol uses the standard ASCII (American Standard Code for Information Interchange) character set, just like typing directly from a keyboard. ASCII protocol has no error-checking or compression features. It is simple, uncomplicated, and is used with simple character-based data. It is not a good protocol for transferring program files.

## Xmodem

Xmodem is the next level of protocol. Xmodem includes error detection, which makes it more suitable for transferring program files. It transfers 128-byte blocks of data and one checksum (error-checking) character. The receiving computer calculates a new checksum and compares it to the one transmitted. If they are the same, the receiving computer transmits an ACK. If they are different, it sends back an NAK, and the transmitting computer then retransmits the data block. The protocol uses parity error checking, which is not perfect. If two errors were to occur—that is, if the first error were to change the parity bit, and the second error were to change it back to its original state—the second would cancel the first, and no error would be reported. The result can be a corrupted file or random characters on the display.

## Ymodem

Ymodem is faster than Xmodem. Ymodem transfers data in 1024-byte blocks; therefore, less time is required to verify data with ACKs and NAKs.

## Zmodem

Zmodem shares all the features found in Xmodem and Ymodem protocols. It also adds a few new features, including crash recovery, automatic downloading, and a streaming file transfer method. This is the protocol of choice for most situations.

### Kermit

The Kermit protocol is rarely used today. It was the first of the synchronous protocols for uploading and downloading data to and from a mainframe computer.

# Handshaking

Did you ever wonder what all the noise that occurs when analog modems or fax machines begin to communicate means? The devices are handshaking, or negotiating, the rules (protocols) of communication. Because all modems and computers are not exactly the same, there must be some way for the two machines to determine how to communicate. That is what happens in that short burst of information between the two modems: Decisions are made about what transmission speed to use (the fastest speed of the slowest device), how the data will be packaged, and which device will control the transfer. If both machines cannot satisfy any of the parameters, the negotiations will fail and both parties will disconnect.

---

**Tip**    If you experience communication difficulty between two modems, be sure that you have not limited one of them to parameters that the other is unable to meet. For example, if one modem has a minimum speed restriction imposed by the software, it might need to be changed before it can communicate with other modems.

---

Connections between a sending device (sometimes referred to as DCE) and a receiving device (DTE) are called *handshaking signals*. They ensure that each sending and receiving device is in sync with the other. The flow control of data between modems is handled by the modems themselves. However, the local flow control between modem and COM port can be set by the user. There are two types of flow control:

- **Hardware flow control.** This takes advantage of some of the extra wires in the serial connection between the modem and the COM port. These wires are used to let the other device know that the DCE is ready to send or receive data. The wires are named RTS and CTS. Hardware handshaking is sometimes referred to as RTS/CTS.

- **Software flow control.** This uses special characters known as XON and XOFF to let the other device know that the DCE is starting to send data or that the data transmission is finished. Software handshaking is slower and not as dependable as hardware handshaking. Only some very old modems use software handshaking. If given a choice, always use hardware flow control.

# Modem Standards

As with every other communication device, standards are needed to ensure that both sides speak the same "language." Modems have their own set of standardized communication conventions.

## Error Detection

Some modems offer various forms of hardware error detection and correction. Such features usually require matching firmware in the modems at both ends.

## Data Compression

Data compression is a means of shrinking files into smaller packets, resulting in faster connections and lower space requirements on the host and client machine for storage. Some modems can perform on-the-fly data compression; both modems must be able to understand the compression for it to work. On-the-fly compression significantly enhances the amount of data sent between modems during a given time period. There are now a variety of industry standards for data compression, based in part on the work done by various Internet-related committees.

## Communication Standards

There were no standards during the early days of modem communication. The only way to ensure data transmission was to place identical modems at the sending and receiving ends of the transmission. Compatibility was a great concern, and proprietary modems were the norm.

Today, modems comply with several standards. There are two sources for these standards:

- Manufacturers have placed specifications of their modem functions in the public domain. These specifications can now be copied and used by any manufacturer. If enough manufacturers use a specification, it becomes a standard on its own merits.
- Standards committees are formed when there is enough interest expressed by users, vendors, or regulatory committees to develop a set of rules for a class of data or modems.

The following material details the standards that evolved with telecommunications. Most of these are obsolete to the average user since the advent of faster devices, alternatives to modems, and the Internet.

## Early Bell Standards

Bell Telephone produced the first generally accepted modem standards (103 and 212A); they developed out of the market-dominant position of the telephone company in telecommunications. To compete, other vendors offered products that would recognize the Bell command set. This scenario occurred more than once with subsequent standards.

## CCITT Standards

The CCITT modem standards are commonly known as *Vdot standards* because each is named using the letter *V* followed by a decimal point and a number. The Vdot standards set out detailed requirements for the use of various modem speeds, incorporation of data-compression schemes, and error correction.

## MNP Standards

The MNP (Microcom Networking Protocol—named for Microcom, the company that developed them) set forth a series of error-correction methods.

## Error-Detection and Data-Compression Protocols

In addition to speed standards, some CCITT standards include error-detection and data-compression protocols. The following table shows the standards that include error detection.

| Standard | Baud | Bps | Type | Comments |
|----------|------|-----|------|----------|
| V.42 | 2400 | 2400 and up | Error correction | |
| MNP 1–4 | 2400 | 2400 and up | Error correction | |
| V.42bis | 2400 | 9600/38.4K | Data compression | V.42 must be present. |
| MNP 5 | N/A | N/A | Both | |

## 56-Kbps Modems

Telephone lines are capable of carrying 56 Kbps of data; however, conversion from analog to digital signals and back comes with a price: a speed limit of 33.6 Kbps. Because many telephone systems are now digital, it is possible to transmit, in some instances, at a full 56 Kbps in one direction. The return data, however, is still limited to 33.6 Kbps. For these reasons, it is unlikely that you can achieve a full data transfer rate with a 56-Kbps modem. To achieve the best performance, the following conditions must be met:

- Digital-to-analog conversion should be limited so that it takes place only once within the network. Each conversion slows the communication process.
- The host must be connected digitally.
- Both modems must support the 56-Kbps technology.

Originally, there were three 56-Kbps modem standards: K56flex, x2, and V.90. Unfortunately, these standards were not compatible at 56 Kbps, so to achieve the highest possible speed, both modems needed to use the same standard. Several companies developed the K56flex standard, and U.S. Robotics developed the x2 standard. Currently, the V.90 standard has replaced both the K56flex and the x2, and most 56-Kbps modems can be upgraded to this standard. If you have a 56-Kbps modem and want to upgrade to V.90, check the manufacturer's Web site for instructions and download the appropriate software.

## Modem Commands

Just like the early computers that needed MS-DOS commands to tell them what to do, modems also need commands. Programmers also needed a standard command set to incorporate the use of modems into their software. Unfortunately, there are no true standard command sets for modems because manufacturers are free to create their own. There is, however, one set of commands that has been accepted as a de facto standard. Most modems today are Hayes-compatible. In the early 1980s, Hayes developed the AT command set.

These commands are very useful as diagnostic tools for today's computer professional. To use these commands, make sure the communication software is loaded and the computer is in terminal mode. Unless the modem is set up to autoconnect (online mode), it will be in command mode and ready to accept AT commands. The following table lists some of the more useful AT commands used by computer professionals.

| Command | Function |
|---|---|
| AT | Lets you know that your modem is plugged in and turned on. The mode should respond with OK. |
| ATE1 | Echoes the command on the screen. |
| ATE0 | Turns off the echo to the screen. Some modems will not run correctly when the echo is on. |
| ATH | Takes the telephone off the hook. Should elicit a reply of OK or 0 from the modem, or a dial tone and an OH indicator if it's an external modem. |
| ATM1 | Turns the speaker on for the dial tone. ATL0 is the lowest volume and ATL2 is medium volume. |
| ATM0 | Turns the speaker off. |
| ATD | Takes the phone off the hook and dials a number if one is included with the command (for example, ATDT555-2222). The second T is for tone; substitute P for a pulse phone. Include a W (ATDTW) to instruct it to wait for a dial tone before dialing. Include a comma anywhere after the command to instruct it to pause before continuing to dial. |
| ATQ0 | Enables result codes. A troubleshooting aid. Type **ATV1** prior to this command and you will get back verbose result codes (OK-BUSY-CONNECT 2400,9600-COMPRESSION:V.42bis). |
| ATQ1 | Disables result codes. |
| ATH, ATH0 | Hangs up the modem. |
| ATX | This resets your modem to a predefined state. You can configure your own reset state. If it wasn't set previously, it can be reset to the factory's default setting. |

## Troubleshooting

It can be very frustrating when a modem does not function as expected. However, you can follow these simple guidelines to determine whether the modem is really broken or something else is the culprit.

| Possible Cause | Possible Solution |
| --- | --- |
| New hardware was added to the computer and now the modem doesn't work. | Check for IRQ and I/O conflicts. |
| New software was added to the computer and now the modem doesn't work. | Check for IRQ and I/O conflicts. Cards that were configured for software can be inadvertently changed by corrupted software or by the installation of new software. |
| The software says there is no modem. | Make sure the software is checking the correct port. Reconfigure or reinstall the software (there might be a corrupt driver). |
| Modem works sporadically. | Try another modem type. Check the phone lines. |
| Modem does not hang up the phone line. | A power surge (often caused by a lightning strike) can cause this problem. If manual disconnect and reconnect allows the modem to disconnect, but it does not automatically drop the connection in the future, replace or repair the modem. |

## Lesson Summary

The following points summarize the main elements of this lesson:

- Modems convert parallel digital data to and from serial analog data.
- Modem speeds are based on bps.
- CCITT (now ITU-T) establishes standards for modem communication.
- AT commands are used to manually communicate with and test a modem.
- Modems can be installed internally or externally.
- The primary modem problem is IRQ conflicts.
- Modems and ISDN TAs do similar things but are not the same kind of device.

# Lesson 2:  The Internet and Web Browsers

Once the domain of academics and defense contractors, the Internet is now a part of everyday life. Browsing for news, chatting with online friends, and exchanging e-mail are common PC activities for young and old.

## After this lesson, you will be able to

- Define how the Internet works
- Define basic Internet-related terms
- Install and configure a browser
- Set up an Internet account

## Estimated lesson time: 45 minutes

## The Internet

The *Internet*, commonly known as "the Net," is the most extensive WAN (wide area network) in the world—a network of networks working together. This relatively new communication technology has begun to affect our lives as significantly as television and the telephone. When most people talk about using the Internet, they talk about which Web sites they have visited or people they have met online.

Most LANs make use of passwords and other forms of security, but the Internet is one of the most open networks in the world. Some common Internet uses include communication; locating lost friends and family; researching information for school or work; and locating businesses, products, or services (such as travel). The Internet can be a valuable resource for virtually anything and everything.

Although detailed knowledge of the inner workings of the Internet is not a requirement of the A+ Certification Exam, you will find questions on the exam on various aspects of its use. In addition, knowing how to find drivers and technical information on vendor Web sites can save time and effort in providing customers with updates and repairs.

### Internet Basics

The Internet is really a collection of services. Let's take a look at the most important services and the major concepts behind them.

## The World Wide Web

When people say they are "surfing" the Net, they are probably visiting the collection of hyperlinked Web sites known as the *World Wide Web* ("the Web" or WWW). These Web sites are located around the world, and their numbers continue to grow by the thousands every day. Each Web site within the Web has a unique address called a URL (Uniform Resource Locator).

**Note**    The Web is not the Internet; it is only part of the Internet. Although it is currently the largest, most popular, and fastest-growing part of the Internet, it represents only a fraction of the Internet services available that include FTP, Gopher, and Telnet.

## Web Sites

The Web is a network of host sites that can be accessed for information. Most pages provide information to clients using the *Hypertext Transfer Protocol* (HTTP— this is the http:// seen in the full address line in a browser).

Pages can be hyperlinked so that, when a user clicks on a text string or image that has been coded as a link, they are shown the contents of the linked page. All Web pages use some derivative of SGML (Standard Generalized Markup Language) to code pages so the browser can "read" the instructions on how to display and link material on the pages. A committee of government and industry experts in networking, information systems, and publishing designed this standard.

A loose form of an SGML application, Hypertext Markup Language (HTML) was designed to tag the content of Web pages. If you choose to view the source code of a Web page in your browser, you can see the markup that tells what each portion of the page is, if it has hyperlinks, and any special information on how to display it.

Some purists lament how open the design of HTML is, but that openness allows for additional plug-ins that let browsers handle animation, sound, streaming video, and other enhancements to the Web experience.

## Browsers

A browser is the most common Internet application for the end user. The two most popular are Microsoft Internet Explorer and Netscape Navigator. These programs "open" Web pages for viewing, can access and download remote files using FTP, and perform other routine online tasks. Figure 15.5 shows a browser in action viewing the Microsoft Web site.

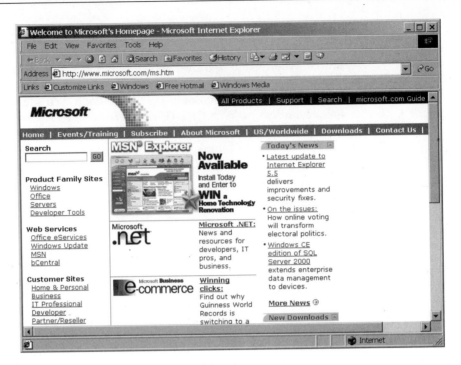

**Figure 15.5**   Surfing the Web with Microsoft Internet Explorer

## Electronic Mail

Electronic mail, usually known as e-mail, is the most commonly used function of the Internet, allowing users to send and receive messages (and files) electronically to and from millions of people all over the world. Electronic mailing lists allow users to join group discussions with people who share their interests. Like regular mail (now often called *snail mail*), e-mail is also sent to an address (a virtual one).

To make use of e-mail, one must have access to an e-mail server, an account on that server, and a program to send and receive messages. Microsoft Windows includes Microsoft Outlook Express as an e-mail client. Several others, like Eudora and Hotmail, are available online. You can also find several products either as stand-alone software or bundled (as in Office 2000) as commercial software products in stores. Virtually all ISPs offer e-mail as part of their packages, and free accounts are available as well.

To set up an account, you will need to know the address information for both the inbound and outbound mail servers (obtained from the provider), as well as the account address (usually in the form of mailto:accountname@provider.ext). The account will have a password that can usually be stored so the user does not have to enter it each time mail is sent or received. Check with the vendor and program documentation for detailed information on setting up specific programs to handle e-mail and connecting to an ISP. (Windows 95 and 98 and Windows Me all include an Internet Connection Wizard that makes it easy to connect to the Internet by prompting you for all of this information.)

**Note**   When setting up programs like Microsoft Outlook, be sure to ask the client if and how often he or she wants mail checked. If the client does not have a permanent connection to the Internet, charges may be made based on the connect time. Checking frequently for e-mail may add to ISP billings.

## FTP

FTP is a special application used for uploading and downloading files to and from the Internet. Programs like Win-FTP and Cute_FTP offer an easy-to-use interface for moving files to a remote computer and are popular with Webmasters. Most new browsers support downloading files via FTP automatically.

## TCP/IP

TCP/IP is the language (network protocol) used by computers to talk to each other over the Net. TCP/IP has also become a common protocol for LANs. Regardless of which operating system or software you use, your commands travel through the Internet in TCP/IP format. The services of the Internet and the Web could not be provided without TCP/IP.

## IP Address

Each machine on a network is given a unique 32-bit address. These addresses are normally expressed in decimal values of 4 bytes, separated with periods—for example, 127.0.0.1. Each position can have up to 256 values, from 0 to 255. Without a unique address, there would be conflicts and chaos. It designates the location of its assigned device (usually an NIC) on the network.

## ISPs

ISPs furnish the connection between dial-up (modem) users and the Internet. Although some are big names with millions of users, there are many more that serve local areas with both dial-up and hosting plans.

## URLs

As mentioned, the URL is the Web's address system. To access a Web site, the user must enter the designated URL on the network. Each URL begins with the character sequence http://. The letters HTTP are an acronym for the Hypertext Transfer Protocol, which identifies the Web site as an address. The rest of the URL is the name of the site. For example, Microsoft's URL is *http://www.microsoft.com.* (Because it is universal, it is seldom necessary to first type the characters "http://" when typing a URL in a browser; most engines take it for granted.)

## Domain

An Internet *domain* is a site with a common general interest or purpose, often run by a single firm or institution. The domain suffix gives a general idea of the site's purpose: .com for businesses, or .edu for educational institutions. The following table lists common Internet domains.

| Domain | Description |
| --- | --- |
| .com | Commercial organizations |
| .net | Internet core networks (also used by some Internet-related enterprises) |
| .edu | Educational institutions |
| .org | Nonprofit organizations |
| .gov | U.S. government nonmilitary institutions |
| .mil | U.S. government armed services |
| .xx | Two-letter country code (for example, .ca for Canada, .de for Germany) |

**Note**    There are several new extensions being added to Web domain names, and the above list is not intended to be a complete listing.

## DNS

DNS (Domain Name System) is the hierarchical naming system used for identifying domain names on the Internet and on private TCP/IP networks. DNS maps DNS domain names to IP addresses, and vice versa. This allows users, computers, and applications to query the DNS to specify remote systems by their domain names rather than by IP addresses.

## DNS Server

A DNS server is a computer that does the job of matching names and addresses in the DNS system.

## Getting Connected

These days, many computer professionals are involved in getting their clients online. Before actually setting up the system, you need to determine just how the computer will access the Internet. Once that was as simple as choosing a modem. Today that job has become a bit more complicated with the advent of faster alternatives to POTS. If the customer is planning to use ISDN, then you will need an ISDN TA. DSL (Digital Subscriber Line) satellite and cable connections will also require special hardware. Some connections, such as DSL and cable, may be "always on," meaning that the computer is constantly connected (when the computer is on). Most modem and ISDN customers make use of dial-in service, and a connection is only active when the user opens an application that accesses the Internet. One practice that is becoming more common is adding a firewall between a computer and the Internet to improve security. A firewall may be another computer or a stand-alone device that acts as a gateway to the Internet, monitoring incoming traffic. It can help prevent the introduction of a virus or attempts to "hack" into the protected system or network. Firewalls have long been employed in network environments.

Most people use a dial-up connection to the Internet via independent ISPs that provide local community-based service to users, but popular national ISPs such as The Microsoft Network (MSN) are useful if you travel because many of them have toll-free numbers for dial-up access or many local numbers throughout the country. Local ISPs are appropriate for customers who are looking for a cost-effective company that offers local (including technical) support.

You also need to consider which browser(s) to set up to "surf" the Internet. Most ISPs (especially local ones) provide only the connection or gateway to the Internet. Others provide their own browser software package. Most ISPs allow you to use your choice of browsers. Some local and national ISPs provide startup software that includes their recommended browser, as well as FTP tools and other Internet utilities. From time to time, Web surfers will encounter pages that work well only with a specific browser or with a specific plug-in like a Flash! player. In this case, it might be necessary to install additional software or more than one browser.

## Using Ping

Anyone installing or troubleshooting an Internet connection should be familiar with using the ping (Packet Internet Groper) application. This utility lets you test the connection between devices using the TCP/IP protocol. When you use ping, it sends a request to a specific IP address and reports whether the target is present and how long it takes to get a reply. Figure 15.6 shows ping in action.

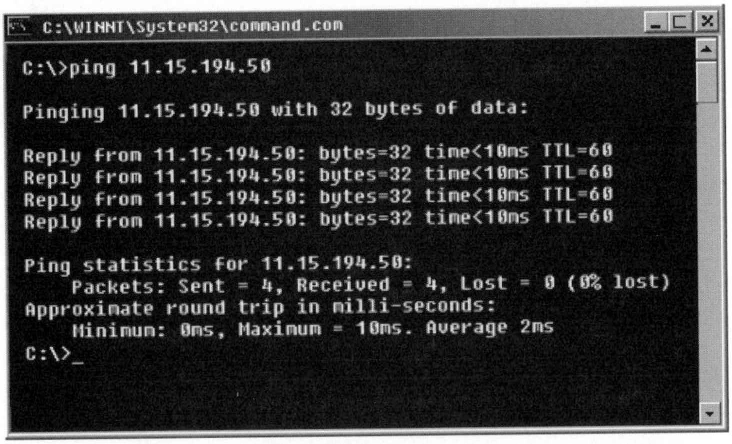

```
C:\WINNT\System32\command.com                          _ □ ×

C:\>ping 11.15.194.50

Pinging 11.15.194.50 with 32 bytes of data:

Reply from 11.15.194.50: bytes=32 time<10ms TTL=60
Reply from 11.15.194.50: bytes=32 time<10ms TTL=60
Reply from 11.15.194.50: bytes=32 time<10ms TTL=60
Reply from 11.15.194.50: bytes=32 time<10ms TTL=60

Ping statistics for 11.15.194.50:
    Packets: Sent = 4, Received = 4, Lost = 0 (0% lost)
Approximate round trip in milli-seconds:
    Minimum: 0ms, Maximum = 10ms. Average 2ms
C:\>_
```

**Figure 15.6**    Using ping to test TCP/IP connections

Under Windows this program can be run in a DOS window accessed by typing **command** in the Run dialog box. The syntax is ping –switches address. For example, entering ping –t 12.12.122.255 would search for and ping TCP/IP address 12.12.122.255 until you press CTRL+C to end the action because you set the –t switch. The following table shows the switches for the ping command.

| Switch | Function |
| --- | --- |
| –a | Resolves addresses to host names. |
| –f | Sets a "Don't Fragment" flag in outgoing packets. |
| –i <TTL> | Specifies the Time to Live for outgoing packets. |
| –j <host-list> | Loose source routing along host-list. |
| –k <host-list> | Strict source routing along host-list. |
| –l <size> | Sends packets to the size set in the brackets. |
| –n <count> | Sets the number of echo requests to the value given within the brackets. |
| –r <count> | Records the route for count hops. |
| –s <count> | Time stamp for count hops. |
| –t | Pings the specified address until stopped. You can view statistics and then continue pinging by pressing CTRL+BREAK. Stop completely without statistics by pressing CTRL+C. |
| –v <TOS> | Specifies type of service. |
| –w | Sets the length of the wait periods (in milliseconds) for a response before showing a timeout error. You may need to set this if the host is slow in responding. |

## Lesson Summary

The following points summarize the main elements of this lesson:

- The Internet is a vast collection of network servers.

- The most active portion of the Internet for the average user is the Web.

- The Internet offers a variety of services, and most can be accessed through a browser.

- Most users make use of a dial-up connection provided by an ISP to access the Internet.

- The Internet uses the TCP/IP protocol and DNS to route traffic.

- Ping is a useful program for checking TCP/IP connections.

# Chapter Summary

The following points summarize the key concepts in this chapter:

- Modems convert parallel digital data to and from serial analog data.
- Modem speeds are based on bps.
- CCITT (now ITU-T) establishes standards for modem communication.
- AT commands are used to manually communicate with and test a modem.
- Modems can be installed internally or externally.
- The primary modem problem is IRQ conflicts.
- The Internet is a vast ad-hoc computer network.
- The most active portion of the Internet for the average user is the Web, but many other services are available as well.
- The Internet gateway most people use is a dial-up connection and a browser.
- The Internet uses the TCP/IP protocol and DNS to route traffic.
- Any technician who services an Internet connection should understand how to use the ping utility to check TCP/IP connections.

# Review

The following questions are intended to reinforce key information presented in this chapter. If you are unable to answer a question, review the appropriate lesson and then try the question again. Answers to the questions can be found in Appendix A, "Questions and Answers."

1. What is the purpose of a modem?

2. Which AT command is used to take the phone off the hook?

3. What is the difference between baud and bps?

4. What is the name of the chip that converts data from parallel to serial?

5. Name three transfer protocols.

6. What is Zmodem? What are its advantages over other protocols?

7. Define handshaking.

8. What are AT commands and how can a computer technician use them?

9. Explain the difference between half-duplex and full-duplex. What makes them different? Where or when is each used?

10. What is the difference between synchronous and asynchronous communication?

11. Why are fax standards different from modem standards?

12. Describe the Internet.

13. What is needed to set up an e-mail account?

14. What is a browser?

15. What does HTTP stand for?

16. What is the ping command used for?

17. What is a DNS server?

18. What is an ISP?

CHAPTER 16

# Operating System Fundamentals

Lesson 1: Operating System Basics .......................... 369

Lesson 2: The Command Prompt and DOS Mode Operations ...... 381

Lesson 3: File Systems ...................................... 397

Chapter Summary ........................................... 406

Review ..................................................... 407

## About This Chapter

In this chapter, we shift our attention from the realm of hardware to the software that lets us put the computer to work. There are literally thousands of software packages on the market, ranging from productivity tools like word processors to simple reminder note functions, but the most fundamental type of software is the operating system.

The operating system provides access to fundamental system services and allows you to configure hardware features. It is responsible for setting up file systems and making use of drivers for display adapters, SCSI (Small Computer System Interface) cards, mouse and keyboard devices, printers, and scanners. Understanding how to effectively use an operating system is a fundamental skill for any computer technician.

## Before You Begin

You should have already read the material on CPUs (central processing units), memory, and hard drive operations, and be familiar with the POST (Power On Self Test) performed every time the computer is turned on. Basic familiarity with Microsoft Windows is recommended; intermediate or expert-level experience is not required. You should be able to perform the basic tasks of navigating the Windows interface, working with files and folders, using a mouse, and using applications like a word processor. Understanding the command prompt is also helpful, but not required.

# Lesson 1:  Operating System Basics

All operating systems share certain basic features and elements. Understanding the inner workings of operating systems is a fundamental job skill for any technician. In this lesson, we examine the development of DOS and the evolution of Windows. We also discuss the basic capabilities operating systems must provide to make full use of system hardware components.

## After this lesson, you will be able to

- Define an operating system
- Explain the fundamental roles the operating system plays in computer operations
- Understand the development of the PC-based operating environment from early DOS to modern Windows systems

## Estimated lesson time: 35 minutes

## The Software Core

Virtually all the time spent working with a computer is spent in the realm of the operating system. With the exception of a few moments after we turn the machine on, every keystroke, every mouse click, and every interaction with peripheral devices is recorded and processed by the operating system. Without it, we would be unable to use any other programs. Most users pay very little attention to the operating system, but computer technicians need to be able to work with it effectively to keep the PC running safely and efficiently. All operating systems share certain basic components and features. The following sections describe these key components, their functions, and some basic considerations in their design and use.

### User Interface

The user interface is one of the most important, yet underappreciated, parts of any operating system. A correctly designed interface allows the user to interact with the computer, accessing its power without having to learn complicated control methods. Today, the Windows-based environment, making use of a mouse, a keyboard, drop-down menus, and scrolling content areas, is the dominant form of user interface.

The majority of Windows-based programs share many of the same commands for functions like adding and moving text and printing, opening, and saving files. This common approach saves time and effort, allowing both programmers and end users to concentrate on the task at hand rather than telling the computer what they want.

## File System Management

The operating system is responsible for creating and maintaining files, placing them on storage media, reorganizing them, ensuring their integrity, and erasing them as needed. The design of the operating system determines the naming convention for files. For example, MS-DOS originally limited the name of a file to eight characters with a three-character extension following a period to denote the file type.

## Device Management

The operating system does not automatically know the nature of the computer components that exist on the system. To control hard drives, accept display information from graphics adapters, or communicate with printers and other peripheral devices, the operating system must be enabled with drivers and command sequences.

The operating system needs to provide methods for preparing storage media, like floppy and hard drives, and to work with its file system. It controls all the machine's hardware and its functions, tracking the status of communications ports, printer ports, and remote devices like Iomega Zip drives or printers; providing memory management; interacting with any TSR (terminate-and-stay-resident) programs; and maintaining the integrity of its own operation.

## Boot and Installation Routines

Most operating systems are loaded as software. They must include boot sequence code that can be accessed during system startup so that they can be loaded into memory and made functional when the computer is turned on. They must be provided with installation routines as well as troubleshooting and recovery techniques for reinstallation in the event components become corrupted during use.

## Error-Handling Capability

Problems ranging from severe damage to simple user error can cause a system to become unstable. A well-designed operating system will be able to detect such problems, display error messages to alert the user, and provide the ability to recover without significant loss of data or corruption of the operating system.

## Housekeeping Utilities

A complete operating system includes software routines for defragmenting hard drives, scanning for viruses, and performing other housekeeping chores that keep the system running at optimal performance.

## Networking Capability

The earliest PC operating systems were designed as single-user environments, but the increasing popularity of workgroup computing and the Internet has made built-in support for networking protocols and a collection of interoperability tools part of any modern operating system.

# A Short History of MS-DOS

The newest versions of Windows are advanced operating systems that build on more than two decades of PC software development, beginning with DOS. There were other operating systems in use during the first days of the PC era, such as CP/M, but the original IBM PC, released in 1981, shipped with an operating system called DOS (disk operating system). It was by far the dominant operating system until it was supplanted by Window 3.1 in 1992, and later by 32-bit versions of Windows, like Windows 95 and Windows NT. Today all popular versions of Windows are 32-bit operating systems.

The modern computer professional must be familiar with MS-DOS because many concepts and conventions used in Windows stem from its predecessor. Several fundamental diagnostic routines require knowledge of user command prompt interaction that will be part of your activities as a computer technician. These include installing a new operating system, formatting a new hard drive, checking for low-level hardware problems, and repairing damage from viruses. In Lesson 2 we examine and work with these programs and the command prompt interface.

There were once many variations of DOS, some with proprietary labels, but today, most references to DOS are synonymous with MS-DOS. The following table provides a thumbnail overview of the history of MS-DOS, showing the development of features as each new version was released. You can use this information to get a general picture of the development of the PC operating system as it matured.

| Version | Introduced | Features |
| --- | --- | --- |
| 1.0 | August 1981 | Distributed on one floppy disk (required 8 KB of RAM [random access memory]). |
| 1.1 | May 1982 | Added support for 320-KB double-sided disks. |
| 2.0 | March 1983 | Introduced support for hard disks, directories, background printing, and the ability to add device drivers. |
| 3.0 | August 1984 | Increased support for hard disks larger than 10 megabytes (MB) and 1.2-MB floppy disks. |
| 3.1 | March 1985 | Added networks and file sharing. |
| 3.2 | January 1986 | Included support for 3.5-inch floppy disks. |
| 3.3 | April 1987 | Added new commands and international support. |
| 4.0 | February 1988 | Added support for hard disks greater than 32 MB, the MEM command, and MS-DOS Shell. |
| 5.0 | May 1991 | Added memory management tools, help, undelete, unformat, and task swapping. This was the last version to come with a printed manual. |

*(continued)*

*(continued)*

| Version | Introduced | Features |
|---------|------------|----------|
| 6.0 | March 1993 | Included new features such as MEMMAKER, multiple boot configurations, Windows Unformat and Undelete, virus protection, and backup. MEMMAKER is a utility used to modify the system's CONFIG.SYS and AUTOEXEC.BAT files so that device drivers and memory-resident programs take up less conventional memory space. |
| 6.2 | October 1993 | Included ScanDisk, Microsoft Diagnostics (MSD) utilities, and enhanced diagnostics. |
| 7.0 | December 1995 | The end of DOS as a stand-alone product. It was relegated to command-level environments included with Microsoft Windows 95 and later editions. |

## Understanding DOS

All versions of DOS had several things in common. First, they were built for a specific class of CPU and computer: The original version of DOS was designed to provide operating system services for the original IBM PC. That machine shipped with either one or two floppy drives and had a port for a cassette drive in the back. The original release of the PC did not include support for adding a hard drive to the system. As Intel processors increased in power and as the PC became a more advanced platform, DOS was extended to take advantage of the new features and capabilities.

In spite of improvements with each new version, MS-DOS was never able to overcome critical limitations. DOS was designed to work as a stand-alone operating system, lacking any native networking support. The need to maintain backward compatibility with early Intel processors forced DOS developers to contend with the severe memory limitations left over from the original 8080 design.

In fact, DOS always had the ability to keep within the hardware limits of the basic PC of its day. That meant a very low memory overhead and a simple user interface that assumed no more than the most basic display system. All versions used a command-line user interface and required few files present on the system to run basic services. The command prompt was a standard part of PC life during the days of DOS for those who did not use Windows (and very few people did until the release of Windows 3.1). The user interface involved simply typing an appropriate command following the prompt in the proper syntax and pressing ENTER.

The command prompt could vary, but the most common form was C:\> (usually known as the C prompt), where the letter stood for the active drive and a flashing cursor line indicated that the system was ready to accept a command. Technicians and power users working on Windows-based systems still need to be comfortable with the DOS command prompt. As you will see in Lesson 2, using this prompt is still a fundamental requirement in setting up a new system or hard drive.

## DOS Boot Sequence and Files

MS-DOS includes three core programs that are required to make a drive or floppy disk bootable and load the operating system into memory:

- **IO.SYS.** The interface between the hardware and the operating system code
- **MSDOS.SYS.** The main operating system code
- **COMMAND.COM.** The interface between the user and the operating system code

These three files can be seen as layers, each taking an area of responsibility. Virtually all operating systems work this way. Because MS-DOS is a relatively simple operating system, examining its approach provides insights into how more complicated operating systems function.

IO.SYS can be considered the lowest layer, acting as an intermediary between the various hardware components and the software environment. MSDOS.SYS is the middle layer. It not only provides key logic but also basic commands for opening and closing files, navigating the file system, and other common tasks. COMMAND.COM provides support for the operating system's direct interaction with the user, accepting commands and performing the necessary steps for execution.

Although these three core files would make a system operational, MS-DOS had limitations. One of the great advantages in the PC design is its open architecture. No two computers have to be exactly alike, so supporting these variations means having custom device drivers, memory configurations, and some way of recognizing and managing exactly what is on each system. Microsoft developers came up with a simple solution: MS-DOS used two optional startup files to process custom commands required by the user, hardware devices, or applications. These files were the following:

- **CONFIG.SYS.** Loads extra hardware and device drivers not built into IO.SYS
- **AUTOEXEC.BAT.** Loads TSR programs selected by the user and sets up environment variables such as TEMP and PATH

Windows uses a boot process that is quite similar to DOS (we look at it later), and some versions can actually use the AUTOEXEC.BAT and CONFIG.SYS files. *Booting the system* is a term that originated in the early days of computer operations, coming from the saying "pulling yourself up by the bootstraps." Here is a summary of the steps involved and how the core files described work.

1. When power is first applied to the system, the computer performs the POST, a series of self-checks stored in permanent read-only memory. The POST code includes instructions that cause the machine to locate and invoke an operating system if it exists.

2. The ROM BIOS (read-only memory basic input/output system) on the motherboard looks for an operating system. It checks for the presence of IO.SYS and MSDOS.SYS. The locations to be checked are defined in the CMOS (complementary metal-oxide semiconductor) and usually involve first searching the A (floppy disk) drive and then the C drive.

3. The operating system processes the CONFIG.SYS file (if present on the boot drive). CONFIG.SYS contains information to configure the system environment, including special memory management overlays and hardware drivers.

4. COMMAND.COM is loaded.

5. The operating system processes the AUTOEXEC.BAT file (if present). AUTOEXEC.BAT loads programs and user-defined settings.

6. If no programs (such as Windows) are invoked by AUTOEXEC.BAT, COMMAND.COM presents the active-drive prompt and waits for a command.

The process of starting from a no-power condition is called a *cold boot*. Occasionally, a system might require a reset—for instance, when the computer locks up or runs out of memory. Resetting can be accomplished without turning off the computer by pressing the CTRL, ALT, and DEL keys at the same time. This is called a *warm boot*.

## The DOS File System

In MS-DOS, the file was the primary unit of data storage on the computer, allowing the system to distinguish what represented a single collection of information from another. Files were organized into directories. File and directory names were up to eight characters long and files could have a three-letter extension following a period. Names were not case-sensitive, and, internally, the system made no distinction between uppercase and lowercase characters in naming conventions. When operating in DOS mode, the same restrictions apply.

Most DOS users quickly came to understand the basic naming conventions of the operating system. Several extensions were universally used and a number of others gained wide acceptance. These naming conventions have carried over into the Windows environment. The following table presents several extensions that all computer technicians should be able to recognize and use.

| Extension | File Type | Used For/Meaning |
|---|---|---|
| .exe | Program/application files | Executable files. |
| .com | Program files | Command files. |
| .sys | System files | To define and configure options. |

*(continued)*

| Extension | File Type | Used For/Meaning |
|---|---|---|
| .bat | Batch files | A text file that can be run to execute a series of commands or launch programs. DOS offered a series of options that could be used to perform a wide variety of tasks automatically. |
| .txt | Text files | Plain ASCII (American Standard Code for Information Interchange) data. |
| .doc | Document files | Word processing file text with formatting. |
| .drv | Driver files | Software that configures a hardware device. |

We return to the command prompt and the programs, functions, and techniques that migrated into the modern Windows operating systems in Lesson 2. Next, we explore how Windows came to replace DOS and dominate the PC market.

## The Evolution of Microsoft Windows

Early editions of Microsoft Windows (through Windows 3.*x*) were not really complete operating systems, but rather operating environments that used MS-DOS as a foundation. Windows was developed to make the computer more developer- and user-friendly by providing a common GUI (graphical user interface) that could be shared by all compatible programs. The GUI uses icons, toolbars, standard menus, and common device drivers to simplify application development and minimize the time it takes a user to learn a new product. The addition of the mouse and enhanced graphics displays extended the reach of the PC into the desktop publishing, education, and graphic arts markets once dominated by specialized workstations and the Apple Macintosh.

Windows Version 1.0 was released in 1985, providing a graphical interface and little else. Version 2.0 followed in 1987, and it was popular in the engineering, design, and graphics and desktop publishing communities. It wasn't until the release of Windows 3.1 in 1992 that this operating environment became popular.

This jump in popularity could be attributed to an increasing software base with applications that overwhelmed the features in the MS-DOS environment: faster graphics cards and improved memory management. The final, most well-known, and most used 16-bit version of Windows was Windows 3.11, released in the fall of 1993.

Microsoft Windows 95 took its name from the year of its release. With it, Microsoft changed more than the naming convention; it changed Windows into a full-fledged 32-bit operating system.

All applications written to meet current Windows standards provide a common user interface, including the following components:

- The menu system offers the same basic commands for file, print, copy, and save operations.
- Selecting text or objects with the pointing device or keystroke commands is done in a consistent manner.
- Clicking and dragging mouse functions are the same.
- The sides of most application areas provide scroll bars for displaying text and graphics not currently visible in the window.
- Windows can be overlapped and resized to make the best use of the screen area.
- Data can be cut and pasted among applications, and data held in one file can be accessed and used by another program.

This common approach shortens the user's learning curve for unfamiliar applications. On a programming level, application developers have access to a toolbox of Windows routines, so they do not have to reinvent the wheel every time they want to invoke a menu or dialog box.

The multitasking capability of Windows allows the user to have more than one application open and switch among them, even cutting and pasting data from one open window to another. DOS was designed to run on 8086 class machines, with a conventional memory limit of 640 KB of RAM. Windows overcomes this restriction by implementing new modes of memory utilization. You should be familiar with how these modes operate for the exam.

## Operating Modes

Early PC operating systems were designed for 8088 processors. As more powerful CPUs became available, the limits of the 8-bit operating environment hindered the development of programs and devices that could make use of more powerful PCs. With the release of 80286 processors, the CPU was able to address more than 1 MB of RAM, thus breaking the DOS barrier. However, the market was still dominated by MS-DOS–based programs that worked within this limit. The release of Windows solved this problem by allowing a CPU to operate in several modes—thus accommodating both the old and new worlds—and fostering a whole new market for memory managers to help overcome configuration hurdles.

## Real Mode

The original purpose of Windows was to provide an MS-DOS–based GUI. The first versions did not include memory-management functions and did not multitask. They were designed only for starting programs and managing files while operating within the MS-DOS limit of 1 MB of RAM. Later versions moved outside the 1-MB limit but continued to support this MS-DOS mode until Windows 3.1 appeared.

This MS-DOS mode, called *real mode,* is now virtually obsolete. However, some older MS-DOS applications and hardware still require the use of real mode. Support of real-mode applications and hardware is part of downward compatibility. Even in the Windows 95 and Microsoft Windows 98 environments, you will encounter terms, such as *real-mode driver,* which refer to operating at this level.

**Note** If any real-mode drivers are loaded in 32-bit versions of Windows, the system will be forced into compatibility mode. This will slow down the machine and limit memory utilization. In general, you should stay in 32-bit mode.

### Standard Mode

Windows 2.0 broke free of the MS-DOS 1-MB barrier by making use of the 286-level *protected mode* of operation. Protected mode Windows could address up to 16 MB of RAM. Although MS-DOS programs could run only in the first megabyte of memory, specialized programs were written that would run in (and only in) the extended memory controlled by Windows. The term *protected mode* refers to the use of protected memory. (Standard mode is run with the processor in protected mode.) Along with Windows protected mode came the now-famous General Protection Fault (GPF). Encountering this error generally means that some portion of the Windows protected mode has been violated (for example, the program is trying to write data outside the portion of memory allocated to it).

Microsoft expanded the concept behind Windows by adding support for standardized graphics, fonts, I/O (input/output) devices, and memory mapping. Together these elements are known as *resources,* with Windows acting as a resource manager. In the MS-DOS environment, application developers handled these tasks themselves. Because Windows has these resources built in, it is an easy environment in which to write programs. By breaking the MS-DOS barrier (engaging 286 protected mode), Windows running in standard mode takes control of many of the hardware functions. This means that programs do not have to write the code directly to control devices; instead they ask Windows to use them.

MS-DOS programs can run only under Windows in real mode. Running 286 protected mode worked well for the special programs, but once in protected mode, it was not possible to return to real mode without resetting the CPU (only the CPU—not the computer). The MS-DOS program would unload when the user switched back to Windows. These versions (1.0 and 2.0) of Windows could run only one MS-DOS program at a time.

### Windows Runtime Version

Certain applications (like Aldus PageMaker) could be purchased with a *runtime version* of Windows. This allowed a program that required a Windows environment to run on a computer that did not have the full version of Windows installed.

### 386 Enhanced Mode

Introduced with the Intel 80386 CPU, the 386 protected mode allowed addressing up to 4 gigabytes (GB) of memory, supported virtual memory, and allowed multiple MS-DOS programs to run simultaneously. Beginning with Windows for Workgroups 3.11, only 386 enhanced mode operation allowed for use of the operating system's features. Real mode was still used in a limited way for advanced diagnostics and development, but this method of operation restricts the system's performance dramatically.

### Windows Resource Management

As mentioned, Windows is a resource manager, and it treats everything in the computer as a resource. Resources include memory, video, serial ports, and sound. All resources are presented to Windows through *device drivers*, files that establish communications between a device and the operating system.

Applications are resource consumers that must request access to any resource using standardized subroutines called the *application programming interface* (API). Another file called a dynamic-link library (DLL) can address the Windows core directly. These small files store subroutines that either come with the compiler that created the application or are created by the programmer. DLL files always end with the extension .dll. Loss or corruption of DLL files will cause an application to lock up or be prevented from loading.

---

**Note**   Some programs come with custom versions of DLLs that overwrite the standard DLL of the same name. If a problem occurs after loading a new application, installing a repair update of Windows might correct the problem, but this can also render the new program useless. In such cases, you will need to consult with the program vendor or check the Microsoft Knowledge Base at *http:/ www.microsoft.com* for more information on a fix.

---

When a program starts, it loads a small piece called a stub in conventional memory. This stub makes a request to the operating system for RAM (usually through a file named KRNL386.EXE), which then allocates the amount of RAM as long as it is available. This area of RAM is known as a *segment,* and its location is stored in a heap. Once loaded, a program can ask for resources as required. As long as there are resources available, Windows will provide them.

RAM is the most important resource that Windows must manage. Windows provides a way to gain memory when there is none using *virtual memory*, the ability to make something other than RAM chips hold data. Windows can create a special file (called a *swap file*) on the hard disk drive to act as a "virtual" RAM chip. Although this allows Windows to access additional resources, the hard drive is much slower than actual RAM. To compensate for this difference in speed, Windows prioritizes programs and caches the less frequently used ones to the slower hard drive, thus allowing the most active program to use the speedier RAM chips.

To get around the problem of resetting the CPU to run an MS-DOS program, later versions of Windows have the ability to run what is known as virtual 8086 mode, an extension of 386 protected mode that allows for the creation of virtual 8086 machines. A virtual 8086 machine is a segment of RAM that operates as if it is an 8086 computer. Windows will run itself in one virtual machine (VM) and allocate another VM to an MS-DOS program. Using several VMs, Windows can overcome the limitations of running only one MS-DOS program at a time.

## Windows for Workgroups 3.11

Microsoft Windows for Workgroups was an upgrade to Windows 3.1. It works and runs like Windows 3.1 with a few enhancements, such as better networking capabilities for sharing files and printers. It also includes two utility programs: Schedule+ and Mail Service.

## Windows 95, Windows 98, and Windows Me

Unlike earlier versions of Windows, Windows 95 became a true operating system in its own right. In addition, Windows 95 ushered in the era of Plug and Play technology, which allows the operating system to detect new hardware automatically. These versions of Windows overcome the limits of DOS and the 640-KB memory limits, can easily be networked, make use of the Internet, and are aimed at the home and general office markets. Windows Me is the most recent mass-market edition of the Windows 9x family and offers improved reliability and recovery, enhanced Plug and Play support, and extended multimedia capability.

## Windows NT

In 1993, Microsoft released another operating system aimed primarily at the professional scientific, engineering, and design markets. When it was first introduced, Microsoft Windows NT was used in relatively simple network installations. Over several revisions, it has been enhanced to support the needs of corporations ranging in size from small to large and, more recently, the needs of the Internet and intranets.

Windows NT Workstation is aimed at the technical and professional user, while the Server editions are designed for robust networking. Both provide high security levels not available in other Windows operating systems. There are several versions of Windows NT, ranging from 3.0 through 4.0. In addition, there are Service

Packs, which provide inline fixes that do not change the version number. Windows NT provides three levels of operating systems in each of the later versions:

- **Professional (replaces Workstation).** A powerful, robust operating system with limited networking to allow the professional user to share printers and files.

- **Server.** A complete LAN (local area network) host with a variety of sophisticated features for managing users and access to printers, files, RAID (redundant array of independent disks) installations, and other shared resources.

- **Advanced Server.** The enterprise edition includes all the tools in the Server edition, as well as additional tools for complex network environments.

## Windows 2000

Microsoft Windows 2000 is the replacement for Windows NT, adding Plug and Play support, better multimedia tools, and advanced Internet support. Like Windows NT, it comes in three versions: Professional (replaces Workstation), Server, and Advanced Server. It dramatically improves Plug and Play support, multimedia capabilities, and management and networking tools.

---

**Note**   Be careful when upgrading to Windows NT or Windows 2000. They are not merely more powerful versions of Windows 98, but more robust, completely new environments. Not all applications and hardware are compatible with them. Be sure to consider all the advantages and disadvantages before making the decision to upgrade. Check the Microsoft Web site at *http://www.microsoft.com* for the latest version of the compatibility list.

---

## Lesson Summary

The following points summarize the main elements of this lesson:

- An operating system provides the interface between hardware and user.

- MS-DOS was one of the first operating systems and was, for a long time, widely accepted as the standard.

- MS-DOS had some major limitations, especially in memory handling and user interface design.

- Early versions of Windows were operating environments that ran on top of MS-DOS.

- There are three files that make up the core operating system of MS-DOS: IO.SYS, MSDOS.SYS, and COMMAND.COM.

- Windows has progressed into a variety of products that offer full access to the features and power of the modern PC, as well as easy networking and a common platform for application design using a standard GUI.

- Windows still uses several DOS programs and the command prompt for several key operations.

# Lesson 2: The Command Prompt and DOS Mode Operations

The command prompt was the familiar PC user interface during the days of DOS. It still plays an important role in the life of a technician, even in the Windows era. This lesson covers the key skills needed to use it effectively.

## After this lesson, you will be able to

- Explain the role of the command-line interface
- Be familiar with key DOS terms
- Use the primary command prompt applications
- Understand the functions of CONFIG.SYS and AUTOEXEC.BAT

## Estimated lesson time: 60 minutes

Lesson 1 presented the basics of operating systems—what they are and what they do. It also provided a summary of the development of mainstream PC-based operating systems: MS-DOS and Windows. This lesson takes us one step further, into the realm of configuring an operating system and using core applications to maintain the system and investigate its performance using command-line applications and tools. It is not intended to be a complete course in command-line operations or all the fine points of the applications that are available from it. Both are well beyond the scope of this book.

**Note**  Bookstores and computer and software stores offer books that describe the various software operating systems. A reference book for each operating system that you work with is a necessary component of a computer technician's library. Microsoft also offers comprehensive documentation on its products, including updates, troubleshooting issues, and so on, as subscription programs.

## The COMMAND Command

MS-DOS, like UNIX, used a command-line or text-based user interface. This means that the user must memorize and type commands to interact with the operating system—not exactly a user-friendly operating system, and part of the reason for the popularity of Windows and its graphical interface. The latest versions of the Windows operating system still incorporate a limited version of DOS, which can be either used as a stand-alone environment or run within a window.

There are some advantages to the simpler text-based interface. It requires no fancy drivers; the display functions are built right into the system hardware. Running in DOS mode eliminates the need for 32-bit drivers and high memory management. That makes it an excellent tool when troubleshooting an ailing PC. When Windows fails, using the command line (often referred to as going into MS-DOS mode) is often the best way to access any recoverable data and begin the repair process. Computer professionals should know how to use and navigate in the DOS environment.

---

**Note**    During the course of this lesson, you are encouraged to actually try using the command line and running many of the examples. For that reason, we recommend reading this chapter in front of a PC. We assume you are using some version of Windows when we walk through an exercise. Keep in mind that some of these actions can alter the system, so be sure you understand any cautions given in the text and how the command will operate.

---

In Lesson 1, we looked at the three core files necessary to load MS-DOS on a system. COMMAND.COM contains the code that provides the actual user interface. By running this command under Windows, you open up a DOS session. You can do that now (regardless of the version of Windows you are using) by going to the Start menu, selecting Run, and typing **command**. A DOS window should open on your desktop with an active prompt.

Type the command **mem**. You can use uppercase, lowercase, or mixed case; DOS commands are not case-sensitive. The result should look somewhat like the example in Figure 16.1, an illustration that shows how the command interface works.

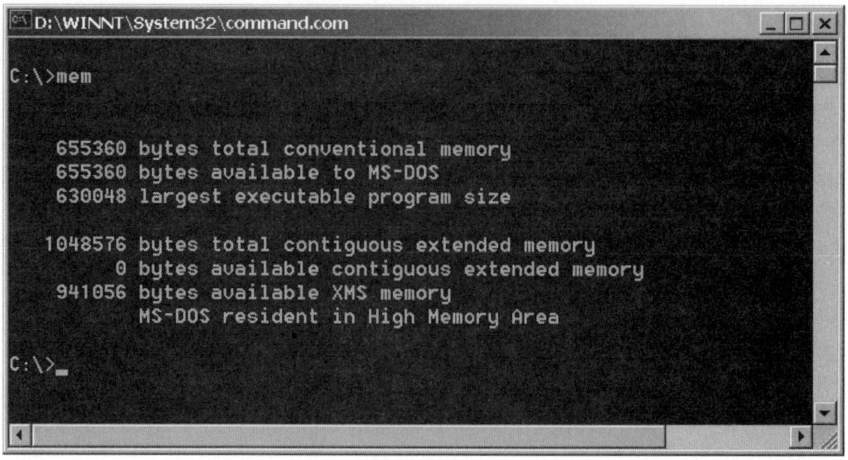

**Figure 16.1**    The command prompt and MEM application

The basic concept of command interface operation is quite simple. You type in a command, and when you press ENTER, the operating system loads and executes the command. That's exactly what happens, as shown in Figure 16.1. The information displayed on the screen shows the memory usage of the current system configuration. It was obtained by the memory command MEM.COM. Once the program has executed, the prompt with a blinking cursor reappears. It shows where characters will appear when you type them and indicates that the system is ready to accept a command.

You can modify the appearance and information presented by the command prompt in several ways to meet your personal preferences and needs. Working with this feature will help you understand how the command interface works and make you more familiar with using it. If you have access to a computer, you should have it running Windows with a DOS session window open. If you are running DOS, you should have an active command prompt with flashing cursor displayed. (The instructions that follow assume that you are working at the computer.) Provide the information displayed on the screen, if you can, to make it easy to follow along.

## Working with the Prompt

Type the command **PROMPT /?** or **HELP PROMPT**, then press ENTER (the syntax varies with the version of Windows or DOS; it's OK to try one and then the other). Commands are shown here in uppercase to make them stand out, but you can type them in uppercase, lowercase, or any combination, as DOS is not case-sensitive. After executing the command, something similar to the following information should be displayed on your screen (the exact information will vary with the version of DOS being used):

```
C:\>help prompt
Changes the command prompt.
PROMPT [text]
text     Specifies a new command prompt.
Prompt can be made up of normal characters and the following special
codes:
  $D   Current date
  $G   > (greater-than sign)
  $N   Current drive
  $P   Current drive and path
  $S   (space)
  $T   Current time
Press any key to continue . . .
```

We used the DOS HELP command to find out how to use the PROMPT command. HELP is an internal command, meaning the user doesn't have to know exactly where it resides; it is always available when the user has a prompt. The listing generated when the program executed started by explaining what the command does. The rather terse reply shows how this command can be used to customize how the prompt appears and the information it provides. The next line shows the syntax that must be used to actually enter the command. In this case, it is the command followed by the desired text that is to be the new prompt. Do not enter the brackets when you actually use the command.

The listings given later show some of the special options that can be added to the text string. The final line in the preceding example, Press any key to continue, tells you that more information on the command is still coming but cannot fit on the screen. You must press a key to display the rest of the information before the system will return an active prompt because the program has not finished executing.

To show you exactly how this command works and make you comfortable with the syntax used at the command line, we will experiment a bit. In the command line type

```
prompt This is the prompt with the time$S$t$g
```

then press ENTER. Your screen should look similar to the following example:

```
C:\>prompt This is the prompt with the time$S$t$g

This is the prompt with the time 9:32:22.43>
```

Here is what happened: The PROMPT command (the first word you typed) executed when you pressed ENTER. The program replaced the exiting prompt with the text and options you selected. The first word is capitalized because it was that way in the text string you typed, and DOS will take literally any character you type and make it part of the new prompt. The $S adds a space, the $t looks up and enters the current system time every time the prompt appears, and the $g produces the > symbol.

Try a few more strings, maybe your name with the date, and so on. Once you feel you understand how the command and the syntax work, change the prompt by typing the command **prompt$P$G** (which will give a prompt that looks like C:\>, where C is the active drive letter), and move on to the next part of the lesson.

## Internal and External Commands

External commands are programs that exist as separate files. To use them you must already be in the directory where the file exists, or tell the system exactly where to find the file by typing in the complete path to its location. You should be familiar with external commands because they are also common to the Windows environment. DOS mode provides several external programs and commands.

In Windows, you also have access to a variety of useful applications and system utilities, such as Windows Explorer, Notepad, System Information, and the Control Panel. DOS mode has its own collection of management tools—the internal commands—that are built into the operating system. These include DIR, the directory command, which displays a list of the files and subdirectories for the location in which it was requested; COPY, which allows you to make a copy of a file and move it to another location; and MEM, used earlier in the chapter, which provides a breakdown of memory use on your computer. Internal commands can be tied to the command prompt warning about where the file resides on the system. The following table lists examples of commonly used internal MS-DOS commands.

---

**Note**  Keep in mind that the exact options and operation of MS-DOS and DOS mode under Windows will vary from version to version.

---

| Command | Function |
| --- | --- |
| CHDIR or CD | Changes the directory (for example, cd\word would take you to the Word subdirectory). |
| CHKDSK | Examines the file allocation table (FAT) and directory structure on a drive, checking for errors and inconsistencies that can keep you from accessing a file. It also locates lost clusters and can convert them into files for later deletion. It can also reclaim wasted space. |
| CLS | Clears the screen. |
| COPY | Copies files or disks. To copy all files from the "myfiles" subdirectory to the A (floppy) drive, the command would be copy c:\myfiles\*.* a: Note that an asterisk (*) designates a wild card in DOS. In this case, you are copying all files with all extensions to the floppy drive. |
| DATE | Changes the system date. |
| DEL | Deletes files (for example, c:\del MYFILE.TXT). |
| DIR | Lists a directory of files. |
| DIR /P | Views directories one page at a time. This allows you to view a subset of the directories when you can't see all of the files on a single screen. (Directories can be quite long.) |
| DIR /W | Displays wide format in columns: Only the filename is listed, not size, date, or time. |
| DIR /W /P | Displays large directories in columns one page at a time. |
| DISKCOMP | Compares two disks. The syntax is: a:\ diskcomp a: b: or diskcomp a: a: (the computer will prompt you to insert the second disk to be compared). |
| MKDIR or MD | Makes a directory. |
| PROMPT | Changes the appearance of the cursor. |
| RENAME or REN | Renames a file. |
| RMDIR or RD | Deletes a directory. This works only if the directory is empty of all files, including hidden ones. |
| TIME | Changes the system time. |
| TYPE | Displays (types) a text file. |
| VER | Displays the version of MS-DOS in use. |

The following table lists examples of commonly used external MS-DOS commands.

| Command | Function |
| --- | --- |
| DISKCOPY | Makes a copy of a complete disk. Requires that both the source and the destination disk have the same format. |
| EDIT | Invokes the text editor program. This program is useful for making changes to text files, such as editing CONFIG.SYS and AUTOEXEC.BAT. |
| FORMAT | Prepares a disk for receiving files. Places a root directory on the disk. |
| FORMAT /S | Formats a disk as a system disk. |
| UNDELETE | Sometimes recovers a deleted file; works only if the disk has not been modified since the file was deleted. |
| XCOPY | Copies the contents of one disk to another disk. Does not require both disks to have the same format. (Note that it will not copy hidden files unless you use the /h switch.) |

Command mode is a good bit different from Windows, in which you can click (or double-click) on an icon to launch a program. In DOS mode, you have to know the name of the program you want to run and the directory where the program resides. There is very little information on the screen, and navigation is much different from within Windows. To use the command interface effectively, you must understand the concept of path and the syntax for entering commands and navigating the file system.

## DOS Mode Navigation and File Management

The DOS file system uses a tree structure for its directories, which is based on a concept of root and branches. The primary volume on a drive is called the *root;* it can contain both files and directories. Each directory creates another *branch,* which can also contain files and directories. A nested directory is a subdirectory of the level above it.

Strictly speaking, all directories in the DOS environment are actually subdirectories of the root directory and must be named. The root directory does not have a name; it is created when you set up the partition(s) on the drive, and it is represented by a backslash (\). A fully qualified path is the entire listing of directories from the root to the file. Look at the status bar in Figure 16.1. D:\WINNT\System32\COMMAND.COM is the full path to the COMMAND.COM file. System32 is a subdirectory of WINNT, which is a subdirectory of the root of the D drive.

The best way to become familiar with directory structure under DOS is to actually work with it. Because DIR is a system-level command, you don't have to provide the full path to it. Open up a command window, if you do not already have one open on your desktop. Type **dir**, and then press ENTER. The result should be similar to the one shown here, which has been edited as an example.

```
C:\WINNT>dir
 Volume in drive C has no label.
 Volume Serial Number is 7CF4-ED00
Directory of C:\WINNT
12/07/2000  06:13a      <DIR>          .
12/07/2000  06:13a      <DIR>          ..
09/06/2000  01:45p             16,214 Active Setup Log.txt
02/22/2000  03:47p                161 mmdet.log
12/07/1999  07:00a             50,960 NOTEPAD.EXE
12/09/2000  08:18a      <DIR>          system32
12/07/1999  07:00a             44,816 twain_32.dll
09/02/2000  07:05a                262 wcx_ftp.ini
              97 File(s)      4,665,353 bytes
              31 Dir(s)  13,901,348,864 bytes free
C:\WINNT>_
```

DIR provides a wealth of information if you know how to read it. The first two lines identify the drive for which the directory was requested, and the third gives the actual location involved. The actual listing of the files is presented as a table with four columns. The leftmost column shows the date on which the file was created; the second column gives the system time at which it was written to disk. The third column indicates if the item is a subdirectory (which is, in reality, a file that holds other files), and the fourth column provides the file size and the name of the file. The final two lines display the total number of files in the directory and their aggregate size in bytes, followed by the total number of subdirectories on the drive and the number of subdirectories with the total amount of free space on the drive.

---

**Note**   DOS does not support Windows long filenames. Some files may appear truncated, with something like a ~1 used to show the fact that the filename is actually different—for example, longna~1.doc. Also be aware that different versions of Windows and MS-DOS will have listings that may vary from the ones shown in this lesson.

---

Notice the first two directory listings. Their names seem to be made up of dots. They are not actually directories but placeholders for navigation. The best way to see how they work and get practice with DOS mode file operations is to create a directory and file, then navigate a bit. To do so, perform the following steps:

1. Change to the C drive, if you are not already logged on to this drive, by typing **C:** at the command prompt.

2. Type in **cd ..** until the prompt shows that you are in the root directory of the C drive with the prompt C:\>.

3. Next, create a directory named Test. Type **md test**. MD is the Make Directory internal command, and test is the name we are giving it. So the syntax is md [new directory name].

4. Use the DIR command and make sure the new directory is there. Now type **DIR test**. The result should look like this:

```
C:\>dir test
 Volume in drive C has no label.
 Volume Serial Number                        is 7CF4-ED00
 Directory of C:\test
12/09/2000  10:04a       <DIR>           .
12/09/2000  10:04a       <DIR>           ..
               0 File(s)              0 bytes
               2 Dir(s)   13,883,142,144 bytes free
C:\>
```

The DIR command gave the contents of Test because you asked it to by following the command with the name of the directory.

5. Now change into that directory by typing **CD test**. CD is the Change Directory internal command.

6. Type **DIR** and press ENTER. You should get the same listing as the Test directory in the active location.

## The PATH Command

Understanding the DOS concept of path and how to use the command of the same name is critical to command-line navigation and running applications in DOS mode. The best way to understand it is by using it. The PATH command displays or sets a search path for executable files. Here is the syntax for using PATH:

```
PATH [[drive:]path[;...][;%PATH%]
PATH ;
```

Type **PATH** without parameters to display the current path. Including %PATH% in the new path setting causes the old path to be appended to the new setting. PATH ; clears all search path settings and directs the system to search only in the current directory. The best way to become familiar with the PATH command is to use it. At a DOS prompt, simply type **path**. Doing so on a computer running Windows 2000 Workstation produces the following result:

```
C:\>path
PATH=C:\WINNT\system32;C:\WINNT;C:\WINNT\System32\Wbem;C:\PROGRA~1\RESOUR~1\
```

Your result will vary based on the way your system is configured. Any programs in any of the listed directories can be run from any location on the machine. Any other programs can only be run in their own native directories or be activated by typing in the full path before the program name. Listings with the ~ as part of the name, like RESOUR~1, are truncated. The name has been shortened because DOS mode does not support the long filenames used in newer versions of Windows.

Experiment with the PATH command until you are comfortable with it, and then move on to the next exercise.

---

**Tip**   Use the PATH command to set the active path to include the drive and directories of any programs you are troubleshooting in command mode. That lets you run them without changing to that location or typing the full path. Once the machine is rebooted, the path will return to its default setting.

---

## Creating a Batch File

To create a new file in your test directory using the COPY command, perform the following steps:

1. Have a DOS window open. Make sure you are still in the test directory with the DIR command by making sure the prompt reads C:\TEST>. (If not, type **CD \Test**.)

2. Type the following at the command prompt:

```
copy con newfile.bat
ver
mem
^Z
```

The ^Z at the end of the list is made by pressing CTRL while you press Z. This writes the file to disk. Be sure to press ENTER after each line to make the line breaks. After you type ^Z, press ENTER. The system should respond with:

```
1 file(s) copied
```

3. Repeat the DIR command. You should see the test file in the directory of C:\Test:

```
12/10/2000  07:22a      <DIR>           .
12/10/2000  07:22a      <DIR>           ..
12/10/2000  07:23a                   38 newfile.bat
             1 File(s)            38 bytes
             2 Dir(s)  14,077,116,416 bytes free
```

4. Now type **newfile**, then press ENTER. You should see the batch file you just created run, showing first the version of Windows being used and then the system memory configuration.

5. Type **CLS** (another internal command) at the prompt; the screen output will clear and you should be back at the C:> in the test directory (C:\Test>).

In this exercise, you created a file by typing commands in a plain ASCII file and giving it the name NEWFILE.BAT. A batch file is a program that will run a series of existing commands or applications when you enter its name at the DOS prompt.

## Renaming a File

By now, you should be getting comfortable with the command prompt. There are some additional skills you should have before taking the exam. One of these is the simple act of renaming the file. The test file we just created doesn't really explain what it does and it is a bit long. To rename a file, perform the following steps:

1. Type **Rename newfile.bat vm.bat** at the command prompt, then press ENTER.

2. As soon as you press ENTER, the name of the file should be changed. You can test this by simply typing **vm.bat** at the DOS prompt.

   The syntax of the rename command should be obvious by now. (You can also use the shortened ren.) Enter the RENAME command followed by the original filename, then the new filename. Next, do a little navigation.

3. At the command prompt type **CD..**  As explained earlier, the directory listing with the two dots is a placeholder for navigation purposes. You use it to move up one level in the directory structure.

4. The prompt should now show that you are in the root directory of the drive. Try running the new file by typing **vm.bat**. Because you are no longer in the directory that contains the file and the operating system does not find it, you should see an error message listing somewhat like this one:

   ```
   C:\>vm.bat
    vm.bat is not recognized as an internal or external command,
   operable program or batch file.
   C:\>
   ```

   The exact wording of the error message will vary based on the versions of DOS and Windows you are using. Earlier versions will simply show "File not found." DOS was never known for verbose help or error messages.

5. To run a program or use a file that is not in the current directory, you must provide the full path to the location of the file when you issue the command. In this case, you can run your batch file by pointing the operating system to the test directory like this: **C:\test\vm.bat**. First provide the drive letter, then use back slashes (\) to tell a system to move down into subdirectories, and finally give the full filename.

6. Try it, then clear the screen with the CLS command.

7. Now move back into the test directory, erase the test file, and remove the new directory to leave your system in the same condition it was in when you started this exercise. Once again, use the CD command to move into another directory. Type the following:

   ```
   cd \test
   erase vm.bat
   cd..
   rd test
   dir
   ```

When you give the ERASE VM.BAT command, depending on the version of DOS you are using, you may be prompted to confirm your command. Just press Y to confirm the operation and continue.

Now run a final directory command to check and make sure that the action has been completed. The directory should not be in the listing.

## Using Edit

At times you may need to edit text files like AUTOEXEC.BAT, CONFIG.SYS, SYSTEM.INI, or other primary configuration files in DOS mode. You could use the COPY command techniques employed earlier, but there is an easier way. All versions of DOS and Windows that you are likely to encounter include a text editor called Edit that you can use to create and modify text files. Figure 16.2 shows Edit open in a DOS window.

**Figure 16.2** Edit, the DOS mode text editor

Any computer technician should be able to operate a basic word processor and should find Edit quite familiar to use. Because of that, we won't dwell on its finer points. There are a few things that you should be aware of, however, if you are not used to the DOS environment:

- If the path to the file you wish to edit is not defined, you will have to enter it to run Edit and display the file you wish to edit.

- Unless you have a mouse driver for DOS mode installed in AUTOEXEC.BAT (or as part of native DOS operation), you will not have mouse support in Edit. Press ALT plus the first letter of the menu desired to open a menu, then the cursor keys and ENTER to select and use a function.

We work with additional DOS commands in the next lesson and in Chapter 17, "Introducing and Installing Microsoft Windows," Chapter 18, "Running Microsoft Windows," and Chapter 19, "Maintaining the Modern Computer," in conjunction with very important troubleshooting techniques. The following table presents a quick reference of some of the important terms and concepts you should be familiar with when working in DOS mode, as well as for the A+ certification exam. Some items are a review of the previous discussion; some expand on the material just presented and will be used as we continue.

| Term | Description |
|---|---|
| Backslash (\) | A symbol used to separate each directory level, for instance C:\Windows\Utilities. For this reason, it is a reserved character and cannot be used as part of a filename. |
| Case sensitivity | The ability of the operating system to distinguish between uppercase and lowercase letters. MS-DOS commands are not case-sensitive. Traditionally, MS-DOS commands have been represented in documentation as uppercase. You can type MS-DOS commands in either uppercase or lowercase (they are shown in this book as uppercase). |
| Cursor | Anytime you are entering data, whether in an application or in an MS-DOS command, the cursor (usually a small flashing line) indicates the place where the next character will be inserted. It is a good idea to always know where your cursor is. |
| Default drive | Each drive in a computer has its own letter designation. The default drive is the active drive. Unless otherwise specified, any commands act on the default drive. The current default drive is indicated by the MS-DOS prompt. For example, if you want to see a directory (the command is DIR) of files on the A drive and the default drive is C, you need to type **DIR A:**. Otherwise, you will see a directory of the C drive. |
| Directory | Directories—known as folders in the Windows and Macintosh environments—are locations for storing files. Every disk contains a main directory known as the *root directory*. Below the root directory is a hierarchical structure of other subdirectories. |
| DOS prompt | The DOS prompt usually displays the active drive letter (for instance, C) and directory. This indicates that the operating system is ready to accept the next command. (The prompt is user-changeable.) |
| Drive pointers | DOS assigns letters to each drive during the boot process. |
| Entering commands | You can type a command and press ENTER to execute it. If you make a mistake, correct it by using the BACKSPACE or DEL keys. Use ESC to start a command again. Press F3 to repeat a command. |
| Error messages | Brief technical messages that are displayed when an error occurs. |
| Filenames (also filespecs) | A filename is made up of three parts—a name of up to eight characters, a period, and an extension of up to three characters. The name can include any number, character, or the following symbols (reserved characters): _ ( ) ~ ' ! % $ & #<br>You cannot use spaces in MS-DOS filenames. |
| Greater than (>) | This symbol is used to indicate that a command can be redirected to an output device. For example, to redirect the directory command to a printer, type **DIR > LPT1**. |

*(continued)*

| Term | Description |
|------|-------------|
| Path | The address to a file. The path consists of the drive name, the location of the file in the directory structure, and the filename (for example, C:\Mystuff\MYFILE.DOC). |
| Prompt | The command prompt–user interface provided by COMMAND.COM to signal to the user that the computer is ready to receive input (for example, C:\> or A:\>). |
| Switches | Many MS-DOS commands can be used with a switch (/ followed by a letter) to invoke special functions. Because no comprehensive MS-DOS manuals are available as part of the shipping product for versions later than MS-DOS 5, when you follow a command with a space and /, a list of parameters and switches available for that command is displayed. |
| Syntax | Syntax is the arrangement and interrelationship of words in phrases and sentences. In computer jargon, it is the correct format in which to type a command. In MS-DOS, every letter, number, and space has a value. The most common problem when typing MS-DOS commands is adding or leaving out a letter or character. Simple typing mistakes are the most common cause for "Bad command or filename" errors. |
| Wildcards | These can be used to expand a search for a file with the DIR command, and allow the user to locate files of a similar type or name. The question mark (?) matches any character in a specified position, and the asterisk (*) matches any number of characters up to the end of the filename or extension. For example, to search for files beginning with the letter A, the command would be DIR A*.* or A?????.* (the second command would find a file that starts with the letter A and any other five characters). |

## Working with CONFIG.SYS and AUTOEXEC.BAT

As mentioned in Lesson 1, the CONFIG.SYS and AUTOEXEC.BAT files can be used during the boot process to execute commands and load legacy drivers in many versions of Windows (although their use diminished beginning with Windows 95). The CONFIG.SYS file is run first. It sets up and configures the computer's user-defined hardware components. The AUTOEXEC.BAT file executes commands and loads TSR programs.

**Note**  TSRs were very popular during the heyday of MS-DOS and were often used to adjust how the operating system used memory. If these programs improperly adjust the system memory stack or cause a conflict, they can cause a variety of difficult to isolate problems. The problem gets worse if more than one program is being used. In the Windows environment, you should generally stay away from using TSRs unless they are absolutely necessary. We cover their operation with different versions of Windows in Chapter 17, "Introducing and Installing Microsoft Windows," and troubleshooting in Chapter 18, "Running Microsoft Windows."

## CONFIG.SYS Commands

The following table lists several CONFIG.SYS settings and their functions. Keep in mind that not all settings are available (or recommended) in all versions of Windows.

| Setting | Function |
| --- | --- |
| BUFFERS | Allocates reserved memory for transferring information to and from the hard disk. |
| COUNTRY | Enables MS-DOS to use country conventions for times, dates, and currency. Example: COUNTRY=044,437,C:\DOS\COUNTRY.SYS. (You do not need to use this in the United States unless you wish to use an alternate convention.) |
| DEVICE | Loads a device driver into memory. Example: DEVICE=C:\DOS\EMM386.EXE |
| DEVICEHIGH | Loads a device driver into upper memory. |
| DOS | Loads part of MS-DOS into upper memory area. Example: DOS=HIGH, UMB |
| FCBS | Specifies the number of file control blocks (FCBs) that MS-DOS can have open at the same time. |
| FILES | Specifies the number of files that MS-DOS can hold open concurrently. Example: FILES=60 |
| INSTALL | Loads a memory-resident program. Example: INSTALL=C:\DOS\SHARE.EXE/F:500 /L:500 |
| LASTDRIVE | Specifies the maximum number of drives the computer can access. Example: LASTDRIVE=Z |
| MOUSE.SYS | Loads a mouse driver. |
| NUMLOCK | Specifies whether the Num Lock key is on or off when MS-DOS starts. |
| SHELL | Specifies the name and location of the command interpreter. The interpreter converts the typed command to an action. The default for MS-DOS is COMMAND.COM. |
| SWITCHES | Specifies special options in MS-DOS. The /n switch will disable the use of the F5 and F8 keys to bypass startup commands (used for security). |

Here is a sample CONFIG.SYS listing:

```
DEVICE=C:\WINDOWS\HIMEM.SYS
DEVICE=C:\DOS\EMM386.EXE NOEMS
DOS=HIGH, UMB
BUFFERS=20
FILES=80
FCBS=4,0
LASTDRIVE=Z
DEVICE=C:\CDROM\NEC2.SYS /D:MSCD001 /V
```

## AUTOEXEC.BAT Commands

The following table lists several commands that are often used in an AUTOEXEC.BAT file.

| Setting | Function |
| --- | --- |
| ECHO | Displays commands as they are executed. ECHO OFF suppresses the display of commands as they are executed. |
| PAUSE | Stops the execution of AUTOEXEC.BAT and displays the message "Strike any key to continue." |
| PATH | Defines the search path for program commands. |
| SET | Displays, sets, or removes MS-DOS environment variables. |
| SMARTDRV | Provides disk caching. |
| KEYB | Configures a keyboard for a specific language. |
| SHARE | Starts the Share program, which will install the file sharing and locking capabilities. |
| DOSKEY | Loads the DOSKEY program. You can use the DOSKEY program to view, edit, and carry out MS-DOS commands that you have used previously. |
| MOUSE.EXE | Loads a mouse driver. |
| PROMPT | Sets the display of the command prompt. |

Here is a sample AUTOEXEC.BAT listing:

```
@ECHO OFF
PATH C:\DOS;C:\WINDOWS;C:\
DOSKEY
SMARTDRV
UNDELETE /LOAD
VSAFE
MSAV
```

**Tip**   Here are a couple of useful tricks to try when working with CONFIG.SYS and AUTOEXEC.BAT. If you want the computer to ignore a command line, type **REM** before that statement. For example, REM MOUSE.EXE would tell the computer to ignore that line, and the MOUSE.EXE file would not be loaded. Before editing existing CONFIG.SYS or AUTOEXEC.BAT files, copy them to a different directory or make a copy of each, but with an .old extension to the filename (AUTOEXEC.OLD and CONFIG.OLD). This way, you will have the current configuration data at hand if something goes amiss.

## Lesson Summary

The following points summarize the main elements of this lesson:

- DOS mode programs offer tools for working with a Windows system that is not properly loading the user interface or 32-bit modes and cannot be repaired using safe mode.

- DOS mode is still used for performing low-level disk operations like partitioning hard drives and running some virus test and recovery programs.

- A+ technicians should know how to navigate in DOS mode and perform basic file operations.

- CONFIG.SYS and AUTOEXEC.BAT are two files that allow custom settings during the boot phase but are not fully supported (or even recommended) with some 32-bit versions of Windows.

# Lesson 3:  File Systems

One of the most important roles that an operating system plays in computer operations is defining and managing the file system. This lesson examines the major file systems in use today. In configuring a system or performing a new upgrade, it is often necessary to choose the appropriate file system for best performance, full access to operating system features, system security, data reliability, and compatibility.

## After this lesson, you will be able to

- Explain the differences among the major file systems used on today's PCs
- Understand why different types of media (magnetic, CD-ROM, and so on) have different file systems and attributes
- Understand how to choose which file system to use on a new hard drive or floppy disk
- Understand file attributes and how they are used

## Estimated lesson time: 40 minutes

## File System Basics

The file system is a component of the operating system that acts as an interface with hardware storage devices, and organizes data on them in a form that can be used by the system and applications. It is not unusual to have several file systems on a modern PC. Part of the reason for this is that different types of storage media often require different types of formatting or translation because of the amount of storage media involved or for compliance with a standard. For example, the size of a hard disk will limit which file system it can use, and CD-ROM devices are manufactured with a specific file system already in place.

The file system defines many things including file naming conventions, file size, and, in some cases, the capacities of the storage products themselves. In the case of products like CD-ROMs, digital video discs (DVDs), and Zip drives, the manufacturer or a standards committee defines the capacities.

Magnetic media like floppy drives and hard disks employ several different types of file systems, depending on the operating system on the target computer. Choosing the right operating system is an important step during the installation or upgrade process.

### Key Terms

The following table provides definitions for key words that are necessary to understand the operation of file systems. Most should already be familiar from earlier lessons, but a quick review is in order.

| Term | Definition |
|---|---|
| Block | A set of contiguous bits that make up a definable quantity of information on storage media. |
| Boot disk | A system device (usually a hard drive, floppy drive, or CD-ROM drive) that is used to start a computer. Usually, but not always, this device also contains the operating system code. |
| Boot sector | The sector on a disk containing a small amount of information that defines the devices layout, identifies the file system, and allows the drive to be declared a boot device. |
| Cluster | The number of disk sectors that can be treated as a single object by the operating system. |
| Dual boot | A hard disk or system that has been configured so that it can operate using more than a single operating system or file system. |
| Encryption | A method of encoding data, usually to prevent unauthorized use, in a form that can be read only by using the decoding mechanism. |
| End-of-file (EOF) marker | This is the last bit of information contained in the file. In the preceding lesson, when you created a batch file, the CTRL+Z character was the EOF marker. |
| File | Data collected and stored as a single unit on some form of mass storage medium. |
| FAT | The linked list system used to track disk space currently in use. This was the fundamental method used by early DOS operating systems, and is still available today in several formats. |
| File format | The way the file content is formatted for individual files within a file system. |
| File handle | An integer value set by the file system to denote an open file. |
| File locking | A feature in a network file system that allows an individual file to be locked so that two instances cannot be open for modification at the same time. |
| Filename | The identifier used to label the individual file for use by the operating system or user. Different file systems have different naming conventions, allowed lengths, and reserve characters that cannot be used in naming a file. |
| Folder | The equivalent of a directory that is used to hold a collection of files in the Windows file system. |
| Format | The act or program used to prepare a disk for use by a file system. Also referred to as a high-level format, it requires that the hardware already be prepared with a low-level format and be partitioned. This usually involves dividing the media into a series of tracks and sectors. |
| Low-level format | An initial preparation of a hard disk used to prepare the media for partitioning and high-level formatting by a file system. Low-level formatting is usually performed using firmware or software provided by the drive or disk controller manufacturer. |

*(continued)*

| Term | Definition |
|------|------------|
| Master boot record | A specific sector on the first partition of the drive containing executable code and information about the operation of the start process for a given operating system. |
| Partition table | Indicates the logical structure (partitions) of a hard disk. Partitions are used to divide a large physical drive into smaller virtual sections. Each section can then be described as a logical drive and have its own individual drive letter. The partition table is kept in the same location as the master boot record. |
| Primary partition | The key partition on a hard disk. Most systems only have one primary partition, which holds the boot sector and operating system. This volume is usually designated the C drive. |
| Sector | The smallest storage unit on a disk. |
| Track | A series of sectors residing on a disk and arranged so that they lie at the same horizontal distance from the center of the disk. |
| Volume | A physical or virtual drive designated on a storage system. |

## Comparing and Choosing File Systems

There are several file systems commonly used on today's PCs. For most users, the operating system of choice is Microsoft Windows, of which several varieties are available, including Windows 95, Windows 98, Windows Me, Windows NT, and Windows 2000. All offer two or more options for choosing a file system. As an A+ technician, you will be expected to help users select the right operating system, install an appropriate file system, and explain the differences among them. The actual choice of which file system to use can involve several factors, as follows:

- Is the computer's storage system to be dedicated to a single operating environment, or will the machine be used for two or more operating systems?

- How many hard drives will be installed on the system?

- What are the sizes of the drives to be used on the system?

- How large are the expected partitions on the hard drives?

- Will the user need to make use of any legacy applications that will not support one of the newer file systems?

- Is the owner interested in using advanced file system features only offered on newer file systems?

- Are there security considerations that require the use of a file system that provides additional controls over access to directories and files?

# FAT-Based File Systems

All modern PCs can use a FAT-based file system. This is a very simple form of file system, named for the fact that it organizes files by listing them in a table. A backup copy is maintained, and both are kept in the root directory of the primary partition. The FAT file system was originally developed for floppy disks, and all versions of Windows still use FAT for that purpose.

There are three basic varieties of the FAT file system in use today. All start with the letters FAT, followed by numbers designating the number of bits required for a single FAT entry. For example, the floppy drive version known as FAT12 uses a 12-bit table. FAT16 was introduced with MS-DOS 3.0 to enable support for large drives. FAT32 is the preferred file system for Windows 95 and later versions and supports long filenames.

FAT-based file systems are quite popular and perhaps the most widely used PC-based file system. Reasons for their popularity include ease of installation, a wide range of management tools, and compatibility with a wide range of operating systems including all versions of Microsoft Windows, OS/2, and many PC versions of UNIX.

## FAT16 and FAT32 Compared and Contrasted

Deciding to use FAT and choosing which version to use was simple in the past. In the days of MS-DOS, FAT16 was just about the only option. FAT32 complicated matters. It offers several enhancements but lacks some of the broad compatibility of its earlier sibling.

The following table compares the various features of FAT16 with FAT32.

| FAT16 | FAT32 |
| --- | --- |
| Widest range of compatibility with operating systems, supported by all versions of DOS, Windows 95, Windows 98, Windows NT, Windows 2000, and several versions of Unix. | Limited compatibility with operating systems. FAT32 for Windows 95 OSR2 (Operating System Release 2) and Windows 98 are only compatible with those operating systems. |
| MS-DOS bootable floppy can be used to boot a problem system and access all files on a viable FAT16 hard drive. | Cannot use a DOS or Windows 95 (other than OSR2) disk to boot and access files on the hard drive. |
| Small system footprint offers performance advantages on volume smaller than 250 MB. | FAT32 allocates disk space more efficiently than FAT16, allowing the system to make more efficient use of disk space. It often allows storing of much more data compared to FAT16. |
| Requires manual intervention to make use of the backup copy of the FAT if the original becomes corrupted. | Can automatically employ a backup copy of a volume's FAT if the master copy becomes corrupt. |

*(continued)*

| FAT16 | FAT32 |
|---|---|
| No backup provided of the boot sector. If the boot sector becomes corrupt, all data on the volume may be lost. | Provides automatic backup of the boot sector, providing a way to possibly recover the volume in the event of a boot sector failure. |
| Individual volume size cannot exceed 2 GB and still maintain full compatibility with all supported operating systems. | Supports drives up to 2 terabytes (TB) in size; largest volume size is 32 GB. |
| No version of the FAT file system provides built-in security or data compression methods. | |
| Offers much better performance if the system must use real-mode MS-DOS or Windows 98 operating in safe mode. | Smaller cluster size can result in faster load times for applications and large data files. |
| Dual boot of DOS and Windows, Windows NT, and Windows 98 is possible with FAT16. | Dual boot with non-FAT32-supported operating systems is not supported. |
| FAT16 is limited in the length of filenames to the 8.3 convention of an eight-character name with a three-character extension and no spaces. | FAT32 supports long filenames of up to 255 characters with the ability to use spaces. |
| FAT16 volumes can be converted to FAT32 using the Drive Converter Wizard. Once done, the drive cannot be returned to FAT16 operation. | |

# The NTFS File System

With the advent of Windows NT, Microsoft introduced the NTFS (NT file system). Like FAT32, it supports long filenames and the use of spaces in names. Unlike FAT, NTFS is optimized for multiuser environments. It provides an extra level of file security, and is more reliable than previous file systems. This technology was improved with the release of Windows 2000. As with the advances in the FAT system, there are some minor incompatibilities among versions due to the changes needed to allow for improved features. As a result, not all file system operations available in the Windows 2000 version of NTFS can be used when accessed by systems running Windows NT. Microsoft recommends using the new version of NTFS on all machines running Windows 2000 unless there is some overriding reason to use an alternate file system. The following lists detail the advantages and disadvantages of the NTFS file system.

## In the Plus Column

- NTFS supports very large volumes up to 2 TB in size.
- It maintains a log that can be used to recover and repair a volume's content in the event of a system failure.
- The root folder volume can hold an unlimited number of files.

- NTFS employs a B-tree file structure resulting in faster file access. B-tree data structures are often used in database applications, allowing the system to quickly trace a record or file using a branching algorithm.

- The advanced compression systems available on NTFS volumes allow users to compact individual files and folders and still read them while they are compressed.

- Both folders and files can be set with security levels that define who can access them, the level of access permitted, and whether or not the file can be accessed over any network. You can set security levels for individual users, groups of users, or all users on the system.

- An administrator can set disk quotas limiting the amount of space that an individual user can use for personal files.

### In the Minus Column

- NTFS volumes are not directly accessible under MS-DOS, Windows 95, or Windows 98.

- NTFS volumes cannot be used as a primary partition for dual boot system configurations with those operating systems.

- For volumes smaller than 400 MB that consist mainly of small files, the additional overhead required for NTFS features may result in slower performance than under a FAT file system.

## File System Size Limitations

Different file systems are available on PCs developed during different points in hardware development. As a result, their capabilities relative to hard disk size mirror the increasing capacity of the hardware at the time the operating system was released. The following table shows the supported volume size and default cluster size for the various operating systems. Keep in mind that under FAT, drives smaller than 16 MB are created using the FAT12 mode. Another consideration is that MS-DOS, Windows 95, and Windows 98 cannot access FAT16 volumes larger than 2 GB.

| Volume Range | FAT16 | FAT32 | NTFS |
|---|---|---|---|
| 7 MB–16 MB | 2 KB | Not supported | 512 bytes |
| 17 MB–32 MB | 512 bytes | Not supported | 512 bytes |
| 33 MB–64 MB | 1 KB | 512 bytes | 512 bytes |
| 65 MB–128 MB | 2 KB | 1 KB | 512 bytes |
| 129 MB–256 MB | 4 KB | 2 KB | 512 bytes |
| 257 MB–512 MB | 8 KB | 4 KB | 512 bytes |
| 513 MB–1024 MB | 16 KB | 4 KB | 4 KB |

*(continued)*

| Volume Range | FAT16 | FAT32 | NTFS |
|---|---|---|---|
| 1025 MB–2 GB | 32 KB | 4 KB | 4 KB |
| 2 GB–4 GB | Not supported | 4 KB | 4 KB |
| 4 GB–8 GB | Not supported | 4 KB | 4 KB |
| 8 GB–16 GB | Not supported | 8 KB | 4 KB |
| 16 GB–32 GB | Not supported | 16 KB | 4 KB |
| 32 GB–2 TB | Not supported | Not supported | 4 KB |

As you can see from the data here, the size of the volume to be formatted and used has a direct bearing on which operating systems are available.

## File System Security

Maintaining the security of files on an operating system is another consideration when choosing a file system. Generally speaking, NTFS offers significant security advantages over other PC-based file systems. FAT offers the advantage of less overhead plus greater OS compatibility and may be better suited when advanced security mechanisms are not needed.

### File Attributes on FAT File Systems

FAT was developed without any direct consideration of multiple users on the system, so designers had no concern about prying eyes. You cannot lock a file so that it can be kept from anyone who has access to the system. Instead of passwords and locked files and directories, FAT offers a set of attributes that provide a method to prevent overwriting files that need to stay in the same form, to hide files from being shown in regular directory listings, and to denote if a file has been backed up. The FAT maintains a marker for each file noting whether or not an attribute is set.

In DOS mode, you can set file attributes using the attribute command. In Windows, you can adjust attributes by right-clicking a file and choosing the Properties option from the shortcut menu. The following listing shows the syntax and options when using the attribute command in DOS mode:

```
ATTRIB [+R | -R] [+A | -A ] [+S | -S] [+H | -H] [[drive:] [path]
filename] [/D]]
```

```
+    Sets an attribute.
-    Clears an attribute.
R    Read-only file attribute.
A    Archive file attribute.
H    Hidden file attribute.
/S   Processes matching files in the current directory (folders)
     and all sub directories.
/D   Processes directories as well as files.
```

## NTFS File and Folder Security

NTFS uses the concept of permissions rather than attributes to control access to files and folders contained within the file system. These vary somewhat from version to version, but regardless of the version, permissions are set using a dialog box that can be accessed by right-clicking on the file or folder involved and choosing the appropriate options from the dialog box. Once set, the permissions apply to both local users and anyone accessing the system over the network. Figure 16.3 shows the Security tab in the AUTOEXEC Properties dialog box. It lists the names of the individuals and roles (such as the system administrator) that have been granted permissions to the file, as well as the permissions involved. Select options by clicking the appropriate button.

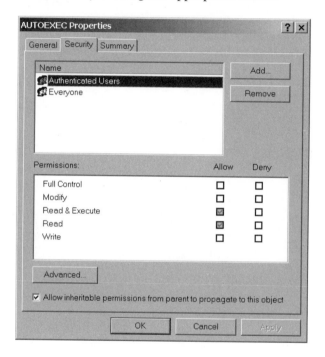

**Figure 16.3**   The Windows 2000 AUTOEXEC Properties dialog box's Security tab

The basic options include Full Control, Modify, Read and Execute, Read, and Write. A more extensive collection of options including who can delete subfolders, create files within a folder, modify permissions, and take ownership of a file or directory are included in the Advanced Permissions dialog box (shown in Figure 16.4), which is accessed from the Properties dialog box by clicking the Advanced button.

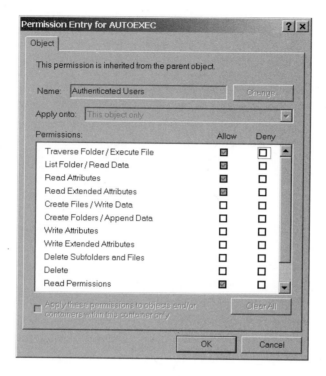

**Figure 16.4**   The Advanced Permissions dialog box

## Lesson Summary

The following points summarize the main elements of this lesson:

- Choosing a file system often involves several variables.

- The size of a hard drive may be the deciding factor in choosing a file system.

- If the system must support more than one operating system, FAT16 may be the only option.

- FAT-based file systems offer wide compatibility, a small footprint, and good performance on small drives.

- NTFS systems provide much better support for large drives and enhanced security.

# Chapter Summary

The following points summarize the key concepts in this chapter:

## Operating System Basics

- An operating system is the interface between hardware and user.

- All operating systems contain several basic features including the need for a user interface, and the ability to manage memory, files, and information between the PC and remote devices.

- PC operating systems have evolved from a very simple command-line interface and management of floppy drive storage to a variety of products that offer full access to the features and power of the modern PC, as well as easy networking and a common platform for application design using a standard GUI.

- Understanding operating system installation, operations, and troubleshooting are key skills for a computer technician.

## The Command Prompt and DOS Mode Operations

- In spite of the advent of new GUIs, knowledge of command prompt operations is a necessary skill for troubleshooting computer problems.

- The command prompt is a basic user interface that accepts a command, executes that command, and returns control to the user.

- There are a number of internal and external commands that are still very useful in diagnosing and configuring an ailing system.

- Edit is an external MS-DOS program that offers the ability to create and edit plaintext files.

## File Systems

- There are a variety of file systems, in several versions, available for PC platform use.

- The most common PC file system is probably FAT16.

- FAT32 offers several enhancements over FAT16, including support for long filenames and larger hard drives. However, it is less compatible with other operating systems.

- NTFS offers many enhanced features over other PC file systems, but it is only compatible with Windows NT, Windows Me, and Windows 2000.

- A single PC system can have more than one file system, but care must be taken in ensuring compatibility and access to files.

- There are a number of factors involved in choosing the correct operating system, including compatibility, hardware configuration, security, networking capability, and the need for the machine to boot in more than one operating system.

# Review

The following questions are intended to reinforce key information presented in this chapter. If you are unable to answer a question, review the appropriate lesson and then try the question again. Answers to the questions can be found in Appendix A, "Questions and Answers."

1. What does DOS stand for?

2. What was DOS created to do?

3. Which version of MS-DOS is bundled with Windows 95?

4. Describe the core operating system files used within MS-DOS.

5. What are the two MS-DOS user-definable startup files and their purpose?

6. Which DOS command is used to show the amount of free space left on a disk?

7. Describe the difference between real mode and protected mode.

8. Which wildcard character can be used to replace a single character in a search string?

9. Explain the operation of the command-line interface.

10. If a user working in DOS mode types a valid command to execute an external program and gets the response "File not found," what is the most common reason for the error message?

11. Your customer wishes to have a machine configured for both the Linux operating system and Microsoft Windows 2000 Professional. The computer has only one hard drive. Identify which file system you would recommend and explain the reasons for your choice.

12. Explain the steps involved in preparing a new hard drive to accept an operating system.

13. Why didn't the designers of the FAT file system provide a method for limiting access to files and folders?

C H A P T E R   1 7

# Introducing and Installing Microsoft Windows

**Lesson 1: The Windows Family** ............................... 411

**Lesson 2: Preparing for Windows Installation** ................... 418

**Lesson 3: Installing Windows** ................................ 425

**Chapter Summary** ......................................... 446

**Review** ................................................. 447

## About This Chapter

This chapter describes the different members of the Microsoft Windows family and covers both the planning and installation procedures of a Windows deployment for both Microsoft Windows 98 and Microsoft Windows 2000 as required for the A+ Certification Exam. It is a prerequisite for Chapter 18, "Running Microsoft Windows," which focuses on operating and managing these popular PC environments. To gain the high level of proficiency required of today's computer professional, you should obtain advanced training in these operating systems and build a library of references after completing this chapter.

---

**Note**   This chapter focuses on the Windows 98 and Windows 2000 operating systems because they are the primary focus on the A+ Exam. Information on Microsoft Windows Me is provided to round out the discussion, but it is not currently covered on the test. Some material on Microsoft Windows 95 and earlier versions of Windows is included because you may be expected to perform upgrades on computers running these operating systems.

---

## Before You Begin

This chapter assumes you are familiar with the Windows operating environment and the material presented in Chapter 16, "Operating System Fundamentals." You should be comfortable using DOS mode and familiar with PC system components.

# Lesson 1:  The Windows Family

In this lesson, we compare the different members of the Windows family from the end-user Windows 98 to the enterprise world of large-scale servers and Windows 2000 Datacenters.

## After this lesson, you will be able to

- Differentiate among the current versions of Windows
- Know the basic features, system requirements, intended users, and uses for the different versions of Windows currently on the market

## Estimated lesson time: 15 minutes

## The Expanding Windows Family

The first edition of Microsoft Windows was released in 1983. It was actually little more than a graphical interface for MS-DOS. Over the next dozen years, Microsoft engineers developed the product into a suite of full-fledged, 32-bit operating systems. The Windows family of products can be divided into two categories: Windows 9*x* versions were offered primarily for use at home and in small offices, and the Windows 2000 series was developed mainly for technical, scientific, network, and enterprise applications.

Although end users are often only familiar with the version of Windows loaded on their computers, as a computer technician you must be familiar with the entire line of current Windows editions. You must be able to recommend the correct product to clients and to install and support it. The following sections provide a quick overview of the Windows operating systems currently on the market.

### Windows 95

Windows 95 was released to the public in the summer of 1995. It represented a change in naming conventions, as Microsoft moved from version numbers, such as Windows 3.1, to a naming system that included the date the new operating system was released. Windows 95 was aimed at the consumer market, but its ease of use quickly made it popular in the business market as well. You may encounter two variations of Windows 95, but no new copies of this operating system are being sold. The original OSR1 version of Windows 95, sold as both a stand-alone product and an upgrade, was the regular, commercial, off-the-shelf product. The updated OSR2 version, adding new hardware support, was only offered as an original equipment manufacturer (OEM) product installed on new PCs. (You couldn't purchase this version without buying a new computer.)

In general, you should recommend an upgrade to a newer version of Windows to any customer bringing in a Windows 95 system for service. These more recent editions of Windows, listed below, offer significant improvements over Windows 95.

## Windows 98

Three years after the introduction of Windows 95, Microsoft released Windows 98. This version of Windows was the first to really take advantage of Plug-and-Play technology. Hardware meeting the Plug-and-Play requirements is automatically detected and configured by the operating system after installation. It eliminated the need to set jumpers and memory addresses for direct memory access (DMA) channels and it added internal support for new hardware standards including USB (universal serial bus) and IEEE (Institute of Electrical and Electronics Engineers) 1394.

Windows 98 also introduced a new generation of support tools, including a maintenance wizard that allows users to schedule automatic execution of disk defragmentation and other routine, recurring tasks. The System Information tool makes short work of checking settings, identifying drivers, and tracking the operation of the computer. We look at these utilities in detail in the next chapter.

The Internet was growing in importance during the development of Windows 98, and the new operating system closely integrated the browser with the operating system. It is also possible to tailor the user interface to make it very similar to browsing the World Wide Web.

## Windows Millennium Edition

The most recent edition of Windows designed for home and general office use shipped in the third quarter of 2000. Once again modifying the naming convention, the product is called Windows Me. It continues the trend in Windows development toward improved ease of use, ease of maintenance, and support for the newest PC hardware.

Windows Me is closely linked with the Internet. Users can elect to have the system automatically updated over the Internet via the Microsoft Web site. The System Restore feature makes it just as easy to undo configuration changes and return a computer to a preupdate condition. Windows help is now presented in a browser window, and the user interface can be tailored to mimic browser operation in many respects. The Windows Media Player is now a full-fledged multimedia tool. Local area networking has been simplified with increased use of wizards for setup of devices like printers and scanners that can be shared. Internet settings can be copied from browser to browser so that multiple computers can share the same logon information and favorites.

Microsoft markets Windows 98 and Windows Me as the best platforms for multimedia, PC gaming, and home network applications. It also offers broader support for consumer PC hardware and software products. These operating systems are designed for installation by the average end user. The hardware requirements are geared to the typical home PC. Given these features, many network administrators have also chosen to make these platforms the operating systems of choice for their average network users.

## Windows NT

Power users and those using computers for scientific and technical applications often require more powerful systems than the average office worker. Network servers require higher degrees of reliability, security, and advanced management tools. To meet those needs, Microsoft developed another series of operating systems, calling the initiative New Technology (NT). The result was the Windows NT platform.

Windows NT is not just an upscale version of Windows 9*x*. It is a completely different operating system, designed to offer faster performance, exceptional reliability, advanced security, scalable performance (multiprocessor, clustered computing), and the ability to operate with a number of different processor families (Intel Pentium, DEC Alpha). Today it is available in both a workstation edition for stand-alone use and a variety of server platforms scaling all the way from small networks to large enterprise and Web farm environments.

Microsoft released Windows NT 3.1 in 1993, in both workstation and server editions. Windows NT 3.51 was released in 1995, offering additional security enhancements and support for POSIX (Portable Operating System Interface for Unix). This version also offered tools for incorporating mixed networks of Windows NT and Novell NetWare servers.

Windows NT 4.0, released in 1996, incorporated a user interface very similar to that of Windows 95. It also extended the range of hardware supported by the operating system. Until this release, Windows NT lacked a range of drivers for scanners, sound cards, and similar desktop components. There are still significant numbers of computers running Windows NT 4.0. The majority of these installations are servers, and the average nonnetworking technician is unlikely to be called on to perform major service to this operating system.

## Windows 2000

Windows 2000 is the successor to Windows NT (during its early development it was called Windows NT 5.0). In spite of the name change, Windows 2000 is built on a solid Windows NT foundation. In many ways, Windows 2000 combines the best of Windows 98 and Windows NT. It offers and extends the multiprocessor support, advanced security and administration tools, NTFS (NT file system), and robust network capability found in Windows NT. Like Windows 98, it provides full support for Plug-and-Play installation of new hardware including USB, IrDA (Infrared Data Association), and IEEE 1394 devices.

Windows 2000 is actually a family of four products that all offer the same basic features, user interface, and core technology. The basic features and differences of these versions are

- **Windows 2000 Professional.** Windows 2000 Professional is considered the desktop version of this operating system. Like Windows 98, it is designed for the single user. It supports dual CPU (central processing unit) operations (SMP, or symmetric multiprocessing), file encryption of sensitive data, automatic system monitoring and advanced troubleshooting tools, NTFS5 support, and dramatically enhanced mobile computing capability over previous versions of Windows NT.

- **Windows 2000 Server.** Windows 2000 Server is the entry-level server platform, replacing Windows NT Server. It extends SMP capability to four CPUs per machine and adds support for Active Directory services. This is the Windows 2000 enhancement to the domain technology found in Windows NT. Active Directory makes it easy to offer network resources and develop group policies to enable secure sharing of resources like storage media, printers, and Internet access. Windows 2000 Server is designed to offer file, print, and Web services in networks that do not need the more robust features and scalability found in the Windows 2000 Enterprise products.

- **Windows 2000 Advanced Server.** Windows 2000 Advanced Server is a powerful departmental server product. It provides support for up to eight CPUs, up to 8 GB of RAM (random access memory), large scale RAIDs (redundant arrays of independent disks), load balancing, and clustering of two servers. This platform is designed for high-traffic networks and e-commerce sites, and it is beyond the scope of the A+ Exam and this training guide.

- **Windows 2000 Datacenter Server.** Windows 2000 Datacenter Server is the most advanced and robust networking platform offered by Microsoft. Like all other Windows networking products, it is only offered through qualified partners who can install and support it. Windows 2000 Datacenter Server is designed for large data warehouses, advanced scientific and engineering applications, and large-scale Web farms. It supports four-way clusters and storage area networks. Like Windows 2000 Advanced Server, it is beyond the scope of this book.

## System Requirements Compared

As you can see, there are quite a few versions of Windows available. The preceding summaries provide a good idea of the intended audience for each product. The server versions of Windows 2000 are aimed at the network environment, rather than the end user. In all likelihood, the most appropriate user for most of those products will be the network administrator. Windows 2000 Professional, Windows 98, and Windows Me are all end-user products. Most users will be quite satisfied with either of the latter two. The more demanding user will find Windows 2000 more satisfying from a performance standpoint, but there is a higher price to pay both in the initial purchase price of the software and in the hardware required to run it effectively. Understanding system requirements is necessary to help users choose the right operating environment and to ensure that it runs effectively.

The following table lists the minimum hardware requirements for the versions of Windows you are likely to encounter as an A+ technician. Keep in mind that many users will actually need a system that exceeds these requirements (especially for technical, multimedia, or graphics applications) to run effectively. Evaluating those needs is a topic for the next chapter.

**Note** Windows 2000 can run on systems based on processors other than the Intel Pentium. However, this table only shows the requirements for Pentium-based systems.

| Hardware | Windows 98 | Windows Me | Windows 2000 Professional | Remarks |
|---|---|---|---|---|
| Processor | 486 DX/66 | Pentium 150 300–400 MHz recommend for full multimedia and video editing | Pentium 133 (Pentium II 300 recommended); will support dual CPUs | Intel Pentium processor with MMX or equivalent required to take full advantage of multimedia. |
| Memory | 16 MB | 32 MB | 64 MB (can support up to 4 GB) | All 32-bit versions of Windows benefit greatly from additional RAM. |
| Disk space | 120 MB | 480 MB | 2 GB with 650 MB free | Typical installations often exceed twice the minimum disk space required. |
| Display system | VGA with 16 colors | VGA or higher | VGA or higher; SVGA Plug-and-Play monitor recommended | Many applications need at least 256 colors, many 24-bit color modes. |
| CD-ROM | Optional | CD-ROM or digital video disc (DVD); 8X or faster drive recommended | CD-ROM or DVD; 12X or faster drive recommended | |
| Input devices | Keyboard and Windows 98-compatible pointing device | | | |
| Other recommended devices | Modem, sound card, and additional RAM, plus network card if the system is to be used as part of a LAN (local area network) | | | |

---

**Note**   The actual products that can be used to meet the system requirements for Windows 2000, and especially for Windows NT, are much more closely defined than those for Windows 98 and Windows Me. Before making a final purchase selection, clients should be advised to make sure that a computer or upgrade component is fully compatible with the operating system. Microsoft publishes a hardware compatibility list that you can use to verify that a given product or computer is certified to work with the operating system. This is much less of a problem with Windows 2000 than with Windows NT, but it is still a necessary precaution. The information is available on the Microsoft Web site.

---

## Some System Configuration Considerations

### How Much RAM Is Enough?

The amount of RAM necessary on any Windows system depends on the user and which applications are to be run. The system requirements are just a starting point. Typical Microsoft Office users can usually work quite well with 32 MB of RAM. Moderate users of the COPY and PASTE commands will need to increase RAM to at least 64 MB. If users require their applications to be a click away (all running at the same time), they will need at least 128 MB of RAM. In the 32-bit Windows world, additional RAM always boosts performance.

### Processing Power Possibilities

The recommended CPUs in the preceding table are obviously the bare minimum. Intended use of the computer is the best guide to the appropriate CPU. For general productivity applications with little or no multitasking, the minimum processor requirement may suffice. This is especially true if a good graphics adapter with its own coprocessor is also installed on the system. Machines slated for use in scientific, technical, and graphics-intensive applications, or machines intended for multitasking will need more power. Machines using multimedia applications will benefit from a Pentium with MMX capability. Remember that adding more RAM often provides a bigger boost than the next bump in CPU power.

### Getting the Picture

A third area for serious consideration during an upgrade or purchase is the quality of the graphics adapter. The strength of the card's coprocessor and the amount of RAM on the adapter affect screen redraw speed, the refresh rate of the display, resolution, and color depth.

### Storage Space

The fourth key component in determining true system requirements is the amount and type of mass storage available. When upgrading an older computer with a new operating system, make sure that there is enough storage space for both the new operating system and anticipated upgrades in application software.

New versions of office suites or graphics applications like Photoshop or CorelDRAW often require much more space than earlier versions.

## Key Points to Remember

- You can never have too much RAM.

- RAM is the key to optimization of Windows.

- The simplest and least expensive way to improve the speed and performance of any computer is to add RAM.

- Moore's Law (from Gordon Moore, cofounder of Intel): Processing power doubles every 18 months.

- Parkinson's Law of Data: Data expands to fill the space available for storage (from the original Parkinson's Law: Work expands to fill the time available).

## Lesson Summary

The following points summarize the main elements of this lesson:

- Microsoft Windows is an evolving platform that has replaced MS-DOS as the principal microcomputer operating environment.

- The Windows market can be segmented into two portions: home and small office, and technical, workgroup, and enterprise.

- Windows 98 and Windows Me are the products of choice for the home environment and business applications where the advanced networking features of Windows 2000 are not required.

- Windows 98 and Windows Me are the best choices for PC games and multimedia. They offer the broadest support for consumer hardware and software packages.

- Windows 2000 offers enhanced reliability and security and a more robust environment that provides MSP ability, improved management and monitoring tools, and scalability from small networks to complex enterprise information centers.

- Choosing the right version of Windows for a given customer or installation requires knowledge of the intended uses, the skill of the users, networking considerations, and the target hardware configuration.

# Lesson 2:  Preparing for Windows Installation

The preceding lesson provided an overview of the Windows operating system. Performing a proper installation involves more than just loading the files and should include proper planning, which is the focus of this lesson. Lesson 3 walks you through the actual setup for both Windows 98 and Windows 2000 in detail. The best way to work with this material is to actually perform the steps on a PC as they are introduced. Most readers should have access to the commercial Windows product. You can also download time-limited versions of the Windows 2000 Professional and Server from the Microsoft Web site to be used for training purposes.

### After this lesson, you will be able to

- Prepare a system for a new Windows installation or upgrade an existing one
- Manage a dual boot configuration

### Estimated lesson time: 45 minutes

## Planning the Installation

We've all heard the old saying "prior planning prevents poor performance." That is especially true when it comes to installing a new operating system. Both Windows 2000 and Windows 98 offer automated setup programs that take virtually all the pain out of the actual process of transferring files and configuring system settings. In many cases, the system can be "successfully" installed by doing little more than running Setup from the distribution CD-ROM. While you could install Windows in this fashion, and Windows would probably run, it probably wouldn't run either as well as or reliably as it should.

Installing either operating system (especially if you're installing both) on a computer requires following a detailed checklist for an optimal and satisfactory result. The following sections walk through the expanded process before, during, and after you run the setup routine. Keep in mind that the job is not finished until the system is properly tuned, all hardware is working properly, and application software is ready to use.

The task headings that follow work equally well for Windows 2000, Windows 98, Windows 95, and virtually any other operating system. Specific information for Windows 2000 and Windows 98 is contained under each heading as appropriate. Some of the tasks are identical; others vary somewhat to take advantage of the strengths of each platform. Having both compared side by side underscores the differences and highlights key features of the two operating environments.

Some platforms are more forgiving than others, reducing the possibility of problems during installation. An old saying from the early days of advanced PC operating systems is, "If a computer is running DOS it only proves that the machine is not on fire." The MS-DOS environment is a very simple design, without multiple processes running in the background. Today's environments must monitor the status and memory usage of several programs at the same time. In general, the more complicated the computer or operating system, the more care must be taken during installation.

# Decide on the Boot Method(s)

Many people are unaware that more than one operating system can run on a single computer. Computer technicians, however, may be called on to install two or even three operating systems on the same machine. Both Windows 98 and Windows 2000 support dual boot operation. Each does so slightly differently, and the exact configuration depends on the operating systems involved. These might include various versions of Windows 95 or Windows 98, one or more editions of Windows 2000, Windows NT, UNIX, and in rare cases, even OS/2.

Dual boot installations require going through all setup steps for an individual operating system setup, and the complexity of ensuring that one installation doesn't damage the other, that file systems are compatible, and that all hardware devices and software required by each operating system are properly accessible.

Before undertaking a multiple operating system configuration, carefully read all relevant documentation for each operating environment. Draw up a compatibility list and make notes on any special requirements. For example, some operating systems allow a dual boot, but only if they are loaded first or last. File systems have to work to the lowest common denominator. For example, you can run a version of DOS or Windows 98 with Windows 2000, but only if you employ a FAT16 file system on at least part of the primary hard drive's primary partition. The older operating systems must reside on this primary partition. You can also use an NTFS partition on the system, but files there will not be accessible when in DOS or Windows 98 mode.

## Windows 2000 Dual Boot Considerations

- You can dual boot Windows 2000 with the following operating systems: MS-DOS, Windows 3.*x*, OS/2, Windows 95, Windows 98, Windows Me, and Windows NT Workstation 3.51 and 4.0.

- Each operating system must reside on a different disk partition.

- In most cases, it is necessary to use the FAT16 file system.

- You need to install application software under each operating system on the computer so that it will be entered in the appropriate registry. You do not have to actually install it to two locations unless you load it on a file system that one of the operating systems can't read. When setting up a dual boot system involving MS-DOS or Windows 95 with Windows 2000 Professional, Windows 2000 Professional must be installed last.

- If you are using a dual boot machine in a Windows NT domain or a Windows 2000 Active Directory network, each operating system must have its own machine name to be properly recognized on the domain.

### Windows 98 Dual Boot Considerations

- The C drive must be a FAT16 partition and include enough free space for the Windows 98 installation.
- The two operating systems must reside in different partitions or hard disks.
- Dual boot systems combining Windows 98 and Windows NT are discouraged because the two operating systems do not use the same registry settings or device drivers. If you choose to attempt this, you need to set up all programs twice, separately loading any required drivers.
- Dual booting Windows 98 and Windows 95 is not possible because both operating systems use the same boot file and the second installation will overwrite the first.
- Windows 98 cannot access files on NTFS partitions, and Windows NT cannot access files on FAT32 drives.

## Confirm Hardware Requirements and Compatibility

As mentioned in the last lesson, to ensure both proper performance and reliability, a computer's system components must meet or exceed the system requirements of the operating system involved. Minimum requirements are just that: minimums (and only in the most basic application environment are they enough to operate efficiently). With Windows 2000, it is also advisable to choose components from Microsoft's hardware compatibility list. In general, with Windows 98 and Windows Me, choosing products that are certified to work with the operating system and display the appropriate certification logo is sufficient.

## Obtain and Perform Updates to Firmware or Components

Before performing an installation, check the system BIOS (basic input/output system) firmware for devices like graphics cards, SCSI (Small Computer System Interface) controllers, and any third-party drivers for updates. It is not uncommon for businesses to update their code to reduce problems or improve performance. Any updates that do not require the operating system should be performed before the installation process begins, and drivers should be made available for those that do.

## Choose Between an Upgrade or a Clean Install

During a clean install, an operating system is installed on a hard disk that is either brand new or has recently been formatted and is currently without an operating system. An upgrade simply adds new components and updates existing ones. Each approach has advantages. The clean install ensures that there is no difficulty with old files and drivers, offering a "fresh start." Depending on the existing operating system, an upgrade can simply transfer many of the existing system settings, user preferences, and network connections to the operating system.

**Note**    Windows 2000 Professional offers a Check Upgrade Only mode in its setup routine. This lets you perform a dry run on the system that reports any possible conflicts that might be encountered during the actual upgrade, including hardware incompatibilities and software that might not operate correctly under the operating system.

## Record and Obtain Information

The next step in preparation is creation of a written record of the system configuration and network settings, along with digital copies of configuration files, a copy of any custom Windows Registry entries, and any other system-specific or general network information required to make a smooth transition.

The reason for this step should be clear. Although Windows 2000 and Windows 98 offer Plug-and-Play installation, not all hardware will be recognized properly, and you may be confronted with device conflicts. In many network environments, you need to know the machine name, domain name, IP (Internet Protocol) address, printer locations, and so on. With an open dialogue waiting for data input, you don't want to have to shut down the machine to obtain the needed information.

If you are performing an upgrade from an existing system, Windows can actually do that work for you. The Windows 95 Device Manager (accessed by double-clicking System in the Control Panel) and the Windows NT Diagnostics tool both offer a feature that lets you print a hard copy of all system settings including DMA and IRQ (interrupt request), drivers used, and memory configurations.

## Back Up Data and Key Files

Any time a new operating system is added to an existing computer, you should make a backup of all data files that the user does not want to lose. There's never a guarantee that the procedure will go smoothly or that data won't be lost.

It is also a good idea to make copies of any batch files, user profile files (like Favorites from the Internet browser), and so on, and save them on a floppy disk so they can be easily migrated to the new system.

## Remove or Disable Possible Conflicts and Verify Existing Settings

Now it's time to eliminate potential trouble spots. Many programs, like antivirus scans, third-party memory managers, TSRs (terminate-and-stay-resident programs), and legacy 16-bit device drivers may interfere with this program or cause it to improperly configure the system. Be especially careful of any third-party disk partitioning software.

If you are upgrading from an earlier version of MS-DOS or Windows that has active CONFIG.SYS and AUTOEXEC.BAT files, remove any unwanted 16-bit or legacy entries, then leave the files in place. Both Windows 98 and Windows 2000 can use those files to make appropriate listings in their registries.

**Note**  There are variations in just how simple and effective the conversion of registry and configurations settings is among different versions of Windows. The process works best when you are moving upstream in the same product series. Windows 98 usually smoothly incorporates settings from Windows 95, and Windows 2000 from Windows NT. Windows 2000 is less effective working with an existing Windows 98 or 95 system. Keep in mind that although the user interface may seem similar, Windows 95 and Windows 98 employ quite different core technology than Windows NT and Windows 2000.

## Prepare the Hard Drive and File System

At this point, you should have a good idea of the file system configuration, how much drive space will be needed, and how the disk(s) will be partitioned. If the primary drive of the operating system is already partitioned using the desired file system, you can proceed directly to the operating system setup. If you are installing Windows 2000 and planning on using the NTFS file system, you can also proceed directly to the Windows 2000 Setup program, which can be used to partition and prepare hard drives during the installation process.

If you plan on using either a FAT16 or FAT32 file system, and need to either create or change partitions, you will have to use the Fdisk utility to prepare the drive. Fdisk is a command-line utility that dates to the early days of MS-DOS. Before using Fdisk, be sure to back up any needed data that exists on the target drive. Any modification using Fdisk immediately results in the destruction of all data on the partition.

**Caution**  Before using Fdisk, be sure that no third-party disk management utilities were used to partition the drive. In most cases, these applications provide translation between the system and the drive to provide support for large drives that exceed the capability of the system BIOS. If they are removed, the drive may not work or may not report all of its capacity. If you suspect the presence of one of these utilities, watch for messages during system startup or look for messages that indicate loading of a driver for the translation software. This does not apply to firmware-level translation like that provided by SCSI host adapters.

## Partitioning a Hard Drive with Fdisk

The Windows 98 and Windows 95 startup disks, along with all versions of MS-DOS, provide copies of Fdisk. If possible, use the same version of the program as the operating system you are installing. (This is not possible with Windows 2000.) The program can be run from inside a DOS command window in Windows 98, but cannot be operated on the drive that was used to boot the system. You will most commonly run the program at a regular DOS command prompt. The complete syntax is

```
FDISK [/STATUS] /X
```

/STATUS displays partition information.

/X indicates that it ignores extended disk access support. Use this switch if you receive disk access or stack overflow messages.

With many versions of Fdisk, if you are working with a hard disk with a capacity greater than 512 MB, you will be asked if you wish to enable FAT32's large drive support. Answering Yes enables the 32-bit FAT file system. If you answer No, the system uses FAT16, which limits partitions to 2 GB, even if it is a larger drive. Although FAT32 offers many enhancements over the older 16-bit mode, as already discussed, it is not widely compatible with other file system formats.

Fdisk provides several options:

- Create a partition or logical drive
- Set the active partition
- Delete partition or logical drive
- Display partition information
- Choose drive (on computers with multiple hard drives)

Make sure you are working on the drive you want to modify if there is more than one physical hard disk on the system. Check the Current Fixed Disk Drive listing. The first fixed disk is followed by the number 1. A second physical drive would be noted with the number 2.

It is best to work in a step-by-step fashion when using this utility. Start by displaying the current partition information and verifying that you're working on the proper drive. Next, delete any unwanted partitions. This must be done in a specific order. Start by removing any non-DOS partitions; then remove any extraneous logical drives in the extended MS-DOS partition. Next, remove the extended partition, and finally the existing primary DOS partition. For example, if you wish to remove the existing primary partition, you must work through all the steps. If you only want to remove one logical drive and an extended partition, you must perform only the first two steps.

Remember that Fdisk is primarily an MS-DOS utility. Although it generally has the ability to remove non-DOS partitions, that is not always true, and you may have to use a third-party product to remove inside partitions.

Once partitions are deleted, you may go through the process of creating a partition to actually use for the new installation. Once that is completed, you need to mark one of the partitions as the primary partition. In general, this is the first partition, which will be the C drive. With some operating systems or in a dual boot configuration, this may not always be true. Once you have completed the modifications, the program verifies the disk integrity and requires a restart of the system.

File allocation table (FAT)-based operating systems require that after partitioning a drive, the media must be formatted using the Format utility. The Format program must be compatible with both the version of DOS that you have used and the operating system to be installed.

With the hard disk and file system prepared, the computer is ready for its new installation and you can start the setup process.

## Lesson Summary

The following points summarize the main elements of this lesson:

- Installing a new operating system requires careful planning.
- Dual boot machines must be configured to properly support both operating systems.
- Upgrade and optimize all system components before proceeding with setup.
- You should back up all important files and make a record of key system settings.

# Lesson 3: Installing Windows

With the effort that goes into preparing for an operating system installation, it might seem that the actual act of running the setup procedure is anticlimactic. In reality, there are a number of options and custom settings that can be used during this procedure to make it more efficient and more reliable, and to help overcome system configuration problems. You can also set several options based on user preferences for the network environment the machine will operate in. This lesson covers in detail the setup routine provided with Windows 98 and Windows 2000. We cover each operating system in turn.

## After this lesson, you will be able to

- Choose the best method for setting up Windows 98 and Windows 2000
- Describe the issues and features with the different types of setup approaches
- Install Windows 98 and Windows 2000
- Troubleshoot problems in installation with both operating systems

## Estimated lesson time: 75 minutes

## Performing a Windows 98 Setup

### Running Setup

Microsoft Windows 98 comes in two versions: one for upgrading an existing version of Windows on the same drive, and another for a new installation. Both assume that you have already prepared the file system as outlined in Lesson 2.

Running an upgrade allows you to maintain settings that already exist under Windows 95, Windows 3.x, or Windows for Workgroups. If you are using one of these operating systems, you should usually run the Setup program from within the Windows interface.

If you do not wish to keep any of the current settings; if you are loading the operating system on a new computer or a freshly prepared disk drive; or if you are recovering from a failed setup procedure, then you should run the program from a command prompt under MS-DOS. The necessary files are available on CD-ROM (preferred) or on floppy disks (special order), or they can be copied to a network location that is available to the target computer. Keep the following points in mind:

- A CD-ROM drive to be used for setup must be accessible from the DOS prompt. The Windows 98 startup disk includes drivers needed to run both typical IDE (Integrated Device Electronics) and SCSI CD-ROM drives. If the CD-ROM is attached to the system via a sound card, it may not be able to run Setup.

- Except for necessary device drivers, network card drivers, and any TSR programs needed to actually operate the systems, no other application should be running when you begin Setup. Be sure to disable any third-party memory managers or antivirus programs.

- Running Setup over a network will require about 170 MB of storage space on the server.

- If you are performing a new installation and have the full Windows 98 package for use on a new computer, it will contain a Windows 98 startup disk. If you are using the upgrade-only package, the program will only operate if you are installing on a machine that already has a recognized operating system for improved upgrade, or if you have the disks for one of those operating systems available to prove that you are performing a legitimate upgrade.

The Windows 98 Setup program is much improved over the version that was provided with Windows 95. The earlier product required 12 steps, and Plug-and-Play technology was in its infancy. It was often necessary to break the installation routine or restart under Windows 95. That problem has largely disappeared with Windows 98, which offers much more robust Plug-and-Play support and a more compact five-step installation.

## Making Use of Windows 98 Setup's Command-Line Switches

There are a variety of options available when running Windows 98 Setup in command-line mode from the DOS prompt that are unavailable when performing installation from within the Windows environment. The following list provides most of the switches in alphabetical order along with an explanation of their function. The syntax is:

`setup /[switch]` at the command prompt.

Many of these commands are very useful in recovering a failed installation or forcing one on a difficult system:

- **/?** Provides help on syntax command-line switches.
- **/C** Don't load the SmartDrive disk cache.

- **/D** Don't use the existing version of Windows for the early phases of Setup. (Use if problems starting Setup could be caused by missing or damaged Windows support files.)

- **/DOMAIN:** *domain_name* This option sets the Windows NT Logon Validation domain used by Client for Microsoft Networks to the value given in *domain_name*.

- **/F** Saves a little memory by prohibiting holding filenames in the local cache, but Setup runs slower.

- **/IC** Performs a clean boot in some versions of Windows. If this is set and KeepRMDrivers=1 is not in the registry, drivers are commented out from the CONFIG.SYS or AUTOEXEC.BAT file. (Commenting out is a way to prevent a line in either of these files from executing. The system will not process any line with the letters REM in front of it. This remains in effect until the next line break, at which point the system will begin processing the commands again.)

- **/ID** Disables the usual check of the target drive for the minimum disk space required to install Windows 98.

- **/IE** Skips the Startup Disk screen.

- **/IF** Performs a "fast" setup. Does not notify setup to look up filenames in the cache.

- **/IH** Runs ScanDisk so you can see the results. Use this switch if the system stalls during the ScanDisk check or if an error results.

- **/IL** Loads a Logitech mouse driver that supports the Logitech Series C mouse.

- **/IM** Skips the check of low conventional memory.

- **/IN** Does not run the networking Setup software. Neither the networking software nor the Networking Wizard screens will appear.

- **/IQ** Skips the check for cross-linked files.

- **/IR** Does not perform an update of the Master Boot Record (MBR).

- **/IS** Skips ScanDisk.

- **/IW** Does not display the License Agreement dialog box.

- **/IX** Does not perform a character set check.

- **/NF** Does not provide a prompt to remove the floppy disk from drive A at the end of the Copying Windows 98 Files To Your Computer Setup step (Step 3). Use this switch when installing Windows 98 from a bootable CD.

- **/NH** Does not run HWINFO.EXE when running Setup from the Windows 95 user interface.

- **/NOSTART** Copies a minimal installation of the required dynamic-link libraries (DLLs) used by Windows 98 Setup, then exits to MS-DOS without installing Windows 98.

- **/NR** Skips the registry check.

- **/PI** Keeps forced configured hardware settings (hardware not using default settings). Some BIOS requires hardware to have a forced configuration to work. By default, Setup removes the forced configuration and some hardware may not work properly after this is done.

- **/PJ** Loads Advanced Configuration and Power Interface (ACPI) by default.

- **/script_*filename*** Uses a script to install Windows 98 automatically; for example, setup MSBATCH.INF specifies that Setup should use the settings in MSBATCH.INF. The full filename must be given and it must be eight characters long with a three-character extension (8.3 filename).

- **/SRCDIR** Specifies the source directory where the Windows 98 Setup files are located.

- **/S *filename*** Load the specified SETUP.INF file when starting Setup.

- **/T:*tempdir*** Specifies the directory where Setup is to copy its temporary files. This directory must already exist, but any existing files in the directory will be deleted.

## The Actual Windows 98 Installation Process

As you can see from the preceding list of switches, there are quite a few options when it comes to installing Windows 98. Depending on the current state of the computer (operating system, and so on) and the options you select, the Setup program will present you with a variety of dialog boxes or prompts during the installation. In spite of the differences, the underlying task remains the same: to discover the computer's configuration, install the appropriate files, and return the system to the user with both the operating system and devices in proper working order. What follows is an overview of the process.

### Confirm the Disk Status

Unless overridden, the first thing Setup does is run ScanDisk. If run from MS-DOS, Setup will run the real-mode version of a program. ScanDisk inspects the directory structure, FAT, and the integrity of the file system. If you are installing from within a 32-bit version of Windows, the program will also fix any long filename errors found.

## Collect Computer and Setup Information

Once the media have been verified, Setup prompts you to provide several pieces of information needed before the files can be copied:

- It makes the user verify agreement with the end user license provisions.

- It prompts the user to enter the product key that verifies that this is a legal copy of Windows 98. Setup cannot continue unless this is properly entered. It is usually found on the back of the CD case. In some cases, the product key step is not required (see Figure 17.1).

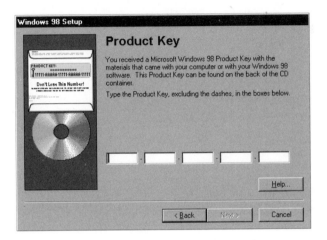

**Figure 17.1**   The Product Key dialog box

- It prompts the user for the directory into which Windows 98 will be installed. Once entered, the program confirms that there is adequate space for the installation. If unsuccessful, you are prompted to specify another location or remove enough files so that Setup may proceed.

---

**Note**   If Windows 98 is set up in a new directory other than the one in which the preexisting version of Windows was already installed, all Windows-based applications will have to be reinstalled because any application-specific DLLs will not be present in the proper Windows 98 directory. Also during this phase, Windows may offer the option to save the existing MS-DOS and Windows system files required to restore the computer to the pre-Windows 98 installation state. This is highly recommended, but requires about an additional 50 MB of hard disk space.

---

Once a directory structure has been set up, the next step is to choose the type of installation to be performed. Four choices are offered. Typical installation provides a standard set of features most suitable for the computer's configuration.

Portable installation includes options useful for laptop users. Compact installation provides a minimal set of features. Custom installation provides another dialog box that lets the installer choose the specific options to be installed. Figure 17.2 shows the dialog box offering these options.

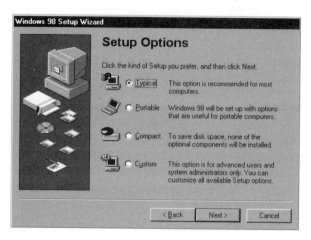

**Figure 17.2**   The Setup Options dialog box

Another dialog box appears, requiring the user to enter his or her name and the company name. When the next button is clicked, the user is given the option to install or remove optional components from the list of features to be copied to the disk.

The next dialog box requests the computer name, workgroup, and physical location of the machine. This name must be unique to the network and can contain up to 15 characters. Names cannot contain punctuation or blank spaces. The workgroup name has the same limitations. The computer description cannot contain commas but can be up to 40 characters in length. This entry is not needed if the computer will not be attached to a network.

Now the user is prompted to provide the geographic location at which the computer will reside. This is used to allow Web sites to deliver content based on the region in which the computer is operated. This step does not occur in all versions of Windows (see Figure 17.3).

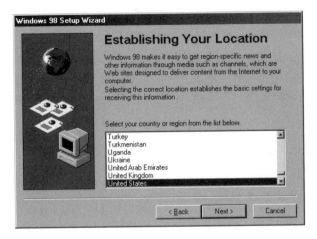

**Figure 17.3**   The Location dialog box

### Create a Startup Disk

This step requires a 1.44-MB floppy disk or two 1.2-MB floppy disks. The Startup disk contains all the real-mode files, CD-ROM device drivers, and utilities needed to start the computer in DOS mode, along with a suite of diagnostic programs. In the event the system uses specialized SCSI drivers or a sound card to access the CD-ROM drive, you will need to manually copy these drivers to the startup disk and adjust the CONFIG.SYS and AUTOEXEC.BAT files for proper operation. The Windows 98 Startup disk should be considered a critical part of your technician toolkit, and understanding its operation is required for both your day-to-day work and for taking the exam. We cover it in detail in Chapter 18, "Running Microsoft Windows."

### File Copy

This stage is when the actual files are extracted from their compressed archive files (noted by a .cab extension) and copied to the hard drive. There is no need for user input during this part of the process.

**Caution**   You should not interrupt the copy process for any reason. If the procedure does not finish normally, the operating system will be in an unstable state and you may have to repeat the process.

### Tuning the Configuration

Once the copy process is done, the computer will be restarted. At this point, Windows goes through a tuning process to set up the system based on the devices found on the computer and any settings migrated from a previous installation of Windows. The program finalizes the Control Panel and Start menu and asks the user to select the proper time zone. Once the process is finished successfully, you will see the Welcoming dialog box, which offers access to information about the features of Windows 98 (see Figure 17.4).

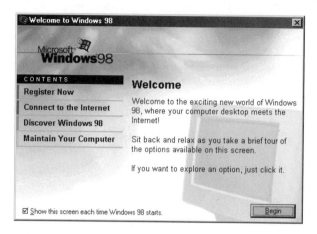

**Figure 17.4** The Welcome To Windows 98 dialog box

### Establish Network Connections

If you have installed Windows 98 over an earlier version of Windows that was already set up on a network, the appropriate network settings and protocols should already be loaded. When Windows reboots after Setup is complete, you should see the appropriate network logon. If you installed Windows into a new directory or performed a clean install, you will have to use the Control Panel/ Network setting to install protocols and configure the network settings in order to make the computer a part of the network.

# Troubleshooting a Windows 98 Installation

If you follow the detailed planning steps covered earlier in this chapter, the majority of Windows 98 installations will execute properly and the system will be ready for use after the Setup routine is completed. However, things don't always go as planned. As a technician, you need to have an understanding of what the routine is doing behind the scenes, and know how to troubleshoot a failed installation. At several points the Setup routine examines the system to determine the hardware and Windows-related software already installed. It generates several files that track the actions taken, creating logs that can be used if either automatic or manual intervention is necessary.

### Using Safe Recovery

Safe Recovery is a process built right into the Windows 98 Setup code. During the entire installation, Windows is tracking virtually every action taken. This information is used if Setup fails in a way that prevents the operating system from loading successfully due to hardware conflicts, software conflicts, failure to meet system requirements, system shutdown during the copying process, or a component failure. Given the wide variation in system configurations, the failure could be due to any number of reasons. Fortunately, automatic Safe Recovery often resolves the problem.

Running Safe Recovery is very simple. If you are sure that Setup has hung the system (there are some components that take a good bit of time to identify and configure; the system may be busy, or not stopped), wait an additional three to four minutes, then press CTRL+ALT+DELETE to restart the computer. If this does not reboot the system, turn off the computer's power, wait ten seconds, and turn the unit back on. Let the boot process continue normally. You may be returned to Setup and offered the Safe Recovery option. If so, select it and proceed with the installation. If not, run Setup again and select the Safe Recovery option when it appears.

**Note**  If you fail to select Safe Recovery when offered the dialog box, Setup will repeat the entire Windows 98 Setup process.

Most setup failures are due to hardware detection and system or software configuration problems. To get around them, Windows uses an iterative process. When a fatal incident occurs, Windows logs the point of failure and bypasses the point at which the failure occurred. This method allows Windows to continue the installation, even when a system has a problematic device. Windows disables the problem product, so it may not show up as properly identified in the Device Manager list. You may be able to make the offending device operational by accessing Device Manager from the Control Panel/System icon and changing the settings manually. If Setup hangs again, repeat the process. If the problem is software-related, the Setup Wizard may suggest removing the software product that is causing problems. In extreme cases Safe Recovery may not be able to fix a problem, and a dialog box will appear telling you that Setup cannot continue. If the message offers a suggestion of the problem's cause, remove the device or software from the system and start Setup from the beginning.

## Beyond Safe Recovery

Sometimes Safe Recovery is not sufficient and manual intervention is required. In such cases, you should first review the planning process to make sure no critical issues have been overlooked. If your system meets all requirements stated by Microsoft and there are no obvious problems, the information generated by the failed installation can help you pinpoint the problem. To use it, you must understand both the Windows hardware detection process and the recovery files generated during installation.

Setup attempts to detect devices that are already installed on the computer when Windows is added to the system. For devices that support the Plug-and-Play initiative, an interactive set of queries is used to identify both the product and its required resources. These devices can include everything from the motherboard, CPU, and BIOS, to display adapters, mouse, and network adapters.

Older devices that do not support the Plug-and-Play initiative are also investigated. Memory addresses, DMA channels, and IRQs are cataloged. During this process, Windows 98 examines device information and settings from files like WINDOWS.INI and CONFIG.SYS. Buses (PCI [Peripheral Component Interconnect], SCSI, and so on) and hardware devices are grouped into classes and listed in the Registry.

Four classes of devices (CD-ROM adapters, network cards, SCSI controllers, and sound cards) are detected using a process known as *safe detection.* Safe detection uses a variety of methods to locate devices that exist on the system within those classes. It can also investigate ROMs for manufacturer identification. During Setup, you can opt to skip certain classes of devices. This is useful if you know a product will cause problems.

## The Setup Log Files

The installation routine creates five files that can be used if the process fails: BOOTLOG.TXT, DETCRASH.LOG, DETLOG.TXT, NETOLOG.TXT, and SETUPLOG.TXT. As you can tell from the file extensions, most of these are ASCII files that can be read with a text editor like Wordpad, Notepad, or Edit. In some cases, Setup actually makes use of these files automatically as it attempts to recover from a failed installation.

BOOTLOG.TXT is a very useful file for more than just installation issues. It creates and holds a record of the entire boot process, including which drivers were loaded and initialized and their status. It is automatically generated during the setup process, but you can also create it by pressing F8 during a regular Windows 98 startup, or using the /b switch if you start Windows from a DOS prompt using the WIN.COM command.

The BOOTLOG.TXT file detects failed initialization of critical virtual device drivers (VxDs), failure to boot from a SCSI hard drive, failure of a critical component to load, and the failure to locate a resource. We look more closely at the options offered with this file in the next chapter.

DETCRASH.LOG is generated if Setup fails during the hardware detection phase. It contains listings that show which detection module was running and the resources that were being accessed when the failure occurred. When the system is restarted, Safe Recovery is invoked and the installation routine proceeds without any additional attempts to discover that class of device. This file is used directly by Setup and is not normally readable by the user.

DETLOG.TXT is generated every time the detection process runs, either during a new Windows installation or by invoking the Add New Hardware Wizard from Control Panel. It is a user-readable version of the information contained in

DETCRASH.LOG. This file is very useful for a technician, because it can quickly pinpoint the likely cause of a device that generates an error during initialization. The following table shows how the entries appear and what they mean.

| Report Category | Provides Information on |
| --- | --- |
| Parameters = "xxxxxx" | Shows the command-line switches specified when Setup was invoked. |
| WinVer = ######## | Shows that environment detection is run. |
| AvoidMem = #####h-#####h | Shows the UMB (upper memory block) address range specified to be avoided during the detection phase (if entered)— for example, AvoidMem=c4000-c800 |
| DetectClass: Skip Class Media | Indicates that detection found no hints that the computer might have a particular class of device present, so it skipped that class. |
| DetectClass: Override | When one or more skip class entries appear in DETLOG.TXT, the Analyzing Your Computer screen is presented during Setup to allow a manual override of the decision. Related DetectClass Override lines appear in DETLOG.TXT for the classes checked. |
| Custom Mode | Describes your selection for the devices the user told Windows 98 not to detect. |
| Devices Verified = | Shows the number of devices verified from the Registry. If the number is 0, there was no existing Registry or it was empty. |
| *System Device Listings* | |
| Checking For | Shows that detection looked for that device, followed by a description of the device or class. If the device is detected, Detected shows its resource information. |
| *Network Adapters Listings* | |
| Checking For | This section lists the attempts to detect network adapters. |
| PROTOCOL.INI Section | If detection finds a PROTOCOL.INI file, it saves the [*net_card*] section in DETLOG.TXT. |
| NCD: Detecting Network Adapter | Detection found a network adapter using safe detection (usually PROTOCOL.INI) and the system had information for verifying this adapter. If verified, a Detected line is included. |

NETLOG.TXT provides a similar readout to DETLOG.TXT, but focuses on network components. It describes what network components were found on the system, including network adapters, protocols, clients, file and print sharing, and protocol bindings.

SETUPLOG.TXT is used to enable Safe Recovery if Windows 98 Setup fails before the hardware detection phase begins. It allows the program to determine exactly when the system stalled, what needs to be repeated, and what should be skipped. This file can be found in the root directory of the boot disk, and it contains listings in the order in which they were executed. If you wish to use this file to manually locate a fault, examine the end of the file. Listings include the type of installation performed, the installation directory, any applications running during the process, errors logged during the process, the system hardware configuration, Registry status, the files copied during Setup, and outstanding issues that need to be completed after the next computer restart.

---

**Note**    DETLOG.TXT and DETCRASH.LOG are both hidden files in the root directory of the primary hard drive. Take care not to delete, move, or rename them. Doing so will eliminate a proper Safe Recovery option, thereby forcing you to repeat the entire installation process.

---

As you can see, the recovery files store a wealth of valuable information you can use in the event of a Setup failure. When confronted with an elusive installation problem, consider opening the appropriate file in a text editor to help pinpoint where the installation failed. You may have to remove, or remove and replace, a problematic hardware product.

Chapter 19, "Maintaining the Modern Computer," covers techniques you can use to troubleshoot a Windows installation when it appears the installation was successful but the system becomes unstable soon after loading the operating system. There are a variety of additional tools available that fall outside the scope of this discussion.

## Performing a Windows 2000 Installation

### Not Quite the Same

Installing the Windows 2000 operating system on a computer is very similar to the process for Windows 98. However, there are a few important differences. Because Windows 2000 is not designed as a mass-market operating system, its designers imposed much more rigid requirements on the hardware used in conjunction with it. Although it offers much wider support than Windows NT for multimedia devices, scanners, and other peripherals, not all such products have Windows 2000 drivers. You cannot assume that a Windows 98 driver will work with Windows 2000. The advantage to this more meticulous approach is a much more reliable operating environment.

The NTFS file system is a good deal more complicated than the FAT file systems found in Windows 98, Windows Me, and earlier Microsoft operating systems. Employing it—which Microsoft recommends with Windows 2000—involves different installation and management procedures.

The more robust security provided within Windows 2000 adds a few extra steps, because user and administrative accounts must be present on the computer for users to gain access to it. There are some other minor differences, but anyone familiar with the Windows 98 installation process should have no difficulty installing Windows 2000.

## Preparation and Planning

Before proceeding with the actual installation, you should go through the planning procedure outlined in Lesson 2, paying particular attention to system requirements. Hardware compatibility is much more important with Windows 2000 than with Windows 95 or Windows 98, and you should be sure that the system components are all included on the Windows 2000 hardware compatibility list if at all possible. A copy of the list is included on the Windows 2000 CD (HCL.TXT, located in the Support folder). If a product isn't listed, you can check the Microsoft Web site at *http://www.microsoft.com/hcl*. The final alternative is to visit the vendor's Web site and see if a Windows 2000 driver or support notes are available there.

It is also a good idea to check the vendor's site to see if new software or device drivers are available for use with Windows 2000. In many cases the drivers provided on the Windows 2000 CD will not be the most current. If new drivers are available, you should obtain them and have them available on floppy disk for use during installation.

## Upgrades and Updates

You should make sure that the major system components—especially the motherboard, display adapter, and hard drive or SCSI controller—have the most recent version of available firmware. For Windows 2000 Plug-and-Play and power management features to work properly, the system bus must support the ACPI standard.

**Caution**   Be extremely careful when upgrading the BIOS on a component. Be certain that the BIOS applies to the product, that it is appropriate and approved for use with Windows 2000, and that you carefully follow all steps in the instructions provided by the manufacturer. Failure to do so can seriously damage the component.

Some software products, especially those that control hardware (like scanners or sound cards), may require updates to work properly with Windows 2000. They also must support 32-bit drivers. Many vendors provide upgrade packs for use with Windows 2000 to convert existing Windows 98 and Windows 95 products. Information on compatibility can be found at *http://microsoft.com/Windows/ professional/deploy/compatible/*.

## Gathering Information

The gathering of information is very similar to that for Windows 98. In addition, you should have available the desired name and initial password for the administrator account that the client wants to use, and the names and initial passwords for new user accounts that you are going to establish during installation. For security reasons, you should recommend that your clients change those initial passwords after installation.

## Upgrade or Clean Install?

If you are installing Windows 2000 on a computer that already has an existing installation of Windows 95, Windows 98, Windows NT Workstation 3.51, or Windows NT Workstation 4.0, you will be offered the option during installation of having Setup save your existing settings and applications for use with the new operating system.

The upgrade process simplifies setup dramatically, as Windows can directly configure a number of settings from the existing configuration. You also don't have to worry about the boot method and how to start the Setup program. Simply install the Windows 2000 CD in the drive and it should automatically bring up a dialog box offering to update the current version of Windows. Click OK to begin the installation. If the dialog box doesn't appear, click on the drive's icon to open the dialog box. When upgrading, Windows 2000 is installed in the same directory as your existing copy of Windows, and many of the files already present on the drive will be overwritten with new versions.

Choosing to perform a clean install on such a system will result in Windows 2000 installing its files in a new folder. If you are installing Windows 2000 on a computer with an unsupported previous operating system, such as a 16-bit version of Windows or OS/2, a new copy must be installed. This means you must set all preferences during installation, and after the process is complete, reinstall any software that requires Windows support.

You may also choose to configure the system to dual boot and support both operating systems, as previously discussed. This approach can be useful if there are older programs or hardware devices that the client wishes to access on the computer that are not supported under Windows 2000.

## CD-ROM, Floppy Disk, or Network Installation?

Windows 2000 can be installed from the distribution CD-ROM, with a combination of floppy disks and the CD-ROM, or from installation files stored on a network drive. The simplest installation is done directly from the CD-ROM, but to do so the computer must be able to boot from the CD-ROM drive. If you are running any supported version of Windows, this is the preferred method.

If a computer does not support a bootable CD-ROM, you can create a set of Windows 2000 boot disks or make the contents of the CD available over a network. If you choose the network approach, the system must be bootable in such a fashion that you can access the network with privileges to use the directory where the files are located. Given the wide range of variables in networks, describing all permutations is beyond the scope of this book. The following section discusses the steps required to create the floppy disks needed for Windows 2000 installation if you choose this method.

### Creating Windows 2000 Setup Disks

If you decide to start Setup from floppy disks, you will need a set of boot disks. Here's how to create them from the distribution CD-ROM. Have a computer with access to a CD-ROM drive running any version of MS-DOS or Windows. Have four blank, formatted, 3.5-inch, 1.44-MB disks and label them Windows 2000 Setup Disks 1, 2, 3, and 4. Place the Windows 2000 CD-ROM into the CD-ROM drive. At a command prompt (either MS-DOS or Windows COMMAND.COM), type **d:\bootdisk\makeboot a:** (where d: is the drive letter of the CD-ROM drive). Insert the first floppy into the primary floppy disk drive (A) when prompted, and follow the instructions when asked to remove and insert the remaining three disks.

## Starting Setup

There are three ways to start the Setup program. As already mentioned, you can perform an upgrade from within a supported version of Windows. You can boot the computer directly into the installation routine using either the distribution CD or the startup floppies. Both of these options turn control immediately over to the routine. The third option is to run Setup from a command line using a variety of switches to invoke the process. As with Windows 98, there are a variety of switches that provide access to the number of sophisticated options that can be used to fine-tune the setup process.

There are two different command-line programs available, depending on which operating system is used to start the computer. WINNT32.EXE is the preferred command used for all 32-bit operating environments. WINNT.EXE is available for use with 16-bit environments. Remember that you must have some version of either MS-DOS or Windows available to start the computer and provide the command prompt. This can be an operating system already installed on the hard drive or it can be a bootable floppy. The Windows 98 Startup disk usually has all files needed to both boot the system and provide the CD-ROM support needed to access the Windows 2000 CD.

The following is the syntax for using WINNT32.EXE:

```
winnt32 [/s:sourcepath] [/tempdrive:drive_letter]
    [/unattend[num]:[answer_file]] [/copydir:directory_name]
    [/copysource:directory_name] [/cmd:command_line]
    [/debug[level]:[filename]] [/udf:id[,UDF_file]]
    [/syspart:drive_letter] [/checkupgradeonly]
    [/cmdcons] [/m:directory_name] [makelocalsource]
    [/noreboot]
```

The options are as follows:

- **/s:*sourcepath*** Specifies the source location of the Windows 2000 files. To simultaneously copy files from multiple servers, specify multiple /s sources. If you use multiple /s switches, the first specified server must be available or Setup will fail.

- **/tempdrive:*drive_letter*** Setup places its temporary files on the specified partition and installs Windows 2000 on that partition.

- **/unattend** Updates the previous version of Windows 2000, Windows NT 4.0, Windows NT 3.51, Windows 95, or Windows 98 automatically. All user settings are taken from the previous installation. Use of this switch affirms reading and accepting the Microsoft License Agreement for Windows 2000.

---

**Note** As a technician you must understand that by using this switch to install Windows 2000 on behalf of a third party, you are confirming that the end user (whether an individual or a single entity) has received, read, and agreed to all of the terms contained in the Windows 2000 Microsoft License Agreement. OEMs may not specify this key on machines being sold to final end users.

---

- **/unattend[*num*]:[*answer_file*]** Performs a fresh installation in unattended Setup mode on computers running Windows NT or Windows 2000. The declared answer file provides Setup with any custom specifications. *Num* denotes the number of seconds delayed between the time that Setup finishes copying the files and the time it restarts the computer. *Answer_file* is the name of the specified answer file.

- **/cmd:*command_line*** Setup carries out the *command_line* program before the final phase of Setup. This happens after the computer has restarted twice and after Setup has collected all the configuration information, but before Setup is completed.

- **/debug[*level*]:[*filename*]** Creates a debug log at the level specified. The log levels are: 0 = severe errors, 1 = errors, 2 = warnings, 3 = information, and 4 = detailed information for debugging. Each level includes the levels below it.

- **/udf:*id*[,*UDF_file*]** Indicates an identifier (*id*) that Setup uses to specify how a Uniqueness Database File (UDF) modifies an answer file (see /unattend). UDF settings override values in the answer file, and the identifier determines which values in the UDF are used.

- **/syspart:*drive_letter*** Setup copies the startup files to a hard disk and marks the disk as active. You can then install them into another computer, and it will automatically start the machine at the next Setup phase. The /tempdrive parameter must be used in conjunction with the /syspart parameter.

- **/checkupgradeonly** Checks the computer for Windows 2000 upgrade compatibility. When used with Windows 95 or Windows 98 upgrades, Setup creates a report named UPGRADE.TXT in the Windows Installation folder. For

Windows NT 3.51 or 4.0 upgrades, the report is WINNT32.LOG in the Installation folder. The report includes information on MS-DOS configuration (including information on the contents in any existing AUTOEXEC.BAT and CONFIG.SYS file that might create problems), unsupported Plug-and-Play hardware, incompatible software products that may require upgrade packs, and software that may have to be reinstalled to work properly. The report also provides valuable links to the Microsoft Web site as appropriate. Before exiting, you are offered the options of saving or printing the report.

---

**Note**   This is a very useful switch that can be used anytime there is a question concerning the compatibility of any component hardware or software when performing an upgrade. Not only does it provide an exhaustive check of the system, but you can use the resulting report to explain needed system upgrades to the client.

---

- **/m:*directory_name*** Setup copies replacement files from an alternate location, if those files are present there, instead of using the files located in the default location.

- **/makelocalsource** Setup copies all installation source files to the local hard disk. This is used when the CD will not be available later in the installation.

- **/noreboot** Setup won't automatically restart the computer after the file copy phase of Winnt32.

The following is the syntax for using WINNT.EXE:

```
winnt [/s:sourcepath] [/t:tempdrive] /u:answer file][/udf:id
[,UDF_file]] [/r:folder][/rx:folder][/e:command][/a]
```

The options are as follows:

- **/s:*sourcepath*** Sets the source location of the Windows 2000 files. It must show the full path, such as x:\[*path*] or \\server\drive[\*path*].

- **/t:*tempdrive*** Places temporary files on the specified drive and installs Windows 2000 on that drive.

- **/u:*answer file*** Used in conjunction with the /s switch, this option performs an unattended setup using an answer file to complete some or all of the prompts normally activated during Setup.

- **/udf:*id* [,*UDF_file*]** Indicates an identifier (*id*) used with a UDF to modify an answer file (see /u entry). Use /udf parameters to override values in the answer file.

- **/r:*folder*** Specifies an optional folder to be installed. The folder remains after Setup finishes.

- **/rx:*folder*** Specifies an optional folder to be copied. The folder is deleted after Setup finishes.

- **/e:*command*** Specifies a command to be executed at the end of graphical user interface (GUI) mode Setup.
- **/a** Enables accessibility options.

# The Step-by-Step Installation Process

No matter which method you use to start the process, the main steps are similar. As with Windows 98, the majority of the steps are performed automatically and are actually transparent to the user. In a clean install from either the CD or the startup disks, the user is first presented with a series of blue screens. For an upgrade, the entire process uses familiar Windows dialog boxes. So long as you undertake proper advanced planning, and the computer where you are loading Windows 2000 has compatible hardware, the actual creation of the new filing system should be simple and straightforward.

### Choosing a File System and Disk Partition

Because Windows 2000 supports a variety of file systems, it will prompt you to specify which you wish to use. If the system will be used only for Windows 2000 operations, Microsoft recommends using NTFS5 for all drives and partitions. This is the only file system that offers full support for all of Windows 2000's features and provides access to all of the security functions. You can upgrade existing FAT and NTFS partitions during the setup process, or later after the new system is up and running.

Keep in mind that you only need to actually create or size the partition that will hold Windows 2000. If you are planning a dual boot system, a total NTFS may not be the best approach. The computer must have a FAT file system on the primary partition for MS-DOS, Windows 95, and Windows 98 access. If you have any existing DriveSpace or DoubleSpace volumes on the system, they must be converted prior to starting an upgrade to Windows 2000. Accessing the new file system using a dual boot system with Windows NT 4.0 requires that the Windows NT system have Service Pack 5 installed.

No matter which file system you choose, it is important make sure there is enough hard disk space available beyond the minimum installation requirements to leave room for system upgrades, utilities, a virtual memory paging file, and any applications planned for that drive.

### Disk Validation and File Copy

Once file system options have been determined, Setup performs an examination of the hard disk partitions, making sure that they are ready to receive the operating system. If that process completes successfully, the appropriate folders are created and the operating system files are uncompressed and copied to the target hard drive. At this point, the computer automatically reboots.

### Primary Device Detection and Information Gathering

From this point on, the setup process continues using the familiar Windows interface. There may be a delay of several minutes while Setup conducts an inspection of the target computer and installs and activates devices like the keyboard and mouse.

Several dialog boxes are then presented to the user to verify the installation key, customize regional settings, collect the user's name and company name, set the computer name and administrative password, collect the date and time settings from the system clock, and obtain information about any existing network, workgroup, and domain environments the new system will be joining.

**Caution**   Be sure to write down both the administrative user account and password immediately. Without the proper information, you will be denied access to the system and will be unable to complete the installation process.

### Operating System Installation

Once all that information is gathered, Setup presents a dialog box offering optional components like IIS (Internet Information Services) and advanced management and monitoring tools. Clicking OK causes the Windows 2000 installer to actually install those operating system components. This step also includes setting up the Start menu configuration, setting Registry entries for the selected components, saving system settings, and removing the temporary files used during the setup process. Once these tasks are complete, Setup restarts the system.

## Postinstallation Tasks

### Setting Up Local User Accounts

The official installation process is now finished, but you must perform some additional tasks before the job is actually complete. When the system restarts, a dialog box appears, allowing access to the system. You must press CTRL+ALT+DELETE to proceed to the user logon screen. This step is a security method to prevent a program from running in the background that can capture logon information.

Pressing the key combination produces a logon screen that asks you for a user name and password. Entering a new name and password creates a basic user account that will provide simple access to this computer. For full rights you must log on using an account that has administrative privileges. At this point the only such account is the one you created during the setup process.

### Joining Networks and Domains

Both the administrative account and the new user account are specific to this computer, and they do not grant access to any network or domain that you have specified during installation. To gain full access to the network you must now join the computer to any desired workgroup or domain and set up the appropriate domain or workgroup user accounts needed to access them. That may require administrative access to the servers for those networks.

### Creating an Emergency Repair Disk

The final task is to create an emergency repair disk (ERD). This disk contains three files needed to restore the original registry created during the setup process. This is a change from Windows NT 4.0, which actually saved a copy of the registry on the ERD.

The Windows 2000 ERD contains the AUTOEXEC.NT, CONFIG.NT, and SETUP.LOG files. AUTOEXEC.NT and CONFIG.NT are used to initialize the MS-DOS environment, and SETUP.LOG lists the files installed by Setup, as well as their CRC (cyclical redundancy check) data for use during the repair process.

The ERD is not a bootable disk, and by itself cannot repair anything. It is the last line of defense if the system becomes corrupted, and the Registry must be restored. The details of this process are covered in more detail in Chapter 19, "Maintaining the Modern Computer."

To create an ERD, click the Start menu and choose Programs/Accessories/System Tools/Backup. Insert an empty, high-density, 3.5-inch floppy disk into the floppy drive. Click the Welcome tab from the open application and follow the prompts to create the ERD disk. When the process is complete, remove the disk, label it with both the date and the computer name, and then store it in a safe place.

# Troubleshooting

Given the rigid hardware compatibility requirements and the thorough nature of the Setup routine, the majority of Windows 2000 installations should perform as the manufacturer intended—without problems. The following sections provide suggested troubleshooting tips in case the process fails.

### Check Hardware and Software

Run a second compatibility check on all components involved in the installation. Make sure that all hardware is actually listed in the hardware compatibility list, and replace any items that are not. If this is an upgrade, make sure that any software already on the system is Windows 2000-compliant. Try running the Setup program with the /u switch and check the compatibility report for any problems. Resolve any reported issues. Inspect the distribution CD-ROMs for any flaws.

### Repeat the Installation

Once you have finished the compliance check, repeat the installation routine. If it fails a second time, you must take further steps to identify and resolve the issue.

### Inspect the Logs

Windows 2000 creates several logs during the installation process that can be accessed with a text editor. They are usually located in the \Winnt directory. They include the following:

- Setupact contains an action log describing every step that Setup performs in chronological order. It also includes the errors that are written into the error log. A quick scan of this file can often pinpoint a device driver that did not load or a file that was not copied.

- Setupapi is a log of the installation of the different device classes on the computer.

- The Events Log can be accessed if the installation completes but you are still having trouble with a service that fails to start. This utility can be accessed from the Control Panel under Administrative Tools. It is covered in more detail in Chapter 19, "Maintaining the Modern Computer."

### Simplify the Hardware Configuration

If you cannot pinpoint the exact problem and suspect it is hardware-related, you can remove components that are not critical to system operation (like a sound card or video capture device) and run the installation program again. Once you have successfully installed Windows 2000, you can add these components individually.

### Use the Recovery Console

Windows 2000 provides a recovery console that can provide basic repairs to a corrupted system, as well as offering command-line access to a variety of utilities for inspecting and repairing components. This program is covered in detail in Chapter 19, "Maintaining the Modern Computer."

## Lesson Summary

The following points summarize the main elements of this lesson:

- Most of the Windows installation process is automated.

- Although similar in appearance, there are fundamental differences between the Windows 98 and Windows 2000 installations.

- If proper planning has been performed, all system requirements met, and proper settings selected, the majority of installations will proceed without problems.

- Although the automated installation routine provided with Windows will satisfy the requirements for most configurations, using the command-line options provides much more control for the experienced user.

- In case of difficulty, both versions of Windows offer a variety of tools to assist in troubleshooting.

# Chapter Summary

The following points summarize the key concepts in this chapter:

### The Windows Family

- The Windows family of operating systems includes a variety of products tailored to the needs of different users and environments.

- Windows 98 and Windows Me are designed for the typical end user. Both offer the broadest range of hardware and software support.

- Windows 2000 is the most robust version of Windows. It offers the most reliability and security of any member of the Windows family.

- The Windows family includes several products designed specifically for network applications ranging from LANs to complex enterprise data centers.

### Preparing for Windows Installation

- Proper planning and system preparation are critical for a trouble-free, optimal Windows installation.

- It is possible to operate more than one operating system on the same computer, but additional care in designing the file system must be taken.

- Windows 2000 requires much more critical evaluation of both the hardware and software components to ensure smooth installation and subsequent operation.

- Prior to beginning the actual installation, make sure that primary hardware components are equipped with a supported BIOS.

- Although the varieties of Windows may all look similar to the end user, each has its own unique hardware requirements.

### Installing Windows

- Superficially, the installation process appears the same for both Windows 98 and Windows 2000. In reality, they are quite different.

- During Setup, the installer must have ready information concerning system configuration and software drivers. You must be ready to answer all prompts needed to configure the system.

- With the maturation of Plug-and-Play technology, most Windows installations proceed without difficulty.

- In the event that an installation does encounter problems, the Windows environment provides a number of tools for troubleshooting and producing a successful outcome.

- The installation process installs the operating system, but additional tasks are often required after the process is completed to set the system up on networks, customize settings, and ensure that third-party applications run successfully.

# Review

The following questions are intended to reinforce key information presented in this chapter. If you are unable to answer a question, review the appropriate lesson and then try the question again. Answers to the questions can be found in Appendix A, "Questions and Answers."

1. List several differences between Windows 98 and Windows 2000.

2. Explain some of the primary considerations in designing a dual boot system.

3. Where can you find information about what hardware can be used with Windows 2000?

4. What is the purpose of the Windows 98 startup disk?

5. What is an ERD?

6. What steps have to be taken to use a compressed drive created under Windows 95 or Windows 98 with Windows 2000?

7. What is Safe Recovery?

8. What is Fdisk?

9. What are the four setup options offered after Windows 98 Setup prepares the installation directory?

10. Can Setup be run for both Windows 98 and Windows 2000 from MS-DOS?

11. What is the purpose of the Check Upgrade Only function during Windows 2000 installation and how is it invoked?

12. What should be the first step in troubleshooting any failed Windows installation?

13. What is the first step required to log on to a Windows 2000 machine (not during installation, but at any time the system is accessed after Setup is complete)? What is the purpose of this step?

14. What are the basic minimum system requirements required to run Windows 2000?

CHAPTER 18

# Running Microsoft Windows

**Lesson 1: How Windows 98 Works** ............................ 450

**Lesson 2: How Windows 2000 Works** ........................ 466

**Lesson 3: Managing Windows** ................................ 474

**Chapter Summary** ........................................... 495

**Review** .................................................... 496

## About This Chapter

This chapter focuses on operating and managing Microsoft Windows 98 and Microsoft Windows 2000 with emphasis on the skills needed for the A+ Certification Exam. To gain the high level of proficiency required of today's computer professional, you should go on to obtain advanced training in these operating systems and build a library of references after completing this chapter.

---

**Note** This chapter focuses on the Windows 98 and Windows 2000 operating systems because they are the primary focus on the A+ Exam.

---

## Before You Begin

This chapter assumes you are familiar with basic use of the Windows operating environment and the material presented in Chapter 17, "Introducing and Installing Microsoft Windows." To get the full benefit of the discussion, work along with the text at a computer with the operating system installed. You should already be comfortable with the Windows user interface, operating in DOS mode, and PC system components. You should also work through the lessons in this chapter in order, as each one builds on the preceding material.

# Lesson 1: How Windows 98 Works

This lesson explains the basic design of the Windows 98 system architecture, how the operating system manages tasks, and the entire system boot process. You should be familiar with the material in this lesson before moving on to Lessons 2 and 3 in this chapter. If possible, you should follow this lesson by performing the actual steps involved in examining the files mentioned on your computer. The same is true for the material presented in Lessons 2 and 3, as well as the material in Chapter 19, "Maintaining the Modern Computer."

---

### After this lesson, you will be able to

- Understand the Windows 98 system architecture
- Understand how Windows 98 handles tasks and allocates memory
- Identify the elements of the boot process and core files of Windows 98

### Estimated lesson time: 55 minutes

---

## The Windows 98 System Architecture

### Basic Functions and Features

Windows 98, like its predecessor Microsoft Windows 95 and the newer Microsoft Windows Me, is a natural successor to the MS-DOS and Microsoft Windows 3.1 environments. It is a true 32-bit operating environment offering improved performance, preemptive multi-tasking and multi-threading operation, advanced hardware support, better operating system stability, and the ability to manage large amounts of memory.

Like Windows 2000, Windows 98 employs dynamic hardware and system environment configuration technology, which makes it easier to install devices or reconfigure the system. This includes support for the Windows Driver Model, allowing both operating systems to share a common driver library.

The operating system can be broadly broken down into two major components: the core and ancillary systems. The Windows 98 core consists of four components: the Graphical Device Interface (GDI), the kernel, the user component, and the user interface. These four elements all have a matching pair of two 32-bit and one 16-bit dynamic-link libraries (DLLs). This allows Windows 98 to use the 32-bit mode of operation to improve performance, also allowing backward 16-bit compatibility for old devices and applications.

All of the ancillary systems operate using 32-bit mode. Windows 98 comes with a collection of 32-bit file system drivers that support FAT16, FAT32, and ISO 9660 format CD-ROM (compact disc read-only memory) discs, and the DVD (digital video disc) Universal Disc Format. The following sections provide a closer look at the four primary components and some key subsystems.

## Graphical Device Interface

The GDI is an imaging system that draws all the objects displayed on the screen or reads the information to devices like printers that can receive graphical output. The GDI is also the component responsible for interacting with the display system and its related drivers. The average user often takes the generation of the user interface for granted; in reality, it is one of the most complex tasks performed by the operating system. Many of the memory problems associated with earlier versions of Windows could be traced back to graphics display problems and GDI management.

## User Interface

The Windows 98 user interface is a 32-bit shell that includes a variety of tools to make use of the file system and gain access to system services. These include My Computer, the Network Neighborhood, and Windows Explorer. All Windows applications can make use of the shell services, including dialog boxes and the ability to list and view files.

## User Component

This core element of the operating system is the I/O (input/output) manager. It receives and routes input from the mouse, keyboard, microphone, and other input devices. It also routes traffic to and from the communications ports, the system timer, and the sound card. In addition, it acts as the output coordinator for the GDI by controlling the output of display elements like menus, dialog boxes, and icons.

## Kernel

The kernel can be thought of as the core of the core of the operating system. It controls all tasks: When an application opens, it is the kernel that invokes the executable file and terminates it when it is done. It loads and manages all DLLs and allocates memory. The kernel is also responsible for all preemptive multi-tasking and multi-threading operations.

## Process Scheduler

The Process Scheduler is responsible for providing system resources. Through proper allocation, it allows multiple applications to run simultaneously. Windows 98 advances the cooperative multi-tasking found in Windows 3.1, which required an application to periodically relinquish access to system services to allow another application to execute. A more elegant approach is preemptive multi-tasking, which Windows 98 uses for all 32-bit applications. The Process Scheduler executes this by dividing the amount of time each application can have to access to the CPU (central processing unit) and other system resources. These time slices are called *threads*, so the term *multi-threaded* can be applied to Windows 98, meaning that an application can have more than one thread open at a time. As a result, Windows 98 is known as a multi-threading, multi-tasking operating system.

### File System Drivers

Like Windows 2000, Windows 98 offers support for the Windows Driver Model (WDM), allowing compatible devices to use the same driver for both operating systems. Its Plug-and-Play feature is much improved over Windows 95, allowing for dynamic hardware configuration and all but eliminating the need for jumpers and manual configuration of adapter cards.

### The Virtual Machine Manager

The Virtual Machine Manager (VMM) oversees the key resources required by both applications and system processes. These include process scheduling, memory management, exception handling (issuing General Protection Faults or GPFs), and mapping access to the system BIOS (basic input/output system), device drivers, and TSR (terminate-and-stay-resident) programs.

The VMM manages the system's virtual machine, the environment in which all system processes operate. All 32-bit applications are provided their own individual virtual machines, as are any MS-DOS programs that run in a protected space. Legacy 16-bit Windows applications are all grouped together in a single 16-bit virtual machine that emulates an 8086 processor. This 16-bit machine is said to be operating in V86 mode.

## The Windows 98 Virtual Memory Model

Using virtual memory, Windows 98 can provide more functional memory to applications than the amount of RAM (random access memory) actually present on the computer. When an application or process needs more memory than is actually available, the operating system moves data between virtual memory and the system's hard disks to free RAM for the active process.

With MS-DOS and versions of Microsoft Windows prior to Windows 95, all processes and active applications shared a single address space. Without the use of special memory managers, all applications and most system code had to reside in the first 640 KB of physical memory (RAM). If any process corrupted the memory stack, the entire system would fail. This memory model significantly limited how much memory was actually available to both the operating system and any application and compromised the integrity of the operating environment.

Windows 98 provides a unique virtual address space for each process or program, using a demand-page virtual memory system that can be as large as 4 GB. Part of the space is reserved for system processes and part is available for use by applications. A process can only access memory that has been specifically allocated for its use. The Windows 98 core components (such as the kernel and the GDI) and shared DLLs are contained in a shared address space. The 4 GB is allocated and used as follows:

- **0–640 KB.** The first 640 KB is reserved for real-mode device drivers and TSRs. This allows backward compatibility for older applications, which expect to see RAM in this location.

- **4 MB–2 GB.** This region is the province of Win32-based applications. Each program is in its own private address space.

- **2 GB–3 GB.** This 1-GB space contains the shared Windows 98 core components and DLLs. This region can be read by any application or process that needs these resources.

- **3 GB–4 GB.** This is the privileged-mode space, holding the system kernel code, which controls and directs access to all hardware and memory addresses.

## The Virtual Memory Swap File System

Obviously, if Windows 98 has the ability to move data between physical memory and virtual memory, there has to be a specially designated file (and file structure) on the hard disk to be used as a "scratch" area. It is known as the *swap file*. When physical memory becomes low, Windows 98 automatically adjusts the size of the swap file and the way virtual memory is allocated. This is a major improvement over Windows 95, which required the user to set the amount of space used by the swap file and designate if it would operate in 32-bit mode. In Windows 98, all this is usually done automatically in 32-bit mode. The user can still override the settings, but this is rarely necessary.

## The Memory Pager

The Memory Pager actually handles moving blocks of data to and from virtual memory into the physical address space by dividing the data in equal blocks known as *pages*. The code contained in specific pages is moved into RAM when needed. This approach allows any given application access to the full 2 GB of memory space provided for it in the Windows 98 memory model.

## DOS Mode Support

DOS mode support allows a legacy application to gain exclusive access to the system resources it needs to operate. Windows 98 does this by creating an exclusive operating environment known as MS-DOS mode. Applications running in this space have access to the resources they need as long as their process is running. This is an exception to the multi-tasking feature mentioned earlier. Windows 98 provides for this by the use of separate virtual machines for each MS-DOS mode session.

## The WDM

The WDM is the device driver architecture that first appeared in Windows 95 OSR2 and has been improved to work with both Windows 98 and Windows 2000. Some drivers originally designed for use with Windows 95 using the WDM may not be compatible with these newer operating systems. This architecture was designed to create a single driver that can be used across the range of Windows operating systems. This offers several benefits: It reduces the cost of providing device drivers, makes devices available on a wider range of platforms, and simplifies distribution.

The WDM architecture is arranged in a series of layers, with a hardware device at the bottom and the applications using it at the top. Figure 18.1 depicts the layout of the architecture, and the following list describes each element's function within it.

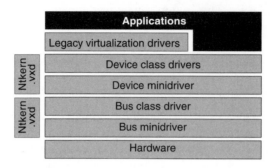

**Figure 18.1**    The Windows Device Model architecture

An individual WDM driver belongs to one of several classes:

- Device class drivers contain class-specific functions. They are not specific to a given piece of hardware or system bus, but provide a more generic function. These are used for classes of products like mice, joysticks, and keyboards.

- Bus class drivers are available for both USB (universal serial bus) and IEEE 1394 buses on a system. They work to speed up communications between the hardware layer and the minidrivers.

- Minidrivers are hardware-specific and generally operate a class of devices operating on a specific type of bus. This class includes support for SCSI (Small Computer System Interface), USB, DVD, IEEE 1394, and network adapters. Minidrivers can be written to support multifunction cards like a video capture card that includes both video and sound functions on a single product. Windows 98 dynamically loads and unloads minidrivers as they are needed or released to save on memory and avoid usage conflicts.

- Virtual device drivers (VxDs) are 32-bit protected mode drivers responsible for managing a system resource (either hardware or software). These drivers do not directly control the hardware device, but act as an interpreter between the hardware and the application, ensuring that only one system process controls the resource at any specific time. Like minidrivers, VxDs are only held in memory when they are actually in use. Some VxDs are also used with legacy hardware and software to allow them to function within the Windows 98 environment.

- NTKERN.VXD is the operating system services layer for Windows 98. This layer is always system-specific and allows the minidrivers to function with more than one operating system. Under Microsoft Windows NT, the operating system services layer is the hardware abstraction layer (HAL).

## 32-Bit VFAT

Disk access is provided through the 32-bit VFAT (Virtual File Allocation Table). Unlike the 16-bit file allocation table (FAT) used before Windows 95, VFAT is a virtual device driver that operates in protected mode. This provides more reliability and works with a greater variety of hardware. Don't confuse 32-bit VFAT with 32-bit FAT, which has to do with how data is stored on a hard disk partition (the cluster size). VFAT has to do with how files are accessed.

Like the older 16-bit FAT, VFAT links clusters of files together. In the old 16-bit system, the largest number of clusters on a drive was 65,525; with 32-bit operation the maximum cluster size is now 268,435,445.

The first 8 bytes of the FAT32 table are reserved for system use. The value of the final byte is normally 0, set to that value during system startup. When you issue a proper shutdown command on the system, the value is changed to 1. If, during startup, Windows detects that the value of the eighth byte is 0, it assumes the system shut down improperly and ScanDisk runs during the boot process.

---

**Note**  VFAT was formerly known as 32-bit file access in Windows 3.1. Don't confuse 32-bit file access with a 32-bit operating environment; they are not the same.

---

## Long Filename Support

In MS-DOS and Windows 3.x, filenames were limited to an 8.3 format; that is, the filename itself was restricted to a maximum of eight characters in length, and the extension to a maximum of three characters in length. Filename and extension are connected by a period, or dot. Beginning with Windows 95, the operating system added long filenames (LFNs) support. The LFN removes the 8.3-filename limitations of older MS-DOS and Windows operating systems. In a regular MS-DOS 8.3 file specification directory, all file records are stored in 32-byte records. Of the 32 bytes, 10 are reserved. The other 22 bytes are used to store information on starting clusters, creation date, and creation time, and 11 bytes are for the filename itself. LFNs exist on FAT partitions by chopping the filename into 12-byte chunks (stealing one of the reserved bytes) and allowing up to 13 chunks, creating a filename of up to 255 characters.

When an LFN is saved, the system creates a short name that conforms to the 8.3 standard. Then, each group of 12 characters is cut off and stored in its own directory section. The directory entries that make up the LFN are called LFN entries. These must be backward compatible with MS-DOS programs and with MS-DOS itself.

**Note**   To make files backward compatible with MS-DOS, Windows takes the first six characters (no spaces) of the filename, adds a tilde (~), a number, and then the extension. If two or more files have the same first six characters, the number is incremented by one for each. For example, two files named LONG FILE NAME ONE.TXT and LONG FILE NAME TWO.TXT would become LONGFI~1.TXT and LONGFI~2.TXT.

To make LFNs compatible with MS-DOS means to make sure that MS-DOS ignores the LFN entries in the directory structure. This is achieved by giving LFN entries the bizarre attribute combination of hidden, read-only, system, and volume label. There is nothing in the MS-DOS code that tells it what to do if it encounters a file with this combination of attributes, so MS-DOS does not interfere with it.

**Caution**   Older disk utilities are incompatible with LFNs and will try to erase the LFN entries. It is critical that any disk utility that tries to diagnose the directory structure, including the Scandisk utility that is included with MS-DOS 6 and earlier, should never be run on a computer with LFNs. The Scandisk versions that come with Windows 98 and Windows Me are compatible with LFNs.

## The Windows 98 Boot Process

Understanding the boot sequence for the operating systems you encounter during your work is a necessary skill. The rest of this lesson is devoted to the sequence of steps that begins when power is supplied to the computer or the RESTART command is issued and ends when control of the system is returned to the user interface. This process can be broken down into three broad phases.

## The BIOS Initialization Phase

During the BIOS initialization phase, the computer's BIOS and the embedded power-on self test (POST) code hold system control. Just how this phase affects Windows depends on the type of BIOS the system has. Older machines that do not support Plug-and-Play enable devices in a static mode based on the device settings. Computers with a Plug-and-Play-enabled BIOS initializes and completes the configuration of the Plug-and-Play-capable devices before the POST begins, resolving possible conflicts. It then looks for the existence of an operating system. At this point, Windows 98 begins taking control of the operating environment.

## Hardware Profile and Real-Mode Driver Loading Phase

The initial phases of Windows 98's startup are actually conducted in real mode. In the real mode environment, Windows 98 operates much like MS-DOS. The Windows 98 IO.SYS is the first system file loaded into memory. It actually incorporates many of the features of the old MS-DOS IO.SYS, as well as much of the functionality of the MS-DOS MSDOS.SYS file. As the following table indicates, it loads many of the core settings that once were the province of CONFIG.SYS.

| Entry | Function |
| --- | --- |
| dos=high | Specifies that MS-DOS is to load in the high memory area (HMA). Also, the upper memory block (UMB) value is included if EMM386 is loaded from CONFIG.SYS. (IO.SYS does not load EMM386.) |
| HIMEM.SYS | Enables access to the HMA and loads and runs the real-mode memory manager. HIMEM.SYS is loaded by default in Windows 98. |
| IFSHLP.SYS | The 32-bit Installable File System Manager uses the services provided by this driver to assist in trapping real-mode file system and network-related application programming interfaces (APIs). |
| SETVER.EXE | Optional TSR-type device included for compatibility. Some MS-DOS-based applications require a specific version of MS-DOS to be running. This file responds to applications that query for the version number and sets the version number required. |
| files= | Specifies the number of file handle buffers to create. This is specifically for files opened using MS-DOS calls and is not required by Windows 98. It is included for compatibility with older applications. The default value is 60. |
| lastdrive= | Specifies the last drive letter available for assignment. This is not required for Windows 98 but is included for compatibility with older applications. If Windows 98 Setup finds this entry, it is moved to the registry. The default value is *z*. |
| buffers= | Specifies the number of file buffers to create. This is specifically for applications using IO.SYS calls and is not required by Windows 98. The default value is 30. |
| stacks= | Specifies the number and size of stack frames. This is not required for Windows 98 but is included for compatibility with older applications. The default value is 9256. |
| shell= COMMAND.COM | Indicates what command process to use. By default, the /p switch is included to indicate that the command process is permanent and should not be unloaded. If the /p switch is not specified, AUTOEXEC.BAT is not processed and the command process can be unloaded when quitting the operating system. |
| fcbs= | Specifies the number of file control blocks that can be open at the same time. You should use this line in CONFIG.SYS only if you have an older program that requires such a setting. The default value is 4. |

During this phase, Windows 98 determines the computer's configuration. It performs a detection sequence that examines IRQs (interrupt requests), the system

BIOS, Plug-and-Play data, and whether the device is actually a laptop docking station. At that point, it loads the MSDOS.SYS settings and processes the CONFIG.SYS and AUTOEXEC.BAT files, if they exist.

Be aware that several files are automatically loaded by IO.SYS in addition to any invoked by any user-defined startup settings: HIMEM.SYS, IFSHLP.SYS, SETVER.EXE, and DBLSPACE.BIN or DRVSPACE.BIN (if DLBSPACE.INI or DRVSPACE.INI exists in the root of the boot drive). You cannot edit or directly adjust IO.SYS without causing it to fail. If you do not wish to load any of these files, they should be renamed.

## Using MSDOS.SYS for Custom Configurations

There is still an MSDOS.SYS file employed in Windows 95 and Windows 98, but it is not the same as in MS-DOS. It actually replaces the functions of CONFIG.SYS. This is the proper place to make custom boot configuration settings unless there is some overriding reason to use CONFIG.SYS and AUTOEXEC.BAT for backward compatibility. They are not actually necessary unless you need to load them to support older MS-DOS applications or hardware.

---

**Note**   If you invoke any primary real-mode drivers using the CONFIG.SYS and AUTOEXEC.BAT files, you may force Windows 98 into real-mode operation for all or part of its functions. This can significantly degrade system performance.

---

The following example shows a very simple MSDOS.SYS file.

```
;FORMAT
[Paths]
WinDir=C:\WINDOWS
WinBootDir=C:\WINDOWS
HostWinBootDrv=C

[Options]
BootMulti=1
BootGUI=1
DoubleBuffer=1
AutoScan=1
WinVer=4.10.1998
;
;The following lines are required for compatibility with other programs.
;Do not remove them (MSDOS.SYS needs to be >1024 bytes).
;xxxxxxxxxxxxxxxxxxxxxxxxxxxxxxxxxxxxxxxxxxxxxxxxxxxxxxxxxxxxxxxxxxxxa
;xxxxxxxxxxxxxxxxxxxxxxxxxxxxxxxxxxxxxxxxxxxxxxxxxxxxxxxxxxxxxxxxxxxxb
```

In Windows 98, you can use a text editor to adjust the settings in MSDOS.SYS just as you could with CONFIG.SYS under DOS. The following table provides a list of entries and their function. You may wish to examine the contents of this file on your system (assuming you are using Windows 98). To do so, you will need to enable viewing hidden files, as MSDOS.SYS is a hidden system file. If the value setting uses a Boolean operator, set it to 1 to enable the option and 0 to turn it off.

**Caution**  Be sure not to change any values you don't completely understand because they will alter the method and ability of the system to start. Normally, when modifying this file you should save the original version under another name so that it can be easily restored if undesirable results are obtained.

| Entry | Description |
|---|---|
| **[Paths] Section** | |
| HostWinBootDrv=c | Defines the location of the boot drive root directory. |
| WinBootDir= | Defines the location of the necessary startup files. The default is the directory specified during Setup; for example, C:\Windows. |
| WinDir= | Defines the location of the Windows 98 directory as specified during Setup. |
| **[Options] Section** | |
| AutoScan= | Enables ScanDisk to run automatically when your computer restarts. The default is 1. When this value is set to 1, ScanDisk prompts you to indicate if you want to run ScanDisk; if you do not respond after 1 minute, ScanDisk runs automatically. Setting this value to 0 disables this feature. Setting it to 2 launches ScanDisk automatically (if needed) without prompting you. |
| BootDelay=$n$ | Sets the initial startup delay to $n$ seconds. The default is 2. BootKeys=0 disables the delay. The only purpose of the delay is to give the user sufficient time to press F8 after the Starting Windows message appears. |
| BootFailSafe= | Enables safe mode for system startup. The default is 0. (This setting is typically enabled by equipment manufacturers for installation.) |
| BootGUI= | Enables automatic graphical startup into Windows 98. This is equivalent to putting the win statement in AUTOEXEC.BAT. The default is 1. |
| BootKeys= | Enables the startup option keys (that is, F5, F6, and F8). The default is 1. Setting this value to 0 overrides the value of BootDelay=$n$ and prevents any startup keys from functioning. This setting allows system administrators to configure more secure systems. |
| BootMenu= | Enables automatic display of the Windows 98 Startup menu, so that the user must press CTRL to see the menu. The default is 0. Setting this value to 1 eliminates the need to press CTRL to see the menu. |

*(continued)*

*(continued)*

| Entry | Description |
|---|---|
| BootMenuDefault=# | Sets the default menu item on the Windows Startup menu; the default is 3 for a computer with no networking components and 4 for a networked computer. |
| BootMenuDelay=# | Sets the number of seconds to display the Windows Startup menu before running the default menu item. The default is 30. |
| BootMulti= | Enables dual-boot capabilities. The default is 0. Setting this value to 1 enables you to start MS-DOS by pressing F4 or by pressing F8 to use the Windows Startup menu. |
| BootWarn= | Enables the safe mode startup warning. The default is 1. |
| BootWin= | Enables Windows 98 as the default operating system. Setting this value to 0 disables Windows 98 as the default; this is useful only with MS-DOS version 5 or 6.x on the computer. The default is 1. |
| DblSpace= | Enables automatic loading of DBLSPACE.BIN. The default is 1. |
| DoubleBuffer= | Enables loading of a double-buffering driver for a SCSI controller. The default is 0. Setting this value to 1 enables double buffering if required by the SCSI controller. |
| DrvSpace= | Enables automatic loading of DRVSPACE.BIN. The default is 1. |
| LoadTop= | Enables loading of COMMAND.COM or DRVSPACE.BIN at the top of 640 K memory. The default is 1. Set this value to 0 with Novell NetWare or any software that makes assumptions about what is used in specific memory areas. |
| Logo= | Enables display of the animated logo. The default is 1. Setting this value to 0 avoids a variety of interrupts that can create incompatibilities with certain third-party memory managers. |
| Network= | Safe mode with networking is not supported in Windows 98. This value should be set to 0 or left blank to disable this feature. |

## Loading CONFIG.SYS and AUTOEXEC.BAT

As mentioned previously, although not recommended, you can use both CONFIG.SYS and AUTOEXEC.BAT to modify how Windows 98 operates. In general, they work just as they did under MS-DOS, but there are some important things to consider and be aware of when using these files:

- Don't include any mouse support in either file. Windows 98 includes internal support for most mice.

- Windows 98 has its own disk caching and double-buffering algorithms, so you do not need to include the SMARTDRV.SYS command in CONFIG.SYS.

- The comspec, path, prompt, net start, and temp settings made via AUTOEXEC.BAT under MS-DOS are now automatically handled by IO.SYS in Windows 98. They can be overridden by AUTOEXEC.BAT without affecting the 32-bit mode operations of Windows 98.

- Do not reference other versions of Windows that might still be on the drive under Windows 98 in the AUTOEXEC.BAT file.

- Be sure the Windows and Windows\Command directories are in any new path statements.

- Device and memory settings should be handled via the System or Device Manager or Registry in Windows 98 whenever possible, avoiding the CONFIG.SYS and AUTOEXEC.BAT files.

## Protected Mode Initialization Phase

Once the real mode components are in place, the startup invokes WIN.COM. This file manages the initial system inspection for 32-bit operation and loads the core Windows operating system components.

The boot process loads a series of static and dynamic VxDs, including VMM32.VXD. This file is a composite VxD that contains the VMM and the real mode loader. It also invokes any other VxDs that reside in the Windows\System\Vmm32 directory. The exact list of VxDs loaded at this point varies based on the machine configuration. It is possible to see which ones are called by examining the [386enh] section of the WINDOWS.INI file.

Once the virtual machine is running, the SYSTEM.INI file is processed, and the system is fined tuned with those settings. Next, the configuration manager is started, employing information from the Plug-and-Play BIOS, or if the system does not have one, by developing its own device list and loading the appropriate drivers. The configuration manager resolves any conflicts and then initializes the drivers. If a conflict cannot be resolved, one or more of the devices may be disabled.

With the hardware structure defined and appropriate VxDs in place, the final system components can be loaded. These include: KERNEL32.DLL (which provides the main Windows 98 components), KRNL386.EXE (which loads device drivers), GDI.EXE and GDI32.EXE (which manage and provide the GUI), and USER.EXE and USER32.EXE (which provide the user interface code).

Those files call on additional resources such as fonts and miscellaneous desktop components (like icons and menus), and handle any secondary settings described in the WIN.INI that were not already processed. This completes the system startup, and a dialog box is presented so that a user may log on to the system and begin using it. (Standalone machines may not have the final prompt if no password is required to use that PC.)

# Alternate Startup Methods and Resources

The initialization scenario depicted in the preceding sections details the normal procedure for starting Windows 98. Technicians and users alike may want to start Windows using another method for a variety of reasons: to load the system into a previous version of MS-DOS, to operate in a command-mode-only environment, or to troubleshoot problems. Windows 98 offers two methods for bypassing the normal startup procedure and gaining access to a command prompt or safe mode.

## The Startup Menu

If the system was shut down improperly, the Startup menu should appear the next time the operating system loads. It can also be invoked manually by pressing CTRL while the system is booting. Choose the appropriate mode for the desired system startup. The exact options available from this menu vary based on the system configuration and the reasons for which it was brought up. The following table shows the most common options and their functions. Note that the Start In Safe Mode With Network option available in Windows 95 has been removed in Windows 98.

| Menu Option | Remarks |
| --- | --- |
| Normal | This invokes the normal startup routine and loads Windows with all the normal startup files and registry values in 32-bit mode. |
| Logged (BOOTLOG.TXT) | Runs system startup, creating a startup log file. |
| Safe Mode | Starts Windows, bypassing startup files and using only basic system drivers. You are provided with minimal support (including a basic VGA display driver) to allow troubleshooting and adjustment of the system configuration files. You can also start this option by pressing F5 or typing **win /d:m** at the command prompt. Booting into safe mode bypasses all secondary startup files, including the registry, CONFIG.SYS, AUTOEXEC.BAT, and the [Boot] and [386Enh] sections of SYSTEM.INI. |
| Step-By-Step Confirmation | Starts Windows, allowing you to confirm or disable startup files line by line. You can also start this option by pressing F8 when the Startup menu is displayed. |
| Command Prompt Only1 | Starts the operating system with startup files and Registry, displaying only the command prompt. |
| Safe Mode Command Prompt Only1 | Starts the operating system in safe mode and displays only the command prompt, bypassing startup files. This has the same effect as pressing SHIFT+F5. |
| Previous Version of MS-DOS | Starts the version of MS-DOS previously installed on this computer. This is only available on computers upgraded from a previous MS-DOS environment. You can also start this option by pressing F4. This option is available only if BootMulti=1 in MSDOS.SYS. |

## The Startup Disk

You can also use the startup disk that was created during the initial system installation or use the Start menu. The startup disk provides the drivers necessary to access the CD-ROM drive, enable 32-bit file system access, and start the system in command mode—even if you can't access the hard drive normally—if it is intact. Booting this way also provides access to a number of utilities that are covered in Chapter 19, "Maintaining the Modern Computer."

## The WIN.COM Command

Once a command prompt is available, you can attempt to load Windows with the WIN.COM command and one or more of its switches to start Windows 98. Keep in mind that you may have to provide the path to the command. It is usually in the C:\Windows or C:\Windows98 directory. The following table shows the WIN.COM syntax and the uses of the switches.

| Switch | Purpose |
|--------|---------|
| /d | Used to start Windows in safe mode with one of the following options to troubleshoot the operating system. |
| /f | Disables 32-bit disk access. This is equivalent to disabling the hard disk controller(s) in Device Manager. Try this if the computer appears to have disk problems or if Windows 98 stalls. This is equivalent to 32BitAccess = FALSE in SYSTEM.INI. |
| /m | Starts Windows 98 in safe mode. |
| /s | Specifies that Windows 98 should not use ROM (read-only memory) address space between F000:0000 and 1 MB for a break point. Try this if Windows 98 stalls during system startup. This is equivalent to SystemROMBreakPoint = FALSE in SYSTEM.INI. |
| /v | Specifies that the ROM routine will handle interrupts from the hard disk controller. This is equivalent to VirtualHDIRQ = FALSE in SYSTEM.INI. |
| /x | Excludes all of the adapter area from the range of memory that Windows 98 scans to find unused space. This is equivalent to EMMExclude = A000-FFFF in SYSTEM.INI. If this switch resolves the issue, you may have a conflict in the upper memory area (UMA) that requires an Exclude statement. |

## The BOOTLOG.TXT File

Windows 95, Windows 98, Windows NT, and Windows 2000 all provide the ability to create a boot log. One of the Start menu options offers the ability to generate this file as the system is started. It is not unusual to have this file run as long as 15 or 20 pages on even a simple system. The following sample shows portions of an actual BOOTLOG.TXT file. As you can see, it depicts in sequence each action the start process makes and whether or not it executes successfully. This file is a powerful tool for determining exactly where a problem with a driver or setup process occurs. In the event of an obscure or difficult problem loading the operating system, it can prove invaluable. We discuss its use further in Chapter 19, "Maintaining the Modern Computer."

```
[000820DF] Loading Device = C:\WINDOWS\HIMEM.SYS
[000820DF] LoadSuccess  = C:\WINDOWS\HIMEM.SYS
[000820DF] Loading Device = C:\WINDOWS\DBLBUFF.SYS
[000820F1] LoadSuccess  = C:\WINDOWS\DBLBUFF.SYS
[000820F1] Loading Device = C:\WINDOWS\IFSHLP.SYS
[000820F1] LoadSuccess  = C:\WINDOWS\IFSHLP.SYS
[00082117] Loading Vxd = VMM
[00082117] LoadSuccess = VMM
[00082116] Loading Vxd = msmouse.vxd
[00082116] LoadSuccess = msmouse.vxd
[00082116] Loading Vxd = dynapage
LoadStart = C:\WINDOWS\fonts\symbole.fon
LoadSuccess = C:\WINDOWS\fonts\symbole.fon
LoadStart = C:\WINDOWS\fonts\smalle.fon
LoadSuccess = C:\WINDOWS\fonts\smalle.fon
LoadSuccess = user.exe
Init = Final USER
InitDone = Final USER
Init = Installable Drivers
InitDone = Installable Drivers
Terminate = User
Terminate = Query Drivers
EndTerminate = Query Drivers
Terminate = Unload Network
EndTerminate = Unload Network
Terminate = Reset Display
EndTerminate = Reset Display
EndTerminate = User
```

## Lesson Summary

The following points summarize the main elements of this lesson:

- Windows 98 is a true 32-bit operating system, which builds on Windows 95 and adds improved performance, reliability, and support for Plug-and-Play technology.

- The operating system can be broadly broken down to two major components: the core and ancillary systems. The core consists of four components: the GDI, the kernel, the user component, and the user interface.

- The WDM allows a single driver to be used across a range of Windows operating systems, including Windows 98, Windows Me, and the various editions of Windows 2000. The WDM architecture is arranged in a series of layers, with a hardware device at the bottom and the applications using it at the top.

- The Windows 98 boot sequence can be broken down into three broad phases: the BIOS initialization phase, the hardware profile and real-mode driver loading phase, and the protected mode initialization phase.

- The Windows 98 boot sequence takes over after the POST and concludes with turning the system over to the user interface.

- Although you can still make use of the AUTOEXEC.BAT and CONFIG.SYS files, their functions have been incorporated directly into the Windows 98 operating system startup processes.

- Safe mode is a means of operation that can be used to troubleshoot a Windows 95 or Windows 98 operating system that fails to load properly.

# Lesson 2:  How Windows 2000 Works

This lesson explains the basic design of the Windows 2000 system architecture, how the operating system manages tasks, and the entire system boot process. You should be familiar with the material in this lesson before proceeding to Lesson 3.

### After this lesson, you will be able to

- Understand the Windows 2000 system architecture
- Understand how Windows 2000 Professional handles tasks and allocates memory
- Identify the elements of the boot process and core files of Windows 2000

### Estimated lesson time: 55 minutes

## The Windows 2000 System Design

To the casual observer the Windows 2000 and Windows 98 operating systems may appear virtually identical. They share a common user interface, use similar file naming conventions, and come from the same manufacturer. However, Windows 2000 is a radically different environment from Windows 98. A quick examination of some of its advanced features highlights how much more robust the design is:

- Windows 2000, like its Windows NT predecessor, is able to run on both CISC (complex instruction set computing, like the Intel Pentium) and RISC (Reduced Instruction Set Computing, like the DEC Alpha)-based CPUs.

- It provides SMP (symmetric multiprocessing) support, allowing the system to use more than one processor at the same time. Windows 2000 Professional supports two processors per platform and other versions in the Windows 2000 family can operate up to 32 processors at the same time.

- Windows 2000 can operate applications written both to the Win32 and the POSIX (Portable Operating System Interface for UNIX) environment.

- The Windows NT advanced file system and other elements of the Windows 2000 environment offer security features not found in Windows 95, Windows 98, and Windows Me.

- A variety of advanced management and customization tools provide the user much more control over the Windows 2000 environment than that found in Windows 98.

- Windows 2000 Professional is built on the same core technology as the Windows 2000 Server platforms, based on Windows NT technology, offering advanced networking controls not found on simple peer-to-peer platforms like Windows 98 and Windows Me.

# Two Modes, Several Subsystems

As an operating system, Windows 2000 can be divided conceptually into the kernel mode and user mode, each containing several subsystems. Functionally, it helps to visualize the entire operating environment as a series of layers. The bottom layer is the physical hardware itself, above that is the kernel mode, on top of that the user mode, and above that rests the applications that use the services provided by the operating system. Figure 18.2 provides a graphical representation of this model. It focuses on Windows 2000 Professional, but can be extended all the way to Windows 2000 Datacenter Server. Keep in mind that many of the server functions of the advanced editions of Windows 2000 may require additional components.

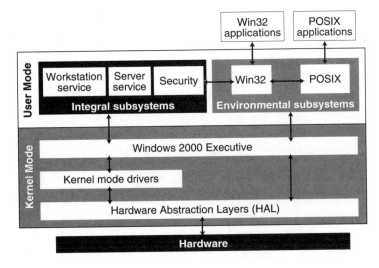

**Figure 18.2**   The Windows 2000 Professional operating system architecture

## Kernel Mode

The kernel mode is the portion of the operating system that has direct access to both the physical hardware devices and the system data that runs on it. This is the layer that provides access to memory and prioritizes access to system resources like memory and hardware devices, so its operations are contained in a protected memory area. The kernel mode consists of several components.

## Hardware Abstraction Layer

The hardware abstraction layer (HAL) is the key to Windows 2000's ability to support multiple processors and to run on platforms built on different CPU architectures. The HAL is responsible for operating the interface among all the different I/O devices on the system, interrupting controllers, and providing platform-specific hardware support for every device on the system. This component operates basically the same way it did under Windows NT.

## Windows 2000 Executive

The Windows 2000 Executive acts as the interface between the HAL and the system components contained in user mode. The components of the Windows 2000 Executive provide core services through a set of internal routines that make sure that two devices, like an application, virtual machine, or CPU, are not allowed to access the same device at the same instant. You can see from the descriptions of Windows 2000 Executive components that follow that the operating system processes in Windows 2000 are more compartmentalized and, therefore, more fault-tolerant than similar functions found in Windows 98 and Windows Me. They are also more extensive.

The I/O Manager processes commands issued through the user mode into I/O request packets and services I/O operations related to device drivers. Its subcomponents include the Cache Manager, which improves disk performance by performing reads to disks in the background and holding recent disk reads in system memory, and low-level device drivers that directly manipulate hardware I/O.

The GDI and Window Manager are the two Windows 2000 System Executive components that manage the display system. Both are contained within the WIN32K.SYS device driver. The GDI component manages the functions required for drawing and manipulating graphics on the screen or graphics that are output directly to devices like a printer. The Window Manager controls screen output and window displays, as well as accepting and forwarding signals from the keyboard and pointing devices to the active application.

Client/server communications are the province of the Interprocess Communications (IPC) Manager. The IPC subsystem requests information from the server functions of the Windows 2000 Executive. The IPC has two components: The local procedure call (LPC) facility handles client/server traffic that exists within a single computer, and the remote procedure call (RPC) facility manages client/server traffic that takes place between two or more computers.

The Security Reference Monitor (SRM) is responsible for enforcing all security policies that are in force on the local computer.

During its operation, Windows 2000 creates a variety of transitory objects including processes (programs or part of a program), threads (a specific set of program commands that can be operated independently), and data structures. The Object Manager is the kernel mode component responsible for keeping track of all these objects during their life span. The actual creation and ending of threads and processes is the task of the Process Manager.

The Plug-and-Play Manager coordinates the operation of Plug-and-Play device drivers among the HAL, the Windows 2000 Executive, the appropriate interface or system buses, and the relevant device drivers. During boot, and in the event of the discovery of new or removed devices, it manages device configuration and initialization or removal of drivers and coordinates their availability with the user mode components.

The Power Manager performs a similar function with power management APIs, coordinating events, generating IRPs (Interrupt Request Packets), and starting and stopping devices that make use of power management functions.

The Virtual Memory Manager provides a private virtual memory address space for each process or thread and protects that space against encroachment by other system objects. The Virtual Memory Manager controls this function for both physical RAM and hard disk space, as well as managing demand paging. These concepts should already be familiar from our discussion of Windows 98.

### Kernel Mode Drivers

The structure and function of device driver operations within Windows 2000 is much more complex than that found within Windows 98. In general, hardware devices are objects managed by the I/O Manager, and the logical, physical, and virtual drivers for devices are represented as objects within the system. Kernel mode drivers act as an interface between the HAL and the Windows 2000 Executive. The direct control of these drivers is the province of the I/O Manager.

Kernel mode drivers are divided into three layers based on their function and how close they come to directly controlling the hardware.

- Low-level drivers are usually used to exert direct physical control over devices like a Plug-and-Play hardware bus. This class of drivers also includes legacy Windows NT device drivers.

- Intermediate-level drivers include WDM drivers like those discussed in the preceding lesson that are employed with Windows 98. These are generally Plug-and-Play function drivers designed to control specific peripheral devices and mini drivers, and they are used for tasks like disk mirroring.

- High-level drivers include those that operate translations between different file system devices such as FAT, NTFS, and CDFS (CD-ROM File System) and the operating system. This class of drivers is known as file system drivers. They cannot act on their own; they depend on support from one or more intermediate-level drivers.

### User Mode

User mode can be thought as a layer of insulation between kernel mode and users and their programs. User mode handles all conversations with the kernel and provides the APIs needed to emulate application and network environments. It is the user mode that enables Windows 2000 to run applications written for Windows 95, Windows 98, MS-DOS, and POSIX. User mode is comprised of a series of subsystems.

There are two primary groups of subsystems: integral and environmental. A good example of the former is a security subsystem, which manages logon requests from users. It manages all the rights and permissions granted to user accounts and controls access to resources. Environmental subsystems might be thought of as the final layer. The most common is the Win32 environment, which acts as an intermediary between legacy Win16 and MS-DOS applications and controls and Win32-based applications running in a Windows 2000 environment.

# The Windows 2000 Boot Process

In many ways, the Windows 2000 Professional boot process is different from that encountered with Windows 98. It is, however, very similar to the process of initialization used by Windows NT. The process can be broken down into seven segments, from turning on the power to presentation of the logon screen. The following sections detail them and describe the key files needed to initialize Windows 2000 Professional operation.

### System Start and POST

This phase of system startup is identical to that of Windows 98, as this portion of the process is hardware dependent.

### BIOS Initialization and Operating System Detection

This phase also is directly under control of the hardware and behaves just as it does in Windows 98. The system BIOS institutes a search for an operating system. In most cases, it searches first on the floppy drive, then the system hard disks. It searches the active partition of the first hard drive and looks for code that loads an operating system. When the Windows 2000 code is located, the startup routine diverges from that of Windows 98 and Windows Me.

### Bootstrap Loading

Microsoft Windows 2000 does not automatically assume that it is the only operating system on the computer. It also does not require that all the primary files reside on the primary partition of the first hard drive, as is the case with MS-DOS, Windows 95, Windows 98, and Windows Me. Instead, it uses a bootstrap loading process to allow the user to choose which operating system to initialize and to locate the required operating system files.

The primary partition of the boot drive on a Windows 2000 computer contains at least four system-specific startup files, and as many as eleven.

These files must be present in the root directory:

- NTLDR
- BOOT.INI

- NTDETECT.COM
- CDLDR

This file must also be present in the root on multiple boot systems:

- BOOTSEC.DOS

This file may exist on systems with very large SCSI or EIDE drives:

- NTBOOTDD.SYS

These files may be in either the root directory or in a subdirectory of the WinNT directory on another drive if you elected to install the operating system on a second drive:

- HYBERFILL.SYS
- NTOSKRNL
- HAL.DLL
- SYSTEM KEY

## Various Device Drivers Needed to Launch the Operating System

NTLDR is responsible for offering a menu with the available operating systems, for taking action based on the selection, and for performing the startup procedures that must take place before the kernel is loaded. To do so, it performs the following tasks:

- It forces the CPU(s) into 32-bit flat memory mode.
- It identifies the type of file systems on the drive (NTFS and/or FAT) and initializes access to the appropriate code to read files on the system.
- It inspects the BOOT.INI for entries that indicate if there is more than one operating system available. If so, it offers a menu allowing the user to select the appropriate operating system. The following listing shows the contents of a BOOT.INI file that offers loading Windows 2000 Professional, the location of the system files (in this case the first partition of the first hard drive), and the Windows 2000 Professional Recovery Console. A 30-second delay is provided before the default system is started.

```
[boot loader]
timeout=30
default=multi(0)disk(0)rdisk(0)partition(1)\WINNT
[operating systems]
multi(0)disk(0)rdisk(0)partition(1)\WINNT="Microsoft Windows 2000
Professional" /fastdetect
C:\CMDCONS\BOOTSECT.DAT="Microsoft Windows 2000 Recovery Console /
cmdcons
```

If the user selects an operating system other than Windows 2000 Professional, control is passed over to the BOOTSECT.DAT file. In the example above, it invokes the Recovery Console located in C:\Cmdcons. During this phase, the user may also invoke the last known good configuration or choose an alternate boot process to perform troubleshooting tasks. If the user does not, NTDETECT.COM is invoked to handle the initial hardware detection phase. NTLDR remains in operation throughout this process.

### Hardware Detection and Configuration

NTDETECT.COM examines the system and reports back, providing the computer ID, hard drive adapter type, graphics adapter, keyboard and pointing device, types of communications and parallel ports, and presence of a floppy drive. In the unlikely event that more than one hardware profile has been established for this machine, the user is offered the option of selecting one at this point. (Hardware profiles are usually only necessary in the event that there is legacy non-Plug-and-Play hardware present on the machine.)

### Loading the Kernel and Preparing to Accept the User

NTLDR begins loading the kernel and the hardware abstraction layer into RAM. At this point, control is passed to the kernel and the user is presented with the Windows 2000 Professional Startup screen. The NTOSKRNL file examines a configuration and collects information about network logons and connections.

The kernel service controller starts any system services that are configured to load automatically, and the registry settings for hardware operation of the local machine are confirmed and initialized. At this point, the user logon screen appears.

### User Logon

Windows 2000, like Windows NT, requires a user to actually log on before system startup is complete. To do so, press CTRL+ALT+DEL and enter any appropriate user account name and password. Windows 2000 provides for two types of users: local and workgroup, or domain.

Local accounts, as the name implies, are those set up directly on the system. The local security subsystem verifies the user account, checks the password, and grants or denies access based on local settings. Workgroup and domain accounts reside on a security server, often a domain controller. The account information and user rights are then verified at the server or an authorized alternate location. Once the account has been validated using one of these methods, the system is operational.

## Lesson Summary

The following points summarize the main elements of this lesson:

- Windows 2000 is a radically different operating system, in both function and design, than Windows 98.

- Windows 2000 is built on the core technology found in Windows NT.

- The Windows 2000 environment is composed of a series of layers that link hardware to applications. It can be broken into two primary segments: the kernel mode and the user mode. Each of these is comprised of a series of subsystems or components.

- Kernel mode is responsible for talking with the physical hardware and managing primary device drivers. It also includes the Windows 2000 Executive, which communicates with user mode.

- The Windows 2000 boot process is significantly different from that of Windows 98 or Windows Me. It is similar to that for Windows NT.

- The Windows 2000 start procedure begins with system power up or restart and finishes only when a user successfully logs on.

- Most of the initial startup process is under the control of the NTLDR program until the kernel is loaded.

# Lesson 3:  Managing Windows

This lesson covers configuring Windows. It builds on the information in the preceding lessons, and it is necessary to understand the material presented in Chapter 19, "Maintaining the Modern Computer." You should follow this lesson at a computer running either Windows 98 or Windows 2000 Professional. The lesson covers both operating systems.

### After this lesson, you will be able to

- Understand the functions of the Registry Control Panel and the Microsoft Management Console
- Understand how to configure system settings and add new hardware using the Control Panel
- Understand basic use of the Windows 2000 Administrative Tools
- Know the fundamentals of how to edit the Registry

### Estimated lesson time: 50 minutes

## Introducing the Windows Registry

Most end users rarely need to adjust system settings or add new hardware to their computers. The majority of routine maintenance and simple repair tasks they need to attend to can be accomplished with the assistance of wizards found in both Windows 98 and Windows 2000. As a technician, however, you need to be familiar with the System Registry and the tools used to work with it: the Windows Control Panel and, in the case of Windows 2000, the Microsoft Management Console (MMC). You will use them on a regular basis to configure, fine tune, and repair your clients' computers.

---

**Note**   The information presented in this lesson serves as more of an introduction than a tutorial. Fully covering all aspects of configuring and managing the Windows environment is beyond the scope of this book. It is recommended that you consult the appropriate Microsoft Resource Kits for the operating systems you work with. These publications include in-depth training and reference materials for the various settings and their uses.

---

Microsoft Windows treats all the devices, device drivers, software services, and applications that use it as objects. The System Registry tracks and makes available to the kernel information on all the those objects, hardware, network settings, user preferences, and storage systems—virtually everything related to system operation.

## A Major Change in Approach

Windows 3.*x* made use of two kinds of initialization (.ini) files: system and private. System initialization files were used to control the Windows environment and included SYSTEM.INI and WIN.INI, and their settings were globally available. Private initialization files were more specific in scope and included CONTROL.INI, PROGMAN.INI, WINFILE.INI, and PROTOCOL.INI, as well as any application-specific .ini files. Initialization files created a bridge between the application and the Windows operating environment.

In addition to .ini files, Windows 3.1 used a host of other text files to manage operations. The files included two holdovers from MS-DOS: AUTOEXEC.BAT and CONFIG.SYS. Some systems had more than 150 files responsible for the operation of the computer and the Windows environment, many of them from third-party providers. This situation often resulted in confusion and erratic, unreliable operation. It also made writing drivers and installation routines much more difficult than necessary.

---

**Note**   The Registry replaces CONFIG.SYS, AUTOEXEC.BAT, and the old .ini files used in versions of Windows 95 and Windows 98 and, to a lesser extent, Windows NT and Windows 2000. Windows 2000 can still read .ini file settings to provide backward compatibility for legacy devices and software. However, whenever possible, use of these files should be avoided.

---

During the development of Windows 3.11, it became apparent that a move away from the .ini files was needed. A new file type was introduced into the programming environment. The file was called REG.DAT, and it was the precursor to the Windows 95 Registry. REG.DAT included information used for drag-and-drop operations, OLE (object linking and embedding), and establishing associations between data files and their programs.

The binary file REG.DAT was bundled with its editor, REGEDIT.EXE. This began the process of centralizing computer operations, but REG.DAT had serious size limitations. It could not exceed 64 KB, the same limit established for the .ini files in Windows 3.11.

Since then, development of the registry concept has matured and, in the modern Windows 98, Windows NT, and Windows 2000 era, knowing how to adjust the Registry settings is as critical for a technician as understanding CONFIG.SYS and upper memory management was in the days of MS-DOS.

## A Critical Central Repository

It's convenient to think of the Widows Registry as "data central." During system startup and regular operation, the kernel, system services, background hardware detection devices for Plug-and-Play operation, device drivers, and applications are checking with the Registry to confirm settings. Anytime you install a new piece of software or hardware, make use of the functions of Control Panel, or do something as simple as changing the View options used to control information display in folders, you are modifying the Registry.

If the Registry becomes corrupt or has the wrong data for an object, it can degrade or even halt system operation. With that in mind, Windows provides work tools and safeguards to make it easy to safely modify settings, while ensuring integrity of the Registry files. There are some differences in the Registry structure and tools provided between Windows 95, Windows 98, Windows Me, Windows NT, and Windows 2000. In spite of that, it is possible to learn the basics of working with the Registry for both families of Windows at the same time. Windows 2000 and Windows NT offer some extra controls and tools that are not found in the Windows 9*x* family.

---

**Note**    For purposes of this discussion, we use Windows 9*x* to refer to Windows 95, Windows 98, and Windows Me, unless otherwise noted. Fully covering all aspects of configuring and managing the Windows environment is beyond the scope of this book. You should assemble a library including the appropriate Microsoft Resource Kits for the operating systems you install and maintain. These publications include additional training and reference materials for the various settings and their uses.

---

The Registry is seen by the operating system as if it was a single data store, but, in reality it is comprised of several files. Hardware- and application-specific settings are stored in one file, user-specific data (such as user profiles) are stored in another, and system-specific policies (which can be used to locally override elements of settings in the other two files) form a third. During system operation, the active elements of the Registry are brought into RAM as a single repository.

# Windows Configuration and Management Tools

## The Windows Control Panel

The most commonly used tool for modifying the Registry or adjusting the system configuration is the Windows Control Panel. The fundamental use and operation of the Control Panel is virtually the same in all versions of Windows. There is a slight difference in the organization and number of tools contained within the Control Panel. The Windows 98 Control Panel contents are very similar to those in Windows 95. Windows 2000 has some additional folders and icons. The Windows Me Control Panel is very similar to that of Windows 2000. Figure 18.3 shows the contents of both the Windows 98 and Windows 2000 control panels. You may wish to work through the rest of this lesson seated at the computer and follow along with the discussion by opening and examining the system tools as they are presented. You can open the Control Panel by accessing the Start menu. Choose Settings, and then choose Control Panel. A window similar to one of those shown in Figure 18.3 should appear.

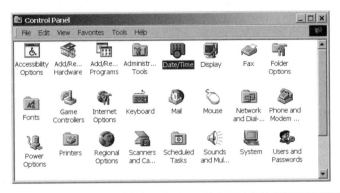

**Figure 18.3**   The Windows 98 and Windows 2000 control panels

As you can see from Figure 18.3, most of the icons are identical in both editions, and many of these are self-explanatory. For example, the Mouse and Game Controllers icons are used to define active buttons, define their use, and perform calibrations.

## Working with System Properties

The System Properties icon is one of the most useful Control Panel components. This utility quickly provides detailed information on the system configuration and often helps pinpoint components that are not working properly or do not have properly functioning drivers. To access it, double-click the System icon, which shows an image of a CPU with monitor, keyboard, and mouse. Figure 18.4 shows the Windows 2000 Professional System Properties utility open to the General tab. The General tab is similar for all the different versions of Windows currently in use, but the other options tabs offered vary. In some cases, they may vary between two computers running identical operating systems, depending on

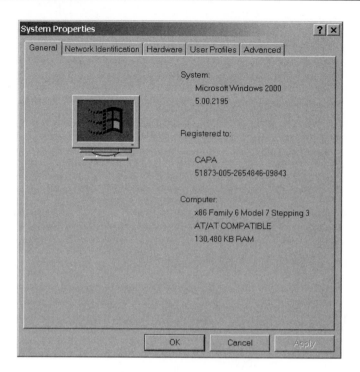

**Figure 18.4**    The Windows 2000 System Properties dialog box

the hardware that is installed. All share one attribute: They quickly let you locate information about specific devices on the system.

The General tab provides three basic pieces of information: the version of the operating system in use; if it is registered and to whom; and a quick run-down of the CPU, computer type, and amount of RAM on the system. The string of numbers in the registration information portion uniquely identifies this installation of Windows and is tied to the registered user. You need this number to call Microsoft for support in connection with this machine.

If you are following along using Windows 2000, click the Hardware tab, and then click Device Manager, found in the middle of the window. In Windows 9x, click the Device Manager tab in the System Properties dialog box. The Windows 2000 Device Manager window is shown in Figure 18.5. Although the detailed appearance of the window that now opens may vary based on the version of Windows being used and the display options set, its basic function remains the same.

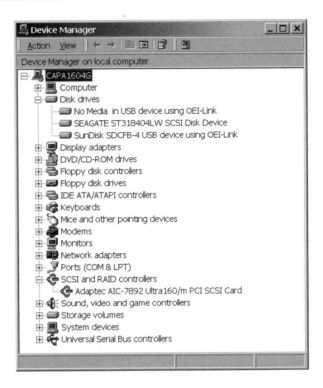

**Figure 18.5**   The Windows 2000 Device Manager

The Device Manager is one of the most useful tools in the Control Panel. It can be used to identify the components on the system, determine if they are considered functional by the operating system, and provide detailed information about the device driver.

The main portion of the Device Manager window contains a series of icons. If a plus sign (+) appears to the left of the icon, you can click on it to see devices and subcategories nested within that listing. For example, in Figure 18.5, both the Disk Drives and SCSI and Raid Controllers listings are open to show their contents. In the information bar just above the main window area in the figure, notice that it says "Device Manager on local computer." This is one difference between Windows 9x and Windows 2000. With Windows 2000, you can use Device Manager to manage the Registry on remote computers if you have the proper administrative credentials to work on the remote system and it is configured to provide this feature. If your work entails providing support to remote computers over a local area network (LAN), you may wish to learn more about this feature.

Right-clicking on a device's icon within the Device Manager window, or within Windows 9x, and clicking on the Properties button with the icon selected brings up detailed information about the specific device. Figure 18.6 shows the details concerning the SCSI hard drive shown in Figure 18.5. The specific information and options provided when you examine the properties vary based on the version of Windows and the specific device being inquired about. Remember that all this information is being pulled directly from the Registry and, in cases where you can modify the information or adjust a setting, the Registry itself is being updated with your changes.

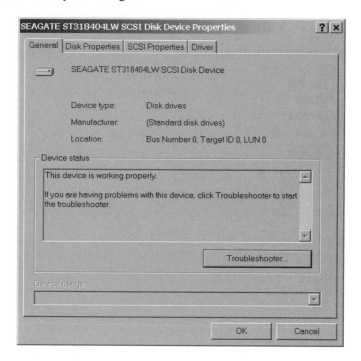

**Figure 18.6**   A typical Device Manager Properties dialog box

This dialog box has tabs of its own, starting with a General tab. Notice the device status area of this dialog box. If the device is shown as working properly, it indicates that Windows is satisfied that the driver can communicate with the device. Depending on the version of Windows and the type of device, you may be offered a Troubleshooting button. Clicking it will usually activate a wizard that will walk you through a series of options to try to resolve any problems you might have with the device.

The Driver tab in Windows 2000, depicted in Figure 18.7, shows how the  Device Manager is increasing in usefulness as Windows matures. Early versions of the operating system did little more than provide the name of the driver file and the date it was produced. As you can see, the newest versions of Windows allow you

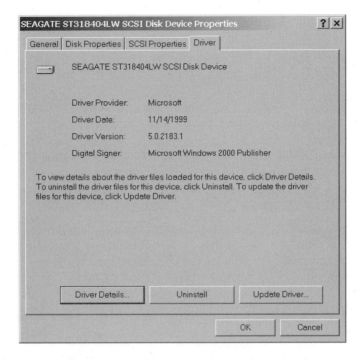

**Figure 18.7**   The Device Manager Driver tab

to inspect more driver details and update or install a driver directly from within the Driver tab if needed. Device Manager has a number of wizards that simplify the process of updating driver information and adding and removing devices in the system.

If the device is not working properly, has been disabled, or has produced a conflict with another device on the system, its icon appears with either a yellow caution or a red warning circle placed over a portion of the icon. Figure 18.8. shows a number of buttons used for obtaining properties, refreshing the device list, removing a device, and printing a report. These tabs are found when working with the Windows 98 Device Manager.

**Figure 18.8**   The Display Properties dialog box

### Alternate Methods of Accessing Control Panel Functions

Windows offers several ways besides the Control Panel to access some Control Panel functions. For example, right-clicking in any open area of the Windows desktop and selecting Properties launches the same Display Properties dialog box. You can also access this dialog box by double-clicking the Display icon in the Control Panel. This utility allows quick adjustment of display adapter settings, changes in the appearance of the desktop, and setup of screen savers and effects. It can be used to troubleshoot display problems, set color depth, and fine-tune the interaction between the graphics adapter and the monitor. The Display Properties dialog box is shown in Figure 18.8.

## The Windows 2000 Administrative Tools

Windows 2000 provides additional tools beyond those found in Windows 98. The easiest way to access these tools is to open up the Administrative Tools folder found inside the Windows 2000 Control Panel. Figure 18.9 shows the basic contents of the Administrative Tools folder. Windows 2000 ships with a common set of administrative tools, but these are only a starting point. Third-party vendors and administrators can build custom consoles and utilities called *snap-ins*.

**Figure 18.9**    The Windows 2000 Administrative Tools folder

### Using the MMC

The MMC provides an easy means of centralizing system administration, managing tasks, and troubleshooting system problems. Figure 18.10 shows a typical Windows 2000 computer management console. It is accessed in the Administrative Tools folder by double-clicking the Computer Management icon. The MMC can be used in conjunction with the Task Scheduler to automate routine tasks. A technician can perform many system support tasks using the tools in the Control Panel, but the MMC generally offers easier access and provides some utilities not available as first-level icons in the Control Panel. This is especially true when it comes to managing storage devices.

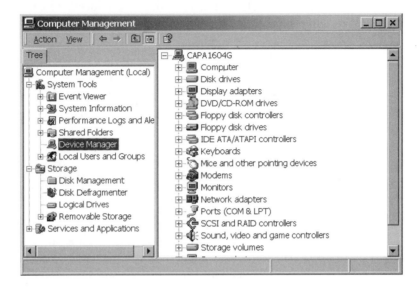

**Figure 18.10**    The Windows 2000 Computer Management console

The console shown in Figure 18.10 is open on the Device Manager. The left window pane shows the tree with the different management applications that are available. The section of the window on the right provides the same functionality the Device Manager does when accessed from within the Control Panel, because the Device Manager has been selected. Right-clicking on a device in the right panel presents the same dialog boxes and options as the Device Manger will from the Control Panel.

Clicking System Information on the left side of the MMC displays a tree structure in the right side of the window, depicting all the devices and services on the system. You can see that it is very easy to use the MMC to quickly examine and work on a system.

The time spent learning to use the MMC is time well spent. Microsoft has shown a commitment to using the MMC as the core of future management tool development. It offers a single user interface for a wide variety of system tools, which has become even more important in a network environment. In addition to the system tools and storage tools shown in our example in Figure 18.10, the server editions of Windows 2000 offer a variety of tools for administering network, Internet, and server services within the MMC.

## Using the MMC to Track System Operation and Performance

During operation, Windows 2000 tracks virtually everything that happens on the system and writes the information to a series of logs. The Event Viewer snap-in shown in Figure 18.11 is used to examine three key log files:

- The system log contains a listing of all internally generated warnings, errors, and critical events related the operation of the system.

- The security log monitors all attempts to access the system, records whether they succeed or fail, and tracks any other security parameters set as part of the system on a policy.

- The application log tracks the operation of programs on the system and contains any errors, warnings, or other events that are specifically tracked for that application.

As you can see in Figure 18.11, the operation of the Event Viewer is similar to that for other snap-ins that operate within the MMC. The Event Viewer tree in the left pane contains three branches, one for each log. Clicking on one of the branches opens the appropriate log in the pane on the right. The entry includes the date stamp for the time the event was launched, the source, and an event code that can be used to aid in troubleshooting or for more information about the type of event. The leftmost column provides the name of the type of event. Those most likely to demand operator intervention are flagged with color-coded icons. In our example, the error messages on the first two lines have red flags with Xs, indicating the failure of a device. Not all warnings actually demand intervention. In this case, a removable storage device merely did not have media installed.

**Figure 18.11**   The MMC Event Viewer

Microsoft Windows 2000, like Windows NT, offers a wide range of performance monitoring and tuning tools. These can be set to actively track in real time virtually every performance indicator of the system, memory usage, and primary systems (like the display, drives, and system processes). The information can be presented in a set of graphs or stored in spreadsheet or database format for later review.

## Windows 2000 Disk Management

The MMC serves another important function. The Disk Management snap-in is used to mount drives, create partitions, set up or convert file systems, and dynamically allocate storage space. These tools far outperform those found in the Windows 9x environment, which are based on MS-DOS.

Windows 2000 supports two types of hard disk storage. Basic storage is identical to that found on most other operating systems. Physical hard drives are partitioned and then initialized for the use of storage. Basic storage uses a program like Fdisk to divide the drive into partitions. Once created, these partitions cannot be modified without destroying the data on them. Dynamic storage is a method of disk utilization unique to Windows 2000. Drives initialized using the dynamic method are set up as a single partition that spans the entire physical disk, but is not limited to a single disk; therefore, a single volume can span several disks. In addition, you can create mirrored and striped volumes to improve performance or combine several of these into a Level-5 RAID (redundant array of independent disks) to increase data security.

All hard drives start as a basic disk, and they can be divided into primary extended partitions as normal. If you plan on dual booting a system with a non-Windows 2000 operating system, the primary partition should be formatted with the FAT file system. Volumes that do not need direct access to that operating system can be formatted using NTFS and become part of a dynamic storage environment.

Figure 18.12 depicts the Disk Management snap-in on a system running Windows 2000 Professional. The system has one dynamic disk, one CD-ROM drive, and two removable devices contained on a smart card reader. The left pane shows a typical MMC tree, the top right pane shows the different volumes on the system, and the pane below shows a graphical representation of the drives. The user can change the content of each of these views.

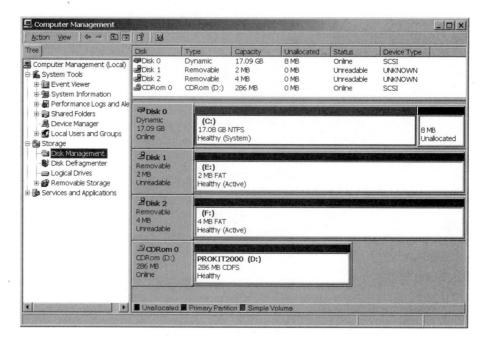

**Figure 18.12**    The MMC Disk Management snap-in in action

When a disk without a partition or formatting is added to the system, it is displayed in the Disk Manager as a foreign disk. Right-clicking on it invokes a wizard that allows you to prepare the disk for use and import the new disk into the system. Basic disks can be upgraded at any time using a similar wizard. Right-clicking on a disk shows all system information concerning the disk, including its capacity, space allocation, type, capacity, status, adapter information, and volume information. Network administrators with appropriate permissions on a Windows 2000 server can use the MMC to manage disks on any other computer running Windows 2000 within the province of the domain or of a trusted domain from any other computer running Windows 2000 on the network.

# Working Directly with the System Registry

## Components of the Windows Registry

The Windows 9*x* Registry consists of six root keys, each of which reflects a different aspect of the configuration. Windows NT and Windows 2000 make use of only five of the keys due to differences in the way the system accesses and holds the Registry in memory.

Like the information display of the MMC, the Registry is presented as a series of trees and branches arranged in a hierarchical order. Each branch of the Registry (known as a *key*) groups information that logically belongs together. All top-level keys are called *root keys* and are defined and named by Windows; these cannot be changed. Root keys are named HKEY_*XXX* and can be followed by several subkeys. All other keys in the Registry are subkeys of these six primary keys. Subkeys can be added, deleted, or renamed. The six primary keys are described in the following sections.

### HKEY_CLASSES_ROOT

In Windows 9*x*, this section of the Registry defines the standard-class objects used by Windows. Do not make any changes to this section unless you are absolutely sure you need to do so! This is a link to the HKEY_LOCAL_MACHINE\ SOFTWARE\Classes, which provides compatibility with the Windows 3.1 registration database. This compatibility is important if you want to run Windows 3.1 16-bit applications in Windows 9*x*. In Windows 2000, this key contains software configuration data, file class associations, and any information needed for OLE support.

### HKEY_CURRENT_USER

This section serves the same functions in both Windows 9*x* and Windows 2000. It defines the current user settings, so it is usually not important for repairing computers. Personalized information like fonts, some icons, and colors can be changed here. This is a link to the HKEY_CURRENT_USERS key. This key provides Windows 9*x* compatibility to applications using the Windows NT Registry structure.

### HKEY_LOCAL_MACHINE

This portion of the Registry contains all the data for the system's non-user-specific configurations (including every device in the computer). This is the largest key in the Registry and the portion where you will perform the bulk of your system edits to optimize Windows performance. Information stored here includes hardware configuration, peripheral devices, installed software, OLE compatibility, software configuration, and Windows operating system configuration. In Windows 9*x* this data is stored in the SYSTEM.DAT file.

### HKEY_USERS

This section of the Registry is where both Windows 9*x* and Windows 2000 keep track of different user settings. If your computer is not configured for multiple users, you will have a single subkey named DEFAULT. If your computer has been configured for multiple users, two profiles are created when you log on: HKEY_USERS\DEFAULT and HKEY_USERS\*user name*\USER.DAT. If it is a two-user system, the other user's settings are held in memory. This makes it impossible to alter user settings without logging on under that user's name and password.

### HKEY_CURRENT_CONFIG

This key handles Plug and Play and contains information about the current configuration of a multiple-hardware-configured computer. On Windows 9*x* machines, this key works in conjunction with HKEY_LOCAL_MACHINE\ Config\\xxxx, where *xxxx* is the subkey that represents the numeric value of the current hardware configuration. On Windows 2000 machines, it contains the data stored with the active hardware profile, which is used to configure device drivers.

### HKEY_DYN_DATA

In Windows 9*x,* this is the Registry data, which is stored in RAM to speed up system configuration. A snapshot of all hardware in use is stored here. It is updated on startup and when any changes are made in the system configuration file. This portion of the Registry is dynamic. It is where V*x*Ds are installed, where Plug and Play hardware information is maintained, and where performance statistics are calculated. Because this information is accessed and changed constantly, this portion of the Registry is never written to the hard disk. It resides in the computer's RAM. This key does   not exist in Windows 2000.

## Accessing and Managing the Registry

Most modifications of the Registry should be done using the Windows Control Panel in the Windows 9*x* environment. With Windows 2000, you should use either the MMC or the Control Panel to modify Registry settings. The fact that the Registry is the central system configuration repository means it is also a key system weakness—once it has been corrupted, it's hard to recover settings if they haven't been backed up. Only very knowledgeable users should directly view or change entries.

You can view or change the entries using one of the two Registry editors that ship with Windows 2000, REGEDT32.EXE or REGEDIT.EXE. Only the latter is included with Windows 9*x*. The Registry itself is stored in binary format, so you can't open, view, or edit the contents directly. Don't look for either editor on the Start menu because they are considered too potent for the average user. You must enter the appropriate command name in the Run dialog box to start the editor. Although both programs ship with Windows 2000, REGEDIT.EXE lacks a security menu and does not support several commands available in REGEDT32.EXE.

You edit the Registry in real time using either of these editors. As soon as you enter a setting, the effect of your action is immediate. During the remainder of this lesson, some examples are shown with the Registry editor open. Be sure not to make any modifications to the Registry itself without being sure of the actions being taken.

**Caution**   Editing the Registry directly can cause serious problems if it is not done correctly. Windows provides the Control Panel, MMC, and Properties dialog boxes for editing the Registry. Microsoft recommends these methods rather than direct editing of the Registry. There are some occasions when may it be necessary to edit the Registry, however, if the system or an application failure totally corrupts a Registry key. If you must edit the Registry, follow all the appropriate procedures for backing up the Registry data and preparing for recovery in the event something goes wrong. Even then, it may not be possible to perform a total recovery. Edit the Registry only as a final resort in the event of a major system failure.

## Using REGEDIT with Windows 9*x*

If you feel you must edit the Registry, then back it up first (see Chapter 19, "Maintaining the Modern Computer," for details on backing up the Registry). The tool used to edit the Registry is REGEDIT.EXE (see Figure 18.13). This program is not included in any of the menus and is not found on the desktop. You must activate REGEDIT.EXE by locating the executable file in the Windows directory in Windows Explorer or by starting the program from the command line using the Run dialog box from the Start menu.

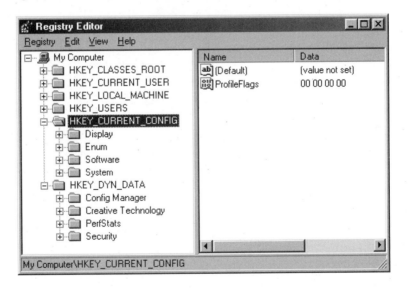

**Figure 18.13**    REGEDIT open in Windows 98

The following table provides an overview of the commands in REGEDIT.

| Menu | Commands | Remarks |
|------|----------|---------|
| Registry | Import Registry File | Allows you to import a Registry file that you've created or modified into the current Registry. Importing a Registry file is often the best way to rescue a corrupted Registry or to replace a damaged Registry with a known good backup. |
| Registry | Export Registry File | Allows you to export a copy of the Registry file to a floppy disk or network location. Exporting a Registry is a crucial step when backing up a Windows 9x system. |
| Registry | Connect Network Registry | Allows you to connect to a user on your network and, if you have the proper authority, modify that user's Registry entries. This is a very powerful feature, but not necessarily one that a majority of users should have access to. |
| Registry | Disconnect Network Registry | Releases the connection to a network user's Registry. |
| Registry | Print | Allows you to print either the entire Registry or one of its keys or branches. |
| Edit | New | Lets you create keys and assign values. |
| Edit | Delete | Lets you delete a key, key value, or value name. |
| Edit | Rename | Lets you rename either a key or value name. |
| Edit | Find | Finds a particular string or key value name. |
| Edit | Find Next | Finds the next value that was defined in the Find command. |
| View | Status Bar | Either hides or shows the status bar at the bottom of the screen. |
| View | Split | Lets you move the split bar (vertical separation) between the Key window (on the left) and the Value window (on the right). |
| View | Refresh | Refreshes the REGEDIT screen. |

**Note**   The Edit command doesn't include the typical Copy, Cut, and Paste options. If you need to copy and paste in REGEDIT, you need to use the Windows keyboard commands. Press CTRL+C for Copy and CTRL+V for Paste. These two commands are a necessity if you do a lot of searching and replacing in the Registry.

## REGEDIT's Dual Purpose

REGEDIT is more than a Windows utility program. It can be used from inside real-mode MS-DOS. This is particularly important if you have a seriously corrupted Registry file and Windows won't start. During installation, Windows 9x puts a copy of REGEDIT.EXE on the startup disk. When running REGEDIT in real mode, it doesn't have an interface—it uses a command-line format to carry out instructions. The following table lists the most common REGEDIT switches.

| Switch | Function |
|--------|----------|
| /? | Displays the REGEDIT command-line syntax |
| /L:system | Provides the location and filename of SYSTEM.DAT |
| /R:user | Provides the location and filename of USER.DAT |
| /E *filename* <regpath> | Creates a Registry (.reg) file |
| /C *filename* | Replaces the entire Registry with the contents of your .reg file |

To use REGEDIT in real mode, you need to tell it where your SYSTEM.DAT and USER.DAT files are located, if they are in a directory other than Windows. These are the two key Windows 9*x* Registry files. Here is the syntax needed to replace an existing, corrupt Registry with the contents of the .reg file you created (remember, this command is typed in full at the MS-DOS prompt):

```
REGEDIT [/L:system] [/R:user] /C filename
```

### Using REGEDIT to Modify the Registry

Remember that before modifying any critical keys in Registry, you should always create a back-up. When you edit the Registry, consider using the Control Panel applications to make Registry edits. The Control Panel is essentially the wizard for updating specific parts of the Registry. A corrupted Registry is not something you can easily recover, and the system may be rendered useless.

You can make edits directly to Registry using either the menu bar commands or the right mouse button. Add keys by simply right-clicking the key you want to add to and entering your information. Windows 9*x* has some restrictions you need to be aware of when adding keys:

- You cannot add a top-level key. Windows 9*x* creates these and you cannot modify the existing entries or create new ones.

- Within a parent key, each subkey name must be unique, but you can use the same subkey name in *different* parent keys.

- Modifying the value section of the Value entry by double-clicking the value in the Value window. After you double-click the value, you will see one of three different dialog boxes.

- Windows 9*x* uses multiple registries for multiuser operations, and it can be difficult to know exactly where pieces of information are stored. The System Policy Editor allows network administrators to locate where information is stored.

## Editing the Registry with REGEDT32 in Windows 2000

You can use REGEDIT to perform basic Registry modification tasks in Windows 2000, but it is not recommended. REGEDT32 is the editor of choice if you must modify the Registry directly. Its menus and commands are quite simple, belying the program's power. The following table provides the primary commands, their locations, and a brief description of how they are used. The rest of the menus and options are either demonstrated in the following exercise, covered in the REGEDIT.EXE material, or are easy enough to understand by their names and menu locations.

| Command | Menu | Remarks |
|---------|------|---------|
| View | Find Key | Searches the Registry for a specific key. Its scan begins at the currently active key and looks in all listings below that. |
| Registry | Save Key | Saves the currently selected key and all subkeys in binary format. The resulting file can then be used with the Restore command to reload those values after testing a modification of the Registry. |
| Registry | Save Subtree As | Saves the current key and other keys in text format. This file is not actually usable by the Registry and cannot be converted into Registry data. |
| Registry | Select Computer | Windows 2000 administrator can gain access to remote computers using this command. Windows 2000 systems allow access by any valid user account on the system. A valid user is defined as someone who has a Registry setting with a value of 1 in the HKEY_LOCAL MACHINE\SYSTEM\ CurrentControlSet\Control\SecurePipeServers\Winreg key of type REG_DWORD. |
| Registry | Restore | This loads the data in a file created with the Save Key command under the currently selected key and overwrites the existing entries. |

**Caution**    The Registry file in Windows 2000 is much larger than that in preceding versions of Windows. As a result, it cannot be backed up as simply as in Windows 98. Recovery procedures are detailed in Chapter 19, "Maintaining the Modern Computer," and should be followed before any attempt to actually edit core components of the Registry.

## Using REGEDT32 to Examine the Registry Contents

With a little care, REGEDT32 can safely be used to examine the Registry. Launch the program by clicking Start, then clicking Run, and then typing Regedit32 in the Run dialog box. A window should open on your desktop similar to the one shown in Figure 18.14. As you can see, this editor opens each key in its own window. The branches are contained in the left pane and the content is displayed in the right pane.

We are now going to take a step that you should take every time you use REGEDT32 or REGEDIT. Open the Options menu and adjust the Read Only option so that there is a check mark in front of it. Remove the check mark from in front of Save Settings On Exit found below it. This precaution prevents you from saving any changes you make.

## Choosing a Registry Section

The subwindows inside the main Registry Editor window each hold one of the five files used by Windows 2000 to store the registry data. Choose the one labeled HK_USERS on Local Machine, and work your way down the hierarchy to the Default\Control Panel\Mouse folder. With the mouse folder selected, you should see a display similar to that shown in Figure 18.14.

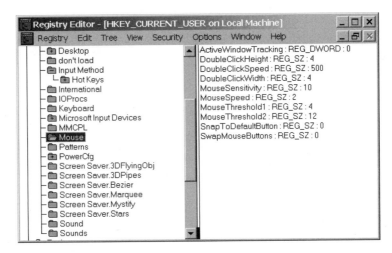

**Figure 18.14**   The HK_Current_User On Local Machine mouse settings shown in REGEDT32

From reading the entries, it is quite easy to see why editing the Registry is not a job for amateurs, and why most settings should be managed from the Control Panel. Most of the mouse settings are the same ones controlled by the Control Panel Mouse utility. Figure 18.15 shows one of the tabs in the Mouse Properties dialog box that controls three of the settings. The Snap To Default option in Figure 18.15 is not selected. In the Registry editor, the SnapToDefaultButton: REG_SZ: has a value of 0. If you access the Mouse Properties dialog box and enable Snap To Default, the value in the Registry changes to 1. If you change the value in the Registry manually to 1, the Snap to Default check box in the Mouse Properties dialog boxes becomes checked.

Obviously, changing a simple mouse setting in error is not likely to bring the average machine running Windows crashing down. Still, it is not wise to make changes to the Registry without knowing exactly what the effect is, and the exact setting and syntax necessary to gain the desired effect. For example, the range for setting mouse double-click speed is quite wide. In our example, it is currently set to 500. Without a reference, it would be difficult to know exactly what the correct range would be.

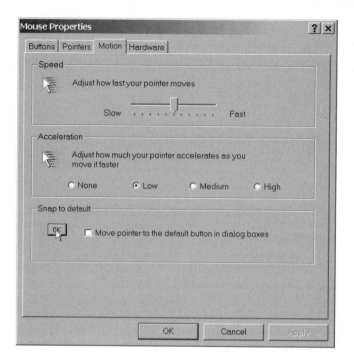

**Figure 18.15**    Local machine mouse settings as shown in the Mouse Properties dialog box

In spite of warnings about the dangers of editing the Registry, the ability to do so is a valuable tool for a technician. In some cases, it is possible make adjustments to the Registry that can save hours of work on rebuilding a system. To become proficient, you should obtain a reference detailing the Registry settings and a manual with further instructions on editing techniques, then practice on a system that is not being used for critical work.

## Lesson Summary

The following points summarize the main elements of this lesson:

- The structure and function of the system Registry is basically the same for all versions of Windows after Windows 95.

- The Registry is a database stored in a binary format containing all the details of the system configuration.

- The preferred way to edit the Registry is to use configuration tools such as the Control Panel and the MMC.

- In the event the Registry must be edited manually, you must do so using the appropriate editor for your version of Windows.

- Addition of elements to the Registry should be handled by properly trained technicians with an appropriate reference.

# Chapter Summary

The following points summarize the key concepts in this chapter:

### How Windows 98 Works

- Understanding the boot process for both the computer hardware and the operating system is key to being able to properly maintain and troubleshoot a system.

- Windows 98 is built on the foundation of MS-DOS and earlier versions of Windows and uses similar startup files.

- Although it is still possible to use configuration files like CONFIG.SYS and AUTOEXEC.BAT to manage Windows 98 system settings, they should only be used if necessary for legacy data.

### How Windows 2000 Works

- Windows 2000 is a completely different operating system from Windows 98, even though the user interface is virtually identical and both operating systems can share many drivers.

- The Windows 2000 system architecture is much more modular in design than Windows 98 and has a completely different set of core files to bring the operating system online.

### Managing Windows

- Both Windows 9x and Windows 2000 use the Registry to enable system configuration.

- The Control Panel and MMC are the preferred ways to edit settings within the Registry. The Registry should not be modified directly unless it impossible to do so with those tools.

- The Registry is a database stored in binary format.

- In the event that the Registry must be edited manually, use the editor provided with the operating system specifically for this purpose.

# Review

The following questions are intended to reinforce key information presented in this chapter. If you are unable to answer a question, review the appropriate lesson and then try the question again. Answers to the questions can be found in Appendix A, "Questions and Answers."

1. What are the core components of the Windows 98 operating system?

2. What is the kernel, and what is its function within the operating system?

3. What is the VMM?

4. What is virtual memory, and what are its benefits?

5. What is the definition of WDM, what is it, and why is it important?

6. What is a minidriver?

7. Briefly explain the two core files needed to boot Windows 98.

8. Can you use CONFIG.SYS and AUTOEXEC.BAT in Windows 98? Are there any special considerations?

9. What is the purpose of the NTLDR program in Windows 2000?

10. What is the purpose of the BOOTLOG.TXT file?

11. What is the HAL, and what is its function?

12. Define the Registry.

13. What is the MMC?

14. What is the preferred editor for working with the system Registry and Windows 2000?

C H A P T E R   1 9

# Maintaining the Modern Computer

**Lesson 1:** **The Right Tools for the Job** . . . . . . . . . . . . . . . . . . . . . . . . . **501**

**Lesson 2:** **Planning and Performing Regular Maintenance** . . . . . . . . . **515**

**Lesson 3:** **Maintaining the Windows System Environment** . . . . . . . . . **524**

**Chapter Summary** . . . . . . . . . . . . . . . . . . . . . . . . . . . . . . . . . . . . . . . . . . **538**

**Review** . . . . . . . . . . . . . . . . . . . . . . . . . . . . . . . . . . . . . . . . . . . . . . . . . . **539**

## About This Chapter

The modern personal computer and its operating system are a far cry from the earliest PCs. The array of sophisticated hardware and the advanced features of the Microsoft Windows environment have become essential parts of everyday home and office life. Keeping this vital tool running efficiently requires the right skills, the right tools, and regular routine maintenance. Properly performed regular maintenance can prevent problems.

This chapter deals with the necessary tools and general practices used in performing such maintenance. Keep in mind that your situation may call for different programs than the one presented here, based on the user population, system configuration, and the tasks for which the computers are used. The information in this chapter is based on the average desktop workstation. Complicated networking environments for advanced operating systems may entail additional procedures.

## Before You Begin

Before starting this chapter, you should read the previous chapters that cover the physical components of a computer and the fundamentals of the Windows operating system. In addition, if you are unfamiliar with the procedures for dealing with the risks of electrostatic discharge (ESD), you should review Chapter 22, "The Basics of Electrical Energy," especially Lesson 2, "Electrostatic Discharge."

# Lesson 1:  The Right Tools for the Job

In this lesson, we look at the tools and resources needed to function effectively as an A+ certified computer technician. Working on computers requires tools and resources in addition to skill. The material in this lesson details the elements of an A+ technician's toolkit. We also review the basic safety considerations that are part of the job when working with electrical and electronic equipment in a repair facility.

### After this lesson, you will be able to

- Identify and describe the basic tools required to be equipped for working on computers
- Describe the outside resources available to make your work more productive and effective
- Explain the safety considerations and basic policies to be used when working with computer equipment

### Estimated lesson time: 20 minutes

## Assembling a Complete Toolkit

Knowledge, preparation, and having the right tools for a task are the primary ingredients for a successful, efficient, and profitable maintenance activity, system upgrade, or computer repair. Before attempting any work on a computer, you should have a good understanding of the procedure or problem at hand. Ten minutes to an hour of preparation can save hours of endless guessing and frustration.

One thing that can make any job easier is having the right set of tools and reference materials on hand at all times. With the availability of information on the Internet and CD-ROM, plus the expansion of the laptop into a full-fledged computer, it's easy to carry a whole library in a small bag and have online access to virtually any driver you might need.

## Tools of the Trade

Nothing is more important than having the right tools for the job. Being an effective computer professional requires owning or having access to four sets of tools:

- **Hardware toolkit.** Common hand and electronics repair tools. Use this to take things apart and put them back together.
- **Software toolkit.** Use this to troubleshoot and correct operating systems, hardware, drivers, and application problems. These days, your software toolkit should also include good, routinely updated virus checkers and a bootable disk with key diagnostic and system files for each operating system you work with.

- **Technical library.** Use this to help you keep track of the ever-growing base of information and provide answers to "I never saw that before" problems.

- **Spare parts.** Keep a basic set of the most commonly replaced computer system components—such as power supply, floppy drive, display card, and cables—so that they can be easily replaced when you're on location. When in doubt, exchanging a problematic part with a known-to-be working part will help you troubleshoot. Be careful to collect only parts that you're sure work. Exchanging a bad part with another bad part won't help the troubleshooting process and can even make matters worse. A "goodie bag" with screws, jumpers, expansion plate covers, and so on can save time when one goes missing.

## Recommended Tools and Resources

A computer professional does not need a large toolbox; only a few basic hand tools and a handful of floppy disks are required to solve most computer problems. Most PCs can be opened and most parts removed and replaced with a pair of screwdrivers. Be careful when working on a proprietary machine, however—special tools are often required. A small canvas bag or a briefcase is generally sufficient to carry everything you need.

The following table lists and describes the hand tools that will meet most needs.

| Tool | Description |
|------|-------------|
| Screwdrivers | Two (one large and one small) flathead (regular) and Phillips (sometimes called a cross) screwdrivers are usually sufficient. Avoid magnetic screwdrivers. Although they are convenient for picking up lost screws, their magnetism can cause problems. A power screwdriver can be a real time-saver when you have new cards to add to several machines. |
| Torx driver | Used to remove the odd star-shaped screws found on some proprietary computers and components. Sizes T-10 and T-15 should meet the needs of most computers. |
| Nut driver | This variation on the screwdriver fits over the hexagonal collar on many computer screws. Sizes 3/16-inch, 7/32-inch, and 1/4-inch will handle most jobs. Sets with snap-on heads that can be adjusted for several sizes are handy. |
| Tweezers | Very convenient for picking up small parts (for instance, screws). You might consider the long plastic variety; these don't conduct electricity and hence won't create any short circuits. |
| Needlenose pliers | Can be used to pick up dropped items and to hold or loosen screws, nuts, and bolts. |
| Chip removers | Although optional, these are very useful when changing video RAM (random access memory) or other (older) RAM chips that are pushed into a socket. |

*(continued)*

| Tool | Description |
| --- | --- |
| Tube or plastic bag for small parts | A short plastic tube (with caps on both ends) will keep loose screws and small parts from getting lost. |
| Compressed air | A can of compressed air is helpful to remove dust. |
| ESD tools | An antistatic wristband is an essential tool. Antistatic mats and antistatic bags are also helpful to reduce the risk of ESD. |
| Multimeter | A small, digital meter that is capable of measuring volts (alternating current [AC] and direct current [DC]) and ohms (resistance or continuity) is all that is needed. |
| Flashlight | A small (bright) light is necessary for illuminating those hard-to-see places. |
| Hemostats | Good for picking up and holding small parts. Straight hemostats will work most of the time. However, curved ones will get into those small places that the straight ones cannot reach. |
| Power-on self test (POST) card | A POST card can be used to see what the error messages during system start are when no data is being sent to the display. |
| Laptop, blank floppies, and CD-ROM folder | This combination can save hours of time. It can be used to download drivers from the Internet. With the right collection of CDs you can access virtually any system file that you might need, the help screens for command syntax, and a wide array of information from the Microsoft Knowledgebase. You can use the blank floppies to move files to and from an ailing computer. Be sure to have a phone cord to connect the laptop modem to the wall jack. |

# Recommended Software

Don't feel compelled to carry an entire arsenal of arcane software. At the same time, assemble a collection of the software that supports the computers you normally work on. That includes the operating system disks and common drivers. Use the items that follow as a guide.

## Bootable Floppy Disk

You should compile and carry bootable floppy disks for each operating system that you encounter. These should contain the following files:

| | | |
| --- | --- | --- |
| ATTRIB.EXE | **FORMAT.EXE (.COM)** | QBASIC.EXE |
| **COMMAND.COM** | HIMEM.SYS | SCANDISK.EXE |
| DEFRAG.EXE | LABEL.COM | SHARE.EXE |
| EDIT.COM | MEM.EXE | SIZER.EXE |
| EMM386.EXE | MEMMAKER.EXE | SMARTDRV.EXE |
| EXPAND.COM | **MSCDEX.EXE** | **SYS.COM** |
| **FDISK.EXE (.COM)** | **MSD.EXE (.COM)** | |

**Note**   These files will barely fit on one 3.5-inch high-density floppy disk. Files listed in bold are essential.

The Microsoft Windows 98 and Microsoft Windows Me startup disks are also a good item to carry. These are bootable disks that load all drivers needed to run a CD-ROM on most PCs, and they include most of the files just listed as well.

**Tip**   The utility MSD.EXE is a good diagnostic tool that can determine which hardware options are installed on a computer system without the need for you to remove the case. MSD.EXE is also a great tool for diagnosing software conflicts.

## Operating System Disks

Make sure copies of the original operating system CDs or floppy disks are available. If it becomes necessary to install one or more components that were left out during the original installation, the computer might require verification of serial numbers from the original disk before any additional files can be installed. Microsoft Windows 95, Windows 98, Windows Me, Microsoft Windows NT, and Microsoft Windows 2000 have associated rescue disks (more about those in the next chapter) in case there are any problems with corrupt files in the operating system. It is a good practice to ensure that you have these disks available.

**Note**   Each Windows 2000 and Windows NT emergency repair disk (ERD) is unique to the computer for which it was created. Therefore, a new one must be made for each computer in service and kept up to date every time the Registry is significantly modified.

## Software Utilities

There are many good-quality utility programs available today that allow the experienced user to find and correct a multitude of problems. However, use caution when "correcting" a problem that has been identified by the software. The software might consider something a problem simply because it does not recognize it, on the assumption that, "if I don't know what it is, it must be bad." In some cases, the cure is worse than the disease. Also, keep in mind that one utility will not solve every problem. As a computer professional, you will do far better to master one good software system than to have a box full of utilities that you don't know how to run effectively. Don't forget good old MS-DOS; it is full of useful commands that are often forgotten or never used.

**Caution**   Older versions of utility programs designed to work with MS-DOS and Windows 3.*x* can wreak havoc on newer versions of Windows. Be especially careful if you're running later versions of Windows 95 or Windows 98 that use the FAT32 file system, because many utilities are designed to handle the traditional FAT16 file system.

You should never run any application to "tune" a system that is not specifically designed for that version of the operating system. That applies especially to advanced 32-bit operating systems such as Windows 98 and Windows 2000.

Another required part of the software toolkit is a set of virus-checking and repairing programs that are compatible with each operating system you work with. Optional additions are disk and video display diagnostic programs.

### Documentation and Manuals

Documentation is another key part of advanced preparation in general, as well as preparation for specific jobs. If adequate documentation is not readily available, your first step is to collect or create it. When you finish a job, don't forget to save an account of what you did, any problems you encountered, and notes on any follow-up required.

## Outside Resources

The computer industry changes so rapidly and is so complex that no one person can hope to master it. When a client has an urgent problem, and the answer is not readily apparent, an outside resource may have the answer at hand. As a technician's career advances, it is important that his or her skills advance along with responsibility. These are just a few of the reasons to develop a set of outside resources to increase your base of knowledge.

### Don't Stop Learning

Continuing education is vital in the computer-repair business. Attending seminars, reading books and magazines, and listening are essential parts of the job. The formal training that you are undertaking should be the beginning of your technical education, not the end. Remember, you will never know everything, and it will often seem that as soon as you've mastered a new technology, it is revised. Knowing how to find the answer is often more important than guessing or thinking you know it all.

### Networking

When you want to increase computers' data-handling capabilities, network them. Remember that you are not the only person interested in fixing computers. Take advantage of every opportunity to make connections with your colleagues in the computer business and in the classroom.

Join a local computer users' group—one can easily be found by asking around local computer stores. These groups are great places to meet and share common interests with others.

Make yourself available to other technicians. The person you help to solve a problem (from your base of knowledge and experience) today will be there to help you tomorrow. The best time to learn about problems and their solutions is before they happen to you.

The range of hardware, operating systems, and software available today makes it impossible for any single person to master every aspect of the personal computer environment. Your experience base, as you encounter problems, will be different from that of your colleagues.

Build a network of technicians with different areas of specialization. Share your specialized expertise with your colleagues and learn from them when the opportunity and need arises.

## Get Connected

Today's computer professional needs to be linked electronically to the Internet. You need Internet access for e-mail, Usenet newsgroups, and the World Wide Web. After all, your goal is to make computers work for others, so put yours to work for you.

## E-Mail

E-mail is a useful way to communicate with technical support people and colleagues. E-mail is asynchronous communication that transcends time zones; a question can be posed at any time of the day, and answered anytime, without fear of inconveniencing the other party. It is also a good method for providing customer service.

## Usenet

Usenet newsgroups are good places to acquire detailed information about computers. In a newsgroup, you can get information from other users. You are more likely to get a frank opinion than to hear "the company line." There are thousands of Usenet newsgroups, and hundreds are dedicated to computers. Be sure to look for FAQ (frequently asked question) lists. They are great for answering basic questions and giving guidance on how to use a particular newsgroup.

Newsgroups are also invaluable when you come across a situation that stumps you. Write up the problem and post it to an appropriate newsgroup (or more than one, but don't cross-post). You may be amazed at the responses you will get from helpful colleagues—everything from "try this" suggestions to the actual solution to your problem from someone who has encountered it before.

## The World Wide Web

The Web has quickly become the best place to get computer information. Most suppliers have a presence on the Web, and they often provide upgrades, patches, and workarounds for problems users encounter with their products. Many maintain technical databases full of information about both their legacy products and the most current ones. This information is usually free, but the fact that it exists is not always advertised. It is not uncommon today for a supplier to post a fix or upgrade on its Web site without notifying registered users.

Finding the correct Web site can often be challenging. A good starting place is a portal site that caters to technicians who frequently upgrade computers. These sites help you search for a source for buying parts and have links to the major computer industry manufacturers.

If you don't have luck with portals, use search engines. You might feel overwhelmed at first with your search results, because responses can literally number in the thousands. Learn how to use "advanced" search techniques and try *suppliername*.com to find the correct domain (it works more often than not).

A good example, and an excellent resource, is *www.microsoft.com.* Go to the support page and access the Knowledge Base. You will find a wealth of information regarding Microsoft products. After you find a good source, don't forget to use the Web browser's Favorites, Bookmarks, or similar features to organize folders with links to the most useful resources you find online. For example, you could create folders for technical support by company or product.

## Commercial Networks

There are a number of major commercial online networks, such as The Microsoft Network (MSN), available. Many of the smaller Internet service providers (ISPs) host forums for computer users, similar to the newsgroups previously discussed. The difference is that they are private, available only to the users of the service. They work similarly to a bulletin board system (BBS) where you can post questions and respond to other postings.

## Practice

Knowledge that does not get used gets lost. Practicing is the only way to keep your skills sharp. However, use caution when trying things out for the first time or when experimenting (especially on someone else's computer). Explaining that you crashed because you were "playing" with a new technique or piece of hardware can be a painful experience for all involved.

However, it doesn't hurt to keep some equipment on hand for the sole purpose of playing. For many technicians, extra equipment at work is rare and their personal machines become their test machines, constantly being ripped apart and experimented on. If a system or two can be kept around for experimentation and education, you can greatly enhance the value of any other training you receive and reduce overall costs. Given the cost of PCs today, a test machine is a worthy addition to your lab.

### Read, Read, and Read Some More

Keep up with the computer industry press. There are many good computer books available, but remember, computer books have a relatively short shelf life. Magazines and subscription services like Microsoft Tech-Net are great resources. Don't forget that most print magazines have online editions, and some excellent magazines exist only online. These e-zines offer in-depth reviews and industry advice long before it appears in hard-copy publications.

Subscribing to a computer magazine usually means that your name appears on a number of mailing lists that are sold to computer companies. If you can overcome sensitivity to privacy issues and tolerate junk mail, the ads that will begin to fill your mailbox offer another way to keep track of new products as they become available.

## Technical Support

You might ask yourself why you need technical support if you are yourself an A+ technician. The answer is simple: You can never know everything. The ability to use technical support wisely is part of your technical growth and part of staying on top. However, the unlimited technical support by phone that we once took for granted is rapidly disappearing. It is being replaced by limited technical support transmitted through e-mail and the Web. This means that increasingly we are expected to get the job done without direct support from the original equipment manufacturer (OEM). Technical support is out there, but it must be used wisely to be cost-effective.

### Telephone Support

Many telephone-based support systems are geared toward novice and home users, not to knowledgeable, well-trained technicians, and many try to walk all callers through basic installation procedures. Exercise patience when talking to someone at this level, who probably had to complete a basic troubleshooting procedure required by his or her employer; that person must follow the rules and procedures of the company. Also, don't be blinded by how much you think you know. The individual providing phone support just might cover something that you missed or lead you in another, more fruitful direction. If the problem remains unresolved, you will usually have to convince support personnel to send you to the next level of support.

After you get to that next level, always ask the "level 2 technician" to give you the phone number for the direct technical-support line. Some technicians are reluctant to give out that number unless the caller promises not to distribute it and not to call about trivial matters. Every computer technician should build up a collection of technical-support phone numbers, including as many direct numbers that bypass the usual voice-mail routing system as possible. The major drawback to technical-support lines is the amount of time callers often spend on hold. If you are going to rely on telephone support, it may be worthwhile to consider priority support for critical incidents. These are fee-based hotlines, often with toll-free numbers that provide quicker service—for a price.

---

**Tip**  It is a good idea to have the problem computer in front of you when you call. Often, you will be asked to follow some basic instructions while you are on the line with the technician. It is more believable to the technician to hear you describe the failure in real time, rather than simply telling the technician that you have already tried the recommended solution to no avail.

---

## Online Support

Online technical support is becoming a better option. Most free phone support today is only provided to registered owners for a limited time. If you want ongoing support, you will have to subscribe to a service or use a pay-as-you-go phone line. Checking vendors' Web sites or online forums on commercial networks such as MSN often provides a solution without the need to contact the company. Many forums have libraries of technical support questions that have been posed about particular products. By searching these libraries, you can often get immediate answers to your questions. Some sites also have troubleshooting "wizards" that walk you through a diagnosis and solution to your problem. If not, post questions and hope for an answer, either from the OEM or from another user.

Remember, if support is essential to you and your OEM does not provide the level of service you need, you can always change OEMs (if you work in a large company, inform your supervisor of the problem). Before taking that step, tell the OEM you are considering another OEM and explain why. You could also point out that if the way you've been treated is typical of their service and support, you will post it as a cautionary tale in a newsgroup or two.

## Working Safely

When working with computers, part of the expanded "toolkit kit" is providing a safe working environment for both humans and the hardware. Computers and their peripheral devices are electronic equipment, so most safety issues relate to electrical power. However, when you work on this equipment, there are several other concerns to take into consideration, as listed in the following table.

| Problem | Prevention |
|---------|-----------|
| Back injuries | Some equipment, such as printers, monitors, and even the computer itself, can weigh several pounds (10–20 pounds or more for newer, larger monitors). This might not seem like much; however, improperly picking up (or dropping) the equipment can result in back or other injuries. Be especially careful when removing a component from its original packaging. These components are generally packaged very tightly to provide protection during transport and can be difficult to remove. |
| Cuts | Be very careful when removing covers from computer components. The frames of the cases are often made of thin metal with sharp edges. Also, poorly cut or stamped parts might still have metal burrs, which are very sharp. Devices such as scanners and monitors have glass components that can break. |
| Tripping | Computers tend to have many cables and wires. If not properly installed, these wires and cables can constitute a serious tripping hazard. Use cable ties to bundle up cables and reduce the "spaghetti" effect. Also avoid running cables under carpets and areas where people walk. |

When installing or working on any equipment, make sure that the work done conforms to all applicable local and national safety codes, such as Occupational Safety and Health Administration (OSHA) and National Electric Code (NEC) standards. Many companies have their own internal safety departments and safety manuals. Be sure that you are familiar with them as well.

## Power and Safety

Power is the primary safety hazard encountered when servicing a computer. Be familiar with the following guidelines when working with electrical devices and components.

### ESD

The primary electrical-power concern when working with computers is ESD. This subject is covered fully in Chapter 22, "The Basics of Electrical Energy." Remember that ESD can destroy sensitive computer parts even when the discharge is imperceptible and harmless to humans. If proper ESD tools are not available, touching the case (specifically, the power supply) while working on the computer or its components provides some protection. However, this only works if the power supply is plugged into a properly grounded electrical outlet. For a review of power supplies and how to work with them, see Chapter 5 "Power Supplies."

### Grounds

When used to refer to electronic equipment, the term *ground* can be confusing. Generally speaking, a ground is any point from which electrical measurements can be made. In most cases, a ground means *earth ground*. With early electrical systems, the earth was used as a path for electrical current to return to its source. This is why telegraphs required only one wire (the earth ground serves as the other conductor). In most instances, the frame of the computer is at ground potential or earth ground, as long as the power cord is installed and connected to a properly grounded system. Some electronic equipment uses a special path or conductor for its ground. This is known as *signal ground* and is not the same as earth ground.

Electronic equipment is both susceptible to and a source of electromagnetic interference (EMI). A properly grounded computer prevents the transmission of EMI and protects itself from other sources of EMI. Unchecked, EMI distorts images on a video display and can corrupt communications equipment and data on floppy disks.

## High Voltages

For the most part, a computer uses ±5 and ±12 volts DC. However, two devices use much higher voltages: power supplies and monitors. With these two exceptions, there are generally no electrical hazards inside a computer.

## Power Supplies

The power supply uses 120 volts AC. This voltage is found inside the power supply case. In most cases, there is no need to open the power supply case and work on the power supply. The cost of a new power supply is low enough that it is generally easier to replace than repair. However, should you decide to open the case, be careful. Remember, the power switch on most computers (usually located on the front of the computer) also uses 110 volts AC to turn the power supply on or off. If you are working on a computer and leave it plugged in to provide proper grounding, this could present a hazard.

## Monitors

Monitors use very high voltages (30,000 volts) to drive the CRT (cathode-ray tube). Remember that monitors are dangerous even when unplugged. They can store this high voltage and discharge it if you touch the wrong parts. Working inside the monitor case should be left to a properly trained technician with the necessary tools.

## Power Safety Guidelines

The following are some general guidelines to observe when working around computers:

- Never wear jewelry or other metal objects when working on a computer. These items pose an electrical threat that can cause short circuits, which can destroy components.

- To avoid spills, never use liquids around electrical equipment.

- Do not defeat the safety feature of the three-prong power plugs by using two-prong adapters.

- Replace any worn or damaged power cords immediately.

- Never allow anything to rest on a power cord.

- Avoid using extension cords. These can become tripping hazards. Also, they may not be rated to carry the current requirements of the system.

- Keep all electrical covers intact.

- Make sure all vents are clear and have ample free-air space to allow heat to escape.

- Some peripheral devices such as laser printers and scanners use high voltages. Before removing any covers or working on any of these devices, be sure to read the manufacturers' manuals carefully.

## Fire

Uncontrolled fire is not pleasant to think about, but it is a fact of life. A workplace fire can be disastrous in terms of both injury to people and lost equipment. Knowing what to do in the event of a fire can save valuable equipment and, most important, lives. Here are a few tips to help prevent fire and protect yourself:

- Fire is fast, dark, and deadly. If a fire is detected, and it cannot be controlled with local resources within 30 seconds, exit at once. Do not delay at the scene; call the fire department from another location—one that is safe.

- Always know the emergency procedures to be carried out in case of fire at your workplace.

- Know the location of the nearest fire exits.

- Know the location of the nearest fire extinguishers and how to use them.

- Don't overload electrical outlets.

Simply knowing the location of a fire extinguisher is of no value unless you know how to use it. If you don't, contact your safety department or local fire department. They will be glad to help you get the training you need. Also, remember that using the wrong type of fire extinguisher can be worse than not using one at all.

There are three basic types of fire extinguishers for nonprofessional use, as shown in Figure 19.1.

### Fire Extinguishers

Type A is used to extinguish ordinary combustibles

Type B is used to extinguish flammable liquids

Type C is used to extinguish electrical fires

**Figure 19.1**   Fire extinguisher types

## Environmental Issues

Many computers and peripheral devices (especially printers) use consumable or recyclable components. To help keep our environment safe, you should be aware of these items and use them properly.

Examples of recyclable items or items that require special disposal are

- Batteries
- Toner and cartridge kits
- Circuit boards
- Chemical solvents
- Monitors (CRTs)

Be sure to follow the manufacturers' recommendations for recycling or disposal of any of these items. Some items, such as toner cartridges, even have prepaid shipping labels so that they can be returned for proper disposal.

When purchasing or using any kind of chemicals (cleaners, for example) that you are not familiar with the proper use and disposal of, be sure to check the material safety data sheet (MSDS). This form that describes the nature of any chemicals manufactured. It includes generic information about the product's chemical makeup and any recognized hazards (including what to do and who to call if there is a problem). These forms are required by law, so ask to see them. Chemical suppliers must provide the purchaser with the MSDS for products, if requested. Also consider purchasing sprays with a manual pump dispenser or compressed air rather than chlorofluorocarbons (CFCs) or other propellants that can be harmful to the environment.

## Lesson Summary

The following points summarize the main elements of this lesson:

- Having the proper tools and resource materials is critical to being an effective A+ technician.

- A complete toolkit includes a variety of simple hand tools, plus the software needed to maintain the classes of computers and the operating systems you will be managing.

- It is a good idea to carry spare parts and a laptop as part of your toolkit. Both can be very useful when repairing a computer with failed components.

- The toolkit can consist of both inside and outside resources. Outside resources may include online support services, dial-up technical support, other technicians, and continuing education.

- Workplace safety is as important as any other resource.

- Don't dally in the event of fire. If it can't be contained quickly, get out and get help.

# Lesson 2:  Planning and Performing Regular Maintenance

Maintenance is not the same thing as repair. Proper maintenance can prevent the need for repairs when performed in a timely fashion. At the same time, performing needed maintenance can sometimes do more harm than good. The old adage "If it isn't broke, don't fix it" applies just as much to computers as it does to a tractor. This lesson covers the basics of developing plans and procedures for performing routine maintenance.

## After this lesson, you will be able to

- Describe the methods and tools available for planning computer maintenance
- Identify and describe the basic system maintenance required for the typical desktop PC
- Extend the useful life of computer hardware
- Avoid major problems caused by unexpected downtime

## Estimated lesson time: 35 minutes

## Developing a Set of Maintenance Plans and Procedures

Computers are devices built on the very concept of logic. A logical approach will go a long way toward keeping them running properly. Having a well-organized, predefined set of plans and procedures covering the different aspects of computer care for every class of computer and operating system you deal with is required to make sure that you offer the same level of appropriate care to all of your clients.

Let's define the terms *plan* and *procedure*. A plan is the broader scope of care, and it can contain several procedures. For example, a periodic maintenance plan can detail the activities and tasks that should take place at regular intervals (daily, monthly, annually, and so on), or relative to some specific activity, like a system upgrade. A procedure is a detailed list of steps that should be performed, often in the form a checklist. This list can also include the necessary tools, parts, and remarks about important issues regarding the procedure.

One way to organize plans and procedures is to have a maintenance policy manual. These policies can be ordered by time since the last regular maintenance, and there should be an appropriate plan for each interval. The monthly plan might include regular disk defragmentation, a performance inspection, a short conversation with a user to ascertain if the system is performing as well as expected, and an update of the master recovery disks. Some of these same procedures might also show up on the semiannual and annual plans. The plan references the procedures, which are kept in a separate part of the folder or another folder altogether. If a change in policy or a change in the operating environment requires changes to a given procedure (perhaps due to new software), then simply updating a machine with the procedure will automatically bring all the periodic plans into compliance.

One of the keys to success is to develop a maintenance program that takes into account the types of computers you will be working on, the needs of the end user, and the best practices recommendations provided by the manufacturers of the hardware and the software vendors. Another critical element of success is putting the plans and procedures into writing and keeping good records of the tasks performed, as well as the computers on which they were performed.

## Automated Tasks

Windows includes some form of Task Scheduler in the current versions. It can be set to automate the performance of many common jobs like disk defragmentation during hours of no or low use.

## Keeping Proper Records

When working with computers, it is as important to work smart as it is to work hard. Being organized and keeping good records is the key to becoming efficient, effective, and successful. How much time does it take you to check current configurations when you install a new card on the same computer or find out what the current version of the operating system is? How long does it take to restore important files when a user accidentally erases them? Spending a few minutes reviewing and updating your records each time you perform routine maintenance or perform an upgrade will save you hours in the long run.

A simple set of records with essential information and a work history for each computer you work on can make identifying tasks, settings, and potential problems much easier. Excel or Access can be used to make virtual quick references. Keeping it on a laptop makes it both easy to maintain and easy to access when out on a call. Be sure to back up the data and keep a hard copy on file for quick reference. The following table provides some suggestions about the information you might want to keep.

| Suggestion | Usage |
| --- | --- |
| Name each computer. | The actual name you choose does not matter, but make it unique and descriptive. One idea is to use the same name that Windows uses to identify the computer on a network. You may have to add some notes about who the related client is or the location. Establish naming conventions to make remembering them easier. Use names in addition to serial numbers. |

*(continued)*

| Suggestion | Usage |
|---|---|
| Document all technical information. | Include the operating system name and version, startup and configuration files, hardware IRQs (interrupt requests), I/O (input/output) base address, direct memory access (DMA) channels, device driver names, processor type and speed, size of cache, RAM (random access memory), BIOS (basic input/output system), monitor, video card, modems, and sound cards. |
| Save startup data to floppy disks (unique data). | Include the startup disk (based on the current version of the operating system), device driver disks, and recovery disks—as required by an antivirus program or system. |
| Keep an incident log. | In your log of events for each computer, include such things as the user, application installations (date and version), upgrades (hardware), and problems (cause of failure and actions taken for resolution). |
| Set up a local and specific maintenance task schedule. | Include in the front part of the log a list of the tasks that are to be performed and how often. Note the dates when they have been performed and by whom. |

## Basic Hardware Maintenance

### Cleaning

For the most part, computer equipment is very reliable and lasts a long time. However, dirt and other airborne contaminants will greatly accelerate the deterioration of computer equipment. Therefore, part of a good preventive maintenance regimen is keeping the equipment clean.

The first step is to be sure that the computer is installed in a computer-friendly environment. This means that it should be in a dust-free (relatively speaking), smoke-free, and humidity-controlled (within a range of 50–70 percent relative humidity) location. Generally, a normal office environment will qualify as computer-friendly. However, a normal office environment is not the only place that we find computers. Many computers are located on a warehouse floor, in a shop, or grouped together with large, industrial equipment.

In the event that the location of a computer is not as desirable as it should be, the frequency of preventive maintenance (cleaning) should be accelerated. In these instances, consideration should be given to establishing a computer-friendly zone around the computer, for instance, installing it into a cabinet and providing a source of clean fresh air. The following table describes what a computer technician should include in a basic cleaning kit.

| Item | Usage |
| --- | --- |
| Lint-free chamois cloth or old t-shirt | A cloth is useful for cleaning the outside surfaces. |
| Cleaning solution | Standard household cleaning solutions (not extra-strength) can be used in moderation. The solution should be applied to a lint-free cloth and then applied to the computer surface. Do not use aerosol sprays. These generally use solvents as a propellant, which can dammage the plastic as well as the electrical components of a computer. |
| Foam swabs | Use these with cleaning solutions to clean small parts such as the wheels inside a mouse. (Cotton swabs are not recommended, because the cotton fibers can come off and be a contaminant themselves.) |
| Antistatic spray | An antistatic spray or solution should follow any cleaning in environments with a risk of ESD. A solution composed of 10 parts water to 1 part common household fabric softener will do. |
| Small paintbrush or small hand-held vacuum cleaner | Use to remove dust from around the computer and inside its cabinet. The vacuum can be used to remove dust from the keyboard and other input devices. |
| Canned air | Use to remove dust from the power supply fan or from inside a computer. These cans can be purchased from any computer supplier; they are made especially for removing dust from electronic equipment. |

**Caution**   Never use liquids to clean inside a computer. Never apply liquids directly to the surface of a computer. Never use solvent-based cleanser or aerosols.

The proper placement or location of a computer relative to its environment is important for ease of maintenance and long life. In summary, a computer should be

- Located in a dust-free and smoke-free environment
- Subjected to controlled humidity (50–70 percent relative humidity)
- Subjected to controlled temperature (do not place too close to a heater or in direct sunlight—avoid temperature extremes)
- Have good ventilation (make sure fan and ventilation vents aren't blocked)

## General Preventive Maintenance

For the most part, the MTBF (mean time between failures) of a computer and its peripheral devices is quite long. By following the general cleaning and safety measures just described, you can extend this time. This section describes several components and their special maintenance requirements.

## Monitors

Monitors require very little maintenance. To keep a monitor in peak condition, use the following guidelines:

- Keep it clean—use periodic cleaning, dusting, and good common sense with a monitor.
- Use simple cleaning solutions, not aerosol sprays, solvents, or commercial cleansers. Don't use window-cleaning sprays on a monitor screen.
- Do not leave unattended monitors on for extended periods of time. Use a screen saver or the computer's power-conservation features to reduce power consumption and (on older models) to prevent burn-in of the monitor screen.
- Don't ever attempt to work inside the cabinet unless you are properly trained to do so.
- Don't tamper with the monitor. Monitors emit x-ray radiation. Changing the settings or operating the monitor with the cover removed can disable the manufacturer's safety devices, thus increasing the hazard.

## Hard Disk Drives

Hard disk drives are another type of device that requires very little intervention to keep running. Mechanical failure of hard drives is rare, and, when it does occur, the solution is generally replacement. We cover operating-system-related maintenance issues in the next lesson. Here are a few suggestions for preventing mechanical problems with hard drives:

- Avoid rough handling.
- Never move a hard disk when it is still spinning.
- Never expose the internal housing to open air.
- Perform regular data backups and disk maintenance tasks.

## Floppy Disk Drives

Floppy disk drives are highly susceptible to failure. This is due mostly to the fact that they are exposed to the environment (through the disk slot) and to mechanical damage from insertion and removal of disks. When they fail, the best solution is usually to replace them because they are inexpensive and simple to install. Here are a few tips to increase the life of floppy drives and disks:

- Do not expose the disks to magnets.
- Never touch the exposed surface of a floppy disk.
- Do not allow smoking near a computer.
- Clean the read/write heads. Special head-cleaning diskettes and solutions such as isopropyl alcohol and methanol that do not leave a residue when they dry

are available. Cotton swabs are not recommended because of the fibers they shed. Use cellular foam swabs or a lint-free cloth.

## Keyboards and Pointing Devices

Keeping a keyboard and mouse clean is the key to prolonging their lives. Never place drinks (coffee, soda, tea, and so on) around a keyboard; spilling liquids is a common cause of keyboard failures. Here are a few tips to increase the life of a keyboard, mouse, or other pointing device:

- Use a handheld vacuum cleaner to remove dust from the small crevices.
- Never use spray cleaners.
- Clean a mouse or trackball by removing the ball and cleaning the rollers (if it has a ball inside).
- When using a light pen, never touch the ends with your finger.

## Printers

Printers are more mechanical than other peripherals and therefore require more attention. Because they use paper, ink, or carbon, printers generate pollutants that can build up and cause problems. Always check the manufacturer's recommendations for cleaning. Following are a few steps for cleaning the most popular types of printers.

### Dot-Matrix Printers

- Adjust the print-head spacing.
- Check the tension on the print-head positioning belt. Use a nonfibrous swab dipped in alcohol to clean the print head.
- Clean the printer's roller surfaces.
- Clean the surface of the platen.
- Clean the gear train of the paper-handling motor.
- Apply light oil to the gears using a foam swab.
- Turn the platen to distribute the oil.
- Apply a light coating of oil to the rails.
- Move the carriage assembly to distribute the oil.

### Ink-Jet Printers

- Adjust the print-head spacing.
- Check the tension on the print-head positioning belt.
- Clean the printer and its mechanism.
- Clean the printer's roller surfaces.

- Clean the surface of the platen.
- Clean the surface of the ink-jet print head.
- Clean the gear train of the paper-handling motor.
- Apply light oil to the gears using a foam swab.
- Turn the platen to distribute the oil.
- Apply a light coating of oil to the rails.
- Move the carriage assembly to distribute the oil.

### Laser Printers

- Vacuum to remove dust buildup and excess toner from the interior. Remove the toner cartridge before vacuuming.
- Clean the laser printer's rollers using a damp cloth or denatured alcohol.
- Clean the gear train of the paper-handling motor using a foam swab.
- Apply light oil to the gears using a foam swab.
- Distribute the oil throughout the gear train.
- Clean the writing mechanism thoroughly using compressed air. If possible, wipe the laser lens with lint-free wipes to remove fingerprints and stains.
- Clean the corona wires using a foam swab dipped in alcohol. Be careful not to break any of the strands because, if you do, your printer will be rendered useless until they are repaired.

## Preventive Maintenance Schedule

There are no universal preventive maintenance schedules that work on every computer. Each schedule must be individualized to meet the needs of the work environment. Use the following suggestions as maintenance guidelines for developing your own polices and procedures.

### Do This Daily

- Back up data.
- Check computer ventilation to ensure that it is clear. Remove any paper, books, or boxes that might impede the flow of air into or out of the computer.

### Do This Weekly

- Clean the outside of the case.
- Clean the screen.
- Run the appropriate disk inspection program for the operating system in use on all hard disks. Windows comes with scheduling programs to help you

accomplish this on a regular basis. Information on these procedures is contained in Lesson 3.

- Run a current antivirus program and check all drives. These programs also come with scheduling features to help you accomplish this on a regular basis. They also remind you when to update the virus list (usually done through the manufacturer's Web site).

- Inspect all peripheral devices.

## Do This Every Time a New Device or Software Application Is Added to the System

- Back up all critical data and system files.
- Update the ERD, Rescue disk, or other core files to a floppy in case of system failure or corruption.
- Store the user license, configuration data, any special settings, and technical support access information in the permanent record file kept for this computer.
- Complete and submit the warranty registration card for this product.

## Do This Monthly

- Clean the inside of the system.
- Clean the inside of any printers.
- Vacuum the keyboard.
- Clean the mouse ball and tracking wheels.
- Defragment all hard disk drives.
- Delete any unnecessary temporary files.

## Do This Every Six Months

- Perform an extensive preventive maintenance check.
- Apply an antistatic solution to the entire computer.
- Check and reseat all cables.
- Run the printer's self-test programs.

## Do This Annually

- Reformat the hard disk drive and reinstall all software. Don't forget to back up data first.
- Check all floppy disk drives.
- Consider an upgrade to your computer. Check to see that your components can handle your workload.

## Lesson Summary

The following points summarize the main elements of this lesson:

- The modern microcomputer is very reliable, but still requires regular care.
- Regular preventive maintenance can reduce the need for repairs.
- Part of preventive maintenance is keeping a computer clean.
- Never use solvent-based cleaners on a computer.
- Never use liquids on the electrical components inside a computer.
- Create and implement a regular maintenance plan for each computer under your care.

# Lesson 3:  Maintaining the Windows System Environment

This lesson describes the basic steps required to provide proper periodic maintenance to the operating system and data files contained on a Windows-based computer.

## After this lesson, you will be able to

- Describe the methods and tools available for performing Windows maintenance
- Identify and describe the basic regular maintenance steps required to maintain the Windows file system
- Inspect, clean up, defragment, and back up data on both Windows 98 and Windows 2000-based computers

## Estimated lesson time: 45 minutes

It's not just the outside of a computer that needs to be cleaned; regular housekeeping of the operating system and hard disks is critical to safe, robust performance. The data on the hard disks also requires periodic maintenance and tidying up. The Windows environment is constantly undergoing change. Every time a file is created, opened, or closed, and every time a new software application or hardware device is added, the content of the file system, and often the nature of the Registry, is changed. Over time, the underlying organization of files on the machine becomes fragmented. This fragmentation reduces system performance because the system must work harder to assemble the files so that they may be used.

Numerous temporary files are also created on the system on a regular basis. These are not always removed as often as they should be and they can clutter the storage system. If a disk used for virtual memory paging gets too full, scratch file size is reduced and overall system performance degrades. User data, along with system files, must be backed up on a regular basis to prevent loss in the event critical files become corrupted or the hard disk fails.

Over time, the magnetic media's format weakens. It must be inspected and refreshed before the aging results in data loss or system failure.

Early versions of Windows lacked robust support for managing these tasks, but that has changed. Both Windows 98 and Windows 2000 offer a variety of tools that can do the job. There is one other preventative maintenance task for which you might want to consider a third-party solution: virus detection and elimination. With the widespread use of the Internet and e-mail, a computer virus can spread faster than the flu. They are also difficult to detect as idle, malicious minds seem to keep finding new routes of infection.

Periodically, Microsoft offers updates to the code for its operating systems, and many vendors offer periodic patches to their software as well. Some of these updates fix specific problems, whereas others are designed for use on virtually every computer running the operating system or program. This type of file update does not necessarily occur at regular intervals, but it is a good idea to regularly check for appropriate updates. When a worthy upgrade is released, it should be deployed on all computers that would benefit from it.

With these topics in mind, we can identify several things that should be done on a regular basis to keep the Windows operating and file systems secure and running at peak performance, and designate an order in which to perform them:

- Provide an appropriate level of virus protection.
- Remove old and unused files on a regular basis and keep adequate open space on disks used for virtual memory.
- Scan the media for errors and fix any problems.
- Defragment the drives.
- Back up files and keep updated recovery disks.
- Periodically check for updates, and apply them as appropriate.

## Virus Protection

Viruses are nasty little programs that can wreak havoc on a computer and its data. The sole purpose of a virus is to replicate itself and make life miserable for computer users. Many viruses are simple annoyances, but some of them can cause irreparable harm to files. Viruses can be caught from various sources including shareware, files downloaded from the Internet, software from unknown origins, and bulletin boards.

There are several different types of viruses:

- File infectors attach themselves to executable files and spread to other files when the program is run.
- Boot sector viruses replace or hide inside the master boot record (or boot sector on a floppy disk). They write themselves into memory any time the computer is booted.
- Trojan horses are disguised as legitimate programs, but, when loaded, they begin to harm the system.
- Macro viruses attach themselves as executable code inside a document (such as a Microsoft Word document) and run when the document is opened. (They can also attach themselves to certain kinds of e-mail.) It used to be true that you couldn't get a virus from opening a document; running a program was required. Unfortunately, this has changed thanks to the widespread use of macros by computer users. Although macros are very valuable, they mean that when you open a document you are running a program.

- Polymorphic viruses are an especially unsettling class of invader. They're designed to modify themselves over time and replicate new forms. This makes them both unpredictable and harder to detect.

There is no sure defense against viruses, and the whole software industry has devoted great effort over the last few years to designing detection and remedial software. These programs can be purchased and downloaded from the Internet or obtained through regular distribution channels. Because viruses change rapidly and new ones appear almost daily, it is best to shop for an antivirus utility that comes with free or low-cost regular upgrades that are easy to apply. The following are some general guidelines for virus programs:

- Make sure your choice is compatible with the specific version of Windows on the system, including any upgrades. The wrong antivirus program might do more damage than good.

- If the computer has a BIOS setting that allows you to disable boot-sector writes (prevent applications from writing to the boot sector of the hard disk), consider enabling it. This setting must be disabled before installing Windows updates and some other programs as well. Keep in mind these BIOS-level virus checkers are very limited in ability and should not be relied on for total protection.

- Viruses are often transmitted by floppy disks. Be careful when reading a floppy disk of unknown origin or using your disk on an unfamiliar machine.

- Currently, many viruses and macro viruses are transmitted over the Internet. Use extreme caution when you download files, especially if they come from sources other than a manufacturer's Web site. The most secure protection against Internet-distributed viruses is to have an antivirus program running at all times (or at least when you're downloading and first running new files).

- Trust no one when it comes to loading programs on your machine. Be aware that any program you load on your computer could contain a virus.

- Be sure to keep your antivirus program updated. Hundreds of new viruses are written and transmitted each month.

When designing an antivirus program, you need to take into consideration the needs of the user and the level of risk. A computer that does not have a connection to the Internet or a LAN (local area network) and rarely receives files from outside sources is at little risk. A file server that gets files from a variety of sources, some downloaded from outside, should be equipped with very robust virus detection. In the latter case, it's good if the software has the capability to alert a system administrator with an e-mail message or page when a virus is detected.

## Disk Cleanup

Cleaning up old files not only saves on media and reduces copy time during backups; it also frees up disk space and improves file system performance. Both Windows 98 and Windows 2000 offer Disk Cleanup wizards available on the System Tools menu that make cleaning up old files on a disk easy. Simply invoke the routine and direct it to the desired drive. Wait for the utility to prepare a list of various temporary files, unnecessary program files, files that have been moved to the Recycle Bin, and Internet files that are cached locally on the disk. You can then determine which of these files you wish to delete. Simply click OK and the files are removed. Figure 19.2 shows the wizard ready to delete the files.

**Figure 19.2**   The Disk Cleanup Wizard operating in Windows 2000 Professional

## Checking Drive Integrity with ScanDisk

ScanDisk is an incredibly useful program, and, in the early days of MS-DOS, many people bought utilities like this to keep their system running properly. It inspects the file system and fixes problems and can do so when the system is in use. ScanDisk is built into all the currently shipping versions of Windows. You should be very careful to make sure that any version of ScanDisk you use is actually the one that is compatible with the version of Windows and the file for the PC to be checked and corrected. On most systems, ScanDisk is available in both a command-line version and one that operates within the Windows graphical user interface (GUI).

The ScanDisk utility can both detect and fix problems on local hard disks, floppy drives, RAM drives, and some memory cards. It works with compressed drives set up using DoubleSpace and DriveSpace, but offers only limited support for third-party compression software. Among the operations you can perform on a ScanDisk are

- Inspecting the physical surface of the drive for bad sectors
- Inspecting the file structure, compression structure, and volume signatures of any compressed drives
- Locating and repairing crossed-linked files and lost clusters
- Verifying the integrity of both FAT16 and FAT32 file systems
- Verifying and repairing problems with the directory tree structure of a drive

ScanDisk operates in two modes: standard and thorough. Standard performs a check of both files and folders; the thorough mode adds an inspection of integrity of the drive's physical surface. You can set ScanDisk to run automatically and fix errors or to prompt you before making any corrections (see Figure 19.3).

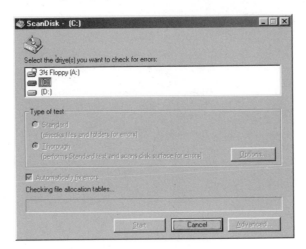

**Figure 19.3**   ScanDisk in action.

Windows 2000 has a similar tool that is accessed in the Properties dialog box for a disk. Open the Tools tab and select the Error-Checking option. Click OK to start the program if the disk is not shared and in use. If it is, the program is automatically run the next time the computer is started.

## Keeping Files Orderly with Disk Defragmenter

An operating system as complex as Microsoft Windows constantly opens and closes files, as do applications and users. Due to design issues, the file systems do not necessarily place data on storage media as a single block when they write a file to disk. As a result, over time, the files on the drive can become severely fragmented (spread out across different sectors of the hard drive). This fragmentation can seriously degrade system performance, as each time a file is opened it must be gathered from several places and stored in memory.

Disk Defragmenter is a utility you access by clicking Start\Programs\Accessories\ System Tools\, and it is found in all current versions of Microsoft Windows. It can be used to analyze a disk and see just how badly fragmented the files are, and then it can rearrange the disk, placing the files in contiguous blocks. The newest versions of Disk Defragmenter have logic that makes them aware of the way the operating system reads executable and dynamic-link library (DLL) files, so they can place clusters in the order they are read. Both of these operations can significantly improve system performance. This utility should be run at least monthly, and more often on busy systems. Any time a computer user complains of a slowdown over regular system performance, fragmentation analysis should be performed. Figure 19.4 shows the Windows 2000 version of the program in operation. As you can see, it works with both NTFS (Windows NT file system) and file allocation table (FAT)-based file systems.

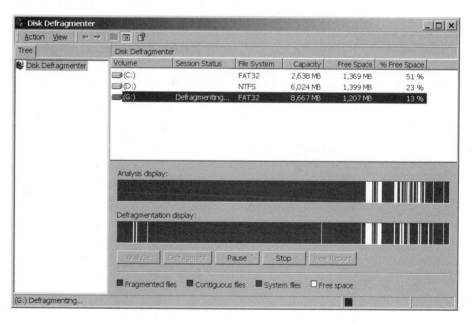

**Figure 19.4**   Disk defragmentation in process.

You can schedule the defragmentation to take place when the computer is not being used, so the speed of its operation is generally not a concern. Some screen savers or other programs that involve disk activity can slow down the operation of the defragmenter, so for best performance they should be disabled during its operation. Windows offers a Maintenance Wizard to automate this and other common disk care tasks.

# File Backups

Hard drives fail. Critical files become corrupted. Data loss is not a matter of if, but when. As a computer professional, one of the most valuable services you can perform is ensuring that your client's critical data is secure. The best way to do that is by developing a good backup plan and making it as automatic as possible. In the days of MS-DOS and in the early days of Windows, Microsoft provided a floppy disk-based backup utility. It was cumbersome to use, and floppy disks were unreliable. Creating a backup volume that spanned from 10 to 20 disks was asking for trouble.

Today, Windows comes with built-in backup software that supports a variety of media. You can back up to tape, another hard drive, or removable media. Third-party vendors provide additional backup software that can write to CD-R (CD-recordable), CD-RW (CD-rewritable), and other forms of inexpensive, high-volume media. Given that today's hard drives provide multigigabyte storage, advanced backup strategies have to be simple and effective.

## Developing a Backup Plan

There are generally accepted practices and common methods used for data backup, and both Windows 98 and Windows 2000 ship with integrated backup software. Tailoring a backup plan that works for individual needs based on this software is a simple process, but must take into consideration the amount of data to be backed up, the frequency of backup, and the equipment available. The various Windows file systems provide an attribute that can be attached to a file to indicate when it was backed up. This can be used to filter which files are copied based on the last time they were backed up or if they have been backed up at all.

There are five different common types of backups based on frequency and which files are added to the archive. With some versions of software, you must select the files manually, whereas in others a wizard or a predefined file list determines what data is moved to the archive. The backup types are

- **Normal backup.** Copies specifically selected files to the archive, no matter when the files were last backed up or if they have been modified. You can choose individual files or entire drives and directories. When instituting a backup plan, the first step should be to create a normal copy of every important file. As each file is copied, it is marked as having been backed up.

- **Straight copy backup.** Similar to normal backup, copies all selected files, whether they've been backed up recently or not. The difference is that it does not mark the file as having been backed up. This is useful if you are making a separate backup copy of a set of files, because it will not exclude them from the next regular backup.

- **Daily backup.** Copies all the preselected files modified on the date the backup was performed. The files are not marked as being copied to the archive.

- **Incremental backup.** Copies just the files that have been created or modified since the last regular backup. This process changes the archives setting on the file when it is copied. Incremental backup is used in combination with normal backup. If it is necessary to restore a drive, the last normal backup is placed back on the volume, followed by the contents of the most recent differential backup.

- **Differential backup.** Archives only those files that do not show that they have been backed up since the last normal or incremental backup.

A backup plan incorporates these different backup methods into a series of regular copies of data that produces an archive refreshed frequently enough to meet the user's needs. In some cases, backups must be very frequent and complete because core data is constantly changing. In other cases, most of the files hardly change at all, so infrequent differential copies may work.

The amount of data and the backup frequency will also dictate the type of hardware to be used. Inexpensive external storage devices like a Zip drive work fine for low-volume applications. For high-volume, high-speed archiving, one or more high-speed SCSI (Small Computer System Interface) tape drives or an equally expensive redundant array of independent disks (RAID) may be employed.

---

**Note**  Be sure both the device and the media are compatible with the operating system, file system, and backup software that will be used on the system.

---

Many companies use a rolling backup plan, which provides a full normal backup of the entire contents of system drives at regular intervals, with incremental or differential backups occurring between those archiving backups.

There is a wide variety of media used for backups. These include various tape formats, optical discs, and hard drives. Magnetic media is notably unreliable. As insurance, many people rotate a series of tapes to be used for a given backup. For example, if backups are done on Monday, Wednesday, and Friday, then a different set of tapes might be used for each day.

## Backup Plan Gotchas

Backup plans are a form of system security, and it is wise to prepare for the unexpected. There are a few things to consider when setting up policies:

- Make sure that your backup copies are stored in a safe, environmentally sound location. It is generally wise to keep a second set off site in the event of fire or other disaster.

- Keep the copies in a secure location. Sensitive data can be stolen from a copy almost as easily as from the computer itself.

- Backups are sometimes your last line of defense against a virus attack. Because some types of viruses can reside on a system for a long time before being detected, it is a good idea to keep one or more long-term backups (from the preceding month or so) available in the case infection and data loss.

- Most backup software is unable to copy files that are currently open and may be trained to skip certain files unless given specific instructions. Be sure the plan includes a method that allows all targeted files to be copied.

- Backup technology changes over time, and so does compatibility. When upgrading hardware, software, or the operating system, be sure that the new components and the old components will work together and allow the restoration of backed up data when needed.

## Backing Up Files with the Bundled Windows Backup Applications

The Windows 98 and Windows 2000 operating systems ship with bundled backup software that is located under System Tools. In Windows 98, you must add it, as it is not automatically installed as part of the regular setup. The features and hardware supported vary from platform to platform. Most offer the ability to predefine jobs, which are collections of files, or drives, that are targeted for backup. This allows you to designate groups of files, which can then be backed up at regular intervals. Most also support the various backup types mentioned earlier. For more information on just which hardware products are supported as backup devices, how to use the program, and the specific feature sets included in a given version of Windows Backup, refer to your operating system help file and related documentation. Figure 19.5 shows the Windows 2000 Backup program at work.

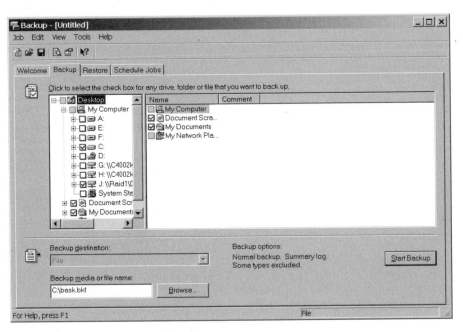

**Figure 19.5** The Windows 2000 Backup utility in action in the backup

**Note** There is a fundamental difference between the Windows 2000 Backup tool and the ones for other versions of Windows (including Windows NT). Windows 2000 organizes backup media in pools managed by the removable storage service. This means you must use a specific piece of media for a given backup job. If you have a weekly backup that is supposed to run every Wednesday, then the machine looks for the media that is attached to that job. If you put in the tape that is supposed to be for the Friday job, it generates an error and the job does not run.

# Backing Up the Registry and Core System Files

One of the most important parts of the system backup is the system Registry. As you learned in the preceding chapter, Windows 95, Windows 98, Windows Me, and Windows 2000 use the Registry to store critical configuration data. Any time you need to edit the Registry, either by adding a new piece of software or hardware, or by using a program like REGEDT32, you should create a full backup of critical system files. These procedures are not the same for Windows 98 and Windows 2000. Both what is backed up and how it is backed up is different.

## Backing Up the Windows 2000 System State Data

In Windows 2000, any time you perform a backup and check the System State option in the Backup Tab, the Registry is backed up automatically. Windows 2000 actually considers more than just the Registry as part of its core file suite, because Windows 2000 needs more than just the Registry data to restore an operating system to the same state as it was at a given point in time. The full set of files is referred to collectively as the system state data, which includes:

- The boot files that we discussed in Chapter 16, "Operating System Fundamentals," under system startup, including various system files and any other files protected by the Windows File Protection (WFP) system.

- Any files contained in the *%system root%*\System 32\ CatRoot\F750E6C3-38EE-11D1-85E5-00C04FC295EE.

- The entire contents of the Registry.

- The database that contains all the registration information for the Component Services Class portion of the kernel.

- Information maintained by the system on the Performance Counter Configuration.

You can also use the Backup Wizard to save the system state data; it offers you the option during its queries. Keep in mind that you must be logged on with administrator privileges or be a member of the backup operators' group to have access to the Backup tool or the Backup Wizard. With the proper permissions, you can back up data files on remote computers over a network, but you can only back up system state data on a local machine.

Whenever you save data with the Backup tool, it is a good idea to have it verify the files (automatically compare the new copy with the original) and to visually inspect the report that it generates by clicking Export. The report is displayed in Notepad, and you can print a copy of the report as a record of the backup. Here is an example portion of such a report:

```
Backup Status
Operation: Backup
Active backup destination: 4mm DDS
Media name: "Media created 01-Jan-01 at 6:34 PM"

Backup of "C: "
Backup set #1 on media #1
Backup description: "Set created 01-Jan-01 at 6:35 PM full normal"
Backup Type: Normal

Backup started on 01-Jan-01 at 6:39 PM.
Backup completed on 01-Jan-01 at 6:58 PM.
Directories: 601
Files: 4833
Bytes: 1,308,086,464
Time: 18 minutes and 30 seconds
Media name: "Media created 01-Jan-01 at 6:34 PM"
```

The italicized text in this example points out three reasons for keeping a copy of the backup report. It provides a record showing the media name for a given backup, so you can quickly locate it in your archive to restore files. It shows that date and type of backup, which can both be used to verify that a scheduled activity took place. It also shows the amount of space used on the media, which is handy for calculating how much space remains on the tape.

## Verifying and Backing Up the Windows 98 Registry

Windows 98 also offers a utility for backing up the registry, built into a program called the Registry Checker. This is a command-line application. Once again, we see that Windows likes to hide Registry-related tools from the casual user—you have to know exactly where and how to find it.

Just as with Windows 2000, it's a good idea to do a backup of the Registry before performing any operation (like installing a new application or piece of hardware). Windows 98 includes a backup utility within a tool that lets you examine the Registry and make sure that it is in proper condition.

To run the Registry checker, open a command-line prompt and run the Start\Run Menu, and type **SCANREGW.EXE** in the Run dialog box. The program first scans the contents of the Registry and makes sure that the files are sound. If everything checks out, it offers to back up the Registry. This makes the program copy the Registry files and store them in a .cab (Windows cabinet) file in the \Windows\Sysbckup directory.

Every time you run the program, it creates a new cabinet. The filenames end in a number, and the most recent version has the highest number just before the .cab extension. Of course, there are more system files than just the Registry to be concerned about, and that leads us to another tool.

## Checking Critical Files with the Windows System File Checker

System files can be corrupted for a variety of reasons, including improper system shutdown, problems with disk media, or a new application improperly overwriting a necessary driver with its version. To minimize both problems and risks associated with this behavior, the Microsoft developers included a combination "guardian angel" and administrator utility.

The WFP system tracks all changes to system files and makes sure that any new files assigned to replace a protected file are valid. It also sends a message to the system administrator when an improper file replacement of one of these protected files is attempted.

There are times you may wish to examine the status of these core system files yourself; for example, if Windows is getting error messages that a certain file is a problem, or some system service starts behaving improperly. The WFP system includes the System File Checker (SFC) utility in both Windows 98 and Windows 2000, which can be run at the command prompt to verify manually the versions of all system files under protection and reload saved copies from a hidden cache.

You can use the SFC to verify the integrity of your system files. Open the SFC, choose Scan For Altered Liles, and click Start. The program reports any files that do not match the SFC DEFAULT.SFC file. If you know a specific system file shown on the list is corrupt or missing or you expect it is the cause of some problem, you can extract it from the Windows installation disk using the SFC Extract option. In SFC, choose Extract One File From Installation Disk, enter the full filename when prompted, and click Start. Then give the program the location of the disk with the file and where you want it to be copied. When you click OK, the SFC extracts the file to the desired location. The SFC options are shown in the table below.

| SFC Option | Function |
| --- | --- |
| Update The Verification information | Update the file data in DEFAULT.SFC. Choose this option when you have updated a system file without running the SFC and are certain that you want to update DEFAULT.SFC to use the updated information about the file the next time the SFC is run. |

*(continued)*

*(continued)*

| SFC Option | Function |
|---|---|
| Restore File | Specify the source location of the file to restore and where to save the new copy of the file. You are also prompted to back up the existing file to the \Windows\Helpdesk\SFC folder. Choose to back up the file in case there are problems using the new file. |
| Ignore | Skip the file. The next time the SFC is run, this file will cause the File Changed dialog box to appear because it was not added to DEFAULT.SFC and it was not restored. |

## Creating Emergency Repair and Startup Disks

Every Windows computer should have either a Startup disk (Windows 95 or Windows 98) or an ERD (Windows 2000 and Windows NT) nearby. The Windows 95 or Windows 98 Startup disk is the same for all computers using that version of the operating system. In other words, you can use the Windows 98 Startup disk for all Windows 98 computers. You can use Windows 98's Startup disk to start a Windows 95 or even a Windows 2000 or Windows NT machine. As long as the file system is compatible, you'll also be able to view and work with files on the computer. You should use the utilities on a disk for only that specific version of Windows with which the system Startup disk was created.

During setup, Windows 95 and Windows 98 offer the option of creating a startup disk. You can also create one at any time by opening up the Control Panel, choosing Add/Remove Programs, and clicking the create Start Up Disk tab. You will need a copy of the distribution CD for that version of Windows and one blank, formatted, floppy disk.

The Windows 2000 and Windows NT ERD is a different matter. These disks are specific for the computer on which they were created. The ERD contains three files: AUTOEXEC.NT, CONFIG.NT, and SETUP.LOG. These are copies of the files with the same name that are contained in the *%SystemRoot%\* Repair folder. The first two files are used to initialize the MS-DOS environment, and the third is used by the Windows 2000/NT emergency repair process.

The ERD should be updated any time a change is made to the structure of the operating system (new drivers, service pack, and so on), or when new hardware is added to the computer.

Windows 2000 has a wizard available to creating your ERD. It is located in Programs\Accessories\System Tools\Backup. Under Windows NT, you must launch the RDISK.EXE program located in the Windows NT directory by clicking Start/Run and entering the command in the Run dialog box. You will need one blank formatted 3.5-inch floppy disk.

The ERD should not be used to repair Registry problems. We cover that process in the next chapter. It should be used if the system becomes so corrupted that you must restore the original Registry created during startup to gain access to the system.

## Lesson Summary

The following points summarize the main elements of this lesson:

- Several routine tasks should be done on a regular basis to keep a Windows-based computer operating securely at peak performance.
- Provide an appropriate level of virus protection.
- Remove old and unused files on a regular basis and keep adequate open space on disks used for virtual memory.
- Scan the media for errors and fix any problems.
- Defragment the drives.
- Back up files and keep recovery disks up to date.
- Periodically check for operating system and driver updates and apply them as appropriate.
- How often these tasks should be performed will vary, based on the user, how the system is used, and the operating environment.

# Chapter Summary

The following points summarize the key concepts in this chapter:

### The Right Tools for the Job

- The tools needed for computer care and repair are quite simple hand tools.
- Your toolkit should include a collection of startup disks and other software needed for the types of machines generally worked on.
- Accurate information is a critical component of a technician's resources.
- Ongoing education is essential.
- Creating a safe working environment is part of the job to protect both you and the equipment.
- Planning can save time and ensure that proper care is provided.
- Documentation tracks work and make follow-ups more effective.

### Planning and Performing Regular Maintenance

- Each class of hardware has its own maintenance tasks and procedures.
- Viruses are a risk to all computers.
- Backups of data must be done in a systematic way on a regular basis.
- The hard drive should be cleaned of old files to improve performance and avoid clutter.
- Regular testing and repair of the file system, as well as defragmenting disks, can improve performance and avoid downtime.

# Review

The following questions are intended to reinforce key information presented in this chapter. If you are unable to answer a question, review the appropriate lesson and then try the question again. Answers to the questions can be found in Appendix A, "Questions and Answers."

1. Name three reasons for adding a laptop computer to your toolkit.

2. What type of solvent should be used to clean the monitor screen?

3. What is a polymorphic virus?

4. What is the ScanDisk program? What is it used for?

5. What is an ERD?

6. What is the best way to remove old, unused files from a Windows-based computer?

7. How does file fragmentation degrade system performance?

8. Define an incremental backup.

9. Explain the difference between a normal and a copy type of backup.

10. Why is it useful to keep long-term archival files, even if you're making regular periodic backups on a short-term basis?

C H A P T E R   2 0

# Upgrading a Computer

**Lesson 1: Computer Disassembly and Reassembly** . . . . . . . . . . . . . **542**

**Lesson 2: Upgrading a Computer** . . . . . . . . . . . . . . . . . . . . . . . . . . **546**

**Chapter Summary** . . . . . . . . . . . . . . . . . . . . . . . . . . . . . . . . . . . . **563**

**Review** . . . . . . . . . . . . . . . . . . . . . . . . . . . . . . . . . . . . . . . . . . . . **564**

## About This Chapter

Computer upgrades are among the most common tasks performed by a computer technician. With new technology being introduced every day, it is a constant struggle to stay up to date. Before you can upgrade or repair a computer, you must know how to take it apart. A thorough understanding of how to disassemble a computer and put it back together is required of any computer professional. This chapter provides guidelines for successfully disassembling, reassembling, and upgrading a computer.

## Before You Begin

Before starting this chapter, you should review the previous chapters that cover the physical components of a computer. Also, if you are not already familiar with the risks and issues concerning electrostatic discharge (ESD), review Lesson 2, "Electrostatic Discharge," in Chapter 22, "The Basics of Electrical Energy."

# Lesson 1:  Computer Disassembly and Reassembly

In this lesson, we look at the tools and practices required by a computer technician to physically take apart a computer and successfully put it back together.

## After this lesson, you will be able to

- Develop a systematic and logical approach to repairing a computer
- Identify procedures for working on a computer
- Identify basic procedures for adding and removing computer components

## Estimated lesson time: 20 minutes

## Preparation

Knowledge and preparation are the primary ingredients for a successful, efficient, and profitable upgrade or repair. Before attempting any work on a computer, it is wise to know what you are working with, and you should have a good understanding of the problem or task at hand. A few minutes of preparation can save hours of endless guessing and frustration.

Documentation is one key to preparation. If adequate documentation is not readily available, your first step is to collect or create it. The Internet is a valuable tool. Make it a habit to check vendor Web sites for updated drivers and information before performing any upgrades or repairs. While there, be sure to download the latest drivers for any new components to be installed. When you finish a job, don't forget to save the documentation, including an account of what you did and any problems you encountered.

### Documentation to Collect Before Starting the Job

The following list provides examples of the types of documentation you should assemble before you begin a repair:

- A computer configuration sheet listing the devices already on the machine, hardware settings (IRQ [interrupt request], ports, and so on), the network configuration, and required passwords for the operating system.
- Copies of the computer and motherboard documentation.
- A list of all installed expansion cards. If possible, include the date on which they were originally installed.
- Copies of the operating system documentation (especially if you are not familiar with the system).
- A plan of action. Writing down a checklist of tasks and related tools and parts before starting a project can help you keep focused and on target. Remember, plans can always change; but, without a plan, you could find yourself wandering aimlessly through the project and perhaps getting sidetracked or lost.

## Questions to Ask Yourself Before Starting the Job

Carefully consider the following questions before you open the case of any computer:

- Is this the right computer?

- Why am I taking it apart?

- Do I have everything necessary to do the job?

- Do I need more information before starting this job?

- Are there any proprietary hardware components in this machine? If so, do I have the right tools, parts, and drivers to complete the job?

- Do any of these tasks require the assistance of a third-party technician—for example, internal monitor adjustments?

# Tools and Components

### Standard Toolkit

You should have a standard toolkit, as described in Chapter 19, "Maintaining the Modern Computer." Most upgrades (unlike some repairs) require very little in the way of tools, most just a simple screwdriver. The toolkit should also contain a DOS—or better yet, the startup disk for your version of Windows to use if you need to boot the system into a DOS command prompt or edit basic configuration files.

### Items Identified During Planning

Assemble the tools and components identified in the planning stage. If the update is a major one, make sure you have properly backed up any user data, as well as the system files and Registry, to be prepared in the event of a serious problem.

### Operating System Disk

Make sure copies of the original operating system disk (or CD) are available. If it becomes necessary to install one or more components that were left out during the original installation, the computer might require verification of serial numbers, installation IDs, or the original distribution disk before any additional files can be installed. You should also create a rescue disk for your version of Windows for the machine you are repairing in case there are any problems with corrupt files in the operating system. It is a good practice to ensure that you have this disk available.

---

**Note**    A rescue disk contains a computer's configuration information, so it is usually unique to the computer for which it was created. Therefore, you should make a new one for each computer you service. It should be updated any time the system configuration is modified.

---

## Disassembly

Disassembling a computer is a straightforward task. In most cases, you need to remove little more than the outer cover of the case to gain access to the memory, expansions slots and cards, and the CPU (central processing unit). Because there are many manufacturers, each seeking to establish its own unique marketing identity, each brand has some custom components or layout. The best strategy for efficient disassembly is locating and using the manual that came with the computer.

Often, manuals don't provide a lot of technical information, but they usually tell you how to remove the cover. The extent to which you have to disassemble a computer depends on the specific problem or repair. Following the procedure outlined here will help you establish a routine for completely and efficiently disassembling most computers:

1. Make a complete backup of necessary operating system and working files.
2. Document the system (hardware and software).
3. Create a clean work area with plenty of room and light.
4. Gather all the necessary tools for the job.
5. Implement all proper safety procedures.
6. Turn off the computer.
7. Disconnect the power cables.
8. Wear an antistatic wrist strap.
9. Locate the screws for the cover—check the manual to discover the location of the screws (sides or back).
10. Remove the screws. It's a good idea to store them in a box or plastic tube to keep them from getting lost.
11. Remove the cover from the computer.
12. Document the location of expansion cards and drives.
13. Remove all the cards and place them in antistatic bags.
14. Document the location and connections for each drive (pay special attention to the red wire on the data cables—this identifies the location of pin 1 on the device and driver).
15. Remove the data and power supply cables.
16. Remove the drives from their appropriate bays—look on their sides for the screws (check the manuals).
17. Remove the motherboard.

## Reassembly

Run the Preassem video located in the Demos folder on the CD accompanying this book to view a presentation of all the hardware components that go into a personal computer.

To reassemble a computer, simply follow the same procedures as for disassembly, but in the reverse order. When installing components, remember the following:

- Do not force connectors into place—if they don't fit easily, they are probably in the wrong place.
- Expansion cards often require some force or side-to-side movement to fit into place, but do not force them.
- When removing cables, remember the pin 1 locations. Check notations on the circuit boards and look for the red wire on the ribbon cables.
- Connect the cables to the drives before installing them in the bays.
- Test the system before replacing the cover.

## Lesson Summary

The following points summarize the main elements of this lesson:

- By following a systematic plan, you can simplify the process of disassembling and reassembling a computer.
- Establishing and maintaining good documentation and having the right hardware and software tools are the keys to a successful upgrade.
- Following safety procedures will ensure that no damage is done to you or the computer.

# Lesson 2: Upgrading a Computer

In today's world of constant change, the task most frequently performed by a computer professional is upgrading old systems to the latest technologies. This ability to expand and upgrade a computer can prolong the life and utility of a system. However, sometimes even the simple addition of a new piece of software can lead to hardware conflicts and the subsequent need for an upgrade, as a computer owner tries to squeeze one more year out of "old faithful." This lesson discusses many aspects of computer hardware upgrades.

### After this lesson, you will be able to
- Describe the principles behind upgrading a computer
- Define the limits of and expectations for upgrading a system

### Estimated lesson time: 30 minutes

Run the Mboard video located in the Demos folder on the CD accompanying this book to view a presentation of a personal computer's motherboard subsystem.

Run the Assembly video located in the Demos folder on the CD accompanying this book to view a presentation of components being assembled into a personal computer.

As discussed in Lesson 1, before you begin to upgrade any computer, you need to document the system. You should create and maintain files that document all computers for which you are responsible. Figure 20.1 provides a sample configuration sheet. Use it as a model to create your own.

*Sample Computer Configuration Sheet*

| Computer Name | |
|---|---|
| BIOS | |

| Primary User(s) | |
|---|---|

| Processor | |
|---|---|

| RAM | | Cache | |
|---|---|---|---|

| Monitor | | Video Card | |
|---|---|---|---|

| Sound Card | | Modem | |
|---|---|---|---|

| Device | IRQ | I/O Base Address | DMA Channel | Device Drivers |
|---|---|---|---|---|
| | 2/9 | | | |
| | 3 | | | |
| | 4 | | | |
| | 5 | | | |
| | 7 | | | |
| | 10 | | | |
| | 11 | | | |
| | 12 | | | |
| | 13 | | | |
| | 15 | | | |

| Drive | Cylinders | Heads | Sector/Track | Capacity | Partitions |
|---|---|---|---|---|---|
| | | | | | |
| | | | | | |
| | | | | | |
| | | | | | |
| | | | | | |

Software Operating System: DOS _ Windows 3.x _ Windows 3.11 _ Windows 95 _ Windows 98 _

Attach copies of:  CONFIG.SYS _           AUTOEXEC.BAT

**Figure 20.1**   Sample configuration sheet

# Memory, Memory, Memory

Does this computer have enough memory? This is the question that most frequently causes users to seek a computer upgrade. As programs and hardware get faster and are required to process more graphics and animation, the need for memory is as important as the need for speed.

Memory upgrades are perhaps the simplest to perform, but they can be very confusing without advance planning. Purchasing the right memory for the job is more than half the process of the upgrade. Before installing memory, there are five things to consider:

- Memory chip format
- Memory speed
- EDO RAM (extended data out random access memory)
- Parity
- Cache memory

The best source of information—which should be checked before obtaining memory—is the documentation that comes with the computer's motherboard. This source generally lists the type of memory required, the proper population scheme, and the location on the motherboard. If this information is not available, open the case and look. Some documentation provides a chart that includes exactly what memory has been installed and what is needed to upgrade to a given level.

---

**Note**   You can add memory with SIMMs (single inline memory modules) or DIMMs (dual inline memory modules).

---

## SIMM Formats

SIMMs come in two basic, physical formats: a 30-pin and a 72-pin chip. Format is the first consideration, because the chips must fit into the motherboard. This configuration, along with the size of the processor, determines how many SIMMs are required to fill one bank.

The 30-pin formats contain memory in 8-bit chunks. This means that a 32-bit processor requires four SIMMs to fill one bank. Typical 32-bit processors consist of two banks of SIMMs and, therefore, eight slots (see Figure 20.2).

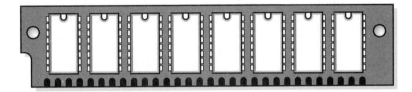

**Figure 20.2**   30-pin SIMM

A 72-pin format is larger and supplies memory in 32-bit chunks. Only one SIMM is required for a 32-bit machine. Pentium processors have a 64-bit data path and require a 72-pin SIMM (see Figure 20.3).

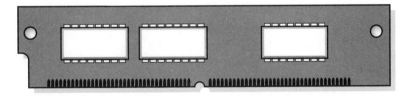

**Figure 20.3**   72-pin SIMM

Memory is normally sold in multiples of 8 MB. However, some older machines will have 8 MB of "on-board" memory (usually soldered in place on the motherboard). When memory is soldered in place, it cannot be changed; however, you can disable it. A computer equipped with this on-board memory can provide 8 MB of memory to the system without having any SIMMs installed in the slots. For such computers, installing 16 MB of RAM (random access memory) would yield a total of 24 MB of RAM; if 64 MB were to be added, the total RAM would be 72 MB, and so on. You won't likely find hardwired memory on a system anymore unless the PC is very old.

## DIMM Formats

DIMMs are much easier than SIMMS to install or remove, because they come in a single card, which is simply pushed into a module slot. The "key" cut into the edge that goes into the slot prevents the card from being inserted the wrong way. The one problem you face is choosing from the wide variety of memory types available. When ordering a new DIMM, you must know exactly the memory type supported by the system on which you wish to install the memory. DIMMs are found in larger memory sizes than SIMMs, ranging to 256 MB and beyond for single cards.

## Memory Speed

*Memory speed* is the amount of time required to access data measured in nano-seconds (ns); each nanosecond equals one billionth of a second. Two important considerations arise when addressing memory speed:

- The lower the number, the faster the chip speed.
- All chips in the same computer should run at the same speed.

Typical chip speeds are 50, 60, 70, and 80 ns. Be sure to check the motherboard documentation or the existing chips to determine the correct speed to use.

## EDO RAM

The EDO RAM chip is used extensively with Pentium processors. This chip can improve read times and overall performance by up to 30 percent. This performance gain is possible because the chip continues to output data from one address while setting up a new address.

## Parity

Parity is used to check the reliability of data. It requires one additional bit (chip). Memory can be purchased with or without parity. With parity, it will cost about 10 percent more. Be sure to check the machine specifications or the existing chips to determine if parity is required. Parity and nonparity chips cannot be mixed; however, some computers allow parity to be turned on or off in the BIOS (basic input/output system) setup.

## Cache

Cache memory can be found as either L1 or L2. The L1 cache is built into the processor and cannot be changed. The L2 cache, on the other hand, can be built into the processor, built onto the motherboard, or sometimes both. In most cases, cache memory is fixed, but some machines allow the L2 cache to be upgraded or expanded. Cache memory is sometimes found on older motherboards (as DIPs, or dual inline packages). Check the motherboard documentation to determine what, if any, upgrades can be made to the cache.

---

**Important**  Take special care when installing DIP chips. They are sensitive to ESD, can easily be installed backwards (look for pin 1 alignment), and the pins can be broken or bent during insertion.

---

## Installing RAM

Installing RAM is a simple process. The only problem is that the slots are not always easily accessible. Sometimes you will need to relocate wires temporarily or even remove expansion cards. This simple procedure usually works:

1. Turn off the computer.

2. Disconnect all external devices (alternating current [AC] power and monitor power).

3. Follow the appropriate ESD safety procedures.

4. Remove the cover of the computer.

5. Locate the SIMM banks and determine that you have the correct size, speed, and quantity of SIMMs.

6. Insert the SIMM in the slot at a 45-degree angle (backwards) and then snap it into the upright position, as shown in Figure 20.4. Be sure that the notch in the SIMM matches the slot. If it doesn't fit easily, it is probably installed incorrectly.

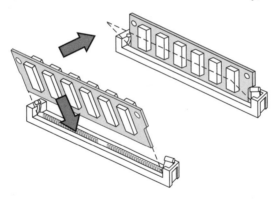

**Figure 20.4**  Installing a SIMM

7. When the SIMM is in an upright position, be sure that the metal retaining clip snaps into position. This clip holds the SIMM in place and must be opened before any SIMM can be removed.

8. Replace any temporarily removed or relocated wires or expansion cards. Check others to make sure they have not been loosened or disconnected.

9. Replace the cover of the computer.

10. Reconnect the power, monitor, and any other needed external devices, and start the computer.

The computer should recognize the new memory and either make the correction or automatically go to the CMOS Setup program. In many cases, you need only exit Setup to save the changes.

# CPU Upgrades

Installing a new CPU is becoming less common as prices of new motherboard/CPU combinations, and even new machines, continue to drop. In many cases, installing additional memory is a more effective upgrade than installing a new CPU. Still, as a technician, you need to know how to update the CPU in an existing machine.

In many cases, upgrading a CPU is as simple as removing the old one and inserting the new one. First, you need to determine whether the CPU can be upgraded and, if so, which CPU upgrade is appropriate. The answer to this question lies in the motherboard, which must have the appropriate socket, data bus, address bus, and crystal to support the new CPU. Consult the documentation that comes with the motherboard—this documentation usually contains a table that defines which CPUs are compatible. If you are unable to find the documentation, or if the processor that you want to install is not listed (because it's of newer vintage than the documentation), consult the motherboard manufacturer by accessing the company's Web site or calling the company's technical support department. Be sure to check on any required jumper settings and BIOS upgrades at the same time.

A small upgrade, going from one level of the same CPU family to another, is usually no problem. However, if you want to upgrade a 386 to a Pentium, or a Pentium to a Pentium III, a new motherboard is the only answer. The same is true if the CPUs are from different chip manufacturers. Refer to Lesson 2, "Replacing and Upgrading a CPU," in Chapter 4, "The Central Processing Unit," for possible scenarios.

## General Procedure for Installing a CPU

Perhaps the most difficult part of upgrading a CPU is determining the limits imposed by the motherboard. However, after that decision is made and you have the new processor in hand, the actual installation is quite easy. Follow this general procedure to install a CPU:

1. Turn off the computer and unplug the power cord.

2. Disconnect external devices (AC power and monitor power).

3. Follow the appropriate ESD safety procedures.

4. Remove the cover of the computer.

5. Locate the socket for the CPU. It could be on the motherboard or on a removable processor card.

6. Remove the old processor. This may require special tools for older processors. Pentium II and III packages are Slot 1 designs, which slide into a slot

much like those used for an expansion card. The original Pentiums (60–166 MHz) and Pentium Pro models usually have a ZIF (zero-insertion-force) socket. Open the ZIF socket by moving the handle to the upright position. (This should not require force.) The CPU can then be easily removed.

7. Install the new processor. Be certain to align the chip properly (this is critical!). Pin 1 on the CPU must fit pin 1 in the socket. There are several ways to identify this pin. Various chip manufacturers, and different versions of a manufacturer's chips, use different methods to mark installation orientation. Slot 1 CPU packages, for example, have a key in the slot, and it fits only one way. Other CPUs have similar schemes appropriate to their socket design. Look for a key pinhole in one corner, a blunt edge on one corner of the socket, a dot, a corner with a pin arrangement that differs from the others, or some other identifying mark. Align this mark with the corner of the socket that contains a blunt edge. If you encounter any resistance or you have to apply any pressure when inserting the CPU, recheck the chip's orientation and alignment, and reinsert the chip. After the chip is in place, secure the ZIF handle, as applicable. You might need to check the documentation to make sure the chip is installed correctly.

8. Set any jumpers or switches on the motherboard. Check the documentation.

9. Replace the cover and power up the computer.

10. Reconnect any peripherals (keyboard, mouse, monitor).

11. Make changes to the CMOS (complementary metal-oxide semiconductor) setup, if required.

Some CPU upgrades also require the installation of a new voltage regulator and cooling fan. Be sure to check the motherboard and CPU documentation for this possibility. Failure to install these parts with the new CPU might destroy it.

---

**Note**  If you are working with a motherboard that has the ability to hold more than one CPU, both CPUs must be of the same type and from the same manufacturer if more than one is actually installed. In addition, on Pentium II and later systems, most such motherboards have a special card that must be inserted in any empty CPU slot, and the appropriate slot must be used for a single CPU configuration.

---

## Expansion Cards

Installing an expansion card is one of the most common system upgrades. Adding faster video cards, adding more ports, or improving sound quality are common reasons for plugging in a new card (see Figure 20.5). Before installing (or purchasing) an expansion card, it is a good idea to make sure it will work in the system to be upgraded, and that appropriate drivers are available for the operating system to be used.

**Figure 20.5**    Motherboard and expansion card

Ask these questions first:

- Is adding a new card the most cost-effective way to make this upgrade, given the type of device and performance or capacity desired? In some cases a USB (universal serial bus) peripheral can offer the same features without requiring the case to be opened.

- Are there any expansion slots available? If no slots of the type required are available, you will have to make some room. To do that, you will need to do one of three things: replace separate, single-port cards with one multifunction card that provides all port connections; use a SCSI (Small Computer System Interface) card and a chain of SCSI devices, if available; or use USB, if available.

- Will the card fit in the type of slot available? Does it match the bus type of the motherboard?

- Are there any available I/Os (input/outputs) and IRQs in the system? If so, write them down.

- Is there enough memory (RAM and hard disk) available to run the device and its software?

- Does the card require a DMA (direct memory access) channel? If so, is one available?

- What are the potential conflicts with other cards and devices?

- Will the operating system support this card? If so, are all the necessary drivers included with the operating system or do they come with the card (or do you need to download the most recent driver from the manufacturer's Web site)?

After you have determined that the expansion card will work, the installation is a simple three-step process:

1. Set any jumpers or switches for IRQ and I/O addresses. (If you are installing the card on a "Plug and Play" PC, the operating system can usually determine a proper IRQ and I/O address without your intervention, although there may be times you will need to adjust this choice because of a conflict with an installed device.)

2. Install the card and cables.

3. Install any software for the card.

Step 1 (IRQ and I/O setup) is perhaps the most confusing and frustrating part. This is especially true if the computer has not been properly documented.

---

**Important**   Be sure to cover all slots. A missing expansion-slot cover can cause a computer to overheat. Be sure that no screws or other items that could possibly short out a component are left loose inside the case after it is closed.

---

### General Procedure for Installing an Expansion Card  (Non–Plug and Play Capable)

Installing a card that is not Plug and Play capable is a bit more complicated than installing one that is:

1. Read the documentation that comes with the card and note any special requirements or limitations before you start the installation.

2. Check the computer documentation (run MSD or other diagnostic program) and determine which IRQs and I/O addresses are available. In Windows, the best way to identify settings is usually the Device Manager.

3. Configure any jumpers or switches on the card (see Figures 20.6 and 20.7). Note that some cards might require changes to prevent conflicts and allow all devices to work.

**Figure 20.6**   Switches

**Figure 20.7** Jumpers

4. Turn off the computer and unplug the power cord.
5. Follow the appropriate ESD safety procedures.
6. Remove the cover of the computer.
7. Install the card in a free slot (see Figure 20.8). Power up the computer, note any conflicts, and make adjustments as necessary. Remember to remove power and use ESD precautions when making changes.

**Figure 20.8** Installing an expansion card

8. Replace the cover.

9. Install any software drivers or applications.

### General Procedure for Installing an Expansion Card (Plug and Play)

The latest technology available for installing expansion cards is called Plug and Play. This is an independent set of specifications, developed by a group of hardware and software companies, that allow the user to make configuration changes with minimal adjustment. Simply install the card, turn on the computer, and use the device.

For Plug and Play to work, the device must be able to identify itself and its system requirements to the system. The operating system then sets the device and makes any other adjustments, such as reconfiguring other devices, as required. For a Plug and Play device to work immediately, you must be sure that the computer hardware—motherboard, BIOS, and other components—the operating system, and the device are Plug and Play–compliant.

---

**Note**  In many systems you must enable Plug and Play features in the system CMOS. Failure to have the right settings makes installing a Plug and Play card a difficult task.

---

## Drives

Installing a new drive is not difficult. However, you must answer a few questions before purchasing a new drive:

- Will the drive physically fit inside the computer? Some desktop cases have only enough space for one hard disk drive, or the available space might be occupied by another device (a CD-ROM drive or floppy disk drive). If there is not enough space, you will have to consider alternatives such as external SCSI drives, USB drives, and parallel port interface drives.

- Will the computer's BIOS and operating system support the size (storage capacity) of the drive?

- Will the drive controller support the new drive? A second or updated controller might be required.

- Are there sufficient cables (data and power) to install the drive?

### Procedure for Installing an IDE Drive

Installing an IDE (Integrated Device Electronics) drive requires some hardware and software preparation to get it running properly. Hardware preparation includes ensuring that you have the correct drive, a place to physically install it, and the proper cables to connect it. Software preparation includes creating a bootable MS-DOS disk containing at least the Format and Fdisk utilities. A Windows 95 or Windows 98 startup disk will do the job. If you don't already have such a disk, be sure to create one before removing an old drive, or have a copy available if installing a new one. Follow these steps to install the drive:

1. Collect all the necessary documentation for the drive and the computer.
2. Back up any data you wish to use again.
3. Turn off the computer and unplug the power cord.
4. Follow the appropriate ESD safety procedures.
5. Open the case of the computer.
6. Set the jumper for the drive. Consult the documentation that came with the drive. It must be set to single use or master or slave. If this is a second drive, both drives might require jumper settings.
7. Connect the cable to the drives. The end connector should be plugged into the master drive. Be sure the cable orientation is correct (pin 1 goes to the red wire).
8. Connect the power cable (see Figure 20.9).

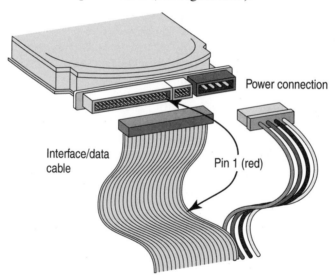

**Figure 20.9**   Cable connections

9. Install the drive in its bay.

10. Reconnect the power, boot up the computer, and run the CMOS setup utility. The CMOS must be set to recognize the new drive. See the manufacturer's documentation for proper configuration. Don't forget that drives larger than 528 MB (approximately) will require logical block addressing (LBA). See Chapter 9, "Basic Disk Drives," and Chapter 10, "Advanced Disk Drive Technology," for more information on disk drive technology.

**Note**  It might be advisable to set up and test a drive before final installation in the bay. Be careful to avoid ESD or placing the drive in a position that will cause excessive heat buildup. Large-capacity drives, especially SCSI and older ESDI (Enhanced Small Device Interface) drives, can generate a lot of heat. It might be necessary to position a small fan to send a current of air over the drive's logic board when running a hard disk drive out of a computer or drive case.

Some larger drives installed in older machines might require the use of disk management software, which usually comes with the drive (in some cases, it's already loaded in the drive). Follow the instructions provided by the manufacturer to extract and use this software. It is especially important to document the use of such software and to make sure it is included on any boot or rescue floppy disk you prepare for such a system.

To complete the installation, perform the following steps:

1. Boot the computer from the bootable floppy disk and run Fdisk to set the partition (or partitions).

2. Format the drive. If it is the only drive or the bootable drive, it must be formatted with the system files.

3. Replace the cover of the computer.

The drive is now ready for software to be installed.

## Operating System Driver Installation

In the days of DOS, installing new device drivers or modifying drivers for existing hardware would have taken up a couple of lessons in a book like this. Windows 98 and Windows 2000 have reduced the need for coverage dramatically. In most cases, Windows recognizes new hardware as long as it conforms to the proper Plug and Play standards. In those instances, Windows may already have the appropriate driver available, or it prompts you for the appropriate disk. Once the files are located, a wizard installs the appropriate drivers, resolves any device issues, and possibly prompts you to restart the system.

In some cases, you may have to manually install an updated driver or manually tell a system what kind of hardware device is being added. This is done using the Add/Remove Hardware Wizard located in the Windows Control Panel. The wizard locates the hardware; when it cannot, it prompts you for the type of device and the driver. You can also get to the settings by using the Device Manager and clicking the Properties tab to install or modify the driver and its settings. To do so, right-click the device, then choose the Update Driver option, and a dialog box similar to the one shown in Figure 20.10 opens.

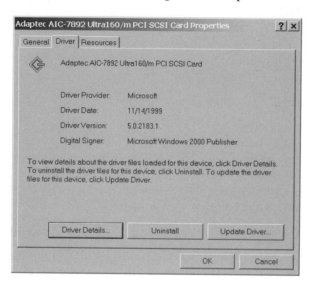

**Figure 20.10**   Device Driver dialog box

## Motherboards

Installing a new motherboard is one way to completely overhaul a computer (see Figure 20.11). In many cases, it is the most inexpensive way to get a new computer. Many of the larger manufacturers use proprietary motherboards that can only be replaced with one made by the same manufacturer to ensure compatibility with other components.

Before deciding to undertake this major overhaul, there are several questions you should answer:

- Will the motherboard fit into the existing case? Check the size and alignment of mounting holes (plastic standoffs that keep the circuitry from contacting the case).
- Does the motherboard have the same built-in COM and LPT ports?
- Does the motherboard have a built-in video card?

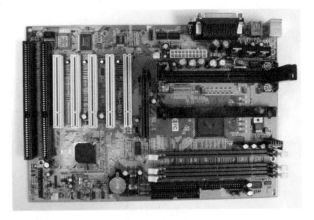

**Figure 20.11**  Motherboard

- Will the existing expansion cards fit the motherboard's expansion bus slots? Are there enough slots available to accommodate the existing cards? The expansion slots should go toward the back of the computer, where the openings are located.

- Is the power connector located on the same side as the power supply? It should be as close to the power supply as possible.

- Will the existing drives (CD-ROM, IDE, or SCSI) work with the controllers on the motherboard?

- Will the memory on the old motherboard work with the new motherboard?

- Will the upgrade meet your current and future requirements?

Installing a new motherboard is a major task and requires complete disassembly, reassembly, and setup of the computer and all its devices. You will put everything covered so far in this lesson into practice when you replace a motherboard. The best advice is to prepare everything ahead of time and to take good notes while disassembling the old motherboard.

## Replacing a Motherboard

Replacing a motherboard is probably the most difficult task (from the perspective of physically replacing parts) that a computer technician will take on. It amounts to no less than building a computer, because it will, in many cases, require complete disassembly first. Although complex, if you carry out the following procedure one step at a time, you should not face any problems:

1. Complete an installation checklist and make sure all the necessary parts are available and will fit into the computer. It's also a good idea to back up all data on the system hard drives and update any rescue disks.

2. Follow the steps for disassembling a computer set out in Lesson 1; these include removing all the screws and standoffs (taking care to keep them in a safe place) and the old motherboard.

3. Check all the settings on the new motherboard.

4. Install the new motherboard. Position the standoffs and make sure they align with the case and the motherboard. Verify that the motherboard is positioned correctly (expansion slots facing the back of the computer). Carefully tighten the screws. Visually check to be sure that the motherboard does not touch the case (see Figure 20.12).

**Figure 20.12**    Motherboard in case

5. Reconnect the case switches. Use the notes taken during disassembly to verify they are in the right place.

6. Follow the steps for computer reassembly set out in Lesson 1.

7. Test the computer to be sure it boots up.

8. Complete the final testing and close the case.

## Lesson Summary

The following points summarize the main elements of this lesson:

- Performing upgrades is one of the computer technician's most commonly performed tasks.

- Good documentation (before and after) is an essential requirement for upgrading.

- A computer technician should be familiar with the steps required to upgrade memory, CPUs, expansion cards, hard drives, and motherboards.

# Chapter Summary

The following points summarize the key concepts in this chapter:

## Computer Disassembly and Reassembly

- Preparation is the key to a successful upgrade or repair. Document the system setup, including hardware and software, using a computer configuration sheet before you begin the project.
- Prepare a plan of action before beginning a project, and stick to it.
- Make sure you have an adequate toolkit, including a bootable floppy disk and any utilities you may need.
- Always create a complete backup of the system you are going to be working on before you begin.
- Implement safety precautions, including ESD prevention.
- Follow the steps for disassembly and reassembly.

## Upgrading a Computer

- Memory upgrades are probably the simplest and most common upgrades performed by a computer technician.
- Installing a new CPU is a common way to upgrade older computers. Installing a new expansion card is another common upgrade.
- Before installing (or purchasing) new parts, make sure the parts will work with the system you intend to upgrade.
- Installing a new hard drive is not difficult. However, certain procedures need to be followed.
- Installing a new motherboard is one way to completely overhaul a computer.

# Review

The following questions are intended to reinforce key information presented in this chapter. If you are unable to answer a question, review the appropriate lesson and then try the question again. Answers to the questions can be found in Appendix A, "Questions and Answers."

1. What bootable floppy disks are needed for a computer professional's toolkit, and why?

2. You are only going to check the memory chips. Do you need to follow ESD safety practices?

3. What is parity?

4. Can the L1 cache memory be upgraded?

5. Your client wants to install an internal modem. How would you determine whether this internal modem could be installed on your client's machine?

6. A friend just got a bargain on a new Plug and Play sound card and wants to install it on a non–Plug and Play computer. Will it work?

7. How do you determine whether to upgrade the CPU or install another motherboard?

8. What is the advantage of Plug and Play?

9. What are the four requirements that must be addressed before installing a new drive in a computer?

C H A P T E R   2 1

# Troubleshooting Techniques and Client Relations

**Lesson 1: Basic Troubleshooting Techniques** .................... **567**

**Lesson 2: Windows Troubleshooting Tools** ..................... **573**

**Lesson 3: Client Relations** ................................... **596**

**Chapter Summary** .......................................... **603**

**Review** ................................................... **604**

## About This Chapter

Although Plug and Play hardware and more mature PC operating systems have taken much of the work out of troubleshooting computers and programs, there are still times when hardware and software don't work correctly. Troubleshooting is as much an art as a science, and we often have to deal with an unhappy or frantic client on a call—one who is worried about his or her data, loss of productivity, and the size of the bill. This chapter covers the care of both the technology and the user by a technician on the job.

Lesson 1 covers general troubleshooting methods. These principles apply to all systems. Lesson 2 goes into the specific tools and techniques used with Microsoft Windows 95, Microsoft Windows 98, and Microsoft Windows 2000, including system recovery. Lesson 3 discusses handling the human component: dealing with the client.

---

**Note**   Be aware that some of these tools can significantly alter the operation of Windows and change configurations drastically. While working with these tools, do not perform any actions unless you understand both the operation and the consequences.

---

## Before You Begin

You should review the previous chapters of this book before tackling this one. Advanced troubleshooting tools are not for the novice. You should be familiar with the operation and configuration of the Windows 95, Windows 98, and Windows 2000 environments. As in the other lessons dealing with software, a basic understanding of the Windows environment, user interface, and the PC is assumed. Some of the material in this chapter has already been introduced and you should already be familiar with it.

Be aware that this is an introduction to troubleshooting techniques, and expertise only comes with experience. Full coverage of the tools involved in troubleshooting for both types of operating systems is well beyond the scope of this volume. For competence, you should supplement these lessons with practice using the tools and techniques presented here. It is a good idea to follow along with the examples and investigate the tools mentioned in this chapter.

# Lesson 1:  Basic Troubleshooting Techniques

### After this lesson, you will be able to
- Identify the steps in defining scope of a computer-related problem
- Understand various troubleshooting techniques
- Apply those techniques to resolve the problem

### Estimated lesson time: 30 minutes

## Troubleshooting

Troubleshooting is perhaps the most difficult task of a computer professional. Frequently, the problems reported are just symptoms, not the cause. It takes investigation to pinpoint the real cause. After you diagnose a problem, you must develop a plan of action to correct the problem. To make matters worse, computers never fail at a convenient time. They fail in the middle of a job or when there is a deadline and the user must have the problem fixed immediately.

Troubleshooting is more of an art form than an exact science. However, to be an efficient and effective troubleshooter, you must approach the problem in an organized and methodical manner. Remember, you are looking for the cause, not the symptom. As a troubleshooter, you must be able to quickly and confidently eliminate as many alternatives as possible so that you can focus on the things that might be the cause of the problem. To do this, you must be organized.

Understanding the following five phases of troubleshooting will help you focus on the cause of the problem and lead you to a permanent fix.

### Phase I: Define the Problem

The first phase is the most critical and, often, the most ignored. Without a complete understanding of the entire problem, you can spend a great deal of time working on the symptoms instead of the cause. The only tools required for this phase are a pad of paper, a pen (or pencil), and good listening skills.

Listening to the client or coworker (the computer user) is your best source of information. Don't assume that just because you are the expert, the operator doesn't know what caused the problem. Remember, you might know how the computer works and be able to find the technical cause of the failure, but the user was there before and after the problem started and he or she is likely to recall the events that led up to the failure.

Ask a few specific questions to help identify the problem and list the events that led up to the failure. You might want to create a form that contains the following standard questions (and other questions specific to the situation) for taking notes:

- Was the computer working properly before this problem occurred?
- When did you first notice the problem or error?
- Was the computer moved recently?
- Have you made any changes to software or hardware?
- Has anything happened to the computer? Was it dropped or was something dropped on it? Was coffee or soda spilled on the keyboard?
- When exactly does the problem or error occur? During the startup process? After lunch? Only on Monday mornings? After using e-mail?
- Can you reproduce the problem or error?
- If so, how do you reproduce the problem?
- What does the problem or error look like?
- Describe any changes in the computer coinciding with the problem (such as noise, screen changes, lights, and so forth).
- Are there any error messages?
- Were there any funny noises or smells present at the time the computer failed?
- Are there current backups of the system and data files available?

If one question leads to another question, determine if the question is really germane. If so, follow up; if not, file it for later review.

At this point, it's often a good idea to examine the computer and verify the client's statements as much as possible. In frustration, people sometimes overlook the obvious or forget important details. On more than one occasion the problem of a "dead computer" has turned out to be a power switch on a surge protector or monitor not turned on. When you examine the computer, reassure the user that you will work to resolve the problem, but don't promise any miracles you can't deliver. If the solution is both obvious and simple, don't make the person feel like they wasted your time. Use it as an opportunity to perform some minor—but useful—periodic maintenance task.

## Phase II: Zero in on the Cause

The next step involves the process of isolating the problem. There is no particular correct approach to follow, and there is no substitute for experience. The best method is to eliminate any obvious problems and work from the simplest problems to the more complex. The purpose is to narrow your search down to one or two general categories. The following table provides 14 possible categories you can use to narrow your search.

| Category | Problem | Symptom |
|---|---|---|
| Electrical power | Electric utility<br>Fuse box<br>Wiring<br>Plugs and cords<br>Power supply<br>Power connectors | Dead computer<br>Intermittent errors on power-on self test (POST)<br>Intermittent lock ups<br>Device not working or not found |
| Connectivity | External cables<br>Internal cables<br>Properly seated cards (chip and boards)<br>SCSI (Small Computer System Interface) chain<br>Front panel wires (lights and buttons) | Device not working<br>Device not found<br>Intermittent errors on a device<br>Device failure or failure to boot<br>Check if improperly connected or real failure or warning |
| Boot | Boot ROM (read-only memory)<br>All products on the hardware abstraction layer (HAL) list (Windows 2000 and Microsoft Windows NT)<br>CMOS (complementary metal-oxide semi-conductor; chip and settings)<br>CMOS battery<br>Flash ROM | Dead computer<br>If not, may not be supported with proper drivers<br>Consistent errors on POST<br>Beep errors<br>CMOS text errors, hard disk drive, floppy disk drive, and video errors |
| Memory | DRAM (dynamic RAM); proper type and setup)<br>DRAM CMOS settings<br>SRAM (static RAM); proper type and setup<br>SRAM CMOS settings<br>Motherboard jumpers | Dead computer<br>Parity errors<br>General Protection Fault (GPF) with consistent addresses<br>HIMEM.SYS errors |
| Mass storage | Hard disk drives, floppy disk drives, CD-ROM drives<br>Zip drives, tape drives<br>Partitions<br>File structure<br>File allocation tables (FATs)<br>Directory structure<br>Filenames and attributes | Error messages:<br>Missing Operating System<br>File Not Found<br>No Boot Device<br>Abort, Retry, Fail |

*(continued)*

*(continued)*

| Category | Problem | Symptom |
|---|---|---|
| Input/output (I/O) | IRQ (interrupt request) settings<br>I/O address<br>Direct memory access (DMA) settings<br>Serial port settings<br>Parallel port settings<br>SCSI settings<br>Card jumper settings | System locks up<br>Device not responding<br>Bizarre behavior from a device |
| Operating system | BUFFERS<br>FILES<br>File Control Blocks (FCBs)<br>Stacks<br>IO.SYS/MSDOS.SYS<br>Set statements<br>Paths and prompts<br>External MS-DOS commands<br>Multiboot CONFIG.SYS | Error messages:<br>Missing Operating System<br>Bad Or Missing Command Interpreter<br>Insert Disk With COMMAND.COM<br>Stack Overflow<br>Insufficient File Handles |
| Applications | Proper installation<br>Proper configuration<br>Knowledge of capabilities<br>Knowledge of bugs, incompatibilities, work-arounds | Application doesn't work properly<br>Application-specific errors<br>Application-specific GPFs<br>Lock ups only in specific application |
| Device drivers | All devices in the Windows Registry, .ini files, CONFIG.SYS, SYSTEM.INI, called in AUTOEXEC.BAT<br>Proper versions<br>Proper configuration | Device lock ups on access<br>Intermittent lock ups<br>Computer runs in safe mode only |
| Memory management | HIMEM.SYS settings<br>EMM386.EXE settings<br>MSDOS.SYS options (Win9x)<br>SYSTEM.INI/WIN.INI<br>Virtual memory<br>Windows resource usage<br>UMB (upper memory block) management | Not Enough Memory error<br>Missing extended memory specification (XMS) and Expanded Memory Specification (EMS)<br>Device lock ups<br>GPFs at KRNL386.EXE<br>GPFs at USER.EXE or GDI.EXE |
| Configuration/setup | Files used for initialization<br>Basic layout of initialized files | Programs refuse to do something they should<br>Missing options in program<br>Missing program or device |

*(continued)*

| Category | Problem | Symptom |
|----------|---------|---------|
| Viruses | Virus-management procedures<br>Knowledge of virus symptoms<br>Virus-removal procedures | Computer runs slow<br>Failure to boot or intermittent lock ups<br>Storage problems<br>Operating-system problems<br>Mysterious symptoms |
| Operator interface | Lack of training or understanding<br>Fear of the computer<br>Poor attitude | "I didn't touch it!"<br>"It always does that!"<br>Multiple users |
| Network | Logon errors<br>Communication errors | User forgets password<br>Expired password<br>Cable or NIC network interface card (NIC) problems |

Be sure to observe the failure yourself. If possible, have someone demonstrate the failure to you. If it is an operator-induced problem, it is important to observe how it is created, as well as the results. Look for error messages, and have a collection handy of the most common error messages for the operating systems you work with. They often will isolate the problem for you.

Intermittent problems are the most difficult ones to isolate. They never seem to occur when you are present. The only way to resolve them is to re-create the set of circumstances that causes the failure. Sometimes, moving step by step to eliminate the possible causes is all you can do. This takes time and patience. The user will have to keep a detailed record of what is being done before and when the failure occurs. In such cases, tell the user not to do anything with the computer when the problem recurs, except to call you. That way, the "evidence" will not be disturbed.

**Tip**  For a totally random, intermittent problem, always suspect the power supply.

## Phase III: Conduct the Repair

After you have zeroed in on a few categories, the process of elimination begins.

## Make a Plan

Create a planned approach to isolating the problem based on your knowledge at this point. Your plan should start with the most obvious or easiest solution to eliminate and move forward. Put the plan in writing! The first step of any plan should be to document and back up.

If possible, make no assumptions. If you must make any assumptions, write them down. You might need to refer back to them later.

### Follow the Plan from Beginning to End

Once a plan is created, it is important to follow it through. Jumping around and randomly trying things can often lead to problems that are more serious. Document every action you take and its results. If the first plan is not successful (it won't always be), create a new plan based on what you discovered with the previous plan. Be sure to refer to any assumptions you might have made.

### Repair or Replace

After locating the problem, either repair or replace the defect. If the problem is software-oriented, be sure to record the "before" and "after" changes.

### Phase IV: Confirm the Results

No repair is complete without confirmation that the job is done. Confirmation involves two steps:

- Make sure that the problem no longer exists. Ask the user to test the solution and confirm client satisfaction.

- Make sure that the fix did not create other problems. You have not done a professional job if the repair has been completed at the expense of something else.

### Phase V: Document the Results

Finally, document the problem and the repair. There is no substitute for experience in troubleshooting. Every new problem presents you with an opportunity to expand that experience. Keeping a copy of the repair procedure in your technical library will come in handy later when the problem (or one like it) occurs again. This is one way to build, maintain, and share experience. The record can also help if there are later questions about the service performed from a client or insurance company.

## Lesson Summary

The following point summarizes the main elements of this lesson:

- Good troubleshooting requires a plan. To be successful, you must stick to your plan. Follow the Five Phase approach.

# Lesson 2:  Windows Troubleshooting Tools

No application or program is perfect. The evolution from MS-DOS to Microsoft Windows 3.*x* to Windows 95 and Windows 98 was neither short nor simple. The current versions of Windows have brought major improvements in the way computers operate and the way we interact with them. Still, expecting the operating system to solve all problems and achieve full compatibility with all hardware is not realistic—there are simply too many different hardware and software manufacturers, each with its unique approach, for one operating system to manage.

As a computer technician, you must understand both the strengths and weaknesses of computer systems (hardware and software) to achieve the best possible performance for your clients. Fortunately, Microsoft has incorporated many tools to help you fine-tune your systems and achieve the best performance. This lesson focuses on some of the methods and tools you can use to identify problems and manage systems.

### After this lesson, you will be able to

- Identify some of the common problems encountered while using Windows
- Understand the general strategy for resolving Windows operating system problems
- Understand the system tools to restore and optimize performance
- Use the proper tool to restore the System Registry
- Troubleshoot problems with MS-DOS applications
- Troubleshoot common printer problems

### Estimated lesson time: 45 minutes

## Basic Windows Troubleshooting Approach

The basic concepts covered in Lesson 1 apply equally well to working with the operating system as they do to hardware problems. Start by gathering information, analyzing the situation, and factoring out any common problems (and resolving them). Then, identify the source of a problem, produce a plan, and execute it. Functionally, there are some differences. Although the electrical engineering skills required to build a computer are quite complex, the final product is a set of components with well-defined operational capabilities. It takes very little training to be able to isolate hardware problems, repair or replace the component at fault, and thus restore the system to proper function.

The operating system is also a marvel of technological design. The complexity of the operating system's design, coupled with its need to interact with the hardware components, means that the problems a technician encounters are diverse and sometimes very difficult to isolate. The following sections provide a quick summary of the steps taken to isolate the problem.

### Gather Information

Start with the user's complaint. Determine if the system has ever worked and if the problem is random or reproducible. Find out as much about the system configuration and the operating system in use as possible. Locate any backups, emergency repair disk (ERD), or other external diagnostic or recovery tools. Find out if the user was presented with any error messages and exactly what was going on when the system failed. If there appears to be a hardware problem, that must be resolved before any work on the operating system proceeds.

### Determine if the System Will Boot and Look for an Obvious Problem

Attempt to start the system. If that works, try to generate the fault yourself. If the system does not boot into normal operation, attempt to boot into safe mode. Identify any obvious problems. If the system boots, determine if you need to move or back up data files for the user before proceeding with repairs.

### Localize and Identify the Problem

It is important to focus on a single issue at a time, even if there are multiple problems on the system. Prepare a list and prioritize the problems. If you've located a simple problem that may resolve the issue, repair it and make sure that there are no other difficulties with the machine.

### Define an Action Plan That Utilizes Appropriate Tools

The only difference in this step between an operating system problem and a hardware problem is the kinds of tools that you will use. Instead of screwdrivers, you will use a variety of software tools provided with the system for much of your diagnosis and repair. A good habit to develop is linking elements of the action plan to specific tools and procedures.

### Resolve the Problem

With the plan in place, the next step is implementation. If you resolve the problem, work with the system until you are sure that there's not an underlying problem that caused the problem you just worked on. The last thing you want is to return on another call right away.

### Minimize Potential for Recurrence

If the problem was due to lack of regular maintenance, operator error, or some other easily identifiable cause, take steps to eliminate the potential for further harm to the system.

## Document Your Work

Both during the operation and at its conclusion, be sure to document your findings, the steps you take, the results, and any requirements for follow-up action. If there are things the user should do, be sure to write them down and present the person with a copy.

# Performing a Differential Diagnosis

To identify a problem and pinpoint a resolution, it's often useful to employ a technique known as *differential diagnosis.* Although this may sound technical and complicated, in reality it is a fancy phrase for examining the behavior of the system, matching that behavior with possible problems, and filtering out the most likely culprit. It is the same technique that physicians employ when attempting to diagnose illness in a human patient. For example, if a person complains of a runny nose and a fever, and it is flu season, then flu is the most likely suspect. The doctor can rule out unrelated problems, but based on the patient's history, the doctor may also need to investigate similar ailments, like an upper respiratory infection.

The same thing holds true for work with computers. If someone complains of a computer that freezes every time a certain application is launched, then that application is a likely starting point for investigation. At the same time, the real problem might lie in a new video driver or a corrupted data file in use by the program. Listening carefully, using a stepby-step procedure to eliminate other potential causes, and experience (not to mention good documentation), in many ways, are your most valuable tools.

In developing a differential diagnosis, you contrast possible causes and work to eliminate all but one. You then validate your assumption by seeing if there is a demonstrable problem with that component. If there is, and fixing it makes the underlying problem disappear, then you have empirical proof that your diagnosis was correct. If not, you must proceed with the process of elimination.

When working on operating system problems, a differential diagnosis can start with observing where in the operational cycle the problem occurs. Break the cycle into three components. System startup begins at the point at which the operating system starts to load and it ends when control is turned over to the user. The operating phase is when both the user and the operating system can use the environment. System shutdown lasts from when a shutdown command is given—or occurs unexpectedly—until the operating system is unloaded from memory. Each phase has both its own most likely causes and its own collection of tools for finding and repairing the problem.

Experience can often be a guide to the problem. If you have a good hunch, check it out as part of the early examination. If it does not pan out, go through the plan in a step-wise fashion.

In some cases, you will find the operating system has been seriously corrupted, or the hard drive has crashed and must be replaced. In such cases, you will have to institute a disaster recovery plan. It is often possible to rebuild the operating system and recover data, but not always. Hopefully, there will be backups of critical data and system files.

There is a natural order to working through these phases. If the operating system starts, you can move on to the operating phase. If the operating system fails to start, you have to resolve that issue before going further.

### Dealing with Startup Issues

Many times the failure to properly load the operating system is actually a hardware problem or difficulty related to new drivers or software. The first step in resolving a problem like this is to identify any changes that have been made to the operating system or the components contained within the computer. You should also ask for copies of the system configuration, emergency startup or recovery disks, and backups of core system files.

While gathering this information, it's a good idea to ask questions that can help identify other causes that might be at work. Even if there is a most obvious cause, it may not be the culprit in this case. Assess the computer skill level of the user. Is it possible that a novice shut down the system improperly or erased critical files? If the system is connected to the Internet or LAN (local area network), or the user has just loaded files from another system, a virus may be at work.

Both Windows 2000 and Windows 98 offer some tools to gain access to the system even when the full-fledged operating environment cannot be loaded. These may not work in all cases, but they usually work if it is only a software issue or if the hardware problem can be resolved without having to reformat the hard disk or replace it. We deal with the actual techniques and tools shortly.

### Operational Issues

Applications, network connections, or system services that do not work are usually isolated problems. The very nature of the problem usually pinpoints the area where the difficulty resides. If the device attached to the system is not working, it may be related to a specific driver or a conflict with another device.

Erratic problems during operation that cannot be directly pinpointed to a specific application or device can be more difficult to diagnose. In most cases, systemwide devices or services like virtual memory or display drivers are likely culprits.

### Shutdown Issues

Computers that unexpectedly hang during normal operation, shift into restart mode without warning, or refuse to close when a proper shutdown command has been given are often some of the most difficult to diagnose and repair. This type of problem can stem from faulty device drivers, runaway system processes or applications, memory management problems, or hardware problems.

# Working Through the Phases

Before actually attempting to boot a system that is exhibiting operating system problems, you should make sure that the computer meets the system requirements for running the operating system involved and that the components are all compatible. This information is available on the Microsoft Web site. While you are checking, you should also obtain the latest drivers for major system components (like the display adapter and any hard disk controllers) if you do not have them with you.

**Tip**   If the user reports an error message you can get details on likely causes and resolutions from the Knowledge Base on the Microsoft Web site. This information is also contained in several reference materials and is available by subscription on CD-ROM from Microsoft.

You should also make sure that the system is receiving adequate, clean power. If there are no obvious hardware problems, you may wish to enable the BIOS (basic input/output system) virus checker or use a third-party program to see if a virus is infecting the system and inhibiting its ability to load the operating system. If the system manages to boot properly, you can proceed to the operating phase.

## System Startup in Safe Mode and Command Mode

During startup you should observe all messages on the screen and make sure that the POST executes properly. Problems during this phase are directly related to hardware in virtually all cases. If new hardware has just been added, try removing it and then restarting the system. If that removal does not fix the problem or there have been no recent additions, you can use an alternate way to start the operating system—safe mode.

Both Windows 98 and Windows 2000 offer a *safe mode*, which loads the operating system with only a minimal set of drivers and a simple 16-color VGA display. To enter this mode press F8 just after the POST concludes. A menu appears, offering several alternate methods of booting the system. This mode is automatically invoked on startup in some versions of Windows if the system was shut down improperly.

If core system files have been corrupted, it may be impossible to gain access to the system even in safe mode. If the hard disk is still functional, you may attempt to start the system in command mode. This is another option on the alternate start menu accessed by pressing F8. If possible, you should try to work within safe mode, rather than using the command mode alone. Safe mode offers access to a wider variety of tools to help isolate and repair problems. Many of the regular Windows system management tools are available in safe mode, whereas in command mode most of the diagnostic and recovery tools are variations on the old MS-DOS utility programs. The Recovery Console, a command mode program available for Windows 2000, is examined later in this lesson.

---

**Note**   Windows 2000 and Windows NT both offer another boot option that brings the system up in the "Last Known Good Configuration." This loads the previous version of the Registry, and may enable a normal system start. Be aware that any new modifications that involve the Registry will be lost. Use it only if you know it won't cause as many problems as it fixes.

---

## Working with the Operating System Management Tools

If you can use safe mode or find another workaround to actually gain entry into the Windows operating environment, there are a variety of tools available to help with troubleshooting and repairing the system. A complete discussion of the tools alone is worthy of a book itself. For our purposes, the following table detailing their functions and a more detailed discussion of the use of the most important ones will suffice. Most of these tools are available by clicking either Start\Programs\Accessories\System Tools, Start\Programs\Accessories\Administrative Tools, or via the Control Panel. Some require command mode access.

| Tool | Operating System | Remarks |
|---|---|---|
| Microsoft System Information (MSI) | Both | This is one of the most useful diagnostic tools available under Windows. It can quickly display virtually every aspect of a system's settings and resources. The exact features available vary with the operating system involved. Anyone working as a technician on any Windows system should become familiar with this tool. In Windows 2000 the MSI is a Microsoft Management Console (MMC) snap-in. It is covered in detail in the next section. |
| Computer Management | Windows 2000 | An MMC snap-in that provides easy access to a variety of maintenance and management tools including the MSI tool mentioned above and Device Manager introduced next. |
| Device Manager | Both | Available by selecting System in the Control Panel, this tool provides some of the same functionality found in the MSI tool, but it does not offer a complete and collected set of reports, or a number of other troubleshooting tools. |
| System Configuration Utility and System Troubleshooter | Both | Often incorporated into the help structure, these tools provide interactive troubleshooting support. By answering questions, the user is presented with various possible resolutions to common problems. |

*(continued)*

| Tool | Operating System | Remarks |
|---|---|---|
| System Services Window | Windows 2000 | This utility is available through administrative tools. It shows what services are running on the machine, their current status, and how they are started. It can be used to stop services for troubleshooting. |
| Microsoft System Recovery | Windows 98 | This is a program that installs a minimal Windows 98 environment that, unlike safe mode, provides full access to 32-bit application programming interfaces (APIs) and device drivers, and works with Microsoft backup to recover files. It is located on the Windows 98 distribution disk in the \Tools\Sysrec directory, with the filename PCRESTOR.BAT. |
| Task Manager | Windows 2000 | The Windows 98 Close Program tool is accessed the same way and offers a very limited subset of Task Manager's features. |
| Windows Maintenance Wizard/Task Scheduler | Both | These are scheduling tools that can be used to automatically run tools such as Backup, ScanDisk, and Disk Defragmenter at regular intervals. There are operating system-specific variations. |
| Dr. Watson | Both | This system utility can be routed to track system events when application faults occur. It creates a log with a .wig extension in the \Windows\Drwatson directory. The log includes an indication of the application that caused the error and the related memory addresses. |
| Boot log | Both | As discussed in Chapter 16, "Operating System Fundamentals," all current versions of Windows can produce a complex log detailing every aspect of system startup. The contents of this log can be examined in a text editor. They are invaluable in trying to track down random system startup problems. |
| Microsoft Backup | Both (not automatically installed in Windows 98) | This program exists in various editions in both Windows 98 and Windows 2000, and can be used to both back up and restore the entire system or selected files. |
| Registry Checker | Both | Both Windows and DOS-based versions of the Registry Checker are available for performing a wide variety of Registry-related tasks including editing, backing up, and restoring this vital system component. |
| Registry Editor | Both | There are two versions of the registry editor. Windows 98 includes REGEDIT, and Windows 2000 includes both REGEDIT and REGEDT32. Ideally, the latter should be run under Windows 2000 for full-featured editing capability. |

*(continued)*

*(continued)*

| Tool | Operating System | Remarks |
|---|---|---|
| MMC | Windows 2000 | The MMC is a single-point interface for operating a variety of system maintenance and troubleshooting tools. Over time, Microsoft intends to make the MMC the standard interface for all such applications. |
| Windows Update | Both | The Windows Update tool offers an online method of quickly identifying and applying updates to various Windows components and related applications such as Microsoft Internet Explorer. It works in conjunction with special Web pages at the Microsoft Web site. |
| Recovery Console | Windows 2000 | The Recovery Console is a special text-mode operating environment separate from the one you're familiar with for DOS operations. In spite of the simple interface, it offers a sophisticated tool to start and stop services, repair the operating system, and fix damaged drive volumes. It allows access to FAT16, FAT32, and NTFS (Windows NT file system) volumes. It is covered in detail later in this chapter. |
| Automatic Skip Driver Agent | Windows 98 | This utility located in the \Windows directory under the name ASD.EXE can be used to detect and skip over device drivers that are interfering with the Windows startup process. |
| IPConfig and Winipcfg | Both | Winipcfg (Windows 98) and ipconfig (Windows 2000) are tools that can provide information about the IP address for the machine. These are two tools that you should practice using for diagnosing network problems related to TCP/IP configuration. |
| Ping | Both | A simple TCP/IP (Transmission Control Protocol/Internet Protocol) test that can check if a computer is on the network by entering the string ping *xxx.xxx.xxx.xxx* where the *xs* are the digits of the IP address. It can be entered at the DOS command prompt. |
| Error messages | Both | Both operating systems provide a variety of messages under all their operating environments to warn the operator of difficulties. The most serious error message is sometimes referred to as the "blue screen of death," which signifies a fatal error that causes a system to stop. In Windows 2000, these error messages bear a code that can be looked up for help in pinpointing the problem and its resolution. They also usually include additional information about what processes, files, and memory addresses were involved in the error. |

*(continued)*

| Tool | Operating System | Remarks |
|------|------------------|---------|
| Event Viewer/ System logs | Windows 2000/both | Windows 2000 provides an Event Viewer, available in the Control Panel, which tracks system, application, and security operations, errors, and faults. Both operating systems provide a variety of logs that track various aspects of system operations and problems. |
| System File Checker | Both | The System File Checker is an application that scans the system and monitors changed, deleted, or corrupt system files. |
| Signature Verification Tool | Both | This tool determines whether a file has a valid digital signature and if the file has been modified since being given that signature. |
| Digital Signature Check | Both | This program allows network administrators to identify whether drivers have been digitally signed by Microsoft. It can be turned on either by using the Policy Editor in Windows 2000 or by direct modification to the Registry. |
| Windows and MS-DOS report tools | Various versions for the specific operating system | User tools that automate the reporting process so a remote technical support service or the on-scene technician can obtain a complete report concerning the system files. |
| Performance Monitor/ System Monitor | Both | In Windows 2000, the Performance Monitor is a tool available through the Control Panel, under Administrative Tools. This is a very sophisticated graphing tool that can monitor the performance of the major system components in great detail. The results can be viewed directly and saved in a spreadsheet and database formats, or using other analysis tools. Results can also be logged. In Windows 98, the System Monitor provides a less sophisticated series of real-time reports about how various system processes are performing. |

**Note**   Many of the tools listed here are available in both operating systems, but that does not mean they are the same. Keep in mind that Windows 2000 and Windows 98 have radically different system architectures. Although they share many common design elements, and many of these utilities both look and work alike, it is important to become familiar with both operating systems and their idiosyncrasies.

# Using the Windows Troubleshooting Tools

## The Windows 2000 Computer Management Snap-In

The Computer Management component of the MMC is a very useful tool for monitoring system events, managing system services, accessing MSI, accessing the Device Manager, and monitoring remote systems. Keep in mind that for full access to all of Computer Management's features, you will need administrator privileges.

Working with the Computer Management console is a good way to become comfortable using the MMC and Windows 2000 diagnostic tools. As you can see in Figure 21.1, the left pane has the familiar tree structure, with details in the right pane. The data is refreshed each time a choice is made with the mouse or keyboard. You can quickly access the Event Viewer, system information, and the majority of the diagnostic tools mentioned in the preceding table by clicking the Tools menu and making a selection. The new MMC interface avoids the back-and-forth hassles of the Control Panel, and the user (with the proper privileges) can customize the contents to suit personal habits or the common tasks performed.

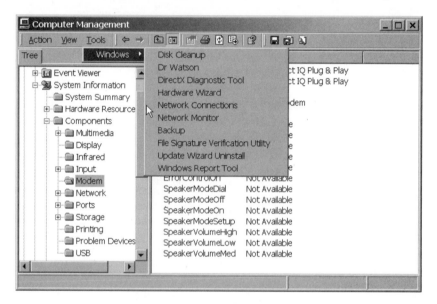

**Figure 21.1**    The Tools menu in the Windows 2000 Computer Management tool

Those following the lesson at a computer will benefit from examining some of the different tools before continuing. Unless you are very familiar with the Registry and computer settings, you should not make any actual modifications at this point.

## Windows 98 MSI Tool

Microsoft Windows Me's system information utility offers a similar interface, but has a more browser-like look and feel (see Figure 21.2). If you open its Tools menu, you will see a similar collection of troubleshooting and diagnostic aids to those in Windows 98. The Windows 98 version still has the classic Windows interface and makes more use of dialog boxes. Anyone familiar with the Windows environment should have little trouble moving among the Windows 2000, Windows 98, and Windows Me versions of these tools.

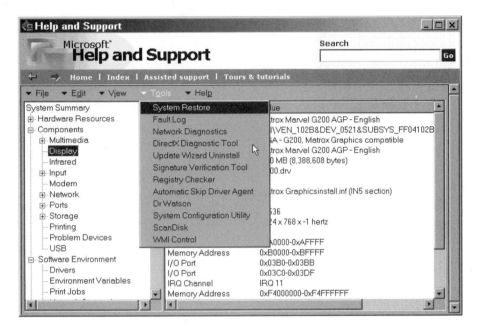

**Figure 21.2**  The Windows System Information tool in Windows Me

## Troubleshooting Windows 98
## with the System Configuration Utility and Device Manager

The Windows 98 operating system offers the System Configuration utility as part of Information Manager, available from the Tools menu. This is a very useful tool for examining startup files and system initialization settings.

If you are having trouble starting a system and can enter safe mode, this should be one of your first stops. Figure 21.3 shows the System Configuration utility open in front of the System Information Manager and the dialog box for the General tab's Advanced Controls option. A series of radio buttons and check marks help you quickly decide which options and settings will be activated during startup and which will be disabled.

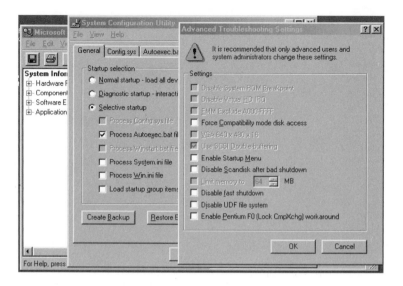

**Figure 21.3**    The System Configuration utility in Windows 98

You can use the System Configuration utility from the Startup menu (press F8 just after POST completes) by selecting the Step By Step Confirmation option to debug problems with Windows startup. You can narrow the problem area by disabling certain options (for example, all options in WIN.INI) during startup using System Configuration. Once you have narrowed the field, enable the offending section and choose a step-by-step confirmation mode. In most cases, the system hangs just after you select the offending driver or device. You can then disable it and resolve the issue in normal startup mode.

---

**Note**    Windows Me moves away from the use of CONFIG.SYS and AUTOEXEC.BAT. The settings that used to be allowed in past versions of Windows 95 and Windows 98 have now all been moved with the Registry and .ini files. If you are using a computer running Windows Me to follow these examples, there will be some differences, just as with Windows 2000. Also, The Create Backup option available under Windows 98 in the General tab of the System Configuration utility has been replaced with a System Restore button.

---

All current versions of Windows offer some version of the Device Manager. In Windows 98, this utility is available as a tab on the System utility found in Control Panel. Windows 2000 places a button in the Hardware tab and makes it available directly through the Computer Management MMC snap-in. If you suspect a hardware device is not loading properly or has stopped functioning, a quick check of the Device Manager will quickly show if this is the case.

If the device is not responding properly, or if there is a problem with the driver, Device Manager tells you by placing a colored marker over the device's icon. A red dot means a critical error has stopped the device from working at all (usually a hardware conflict with another device or a memory error), while a yellow dot indicates a less serious problem. Figure 21.4 shows Device Manager open.

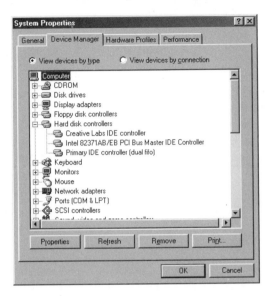

**Figure 21.4**   Device Manager

Look for phantom devices. If a device is incorrectly configured or incorrectly communicating with the operating system, you may see a device shown that is not really on the system—or a real one may appear twice. If Windows does not know exactly what device it is, it may represent it with an icon shaped like a question mark. You can use Device Manager to investigate whether Windows is seeing the proper driver and whether it is working. It also shows hardware-specific conflicts that it can recognize. These kinds of errors occur most often with problems with Plug and Play compatibility for legacy devices. If newer drivers are available, remove the older driver, then try installing the newer one. If you see multiple devices listed where only one exists on the system, right-click each one and select Remove. Reboot the system and see if the problem has been resolved; if not, you may have to work deeper in resolving the settings on the individual device. This can all be accomplished within Device Manager.

## Shutdown and Related Problems

Shutting down Windows improperly can leave a system in an unstable state and corrupt important files. Clients should be educated so they understand that if a computer is not shutting down properly, the underlying problem can lead to serious consequences. The issue should be resolved, rather than just shutting off the computer and denying it power. Many times a system hangs during shutdown due to an application that is not properly releasing control or a runaway process. Two of the most valuable tools for resolving these problems are selective startup and the Windows 2000 Task Manager.

At first, it may seem strange to use startup options to resolve a shutdown issue, but by selectively choosing which options are installed on the system during operation, you can help isolate the problem. If a feature is disabled and the system begins to shut down normally, odds are you've found the offending component. The exact course of action will vary based on what is wrong with it.

Windows 2000 offers Task Manager, a utility that is not available in Windows 9*x*. You can access this utility by pressing CTRL+ALT+DEL while the system is running. It offers three tabs: Applications, Processes, and Performance. Task Manager lets you quickly see which applications and processes are running and how the system is using CPU (central processing unit) and memory resources. Extremely high CPU usage is an indication that something is not running right or that the system is running low on resources and needs to be reconfigured. If you suspect an application is causing a problem, close it and observe the relative change in system resources. Task Manager is shown in Figure 21.5 with the Processes tab selected and in 21.6 with the Performance tab selected.

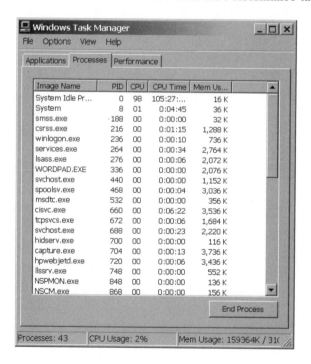

**Figure 21.5**   The Windows 2000 Task Manager with the Processes tab selected

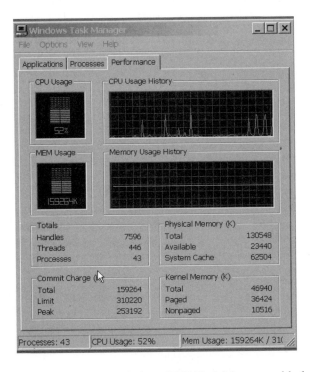

**Figure 21.6** The Windows 2000 Task Manager with the Performance tab selected

You can also use Task Manager to shut down a runaway application or process that refuses to close normally. In Windows 9x there is a less functional Close Program utility that merely lets you end a specific task or shut down the computer.

## Resource Loss and System Monitoring

The Task Manager Performance tab provides a way to quickly see how busy the system is in real time. You can leave it running on top of other applications to track just how starting and stopping a program or service taxes the system. Windows 2000 offers a very sophisticated performance meter in the Control Panel. Using this sophisticated tool takes some study, but is worth the effort if you work on Windows 2000 systems often and especially if you work on the server versions of the product.

## The Windows 98 System and Resource Monitor

Windows 98 also offers performance metering similar to that offered by Task Manager in two separate utilities, System Monitor and Resource Meter. System Monitor provides real-time reports about how various system processes are performing. It displays various functions in a line, bar, or a numeric graph. To run System Monitor, from the Start menu, select Programs, Accessories, System Tools, and System Monitor. By default, the System Monitor shows only the Kernel

Process Usage setting (the percentage of time the processor is busy). You can control the items you monitor by selecting Add Items from the System Monitor Edit menu or by clicking the Add Items button in the toolbar. Two useful items are the kernel (which tracks CPU usage) and the Memory Manager (which tracks allocated memory, cache size, and swap file size), shown in Figure 21.7.

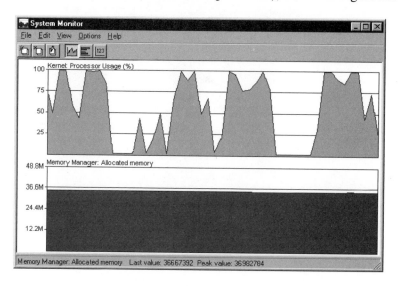

**Figure 21.7.**   Windows 98 System Monitor

Both tools can help you determine whether it's time to upgrade a computer. For example, start the computer and open all the files and applications that are normally used at the same time. Turn on System Monitor and run the system for a while. If the processor is constantly running at more than 75 percent, it might be time to upgrade. Also, if the total allocated memory (RAM, swap file, and cache) exceeds the amount of RAM in the system, it might be time to get more RAM.

## Resource Meter

The Resource Meter is used to monitor (in real time) the use of system resources. When activated, it adds a small bar graph to the system tray indicating the percentage of free resources based on the computer's total resources. As the bar gets smaller (fewer resources available), it changes color to indicate a potential problem. If the color changes to yellow, this means that resources have dropped to 30 percent. If the color changes to red, the resources have dropped to 15 percent. If the resources drop to 10 percent, Windows warns you that the computer is in imminent danger of hanging (unable to respond to user input), so you must close some applications to avoid losing data.

For more details, hold the mouse over the Resource Meter icon for a second or two. This activates a banner showing the individual resource percentages. You can also double-click the icon to display the Resource Meter dialog box, shown in Figure 21.8.

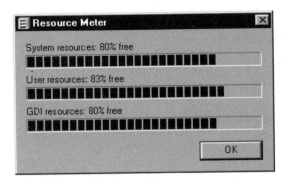

**Figure 21.8**   Resource Meter dialog box

System monitoring tools are valuable applications for both troubleshooting and evaluating the need for a system upgrade. You might use these tools if a customer complains of getting out-of-memory errors or if the computer's disk drives seem to run all the time. By monitoring memory use, you can determine how much memory is required to run all the applications and which applications are consuming the most memory. From that information, you should be able to determine the best course of action. If a client is trying to decide whether or not to upgrade a processor, you can also monitor the CPU kernel to determine just how busy it is. If it is working more than 80 percent of the time, a new processor might be warranted.

# Registry Recovery

Registry recovery is a necessary skill for any technician working regularly in the Windows environment. As with hard disk failure, Registry corruption is a fact of life. The steps that must be taken to restore a corrupted or damaged Registry vary based on whether the computer is using Windows 98 or Windows 2000.

### Troubleshooting Windows 9x Registry Startup

Each time a Windows 9x system is started, the Registry Checker automatically inspects and backs up the Registry. If it finds errors, the Registry Checker first tries to fix a problem itself by restarting the computer and examining the current Registry file in scan mode. If possible, it fixes any errors and then starts the operating system normally.

If the fault creates a situation where there's not enough memory to properly run the Registry Checker, you are prompted to reboot the system and run the program yourself. To do so you must start it at a DOS prompt with the /fix option. Reboot the system and press F8 as soon as the POST is completed. Choose the

Start With Command Prompt Only mode option, and type **scanreg /fix** when the DOS prompt appears.

## Restoring the Registry in Windows 9x for a Backup Copy

If a Registry currently in use is fatally flawed or cannot successfully boot the system, you have to replace it with a backup copy. You will need to restart the system in MS-DOS mode. Once you are at the prompt, start the Registry Checker in restore mode by typing **scanreg /restore**. The program starts and displays a list of the compressed Registry files, along with the date and time on which they were created. Beside each file listing you will see either the words *started* or *not started*. This indicates whether that copy of a backup Registry has ever actually started Windows successfully.

Select the last known good backup of the Registry. If you recently installed new hardware, which may be causing the problem, you may wish to remove it from the system before attempting the registry repair. Registry files are stored with filenames of RH*XXX*.CAB, where the *x*s stand for a sequential number that is attached to the filename. The system default for a maximum number of Registry backups is five, although an administrator can change this using the Scan Registry program.

## The Windows 2000 Recovery Console

Windows 2000 uses the Recovery Console to restore a damaged or corrupted Registry. Be aware that for this process to work you must regularly create an ERD every time a significant change is made to the system that modifies the Registry. If you use the ERD that was made when the system was first installed, the Registry is set back to the initial version at the time setup was complete. This means that any changes to the system are lost. If this produces conflicts that cannot be resolved due to subsequent changes to the operating environment or the computer configuration, the system still may not start.

If you ever intend to use the Recovery Console, it is a good idea to install it before problems occur. Remember it is not automatically installed during a normal Windows 2000 setup. See Chapter 20, "Upgrading a Computer," for information on how to install Recovery Console.

**Caution**   This procedure should only be used if you're certain that the Registry file must be restored and you are certain that the restored version of the Registry will not damage the computer. Improperly used, this procedure can cause loss of data and potentially even damage to the hardware. Before proceeding, you should rename the existing files in the *%system%*\ Repair\Config folder that you intend to restore. If the initial process fails, this may give you a second chance to make the change.

To perform the procedure, start the system and start the Recovery Console rather than the regular operating system.

At the command prompt type:

**cd repair\regback**

**copy *filename drive*:\\*systemroot*\system32\config**

In the second string, the word *filename* should be replaced with the name of the file you wish to restore from the backup. The word *drive* should be replaced with the letter of the drive on which the file exists, and *systemroot* should be replaced with the directory in which your Windows 2000 operating system is installed.

To completely restore the Registry you must copy the following files from the backup directory: Default, SAM (Security Account Management), Security, Software, and System. Once you've finished copying the files, make sure that they were copied by examining the date and time stamps with a backup copy you moved to a safe location before starting the process. If everything matches up, exit the Recovery Console by typing **exit** and restart the system.

## MS-DOS Application Incompatibilities

In spite of attempts to make Windows 9*x* and Windows 2000 backward compatible, they can still experience problems running MS-DOS applications. Most MS-DOS applications run better in newer versions of Windows than in Windows 3.11 thanks to improved memory management, but very few users pushed the envelope by running MS-DOS applications with earlier versions of Windows. (Most users simply updated their applications and learned to use the new software.) Often, MS-DOS applications refuse to run under Windows because they cannot find a version of MS-DOS they recognize. Some older MS-DOS applications make use of system resources in ways that are not compatible with Windows 9*x* or Windows 2000 and will not run. They can also hang the system if they are started in some rare cases.

### Wrong MS-DOS Version

One of the most common causes for MS-DOS and Windows application crashes in Windows 95 and 98 is that many applications check the version number of MS-DOS before running. If the software reads the wrong version number or a version number in the wrong range, an error occurs and the program crashes. To get around this, Windows 95 and 98 "lies" to applications and passes the right version number.

To achieve this, Windows needs a bit of help tricking MS-DOS programs. Include the following line in the CONFIG.SYS file (remember, lines in CONFIG.SYS overwrite IO.SYS and SYSTEM.DAT commands):

```
device=c:\windows\setver.exe
```

With SETVER.EXE loaded, Windows 95 and 98 report an appropriate version number to your MS-DOS application.

Tricking an old Windows 3.x application is a two-step process. First, find the module name for the application that is crashing. To find an application's module name, start Windows Explorer and then right-click the application's executable (.exe) file. Using QuickView, find the module name. For example, the module name for Microsoft Word is winword.

---

**Note** QuickView is not included in a typical Windows 95 and 98 installation. To load QuickView, open the Control Panel and double-click the Add/Remove Programs icon. In the Add/Remove Programs dialog box, click the Windows Setup tab, then select Accessories. Click Details, check QuickView on the Components list, click OK, then follow the on-screen prompts to install QuickView.

---

Next, add a section to your Windows 95 and 98 WIN.INI file. Open WIN.INI using a text editor and add the following lines:

```
[Compatibility]
compiled_module_name = 0x00200000
```

For example, you would add:

```
winword = 0x00200000
```

## Other MS-DOS Workarounds

Often, MS-DOS applications fail to execute because of missing drivers or the presence of Windows itself. By using the Properties tab of a program's .exe file, you can modify many of the settings that cause your program to fail. To perform this modification, perform the following steps:

1. Open Windows Explorer and find the troublesome MS-DOS .exe file.
2. Right-click that file and select Properties.
3. Click the Program tab.
4. Click Advanced. The Advanced dialog box presents the following options:
   - **Prevent MS-DOS-Based Programs From Detecting Windows.** This hides Windows in memory so MS-DOS programs can't detect it.
   - **Suggest MS-DOS Mode As Necessary.** This is an on-the-fly MS-DOS-mode diagnostic. If Windows detects an application that's likely to run better in MS-DOS, it starts a wizard so that you can customize the application to run in MS-DOS.
   - **MS-DOS Mode.** If this option is selected, the application runs in MS-DOS mode. Within this setting are three additional options:

- **Warn Before Entering MS-DOS.** When entering MS-DOS mode, you should close any open Windows applications and files. This warns you to save files and close any applications that are running.
- **Use Current MS-DOS Configuration.** This uses all the current system settings that have been passed along, including settings in CONFIG.SYS, AUTOEXEC.BAT, IO.SYS, and the Registry.
- **Specify A New MS-DOS Configuration.** This allows you to modify CONFIG.SYS and AUTOEXEC.BAT for MS-DOS mode.

This Properties tab is the Windows 9*x* replacement for the .pif files used in Windows 3.*x*. There are five other tabs for configuring the properties of this MS-DOS application, as follows:

- **General.** Provides the statistics of the file.
- **Font.** Specifies the type of font you want to use.
- **Memory.** Configures expanded and extended memory requirements.
- **Screen.** Offers options for running inside a window or full screen.
- **Misc.** Provides miscellaneous settings.

## Printing Problems

It's frustrating when a printer prints random characters or only part of the data or—worst of all—won't print at all. To help resolve such problems, Windows 9*x* offers the Print Troubleshooter. This tool can be found in Windows 9*x* Online Help. Click the Start menu, then select Help. Windows Online Help opens. Click the Contents tab, select Troubleshoot, and display the topic: If You Have Trouble Printing. The troubleshooter asks a series of questions that lead you through the problem and—hopefully—provides a solution.

If the Print Troubleshooter doesn't solve the problem, you can try the Enhanced Print Troubleshooter (EPTS) that ships with some versions of Windows. This program is found on the distribution CD in the EPTS folder. Copy it with its files from the CD to the hard disk drive. Then start the program EPTS.EXE. This program operates in the same way as the standard version, but is much more detailed.

The following are some further troubleshooting tips if the printer won't print:

- Make sure the power is turned on and the printer is online.
- Check the cable connections.
- Verify that the printer has paper.
- Clear any paper jams.
- Clear the print buffer by turning the printer off and restarting it.
- Make sure the driver and the printer are in the same mode.

- Send a print job directly to the printer (not from an application). Go to an MS-DOS prompt and send a text file directly to the printer, thus bypassing any application.
- Try printing from another application (a simple one, such as Notepad).
- Delete and reinstall the printer.
- Try printing to a file and then copy the file to the printer port.

If the printer takes a long time to print, try these troubleshooting tips:

- Make sure spooling is enabled and that Windows is spooling.
- Make sure the drive on which Windows is installed has enough disk space.
- Defragment the hard disk.
- Check if there are sufficient system resources.
- Upgrade the printer driver if a newer one is available (check the Web site of the printer's manufacturer).
- Make sure Windows is sending TrueType fonts as outlines and not bitmaps (check the Fonts tab of the printer's properties sheet).

If your printouts contain random characters, try these troubleshooting tips:

- Be sure the printer language and type is correctly identified for the job.
- Verify that there is enough printer memory to carry out the job. It's not always easy to tell how much printer memory you need—the printer may just give you an out-of-memory error. It may be useful to either eliminate graphics from the document or select a lower print resolution (you can configure the printer from the application's Print dialog box). This can both speed up printing and possibly eliminate errors due to limited printer memory.
- Print directly to the printer. Go to an MS-DOS prompt and send a text file directly to the printer, thus bypassing any application.
- Use raw spooling instead of Enhanced Metafile Spooling (EMF).
- Print one job only at a time.
- Make sure the printable region isn't larger than what is supported by the printer.

If the File menu's Print command is dimmed, try this troubleshooting tip:

- Verify that a printer driver is installed.

If you cannot print from an MS-DOS program, try the following tip:

- In the printer's properties sheet, deactivate Spool MS-DOS Print Jobs.

## Lesson Summary

The following points summarize the main elements of this lesson:

- Diagnosing operating system issues involve the same step-wise approach as used to deal with hardware problems.
- The Windows platform offers a variety of tools for inspecting, testing, and configuring the operating system.
- If you can bring the operating system into full Windows operating mode, the device manager and MMC offer a variety of ways to investigate and adjust system hardware.
- Safe mode offers a method to bypass 32-bit operation and gain access to system tools.
- DOS mode offers the command prompt, which can be used to run a variety of tools that do not require the Windows GUI. To become an effective A+ technician, one must practice with these various tools on a regular basis. Experience develops both skill with tools and the ability to quickly pinpoint a problem.

# Lesson 3:  Client Relations

Whether you're in business for yourself or part of a large organization, there is more to becoming a computer professional than just fixing computers. Lesson 1 focused on how to stay on top of your profession. This lesson focuses on perhaps the most important element of the professional configuration—the customer. Remember that whether you are a consultant, a contractor, or a staff member of a large organization, you are working on an individual's computer and that individual is your customer. Your customers are your business.

### After this lesson, you will be able to

- Identify the level of support needed to resolve a problem
- Put techniques for offering good customer service to use

### Estimated lesson time: 15 minutes

## Getting Organized and Keeping Records

Repairing computers can be a time-consuming job. When a computer goes down or has some kind of glitch, the owner or operator is inevitably in the middle of a major project and rarely has the time or patience to address the problem. Therefore, being an efficient and effective service provider is as important as being able to resolve hardware or software problems. It is as important to work smart as it is to work hard. Being organized and keeping good records is the key to becoming efficient, effective, and successful.

How much time does it take you to check IRQs every time you install a new card on the same computer? Do you spend too much time rebuilding CONFIG.SYS and AUTOEXEC.BAT files when an end user accidentally erases them? Spending a few minutes reviewing and updating your records each time you install a new system or perform maintenance can save you hours in the long run.

Keep a simple set of documents that contains essential information for each computer you work on. Create a database, spreadsheet, or word processing file to make updating easy. Be sure to back up the data and keep a hard copy on file for quick reference. The following table provides some suggestions about the information you might want to keep.

| Suggestion | Usage |
| --- | --- |
| Name each computer. | The name you choose does not matter, but make it unique and descriptive. Establish naming conventions to make remembering them easier. Use names in addition to serial numbers. |

*(continued)*

| Suggestion | Usage |
|---|---|
| Document all technical information. | Include the operating system name and version, CONFIG.SYS, AUTOEXEC.BAT, IRQs, I/O base address, DMA channels, device driver names, processor type and speed, size of cache, RAM, BIOS, monitor, video card, modems, and sound cards. |
| Save startup data to floppy disks (unique data). | Include the startup disk (based on the current version of the operating system, AUTOEXEC.BAT, and CONFIG.SYS), device driver disks, and recovery disks—as required by antivirus programs or the system. |
| Keep an incident log. | In your log of events for each computer include such things as the user, application installations (date and version), upgrades (hardware), and problems (cause of failure and actions taken for resolution). |

# Levels of Support

In an organization or corporate environment with a large number of computers and peripheral devices, it is often wise to separate support functions into several levels or categories. Depending on the size of the organization and the degree of knowledge of the end users, some technical support can be delegated or handled over the phone. By properly delegating responsibility for technical support, you can avoid being tied up with trivial problems, saving time for you and your end users.

## Level 1: Designated, On-Site User

It is usually possible to designate someone within each department or section to handle simple technical-support questions. Find someone with a basic familiarity with computers and designate that individual as the key contact. He or she can handle many of the trivial problems that often plague inexperienced users (for instance, the computer, mouse, keyboard, or printer is not plugged in) and can also handle basic maintenance (such as performing backups). By delegating these tasks locally, you can ensure that technical support will be available when more serious problems arise. You will also have a knowledgeable source on-site to be your eyes and ears.

How you apply this level of support depends on your situation. If, for example, you are an independent consultant or working at a service desk for a computer supplier, you most likely will be dealing with the owner or user and this won't apply.

## Level 2: Telephone Support

Handle as many problems as possible over the phone. Phone support offers the quickest solution to many common problems. In addition, by getting as much information about the problem as possible over the phone, you can be sure to have the right tools on hand and an appropriate plan if and when you arrive on the scene.

### Level 3: On-Site Service

For those jobs that cannot be handled over the phone, you need to decide whether to service the machine on-site or bring it back to your own workspace. Consider these questions when making this decision:

- Will your repairs interfere with your end user's work?
- Will the end user's location interfere with your work?
- Is the computer in a high-traffic area?
- Is there a lot of activity in the area?
- Will the end user want to help? (Also consider whether or not this would be a benefit.)
- Do you have enough space to do the work?

---

**Tip**    If the work will take more than a few minutes, you might do better to take the machine back to your own workspace.

---

## Spare Parts

Having available a large supply of spare parts can definitely shorten the time to complete a repair; however, having too many spare parts can be a problem as well. Maintaining a large inventory is expensive, especially if you have 100 items that just became obsolete. You need to keep spare parts in stock and you need to manage them. Consider the following tips when determining how to manage your spare parts inventory:

- Know the frequency of failures and, therefore, the number of replacements you are likely to need for your organizational situation.
- Know how long it takes to get replacements and order appropriately.
- Know your suppliers and how quickly they can provide parts when you need them. This way you can keep only what you need on your shelf.
- Buy spare components in bulk whenever possible, especially inexpensive components such as floppy disk drives, cables, mouse devices, ink-jet cartridges, and so forth.
- Standardize your parts to keep your inventory small (see the next section).

## Standardization

Standardizing equipment is very desirable in large organizations. It reduces the number of spare parts required and simplifies installations. However, it is not always possible. Many organizations purchase equipment, such as computers, solely on the basis of the best price available at the time of purchase. Therefore, whichever manufacturer happens to be offering a special deal at that time is likely to get the contract. As a result, the organization eventually assembles a wide assortment of computer equipment, making standardization difficult.

In cases such as this, you can standardize what you have control over and group the rest as best as you can. If you have several identical systems, by using an identical configuration with standard CONFIG.SYS, AUTOEXEC.BAT, and IRQ assignments, you can simplify the troubleshooting process. Even if you have many computers with little in common, adopting certain standards can be worthwhile. For example, establish common IRQs for standard equipment such as modems, sound cards, network cards, and mouse and SCSI devices.

# Customer Service

The bottom line in computer repair is customer service. Whether you work for a large organization or as an independent consultant, the end user is your customer. This section discusses general guidelines for setting up and managing customer service.

## Support Calls

There are generally two methods for handling initial support calls to a technical service department. The first method, and perhaps the most common, is the help desk. Each call is routed through a central location or phone. At this point, the call is evaluated, classified according to the nature and urgency of the problem, and then routed to the appropriate member of the support team for action.

In the second method, any member of the support team can respond to a call and attempt to solve the problem. If that fails to resolve the issue, the problem is passed on to a more knowledgeable team member for action.

It is at this stage that you have the opportunity to put your customer service skills to use. The person who calls you will be sensitive not only to how you resolve the technical problem, but how you treat that individual personally. Chances are that if someone needs to call you, that person's day is already going badly. Your demeanor and expertise can improve it or make it worse. This is especially important if you are in business for yourself; it can mean the difference between building your business with repeat calls and referrals—or bankruptcy.

When you receive a call requesting technical support, going through the following four simple steps should lead to a successful conclusion of the encounter.

- **The greeting.** During this stage, which should be as brief as possible, your purpose is to establish the identity of the caller and the nature of the problem. In some cases, it can also lead to initiating a work order or tracking code to follow and record the event. Following good telephone etiquette is critical, especially if it is your business and your caller is a potential customer who is shopping around for a computer repair professional. This is likely to be your potential customer's first impression of your company.

- **The description.** During the second stage, your task is to obtain a description of the problem. It is important to avoid any miscommunication. Try to pick up audible clues (note significant points, caller's level of expertise, and sense of urgency) and guide the conversation (keep it focused). However, appreciate that you, not the caller, are the expert. Don't become frustrated (or sound frustrated) by the caller's lack of understanding of the problem. After all, if the exact problem were known already, chances are you would not be needed to fix it.

- **The interview.** Use this stage to ask questions. (See "Troubleshooting" in Lesson 1.) Keep your questions short, logical, and as simple as possible. This is not the time to try to impress a customer with your expertise. Keep your questions at a level that will not confuse or intimidate the caller.

- **The closure.** By the fourth stage, the end of the conversation, you should be able to assess and evaluate the information. You should provide the client with a plan of action, including what the next step will be, who will be handling the problem, and when they should expect action.

Take the time to create a form or a database for tracking calls that provides a source of information for future use. Basing the form on keywords chosen to describe the problem briefly allows easy creation of reports.

## Reports and Logs

If you work independently, you should also keep a client profile log that includes a few paragraphs describing each of your clients and their business. Include notations of any relevant facts about clients that you can use in future conversations with them. Also take note of any client plans for future expansion or equipment upgrades that might require your help. It is best to get in the habit of writing this down as soon as possible after your service call, when the important details and observations are still fresh in your mind.

Referrals are the lifeline of any small business. If you feel that your client is satisfied with your work, do not hesitate to ask for referrals and ask if you can use the client's name as a reference. Keep a written record of referrals you receive and contact the referred individual with a phone call or letter as quickly as possible. Also, leave a few business cards with your clients and encourage them to give the cards to anyone who might need your services. Call your clients within a few days after you have serviced their equipment to confirm that their problems have been resolved. They will appreciate it. Technicians who work in a corporate setting find this procedure helpful as well.

## Difficult Clients and Coworkers

You will inevitably encounter difficult clients or coworkers. Keep in mind that it is your job to identify and try to resolve these problems, too, not just those that are mechanically based. The following are a few suggestions for handling difficult clients and coworkers:

- If the user needs training, ensure that information about appropriate courses is available. If the individual is one of your coworkers, speak to the user's manager and identify training needs. If it is a client, gently point out the benefits of obtaining specific training or offer some of your time and expertise for tutoring.

- If the client has difficulty remembering instructions, put them in writing. Give the client a memo or sheet with written instructions—and save the instructions for future use.

- Dealing with technophiles (those who think they are experts) can be a challenge. The best approach is to listen carefully and make them part of the solution, not part of the problem. Remember, they came to you for help. In a corporate or large organizational setting, start an advanced users group and make them responsible for developing solutions, or at least for being part of the solution.

- Require users who are coworkers that constantly complain about trivial problems to put them in writing. Include their notes as part of your records. If those complaining are your clients, charge them for your time.

## Escalating Problems

Because new devices and software are introduced every day, it is not uncommon to encounter problems that are outside the scope of the support group or your current level of experience. In such cases, addressing the problem requires gaining the assistance of the hardware or software supplier. Whether you turn to a more experienced team member or an original equipment manufacturer (OEM), be sure to track the progress of the problem and who retains responsibility.

Of course, if you are an independent service person, you are responsible for doing the research to find a solution to the problem. Keep a record of your resources (phone numbers, individual and company names, Internet addresses, documentation sources) for future reference.

If the problem is resolved by making previously undocumented changes (such as a patch or upgrade by the OEM), be sure to pass along the information to other team members. Also, be sure to keep good documentation of the solution because you may need it for future reference.

## Conclusion

After a service call is concluded (successful or not), there is one more action to take: Document the closure. Make this report as detailed as possible. Include what was done to resolve the problem—or what steps were taken to try to resolve the problem—and the results of your efforts. If the problem was not resolved, explain to the user why it could not be fixed and provide some alternatives. This might include advising the user to return the computer to the dealer from which it was purchased, if it is a relatively new unit. If you are unable to resolve the problem, do not be afraid to pass it on to someone with more experience or someone who specializes in that type of problem.

## Lesson Summary

The following points summarize the main elements of this lesson:

- The customer is most important.
- Keep good records.
- Technical support can be provided at three levels: through a designated on-site user, telephone support, or on-site service. Categorizing jobs by these levels makes your work more efficient.

# Chapter Summary

The following points summarize the key concepts in this chapter:

## Basic Troubleshooting Techniques

- Effective troubleshooting requires approaching the problem in an organized and methodical manner.

- Gather information from the user and the computer before zeroing in on a specific cause.

- Make a plan and stick to it, and don't forget to document!

## Windows Troubleshooting Tools

- Windows 2000 and Windows 98 are two different operating systems, but they share many common troubleshooting tools.

- Two very valuable tools are system information and the Device Manager.

- To effectively troubleshoot the Windows environment you must understand the boot process and the functions of the Registry.

- The basic principles of troubleshooting apply to operating system problems the same way as they do to hardware issues.

- Maintaining a healthy Registry and keeping good backups of these critical files is an important part of maintaining a secure Windows system.

## Client Relations

- Good record-keeping is a key to becoming an efficient and effective service provider.

- Recognize the three levels of support—designated on-site user, telephone support, and on-site service—and know how to delegate to the appropriate level.

- Providing outstanding customer service is critical to being a successful computer technician.

# Review

The following questions are intended to reinforce key information presented in this chapter. If you are unable to answer a question, review the appropriate lesson and then try the question again. Answers to the questions can be found in Appendix A, "Questions and Answers."

1. What is the tool used to restore the Registry in Windows 9*x*? Is it the same as the one used in Windows 2000?

2. What are the five phases of troubleshooting?

3. How important is record-keeping?

4. Explain some possible uses for the Windows 2000 Task Manager in troubleshooting, and name a corollary tool available in Windows 98.

5. What are the three levels of technical support?

6. What is the purpose of the ping command, and how do you use it?

7. Why is it important to standardize equipment in large organizations?

8. What four stages should you go through when you receive a service call?

9. Describe some ways of coping with a difficult client or coworker.


10. Explain some of the skills and challenges involved in troubleshooting.

CHAPTER  2 2

# The Basics of Electrical Energy

Lesson 1: Power .......................................... 608

Lesson 2: Electrostatic Discharge ............................ 624

Lesson 3: Safety and Electrical Power ........................ 627

Chapter Summary .......................................... 629

Review ................................................... 630

## About This Chapter

Computers run on electrical energy. Without it, a computer might as well be a paperweight. Because every component of a computer needs power to run (whether plugged into a wall outlet or a battery), a computer professional must understand the basic principles that govern electricity and electrical energy. This chapter introduces you to these principles.

## Before You Begin

There are no prerequisites for this chapter.

# Lesson 1: Power

The energy or power to drive a computer is derived from electricity. Whether it uses 110 volts alternating current (AC), the U.S. standard; 220 volts AC, the European standard; or direct current (DC) from a battery, a computer is useless without a steady, reliable source of power. When we encounter problems with a computer, it is crucial to be able to test the entire power system. This lesson covers the basics of power and electricity.

### After this lesson, you will be able to

- Explain the difference between electricity and electrical energy
- Define the terms used to measure electrical energy
- Identify basic electric and electronic components
- Perform basic and advanced electrical energy tests

### Estimated lesson time: 45 minutes

## Understanding Electricity and Electrical Energy

What is electricity? The meaning of the word varies with the user. Electricity to physicists is the primal property of nature, and they call the power delivered at the wall socket and stored in batteries electrical energy. Most people, including computer technicians, are less fussy, often using the term *electricity* to refer to both:

- The form of energy associated with moving electrons and protons
- The energy made available by the flow of electric charge through a conductor

For our discussion, we talk mainly about the flow of energy used to run computers—electrical energy—and do not worry about the fine points of scientific philosophy.

### Some Definitions

For our discussion we employ the following definitions:

- **Electricity.** The form of energy associated with charged particles, usually electrons.
- **Electric charge.** When charged particles move in tandem, they generate fields, producing energy.
- **Electrical circuit.** The path taken by an electrical charge.
- **Electric current.** When an electric charge is carried, or flows through a conductor (like wires), it is known as a current. A current-carrying wire is a form of electromagnet. Electric current is also known as *electron flow*.

- **Power.** The rate at which an amount of energy is used to accomplish work. Electrical power is measured in watts, which is determined by multiplying voltage by current.

- **Conductors.** Materials that can carry an electrical current. Most conductors are metals.

- **Resistance.** A quality of some materials that allows them to slow the speed of an electrical current, producing heat, and sometimes light, in the process.

- **Insulators.** Materials that prevent or retard the electrical current of electrons.

- **Ampere.** A measurement of current strength, equal to 1 coulomb per second.

- **Coulomb's law.** Two charges will exert equal and opposite forces on each other. Opposite charges attract and like charges repel.

- **Ohm.** A unit of electrical resistance. Ohm's law states that voltage is equal to the product of the current times the resistance, or voltage = current × resistance.

- **Volt.** The unit of electromotive force, or potential energy, that, when steadily applied against a resistance of 1 ohm, produces a current of 1 ampere.

- **Voltage.** The potential energy of a circuit.

## Ohm's Law

In addition to defining terms, we need to understand some basic principles that are applied in testing electrical devices. One formula that all computer professionals should know is *Ohm's law*. All basic power calculations can be performed from this formula or a derivation of it.

Ohm's law states that the current (electrons) flowing through a conductor, or resistance, is linearly proportional to the applied potential difference (volts). A conductor is any medium, usually metal, that allows the flow of electrical current. Resistance is any device or medium that resists the flow of electrons. In mathematical terms, this means:

Resistance: $R = V/I$

Current: $I = V/R$

Volts: $V = IR$

In these formulas, $R$ = resistance in ohms ($\Omega$), $V$ = voltage, and $I$ = current in amperes.

---

**Note**    In some cases, you may find E used instead of V in formulas expressing Ohm's law. The E stands for electromotive force, and is often used by engineers as a more precise technical term for their measurements.

---

By memorizing any one of these formulas, the other two can be easily derived using simple algebra. For example, the voltage (potential energy of the circuit) is equal to the amperage (the current or flow of electricity) multiplied by any resistance to that flow of electricity. The more resistance there is in a circuit, the lower the current flow for a given voltage.

## Personal Computers and Electrical Power

That personal computers (PCs) use electrical power to operate is no surprise, even to the casual user. The technician must understand the different types of electrical energy and how they work inside the PC. A PC's electrical power can come from a wall outlet, in the form of AC, or from a battery in the form of DC.

### AC Power

AC power is what most people think of as electricity. It comes from the wall and powers most of our lights and household appliances.

AC power is man-made, using generators. As the wire coil inside the generator rotates, it passes by each pole of unit magnet(s) producing an electric current. When it passes the opposite pole, the current reverses, or *alternates*, the direction of flow (see Figure 22.1). The number of revolutions made by the generator per minute is called its *frequency*. In the United States, power companies run their systems at 60 turns per second to produce a high-voltage, 60 Hz (cycles per second) AC as they rotate. The power system drops the voltage in stages before it is connected to the consumer's home or business.

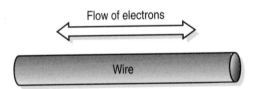

**Figure 22.1**   Flow of electrons

The power company delivers AC power to our homes or businesses with three wires. Two of the wires are *hot*, meaning that they carry a charge. One, the bare wire that runs from the breaker box to the power pole, is *neutral*. The measured voltage between the two hot wires is between 220 and 240 volts AC (VAC), and the measured voltage between either of the hot wires and the neutral wire is between 110 and 120 VAC. These voltages, which are called *nominal* voltages, can vary by plus or minus (±) 10 percent (see Figure 22.2).

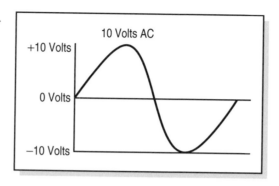

**Figure 22.2** AC volts

Typical electrical outlets are connected between one of the hot wires and the neutral wire. These outlets are usually three-prong connections. The smaller rectangular hole is the hot, the larger rectangular hole is the neutral, and the small round hole is called the *ground*. The ground wire is used as a safety wire. In the event of a short circuit, a large flow of current (amps) is discharged all at one time. This short, strong flow of current will burn out circuits unless it can be safely sent somewhere else. Electricity will always seek the path of least resistance to ground. By providing this wire, a short circuit will cause less damage by providing a path for safe dissipation of the current. To provide a safe working environment for the computer and yourself, make sure that the ground wire is properly installed.

Older structures might have two-wire electrical outlets without the ground wire. An electrical outlet without grounded plugs and the third ground wire is unacceptable for use with a computer (see Figure 22.3). An extension cord without a ground wire is also unacceptable.

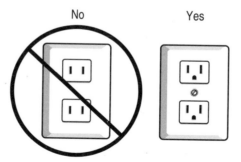

**Figure 22.3** The proper type of outlet includes a ground

**Caution**   A short circuit can cause physical damage to equipment and personnel. It can cause a fire, component damage, permanent disability, or even death. The ground plug provides a direct connection to ground, giving the electricity an alternate path away from equipment and people.

## DC Power

AC is used for transporting low-cost power to end users. However, a computer's electronic components won't run on AC power—they need a steady stream of DC. The PC's power supply performs several tasks, but the main function is to convert AC into DC. A computer's power supply combines two components to handle this job: a *step-down transformer* and an *AC/DC converter*. The AC adapters used for laptop computers, many low-cost ink-jet printers, and many other consumer electronics do the same thing—turn AC into lower voltage DC.

As we have seen, DC is electrical energy that travels in a single direction within a circuit. (The electrical energy in a thunderstorm is another example, but not very practical to electronic applications.) DC current flows from one pole to another, hence it is said to have *polarity* (see Figure 22.4). The polarity indicates the direction of the flow of the current and is signified by the + and – signs (see Figure 22.5).

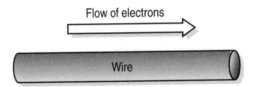

**Figure 22.4**   DC power

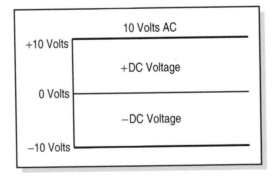

**Figure 22.5**   DC voltage

# Measuring Electricity

A computer professional should know how to use a multimeter—sometimes called a volt-ohm meter (VOM) or a digital volt-ohm meter (DVOM). An electrical test meter is probably the best (and most practical) tool for troubleshooting electrical problems. It is not necessary to be an electronic technician to use this tool effectively.

## The Multimeter

A multimeter is used to measure several aspects of electricity. All multimeters are designed to provide at least four major measurements:

- AC voltage
- DC voltage
- Continuity
- Resistance

A multimeter consists of two probes, an analog or digital meter, and a multiposition switch to select the type of test you wish to perform.

## Testing AC Power

In any new building installation, failure to properly test AC outlets can result in damaged or destroyed equipment, as well as possible injury and electrocution. In the event a wiring error was made that causes the voltage to be outside of the specifications (either two high or too low), problems are sure to arise. Don't take for granted that the building power supply provides the correct voltage or that all of the other inputs are wired correctly.

When testing an AC power source, check these three things:

- Is the hot wire sending the correct voltage, and is it wired to the correct pin?
- Is the neutral wire connected to ground and to the correct pin?
- Is the ground wire connected to ground and to the correct pin?

## Testing AC Outlets with a Multimeter

The first step when testing an AC outlet is setting up the multimeter. Then you need to know how to read the meter. You can also use special equipment if the multimeter does not provide enough information.

## Setting Up the Meter

Basic multimeter usage with AC circuits is quite straightforward:

1. Attach the black test lead to the negative (–) marked hole. In some low-cost meters, leads are permanently attached to the meter.

2. Attach the red test lead to the volts (+) hole. Be careful—if this lead is placed in the wrong hole (ohm or amp) it can cause permanent damage to the meter.

3. Set the selector switch to AC volts (this choice is often denoted by red lettering). If there are multiple selections, use the highest setting possible (if voltage is unknown), or select one level higher than the estimated voltage. For standard household outlets, 200 VAC is a good selection. Some digital meters use "auto-range" and don't need any selection except AC volts.

### Reading the Meter

After the meter is set up, you are ready to test a wall outlet. There are three tests to perform. With AC voltage, it does not matter which lead is placed in which connector.

- **Hot to neutral.** Place one lead in hot (smaller of the two vertical slots) and the other in neutral (larger of the vertical slots). The reading should be between 110 and 120 VAC.

- **Hot to ground.** Place one lead in hot (smaller of the two vertical slots) and the other in ground. The reading should be between 110 and 120 VAC.

- **Neutral to ground.** Place one lead in neutral (larger of the two vertical slots) and the other in ground. The reading should be 0 volts.

### Using AC Testers

An alternate method for testing electrical outlets is to use an AC tester. These small devices are made especially for testing outlets and can be purchased at any home improvement or electronics outlet store. By simply inserting the tester into an outlet, all voltages for all combinations can be tested at the same time. Many testers provide several light-emitting diodes (LEDs) that tell whether or not each function passes the test. This device is not as accurate as a multimeter, but it is more convenient. It will provide a pass–fail indication rather than an accurate voltage reading.

### Testing AC Ripple

The function of the power supply is to convert AC to DC voltage. When it is working properly, a pure DC signal will be produced. However, sometimes, as the power supply ages, its ability to produce pure DC falters. A power supply uses electrolytic capacitors (discussed later in this lesson) to filter or smooth the voltage after it has been converted from AC to DC. These capacitors are second only to fuses as the part of a power supply most likely to fail. When an electrolytic capacitor begins to fail, it allows more and more AC voltage to pass through. This small amount of AC voltage is superimposed on top of the DC voltage and called *noise* or *ripple*. To test for ripple, set a meter to read AC. Then connect a .1µfd (microfarad) capacitor to the red lead. With the power turned on, measure the DC voltage. Any ripple present will be displayed as AC voltage.

## Testing Resistance

*Resistance* is an opposition to the flow of current through a conductor and is measured in ohms ($\Omega$). To find out the level of resistance, place one lead of the meter on each side of the circuit or component to be measured. Keep in mind that measuring a component while it is still soldered in its circuit can lead to inaccurate readings—other components connected to the circuit can affect the total resistance. Unlike voltage checks, you should test resistance with the power off. If a meter is set up to read resistance, you will damage it if you connect it to an electrical outlet.

**Note** Be careful when measuring resistance. If the meter is set too high or the resistance is too high for the meter, you will get an inaccurate reading. Also, before taking a measurement, be sure that any charge stored in a capacitor is properly discharged. Refer to the applicable product manual for details.

## Testing Continuity

*Continuity* is a term used to indicate whether or not a connection exists between one point in a circuit and another. It is used to determine the presence of breaks in wires and electrical circuits.

If no continuity setting is available, use the resistance setting (see the previous section). If the multimeter measures infinite resistance, there is no continuity. This indicates a break in the line. If the multimeter shows little or no resistance, there is continuity and the circuit is complete.

### Testing DC Voltage

Testing for DC voltage is the same as testing for AC voltage, with one important difference: DC voltage is sensitive to polarity. As mentioned earlier, DC voltage has a positive pole (+) and a negative pole (−). When measuring DC voltage, it is important to place the positive (red) lead on the positive side and the negative (black) lead on the negative side of the circuit. If the leads are positioned backward, the polarity of the reading will be the opposite of what it should be.

**Caution** When using an analog meter (one with a dial and needle), connecting the leads backward will cause the needle to move in the opposite direction, possibly damaging the meter.

## Testing a Power Supply

Many computer problems blamed on the operating system or hardware component are really power problems (see Chapter 5, "Power Supplies"). In some cases, it is the power produced and transmitted by the electric utility that will require line conditioning. The quickest way to resolve this is by adding a quality UPS (uninterruptible power supply) with line conditioning circuits (discussed in

Lesson 2 of Chapter 5, "Power Supplies"). Before adding one, test the power supply to make sure it is functioning properly.

**Note** Find out if the client is having any problems with flickering lights or intermittent problems with other appliances, or if he or she is using a power strip with too many connections for the rated use. Improper loading of the circuit, not the PC itself, can be the problem.

A bad power supply can cause intermittent lockups and unexpected computer reboots. Erratic problems encountered during booting and changed or erased CMOS (complementary metal-oxide semiconductor) information can also be traced to a failing power supply. Bad power supplies have been known to destroy data on mass-storage devices (such as hard drives, tape drives, and so on). There are two types of tests for power supplies: a basic test used to verify voltages and an advanced test for checking its internal components.

### Basic Voltage Test

The only purpose of this test is to verify the existence and value of voltages. With time, most power supplies show their age by a reduction in voltage. This voltage drop will show itself in both the 5-volt and the 12-volt outputs, but is more pronounced on the 12-volt side.

### Prepare the Meter for the Test

Again, meter preparation is quite simple:

1. Connect the black lead to the common (–) connector and the red lead to the voltage (+) connector.

2. Turn the test selector to DC volts. If the meter has an AC/DC switch, be sure it is set to DC. If the meter does "auto-range," set the range to 15–20 volts.

### Testing the Voltages

The best place to check voltage is at the power supply's P8/P9 or ATX power connectors (see Chapter 5, "Power Supplies"). For P8/P9 systems, use the following instructions:

1. Place the meter's black (ground) lead on the black wire connection and its red (positive) lead on the yellow (+12 volt) connection.

2. Record the voltages. A good power supply will provide a voltage between 11 and 13 volts DC.

3. Replace the power supply if the voltage reading is less than 10.

**Note** Be sure to reverse the leads when using an analog meter to check negative voltages. This is not necessary with a digital meter because it will simply show a negative sign with the reading.

## When No Voltage Is Present

If you have completed the basic voltage test and no voltage is present, the problem may not be the power supply. It might, instead, be caused by an excessive load on the system due to another piece of hardware. To determine if that is the case, try the following procedure.

## Isolating the Problem

First you should test the hardware:

1. Disconnect the Molex leads from the power supply.
2. Connect the meter leads, as described in the previous sections.
3. Turn off the AC power.
4. Disconnect all the Molex plugs from the devices.
5. Turn the power back on. If power is present at the motherboard, one of the devices is bad and is causing a drain on the power supply.
6. Reconnect each Molex plug, one at a time, and test the power. When the power drops out, you have located the offending device.

## Advanced Testing

The basic test is designed to quickly isolate the power supply as a problem. In most cases, if the test proves the power supply to be defective, it may be more cost-effective to replace the power supply than to try to repair it. Advanced testing requires a working knowledge of power supplies and removal of the power supply and its cover.

There are three sections to a power supply: the switching network, the transformer, and the voltage regulator (see Figure 22.6).

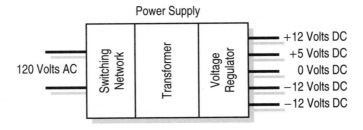

**Figure 22.6**   Power supply

## The Switching Network

AC power coming from the power company is imperfect. It is not uncommon to have sudden increases in voltage called *spikes* or decreases in voltage called *sags* (see Chapter 5, "Power Supplies").

To smooth out the power sent to the electronic components, a PC has basic line conditioning capability—a *switching network*. The better the power supply, the more sophisticated the network. The main components found in a switching network are a fuse, capacitors, rectifiers, and switching transistors.

The switching network performs the following three tasks:

- Filters electrical noise (spikes, sags)
- Eliminates frequency changes (ensuring that current stays at a constant 60 cycles)
- Converts AC *sine wave* signals to AC *square wave* signals

### The Transformer

The *transformer* reduces the voltage of the *square wave* DC into separate 12-volt and 5-volt square wave AC circuits (see Figure 22.7).

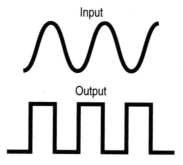

**Figure 22.7** Transformer voltage

### The Voltage Regulator

The *voltage regulator* receives the low-voltage AC outputs of the transformer and converts them to clean DC power. The main components in this section are rectifiers, capacitors, and coils.

The voltage regulator performs three functions:

- It uses rectifiers (diodes) to convert the square wave AC output of the transformer into DC output (see Figure 22.8).
- It regulates the voltage to a constant output level and uses capacitors to remove any ripples that are present.
- It monitors the amount of current used by the computer circuits and adjusts the switching network using a special circuit called the *feedback circuit*. This compensates for variations in load on the power supply.

12 Volt AC          12 Volt DC

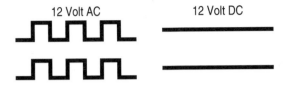

**Figure 22.8**   Regulator section voltage

**Caution**   Do not open the power supply while it is plugged in, and do not open the power supply until it has been discharged. The power supply can carry dangerous levels of power even when disconnected. Only a properly trained technician should ever open a PC power supply. Given the cost of a power supply, there is no good reason to disassemble one; defective units should be replaced.

## Electronic Components

As a computer professional, you should be familiar with the more common types of electronic components found in a computer design.

### Fuse

Before the advent of the circuit breaker, fuses were common in the home and office. A fuse serves one purpose—to fail, and thus cut the flow of power in the event of a current load that has exceeded the safe capacity that the system components can absorb. Fuses come in many shapes and sizes, but a PC fuse is almost always a small, clear, glass tube with metal caps on each end and a wire inside the tube to electrically connect the two caps (see Figure 22.9). In general, the thicker the wire, the more current a fuse can conduct before failing. When a fuse fails, the wire will melt or be broken. You can check for a "blown" fuse by determining if the wire is intact or broken. The amperage (A) rating (stamped on the metal cap) indicates the maximum current the wire is rated to conduct. Be sure not to exceed to the rated limits of the PC design for a fuse, because an excess power load can damage or destroy the system.

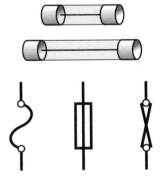

**Figure 22.9**   Fuses

If a fuse in a specific location fails more than once or repeatedly, the system is being overloaded, and you need to isolate the problem causing the failure. Fuses are often found on power supplies and many external components. If a fuse fails, first try to replace it with another fuse of the same rating. If the replacement also fails, the fault probably lies with the motherboard or another internal component.

## Capacitors

A *capacitor* is an electrical component used to hold an electrical charge. In photography, electronic flashes use capacitors to build up power before a picture is taken and to vary the amount of power used in a flash to control the exposure. In PCs, they are often used to regulate the flow of current to areas of the system circuits for a short period of time. Some are fixed-capacity models, whereas others can absorb or hold variable amounts of power. The amount of electrical current a capacitor can control is called *capacitance,* measured in microfarads (see Figure 22.10).

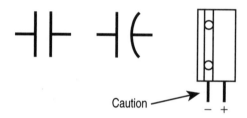

**Figure 22.10**   Capacitors

Most PC power supplies employ an *electrolytic* capacitor. These devices are able to retain a significant charge for long periods. You should work with such components only if you are properly trained to release any residual charge before disconnecting, testing, removing, or replacing one. Failure to follow safe procedures can result in injury or death to you and damage to the system. These capacitors have a distinct polarity (negative and positive) to their two leads.

---

**Caution**    Before you test a capacitor you must discharge the power supply. Failure to discharge can create a serious hazard to you and your equipment.

---

## Rectifiers and Diodes

*Rectifiers* are devices that convert AC power into a DC form (rectification). A *diode* is a device that lets current flow in only one direction (see Figure 22.11). Two or more diodes connected to an AC supply will convert the AC voltage to DC voltage.

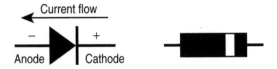

**Figure 22.11**   Diodes

Single diodes are generally used to convert AC to pulsating DC (see Figure 22.12). Two diodes working in parallel produce half-wave rectification, resulting in a pulsating DC. Four diodes produce full-wave rectification, with a continuous stream of pulses.

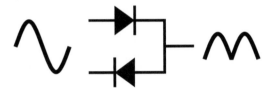

**Figure 22.12**   Half-wave rectifier

Normally, a computer technician does not test at this level; however, diodes can be tested with a multimeter. With the power turned off, test for resistance across both leads of the diode. Then reverse the leads of the multimeter and test again. A good diode will exhibit low resistance in one direction and high resistance in the other.

## Transistors

The invention of the compact, power-efficient, and reliable transistor transformed the modern electronics industry, replacing bulky, power-hungry, and temperamental vacuum tubes. Transistors are basically a pair of diodes connected in series with an on–off switch (see Figure 22.13). Varying the voltage sent to a transistor turns the switch on or off. Early computers used vacuum tubes as switches and were so large that technicians could actually step inside the larger ones to plug in or remove the tubes to program them.

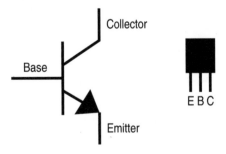

**Figure 22.13**   Transistors

Transistors can be tested, although, this often requires special equipment. Due to the reliability of transistors, a computer technician normally does not need to perform this level of testing.

## Transformers

The most common forms of electrical transformers are step-down or step-up devices. A step-down transformer decreases the transformer's voltage on the output side; a step-up model increases it. Both have a primary wire coil connected to other coils—secondary coils—joining two or more AC circuits.

Electronic transformers generally contain stacks of thin metal-alloy sheets, known as *laminations,* with coils of copper wire wound around them. They are commonly employed in a circuit along with a rectifier that, as we have seen, supplies DC power to the equipment. In the PC power supply, the transformer's secondary coils are used to provide 12-volt, 5-volt, and 3.3-volt outputs used by various components (see Figure 22.14).

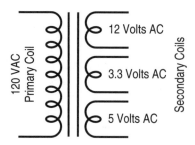

**Figure 22.14**   Transformer

## Testing a Transformer

As noted, a transformer is made up of several coils of wire. Because each coil in the transformer is continuous, each can also be tested for continuity. Follow these steps:

1. Disconnect the power.
2. Discharge all capacitors.
3. Check the bottom of the circuit board of the power supply to be sure all leads have been disconnected. The primary connections, as well as the secondary connections, can be located below the transformer.
4. Configure the multimeter to measure continuity (or resistance).
5. Simultaneously touch each lead of the multimeter to one of the pairs of contacts.

A good transformer will show a reading of low resistance. A very high reading could indicate that one of the coils is broken.

### Inductors (Coils)

*Inductors,* commonly called *coils* because of their shape, are loops of conductive wire (see Figure 22.15). Current passing through the inductor sets up a magnetic field. This field reduces any rapid change in current intensity. Inductors can also be used to distinguish between rapidly and slowly changing signals in a circuit.

**Figure 22.15**    Coil

### Testing a Coil

Because an inductor is simply a wire coil, it can be tested for continuity in much the same way a transformer is tested.

Visually inspect the wire for deterioration. If it shows signs of breakage or burned areas, it should be replaced. If the wire looks good, follow up with a conductivity test. Turn the system power off. Disconnect one lead to the coil (this might require a soldering iron) and connect one meter lead to each end of the coil. A null or low reading indicates continuity. A reading of high or infinite resistance indicates a lack of continuity. Replace the coil.

## Lesson Summary

The following points summarize the main elements of this lesson:

- Ohm's law is the basic formula for power calculations.
- There are two types of power: AC and DC.
- A multimeter is used to measure volts, amps, continuity, and resistance.
- A computer technician should be familiar with the various electronic components found on a power supply circuit board.
- In a new installation, a computer technician should never assume that the power supplied in the wall outlets is correct. Always test and be sure.
- Be careful with large electrolytic capacitors. They can store electrical charges and must be discharged before it is safe to work with them.

# Lesson 2:  Electrostatic Discharge

This lesson discusses a phenomenon that can damage or ruin sensitive electronic equipment—electrostatic discharge (ESD), sometimes referred to as static electricity. Fortunately, it is one of the easiest things to protect against.

---

### After this lesson, you will be able to

- Define ESD
- Avoid ESD

### Estimated lesson time: 15 minutes

---

## Causes of ESD

The human body has an electric field and, under the right (and very easy to obtain) conditions, can generate a tremendous amount of voltage, often referred to as static electricity.

ESD occurs when an imbalance in the amounts of positive and negative electrical charges on the surface of an object is released. The most dramatic example of ESD is lightning, which splits trees as easily as it lights up the sky. The amount of energy released when you touch a metal object can be quite large. The buildup of energy with nylon clothes can easily reach 21,000 volts. About 750 volts are required to produce a visible spark with ESD, and a mere 10 volts or so can ruin a computer chip.

The actual amount of energy in a given ESD event depends on the types of materials involved (wool fabrics generate less than nylon), the humidity (low humidity offers less resistance to the discharge), the amount of physical energy (friction) involved, and how quickly the energy is released.

---

**Note**    ESD does not have to be seen (as a spark) to do damage to electronic components. Voltages lower than 10 volts can damage some parts.

---

### ESD Damage

Over the years, engineers have produced smaller and smaller components, which operate at lower and lower voltages. Their goal is to reduce size, cost, and operational heat production. Those are worthy goals but, because of reduced component size, they present a smaller target with less resistance to power surges. This makes the parts more susceptible to damage from ESD.

The amount of damage and resulting problems caused by ESD can be divided into three categories:

- **Catastrophic failure.** This is sometimes referred to as "frying" or "smoking" a part because of the heat (and sometimes the noise and smoke) generated during the failure. Mishandling and misapplication of a power source, cable, or test instrument are the most likely causes. Care in opening, installing, cabling, and testing are the best ways to prevent this type of ESD damage.

- **Upset failure.** An ESD can produce an erratic fault in a component. This kind of problem is very difficult to detect and repair because the failure is intermittent. It is easy to blame the operating system or a program operation for the data loss or system crash. The best way to diagnose and correct this type of problem is to remove and replace suspected parts until the failure stops appearing.

- **Latent failure.** This type of failure weakens the actual transistor. The affected part will seem normal in most operations and will frequently pass quality control and conformance tests. Like upset failures, these can be very difficult to isolate.

## Preventing ESD

Prevention is the best defense against ESD, and the first step in prevention is to understand the source. The leading cause of ESD damage is improper handling of electronic devices. A semiconductor device can be damaged by ESD during handling before it is installed.

The key to ESD prevention is to keep all electronic components—and yourself—at a common electrical potential. This usually means ground potential, or zero volts. Maintain a habit of "grounding" yourself to the computer chassis whenever you attempt a repair. There are times when it is not practical, or convenient, to wear a ground strap. At such times, touching part of the metal chassis before removing devices will bring you and the computer chassis to a common voltage. Don't move around while installing or handling a part; doing so can generate additional voltages, negating any effort you have made to eliminate ESD.

All repair shops and workbenches should have proper ESD suppression devices, and technicians should use them whenever working with exposed parts. These devices include:

- **Antistatic mats.** Nonconducting pads placed on the work surface and on the floor in front of the work area.

- **Antistatic wristband.** A wristband with a grounding strap connected to the chassis of the PC.

- **Antistatic pouches.** A sealed, antistatic pouch used to store any sensitive electronic device, including hard disk drives, when they are not installed in a computer.

- **Antistatic pad.** An insulating foam pad in which individual chips with exposed pins should be embedded when they are not installed in a computer.

---

**Caution**    AC voltage can kill. Although the power used by the computer components is no more than 12 volts DC, many computers have 110 VAC wired from the power supply to the on–off switch at the front of the computer case. This wiring can present a hazard. Never disconnect or remove boards from a computer with the power applied. This can damage the components.

---

**Caution**    Safety precautions are different for computer monitors. Never work on a monitor with the cabinet removed, power applied, and a wrist strap on; a wrist strap coming in contact with the high-voltage wire (30,000 volts) can cause electrocution.

---

## Lesson Summary

The following points summarize the main elements of this lesson:

- ESD damages computer components.
- ESD can occur without detection.
- ESD can be prevented.

# Lesson 3:  Safety and Electrical Power

Computers are electronic equipment and therefore consume electricity. Although most components in a computer operate on low voltages—in the safe range between 3.3 and 12 volts DC—the main power source and the monitor use high voltages. This lesson sets out some basic high-voltage electrical safety guidelines.

## After this lesson, you will be able to

- Identify high-voltage hazards
- Define some common guidelines for electrical safety

## Estimated lesson time: 5 minutes

## Electrical Safety Is Your Responsibility

Standard wall outlets in the United States provide a nominal 120 VAC and are rated to deliver currents between 15 and 20 amps. Under certain conditions, it is possible to receive a lethal shock from much lower voltages than these. Inside a computer, and especially inside the monitor, voltages as high as 30,000 volts can exist even after the power is turned off.

It is vital to follow basic electrical safety guidelines when servicing a computer. There is no substitute for common sense. However, here are a few tips:

- When in doubt about the correct way to safely service a part of a computer, don't do it. Have an experienced professional do the necessary work.
- Always use grounded outlets and power cords.
- Switch the power off and disconnect all equipment from its power source before removing any covers.
- Always replace blown fuses with fuses of the correct rating and type.
- Do not work alone—you might need help in an emergency.
- Remove all jewelry and any wristwatch. These are conductors that can cause short circuits.
- Have trained personnel service computer power supplies and monitors; these devices use and store potentially lethal voltages (often for days or longer).
- Work with one hand. Using two hands can cause a direct circuit, via your heart, from one object to another.

In the United States, common AC wiring uses the color coding given in the following table.

| Connection | Color |
| --- | --- |
| Live or hot | Black |
| Neutral | White |
| Ground | Green or bare copper |

**Caution**   Color codes for AC wires and DC wires can be different. For example, the *ground* wires on the P8 and P9 connector for an AT-style motherboard are black.

## Lesson Summary

The following point summarizes the main elements of this lesson:

- Electrical safety is your responsibility. Be sure to follow all safety guidelines listed for the devices you work with, and do not work inside of products such as monitors or power supplies without special training.

# Chapter Summary

The following points summarize the key concepts in this chapter:

## Power

- Ohm's law states that the current flowing through a conductor, or resistance, is linearly proportional to the applied potential difference (volts).

- Electricity is delivered to our homes and businesses as AC. Computers use DC.

- Electricity always seeks the path of least resistance to ground. An electrical outlet or an extension cord without a ground wire is unacceptable for use with a computer.

- A multimeter is an instrument used to measure electrical voltage, current, resistance, and continuity.

## Electrostatic Discharge

- ESD depends on the types of materials and the amount of friction involved, the humidity, and how quickly the energy is released. ESD can cause damage to computer parts. Always take preventive measures when working around a computer.

## Safety and Electrical Power

- It is vital to follow basic electrical safety guidelines when working around electrical and electronic devices. Remember, electrical safety is your responsibility.

# Review

The following questions are intended to reinforce key information presented in this chapter. If you are unable to answer a question, review the appropriate lesson and then try the question again. Answers to the questions can be found in Appendix A, "Questions and Answers."

1. What is Ohm's law?

2. What is the formula for Ohm's law for voltage?

3. What is the difference between AC and DC?

4. What instrument is used to measure the various components of electricity?

5. How do you test for continuity?

6. What is AC ripple? How do you test for it?

7. Describe ESD and how to prevent it.

8. What is a latent failure? What makes it especially troublesome?

9. What is a catastrophic failure?

10. When working with a computer, when is it acceptable to use an AC power supply that is not grounded?

APPENDIX   A

# Questions and Answers

## Chapter 1

Page 10

1. Give an example of an early electronic computer.

   **Among the early electronic computers were the Atanasoff-Berry Computer (ABC), ENIAC (Electronic Numerical Integrator and Computer), and Colossus.**

2. What are the three roles that today's computer service professional needs to assume?

   **Today's computer professional needs to be a technician, a scholar, and a diplomat.**

## Chapter 2

Page 23

1. What is the definition of a bus in a computer?

   **A computer bus is a group of electrical conductors (usually wires) running parallel to each other. These conductors can be copper traces on a circuit board or wires in a cable. Usually, they are found in multiples of eight (8, 16, 32, 64, and so on).**

2. What is the purpose of the computer bus?

   **The purpose of the computer bus is to provide a common path to transmit information, in the form of code, to all parts of the computer.**

3. Define the term *decimal*.

   **Decimal, as it is used in this book, refers to the decimal numbering system, based on the ten numbers between 0 and 9.**

4. Describe the difference between serial and parallel communication.

   **Serial communication sends each piece of information one bit at a time on one wire, and parallel communication sends as many bits of information at a time as there are parallel wires.**

5. What is binary code language?

**Binary code language is computer language. The language is called binary because it is based on two states or numbers (0 and 1) represented by a switch condition being set either on or off.**

6. How does ASCII use binary code to represent numbers or characters?

**Computers use the binary system for communication, based on 8 bits (or 1 byte) of information being transmitted at one time. To support this, a standard code called ASCII (American Standard Code for Information Interchange) was developed as the basis for computer communication. Basic ASCII consisted of 128 binary codes that represented the English alphabet, punctuation, and certain control characters.**

7. Define a bit.

**A bit is the smallest unit of information that is recognized by a microcomputer. It is similar to a light bulb in that it can exist only in two states—it is either on or off.**

8. Define a byte.

**A byte is a group of 8 bits. To represent one character of information requires 1 byte.**

9. Which decimal number does the following binary number represent: 00001001?

**This binary number represents the decimal number 9.**

10. What do 1s and 0s represent in computer operation?

**1s and 0s represent voltage to a computer: The absence of voltage represents a 0 bit, and the presence of voltage represents a 1 bit.**

11. Computer buses are usually made of multiples of _____ wires or traces.

**Computer buses are usually found in multiples of 8 wires or traces.**

# Chapter 3

Page 38

1. Describe the three stages of computing and the role of each.

**The three stages of computing are input, processing, and output. Input receives data from outside the current process, or the machine. Processing is the phase where the data received from input is operated on by the application code. Output is the result of the process. The output may actually be the input for another process.**

2. What is the purpose of the central processing unit (CPU)?

**The central processing unit (CPU) is the heart and brain of the computer. This one component or "chip" does all the number crunching and data management.**

3. Describe two devices that process information inside a computer.

**The CPU and the chip set process information inside a computer.**

4. What is a chip set?

**A chip set is a group of computer chips or ICs (integrated circuits) that, when working in harmony, manage and control the computer system.**

5. Name and describe three input devices.

**The mouse, keyboard, microphone, and scanner are examples of input devices. The keyboard accepts character data that is converted from impulses into an inert value, representing the character on the individual key. A microphone converts analog pulses into a digital format that can be used or stored by the computer. A scanner uses an optical array to convert data into a graphic format that can be used or edited.**

6. What type of device is a scanner?

**A scanner is an input device.**

7. Describe three output devices.

**The printer, monitor, and speakers are examples of output devices. A printer produces a hard copy form of the contents of a file, the monitor produces a visual representation of the user interface, and the speakers convert digital information into an analog form that is understood as sound by the human ear.**

8. What is I/O?

**Many devices can handle both input and output functions. These devices are called I/O devices.**

9. Name three I/O devices.

**The floppy disk drive, hard disk drive, modem, and network interface card are examples of I/O devices.**

# Chapter 4

Page 74

1. What is the language of the computer?

**Binary code is the language of the computer.**

2. What is an external data bus?

**The external data bus is the primary bus for handling the flow of data. All devices that process data are connected to the external data bus.**

3. Describe an integrated circuit (IC).

**An integrated circuit is an electronic device consisting of many miniature transistors and other circuit elements (resistors and capacitors, for instance).**

4. Define a clock cycle.

**The timing for all activities within a computer is set by the computer's clock (but not the one that keeps the date and time). Each pulse of voltage produced by the clock is called a clock cycle.**

5. What are the advantages of a Pentium processor over a 486?

**Many improvements were made to the Pentium chip that made it superior to the 486, including:**

- **Faster speeds**
- **A 32-bit address bus and 32-bit registers**
- **A 64-bit data path to improve the speed of data transfers**
- **A dual pipeline, 32-bit data bus that allows the chip to process two separate lines of code simultaneously**
- **A write-back cache of at least 8 KB for data and an 8 KB write-through cache**
- **Branch prediction—the program cache attempts to anticipate branching within the code**

6. What is the difference between SX and DX in a 386 chip?

**The 80386DX was a true 32-bit processor with a 32-bit external data bus, 32-bit registers, and a 32-bit address bus (enabling 4 GB of memory to be accessed). The 80386SX was similar to the DX except that it had a 16-bit external data bus and a 24-bit address bus (it could address only 16 MB of memory).**

7. Which computers use the Motorola 68040 chip?

**Some Apple Macintoshes use the Motorola 68040 chip.**

8. Define microprocessor.

**A microprocessor is an integrated circuit that contains a complete CPU on a single chip.**

9. In computer code language _____ means on and _____ means off.

**In computer code language the number 1 means on and the number 0 means off.**

10. Define clock speed.

**Clock speed, a main selling point for today's PC computer, is the system clock rate, measured in megahertz (MHz). One MHz equals 1 million cycles per second. Clock speed is the number of times per second that a computer can process an instruction.**

11. What is the function of the address bus?

**The CPU accesses memory through an additional bus called the address bus. The number of conductors in the address bus determines the maximum amount of memory that can be used by the CPU.**

12. Microprocessor chips (CPUs) are manufactured in a variety of sizes and shapes. Name as many different kinds as possible.

**Examples of chip packages are DIP, PGA, PLCC, and PQFP.**

13. Name the basic types of CPU sockets.

**The LIF and ZIF sockets are the two basic CPU sockets. The Pentium II and later Intel processors use Slot 1 sockets.**

14. If a customer brought you an old Pentium 60-based computer and asked you to install a new processor, what would your advice be?

**Consider upgrading the CPU and motherboard to a newer CPU and matching motherboard.**

# Chapter 5

Page 90

1. Explain the differences among spikes, surges, and sags.

**Spikes and surges are brief, but often catastrophic, increases in the voltage source (very high voltage for a very short time). These can be caused by the power source (the local power company) but most often are caused by lightning strikes. A spike (or transient) is a very short over-voltage condition measured in nanoseconds, while a surge is measured in milliseconds. A sag is a brief decrease of voltage at the source.**

2. What are the two types of power supply connectors to the motherboard?

**AT style with two plugs—P8 and P9, and the ATX style with a single connector.**

3. What are the two types of power supply connectors for devices such as drives?

**The Molex, a 5-volt connector, is used for hard disk drives, and the mini 3.3 volt is used for floppy disk drives and similar devices.**

4. Name two benefits of having a UPS on a system.

**The UPS (uninterruptible power supply) provides the user some time to save data and properly shut down a system in the event of a power outage. The UPS also conditions the line in the event of a spike or surge.**

5. Describe the difference between a brownout and a blackout.

**A brownout is a decrease in the voltage in the power supply. A blackout is a total power failure.**

6. When you purchase a UPS, what is the most important thing to consider?

**The UPS offers enough time to power the computer until all data can be saved and the computer can be properly shut down.**

7. Will any surge suppressor provide protection against lightning strikes?

**No, surge suppressors offer limited protection, and this decreases with age. Also, nothing can totally protect against a nearby full-force lightning strike.**

8. What is the best defense against spikes caused by lightning?

**To protect against spikes from lightning, unplug your computer from the wall outlet.**

9. What is the most important thing to remember when connecting a P8 and P9 connector to a motherboard?

**The black (ground) wires must be installed next to each other.**

10. Explain the difference between the mini connector and the Molex connector.

**The Molex connector is the most common connector and is used primarily for devices that need both 12-volt and 5-volt power, such as older floppy disk drives, hard disk drives, and CD-ROM drives.**

**The mini connector is used primarily on 3.5-inch floppy drives. Most systems provide a mini connector.**

11. Describe the best way to make sure a new power supply matches the one you are replacing.

**Take the old one with you and match its physical size, as well as the power ratings and number of connectors, to the new one.**

12. What is the primary use of mini connectors?

**Mini connectors are primarily used for 3.5-inch floppy disk drives.**

13. A computer power supply has both 5-volt and 12-volt outputs. The 5-volt output is used to power _____, and the 12-volt output is used to power _____.

**The 5-volt output is used to power devices that manage data only, and the 12-volt output is used to power devices that have moving parts, such as drives and fans.**

# Chapter 6

Page 117

1. What is the main function of the motherboard?

**The motherboard is the primary card in the computer. It defines the limits for CPU type, speed, memory, and expandability.**

2. Name the typical chips found in a chip set.

**A motherboard comes with several chips soldered in place. They constitute the chip set and are designed to work with the CPU. These chips are highly complex and coordinated ICs that help the CPU manage and control the computer's system. Included in the chip set are the clock generator, bus controller, system timer, interrupt controller, DMA controller, CMOS, and keyboard controller.**

3. What is EMI?

**EMI stands for electromagnetic interference. EMI is the same thing as radio frequency interference (RFI), but EMI is a newer term. EMI is con-**

sidered to be any radio frequency that is emitted from an electrical or electronic device that is harmful to the surrounding equipment or that interferes with the operation of another electrical or electronic device.

4. What are ROM chips used for?

ROM chips are used extensively to program the operation of computers, but ROM plays a limited role in the PC; it holds the BIOS information used to describe the system configuration and the instructions for performing the POST routine.

5. Name the three types of ROM chips.

The first type of ROM chip is called the core chip and includes hardware that is common, necessary, and unchanging. The second type of ROM chip is hardware that is common, necessary, and changeable; these chips are called updatable chips. The third type of chip includes any chip other than the first two types of chips.

6. Describe what makes the CMOS special.

The CMOS chips are updatable, and that makes them special. They do not store programs like other ROM chips do; they store only data that is used by the BIOS for the programs needed to communicate with changeable hardware. The CMOS chip also maintains date and time information when the computer is powered off.

7. How can a technician use the POST beep codes?

The purpose of the first POST (power-on self test) is to check the most basic components. Because the video integrity has not been confirmed, any errors that occur in this phase are indicated by a series of beeps. A technician can use the beep codes to interpret any problems that occur before the video is confirmed.

8. What is a device driver?

A device driver is a program that acts as an interface between the operating system and the control circuits that operate the device.

9. What information is contained in the CMOS?

Typically, the CMOS contains at least the following information: floppy and hard disk drive types, CPU and memory size, date and time, and serial- and parallel-port information.

10. Define the POST and describe its function.

Every time a computer is turned on or reset, the entire system is reset. From this on or reset state, it begins to carry out software instructions from its BIOS program. The first set of instructions it initiates is a special program (stored on a ROM chip) called the power-on self test (POST). The POST sends out standardized commands that check every device (in more technical terms, it runs an internal self-diagnostic routine).

# Chapter 7

Page 144

1. What is hexadecimal shorthand used for?

   **Hexadecimal shorthand (hex, for short) is a numbering system used by designers and programmers to simplify the representation of numbers and notations. Known as "base-16 mathematics," it is a complete numbering system based on 16 instead of 10. Just as in the base-10 system, you can add, subtract, or do trigonometry with hex.**

2. Define the following terms: conventional memory, expanded memory, extended memory, HMA, shadow RAM.

   **Conventional memory is the first 640 KB of memory in a computer. The first 1 MB of memory was divided into two sections: 384 KB of RAM (designated upper memory) for running the computer (BIOS, video RAM, and ROM) and 640 KB for applications (designated).**

   **Expanded memory is memory that conforms to the EMS specification, developed by Lotus, Intel, and Microsoft. It requires a special device driver. EMS is accessed through 64-KB blocks of the upper memory.**

   **Extended memory is any memory beyond the first 1 MB.**

   **HMA is the first 64 KB of extended memory on machines with 80286 or higher processors.**

   **Shadow RAM rewrites (or shadows) the contents of the ROM BIOS and/or video BIOS into extended RAM memory (between the 640-KB boundary and 1 MB). This allows systems to operate faster when application software calls for any BIOS routines.**

3. Describe the difference between ROM and RAM.

   **ROM is read-only memory and cannot be changed. It is usually used for BIOS or other data that cannot be lost if the power is off.**

   **RAM is random access memory and is constantly changing. It is used as the main working memory for a computer. RAM memory is lost if the power is turned off.**

4. How many 30-pin SIMM boards are required for one bank of memory on a computer with a 486 processor?

   **Because a 486 computer has a 32-bit external data bus, it requires four 30-pin SIMMs per bank. Remember, a 30-pin SIMM is only one byte (8 bits) wide; therefore, you need to divide the width of the bus by the width of the SIMM—that is, 32 bits (the width of data bus) divided by 8 (the number of bits per SIMM module).**

5. What is the difference between write-through and write-back cache?

   **Some caches immediately send all data directly to RAM, even if it means hitting a wait state. This is called write-through cache. Some caches store the data for a time and send it to RAM later. This is called a write-back cache.**

6. What is DRAM?

   **DRAM (dynamic random access memory) is volatile memory that works only when the computer has power. This is the "scratch pad" that the CPU uses to manipulate data.**

7. Define access speed.

   **The time required to complete a memory read or to write actions is known as the access speed of the memory chip. This time is usually very small and is measured in nanoseconds (one-billionth of a second—abbreviated as ns). The faster the chip, the smaller the access-speed number.**

8. Describe the major difference between SIPPs and SIMMs.

   **A SIPP (single inline pin package) is a printed circuit board with individual DRAM chips mounted on it. SIMMs (single inline memory modules) are the new generation of memory chips. They are similar to SIPPs, with one exception—SIMMs have no pins, as such. 30-pin SIMMs have 30 contacts along the edge.**

9. Define cache memory.

   **To cache means to set something aside, or to store nearby, for anticipated use. Mass storage (disk drives) is much slower than RAM, and RAM is much slower than the CPU. Caching increases the speed of the system by creating special storage areas in high-speed memory.**

10. One of the differences between DRAM and SRAM is that SRAM does not have to be refreshed. What does this mean, and how does it affect the cost of each type of chip?

   **Refreshing means that the information must be updated constantly or it will be lost. SRAM does not require that extra step that can slow things down (nothing can access the memory during a refresh). Because SRAM is faster, the circuitry required is more expensive.**

# Chapter 8

Page 177

1. Why does a computer need an expansion bus?

   **Expansion slots on the motherboard are standardized connections that allow the installation of any device not soldered to the motherboard. By providing this connection to the expansion bus, computers can be customized to meet the requirements of the user.**

2. Name the available expansion buses.

   **The available expansion buses are: ISA, MCA, EISA, VESA, AGP, and PCI.**

3. What happens if two non-PCI devices use the same I/O address?

   **The computer will lock up.**

4. How many IRQs are available on most PCs?

   **There are 15 IRQs available, although some of them are permanently assigned and, therefore, unavailable for use.**

5. Under what conditions would a second modem—installed and assigned to COM3—not work?

   **If the first modem had been using COM1, the failure would be the result of an IRQ conflict. Devices assigned to COM1 and COM3 both make use of IRQ4. If the first modem has already been assigned to COM1, a conflict will occur when both modems make use of IRQ4.**

   **One solution is to assign COM3 an available interrupt, such as IRQ10.**

6. Identify the two divisions of the external data bus and describe the purpose of each.

   **The two divisions of the external data bus are the system bus and the expansion bus. The system bus supports the CPU, RAM, and other motherboard components. The system bus runs at speeds that support the CPU.**

   **The expansion bus supports any add-on devices via the expansion slots.**

7. What is the standard that governs computer buses?

   **IBM established the ISA industry standard, thus generating the market for "clones." The term ISA (Industry Standard Architecture) did not become official until 1990.**

8. What is the difference between ISA and EISA cards?

   **EISA uses a double slot connector that is compatible with ISA devices. Physically, the EISA bus is the same size and looks similar to the ISA. However, they differ in the number of contacts and the depth of the slot. On close inspection, you can see a double set of contacts (one above the other).**

9. Why was VESA created?

   **The Video Electronics Standards Association (VESA) is a trade association of display-adapter vendors. It was created to address the need for faster video to support the increased demands of new graphical operating systems like Windows and OS/2. These environments called for far better graphics and color management than the older character-based operating systems like MS-DOS.**

10. What is bus mastering?

    **Bus mastering allows a device to gain control of the bus to perform special tasks without processor intervention.**

11. Describe ways in which the PCI bus is better than previous technologies.

    **The PCI (Peripheral Component Interconnect) bus was designed by Intel to be a stronger, more flexible alternative to the current expansion buses**

while maintaining backward compatibility. It is CPU-independent, so it is better than the VL bus and is not limited to use in 486-based computers.

12. How does the CPU use I/O addresses?

**The CPU uses the unique address (actually a block of addresses) to communicate with a device in the system using the bus.**

13. What is the I/O port address of COM2?

**The I/O port address of COM2 is 2F8.**

14. What are the functions of IRQs?

**An IRQ is used by a device to send a request to the CPU for permission to transmit data so that all devices do not attempt to communicate at the same time.**

15. List as many of the standard IRQ assignments as you can.

**Here is a list of IRQ assignments. How many did you get?**

| IRQ | Function |
| --- | --- |
| IRQ 0 | System timer |
| IRQ 1 | Keyboard controller |
| IRQ 2/9 | Available |
| IRQ 3 | COM2, COM4 |
| IRQ 4 | COM1, COM3 |
| IRQ 5 | LPT2 |
| IRQ 6 | Floppy disk controller |
| IRQ 7 | LPT1 |
| IRQ 8 | Real-time clock |
| IRQ 10 | Available |
| IRQ 11 | SCSI/available |
| IRQ 12 | Available |
| IRQ 13 | Math coprocessor |
| IRQ 14 | Primary IDE controller |
| IRQ 15 | Secondary IDE controller |

16. What is the function of the DMA chip?

**The only function of the DMA chip (8237) is to move data. It handles all data passing from peripherals to RAM and vice versa.**

17. Why is it important not to assign an IRQ to more than one device?

**If two devices have the same IRQ and try to communicate with the CPU at the same time, the resulting conflict will lock up the computer.**

18. What is the difference between COM ports and LPT ports?

    **COM ports are for serial communications, and LPT ports are parallel ports normally used with printers.**

19. Why is it important to document IRQs, DMAs, and I/O addresses?

    **Because these three things cause more conflicts than perhaps anything else in a computer, you will be able to reduce installation times and correct conflicts.**

20. Identify as many cables and connectors as you can.

    **Here is a table of connectors. How many did you get right?**

    | Name | Uses |
    | --- | --- |
    | DB-9 | Serial ports—external modem, mouse, printer |
    | DB-25 | Parallel port—printer, scanner, removable drive |
    | RJ-11 | Standard telephone connector—2 wires |
    | RJ-12 | Standard telephone connector—4 wires—used with dual phone connections |
    | RJ-45 | Network connector |
    | PS/2 (mini-DIN) | Mouse, scanners |
    | Centronics | Printers |
    | USB | Universal serial bus—technology that allows multiple peripherals to be attached to one cable |

21. What type of connector is used for a parallel port on the computer?

    **A 25-pin female connector is used for a parallel port on the computer.**

22. Describe a null-modem cable.

    **Null-modem cables are used to directly connect two computers together without the need for a modem. The transmit and receive wires in the cable (wires 2 and 3) are switched to make the computers "think" they are using modems.**

23. What type of connector is used for a parallel port on the printer?

    **The most common parallel connector on the printer is the Centronics connector.**

24. Describe a USB connector.

    **A USB connector is an interface that conforms to the Uniform Serial Bus standard. This Plug-and-Play interface allows connection of a variety of devices and is becoming very popular for attaching keyboards, mass storage devices, and multimedia products, such as video cameras, to the PC.**

# Chapter 9

Page 217

1. What is the purpose of an IDE drive?

   **The IDE (Integrated Drive Electronics) drive was introduced in the early 1990s. The IDE quickly became the standard for general-purpose computers. The purpose of the IDE specification was to increase data throughput, support non-hard disk drive storage devices, increase the capacity of hard drives beyond the 528-MB barrier, and allow connection of up to four devices instead of only two.**

2. How many drives can be connected to a single IDE connector?

   **Two drives can be connected to one IDE connector.**

3. What is the best method of determining the number of drives available on a computer?

   **The best method of determining the number of drives available on a computer is to run the CMOS setup program. Originally, the CMOS would only allow for two drives. Later versions allow up to four drives.**

4. What three things should be checked when a floppy disk drive fails?

   **Three things to check when a floppy disk drive fails are the floppy disk itself (not the drive), the CMOS setup, and the drive controller/power supply cables.**

5. What is the best way to ensure long life from a floppy disk drive?

   **To ensure long life from a floppy disk drive, keep it clean.**

6. When you purchase a new floppy disk drive controller, what can you expect to receive with it?

   **Floppy disk drive controller cards also include some or all of the following: hard disk drive controllers, serial ports, parallel ports, and game ports. If the new card contains any ports that duplicate ports already present elsewhere on the computer (on the motherboard, for instance), a potential conflict exists, and you should disable the duplicates prior to installation.**

7. Other than physical size, what are the only differences between a 5.25-inch floppy disk drive and a 3.5-inch floppy disk drive?

   **The only difference between a 5.25-inch and a 3.5-inch drive (other than physical size) is that a 5.25-inch drive has a slot connector and a 3.5-inch drive has a pin connector for engaging and spinning the disk.**

8. What type of cable is used to connect a floppy disk drive to the external data bus?

   **All floppy disk drives are connected to the motherboard (external data bus) by a 34-conductor ribbon cable. This cable has a seven-wire twist in lines 10 through 16. This ensures that when two floppy disk drives are attached, the drive-select and motor-enable signals on those wires can be**

inverted to "select" whichever drive becomes the active target. The other wires carry data and ground signals.

9. What is the proper way to install a floppy disk drive cable?

**The connector end of the cable, with the twist, always goes toward the drives.**

10. To which pin must the number 1 wire of the floppy disk drive cable be connected?

**This red (or sometimes blue) wire is connected to the number 1 pin on the drive's controller connector. (The number 1 pin is usually located next to the power connection.)**

11. You've received the following error message: "General failure reading Drive A:". What is the most likely problem?

**The CMOS settings for the A drive are the most likely cause. Always double-check the CMOS if you are experiencing a recurrent drive failure. Checking is quick, easy, and can save you time.**

12. Are floppy disk controllers sensitive to ESD?

**Yes, floppy disk controllers are sensitive to ESD (electrostatic discharge).**

13. You receive an error message that ends with "Abort, Retry, Fail?". What is the most likely cause of the error?

**This error message indicates a failure to read the drive. These errors are the easiest to fix and can usually be attributed to a bad sector on the drive.**

14. Why is a voice coil actuator arm better than a stepper motor actuator arm?

**A voice coil actuator arm has several advantages over the stepper motor actuator arm. The lack of mechanical interface between the actuator arm and the motor provides consistent positioning accuracy. When the drive is shut down (the power is removed from the coil), the actuator arm (which is spring-loaded) moves back to its initial position, thus eliminating the need to park the head. In a sense, these drives are self-parking.**

15. Define hard disk drive geometry.

**Hard disk drives are composed of one or more disks, or platters, on which data is stored. The geometry of a hard drive is the organization of data on these platters. Geometry determines the maximum storage capacity of the drive.**

16. What is the best way to determine the geometry of an unknown drive?

**The geometry or type of many hard disk drives is labeled directly on the hard drive itself.**

17. Describe HDI.

**Head to Disk Interference (HDI) is another term for head crash.**

18. BIOS limits the number of heads to _____.

   **The maximum number of heads is 16.**

19. BIOS limits the number of cylinders to _____.

   **The maximum number of cylinders is 1024.**

20. How many bytes of data does a sector hold?

   **One sector holds 512 bytes of data.**

21. What is the maximum number of sectors per track?

   **The maximum number of sectors per track is 63.**

22. What does CHS stand for?

   **CHS stands for cylinders, heads, and tracks per sector.**

23. What type of drive is standard on today's personal computer?

   **The IDE is the standard drive on today's personal computers.**

24. Name the characteristics of the three different hard disk drive types.

   **The first hard disk drives for personal computers used the ST-506/412 interface. The ST-506/412 was the only hard drive available for the IBM computer and the first to be supported by the ROM BIOS chip on the motherboard.**

   **The Enhanced Small Device Interface (ESDI) was introduced in 1983 by the Maxtor Corporation. Beginning with this drive, most controller functions were incorporated directly onto the hard disk drive itself.**

   **The Small Computer System Interface (SCSI) has been around since the mid 1970s in one or another form. Apple adopted the SCSI as its expansion bus standard. The SCSI bus functions as a communications pathway between the computer system bus and the SCSI device controller.**

25. What is a partition? What are the two types of partitions?

   **Partitions are logical divisions of a hard disk drive. A computer might have only one physical hard drive (called hard drive 0), but it can have anywhere from 1 to 24 logical drives, called C to Z.**

   **There are two types of partitions: primary and extended.**

26. Define a cluster.

   **A cluster is a combined set of contiguous sectors, which the FAT treats as a single unit. The number of sectors in each cluster is determined by the size of the partition. There can never be more than 64,000 clusters.**

27. What is the FAT and how does it work?

   **The FAT (file allocation table) is simply an index that keeps track of which part of the file is stored in which sector. Each partition (or floppy disk) has two FATs stored near the beginning of the partition. These FATs are called FAT 1 and FAT 2. They are identical. Each FAT can be looked at as a two-column spreadsheet.**

28. What is fragmentation?

**Fragmentation is the scattering of parts of the same disk file over different areas of the disk. When files are scattered all over a drive in noncontiguous clusters they are said to be fragmented.**

29. How can you minimize the impact of a hard disk drive failure?

**To minimize the impact of a hard disk drive failure, perform comprehensive, frequent backups, and save a copy of the boot sector and partition table.**

30. What is the function of ScanDisk?

**ScanDisk performs a battery of tests on a hard disk. These include looking for invalid filenames, invalid file dates and times, bad sectors, and invalid compression structures. In the file system, ScanDisk looks for lost clusters, invalid clusters, and cross-linked clusters.**

# Chapter 10

Page 254

1. Name four methods of overcoming the 528-MB hard disk limitation.

**The first method utilizes Logical Block Addressing (LBA mode)—a means of addressing the physical sectors on a hard disk drive in a linear fashion.**

**The second method utilizes Enhanced CHS—a standard that competes with LBA. This standard allows drives to be manufactured a little faster and more easily than LBA.**

**The third method utilizes Fast ATA, which uses PIO mode 3, and Fast ATA-2, which uses PIO mode 4.**

**The fourth method utilizes logical cylinders, heads, and sectors (L-CHS)—a value used by the operating system to determine the size of the hard drive.**

2. How do multiple block reads speed up a computer?

**The ATA standard requires each drive to activate its IRQ every time it sends one sector of data. This process helps to verify good data transmission, but it slows down the computer. Multiple block reads speed up the process by reading several sectors of data at a time.**

3. How many devices can be installed on a SCSI chain?

**Eight devices can be installed on a single SCSI-1 chain. However, one of those devices must be reserved for the SCSI controller. SCSI-2 and later host adapters allow up to 16, with one reserved for the host adapter. Some SCSI cards offer multichannel support and can handle even more.**

4. What is the effect of improper termination on a SCSI chain or device?

**Improper termination can cause a failure to boot, the "disappearance" of a device from the SCSI chain, erratic behavior, and—in extreme cases—can even destroy a SCSI device.**

5. Sometimes the SCSI device driver conflicts with other drivers. What steps need to be taken to resolve the problem?

   **Often, the only way to tell if there will be a conflict is to try the driver and see what happens. Remember to document every step you take so that you can undo any changes. Load only the device drivers for the SCSI devices.**

   **If the problem occurs, use the F8 key to determine which driver conflicts. (Press F8 when starting MS-DOS or Windows 95 or 98—this will allow step-by-step confirmation of the startup process.)**

   **If the device driver is an executable file, try running it with the "/?" option. This will usually show a variety of command-line switches for the device driver (for example, "MOUSE.EXE /?").**

6. Describe three advantages of using a CD-ROM drive.

   **Advantages of using CD-ROM drives include: large storage capacity, sturdiness, portability, and the fact that data on the disk cannot be changed.**

7. What are the four steps required to install a CD-ROM drive?

   **1. Install the drive controller card, if needed.**

   **2. Install the CD-ROM drive in the computer case.**

   **3. Attach the data and power cables.**

   **4. Install the necessary drivers and set up the CD-ROM drive.**

8. Is a 16X CD-ROM drive 16 times faster than a 1X? Why?

   **No, it is not. The 16X CD-ROM data transfer rate will be 16 times faster, but the mean access time is not 16 times faster.**

9. How would you determine which type of CD-ROM drive to install in a computer?

   **You first have to determine whether or not there is room inside the case and if there are any available IDE controller connections. If not, then consider an external drive. If you want a SCSI controller, you will have to make sure there is an available slot in the expansion bus.**

10. Why would you use the MSCDEX.EXE real-mode driver with Windows 95?

    **Windows 95 and 98 use virtual drivers and do not need the MSCDEX.EXE real-mode driver. However, if you intend to use a CD-ROM drive in the MS-DOS mode (from a bootable disk), the real-mode drivers will have to be installed and added to the CONFIG.SYS and AUTOEXEC.BAT files of the boot disk.**

11. Instead of using magnetic energy for storing data, a CD-ROM uses
    _____ technology.

    **A CD-ROM uses laser technology.**

12. Name some possible controller card combinations.

**There are several ways to combine controller cards: Use the secondary IDE controller on the motherboard; use a new controller card (supplied with the CD-ROM); use an existing SCSI chain; use a SCSI host adapter; create a new SCSI chain; or use an existing sound card with a CD connection.**

13. What software is required for a CD-ROM drive installation?

**The driver that came with the CD-ROM and the Microsoft MSCDEX.EXE program are two files often required for a CD-ROM drive installation. The exact files and drivers will vary with the operating system and, in some drives, may require special drivers to fully take advantage of advanced features.**

# Chapter 11

Page 281

1. Describe the three elements that make up one dot of color.

**One dot of color is made up of three smaller dots: one red, one green, and one blue.**

2. What is the advantage of interlacing? Is it worth doing?

**Interlacing is a way of arranging a video display so that the CRT sweeps all the odd-numbered rows and then all the even-numbered rows (or vice versa). The intention of interlacing is to reduce the flicker on the screen by increasing the refresh rate (in other words, scanning the screen twice as often). An interlaced monitor can be well-suited for stand-alone servers or computers that run for long hours unattended. It might be a good choice when there will be little interaction by an operator or when cost is a primary factor. Interlacing should be avoided for normal use, because it can lead to eyestrain and headaches.**

3. Should a monitor be turned on and off or left on all day?

**The most basic form of power management is to turn off the monitor, using the power switch. At the same time, the CRT is the most expensive component of a monitor and can be damaged when it is turned on and off too frequently. Because these two concepts contradict each other, there is no single correct answer. You will have to make a decision based on the customer's individual circumstances.**

4. What is the "standard" type of video card used with today's computers?

**Some variation of the SVGA video card is used on most computers sold today.**

5. What is the formula for calculating the required memory for a monitor–video card combination?

**The formula is: video memory requirement = horizontal pixels × vertical pixels × color depth.**

6. What does CRT stand for?

**It stands for cathode-ray tube.**

7. What are HRR and VRR?

**The number of times per second an electron beam sweeps is called the refresh rate. The speed at which the electron beam completes one horizontal trace is known as the horizontal refresh rate (HRR). The time taken by the monitor to complete all horizontal traces and return to the top of the screen is the vertical refresh rate (VRR).**

8. Define resolution.

**Resolution is the measurement of image detail produced by a monitor or printer. Monitor resolution is expressed as the number of horizontal pixels by the number of vertical pixels.**

9. What is bandwidth?

**With computer monitors, bandwidth is the maximum number of times per second an electron gun can be turned on and off. Bandwidth is measured in megahertz (MHz—millions of cycles per second). A typical value for a high-resolution, 17-inch color monitor would be around 100 MHz.**

10. Why is it dangerous to open the monitor's cover?

**The CRT part of a monitor acts like a large capacitor and is capable of holding a very large charge (30,000 volts). (You should therefore leave monitor repair to a specially trained professional technician.)**

11. Name four common sources of video problems.

**The video-signal cable, video controller card, video-driver software, and the monitor are the four primary sources of video problems.**

12. Explain one similarity and one difference between VRAM and WRAM.

**Both offer dual port reads and writes, but WRAM is faster and less expensive.**

13. What is a raster?

**Video data is displayed on the monitor by sweeping the electron gun(s) in a series of horizontal lines or traces across the display. The line created by each sweep is called a raster. The number of rasters is used to describe the vertical resolution of a monitor.**

14. What type of connector is used for an SVGA monitor?

**The PGA, VGA, and SVGA monitor each use a 15-pin, three-row, female DB connector.**

15. Explain the advantages of a TFT active-matrix display over a passive-matrix display.

**The TFT screen is brighter and has better contrast than the older, passive displays. TFT provides much better image quality for a system used in an environment with glare or high levels of illumination.**

# Chapter 12

Page 298

1. Name the three most common types of printers and describe their advantages and disadvantages.

   **Impact printers produce an image on paper by physically striking an inked ribbon against the surface of the paper. The advantages of impact printers are that they tend to be inexpensive and print at a relatively high speed. Impact printers were very popular in the late 1980s. Some disadvantages of impact printers are lower print quality and noise.**

   **Ink-jet printers have replaced dot-matrix printers at the low end of the market. Many computer manufacturers and large computer stores offer ink-jet printers along with computers as part of package deals. They produce good-quality printing and are relatively fast, while requiring little maintenance beyond replacing the cartridge. What makes them attractive is their ability to easily produce color, as well as standard black-and-white images. High-quality, color ink-jet output requires the use of special ink-jet papers to obtain the full color of the inks. Other papers may lose color due to ink absorption or dulling by a matte surface.**

   **Laser printers have become one of the most popular types of printer for home use and are a must for most office environments. They produce high-quality, high-speed printing. Early laser printers were notorious for generating lots of heat and consuming lots of power.**

2. The dot-matrix printer is an _____ printer. Name at least one advantage of this type of printer. Name at least one disadvantage.

   **A dot-matrix printer is an impact printer. Its main advantages are its ability to print forms (multiple pages), its high reliability, and its low operating cost. Its disadvantages are its noise, slow speed, and generally low-quality (by today's standards) images.**

3. What are the six steps of laser printing?

   1. **Clean the drum.**
   2. **Charge the drum.**
   3. **Write the image.**
   4. **Transfer the toner.**
   5. **Transfer the image.**
   6. **Fuse the image.**

4. Which components are usually included in a laser printer's replaceable toner cartridge? Why?

   **Many of a laser printer's critical components, including those that experience the most wear and tear, are incorporated into the toner cartridge. The most important is the photosensitive drum. By incorporating these components into the toner cartridge, chances of failure are reduced because the primary-wear components are constantly replaced.**

5. What causes black spots to appear on a document that has been printed on a laser printer? How can this problem be resolved?

**If residual particles remain on the drum, they will appear as random black spots and streaks on the next printed page. The drum will need to be cleaned to clear this problem. This operation requires care and is often done by using canned air. Avoid touching the surface with your bare fingers to prevent leaving fingerprints or burning your fingers on a hot unit.**

6. In addition to the cost of the printer, what other costs should be considered when purchasing a printer?

**You should always consider the total operating cost, including the cost of paper and ink or toner.**

# Chapter 13

Page 312

1. Name the three main types of portable computers.

**The three types of portable computers are laptop, notebook, and subnotebook, or palmtop, computers.**

2. What is a docking station?

**Docking stations (also known as docking ports) are specialized cases that allow entire notebook computers to be inserted within them. This allows the notebook to be connected to desktop I/O devices such as full-sized keyboards, CRT monitors, and network connections.**

3. What is the purpose of PC Cards?

**In order for laptop and notebook computers to have the same degree of expandability that is associated with desktop computers, the Personal Computer Memory Card International Association (PCMCIA) established several standards for credit-card-sized expansion boards that fit into small slots on laptop and notebook computers.**

4. Describe the different PC Card types.

**There are four types of PC Cards:**

**Type I is the original computer-card standard and is now referred to as the Type I standard. These cards are used only for memory. Type I cards are 3.3 mm thick.**

**Type II cards support most types of expansion devices (such as communication hardware or network adapters). Type II cards are 5 mm thick.**

**Type III cards are primarily for computers that have removable hard disk drives. This standard was introduced in 1992. Type III cards are 10.5 mm thick, but they are compatible with Type I and Type II cards.**

**Type IV cards are intended to be used with hard disk drives that are thicker than the 10.5 mm Type III card.**

5. How do you configure a computer card?

**A PC Card is part of the Plug and Play standard. Plug and Play-compatibility provides the means to add components without turning off or rebooting the computer in computers with compatible operating systems. PC cards are not configured with jumper settings (because they don't have any) but with software.**

6. What are the two kinds of displays found on laptop computers?

**The two types of displays found on laptop computers are active-matrix and dual-scan.**

7. Why is heat dissipation a concern in computer-chip technologies for portable computers?

**In desktop systems, CPU heat is dissipated with the use of cooling fans housed inside the case. There is no room for this solution in a portable system, so manufacturers have addressed this problem in the packaging of the chip itself.**

8. With the exception of Macintosh, what drives are standard in a portable computer?

**Except for the size and packaging, hard disk drive technology is similar to desktop technology. EIDE drives are standard in portables, with the exception of Macintosh, which uses SCSI.**

# Chapter 14

Page 332

1. Name the three basic elements required to create a network.

**The three basic elements required to create a network are connection, communication, and services.**

2. The primary benefit of a LAN is its ability to share resources. Name some of the other benefits of networking.

**In addition to the ability to share resources, LANs are resilient, acting as communication gateways.**

3. What is the difference between a peer-to-peer and a server-based network?

**In a peer-to-peer network, each computer acts as a server or a client depending on the user's needs. Each user, or workstation, establishes its own security and determines which resources are available to other users.**

**In a server network, a central server (dedicated computer) manages access to all shared files and peripherals. This is a secure environment suitable for most organizations.**

4. Name the three network topologies.

**The three network topologies are star, bus, and ring.**

5. What types of cabling do thin Ethernet and UTP cabling use?

**Thin Ethernet uses a round BNC connector and UTP uses an RJ-45 connector (similar to a telephone jack).**

6. What is the function of a network interface card?

**Network interface cards (NICs) link the computer to the network cable system. They provide the physical connection between the computer's expansion bus and the network cabling.**

7. Name the three main types of network cabling. What are their advantages?

**Twisted-pair cable is very common, easy to install, and inexpensive.**

**Coaxial cable is found in two types: thin (ThinNet) and thick (ThickNet). When compared to twisted-pair, coaxial cable is the better choice even though it costs more. It is a standard technology and resists rough treatment and electromagnetic interference (EMI). Although more resistant, it is still susceptible to EMI and eavesdropping.**

**Fiberoptic cable is made of light-conducting glass or plastic fibers. It carries data signals in the form of modulated pulses of light. Although it is no less expensive (in both installation and cable cost) than twisted-pair or coaxial cable, it has advantages. It is immune to EMI or detection outside the cable. It supports very high bandwidths (the amount of information the cable can carry) and can handle thousands of times more data than twisted-pair or coaxial cable.**

8. What is the purpose of network protocols?

**A network protocol is a set of rules governing the way computers communicate over a network. In order for computers using different software to communicate, they must follow the same set of networking rules and agreements, or protocols. A protocol is like a language. Unless both computers trying to communicate are "speaking" and "listening" in the same language, no communication will take place.**

9. Describe the functions of a router, a bridge, and a gateway.

**Bridges work like repeaters but offer additional advantages. They can isolate network traffic or problems. The traffic within a segment will not be sent to the entire network unless its destination is in another segment. Bridges can also link unlike segments (Ethernet and token ring).**

**Routers provide interconnectivity between like and unlike devices on the LAN and WAN. Routers work like bridges, but can connect networks using different protocols and can select the best route from network to network based on traffic load. Routers route data based on factors such as least-cost, minimum delay, minimum distance, and least congestion. Routers are generally used to create a WAN and to connect dissimilar networks.**

Gateways provide as much interconnectivity and even greater functionality than routers and bridges do. A gateway usually resides on a dedicated computer that acts as a translator between two completely dissimilar systems or applications. Since a gateway is both a translator and a router, it tends to be slower than bridges or routers. Gateways also provide access to special services such as e-mail or fax functions.

10. What is the most widely used network protocol?

TCP/IP is the most widely used network protocol. It is the protocol of the Internet.

11. What is the difference between a LAN and a WAN?

A LAN is a local area network; it is usually confined to a limited space such as a building or a room. A WAN is a wide area network and can span long distances (even worldwide).

12. Your network is showing signs of reduced bandwidth. What is causing this problem?

This type of problem is called a bottleneck. A bottleneck on a system is the resource that limits the rate at which a task can be completed. If your task uses the processor, network, and disk resources, and spends more of its time transferring data to and from the disk, you might have a memory bottleneck. A memory bottleneck might require adding more RAM.

13. Besides A+ Certification, what are some of the other computer-related certifications available?

Several vendors have their own programs to validate the level of ability of technicians. Microsoft offers the MSCE, and Novell the CNE.

# Chapter 15

Page 335

1. What is the purpose of a modem?

A modem is a peripheral device that enables computers to communicate with each other over conventional telephone lines and through wireless communication.

2. Which AT command is used to take the phone off the hook?

The ATH command takes the phone off the hook.

3. What is the difference between baud and bps?

Baud is limited to 2400 cycles per second. Baud rate is limited by the capability of copper wires to transmit signals. Bps represents the actual number of data bits that can be transmitted per second.

4. What is the name of the chip that converts data from parallel to serial?

This chip is called a UART (universal asynchronous receiver-transmitter).

5. Name three transfer protocols.

**Three protocols for synchronous communication are Xmodem, Ymodem, and Zmodem.**

6. What is Zmodem? What are its advantages over other protocols?

**Zmodem shares all the features found in Xmodem and Ymodem protocols. It also adds a few new features, including crash recovery, automatic downloading, and a streaming file-transfer method. It is the protocol of choice for most telecommunication operations.**

7. Define handshaking.

**Handshaking is the negotiation of the rules (protocols) of communication between two modems.**

8. What are AT commands and how can a computer technician use them?

**AT commands are text commands that can be used to provide instructions to a modem. They are all preceded by the letters "AT." These commands are very useful as diagnostic tools for today's computer professional. To use these commands, make sure the communication software is loaded and the computer is in terminal mode. Unless the modem is set up to autoconnect (online mode), it will be in command mode and ready to accept AT.**

9. Explain the difference between half-duplex and full-duplex. What makes them different? Where or when is each used?

**In half-duplex, the RJ-11 plug has only two wires; therefore, only one signal can be sent or received at a time. Half-duplex is used to send messages in only one direction, like a fire alarm signal.**

**In full-duplex, the RJ-12 plug uses four wires (for two phones). It is the same size as the RJ-11 but with two additional wires. This enables users to send and receive data simultaneously.**

10. What is the difference between synchronous and asynchronous communication?

**Asynchronous communication is data transmission in which the length of time between characters may vary. Timing is dependent on the actual time it takes for the transfer to occur. This differs from synchronous communication, which is timed rigidly by an external clock.**

**Synchronous communication is a form of communication in which blocks of data are sent at strictly timed intervals. Because of this timing, no start or stop bits are required. Synchronous communication is more reliable than asynchronous and, therefore, more widely used.**

11. Why are fax standards different from modem standards?

**Faxes involve a different technology from that used by modems and are developed by different standards committees and operate on technology defined in a different standard than modems. A fax can be a stand-alone**

machine or incorporated into a computer. Computer faxes allow you to use the same format as picture reproduction (they paint a page of black-and-white pixels).

12. Describe the Internet.

The Internet is the outgrowth of a U.S. Department of Defense (DoD) program that linked DoD, academic institutions, and U.S. National Laboratories into a wide area network called ARPANET (Advanced Research Projects Network). During the 1970s and 1980s, a set of standards was developed to exchange a wide range of data. In the 1990s the system was turned over to the public domain. The World Wide Web is the part of the Web most users see, which uses a number of technologies built on HTML, including XML. Both are subsets of SGML, one of the standards developed in conjunction with the original project.

13. What is needed to set up an e-mail account?

Email accounts require a valid account on a mail server, a client program to send and receive messages, and client configuration so it can talk to the server. An ISP usually provides the information needed to configure the client concerning the server address.

14. What is a browser?

A browser is a software program that acts as both a client to a Web server and a interface for surfing the Internet. It usually supports a variety of protocols for viewing Web pages, downloading files, sending and receiving e-mail, and chatting online.

15. What does HTTP stand for?

Hyper Text Transmission Protocol. It is the basic protocol used to display pages on the World Wide Web.

16. What is the ping command used for?

Ping allows a user to send a test signal to a remote IP address to see if there is a valid working path between the remote machine and the user PC, and to see if a given IP address is active on the network.

17. What is a DNS server?

The DNS server maintains a lookup table that allows users to locate a node on a network (like the Internet) by using a domain name rather than the IP address.

18. What is an ISP?

An ISP is a company or server that offers Internet access over a remote connection, often by telephone/modem dial-up. Most offer Web site hosting as well.

# Chapter 16

Page 407

1. What does DOS stand for?

   **DOS stands for disk operating system.**

2. What was DOS created to do?

   **The original version of DOS was designed to support the operation of floppy disk drives.**

3. Which version of MS-DOS is bundled with Windows 95?

   **The version of MS-DOS bundled with Windows 95 is referred to as MS-DOS 7.0.**

4. Describe the core operating system files used within MS-DOS.

   **IO.SYS is the interface between the hardware and the operating system, MSDOS.SYS contains the main operating system code, and COMMAND. COM is the interface between the user and the operating system.**

5. What are the two MS-DOS user-definable startup files and their purpose?

   **CONFIG.SYS loads extra hardware and device drivers not built into IO.SYS, and AUTOEXEC.BAT loads environment variables such as TEMP and PATH as well as running any other batch file commands.**

6. Which DOS command is used to show the amount of free space left on a disk?

   **DIR (directory) returns a list of all the files on the drive and indicates the amount of free space available.**

7. Describe the difference between real mode and protected mode.

   **MS-DOS operates with a 1-MB memory limit called real mode. Windows broke out of the MS-DOS 1-MB barrier by engaging 286-level protected mode (Windows 2.0). Protected mode Windows could address up to 16 MB of RAM. Although MS-DOS programs could run only in the first megabyte of memory, specialized programs were written that would run in (and only in) the extended memory controlled by Windows. Protected mode refers to using protected memory.**

8. Which wildcard character can be used to replace a single character in a search string?

   **The single-character wildcard is the question mark (?).**

9. Explain the operation of the command-line interface.

   **The command-line interface accepts user input typed in via the keyboard, executes the command, and returns control to the user by returning a prompt.**

10. If a user working in DOS mode types a valid command to execute an external program and gets the response "File not found," what is the most common reason for the error message?

**To execute an external command the file must either be in the current directory or located in a directory declared in the path. Otherwise, the command must be preceded by the fully qualified path to the command, such as C:\Windows98\Command\EDIT.COM.**

11. Your customer wishes to have a machine configured for both the Linux operating system and Microsoft Windows 2000 Professional. The computer has only one hard drive. Identify which file system you would recommend and explain the reasons for your choice.

**FAT16 is the proper choice for the boot partition because it is the only file system compatible with both operating environments. Depending on the size of a hard disk it may be desirable to partition a second volume on the hard drive with NTFS to provide access to the advanced security features and performance enhancements of the newer file system.**

12. Explain the steps involved in preparing a new hard drive to accept an operating system.

**First, the drive must be low-level formatted. The manufacturer often does this during the production of the drive itself. If not, it will require software for this routine provided by the manufacturer. Once the system is completed, the drive must be partitioned and one partition must be designated as the boot partition or primary partition. Finally, a high-level format prepares the drive for the specific operating system and file system to be used.**

13. Why didn't the designers of the FAT file system provide a method for limiting access to files and folders?

**The FAT file system was designed as a single-user environment. Password protections and other forms of network security were not engineered into the design.**

# Chapter 17

Page 447

1. List several differences between Windows 98 and Windows 2000.

**Windows 98 is designed for the mass consumer market. It supports a wider range of hardware, is simpler to manage, and has less demanding system requirements. Windows 2000 is designed for use in more demanding environments, offers improved reliability and enhanced security, and supports multiprocessor operation.**

2. Explain some of the primary considerations in designing a dual boot system.

**A dual boot configuration offers the advantage of using products that are supported by both operating systems on a single computer. To do that,**

the hardware and file system must be capable of operating in both environments. Because Windows 98 and Windows 2000 have different system requirements, care must be taken in selecting components. During installation, drive partitions and file system layout must be designed so that files can properly be accessed by both the user and the operating system.

3. Where can you find information about what hardware can be used with Windows 2000?

**The Windows 2000 distribution CD contains a copy of the hardware compatibility list that was current at the time the disk was created. An updates list can be found on the Microsoft Web site.**

4. What is the purpose of the Windows 98 startup disk?

**The Windows 98 startup disk can be used to boot a system and obtain access to a command prompt and the CD-ROM drive. It also contains a variety of utilities that can be used to troubleshoot a system with problems, investigate the file system, and perform basic maintenance on the hard drive. The Windows 98 startup disk should be part of every technician's repair kit.**

5. What is an ERD?

**This is the Windows 2000 emergency repair disk. It contains files needed to restore the Registry to the same state as when the disk was created. The ERD is used as part of the emergency repair procedure if the Registry becomes corrupted or the file system becomes unstable.**

6. What steps have to be taken to use a compressed drive created under Windows 95 or Windows 98 with Windows 2000?

**Compressed drives created using Windows 95 and Windows 98 cannot be used directly with Windows 2000. You must first uncompress the drive before proceeding with the Windows 2000 setup.**

7. What is Safe Recovery?

**Safe Recovery is a Windows 98 feature that automatically attempts to recover from a failed setup. It makes use of the information logged during the preceding attempt to avoid failing at the same point. It may be necessary to manually install devices that were skipped because of the need to use Safe Recovery.**

8. What is Fdisk?

**Fdisk is a DOS, Windows 95, and Windows 98 utility used to create a partition on a hard drive. It can also be used to display the partition information, assign a volume label, and set an active DOS partition.**

9. What are the four setup options offered after Windows 98 Setup prepares the installation directory?

**Typical, Portable, Compact, and Custom are the four choices. Typical is the default option. Portable provides features normally desired by laptop**

users. Compact uses the least possible disk space. Custom allows the user to choose which components are actually installed.

10. Can Setup be run for both Windows 98 and Windows 2000 from MS-DOS?

    **Yes, Setup can be run for both operating systems. The user will need access to the CD-ROM drive, and the installation program must be manually invoked from the command prompt. In the case of Windows 98, this is WIN.EXE. For Windows 2000 you must use a 16-bit version of the installer named WINNT.EXE.**

11. What is the purpose of the Check Upgrade Only function during Windows 2000 installation and how is it invoked?

    **Check Upgrade Only is a process built directly into the installer that allows you to run a compatibility test of the system and software before actually performing the installation. Is invoked by using the command line switch /checkupgradeonly.**

12. What should be the first step in troubleshooting any failed Windows installation?

    **Recheck all required system components and make sure that the product and the target system are compatible with the operating system involved.**

13. What is the first step required to log on to a Windows 2000 machine (not during installation, but at any time the system is accessed after Setup is complete)? What is the purpose of this step?

    **The user must press the CTRL+ALT+DELETE keystroke combination to access the user logon screen. This part of the Windows NT and Windows 2000 security check ensures that no processes are running in the background that might capture user information for use by a hacker.**

14. What are the basic minimum system requirements required to run Windows 2000?

    **The system requirements are a Pentium-class processor, 64 MB of RAM, a VGA display, a keyboard, and a mouse. In addition, all those elements should be contained on the most recent hardware compatibility list.**

# Chapter 18

Page 496

1. What are the core components of the Windows 98 operating system?

    **The Windows 98 core consists of four components: the GDI, the kernel, the user component, and the user interface.**

2. What is the kernel, and what is its function within the operating system?

    **The kernel can be considered the heart of the operating system. It starts and stops all tasks, starts and stops DLLs, allocates memory, and acts as the interface between the hardware and the user.**

3. What is the VMM?

**This is the Windows 98 component that manages the key resources needed by applications and system processes. The virtual machine is the environment where system processes and applications actually operate. In Windows 98, all 32-bit applications are provided within a complete 32-bit virtual machine, and legacy Windows applications operating in 16-bit mode share a single virtual machine.**

4. What is virtual memory, and what are its benefits?

**Virtual memory is the use of disk storage space as a "scratch pad" for system RAM. By moving data between virtual memory and RAM, the system's functional memory can be larger than the actual physical RAM present on the system. Under Windows 98, the use of virtual memory allows for an operating environment up to 4 GB in size.**

5. What is the definition of WDM, what is it, and why is it important?

**WDM is the Windows Driver Model, which allows developers to design a common driver for both Windows 98 and Windows 2000 environments. Using a common model gives both operating systems access to a wider range of hardware with less expense on the part of the manufacturer. This results in more functionality at lower cost.**

6. What is a minidriver?

**Minidrivers are a class-specific set of drivers. They can be used to support a range of devices, such as SCSI-based hardware or Twain-compliant scanners.**

7. Briefly explain the two core files needed to boot Windows 98.

**IO.SYS is very similar to the file of the same name in MS-DOS. In addition, it incorporates many of the customization features found in CONFIG.SYS in the older operating system. These settings are not directly modifiable by the user, but they can be adjusted by modifying the other start file, MSDOS.SYS. Although it shares the same name, it is not the same as the file in MS-DOS. It actually replaces the functions of CONFIG.SYS. This is the proper place to make custom boot configuration settings unless there is some overriding reason to use CONFIG.SYS and AUTOEXEC.BAT for backward compatibility.**

8. Can you use CONFIG.SYS and AUTOEXEC.BAT in Windows 98? Are there any special considerations?

**Yes, they can be used in Windows 98, but they are not recommended except to enable backward compatibility for legacy equipment or software. If they are used, the following actions should be taken: Don't enable any mouse drivers or disk caching software. Don't reference older versions of Windows or MS-DOS. Be sure the path to the current Windows directory is included in any path statements. Leave any hardware customization settings to be handled by the Registry whenever possible.**

9. What is the purpose of the NTLDR program in Windows 2000?

**This file is a key startup manager for Windows 2000, and must reside in every directory of the primary disk partition. It controls system startup until the kernel is loaded or another operating system has been invoked if the machine has a dual-boot system. If this file is not present or has become corrupted, Windows 2000 cannot load.**

10. What is the purpose of the BOOTLOG.TXT file?

**This is an optional startup file that tracks every step in the boot process for both Windows 98 and Windows 2000. It is a plain text file that can be viewed with any text editor to see which boot processes succeeded or failed and to identify any critical components that might be keeping the system from booting.**

11. What is the HAL, and what is its function?

**This is the hardware abstraction layer found in Windows 2000 and Windows NT, which is a core part of the kernel. It can be considered the lowest level of the operating system, and it connects directly to the hardware devices attached to the system. That allows Windows 2000 and Windows NT to support different families of CPUs. The HAL manages the I/O interfaces between all the I/O devices on the system.**

12. Define the Registry.

**In all versions of Windows starting with Windows 95, the Registry has been the central device and system settings repository. A binary database, it is not directly accessible to most users, but it can be modified through a series of tools and wizards. It is a vital system component. If it becomes corrupted, the system may not work properly or at all.**

13. What is the MMC?

**The MMC is the Microsoft Management Console. It is a new user interface that provides easy access to system configuration data and controls. It includes the same functionality currently available under the Control Panel and offers a number of unique advantages to the administrator.**

14. What is the preferred editor for working with the system Registry and Windows 2000?

**REGEDT32 is the preferred Registry editing tool in Windows 2000, replacing REGEDIT from Windows 9x. Although REGEDIT is still available in Windows 2000, it lacks the security controls and several other functions needed to totally manipulate the Windows 2000 Registry.**

# Chapter 19

Page 539

1. Name three reasons for adding a laptop computer to your toolkit.

**A laptop provides an easy way to carry a wide variety of documentation and drivers, it offers Internet access for obtaining drivers and patches,**

and it allows you to maintain a portable database of client and computer care records.

2. What type of solvent should be used to clean the monitor screen?

**No solvent should be used on the glass surface of the monitor.**

3. What is a polymorphic virus?

**They are an especially troubling class of invader that is difficult to eradicate. They can modify themselves over time and replicate into new forms. This makes them both unpredictable and harder to detect.**

4. What is the ScanDisk program? What is it used for?

**ScanDisk is a disk utility that both examines the surface of the hard drive for physical defects and inspects and repairs the file system.**

5. What is an ERD?

**This is the emergency repair disk used by Windows NT and Windows 2000 to restore the system Registry to its original installation state in the event that the computer cannot be started.**

6. What is the best way to remove old, unused files from a Windows-based computer?

**Both Windows 98 and Windows 2000 offer a Disk Cleanup Wizard. This program automatically locates files and offers a number of methods for quickly cleaning up the computer.**

7. How does file fragmentation degrade system performance?

**When files are badly fragmented, it takes longer for the operating system to load the necessary data input into memory. Disk fragmentation also causes more wear and tear on mechanical parts of the drive, as their heads must move further and faster than they would if the files were all stored in continuous clusters.**

8. Define an incremental backup.

**An incremental backup copies just the files created or modified since the last regular backup and changes the archive setting on the file when it is copied.**

9. Explain the difference between a normal and a copy type of backup.

**Normal backups copy specific files to an archive no matter what the archive setting is for the files. As each file is copied, it is marked as having been backed up. A copy backup is similar, but it does not mark the file as having been backed up. This is useful if you are making a separate backup copy of a set of files but do not want to exclude them from the next regular backup.**

10. Why is it useful to keep long-term archival files, even if you're making regular periodic backups on a short-term basis?

**Backups are sometimes your last line of defense against a virus attack because some types of viruses can reside on a system for a long time before being detected.**

11. What is the Windows File Protection system?

**The Windows File Protection system tracks all changes to system files and makes sure that any new files assigned to replace a protected file are valid. It also sends a message to the system administrator whenever an improper file replacement of one of these protected files is attempted.**

# Chapter 20

Page 564

1. What bootable floppy disks are needed for a computer professional's toolkit, and why?

**One bootable floppy disk is needed for every operating system that you will be working on that also contains the basic drivers. A Windows 95 or Windows 98 Startup disk is also a good addition.**

2. You are only going to check the memory chips. Do you need to follow ESD safety practices?

**Always use ESD safety practices.**

3. What is parity?

**Parity is used to check the reliability of data. Parity requires one additional bit (chip). Memory can be purchased with or without parity. Parity adds about 10 percent more to the cost of memory. You cannot mix parity and nonparity chips.**

4. Can the L1 cache memory be upgraded?

**No, it is a part of the CPU core itself.**

5. Your client wants to install an internal modem. How would you determine whether this internal modem could be installed on your client's machine?

**First, the machine must have an available expansion slot. Second, there must be available resources such as IRQ and an address.**

6. A friend just got a bargain on a new Plug and Play sound card and wants to install it on a non–Plug and Play computer. Will it work?

**Possibly, but it will have to be manually configured through either software or by setting jumpers. Many Plug and Play cards do not have jumpers.**

7. How do you determine whether to upgrade the CPU or install another motherboard?

**First, you must evaluate the existing motherboard to see if it can be upgraded and then determine the best CPU that you can use. Second, you**

must determine the needs of the customer, particularly whether the CPU upgrade will meet the customer's operational requirements.

8. What is the advantage of Plug and Play?

**Plug and Play is an independent set of specifications developed by a group of hardware and software companies to make it all but automatic to add new compliant hardware to a PC. This specification allows the user to make configuration changes with minimal adjustments. The user simply installs the card, turns on the computer, and uses the device.**

9. What are the four requirements that must be addressed before installing a new drive in a computer?

- **Will the drive physically fit inside the computer?**
- **Will the computer's BIOS and operating system support the size (storage capacity) of the drive?**
- **Will the drive controller support the new drive?**
- **Are there sufficient cables (data and power) to install the drive?**

# Chapter 21

Page 604

1. What is the tool used to restore the Registry in Windows 9x? Is it the same as the one used in Windows 2000?

**The Registry Checker is the preferred tool used to restore the Registry in Windows 98. Windows 2000 actually offers a separate operating environment, called the Recovery Console, to perform this task.**

2. What are the five phases of troubleshooting?

**Phase 1 is to define the problem, Phase 2 is to identify the cause, Phase 3 is to make the repair, Phase 4 is to confirm the repair, and Phase 5 is to document the incident.**

3. How important is record-keeping?

**Good record-keeping is essential if you are to become successful at your profession. Record-keeping is the process by which you keep track of which techniques worked and which did not work. In short, it becomes your experience database. Good records save you valuable time in the long run.**

4. Explain some possible uses for the Windows 2000 Task Manager in troubleshooting, and name a corollary tool available in Windows 98.

**The Task Manager can be used to see what applications and processes are currently running on the system. It also provides a snapshot of current resources being used. This information can be valuable if the system slows down unexpectedly, and it can also be used to isolate which application or process might be overutilizing resources or corrupting memory. A less robust, but similar tool in Windows 9x is the Resource Meter.**

5. What are the three levels of technical support?

**Level 1 is to provide local support by assigning a knowledgeable person on-site to address minor problems. Level 2 is to provide telephone support. Level 3 is to provide on-site support.**

6. What is the purpose of the ping command, and how do you use it?

**The ping command is used to test and verify TCP/IP connectivity. It reports if a computer can be reached from the current location. The simple syntax used is to type ping at a DOS prompt, followed by the desired IP address.**

7. Why is it important to standardize equipment in large organizations?

**Standardization of equipment in large companies reduces the number of spare parts required and simplifies installation and maintenance.**

8. What four stages should you go through when you receive a service call?

**The four stages of a service call are the greeting, the description, the interview, and the closing.**

9. Describe some ways of coping with a difficult client or coworker.

**If the individual needs training, ensure that they have information about available courses. If the individual is a coworker, speak to the person who supervises them and identify their training needs. If the individual is a client, gently suggest that it would be beneficial to obtain specific training. Send the client a memo or instruction sheet to follow, and save the instructions for future use. Dealing with technophiles (or those who think they are experts) can be a challenge. The best option is to listen carefully and make the individual part of the solution, not part of the problem. Remember, that person came to you for help.**

10. Explain some of the skills and challenges involved in troubleshooting.

**Troubleshooting is one of the most demanding aspects of a computer technician's job. To be performed successfully, it requires excellent listening skills, a systematic approach, a firm grasp of methods and techniques used to resolve problems, problem-solving skills, and knowledge of both computer hardware and operating systems. To be a successful troubleshooter, you must also be able to interact effectively with a client who may be distraught over the possibility of loss of data or productivity.**

# Chapter 22

Page 630

1. What is Ohm's law?

**Ohm's law states that the current (electrons) flowing through a conductor, or resistance, is in linear proportion to the applied potential difference (volts).**

2. What is the formula for Ohm's law for voltage?

   **The formula for Ohm's law is voltage is equal to the current multiplied by the resistance (V = I R).**

3. What is the difference between AC and DC?

   **AC is alternating current in which the voltage varies from positive to negative. DC is direct current in which the voltage stays the same all the time.**

4. What instrument is used to measure the various components of electricity?

   **The instrument used to measure the various components of electricity is VOM—Volt-Ohm Meter (sometimes referred to as Digital Volt-Ohm Meter [DVOM]).**

5. How do you test for continuity?

   **Continuity is a term used to indicate whether or not there is a connection from one point to another. It is used to determine the presence of breaks in wires and electrical circuits. If no continuity setting is available, use the resistance setting. If the multimeter measures infinite resistance, then there is no continuity, indicating a break in the circuit. If the multimeter shows little or no resistance, then there is continuity and the circuit is complete.**

6. What is AC ripple? How do you test for it?

   **A power supply converts AC to DC voltage. When working properly, a pure DC signal will be produced. Sometimes, however, as the power supply ages, its ability to produce pure DC falters. A power supply uses capacitors to filter or smooth the voltage after being converted from AC to DC. These capacitors are second only to fuses as the part of a power supply most likely to fail. When a capacitor begins to fail, it allows more and more AC voltage to pass through. This AC voltage is superimposed on top of the DC voltage and is called noise or ripple.**

   **To test for ripple, set a meter to read AC. Then connect a .1μfd capacitor to the red lead. With the power turned on, measure the DC voltage to ground. Any ripple present will be displayed as an AC voltage.**

7. Describe ESD and how to prevent it.

   **Just as high voltages generated by electrical and electronic equipment can do severe damage to humans, high voltages generated by humans can do damage to computers. We have all seen what a short circuit can do to electrical equipment (smoke, fire, and destruction). Electrostatic discharge (ESD) is an unseen (and sometimes unheard) force, created by humans, that is just as deadly to a computer.**

   **The key to ESD prevention is to keep all electronic components and yourself at the same electrical potential. This usually means ground potential or zero volts. Maintain a habit of "grounding" yourself to the computer**

chassis whenever you attempt a repair. **An ESD wrist strap is the tool most commonly used by technicians to prevent ESD.**

8. What is a latent failure? What makes it especially troublesome?

**This type of ESD problem occurs when a transistor junction becomes weakened. A transistor in this condition may pass all quality tests but, over time, will generate poorer system performance and eventually fail completely.**

9. What is a catastrophic failure?

**Catastrophic failure is the destruction of a part because of the heat generated during the mishandling and misapplication of a power source, cable, or test instrument.**

10. When working with a computer, when is it acceptable to use an AC power supply that is not grounded?

**It is never acceptable to use an AC power supply that is not grounded.**

APPENDIX   B

# Table of Acronyms

This appendix presents many of the acronyms used in this book. Be aware that—as with all acronyms—some have more than one meaning, depending on the context.

| | |
|---|---|
| AC | alternating current |
| AGP | Accelerated Graphics Port |
| ALU | arithmetic logic unit |
| ANSI | American National Standards Institute |
| ASCII | American Standard Code for Information Interchange |
| ASPI | Advanced SCSI Programming Interface |
| BBS | bulletin board system |
| BIOS | basic input/output system |
| BPS (bps) | bits per second |
| CAM | Common Access Method |
| CCITT | Comité Consultatif International Télégraphique et Téléphonique |
| CD-ROM | compact disc read-only memory |
| CGA | Color/Graphics Adapter |
| CHS | cylinder, head, and sector |
| CISC | complex instruction set computing |
| CMOS | complementary metal-oxide semiconductor |
| COM port | serial communications port |
| CPU | central processing unit |
| CRT | cathode-ray tube |
| DC | direct current |
| DDE | Dynamic Data Exchange |
| DIMM | dual inline memory module |
| DIP | dual inline package |
| DLL | dynamic-link library |
| DMA | direct memory access |

| | |
|---|---|
| DOS | disk operating system |
| Dpi | dots per inch |
| DPMI | DOS Protected Mode Interface |
| DPMS | Display Power Management Signaling |
| DRAM | dynamic random access memory |
| DTE | Data Terminal Equipment |
| DVD | digital video disc |
| EDB | external data bus |
| EDO | extended data out |
| EGA | Enhanced Graphics Adapter |
| EIDE | Enhanced Integrated Drive Electronics |
| EISA | Extended Industry Standard Architecture |
| EMI | electromagnetic interference |
| EMS | Expanded Memory Specification |
| ESD | electrostatic discharge |
| ESDI | Enhanced Small Device Interface |
| ETX | end-of-text |
| FAT | file allocation table |
| FPM | fast page-mode |
| FTP | File Transfer Protocol |
| GB | gigabyte |
| GDI | Graphical Device Interface |
| GPF | General Protection Fault |
| GUI | graphical user interface |
| HMA | high memory area |
| HRR | horizontal refresh rate |
| HTTP | Hypertext Transfer Protocol |
| I/O | input/output |
| IDE | Integrated Device Electronics |
| IEEE | Institute of Electrical and Electronics Engineers |
| IOR | input/output read wire |
| IOW | input/output write wire |
| IP | Internet Protocol |
| IPX/SPX | Internetwork Packet Exchange/Sequenced Packet Exchange |
| IRQ | interrupt request |
| ISA | Industry Standard Architecture |

| | |
|---|---|
| ISDN | Integrated Services Digital Network |
| ISO | International Organization for Standardization (often incorrectly identified as International Standardization Organization) |
| ISP | Internet service provider |
| ITU-T | International Telecommunications Union—Telecommunication Standardization Sector |
| KB | kilobyte |
| LAN | local area network |
| LBA | Logical Block Addressing |
| LIM | Lotus/Intel/Microsoft |
| LPT | line printer, now refers to a parallel printer port |
| MB | megabyte |
| MCA | Micro Channel Architecture |
| MCC | memory controller chip |
| MDA | Monochrome Display Adapter |
| MDRAM | Multibank DRAM |
| MFM | modified frequency modulation |
| MHz | megahertz |
| MMC | Microsoft Management Console |
| MOS | metal-oxide semiconductor |
| MSD | Microsoft Diagnostics |
| MTBF | mean time between failures |
| NDIS | Network Driver Interface Specification |
| NetBIOS/ NetBEUI | Networked Basic Input/Output System/NetBIOS Enhanced User Interface |
| NIC | network interface card |
| NTSC | National Television Standards Committee |
| OLE | object linking and embedding |
| PC | personal computer |
| PCI | Peripheral Component Interconnect |
| PDI | post DMA-IRQ card |
| PDL | page-description language |
| PGA | pin grid array or Professional Graphics Adapter |
| PIO | Programmed Input/Output |
| PLCC | plastic leadless chip carrier |
| PM | preventive maintenance |
| POST | power-on self test |

| | |
|---|---|
| POTS | Plain Old Telephone Service |
| PPP | Point-to-Point Protocol |
| PPTP | Point-to-Point Tunneling Protocol |
| PQFP | plastic quad flat pack |
| RAID | redundant array of independent disks |
| RAM | random access memory |
| RISC | Reduced Instruction Set Computing |
| RLL | run-length limited |
| ROM | read-only memory |
| SCSI | Small Computer System Interface |
| SDRAM | synchronous dynamic random access memory |
| SGRAM | synchronous graphics RAM |
| SIMM | single inline memory module |
| SIPP | single inline pinned package |
| SMM | System Memory Management |
| SPA | Software Publishers Association |
| SRAM | static random access memory |
| TB | terabyte |
| TCP/IP | Transmission Control Protocol/Internet Protocol |
| TSR | terminate-and-stay-resident program |
| UART | universal asynchronous receiver-transmitter |
| UMB | upper memory block |
| UPS | uninterruptible power supply |
| USB | universal serial bus |
| VESA | Video Electronics Standards Association |
| VGA | Video Graphics Adapter |
| VLB | VESA local bus |
| VOM | volt-ohm meter |
| VPN | virtual private network |
| VRR | vertical refresh rate |
| WAN | wide area network |
| WFP | Windows File Protection |
| WRAM | window random access memory |
| XMS | extended memory specification |
| ZIF | zero-insertion-force |

# Glossary

## A

**access speed** The time required to complete read or write instructions as required by the memory controller chip. Usually measured in nanoseconds (ns) for memory chips and milliseconds (ms) for disk drives. Most manufacturers rate average access time on a hard disk as the time required for a seek across one third of the total number of cylinders plus one half of the time for a single revolution of the disk platters.

**address bus** A group of parallel conductors (circuit traces) found on the motherboard that are used by the CPU (central processing unit) to "address" memory locations. Determines what information or code is sent to or received from the data bus.

**AGP (Accelerated Graphics Port)** An Intel-designed expansion port found on Pentium II and later computers that allows a separate data path for display adapters.

**ampere** A measurement of electrical current strength.

**ASCII file** Commonly used term to refer to a text file that contains only data as set forth by the **American Standard Code for Information Interchange** to conform to their standard.

**asynchronous** Not synchronized—the computer is free to transmit any number of characters at any time. The bits constituting a single character are transmitted at a fixed rate, but the pauses between transmissions can be of any duration.

**attachment** A file attached to e-mail; most e-mail clients allow the user to append files (for instance, graphics files like .gif or .jpeg files) to e-mail as a handy way of sending information to other people.

## B

**backslash (\)** Symbol used to separate each directory level, for instance C:\Windows\Utilities. For this reason, it is a reserved character and cannot be used as part of a filename.

**bandwidth** Used in several ways to denote the amount of data or load capacity of a medium. (1) The range of frequencies that an electronic system can transmit. High bandwidth allows fast transmission or the ability to transmit many signals at once. (2) On a monitor screen, a higher bandwidth provides a sharper image. (3) The rate at which data can be sent over a modem or other telecommunication device.

**battery** A power source for use outside or as an alternate to electricity. Prevents unique information about the setup of the computer from being lost when the power is turned off. Also maintains the external clock time (not to be confused with the CPU's clock).

**baud** Roughly speaking, a measurement of how fast data can be sent over telephone lines.

**BBS (bulletin board system)** A local computer system that is not part of the Internet. It allows users to dial in and chat with others and download or upload files.

**binary file** A file type in the form of pure data (1s and 0s) that needs to be converted to an image, sound, or application to be used. *See also* ASCII file.

**binary system** The language used by computers that is based on something being either on or off. There are only two digits used in binary language: 1 equals on, and 0 equals off.

**BIOS (basic input/output system)** Software that includes the initialization programs stored on ROM (read-only memory) chips. Used during the startup routine to check out the system and prepare to run the hardware.

**bit**  The smallest unit of information that is recognized by a microcomputer. Shorthand term for binary digit. There are only two possible binary digits: 0 and 1.

**Bi-Tronics**  A modified Centronics connection created by Hewlett-Packard. It utilizes bidirectional communication, allowing the printer to send messages to the computer (for example, out of paper, paper jam, and so forth).

**boot partition**  A hard disk partition containing the portion of the operating system needed to launch the operating environment.

**boot up**  To start a computer; drawn from the phrase "pulling oneself up by one's own bootstraps."

**bps (bits per second)**  The speed at which a modem transmits data. Typical rates are 14,400, 28,800, 33,600, and 56,600 bps. This represents the actual number of data bits that can be transmitted per second.

**bridge**  A device that provides communication between two or more network segments, thereby forming one logical network.

**broadband**  A network with high bandwidth (sometimes defined as greater than 256 bps).

**browser**  Software used to navigate the World Wide Web, such as Microsoft Internet Explorer and Netscape Navigator.

**bulletin board system**  *See* BBS (bulletin board system).

**bus**  The main communication avenue in a computer. It consists of a set of parallel wires that are connected to the CPU (central processing unit), memory, and all input/output devices. The bus can transmit data in either direction between any two components. If a computer did not have a bus, it would need separate wires to connect all the components.

**bus mastering**  The ability of a device to control its own data bus, only making use of the main system bus when data must be sent to the CPU or another device. This reduces CPU and system bus traffic, improving overall performance.

**bus network**  A network in which all computers are connected to a single linear cable. Both ends of the cable must be terminated. Because there is no central point, it is harder to isolate problems in a bus network than in a star network topology.

**byte**  A group of 8 bits that represents 1 character of information (for instance, pressing one key on the keyboard). A byte is the standard unit for measuring memory in a microprocessor. Memory size is measured in terms of kilobytes (KB) or megabytes (MB). 1 KB of RAM is 1024 bytes; 1 MB is approximately one million bytes.

# C

**cache**  A place where data is stored so that it does not need to be read from a slower device. Copies of frequently used disk sectors are stored in RAM (random access memory) so they can be accessed without accessing the hard disk.

**case sensitivity**  The ability of the operating system to distinguish between uppercase and lowercase letters. MS-DOS commands are not case-sensitive; UNIX commands are.

**cathode-ray tube**  *See* CRT (cathode-ray tube).

**CD-ROM (compact disc read-only memory)**  A disc similar to an audio compact disc containing computer data.

**central processing unit**  *See* CPU (central processing unit).

**CGA (Color Graphics Adapter)**  An early color graphics adapter standard with resolutions of 320 pixels by 200 pixels or 640 × 200. CGA supported no more than four colors.

**chip** The ultimate integrated circuit; contains the complete arithmetic and logic unit of a computer. *See* microprocessor.

**chip set** A group of computer chips or integrated circuits (ICs) that, when working in harmony, manage and control the computer system. This set includes the CPU (central processing unit) and other chips that control the flow of data throughout the system. Typical chip sets consist of a bus controller, a memory controller, data and address buffer, and a peripheral controller.

**CISC (complex instruction set computing)** A computer with many different machine-language instructions.

**client** A computer that connects to a network and uses the available resources provided by the server.

**clock** Establishes the maximum speed at which the processor can execute commands. Not to be confused with the clock that keeps time.

**clock speed** Measured in megahertz (MHz)—millions of cycles per second—it is the speed at which a clock can cycle, or how fast a CPU (central processing unit) can execute a command. With faster CPUs, the term is now migrating to gigahertz (GHz).

**clone** A term that derives from the early days of personal computing used to denote a computer compatible with, but not manufactured by, IBM.

**clusters** A unit of storage on a mass-storage device such as a hard disk drive or CD-ROM. On a hard drive, a cluster usually consists of two to eight sectors. The actual amount of data a cluster can hold is dependent on the operating system and controller type.

**CMOS (complementary metal-oxide semiconductor)** A form of read-only memory chip that gets its name from the way it is manufactured and not the information it holds. CMOS chips are used to store data that is read by the BIOS (basic input/

output system) to obtain information on hardware configurations.

**CMOS battery** Prevents unique information about the setup of the computer from being lost when the power is turned off. Also maintains the external clock time (not to be confused with the CPU's clock).

**coaxial cable** Made of two conductors that share the same axis. The center is a relatively stiff copper wire encased in insulating plastic. A wire-mesh tube around the insulation serves as shielding. The outside is a tough insulating plastic tube.

**code** A way of representing information on a machine or in some physical form so that the information can be placed on the external data bus to be read by all devices. Also, statements (source code) written in a programming language that are compiled into executable instructions (object code).

**cold boot** The process of restarting a computer after it has been powered down.

**COM1, COM2** The names assigned to the first two serial ports on a PC.

**command mode** The character mode used in an operating system such as Microsoft Windows, MS-DOS, or UNIX that has a prompt where the user enters commands.

**compression** "Squeezing" a file down in size by getting rid of all the bits that are not really needed. Many files (especially those with graphics) are very large and require a long time to travel over the Internet, so they are best compressed before sent.

**conferences** Different areas of conversation in an e-mail system that are topic-specific rather than individualized.

**conventional memory** The memory area between 0 and 640 KB that is designated for running MS-DOS and MS-DOS applications.

**coprocessor** A separate circuit inside a computer that adds additional functions to the CPU (central processing unit) or handles extra work while the CPU is busy.

**CPU (central processing unit)** The part of a computer that controls the arithmetic and logical operations and decoding and executing instructions.

**CRT (cathode-ray tube)** The main component of a monitor. One end of the tube is a very slender cylinder containing an electron gun(s). The wider end is the display screen.

**cursor** When entering data, whether in an application or at an MS-DOS command prompt, the cursor (often a small flashing line) indicates the place at which the characters will be inserted.

# D

**data bus** A group of parallel conductors (circuit traces) found on the motherboard that is used by the CPU (central processing unit) to send and receive data from all the devices in the computer. Also called the external data bus.

**Data Communications Equipment (DCE)** The receiver in a telecommunications connection.

**DDE (Dynamic Data Exchange)** A Microsoft Windows data exchange protocol that allows for the automatic updating of a file or open application when the source is modified.

**default drive** The active drive on the computer. Each drive has its own letter designation. Unless otherwise specified, any commands are performed on the default drive.

**defragmentation** Running a program to organize the files on a hard disk so that the various clusters of data for each file are once again contiguous. This helps to speed up the hard disk.

**device driver** A program that extends the operating system to support specific devices.

**direct memory access (DMA)** Allows a peripheral device to access the memory of a computer directly, without going through the CPU (central processing unit). This speeds up the transfer of data to or from external devices.

**directory** A location where files are grouped together on the disk. In the Microsoft Windows environment and Apple Macintosh operating systems, these are known as folders.

**DLC (Data Link Control)** A protocol developed by IBM to connect token-ring-based workstations to IBM mainframe computers. Printer manufacturers have adopted the protocol to connect remote printers to network print servers.

**DMA** *See* direct memory access (DMA).

**DOS (disk operating system)** A text-based operating system used by most early PCs to manage hardware, data, and applications.

**DOS prompt** Displays the active drive letter (for instance, C:) and directory. This indicates that the operating system is ready to accept the next command.

**DOS Protected Mode Interface (DPMI)** Specification that allows multiple applications to access extended memory at the same time. Most memory manager producers and application developers have endorsed this standard. Microsoft Windows uses the DPMI specification.

**download** The ability to transfer a file from a remote computer to your computer.

**dpi (dots per inch)** Units used to measure the resolution of images on many printers and scanners. Keep in mind that dpi is an exact measurement in laser printers but often used as an approximation in ink-jet printers.

**DRAM (dynamic random access memory)** Memory that requires a refresh signal to be sent to it periodically.

# E

**ECC (error-correction coding)** The use of a code to verify or disprove that a data string received is the same as the data sent.

**ECP (Enhanced Capabilities Port)** Developed by Hewlett-Packard and Microsoft. It features 2 MB per second data transfer and bidirectional 8-bit operation. ECP specifies whether transmitted information consists of data or commands for the peripheral.

**EGA (Enhanced Graphics Adapter)** An improvement on the older CGA standard. Supports a resolution of up to 640 pixels × 350 pixels at 16 colors in text-only mode or 640 × 200 at 2 colors in graphics mode. The EGA standard was not fully backward-compatible with CGA and MDA (Monochrome Display Adapter).

**e-mail (electronic mail)** The transmission of messages by computer from one person to another, often via the Internet.

**EMS (Expanded Memory Specification)** A technique, developed by Lotus/Intel/Microsoft (LIM), that adds addressable memory to a computer system, overcoming the original MS-DOS upper memory limit. The LIM EMS uses a 64-KB section of memory (usually in upper memory) to provide a "window" into which data can be written. Once in this area, the data can be transferred to the expanded memory. The memory chips are located on an expansion card installed inside the computer.

**Enhanced IDE (EIDE)** A standard developed to increase the size of available disk drives and the speed of data transfer between the host and the disk drive. *See also* IDE (Integrated Device Electronics).

**EPP (Enhanced Parallel Port)** Features 2 MB per second data transfer rates, bidirectional 8-bit operation, and addressing to support multiple (daisy-chained) peripherals on a single computer.

**error messages** Brief technical messages that are displayed by an application or operating system when an error occurs.

**Ethernet** A type of local area network in which communication takes place by means of radio frequency signals carried by a coaxial cable.

**expansion buses** Provide the connection between expansion cards (drive controllers, video cards, modems, and so forth) and the system bus.

**expansion slots** Specialized sockets that allow additional devices (circuit boards/adapter cards) to be attached to the motherboard (by means of the expansion bus). These are used to expand or customize a computer. They are an extension of the computer's bus system.

# F

**fiber-optic cable** A cable that is made out of light-conducting glass or plastic fibers. Multiple fiber cores can be bundled in the center of its protective tubing.

**filenames (also filespec)** Ways to designate files. A traditional DOS filename is made up of three parts—a name of up to eight characters, a period, and an extension of up to three characters. The name can include any number, character, or the following symbols: _()~'!%$&#. For example: MYFILE.DOC. Spaces cannot be used in MS-DOS filenames. Long filenames used in newer operating systems can be much longer and include spaces.

**File Transfer Protocol (FTP)** (1) An application used for transferring files to and from another computer, usually over the Internet. (2) The protocol by means of which these transfers take place.

**floppy disk drive**  Low-capacity magnetic removable storage drive.

**form factor**  The standard physical configuration of a typical device such as a motherboard or a 3.5-inch hard disk drive.

**fragmentation**  Scattering of data in files throughout a disk drive caused by the continual addition and deletion of files. Although not harmful to the computer, fragmentation slows down a hard drive because it causes the computer to access two or more places to retrieve a file. (You can alleviate this problem by running a defragmentation program.)

# G

**gateway**  A link between different computer networks. It is usually a computer that acts as a translator between two completely dissimilar systems. Because it is both a translator and a router, it is usually slower than a bridge or router alone.

**General Protection Fault (GPF)**  An error that occurs in Microsoft Windows when a program tries to access a memory location that is not allocated to it.

**Gopher**  A system of information retrieval that "digs" down through layers of menus to reach what you want. A Gopher system is generally text-based and is best for finding documents buried in archives such as university libraries. Some Web sites offer access to Gopher, but it has largely been replaced by information archives on Web sites.

# H

**horizontal refresh rate (HRR)**  The speed at which the electron beam in a CRT completes one horizontal trace.

**HTML (Hypertext Markup Language)**  An application of SGML (Standardized General Markup Language) used to create Web pages.

**HTTP (Hypertext Transfer Protocol)**  The protocol used to transmit data in the HTML (Hypertext Markup Language) format.

# I

**icon**  A small picture on a computer screen used in Windows (or other graphical operating system) to represent a group of files, an object, or operations. A user accesses the item he or she wants by clicking on the picture with the mouse.

**IDE (Integrated Device Electronics)**  The most common standard for interfacing hard disk and CD-ROM drives in the PC environment. Much of the actual work of controlling the hard disk drive is handled by the system BIOS. This reduces hardware cost but introduces an overall system performance penalty during I/O (input/output) operations. *See also* Enhanced IDE (EIDE).

**integrated circuit (IC)**  An electronic device consisting of many miniature transistors and other circuit elements (resistors, capacitors, and so forth).

**internal cache**  High-speed memory built into the processor to store frequently used data. This bypasses the need to access slower devices such as RAM (random access memory) or hard drives.

**Internet**  A system that links computer networks all over the world.

**I/O address**  A unique name assigned to each device that allows the CPU (central processing unit) to recognize the device with which it is communicating.

**IP (Internet Protocol)**  The protocol used to define how data is transmitted over the Internet.

**IP address (Internet Protocol address)** A unique address that identifies every network and host on the Internet. (A host is defined as the TCP/IP network interface within the computer, not the computer itself—a computer with two network cards will have two IP addresses.)

**IPX/SPX (Internetwork Packet Exchange/ Sequenced Packet Exchange)** NetWare core protocol developed by Novell in the early 1980s.

**IRQ (interrupt request)** A wire used by the CPU (central processing unit) to control the flow of data. It prevents devices from trying to communicate with the CPU at the same time by "interrupting" and temporarily stopping the CPU to deal with a particular request.

**ISA (Industry Standard Architecture)** One of several common expansion slot and card designs.

**ISDN** A telecommunication standard that allows a channel to carry voice and data in digital form over a single line.

**ISO (International Organization for Standardization)** Groups of experts drawn from the industry that set standards for various technologies. The work of these teams has led to development of SCSI (Small Computer System Interface), SGML and Internet standards, as well as the ASCII character set.

**ISP (Internet service provider)** A host computer that users can dial into over a modem to connect to the Internet.

# K

**keyboard** A primary input device much like a typewriter, used for entering text and command function shortcuts into a computer.

**kilobyte (KB)** A unit of memory equal to 1024 characters or bytes (1 KB = one kilobyte).

# L

**LAN (local area network)** A network that covers a limited distance (such as a single building or facility) to allow computers to share information and resources.

**link** Means, also known as a hyperlink, by which a reader is moved to a different location on the Internet when the link is activated. When text is used for a hyperlink, it is often colored differently from the body text of the page so it stands out.

**local bus** A separate bus in the computer designed to provide extra-fast access to the CPU (central processing unit) for certain devices, such as video cards.

**logging on** Means by which—when connecting to a remote computer—the host computer (the one that is called) gives permission to connect. The process of sending the appropriate information to sign on is called logging on. Often a user name and password are required.

**LPT1, LPT2, LPT3** The names assigned to the parallel printer ports on a PC.

# M

**mailing list** A list of subscribers to a particular discussion group. This database can also be used to distribute e-zines (electronic magazines).

**mainboard** *See* motherboard.

**MDA (Monochrome Display Adapter)** Displays text only at a resolution of 720 pixels × 350 pixels. An MDA is perfect for use with MS-DOS-based word-processing and spreadsheet programs. The MDA uses a 9-pin male connector.

**megabyte (MB)** An amount of computer memory equal to $2^{20}$. 1,048,576 bytes = 1024 kilobytes. One megabyte can store more than one million characters.

**megahertz (MHz)** One million hertz (one million cycles per second). A measurement of CPU clock speed.

**memory** The area within a computer where information is stored while being worked on. It stores information (in the form of data bits) that the CPU (central processing unit) and software need to keep running.

**Micro Channel Architecture (MCA)** A short-lived, 32-bit expansion bus that was a proprietary design of IBM used on the IBM PS/2 computer. By abandoning the open design of the existing PC market, IBM limited the willingness of developers and buyers alike to use MCA.

**microphone** Just like the microphone on a tape recorder. Allows input of voice or music to be recorded and saved to a computer file.

**microprocessor** An integrated circuit containing the entire CPU (central processing unit) of a computer, all on one chip, so that only the memory and I/O (input/output) devices need to be added.

**Microsoft Control Panel** The new interface for system management tools that was introduced with Microsoft Windows NT. It offers a single interface to access and utilize a variety of tools.

**miniconnector** A type of power supply connector primarily used on 3.5-inch floppy disk drives.

**modem (MOdulator/DEModulator)** Converts computer data to information that can be transmitted via wires (telephone, ISDN, fiber optics) and wireless communication. Allows communication between computers over long and short distances.

**Molex connector** Type of power supply connector primarily used for devices that need both 12-volt and 5-volt power (floppy disk drives). The most common type of connector.

**monitor** The primary output device, which resembles a television set. It visually displays text and graphics.

**motherboard** Also known as a PWB or printed wiring board, it is the large circuit board found inside the computer. For all practical purposes, it is the computer. It contains the following items: chip set, data bus, address bus, expansion slots, clock, battery, and memory.

**mouse** Device used with graphical environments to point and select objects on the system's monitor. They come in a variety of shapes and sizes.

**MTBF (mean time between failures)** A standard means by which vendors estimate the expected life span of a given product line.

**multitasking** The operation of more than one application at what appears to be the same time on the same PC. The CPU (central processing unit) quickly switches between the various programs, making it possible to work in more than one program at once.

# N

**nanosecond (ns)** One-billionth of one second. The time increment used to measure access speed of the memory chip.

**NetBIOS/NetBEUI (networked basic input/output system/NetBios Enhanced User Interface)** A local area networking protocol developed by IBM and refined by Microsoft; originally, the native protocol for LAN Manager and Windows NT. IBM developed NetBIOS as a way to permit small groups of computers to share files and printers efficiently. NetBIOS is the original edition; NetBEUI is an enhanced version for more powerful networks in the 32-bit operating system.

**network** A group of computers connected together to share data and resources.

**network card** An expansion card that connects a computer to a group of computers so they can access information and programs. Also known as a network interface card (NIC) and network adapter card.

# O

**offline** Networked computers that are not actively connected so that transmission of data is not possible.

**offline reader** A program to display e-mail messages that have been downloaded to a computer.

**ohm** A unit of electrical resistance.

**online** The state in which two or more computers are connected to each other, making data transmission possible.

**operating system** The program that controls a PC and makes it possible for users to run their own applications. The operating system provides the built-in routines that allow the computer to recognize commands, manage files, connect devices, and perform I/O (input/output) operations.

# P

**packet** A group of consecutive characters transmitted from one computer to another over a network.

**parallel** The transmission of several bits at the same time over separate wires.

**parity bit** A very basic type of error-correcting code that uses the value of an extra bit sent at the end of a data string. The bit must have a set value based on an algorithm to verify that the data at the receiving end is correct.

**path** The address to a file. The path consists of the drive name, the location of the file in the directory structure, and the filename. Example: C:\Mystuff\MYFILE.DOC.

**peer-to-peer network** A network in which each connected computer acts as either a server or a client depending on the users' needs. Each user or workstation establishes its own security and determines which resources are available to other users. These networks are limited in size, usually no more than 15 to 20 workstations.

**peripheral** An external device connected to a computer such as a printer, scanner, modem, or joystick.

**persistence** The amount of time a pixel stays visible on a monitor screen, which is a factor of the decay of activity in the phosphor coating.

**pixel** Short for "picture element." One of the dots that make up a graphical image.

**plotter** Similar to a printer, but uses pens to draw an image. Used most often with graphics and drawing programs.

**port** Specific channel used by a network service. For example, Gopher often uses port 70, while some Web sites use port 80.

**power** The strength or force actually put forth by electricity. Electrical power is measured in watts, which is measured by multiplying voltage by current.

**power supply** Takes alternating current (AC) power from a local source (a wall outlet) and converts it to direct current (DC) for on-board electronics use.

**printer** A peripheral device that transfers computer output to paper or other form of hard copy.

**Professional Graphics Adapter (PGA)** An adapter that was originally marketed to the engineering and scientific communities. It was expensive and required three ISA (Industry Standard Architecture) slots when fully configured. This system offered 3-D rotation and 60 frames per second animation. It used a 15-pin, three-row, female

DB-type connector. It gained limited use in CAD environments, but was quickly replaced by better mass-market solutions.

**prompt** The command prompt—a user interface provided by COMMAND.COM in MS-DOS to signal to the user that the computer is ready to receive input (for example, C:\> or A:\>).

**protected mode** A mode introduced with 80286 processors that used an operating system like OS/2 or Windows to allow creation of virtual machines. These provided the functionality of a standard computer in real mode but allowed multiple tasks to take place at the same time. The term refers to the fact that processor, memory, and other hardware are "protected" from the software applications by the operating system, which allocates the memory and processor time.

**protocol** A set of rules that govern the transfer of information. The format used to upload or download files to allow two different computers to communicate in a standard format.

# R

**RAID (redundant array of independent disks)** The combining of several drives using either hardware or software controls to make them seem to be one drive.

**RAM (random access memory)** The main memory where a computer temporarily stores data.

**read-only memory** *See* ROM (read-only memory).

**real mode** An MS-DOS mode in which a computer can perform only one operation at a time and an application expects full control of the system. Real mode operates within the MS-DOS 1-MB limitation.

**register** Temporary memory storage areas located inside the CPU (central processing unit).

Used to hold the intermediate results of calculations or other operations.

**Registry** A file or set of files in Microsoft Windows 95 and later versions that stores information about a computer's hardware and software configuration.

**repeater** A device that works like an amplifier; it increases or boosts a signal to allow transmissions over longer distances.

**resolution** A measurement of the detail of images produced by a monitor or printer. Normally measured by a horizontal and vertical number of pixels for monitors or dpi (dots per inch) for laser printers. The higher the number, the better the quality and the more memory required by the system.

**ring network** A type of network in which all the servers and clients are connected in a closed loop.

**RISC (Reduced Instruction Set Computing)** Uses a smaller and simpler set of instructions to control the processor, thereby greatly enhancing the processing speed.

**ROM (read-only memory)** Computer memory that contains instructions that do not need to be changed, such as operating system startup instructions. The computer can access data from ROM but cannot put new data into it.

**router** A device that works like a bridge but is able to select the best route from network to network based on traffic load. A router can also connect dissimilar networks.

# S

**scanner** A peripheral that converts information from the written page (or a printed graphic) to digital information that can be used by the computer. Works in a manner similar to the scanning process in a photocopy machine.

**scanning** A process that converts a photograph, graphic, or text image found on paper into an electronic computer file.

**SCSI (Small Computer System Interface)** A standard way of interfacing a computer to disk drives and other devices that require high-speed data transfer. Up to 16 SCSI devices, including the host adapter, can be connected in a daisy chain fashion. These devices can be hard disk drives, CD-ROMs, scanners, or printers. SCSI is the only common computer interface that allows adding both internal and external devices on the same chain. (Pronounced "scuzzy.")

**search engine** A program that searches indexes of Internet addresses using keywords. There are hundreds of search engines located on servers throughout the Internet. Popular search engines include AltaVista, Yahoo, HotBot, and Excite.

**serial** Transmission of one bit at a time over a single wire.

**server** The computer that runs the network operating system, manages security, and administers access to resources; strictly speaking, any computer that stores information and allows outside users to get copies of that information.

**server network** This type of network requires a central server (dedicated computer) to manage access to all shared files and peripherals.

**shadow RAM** Many high-speed motherboards use shadow RAM to improve the performance of a computer. Shadow RAM rewrites (or shadows) the contents of the ROM BIOS and/or video BIOS into extended RAM (between the 640-KB boundary and 1 MB). This allows systems to operate faster when application software calls BIOS routines. In some cases, system speed can be increased up to 400 percent.

**software** Any program (set of instructions) that causes a computer to carry out a task or function.

**spooling** Holds computer output before sending it to a printer. This enables the main program to run more quickly because the print spooler handles output. The print spooler then distributes output to the printer at the proper speed.

**star network** A type of network configuration in which all computers are connected to a central point called a hub. The hub collects and distributes the flow data within the network. In large networks, several hubs may be connected. This is the easiest form of network topology to troubleshoot because all information goes through a hub, making it easier to isolate problems.

**superscalar** Technology found in Pentium processors allowing the Pentium to have two instruction pipelines, thereby increasing the speed of processing.

**surge suppressor** Used to prevent large power spikes (such as from lightning) from damaging a computer.

**SVGA (Super Video Graphics Array)** A video standard. The minimum requirement for SVGA compatibility is 640 pixels × 480 pixels at 256 colors. At the low end, typical SVGA systems are operated at 800 × 600 at any color depth. Today, most SVGAs run at 1024 × 768 at 256 with 64 K colors or better.

**switch box** Allows the user to manually (or automatically) switch cable connections so that one computer can use several different printers or devices with one parallel port.

**synchronous** Form of computer communication in which data is transmitted in packets containing more than one character. This is faster than asynchronous transmission because there is no start/stop bit between each individual character.

**syntax** Specific rules that prescribe how the symbols of a programming language can be written to form meaningful statements that will be understood by the PC.

**sysop (system operator)** The system operator of a small BBS (bulletin board system). (Pronounced "SIS-op.")

**system bus** Supports the CPU (central processing unit), RAM (random access memory), and other motherboard components that provide the controlling element to the computer. It is responsible for coordinating the operation of the individual system components and central to the communications system of a computer. Also called the control bus.

**system crystal** Determines the speed at which a CPU (central processing unit) is operated (sets the clock speed); it is usually a quartz oscillator.

# T

**tape drive** A high-capacity removable magnetic data storage device ideal for backups and retrieval of large amounts of data. Works like a tape recorder and saves information in a linear format.

**TCP/IP (Transfer Control Protocol/Internet Protocol)** The name given to a collection of protocols that were designed in the 1970s for use on the large-scale mixed platform that became the Internet.

**telecom software** An application that allows two computers to communicate. Both computers must use compatible software for communication to take place.

**telecommunications** The ability to transmit data over telephone lines to a remote computer.

**telnet** A terminal emulation program that allows you to log on to another computer system over the Internet. You can then run programs on that machine as though you dialed in directly.

**topology** The layout scheme that describes the way in which network nodes are wired in relation to each other.

**transistor** An electronic device that allows a small current in one place to control a larger current in another place; commonly used as amplifiers in radio and audio circuits.

**TSR (terminate-and-stay-resident program)** A computer program, also known as a memory-resident program, that remains in memory after being run so that it can be called up later. These extend the capabilities of the operating system or provide "pop-up" functions (such as a calendar or calculator) that can be brought up in the middle of another program without disturbing that program. These programs were popular in the days of MS-DOS, but lead to numerous problems due to memory usage conflicts.

**twisted-pair cable** Consists of two insulated wires twisted around each other to form a pair. One or more twisted pairs are used in a twisted-pair cable.

# U

**UMA (upper memory area)** The area from 640 KB to 1024 KB that is designated for hardware needs such as video RAM, BIOS, and memory-mapped hardware.

**UMB (upper memory block)** Unused spaces in upper memory that can be divided into blocks. These empty blocks have no RAM associated with them and are simply reserved space. This unused space is valuable because, unlike expanded and extended memory, MS-DOS can run programs in UMB.

**upload** The ability to transfer (send) a file from one computer to a remote computer.

**UPS (uninterruptible power supply)** Acts as both a surge suppressor and a power leveler to provide the computer with a constant source of power. It also provides power during a power failure or interruption so the user can safely save data before shutting down.

**USB (universal serial bus)** A new external expansion bus that is popular for use with low-speed mass storage devices such as Zip drives, modems, and printers.

**Usenet** The vast collection of discussion groups and newsgroups on the Internet.

# V

**vertical refresh rate (VRR)** The speed at which a monitor completes all vertical traces.

**VGA (Video Graphics Array)** A graphics adapter that offers 16 colors at a resolution of 640 pixels × 480 pixels. To gain more colors, VGA uses an analog video signal instead of a digital signal. With the analog signal, the VGA standard is able to provide 64 distinct levels for each color, giving users $64^3$ or 262,144 possible colors. It uses a 15-pin, three-row, female DB-type connector.

**Virtual Control Program Interface (VCPI)** A memory management specification that accesses extended memory for MS-DOS-based applications. It allows only one application to control extended memory and does not support multitasking. Windows is not compatible with the VCPI specification.

**virtual memory** Hard disk space that can be used as additional memory for holding data not immediately required by the processor.

**volts** The unit of electromotive force, or the potential energy, that will produce a current of 1 ampere when steadily applied against a resistance of 1 ohm. Voltage is also considered the potential energy of a circuit.

# W

**WAN (wide area network)** A network that spans a large geographical area. The network is connected by means of telephone lines, ISDN (Integrated Services Digital Network) lines, DSL, cable, radio waves, or satellite links.

**warm boot** The process of restarting a computer that is already running by holding down the CTRL, ALT, and DELETE keys simultaneously. It can also refer to choosing a Shut Down And Restart option in Microsoft Windows 9x or Windows NT.

**wildcards** A keyboard character that represents one or more characters in a string, usually for specifying more than one file by name. The question mark (?) matches any character in a specified position, and the asterisk (*) matches any number of characters up to the end of the filename or extension.

**Windows File Protection** A background service in Windows 9x, Windows NT, and Microsoft Windows 2000 that tracks any modification to core system files and warns of potential problems.

**word** The largest amount of data that can be handled by the microprocessor in one operation and also, as a rule, the width of the main data bus.

# X

**XMS (extended memory specification)** RAM (random access memory) above the 1-MB address. Extended memory is accessed through an extended memory manager (HIMEM.SYS for DOS).

# Index

## A

abacus, 2
ABC (Atansoff-Berry Computer), first digital computer, 4
Accelerated Graphics Port (AGP), 154–155
access speeds
    CD-ROM/DVD drives, 227
    RAM and, 122–123
AC/DC converters, 612
ACPI (Advanced Configuration and Power Interface), 310
AC power
    overview of, 610–611
    safety and, 626
    testing with multimeter, 613
AC ripple, 614
AC testers, 614
active-matrix displays
    overview of, 268
    portable computers and, 303–304
active memory, defined, 120
active partitions, defined, 208
actuator arms, 192–193
adapter cards
    CD-ROM/DVD drives, 225
    SCSI drives, 249
Add New Hardware Wizard, CD-ROM/DVD installation, 230
address bus
    CPUs and, 47–48
    first generation Pentiums and, 60–61
    microprocessors and, 50
    processing components and, 31
address/request, parity protected, 64
Advanced Configuration and Power Interface (ACPI), 310
Advanced Power Management (APM), 310
Advanced Server, Windows NT, 380
Advanced tab, CMOS setup, 106

Advanced Technology Attachment (ATA), 233, 236
Advanced Technology Attachment/ Common Access Method (ATA/CAM), 197–198
AGP (Accelerated Graphics Port), 154–155
ALU (arithmetic logic unit), microprocessor design and, 44
AMD
    CPU development by, 62
    as Intel competitor, 62
American Megatrends (AMI)
    BIOS market dominance by, 104
    BIOS setup program of, 105
    POST beep codes, 113
American Standard Code for Information Interchange (ASCII)
    computer codes and, 45
    information transfer protocols, 350
    overview of, 17
    printers and, 285
    tables for, 18–19
AMI. See American Megatrends (AMI)
analytical engine, computer development and, 3
antistatic devices, 625–626
APM (Advanced Power Management), 310
application logs, 484
arithmetic logic unit (ALU), microprocessor design and, 44
ASCII code. See American Standard Code for Information Interchange (ASCII)
asynchronous communication
    overview of, 342
    using parity bits for error detection, 343
ATA (Advanced Technology Attachment), 233
ATA/CAM (Advanced Technology Attachment/Common Access Method), 197–198
ATA/DMA drives, 238
Atansoff-Berry Computer (ABC), first digital computer, 4

AT Attachment Packet Interface (ATAPI)
    disk drives and, 234
    EIDE upgrades and, 235
AT command, 353
AT power supplies
    AT motherboard connections, 80–82
    overview of, 78
ATX power supplies
    ATX motherboard connections, 82–83
    overview of, 78
audio capability
    audio out cable, 229
    CD-ROM/DVD drives, 226
autodetection, CMOS, 202–203
AUTOEXEC.BAT
    CD-ROM/DVD installation and, 229–230
    commands for, 395
    CONFIG.SYS and, 460–461
    DOS boot sequence and, 373–374
    overview of, 393
    Windows Me and, 584
automated tasks, maintenance, 516
Award BIOS
    market dominance by, 104
    setup program for, 105

## B

backslash, use of, 392
backups
    file backups, 530–533
    file backups, planning, 530–531
    file backups, setting policies, 531–532
    file backups, utilities for, 532–533
    registry backups, 534–535
    system state backups, 533–534
    types of, 530–531
    Windows installation and, 421
Backup Wizard, 533
bandwidth
    cable specification and, 325
    defined, 261
    troubleshooting reductions in, 328

banks, memory chips and, 126

basic input/output system. *See* BIOS (basic input/output system)

batch files
  creating, 389
  renaming, 390–391
  Windows installation and, 421

batteries
  CMOS, 109–110
  lithium ion batteries, 308
  portable computers and, 309
  processing components and, 31
  types of, 308

baud rate
  defined, 336
  modems, 348

BBS (bulletin board system), 337

beep codes, POST test, 112–113

Bell commands, 352

binary notation, 13–16
  bits/bytes and, 13
  computer codes and, 45
  counting in, 14–15
  defined, 13
  hexadecimal code and, 134–135
  parallel and serial devices and, 16
  system of, 14

BIOS (basic input/output system). *See also* ROM (read-only memory) BIOS
  8.4-GB barrier, 237
  32-bit access, 241–242
  classes of, 101–102
  CMOS setup procedures for, 103–109
  defined, 101
  determining manufacturer of, 104
  EIDE drive installation and, 239
  shadow RAM and, 139–140
  Windows 2000 initialization phase and, 456, 470
  Windows installation and, 420

Bi-Tronics, parallel printer cables, 171

bits
  binary notation and, 13
  bps defined, 337
  defined, 349

bits *(continued)*
  value of, 13

blackouts, defined, 86

blocks, defined, 398

bootable floppy disks (boot disks)
  creating, 205
  defined, 398
  software tools and, 503–504

boot drive, Windows 2000, 470–471

BOOT.INI files, 470, 471

BOOTLOG.TXT files, 434, 463–464

boot partitions
  corrupted information and, 215
  defined, 208

boot process. *See also* dual booting
  DOS, 373–374
  operating systems and, 370
  Windows 98, 455–461
  Windows 98, BIOS initialization phase, 456
  Windows 98, hardware and real-mode driver loading phase, 456–458
  Windows 98, loading CONFIG.SYS and AUTOEXEC.BAT, 460–461
  Windows 98, protected mode initialization phase, 461
  Windows 98, using MSDOS.SYS for custom configurations, 458–460
  Windows 2000, 470–472

boot sector, 206, 398

bootstrap loading process, Windows 2000, 470–471

bottlenecks, defined, 328

bps (bits per second)
  defined, 337
  modem speed and, 348

branch directories, 386

branch predictions, 60

branch target buffer (BTB), 63

bridges, function of, 327

brownouts, 86

browsers
  defined, 337
  overview of, 357

BTB (branch target buffer), 63

bulletin board system (BBS), 337

burst mode, 153

bus cycle
  defined, 122
  memory configuration and, 125–126

bus mastering, 153

bus system. *See also* expansion buses
  address bus, 31, 47–48
  data bus, 31
  Dual Independent Bus architecture, 64
  function of, 20–21

bus topology
  Ethernet and, 325–326
  overview of, 318

bytes, 13

# C

cables, 170–175
  CD-ROM/DVD drives, 228–229
  floppy disk drives, 183–184
  FPDs, 268–269
  hard disk drives, 199–200
  identifying, 174
  Internet connections, 360–361
  keyboards, 173–174
  monitors, 264, 278
  networks, 322–325
  null modems, 173
  parallel printers, 170–172
  SCSI drives, 173, 249–250
  serial ports, 172–173
  summary of, 175
  troubleshooting, 174–175, 278

cache bus, Pentium II, 64

cache memory
  defined, 130–131
  microprocessor development, 50
  overview of, 550
  Pentium processors, 60–61, 62
  static RAM (SRAM), 131
  types of memory and, 130–133

capacitors, 620

carrier rings, 57

Carrier Sense Multiple Accesswith Collision Detection (CSMA/CD), 325
cascading, devices, 163
case, computer, 36, 94–96
case sensitivity, 392
cathode-ray tubes (CRTs)
    cleaning, 264
    comparing with FPDs, 267
    costs of, 261
    overview of, 258–260
CCITT (Comité Consultatif International Télégraphique et Téléphonique)
    overview of, 353
    rates designated by, 349
    speed standards of, 348
CCS (Common Command Set), SCSI-2, 244
CD (Change Directory) test, 388
CD-ROM/DVD drives, 222–232
    access time, 227
    advantages of, 222–223
    audio capability, 226
    CD recorders and, 34

    connecting, 225–226
    development of, 222–223
    DVD formats, 225
    input components for, 30
    multimedia and, 231
    portable computers and, 306
    standards, 223
    summary, 253–255
    technology of, 224
    video-capture software, 231–232
CD-ROM/DVD drives, installing
    controller cards, 228
    internal drives, 228–229
    overview of, 227
    software setup, 229
    Windows 3.x and, 229–230
    Windows 95, Windows 98, Windows Me and, 230
    Windows NT, Windows 2000 and, 230–231
CD-R technology, 224

central processing units (CPUs), 39–75
    address bus, 47–48
    clock speeds, 45–46, 58–59
    codes for, 45
    components of, 30–31
    design of, 44
    external data bus, 40–41
    heat sinks and fans, 59
    history of, 43
    illustration of, 26
    installing, 69–72
    integrated circuits on, 43
    memory and, 47–48
    microprocessor design and, 44
    overview of, 27–28
    portable computers and, 56–57, 304–305
    real mode vs. protected mode, 53–54
    recommended for Windows, 415–416
    SIMMs and, 58
    summary, 73–75
    terminology of, 42–49
    transistors for, 42–43
    upgrading, 68–72, 552–553
    use of registers by, 44
    virtual memory and, 53
    working of, 49–50
central processing units (CPUs), types of
    IBM PC AT, 52–53
    Intel 386SX, 55–56
    Intel 486SX, 58–59
    Intel 80286, 52–53
    Intel 80386, 54–55
    Intel 80486, 57
    Intel 8086 and 8088, 50–52
    Intel Pentiums, Celeron models, 65–66
    Intel Pentiums, competitors, 62
    Intel Pentiums, on-board cache, 62
    Intel Pentiums, overview, 59–61
    Intel Pentiums, Pentium II, 63–64
    Intel Pentiums, Pentium III, 66
    Intel Pentiums, Pentium MMX, 63
    Intel Pentiums, Pentium Pro, 62–63

central processing units (CPUs), types of (continued)
    Intel Pentiums, superscalar technology, 61–62
    Intel Pentiums, Xeon line, 66
    Motorola, 66–67
Certified Novell Administrator (CNA), 328
Certified Novell Engineer (CNE), 328
CGA (Color/Graphics Adapter) card, 270
Check Upgrade Only mode, Windows 2000 Professional, 421
chip sets
    modems and, 340–341
    overview of, 99–100
    processing components and, 30
CHS values
    advanced disk drives and, 236
    early hard disk drives and, 235
    EIDE drives and, 239
    overview of, 196
cleaning kit, 517–518
clean install, defined, 420–421
client relations, 596–602
    customer service, 599–602
    customer service, difficult clients and coworkers, 600–601
    customer service, problem escalation, 601
    customer service, reports and logs, 599–600
    customer service, support calls, 599–600
    documentation and, 596–597
    levels of support, 597–598
    spare parts, 598
    standardizing equipment, 598–599
clocks, processors
    cycles of, 45
    developments in speed of, 55
    doubling, 58–59
    first generation Pentiums and, 60
    microprocessor development and, 50
    overview of, 46
    processing components and, 31
    superscalar technology and, 61–62

clones, defined, 52

clusters
  defined, 398
  hard disk drive installation and, 209

CMOS (complementary metal-oxide
    semiconductor), 103–109
  accessing BIOS programs, 105–109
  batteries, 109–111
  clock, 110
  errors, 214
  installing hard disk drives, 200–204
  maintaining, 109
  nonvolatile memory and, 120
  power supply failures and, 616
  settings for floppy disk drives, 185
  typical setup for updating, 104–105
  updateable chips and, 102–103
  updating, 103–109
  virus checker, 107

CNA (Certified Novell
    Administrator), 328

CNE (Certified Novell Engineer), 328

coaxial cables, 323–324

coils (inductors), 623

cold boot, 374

color
  depth of, 271–272
  display adapters and, 272–274

Color/Graphics Adapter (CGA)
    card, 270

Colossus I, first digital computers, 4

Comité Consultatif International
    Télégraphique et Téléphonique.
    See CCITT (Comité Consultatif
    International Télégraphique et
    Téléphonique)

COMMAND.COM program, 373–374

Command Mode, system start up in,
    577–578

command prompt
  COMMAND command, 381–383
  DOS and, 372
  DS mode navigation and, 386–388
  Edit (text editor), 391–393
  external, 384, 386
  HELP command, 383
  internal, 384–385

command prompt *(continued)*
  PATH command, 388–391
  PROMPT command, 383–384
  summary and review, 406–408

Common Command Set (CCS),
    SCSI-2, 244

common mode failures, networks, 328

common-mode noise, 247

communication, electronic. *See*
    electronic communication

Communications Port (COM1)
    Properties dialog box, 341

compact installation, defined, 430

compatibility mode. *See* real mode

complementary metal-oxide
    semiconductor. *See* CMOS
    (complementary metal-oxide
    semiconductor)

COM ports
  COM1, 341
  overview of, 167–168

compression
  data, 352
  disk compression, 211–212

computer cards, 302

computer cases, 36, 94–96

computer maintenance. *See*
    maintenance

Computer Management icon, 482–483

Computer Management snap-in,
    581–582

computers, development of, 1–10
  abacus, 2
  ABC (Atansoff-Berry Computer),
    first digital computer, 4
  analytical engine and
    pre-electronics, 3
  digital electronic computers, 4–7
  first electrically driven, 3
  role of computer service
    professionals, 8
  summary, 9–10

computers, disassemble/reassemble,
    541–545
  disassembling, 544
  preparation for, 542–543
  reassembling, 545
  tools and components, 543

computer service professionals, 8

CONFIG.SYS, 393
  AUTOEXEC.BAT and, 395,
    460–461
  CD-ROM/DVD installation,
    229–230
  commands for, 394
  DOS boot sequence and, 373–374
  EIDE installation, 240
  overview of, 393
  Windows Me and, 584

configuration sheet, for system, 547

connections
  Internet, 360–361
  LANs, 315–316
  overview of, 314
  WANs, 316

connectivity, errors, 214–215

connectors, 170–175. *See also* cables
  floppy disk drives, 184
  identifying, 174
  keyboards, 173–174
  null modems, 173
  parallel printers, 170–172
  SCSI devices, 173, 249–250
  serial ports, 172–173
  summary of, 175
  troubleshooting, 174–175
  USB devices, 157

connectors, power supplies, 80–84
  AT motherboards, 80–82
  ATX motherboards, 82–83
  extenders, 84
  mini connectors, 84
  mini plugs, 84
  molex connectors, 83
  splitters, 84

continuity, testing, 615

controller cards
  CD-ROM/DVD drives, 228
  EIDE drives, 238–239
  memory and, 122

Control Panel, 476–481
  accessing, 482
  introduction to, 474
  modifying Registry, 488–489

Control Panel *(continued)*
   updating Registry, 491
   working with System Properties
      icon, 477–481
control unit (CU), microprocessor
   design, 44
conventional memory, defined, 137
cooling. *See* fans
core chips, BIOS, 101–102
coronas, laser printers and, 291–292
costs
   comparing CRTs and FPDs, 267
   CRT picture area, 261
   display systems, 277
   ink-jet cartridges, 289
   multimedia cards, 274
   printers, 285
   SCSI, 248
CRTs. *See* cathode-ray tubes (CRTs)
crystal speed, clocks, 46
CSMA/CD (Carrier Sense Multiple
   Access with Collision
   Detection), 325
CU (control unit), microprocessor
   design, 44
cursor, defined, 392
customer service, 599–602
   difficult clients and coworkers,
      600–601
   problem escalation, 601
   reports and logs, 599–600
   support calls, 599–600
custom installation, defined, 430
cylinders
   CHS values and, 196
   hard disk drives and, 194–195, 235
Cyrix, CPUs, 62

**D**

data buses. *See* expansion buses;
   external data bus
data compression, 352
data-flow analysis
   defined, 63
   Pentium IIs and, 64
Data Link Control (DLC)
   protocol, 327

data, storing
   advantages of CDs, 223
   CD-ROM technology for, 224
   hard disk drives and, 191
   hard disk drives vs. CD-ROMs, 224
   upgrading Windows and, 416–417
data transfer, DMA mode, 237
data transfer rate
   CD-ROM/DVD access time, 227
   early hard disk drives, 234
   noise and, 247
   SCSI-2, 245
   troubleshooting in networks, 328
date calculations, 46
DC power
   overview of, 612
   testing voltage, 615
DDO (Dynamic Drive Overlay)
   software, 240
DEFRAG command, 211
defragmentation
   Disk Defragmenter, 528–530
   Disk Defragmenter, accessing, 529
   Disk Defragmenter, function of,
      528–529
   Disk Defragmenter, scheduling,
      529–530
   hard disk drives, installation
      and, 211
   operating systems and, 370
   troubleshooting networks, 328
degaussing, monitors, 263–264
depth value, memory capacity and, 127
DETCRASH.LOG, 434
DETLOG.TXT, 434–435
Device Driver dialog box, 560
device drivers
   CD-ROM/DVD, 229–230
   defined, 111
   displays, display adapters and,
      275–276
   displays, improper image formation
      and, 264
   displays, troubleshooting, 278
   hard disk drives, 519
   interrupt requests and, 162
   laser printers, 292

device drivers *(continued)*
   loading, 111–112
   usable memory and, 141
   Windows 95, 98, Me, 230
   Windows 2000, 437, 471–472
device management, 370
Device Manager
   Control Panel and, 478–481
   troubleshooting display
      systems, 278
   troubleshooting with, 584–585
DIB (Dual Independent Bus)
   architecture, Pentium II, 64
differential diagnosis, 575–577
   operational issues, 576
   overview, 575–576
   shutdown issues, 576–577
   startup issues, 576
digital communication, modems
   and, 341
Digital Subscriber Line (DSL),
   connecting to Internet, 360
digital volt-ohm meter (DVOM).
   *See* multimeter
DIME (Direct Memory Execute), 155
DIMMs. *See* dual inline memory
   modules (DIMMs)
diodes, 620–621
DIP. *See* dual in-line package (DIP)
DIP switches, setting I/O
   addresses, 161
DIR command, 386–388
Direct Memory Access (DMA). *See
   also* Ultra DMA drives
   ATA/DMA drives, 238
   data transfer modes, 237
   managing, 167
   setting channels, 166
Direct Memory Execute (DIME), 155
directories
   CD (Change Directory) test, 388
   defined, 392
   DS mode navigation and, 386–388
   of MD (Make Directory) test, 387
   setting up Windows 98 for
      installation, 429
disassembly, computers, 544, 563

Disk Cleanup wizards, cleaning up old files, 527

disk compression, 211–212

Disk Defragmenter, 528–530
  accessing, 529
  function of, 528–529
  scheduling, 529–530

disk drives. *See* by type

Disk Management snap-in, Windows 2000, 485–486

display adapters, 270–276
  advanced display systems and, 272
  evolution of, 270–272
  high color, true color, photo-realism and multimedia displays, 272–274
  troubleshooting, 278
  video memory and, 274–276

display coprocessors, 271–272

display drivers
  display adapters and, 275–276
  improper image formation and, 264
  troubleshooting, 278

Display Power Management Signaling (DPMS), 262

Display Properties dialog box, 482

display systems
  advanced, 272
  basic operation of, 258–261
  choosing, 262, 277–278
  FPDs, 266–269
  FPDs, comparing with CRTs, 266–267
  FPDs, installing and maintaining, 268–269
  FPDs, technology of, 268
  FPDs, types of LCD displays, 267–268
  high color, true color, photorealism, and multimedia displays, 272–274
  monitors, 257–265
  monitors, basic operation of, 258–261
  monitors, considerations in choosing, 262
  monitors, high voltage hazards and, 511

display systems *(continued)*
  monitors, maintenance of, 264–265
  monitors, output components overview, 32
  monitors, power-saving features of, 262
  monitors, preventative maintenance, 519
  monitors, safety and, 626
  monitors, tuning, 262–264
  screens, active-matrix, 303–304
  screens, dual-scan, 303
  screens, portable computers, 303
  summary and review, 280–282
  troubleshooting, 278–279
  video memory and, 274–276

DLC (Data Link Control) protocol, 327

DMA. *See* Direct Memory Access (DMA)

DNS (domain name system), 360

docking ports, 301

documentation
  client relations and, 596–597
  computer assembly/disassembly and, 542
  software tools and, 505
  troubleshooting and, 572

domain name system (DNS), 360

DOS mode. *See also* MS-DOS
  boot sequence, 373–374
  command prompt, 373
  file system, 374–375
  navigation and file management, 386–388
  summary, 406–408
  support for, 453
  terminology of, 392–393
  understanding, 372–375

DOS prompt, 392

dot-matrix printers
  maintaining, 520
  overview of, 287–288

dot pitch, 261

download, defined, 337

DPMS (Display Power Management Signaling) modes, 262

DRAM. *See* dynamic RAM (DRAM)

drive pointers, 392

drivers. *See also* device drivers
  operating systems, 559–560
  real-mode driver loading phase, 456–461

drives. *See* by type

drums, laser printers
  cleaning and charging, 293
  photosensitivity of, 291
  transferring toner to, 293

DSL (Digital Subscriber Line), connecting to Internet, 360

DTMF (Dual Tone Multiple Frequency), 337

dual booting. *See also* boot process
  defined, 398
  Windows installation and, 419–420

Dual Independent Bus (DIB) architecture, Pentium II, 64

dual inline memory modules (DIMMs)
  adding memory and, 126
  formats, 550
  overview of, 130

dual in-line package (DIP)
  core chips and, 102
  protected vs. real modes and, 52, 54
  switches for setting I/O addresses, 161

dual-scan displays, 303

Dual Tone Multiple Frequency (DTMF), 337

duplexing, printers, 286

duty cycle, defined, 285

DVD drives. *See* CD-ROM/DVD drives

DVD-RAM/RW format, 225

DVD-R format, 225

DVD-ROM format, 225

DVD video format, 225

DVOM. *See* multimeter

Dynamic Drive Overlay (DDO) software, 240

dynamic execution, defined, 63

dynamic RAM (DRAM). *See also* random access memory (RAM)
  adding memory and, 126
  comparing costs of SRAM with, 131

dynamic RAM (DRAM) *(continued)*
defined, 121
display coprocessors and, 271–272
purchasing, 127
SIPPs and, 124

# E

ECC. *See* error-correction
coding (ECC)
ECP (Extended Capabilities Port),
parallel printers, 171
Edit (text editor), using, 391–393
EDO RAM (extended data out random
access memory), 274–275, 550
EGA (Enhanced Graphics Adapter)
card, 270–271
EIDE drives. *See also* IDE/EIDE
(Integrated Device Electronics)
hard disk drives
advanced hard disk drives, 235
connecting CD-ROM/DVD drives
with, 226
DVD technology and, 224
early limitations of, 233–235
installing, 238–241
overview of, 233–234
portable computers and, 306
upgrading, 235
EISA (extended ISA), 151–152
ELDs (electroluminescent
displays), 268
electricity vs. electrical energy, 608
electroluminescent displays
(ELDs), 268
electromagnetic interference (EMI), 94
electron guns, 258
electronic communication, 11–24
ASCII code for, 17–19
asynchronous, 342
binary math terms for, 13–16
computer bus system and, 20–21
digital, 341
early forms of, 12–13
laser printing and, 292–293
modems and, 339–340, 352–353
networks and, 314
protocols for, 342

electronic communication *(continued)*
summary, 22–24
synchronous, 342
electronic components, 619–623
capacitors, 620
fuses, 619–620
inductors (coils), 623
rectifiers and diodes, 620–621
transformers, 622
transistors, 621–622
electronic mail. *See* e-mail
(electronic mail)
Electronic Numerical Integrator and
Computer (ENIAC), first
digital computers, 4
electrostatic discharge (ESD), 624–626
causes of, 624
damage caused by, 624–625
handling CPUs and, 72
handling SIMMs and, 125, 128
modem installation and, 346
power hazards and, 510
preventing, 625–626
summary, 629
e-mail (electronic mail)
computer maintenance and, 506
overview of, 358–359
embedded servo, low-level formatting,
204–205
emergency repair disk (ERD)
creating and updating, 504
files on, 536
functions of, 537
updating, 536
Windows 2000/NT and, 444,
536–537
EMI (electromagnetic interference), 94
emissions, CRTs and FPDs, 267
EMS (Expanded Memory
Specification), 137–138
encryption, 398
end-of-file (EOF) marker, 398
Enhanced CHS translation, 236
Enhanced Graphics Adapter (EGA)
card, 270–271
Enhanced IDE (EIDE). *See*
EIDE drives

Enhanced Parallel Port (EPP), 171
Enhanced Print Troubleshooter
(EPTS), 593
Enhanced Small Device Interface
(ESDI) drives, 197
ENIAC (Electronic Numerical
Integrator and Computer), first
digital computers, 4
environmental issues
computer requirements, 517
safety and, 513–514
EOF (end-of-file) marker, 398
EPP (Enhanced Parallel Port), 171
EPTS (Enhanced Print
Troubleshooter), 593
equipment, standardizing, 598–599
erase lamp, laser printers and, 292
ERD. *See* emergency repair
disk (ERD)
ergonomics, comparing CRTs and
FPDs, 267
error-correction coding (ECC)
memory and, 122
Pentium II developments and, 64
errors
floppy disk drives, 186
getting error message details, 577
hard disk drives, 213–216
isolating problems, 115
messages, 392
modems, 352
operating systems, 370
POST codes, 114
SIMMs, 130
using Xmodem, 350
ESD. *See* electrostatic discharge (ESD)
ESDI (Enhanced Small Device
Interface) drives, 197
Ethernet
cables, 323
LAN communication and, 325–326
networks, 318
even parity, 343
Events Log, 445
Event Viewer snap-in, 484
Expanded Memory Specification
(EMS), 137–138

expansion, SCSI hard disk drives, 245
expansion buses, 148–158
  accelerated graphics port, 154–155
  development of, 148–149
  extended ISA, 151–152
  function of, 40
  IEEE 1394 Firewire High-
    Performance Serial
    Interface, 156
  industry standard architecture,
    149–150
  micro channel architecture, 150–151
  Peripheral Component Interconnect,
    153–154
  processing components and, 31
  Universal Serial Bus, 156–157
  VESA local bus, 152–153
expansion cards, configuring, 159–169
  COM and Ports, 167–168
  DMA, 166–167
  installing, 169
  I/O addresses, characteristics of,
    159–161
  I/O addresses, managing, 161–162
  I/O addresses, setting, 161
  IRQs, 162–165
expansion cards, upgrading, 553–557
  non-Plug and Play, 555–557
  Plug and Play, 557
  questions to ask, 554
  steps in adding, 555
expansion slots. See expansion buses
Extended Capabilities Port (ECP),
    parallel printers, 171
extended data out random access
    memory (EDO RAM), 274–
    275, 550
eXtended Graphics Array (XGA), 273
extended ISA (EISA), 151–152
extended memory specification
    (XMS), 137
extended partitions, 206–207
eXtended Technology (XT), IBM, 52
extenders, defined, 84
external cache (L2), 132
external commands, 384–386

external data bus
  first generation Pentiums and, 60–61
  microprocessor development and, 50
  overview of, 40–41
  parts of, 149
  processing components and, 31
external modems
  analog, 343–344
  installing, 347

**F**

F8 key, SCSI devices, 247
fans
  computer cases and, 95
  CPU development and, 59
Fast ATA, 236
fast page-mode RAM (FPM RAM),
    274
FAT (file allocation table), 208–210,
    400–403
  defined, 398
  file attributes on, 403
  file system security, 402–403
  file system size limitations, 402–403
  NTFS and, 401–402
  overview of, 208–209
  sectors and clusters, 209
  workings of, 210
FAT16
  comparing FAT32 with, 400–401
  installing Windows using, 422
  utilities, 505
FAT32
  comparing FAT16 with, 400–401
  disk compression and, 210–212
  installing Windows using, 422
  using, 210
  utilities, 505
fatal errors, power-on self test
    (POST), 114
fax modem
  overview of, 346
  speeds, 349
fdisk utility
  installing Windows, 422–424

fdisk utility (continued)
  partitioning with, 206–209
fiberoptic cables, 324
file allocation table. See FAT (file
    allocation table)
file backups, 530–533
  planning, 530–531
  setting policies, 531–532
  utilities for, 532–533
file formats, 398
file handle, 398
file locking, 398
filenames
  defined, 392, 398
  LFN support for Windows 98,
    455–456
filespecs, 392
file systems, 397–405
  basics of, 397–399
  comparing and choosing, 399–402
  defining files, 398
  DOS-based, 374–375
  FAT-based, 400
  managing, 370
  security of, 403–405
  size limitations of, 402–403
  summary, 405–408
  Windows 98, 452
  Windows 2000, 442
  Windows NT, 401–402
File Transfer Protocol (FTP), 350, 359
fire hazards, 512–513
  extinguishers for, 513
  preventing, 512
firewalls, 360–361
Firewire, expansion buses and, 156
firmware. See BIOS (basic input/
    output system)
fixed disks, 191
flash BIOS, 101
flash ROM, 101
flat-panel displays (FPDs), 266–269
  choosing, 277–278
  comparing with CRTs, 266–267
  installing and maintaining, 268–269

flat-panel displays (FPDs) *(continued)*
  LCD displays and, 267–268
  portable computers and, 300
  technologies of, 268
flip-flop circuits, 131
floating-point unit (FPU),
    Pentium II, 64
floppy disk drives, 182–189
  basics of, 182–185
  errors with, 186–188
  I/O devices and, 33
  preventative maintenance of,
    519–520
  problems with, 185–186
  replacing, 188
  summary, 216–218
floppy disks
  creating bootable, 205
  installing Windows 2000 with,
    438–439
flux reversals, 191
FM (frequency modulation), 191
folders, defined, 398
fonts, printers and, 285
formatting
  defined, 208, 398
  high-level, 208
  low-level, 204–205
  using FORMAT command, 204
FPDs. *See* flat-panel displays (FPDs)
FPM RAM (fast page-mode
    RAM), 274
FPU (floating-point unit),
    Pentium II, 64
fragmentation. *See also*
    defragmentation
  installing hard disk drives and, 211
  troubleshooting networks, 328
frequency modulation (FM), 191
FTP (File Transfer Protocol), 350, 359
full-duplex jack, 346
fuser rollers, laser printers, 292
fuses, 619–620

**G**

gateways, 327
GBs (gigabytes), 13
GDI (Graphical Device Interface), 451
General tab, System Properties,
    478–479
geometry, hard disk drives,
    193–196, 203
ghosting, 296
gigabytes (GBs), 13
Graphical Device Interface (GDI), 451
graphics, evaluating printers and, 284
graphics adapters, 416. *See also*
    display adapters
grounds, electrical
  defined, 611
  power hazards and, 511–512

**H**

HAL (hardware abstraction layer), 467
half-duplex jack, 346
handheld computers, 301
handshaking, communication
    devices, 351
hand tools, maintenance with, 502–503
hard disk drives, 190–216
  actuator arms, 192–193
  comparing with CD-ROMS for data
    storage, 224
  data storage, 191–192
  geometry of, 193–196
  I/O devices and, 33
  partitions, installing
    Windows 2000, 442
  partitions, preparing for Windows
    installation and, 422–424
  physical characteristics of, 190–191
  portable computers, 306
  preventative maintenance, 519
  summary of, 216–218
  types of, 196–198
hard disk drives, advanced, 233–242
  breaking 8.4-GB barrier, 237–238
  breaking 528-MB barrier, 235–237

hard disk drives, advanced *(continued)*
  early limitations of, 233–235
  EIDE drives, installing, 238–241
  EIDE drives, upgrading, 235
  FAT32, 241–242
  multiple block reads, 241
  summary of, 253–255
  Ultra DMA drives, 237–238
hard disk drives, installing
  cabling for, 199–200
  CMOS setup, 200–204
  disk compression, 211
  file allocation tables, 208–210
  fragmentation, 211
  high-level formatting, 208
  low-level formatting, 204–205
  maintaining, 212–215
  overview, 198–199
  partitioning, 205–208
  sectors and clusters, 209
hard disk drives, upgrading, 557–559
  IDE drive, 557–559
  questions to ask, 557
hardware
  cleaning, 517–518
  compatibility, comparing Windows
    systems, 415–416
  compatibility, Windows 2000, 437
  flow control, 351
  loading phase, 456–461
  troubleshooting Windows 2000
    installation, 444
hardware abstraction layer (HAL), 467
hardware acceleration. *See* display
    coprocessors
HDI (head-to-disk interference), 193
head crash, 193
heads
  528-MB limit and, 235
  actuator arms, 192–193
  CHS values and, 196
  hard disk drives and, 194
head-to-disk interference (HDI), 193
heat sinks, CPUs, 59
HELP command, 383–384

hertz, defined, 78

hexadecimal code
  I/O addresses and, 161
  memory mapping using, 134–135

high-level formatting, hard disk
    drives, 208

high memory area (HMA), extended
    memory and, 138

High Sierra specification (ISO 9660
    standard), CD-ROM/DVD, 226

HIMEM.SYS, 138–138

HKEY_CLASSES_ROOT, 487

HKEY_CURRENT_CONFIG,
    487–488

HKEY_CURRENT_USER, 487

HKEY_DYN_DATA, 488

HKEY_LOCAL_MACHINE, 487

HKEY_USERS, 487

HMA (high memory area), extended
    memory and, 138

horizontal refresh rates, monitors, 259

HTML (Hypertext Markup
    Language), 357

HTTP (Hypertext Transfer Protocol),
    357, 359

**I**

IBM
  development of AT (Advanced
    Technology), 52–53
  development of MCA (micro
    channel architecture), 150–151
  development of XT (eXtended
    Technology), IBM, 52
  early features of, 52
  ISA design problems and, 150

IC. *See* integrated circuits (IC)

IDE/EIDE (Integrated Device
    Electronics) hard disk drives
  autodetection, 202–203
  cabling requirements for, 199–200
  comparing with SCSI, 246
  early limitations of, 233
  incompatibility with some CD-R
    technologies, 224
  installing, 557–559
  installing CD-ROMs and, 229

IDE/EIDE (Integrated Device
    Electronics) hard disk drives
    *(continued)*
  low-level formatting and, 204
  overview of, 197–198, 233–234
  sound cards with CD-ROM
    controllers and, 226

IDENTIFY DRIVE command, CMOS,
    202–203

IEEE
  1284 printer modes, 171
  1394 Firewire High-Performance
    Serial Interface, 156
  printer cabling standards of, 170

image formation
  improper, 264
  monitors and, 259

inductors (coils), 623

industry standard architecture (ISA)
  comparing EISA with, 151–152
  expansion buses and, 149–150

information transfer protocols,
    modems, 350–351

initialization (.ini) files,
    Windows 3x, 475

ink-jet printers
  overview of, 288–290
  preventative maintenance, 520–521

input
  components for, 29–30
  illustration of, 26
  overview of, 27–28

input/output (I/O) devices
  limitations of early hard disk drives
    and, 233
  microprocessor design and, 44
  output overview, 33–34

input/output (I/O) manager, Windows
    98, 451

Input/Output Read (IOR) wire, 159

Input/Output Write (IOW) wire, 159

Institute of Electrical and Electronic
    Engineers (IEEE). *See* IEEE

instruction pipeline, 61

INT (interrupt) wire, 162

INTA (interrupt acknowledge), 162

integrated circuits (IC)
  CPU and, 43

integrated circuits (IC) *(continued)*
  defined, 40
  notebook computers and, 301

Integrated Device Electronics. *See*
    IDE/EIDE (Integrated Device
    Electronics) hard disk drives

Integrated Services Digital Network.
    *See* ISDN (Integrated Services
    Digital Network)

Intel microprocessors
  4004, 43
  8008, 43
  80286, 52–53
  80386, 54–55
  80386SX, 55–56
  80486, 57
  80486SX, 58–59
  8080, 43
  8086, 50–52
  8088, 50–52, 270
  Celeron, 65–66
  competitors and, 62
  development of, 50
  Pentium, Xeon line, 66
  Pentium 75, 61
  Pentium III, 66
  Pentium Pro, 62

internal caches (L1)
  first generation Pentiums and, 60–61
  memory and, 131
  microprocessor development and, 50

internal commands, 384–386

internal modems. *See* modems

International Organization for
    Standardization (ISO),
    223–224, 226

Internet, 356–365
  browsers, 357
  defined, 337
  DNS and, 360
  electronic mail (e-mail), 358–359
  FTP and, 359
  getting connected, 360–361
  IP addresses, 359
  ISPs, 359
  overview of, 356
  summary, 363–365

Internet *(continued)*
TCP/IP and, 359
troubleshooting with ping utility, 361–362
URLs, 359
Web sites, 357
Windows 98 features, 412
Windows Me features, 412
World Wide Web and, 357. *see also* Internet
Internet Protocol. *See* IP (Internet Protocol)
Internet server, 337
Internet service provider. *See* ISP (Internet service provider)
Interprocess Communications (IPC) Manager, Windows 2000, 468
interrupt acknowledge (INTA), 162
interrupt requests. *See* IRQs
interrupt (INT) wire, 162
I/O addresses
EIDE upgrades and, 235
managing, 161–162
overview of, 159
setting, 161
standard PC I/O assignments, 160–161
IOCHRDY, setting up PIO mode, 241
I/O devices. *See* input/output (I/O) devices
I/O (input/output) manager, Windows 98, 451
IOR (Input/Output Read) wire, 159
IO.SYS program, 373–374
IOW (Input/Output Write) wire, 159
IP (Internet Protocol)
addresses, 359
defined, 337
IPC (Interprocess Communications) Manager, Windows 2000, 468
IRQs
drive settings, 241
EIDE upgrades and, 235
expansion cards, 162–165
overview of, 162–164
preventing conflicts, 168
setting, 165
typical assignments, 165

ISA. *See* industry standard architecture (ISA)
ISDN (Integrated Services Digital Network)
connecting to Internet with, 360
defined, 337
terminal adapters and, 336, 343–344
ISO (International Organization for Standardization), 223–224, 226
ISP (Internet service provider)
connecting to Internet with, 361
defined, 337
overview of, 359

**J**

jacks, types of, 345–346
jumper settings
computer upgrades and, 556
installing CD-ROM on IDE style drive, 229
installing hard disk drives, 200
I/O addresses, 161

**K**

KBs (kilobytes), 13
Kermit protocol, 351
kernel mode
Windows 98, 451
Windows 2000, 467, 469
keyboards
cables for, 173–174
input components and, 29
portable computers and, 307
preventative maintenance of, 520
key groups, 486
keystone, monitor adjustments and, 263
kilobytes (KBs), 13
kilohertz, 78
Knowledge Base, 507, 577

**L**

L1 cache. *See* internal caches (L1)
landing zone, 196
lands, CD-ROM technology, 224

landscape, printing, 285
LANs (local area networks)
benefits of, 315–316
bus topology, 318
communication over, 325–326
Device Manager and, 479
extending, 327
ring topology, 318–319
star topology, 317
laptops
CPU development and, 56–57
overview of, 300–301
laser printers
components of, 290–292
laser beam of, 291
mechanics of, 292–295
preventative maintenance, 521
troubleshooting problems of, 295–296
LBA translation standards. *See* Logical Block Addressing (LBA)
LCD displays
flat-panel displays and, 267–268
laptops and, 300
portable computers and, 303
LCHS (logical cylinders, heads, and sectors), 236
LEDs (light-emitting diode) displays, 267
LFN (long filename support), 455–456
LIF (low-insertion-force) socket, 69–70
light-emitting diode (LED) displays, 267
line print terminal port (LPT), 168, 285
Liquid Crystal Displays (LCD). *See* LCD displays
lithium ion batteries, 308
local area networks. *See* LANs (local area networks)
logging on, defined, 337
Logical Block Addressing (LBA)
EIDE drives, 235, 239
overview of, 236
logical cylinders, heads, and sectors (LCHS), 236

logical drives
  defined, 203
  partitioning and, 205–206
logical unit numbers (LUNs),
  SCSI, 251
logic circuits, laser printers and,
  290–291
logs
  application logs, 484
  customer service, 599–600
  Events Log, 445
  security log, 484
  Setupact log, 445
  Setup log files, 434–435
long filename support (LFN), 455–456
low-insertion-force (LIF) socket,
  69–70
low-level formatting
  defined, 398
  installing hard disk drives and,
    204–205
LPT (line print terminal port) ports,
  168, 285
LUNs (logical unit numbers),
  SCSI, 251

# M

mainboard. *See* motherboard
maintenance, plans and procedures,
  515–517
  automated tasks, 516
  cleaning hardware, 517–518
  keeping records and, 516–517
  overview of, 515–516
  preventative, 518–521
  preventative, floppy disk drives,
    519–520
  preventative, hard disk drives, 519
  preventative, keyboards and
    pointing devices, 520
  preventative, monitors, 519
  preventative, printers, 520–521
  preventative, scheduling, 521–522
  summary, 538
maintenance, tools, 501–514
  environmental issues, 513–514
  hand tools, 502–503

maintenance, tools *(continued)*
  outside resources, 505–508
  outside resources, continuing
    education, 505
  outside resources, networking,
    505–507
  outside resources, study, 508
  outside resources, World
    Wide Web, 507
  safety, 509–513
  safety, fire hazards, 512–513
  safety, power hazards, 510–512
  safety, problems and
    prevention, 510
  software tools, 501, 503–505
  software tools, bootable floppy disk,
    503–504
  software tools, documentation and
    manuals, 505
  software tools, operating system
    disk, 504
  software tools, utilities, 504–505
  summary, 538
  technical support, 508–509
  technical support, online
    support, 509
  technical support, telephone
    support, 508–509
  types of toolkits for, 501–502
maintenance, Windows, 524–537
  creating ERD and startup disks,
    536–537
  Disk Cleanup wizards, 527
  Disk Defragmenter, 528–530
  file backups, 530–533
  file backups, back up utilities,
    532–533
  file backups, planning, 530–531
  file backups, setting policies for,
    531–532
  overview of, 524–525
  registry backups, 534–535
  ScanDisk, 527–528
  System File Checker, 535–536
  system state back up, 533–534
  virus protection, 525–526
maintenance wizard
  automating maintenance with, 530

maintenance wizard *(continued)*
  Windows 98 and Windows Me, 412
Make Directory (MD) test, 387
manuals. *See* documentation
mapping, memory, 134–142
master boot record, 399
master position, installing EIDE
  drives, 239–240
material safety data sheet (MSDS), 513
MBs. *See* megabytes (MBs)
MCA (micro channel architecture),
  150–151
MCPS (Microsoft Certified Product
  Specialist), 328
MCSE (Microsoft Certified Systems
  Engineer), 328
MD (Make Directory) test, 387
MDA (Monochrome Display Adapter),
  270–271
MDRAM (multibank DRAM), 275
mean time between failures (MTBF),
  extending, 518
megabytes (MBs)
  measuring memory, 122
  value of, 13
megahertz, 78
MEM.COM
  command prompt and, 382
  determining usable memory, 141
memory, 119–145. *See also* random
  access memory (RAM)
  allocation, 136–140
  cache, external (L2), 132
  cache, internal (L1), 131
  cache, write-back vs.
    write-through, 132
  configuring, 125–126
  controllers, 122
  CPUs and, 47–48
  data transfer rate and, 234
  defining, 120
  determining useable, 140–142
  DIMMs, 130
  display coprocessors and, 271–272
  hexadecimal code and, 134–136
  identifying amount of, 124
  mapping, 134–142

memory *(continued)*
  microprocessor development and, 50
  nonvolatile vs. volatile, 120
  Pentium IIs and, 64
  portable computers and, 305–306
  printers and, 285
  processing components and, 31
  ROM, 121
  SCSI host adapters and, 248
  SIMMs, 30-Pin, 124
  SIMMs, 72-pin, 127–128
  SIMMs, installing, 128–130
  SIMMs, specifying, 127
  SIPPs, 124, 127
  SRAM, 131
  video, 274–275
  virtual, 54, 452–456
  voltage and, 128
memory managers
  defined, 54
  expanded memory and, 138
  SCSI hard disk drives and, 248
memory pager, 453
memory upgrades, 548–552
  cache memory and, 550
  chip formats, DIMMs, 550
  chip formats, SIMMs, 548–549
  EDO RAM and, 550
  installing, 551–552
  parity and, 550
  speed of, 550
MFM (modified frequency
    modulation), 191
micro channel architecture (MCA),
    150–151
Microcom Networking Protocol
    (MNP) standards, 353
microphone, input components, 30
microprocessors. *See also* central
    processing units (CPUs)
  defined, 40
  design system of, 44
  development of, 50–67
  early history of, 43
  technology of, 49–50
Microsoft Certified Product Specialist
    (MCPS), 328

Microsoft Certified Systems Engineer
    (MCSE), 328
Microsoft DOS. *See* MS-DOS
Microsoft Knowledge Base, 507, 577
Microsoft Management Console
    (MMC), 477–481
  Administrative Tools, tracking
    system operation, 484–485
  Administrative Tools overview,
    482–483
  introduction to, 474, 482
  modifying Registry settings with,
    488–489
Microsoft Windows, 409–417
  386 enhanced Mode and, 378
  comparing system requirements,
    414–416
  defining objects in, 474
  Driver Model (WDM) and, 452
  Media Player and, 412
  operating modes of, 376
  overview of, 375–376
  real mode of, 376–377
  resource management with, 378–379
  runtime version of, 378
  standard mode of, 377
  system configuration considerations,
    416–417
  user interfaces and, 369
  Windows family, 375–380, 411–414
Microsoft Windows, installing,
    418–446. *See also* Microsoft
    Windows 2000, installing;
    Microsoft Windows 98,
    installing
  backing up data and key files, 421
  choosing upgrade or clean install,
    420–421
  deciding on boot method(s),
    419–420
  firmware or component updates, 420
  hardware requirements and
    compatibility, 420
  planning, 418–419
  preparing hard drive and file system,
    422–424
  recording and obtaining
    information, 421

Microsoft Windows, installing
    *(continued)*
  removing conflicts and verifying
    existing settings, 421–422
  summary, 446–448
Microsoft Windows, managing,
    474–493
  central repository and, 475–476
  Control Panel and, 476–477, 482
  major changes in approach to, 475
  REGEDIT, Windows 9*x*, 489–491
  REGEDT32, Windows 2000,
    491–494
  Registry and, 474, 486–489
  summary, 495–497
  System Properties and, 477–481
  Windows 2000 administrative tools
    and, 482–486
Microsoft Windows, troubleshooting.
    *See* troubleshooting, Windows
Microsoft Windows 3.*x*
  enabling 32-bit file access on,
    241–242
  installing CD-ROM/DVD drives,
    229–230
  transitioning from initialization to
    registry files, 475
  Workgroups 3.11 and, 379
Microsoft Windows 95
  Device Manager, 421
  evolution of, 379–380
  history of, 411
  installing CD-ROM/DVD drives
    on, 230
Microsoft Windows 98, 450–465
  boot process, BIOS initialization
    phase, 456
  boot process, hardware and real-
    mode driver loading phase,
    456–458
  boot process, loading CONFIG.SYS
    and AUTOEXEC.BAT,
    460–461
  boot process, protected mode
    initialization phase, 461
  boot process, using MSDOS.SYS
    for custom configurations,
    458–460
  Device Manager, 584–585

Microsoft Windows 98 *(continued)*
evolution of, 379–380
features of, 412
MSI tool, 582–583
startup methods, 462–464
summary, 495–497
system architecture, 450–452
System Configuration utility,
583–584
virtual memory model in, 452–456
Microsoft Windows 98, installing
command-line switches for,
426–428
dual booting and, 420
hardware requirements for, 415–416
installing CD-ROM/DVD
drives, 230
process of, 428–432
setting up in a new directory, 429
setup process, 425–426
troubleshooting, 432–436
Microsoft Windows 2000, 466–473
Administrative Tools, 482–486
Backup utility of, 532–533
boot process for, 470–472
Computer Management snap-in,
581–582
evolution of, 380
Executive edition, 468–469
features of, 413
kernel and user modes for, 467–470
Professional edition, 380
Professional edition, Check Upgrade
Only mode, 421
Professional edition, operating
system, 466–467
Professional edition, overview of,
413–414
Recovery Console, 590–591
servers, Advanced Server, 414
servers, Datacenter Server, 414
servers, Server, 414
summary, 473, 495–497
system design of, 466–467
Task Manager, 586–587
types of hard disk storage, 485–486

Microsoft Windows 2000, installing
creating setup disks, 439
dual booting and, 419–420
gathering information for, 437–438
hardware requirements,
415–416, 420
installing CD-ROM/DVD drives,
230–231
method of, 438–439
overview, 436–437
post installation tasks, 443–444
preparation and planning for, 437
preparing hard drive and file system,
422–424
running setup, 439–442
step-by-step process of, 442–443
troubleshooting, 444–445
upgrade vs. clean install, 437–438
upgrade vs. update, 437
Microsoft Windows Me
evolution of, 379–380
features of, 412
installing CD-ROM/DVD
drives, 230
moving away from CONFIG.SYS
and AUTOEXEC.BAT, 584
Microsoft Windows NT. *See also*
NTFS (NT file system)
evolution of, 379–380
hardware requirements for, 415–416
history and features of, 413
installing CD-ROM/DVD drives,
230–231
NT Diagnostics tool and, 421
MIDI (Musical Instrument Digital
Interface), 226
mini connectors, 84
mini plugs, 84
MMC. *See* Microsoft Management
Console (MMC)
MNP (Microcom Networking
Protocol) standards, 353
modems, 336–355
asynchronous communication
and, 342
commands for, 354
communication with, 339–340

modems *(continued)*
defined, 336, 337
digital communication and, 341
fax speeds of, 349
handshaking with, 351
hardware for, 343–346
information transfer protocols for,
350–351
installing, 346–347
I/O devices and, 33
ISDN terminal adapters and,
343–344
multifunction, 346
parity and, 343
RS-232 cables, 345
RS-232 port, 344–345
serial/parallel conversion and,
340–341
speeds of, 348–349
standard conventions for, 352–353
summary of, 363–365
synchronous communication
and, 342
telephone-lines and, 345–346
terminology for, 336–338
troubleshooting, 355
types, 56-Kbps, 353
types, external analog, 343–344
types, internal, 343
types, USB, 343
modified frequency modulation
(MFM), 191
Molex connectors
CD-ROMs and, 228
connecting to peripheral
hardware, 83
floppy disk drives and, 184
monitors, 257–265. *See also* display
systems
basic operation of, 258–261
choosing, 262
high voltage hazards and, 511
maintenance of, 264–265
output components and, 32
power-saving features of, 262
preventative maintenance of, 519

monitors *(continued)*
    safety and, 626
    tuning, 262–264
Monochrome Display Adapter (MDA),
        270–271
Morse code, 12–13
motherboards, 93–117
    AT-style, 80–82
    ATX-style, 82–83
    chip sets for, 99–101
    CMOS, accessing BIOS programs,
        105–109
    CMOS, battery for, 109–111
    CMOS, maintaining, 109
    CMOS, typical setup for, 104–105
    CMOS, updating, 103–109
    computer cases and, 94–96
    function of, 40–41
    loading device drivers, 111–112
    manufacturers for, 104–105
    overview of, 93, 97–98
    power-on self test (POST) and,
        112–115
    processing components and, 30
    questions to ask before upgrading,
        560–561
    ROM BIOS and, 111
    summary of, 116–117
    upgrading, 561–562
mouse
    input components and, 29
    preventative maintenance of, 520
Mouse Properties dialog box, 493–494
MPC (Multimedia PC), 231
MSD.EXE, using for diagnostics, 504
MS-DOS, 591–593. *See also*
        DOS mode
    commonly used commands for,
        384–386
    compatibility problems of, 52
    determining usable memory,
        140–141
    Expande d Memory Specification
        (EMS) and, 138
    high memory area and, 138
    history of, 371–372

MS-DOS *(continued)*
    loading device drivers, 111–112
    Protected Mode Interface
        (DPMI), 137
    real mode and, 139
    troubleshooting, workarounds,
        592–593
    troubleshooting, wrong version,
        591–592
MSDOS.SYS
    custom configurations of Windows
        98, 458–460
    DOS boot sequence and, 373–374
MSDS (material safety data sheet), 513
MSI tool, 582–583
MTBF (mean time between failures),
        extending, 518
multibank DRAM (MDRAM), 275
multifrequency monitors, 259–260
multifunction modems, 346
multimedia
    defined, 231
    standards, 231
Multimedia PC (MPC), 231
Multimedia PC Marketing
        Council, 231
multimeter, 613–614
    measurements with, 613
    reading, 614
    setting up, 613–614
    testing power supplies with,
        616–617
multiple block reads, 241
multiple branch prediction,
        Pentium II, 64
MultiSync, monitors, 259–260
multi-threaded, defined, 451
Musical Instrument Digital Interface
        (MIDI), 226

## N

nanoseconds (ns), 122
NetBEUI (NetBIOS Enhanced User
        Interface), 326
NetBIOS (Networked Basic Input/
        Output System), 326

NETLOG.TXT, 435
Networked Basic Input/Output System
        (NetBIOS), 326
networking
    computer maintenance and, 505–507
    operating systems and, 370
network interface card (NIC)
    defining, 314
    fiberoptic cable systems, 324
    installing and configuring, 320–322
    I/O devices, 33
network medium, defined, 314
network operating system (NOS), 319
network protocols, list of, 326–327
networks, 313–333
    basic requirements of, 314–315
    cabling of, 322–325
    certification and, 329
    defined, 314
    interface cards (NICs) and, 320–322
    LANs, communications, 325–326
    LANs, extending, 327
    LANs, overview, 315–316
    maintaining and
        troubleshooting, 328
    network operating system
        (NOS), 319
    protocols for, 326–327
    summary of, 330–333
    topology of, 317–319
    types of, 316
    WANs, 316
    Windows 98 installation, 432
    Windows 2000, installing and
        accessing networks on,
        443–444
    Windows 2000, installing networks
        from, 438–439
    Windows 2000, networking with,
        413–414
nibble, value of, 13
nickel cadmium batteries, 308
nickel metal hydride batteries, 308
noise
    defined, 247
    SCSI hard disk drives and, 247

nonfatal errors, power-on self test (POST), 114

nonvolatile memory
overview of, 120
ROM and, 121

notebook computers, 301

ns (nanoseconds), 122

NTDETECT.COM files
bootstrap loading, 471
hardware detection and configuration, 472
loading Windows 2000 Professional using, 472

NTFS (NT file system), 401–404. *See also* Microsoft Windows NT
file size limitations, 402–403
file systems and, 401–402
folder security and, 404
installing Windows 2000 and, 422
overview of, 401–402

NTLDR files, Windows 2000
bootstrap loading, 470–471
loading kernel, 472
loading Windows 2000, 471–472

null modem cables, 173

numeric error codes, power-on self test (POST), 114

**O**

Object Manager, Windows 2000 Executive, 468

odd parity, 343

ODPR (overdrive processor replacement), 71

offline, defined, 337

offline reader, defined, 337

Ohm's law, 609–610

on-board cache, Pentiums, 62

online, defined, 337

online support, computer maintenance and, 509

operating modes, Microsoft Windows, 376

operating system disk
computer assembly/disassembly and, 543

operating system disk *(continued)*
software tools and, 504

operating systems, 367–408
COMMAND prompt, 381–386
comparing and choosing, 399–402
CONFIG.SYS and AUTOEXEC.BAT and, 393–395
detecting, 470
drivers for, 559–560
FAT-based file systems and, 400
file system, basics, 397–399
file system, security, 403–405
file system, size limitations, 402–403
list of management tools for, 578–581
MS-DOS, navigation and file management and, 386–388
MS-DOS, overview, 371–372
MS-DOS, understanding, 372–375
NTFS file system and, 401–402
PATH command, 388–391
software core of, 369–370
summary, 406–408
using Edit (text editor), 391–393
Windows 95, 98, Me, and NT, 379–380
Windows 2000, 380, 443
Windows, evolution of, 375–379
Windows for Workgroups 3.11, 379

operational issues, troubleshooting, 576

output
components for, 32–34
illustration of, 26
overview of, 27–28

outside resources, 505–508
continuing education, 505
networking, 505–507
study, 508
World Wide Web, 507

overdrive processor replacement (ODPR), 71

**P**

P8 connectors, AT motherboards, 80–82

P9 connectors, AT motherboards, 80–82

Packet Internet Groper (ping), 361–362

palmtop (subnotebook) computers, 301

paper capacity, printers, 284

paper feeding, laser printers, 293

paper transport, laser printers, 290

parallel conversion, modems and, 340–341

parallel devices, binary language and, 16

parallel pin assignments, 172

parallel printer cables, 170–172, 286

parity
checking data reliability with, 550
defined, 122
modems and, 343

partitions, 205–208. *See also* sectors
active partitions, 208
boot partitions, 208, 215
corrupted information and, 215
extended, 206–207
file allocation tables and, 209
hard disk drives, 422–424, 442
overview of, 205
primary partitions, 206–208, 399

partition table, 399

passive-matrix displays (PMDs)
overview of, 268
portable computers and, 303

passwords, Windows 2000
installing, 443
logon and, 472

path, file access, 393

PATH command
creating batch files, 389
overview of, 388–391
renaming files, 390–391

PC Cards, 302

PCHS (physical cylinders, heads, and sectors), 236

PCI (Peripheral Component Interconnect), 153–154, 304
PC I/O port address assignments, 160–161
PCL, printers, 285
PCMCIA (Personal Computer Memory Card International Association), 302
PCs (personal computers), 25–38, 610–612
    AC power and, 610–611
    DC power and, 612
    input components, 29–30, 33–34
    input, processing and output stages, 26–28
    output components, 32–34
    processing components, 30–31
    summary, 37–38
    support hardware for, 35–36
PDPs (plasma display panels), 268
peer-to-peer network, 316
Pentium processors
    history of, 59–61
    on-board cache and, 62
    Pentium 75, 61
    Pentium II, 63–64
    Pentium III, 66
    Pentium MMX, 63
    Pentium Pro, 62–63
    superscalar technology and, 61–62
    Windows hardware requirements and, 415–416
    Xeon line, 66
Peripheral Component Interconnect (PCI), 153–154, 304
peripherals, 32
persistence rate, 259
personal computers. See PCs (personal computers)
PGA (pin grid array)
    defined, 71
    inserting, 55–56
PGA (Professional Graphics Adapter), 272
Phoenix BIOS
    market dominance of, 104
    POST beep codes, 113

Phoenix BIOS (continued)
    setup program for, 105–108
phosphor coating, 258
photosensitive drums, laser printers, 291
physical drives, 203
pin assignments, parallel, 172
pincushion, adjusting monitor display, 263
ping (Packet Internet Groper), 361–362
pin grid array (PGA)
    defined, 71
    inserting, 55–56
PIO (Programmed Input/Output) modes
    installing EIDE drives and, 240–241
    overview of, 234
pipelines
    floating-point unit (FPU) and, 64
    superscalar technology and, 61–62
pits, CD-ROM technology, 224
pixels
    defined, 259
    display coprocessors and, 271–272
    screen resolution and, 260–261
Plain Old Telephone Service (POTS), 338
plasma display panels (PDPs), 268
plastic leadless chip carrier (PLCC)
    386 packaging and, 55
    CPU development and, 54
plastic quad flat pack (PQFP) mounts, 56–57
PLCC. See plastic leadless chip carrier (PLCC)
plotters, output components, 32
Plug and Play
    CD-ROMs/DVDs, 230
    expansion cards, 557
    SCSI hard disk drives, 245
    setting I/O addresses, 161
    Windows 98, 412, 433–434
    Windows 2000, 413
Plug-and-Play Manager, Windows 2000 Executive, 468–469

PMDs. See passive-matrix displays (PMDs)
pointing devices
    portable computers and, 307
    preventative maintenance, 520
polarity, electrical, 612
portable computers, 299–312
    batteries, 308–309
    computer cards, 302
    displays for, 303–304
    hard disk drives, 306
    keyboards, 307
    memory, 305–306
    overview of, 300
    pointing devices, 307
    ports, docking, 301
    ports, USB, 307
    power management, 309–310
    processors, 304–305
    removable media, 306
    screen resolution, 304
    summary, 311–312
    types of, 300–301
    voltage reduction, 305
portable installation, defined, 430
portrait, printers, 285
ports
    COM ports, 168, 341
    LPT ports, 168, 285
    overview of, 167–168
    RS-232 port, 344–345
    serial ports, 172–173
POST. See power-on self test (POST)
PostScript printers, 285
POTS (Plain Old Telephone Service), 338
power, electric, 608–623
    electronic components, 619–623
    electronic components, capacitors, 620
    electronic components, fuses, 619–620
    electronic components, inductors (coils), 623
    electronic components, rectifiers and diodes, 620–621

power, electric *(continued)*
  electronic components, transformers, 622
  electronic components, transistors, 621–622
  measuring, 613–615
  measuring, testing AC ripple, 614
  measuring, testing continuity, 615
  measuring, testing DC voltage, 615
  measuring, testing resistance, 615
  measuring, using AC testers, 614
  measuring, using multimeter, 613–614
  Ohm's law, 609–610
  personal computer (PC), 610–612
  personal computer (PC), AC power, 610–611
  personal computer (PC), DC power, 612
  power supplies, 615–619
  power supplies, advanced testing, 617–619
  power supplies, isolating problems, 617
  power supplies, voltage test, 616–617
  safety, ESD and, 510
  safety, grounds and, 510–511
  safety, guidelines for, 511–512
  safety, high voltage hazards and, 511
  safety, overview, 627–628
  summary, 629
  terminology, 608–609
power hazards, 510–512
Power Manager, Windows 2000 Executive, 469
power-on self test (POST)
  beep codes and, 112–113
  computer cards and, 115
  DOS boot sequence and, 373–374
  error codes, 114
  fatal and nonfatal errors, 114
  identifying amount of memory during, 124
  motherboards and, 112–115

power-on self test *(continued)*
  SIMMs installation and, 130
  troubleshooting, 113–114, 278
  video test error messages, 114
PowerPC processor, 67
power-saving
  monitor features for, 262
  monitor maintenance and, 264
  portable computers and, 309–310
power supplies, 77–91, 615–619
  advanced testing, 617–619
  AT motherboards, 80–82
  ATX motherboards, 82
  connections, overview, 80
  connections, peripheral hardware, 83–84
  extenders, 84
  floppy disk drives, 184
  high voltage hazards, 511
  laser printers, 292
  mini connectors, 84
  mini plugs, 84
  molex connectors, 83
  overview of, 78
  power failures and, 86
  power protection devices, 87–88
  sizes of, 79
  splitters, 84
  summary, 89–91
  support hardware and, 35
  troubleshooting, 86–88, 617
  voltage test, 616–617
  wattage, 80
Power tab, CMOS, 108
PQFP (plastic quad flat pack) mounts, 56–57
preventative maintenance, 518–521.
  *See also* maintenance
  floppy disk drives, 519–520
  hard disk drives, 519
  keyboards and pointing devices, 520
  monitors, 519
  printers, 520–521
  scheduling, 521–522

primary corona, laser printers, 291
primary partitions, 206–208, 399
printers, 283–298
  common terms used, 285–286
  dot-matrix, 287–288
  evaluating, 284–285
  impact, 286
  ink-jet, 288–290
  laser components, 290–292
  mechanics of laser, 292–295
  output components and, 32
  parallel printer cables, 170–172
  preventative maintenance, 520–521
  printer ports, 286
  problems with, 593–595
  resolution, 284
  summary, 297–298
  troubleshooting laser problems, 295–296
Print Troubleshooter, 593
private initialization files, 475
processors, portable computers, 304–305. *See also* central processing units (CPUs)
Process Scheduler, Windows 98, 451
Professional Graphics Adapter (PGA), 272
Programmed Input/Output.
  *See* PIO (Programmed Input/Output) modes
prompt command
  defined, 393
  overview of, 383–384
protected mode
  memory and, 139
  Microsoft Windows and, 377, 461
  MS-DOS and, 137
  vs. real mode, 53–54
protocols. *See also* by individual names
  communication, 342, 350
  defined, 338
  network, 326–327
proxy servers, 338

# R

radiation emissions, CRTs and FPDs, 267
radio frequency interference (RFI), 94
random access memory (RAM), 121–133
  access speeds, 122
  CPUs and, 47–48
  defined, 137
  determining usable memory, 140–141
  ECC and, 122
  installing, 551–552
  microprocessor development and, 50
  Microsoft Windows requirements, 416–417
  packaging, 123–124
  parity and, 122
  virtual memory and, 53, 452
raster lines
  function of, 259
  laser printers and, 293
RDISK.EXE, 536
read-only memory. *See* ROM (read-only memory) BIOS
real mode
  conventional memory and, 137
  memory and, 139
  Microsoft Windows and, 376–377, 461–462
  vs. protected mode, 53–54
  REGEDIT.EXE in, 490–491
reassembly, computers, 545, 563
record keeping
  client relations and, 596–597
  maintenance and, 516–517
Recovery Console
  restoring Registry with, 590–591
  troubleshooting Windows 2000 installations, 445
rectifiers, 620–621
refresh rates
  defined, 121
  monitor maintenance and, 264
  monitors and, 259–260
  troubleshooting, 278

REG.DAT, 475
REGEDIT.EXE
  commands for, 491–492
  commands in, 490
  dual purpose of, 490–491
  modifying Registry with, 488, 491
  Read Only, 492
  Save Settings On Exit, 492
  using with Windows 9x, 489
REGEDT32.EXE, 491–494
  choosing Registry section, 493–494
  Read Only, 492
  Save Settings On Exit, 492
  Windows 2000 backups and, 533
registers
  CPUs and, 44
  first generation Pentiums and, 60–61
  microprocessor development and, 50
Registry, 474–494, 589–591
  accessing and managing, 488–489
  Administrative Tools, 482–486
  backing up, 534–535
  components of, 486–488
  Control Panel, accessing, 482
  Control Panel, introduction, 474
  Control Panel, Systems Properties icon, 477–481
  overview of, 475–476
  Recovery Console, 590–591
  REGEDIT.EXE, 488–491
  REGEDT.32, 491–494
  Registry Checker, 534–535, 589–590
  replacing earlier Window ini. files and, 475
removable media, portable PCs, 306
repeaters, function of, 327
reports, customer service, 599–600
rescue disk, updating, 543
resistance, testing, 615
resolution
  defined, 260
  enhancing, 285
  monitor maintenance and, 264
  portable computer screens and, 304
  printers and, 284, 294–295

Resource Meter, troubleshooting with, 588–589
RFI (radio frequency interference), 94
ring topology, 318–319
RLL (run-length limited) encoding, 191
ROM (read-only memory) BIOS, 101–117
  chips with, 111
  CMOS, accessing, 105–109
  CMOS, battery, 109–111
  CMOS, maintaining, 109
  CMOS, typical setup for, 104–105
  CMOS, updateable chips in, 102–103
  CMOS, updating, 103–109
  core chips, 101–102
  defined, 101
  function of, 121
  loading device drivers, 111–112
  overview of, 101–103
  power-on self test (POST), 112–115
  shadow RAM and, 139–140
  summary, 116–117
root files, 386
root keys, 486–487
routers, function of, 327
RS-232 ports, 344–345
run-length limited (RLL) encoding, 191
runtime version, Microsoft Windows, 378
R/W heads, actuator arms and, 192–193

# S

safe detection, 434
Safe Mode, 577–578
Safe Recovery, 432–433
Safe Start approach, power-on self test (POST), 114
safety, 509–513
  electric power, 510–512, 626–628
  electromagnetic interference, 94
  fire hazards, 512–513
  handling CPUs and, 71

safety *(continued)*
  monitor maintenance and, 264
  monitors, 626
  power supplies, 80
  problems and prevention, 510
  SEC package/slot upgrades, 72
sags, power, 86, 617–618
SCAM (SCSI configured auto-
    magically), 246
ScanDisk, 527–528
  functions of, 528
  installing Windows 98 using, 428
  maintaining disk drives with,
    213–214
  operating modes of, 528
  versions of, 527
scanners, input components, 29
SCANREGW.EXE, 534–535
scheduling
  Disk Defragmenter, 529–530
  preventative maintenance, 521–522
screen prompts, power-on self test
    (POST) and, 112–113
SCSI (Small Computer System
    Interface) drives, 243–252
  adapter cards for, 226, 249
  advanced management, 246
  cables, 173
  CD-ROM/DVD drives and, 229
  connect/ disconnect, 246
  costs and benefits of, 248
  errors and, 214
  file allocation tables and, 208
  future of, 248
  high performance products and, 245
  history of, 243
  IDE compared with, 246
  installing, 248–250
  logical unit numbers, 251
  memory management, 248
  noise and, 247
  overview of, 197–198
  Plug and Play installation, 245
  SCAM support, 246
  SCSI-1, 243–244
  SCSI-2, 244–245

SCSI *(continued)*
  SCSI-3, 245
  setting IDs, 249–251
  setting up subsystem for, 248–250
  simple expansion, 245
  summary, 253–255
  tag command queuing, 246
  termination, 251
  troubleshooting conflict, 247–248
SCSI configured auto-magically
    (SCAM), 246
SDRAM (synchronous DRAM), 121
SEC (single edge connector), Pentium
    II, 64, 71–72
secondary controllers, EIDE drives
    and, 238–239
sectors. *See also* partitions
  corrupted boot and partition
    information, 215
  defined, 399
  file allocation tables and, 208
  hard disk drive installation and, 209
sectors per track
  CHS values and, 196
  early hard disk drives and, 235
  overview of, 195
security
  file system security, 402–405
  folder security and, 404
  updating CMOS and, 106, 108
security log, MMC, 484
Security Reference Monitor (SRM),
    Windows 2000 Executive, 468
Security tab, CMOS, 106, 108
serial conversion, modems and,
    340–341
serial devices, 16
serial port cables, 172–173
servers
  network, 316
  proxy servers, 338
  Windows 2000, 414
Setupact, 445
Setupapi, 445
Setup log files, 434–435
SETUPLOG.TXT, 435–436

Setup program, Windows 2000,
    439–442
SFF (Small Forms Factor)
    standards, 234
SGML (Standardized Generalized
    Markup Language), 357
shadow RAM, 139–140
shielded twisted pair (STP) cables, 322
shutdown problems, 576–577,
    585–587
SIMD (single-instruction multiple-
    data) stream processing, 63
single edge connector (SEC), Pentium
    II, 64, 71–72
single inline memory modules
    (SIMMs)
  30-pin, 124–125
  72-pin, 127–128
  adding memory and, 126
  installing, 128–130, 551
  overview of, 548–549
  SIPPs and, 127
single inline pinned package (SIPPs)
  specifying, 127
  using for memory, 124
single-instruction multiple-data
    (SIMD) stream processing, 63
slave position, EIDE drives, 239–240
Small Forms Factor (SFF)
    standards, 234
SMM. *See* system memory
    management (SMM)
SMP (symmetric multiprocessing), 466
software. *See also* operating system
  CD-ROM/DVD drives, 229,
    231–232
  laser printers, 292
  unauthorized, 328
  utilities, 504–505
  Windows 2000, installing and
    upgrading, 437
  Windows 2000,
    troubleshooting, 444
software core, 369–370
software flow control, 351
software tools, 501, 503–505
  bootable floppy disk, 503–504

software tools (continued)
documentation and manuals, 505
operating system disk, 504
utilities, 504–505
sound cards, 226, 229
spare parts
computer maintenance and, 502
managing inventory of, 598
speakers, output components, 32
speculative execution, Pentium II, 64
speed. See also clocks, processors
32-bit access, 241–242
cables and, 325
first generation Pentiums and, 60–61
modems, 348–349
printers, 284
RAM access, 122–123
SPGA. See staggered pin grid array
(SPGA)
spikes
defined, 86
switching network and, 617–618
splitters, defined, 84
SRAM, 131
SRM (Security Reference Monitor),
Windows 2000 Executive, 468
ST506 hard disk drives
cabling requirements for, 199
overview of, 197
staggered pin grid array (SPGA)
defined, 71
inserting, 56
Standardized Generalized Markup
Language (SGML), 357
standard mode, Windows, 377
standards
Advanced Technology Attachment
(ATA), 233
CD-ROM, 223–224, 226
computer cards, 302
LBA translation, 235
modems, 352–353
Multimedia PC Marketing Council
and, 231
power management, 310
Small Forms Factor (SFF), 234

start bits, 342
star topology, 317
startup disks
Windows 95/98, 431, 463, 536–537
Windows 98 and Windows Me, 504
startup issues, troubleshooting, 576
Startup Menu modes, Windows 98,
462–464
BOOTLOG.TXT file, 463–464
startup disk, 463
WIN.COM command, 463
static RAM (SRAM), 131
step-down transformers, PC power
supplies, 612
stepper motor actuator arms, 192
stop bits, 342
storing data. See data, storing
STP (shielded twisted pair) cables, 322
subkeys, defined, 487
subnotebook (palmtop) computers, 301
Super Video Graphics Array (SVGA)
color and, 272–274
overview of, 272
surges, 86
surge suppressors, 35, 87
SVGA. See Super Video Graphics
Array (SVGA)
swap file system, 453
switches
computer upgrades and, 555
defined, 393
Windows 98 installation and,
426–428
Windows 2000 installation and,
439–442
switching network, 617–618
symmetric multiprocessing (SMP), 466
sync bites, 342
synchronous communication, modems
and, 342
synchronous DRAM (SDRAM), 121
syntax, defined, 393
system bus
external data bus and, 149
Pentium II and, 64
System Configuration utility, 583–584

system crystal, clock speed and, 46
System File Checker
checking integrity of system files
with, 535
options of, 535–536
System Information tool, Windows 98,
412, 583
SYSTEM.INI file, 241–242
system initialization files, 475
system memory management (SMM)
CPUs and, 58
defined, 121
System Monitor, 587–588
System Properties icon, 477–481
System Registry. See Registry
system state back up, 533–534

T

tag command queuing, SCSI, 246
Tape Carrier Packaging processor,
304–305
tape drives, 34
Task Manager, 586–587
Task Scheduler, 516
TCP/IP (Transmission Control
Protocol/Internet Protocol)
defined, 338
overview of, 359
as standard network protocol, 326
using ping to test connections,
361–362
technical library, computer
maintenance and, 502
technical support, 508–509, 596–597
levels of, 597
online support, 509
telephone support, 508–509
technicians, computer, 8
telecommunications, 338
telephone-line basics
multifunction modems and, 346
overview of, 345–346
telephone support, 508–509
terminate-and-stay-resident (TSR)
programs, 140–141, 393

termination, SCSI technology, 249, 251–252

testing. *See also* power-on self test (POST)

AC ripple, 614

CD (Change Directory) test, 388

connections, 361–362

continuity, 615

DC voltage, 615

Make Directory (MD) test, 387

power supplies, advanced testing, 617–619

power supplies, voltage test, 616–617

resistance, 615

transformers, 622

text editors, troubleshooting with, 445. *See also* Edit (text editor), using

text error codes, power-on self test (POST), 114

TFTs (thin film transistors)

active-matrix displays and, 268

portable computers and, 303–304

ThickNet cables, 323

thin film transistors. *See* TFTs (thin film transistors)

ThinNet cables, 323

threads, defined, 451

time, access, 227

time calculations. *See also* clock

clocks and, 46

CMOS battery and, 110

token ring networks

defined, 318–319

Ethernet and, 326

toner, laser printers

cartridges, 291

fusing, 294

transferring to drums/paper, 293

toolkits

computer assembly/disassembly and, 543

types of, 501–502

topology, network, 317–319

bus topology, 318, 325–326

ring topology, 318–319

star topology, 317

trackballs, 306

trackpads, 306

trackpoints, 306

tracks, defined, 399

traffic overloads, 328

transfer corona, laser printers and, 292

transformers

function of, 618

testing, 622

transistors

CPU technology and, 42–43

electronic components and, 621–622

microprocessor development and, 50

Transmission Control Protocol/Internet Protocol. *See* TCP/IP (Transmission Control Protocol/Internet Protocol)

transparencies, laser printers and, 296

troubleshooting

cables and connectors, 174–175

display systems, 278–279

dot-matrix printers, 287–288

ink-jet printers, 289–290

laser printers, 295–296

modems, 355

networks, 328

power-on self test (POST) and, 113–114

problem categories, 569–571

SCSI devices, 247–248

Windows 98 installation, 432–436

Windows 2000 installation, 444–445

troubleshooting, Windows, 573–595

basic approach, 573–575

Command Mode and, 577–578

differential diagnosis, 575–577

MS-DOS incompatibilities, 591–593

operating system management tools, 578–581

operational issues, 576

printing problems, 593–595

Recovery Console, 590–591

Registry Checker, 589–590

Resource Meter, 588–589

Safe Mode and, 577–578

shutdown issues, 576–577, 585–587

startup issues, 576

troubleshooting, Windows *(continued)*

System Monitor, 587–588

Task Manager, 586–587

tools for, 581–585

troubleshooting techniques, 567–572

phase 1-problem definition, 567–568

phase 2-isolating the cause, 568–571

phase 3-conducting repair, 571–572

phase 4-confirming results, 572

phase 5-documenting results, 572

troubleshooting tools, 581–585

Computer Management snap-in, 581–582

Device Manager, 584–585

MSI tool, 582–583

System Configuration utility, 583–584

true color operation, 272–274

trunks, defined, 318

TSR (terminate-and-stay-resident) programs, 140–141, 393

TV out, multimedia, 274, 277

TV tuners, multimedia, 274, 277

twisted-pair cables, 322–324

## U

UARTs (universal asynchronous receiver-transmitters), 340–341

Ultra DMA drives

advanced hard disk drives, 237–238

installing, 238

Ultra DMA/33, 238

Ultra DMA/66, cabling for, 199–200

Ultra DMA/66, low-level formatting, 204

Ultra DMA/66, overview of, 238

UMA (upper memory area), 140

uninterruptible power supply (UPS), 36, 87–88

universal asynchronous receiver-transmitters (UARTs), 340–341

universal serial bus (USB)

modems and, 343

overview of, 156–157

portable computers and, 307

upgrading
  BIOS, 101–102
  vs. clean install, 420–421
  computers, 546–547
  CPUs, considerations for, 68–69
  CPUs, inserting with LIF socket,
    69–70
  CPUs, overview, 552–553
  CPUs, SEC package/ slot, 71–72
  drives, 557–559
  drives, IDE drive, 557–559
  drives, questions to ask, 557
  expansion cards, 553–557
  expansion cards, non-Plug and Play,
    555–557
  expansion cards, Plug and Play, 557
  expansion cards, questions to
    ask, 554
  expansion cards, steps in
    adding, 555
  memory, 548–552
  memory, cache, 550
  memory, DIMM formats, 550
  memory, EDO RAM, 550
  memory, installing RAM, 551–552
  memory, parity, 550
  memory, SIMM formats, 548–549
  memory, speed of, 550
  motherboards and, 560–562
  operating system drivers, 559–560
  sample configuration sheet, 547
  summary of, 563
  Windows 98, 425–426
  Windows 2000, 437–438
U pipeline, 61–62
uploads, defined, 338
upper memory area (UMA), 140
UPS (uninterruptible power supply),
  36, 87–88
URLs, 359
USB. See universal serial bus (USB)
Usenet newsgroups, computer
  maintenance and, 506–507
user accounts, Windows 2000,
  443, 472
user component, Windows 98, 451

user interface
  laser printers and, 291
  operating systems and, 369
  Windows 98, 451
user mode, Windows 2000, 469–479
user type, CMOS setup, 202
UTP cables, 322–323

V

VCDFSD.VXD, 230
Vdot standards. See CCITT (Comité
  Consultatif International
  Télégraphique et
  Téléphonique)
vertical refresh rates, monitors, 259
VESA local bus (VLB), 152–153
VFAT.386, 241–242
VGA (Video Graphics Adapter), 272
video-capture software, 231–232
video cards. See display adapters
video controllers. See display adapters
Video Graphics Adapter (VGA), 272
video memory, 274–275
video RAM (VRAM)
  graphics intensive applications
    and, 277
  overview of, 274
Virtual Machine Manager (VMM),
  Windows 98, 452
virtual machines, 54
virtual memory, 53
Virtual Memory Manager, Windows
  2000 Executive, 469
virtual memory model, Windows 98,
  452–456
  32-bit VFAT, 455
  DOS mode support, 453
  long filename support, 455–456
  memory pager, 453
  swap file system, 453
  WDM architecture and, 453–455
virtual real mode, 54
virus checkers
  operating systems and, 370
  tips on, 107

viruses, 525–526
  protection guidelines, 526
  types of, 525–526
VLB (VESA local bus), 152–153
VMM (Virtual Machine Manager),
  Windows 98, 452
voice coil hard disk drive, 192–193
voice mail, 346
volatile memory, 120. See also random
  access memory (RAM)
voltage
  installing memory and
    checking, 128
  portable computers and, 305
voltage regulator module (VRM), 71
voltage regulators, 618–619
voltage test, power supplies and,
  616–617
volt-ohm meter (VOM). See
  multimeter
V pipeline, 61–62
VRAM. See video RAM (VRAM)
VRM (voltage regulator module), 71

W

WANs (wide area networks)
  Internet and, 356–363
  overview of, 316
warm boots, 374
wattage, power supplies and, 80
WDCTRL, 32-bit access and, 241–242
WDM (Windows Driver Model),
  452–455
Web browsers. See browsers
Webmasters, 338
Web sites, 357
wide area networks. See WANs (wide
  area networks)
width, adjusting monitor's, 263
width value, memory capacity and, 127
wildcards, 393
WIN.COM command,
  Windows 98, 463
window random access memory
  (WRAM)
  graphics intensive applications
    and, 277

window random access memory
(*continued*)
overview of, 275
Windows. *See* Microsoft Windows
Windows Driver Model (WDM),
452–455
WINNT.EXE, 441–442
WINNT32.EXE, 439–441
World Wide Web. *See also* Internet
computer maintenance and, 507
overview of, 357
WRAM. *See* window random access
memory (WRAM)
write-back caches
first generation Pentiums and, 60–61
memory and, 132
write compensation value, 195
write-through caches
first generation Pentiums and, 60–61
memory and, 132

## X

Xeon, Pentium, 66
XGA (eXtended Graphics Array), 273
Xmodem protocol, 350
XMS (extended memory
specification), 137
XT (eXtended Technology), IBM, 52

## Y

Yellow Book standards, 226
Ymodem protocol, 350
yoke, defined, 260
Y power splitter cable, 228

## Z

zero-insertion-force (ZIF) mounts, 56,
70–71
Zip drives, 306
Zmodem protocol, 350

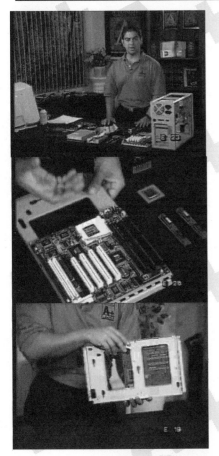

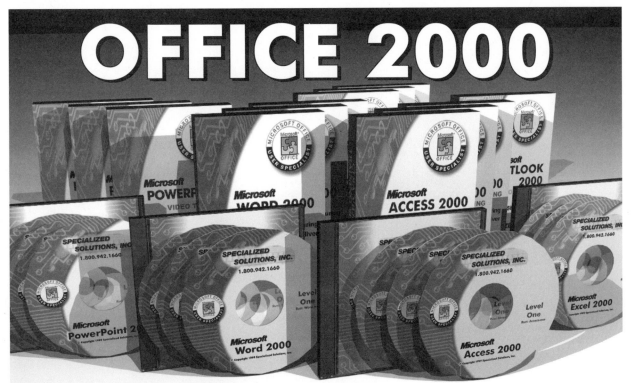

# MICROSOFT LICENSE AGREEMENT

Book Companion CD

**IMPORTANT—READ CAREFULLY:** This Microsoft End-User License Agreement ("EULA") is a legal agreement between you (either an individual or an entity) and Microsoft Corporation for the Microsoft product identified above, which includes computer software and may include associated media, printed materials, and "online" or electronic documentation ("SOFTWARE PRODUCT"). Any component included within the SOFTWARE PRODUCT that is accompanied by a separate End-User License Agreement shall be governed by such agreement and not the terms set forth below. By installing, copying, or otherwise using the SOFTWARE PRODUCT, you agree to be bound by the terms of this EULA. If you do not agree to the terms of this EULA, you are not authorized to install, copy, or otherwise use the SOFTWARE PRODUCT; you may, however, return the SOFTWARE PRODUCT, along with all printed materials and other items that form a part of the Microsoft product that includes the SOFTWARE PRODUCT, to the place you obtained them for a full refund.

## SOFTWARE PRODUCT LICENSE

The SOFTWARE PRODUCT is protected by United States copyright laws and international copyright treaties, as well as other intellectual property laws and treaties. The SOFTWARE PRODUCT is licensed, not sold.

1. **GRANT OF LICENSE.** This EULA grants you the following rights:

   a. **Software Product.** You may install and use one copy of the SOFTWARE PRODUCT on a single computer. The primary user of the computer on which the SOFTWARE PRODUCT is installed may make a second copy for his or her exclusive use on a portable computer.

   b. **Storage/Network Use.** You may also store or install a copy of the SOFTWARE PRODUCT on a storage device, such as a network server, used only to install or run the SOFTWARE PRODUCT on your other computers over an internal network; however, you must acquire and dedicate a license for each separate computer on which the SOFTWARE PRODUCT is installed or run from the storage device. A license for the SOFTWARE PRODUCT may not be shared or used concurrently on different computers.

   c. **License Pak.** If you have acquired this EULA in a Microsoft License Pak, you may make the number of additional copies of the computer software portion of the SOFTWARE PRODUCT authorized on the printed copy of this EULA, and you may use each copy in the manner specified above. You are also entitled to make a corresponding number of secondary copies for portable computer use as specified above.

   d. **Sample Code.** Solely with respect to portions, if any, of the SOFTWARE PRODUCT that are identified within the SOFTWARE PRODUCT as sample code (the "SAMPLE CODE"):

      i. **Use and Modification.** Microsoft grants you the right to use and modify the source code version of the SAMPLE CODE, *provided* you comply with subsection (d)(iii) below. You may not distribute the SAMPLE CODE, or any modified version of the SAMPLE CODE, in source code form.

      ii. **Redistributable Files.** Provided you comply with subsection (d)(iii) below, Microsoft grants you a nonexclusive, royalty-free right to reproduce and distribute the object code version of the SAMPLE CODE and of any modified SAMPLE CODE, other than SAMPLE CODE, or any modified version thereof, designated as not redistributable in the Readme file that forms a part of the SOFTWARE PRODUCT (the "Non-Redistributable Sample Code"). All SAMPLE CODE other than the Non-Redistributable Sample Code is collectively referred to as the "REDISTRIBUTABLES."

      iii. **Redistribution Requirements.** If you redistribute the REDISTRIBUTABLES, you agree to: (i) distribute the REDISTRIBUTABLES in object code form only in conjunction with and as a part of your software application product; (ii) not use Microsoft's name, logo, or trademarks to market your software application product; (iii) include a valid copyright notice on your software application product; (iv) indemnify, hold harmless, and defend Microsoft from and against any claims or lawsuits, including attorney's fees, that arise or result from the use or distribution of your software application product; and (v) not permit further distribution of the REDISTRIBUTABLES by your end user. Contact Microsoft for the applicable royalties due and other licensing terms for all other uses and/or distribution of the REDISTRIBUTABLES.

2. **DESCRIPTION OF OTHER RIGHTS AND LIMITATIONS.**

   - **Limitations on Reverse Engineering, Decompilation, and Disassembly.** You may not reverse engineer, decompile, or disassemble the SOFTWARE PRODUCT, except and only to the extent that such activity is expressly permitted by applicable law notwithstanding this limitation.

   - **Separation of Components.** The SOFTWARE PRODUCT is licensed as a single product. Its component parts may not be separated for use on more than one computer.

   - **Rental.** You may not rent, lease, or lend the SOFTWARE PRODUCT.

- **Support Services.** Microsoft may, but is not obligated to, provide you with support services related to the SOFTWARE PRODUCT ("Support Services"). Use of Support Services is governed by the Microsoft policies and programs described in the user manual, in "online" documentation, and/or in other Microsoft-provided materials. Any supplemental software code provided to you as part of the Support Services shall be considered part of the SOFTWARE PRODUCT and subject to the terms and conditions of this EULA. With respect to technical information you provide to Microsoft as part of the Support Services, Microsoft may use such information for its business purposes, including for product support and development. Microsoft will not utilize such technical information in a form that personally identifies you.

- **Software Transfer.** You may permanently transfer all of your rights under this EULA, provided you retain no copies, you transfer all of the SOFTWARE PRODUCT (including all component parts, the media and printed materials, any upgrades, this EULA, and, if applicable, the Certificate of Authenticity), **and** the recipient agrees to the terms of this EULA.

- **Termination.** Without prejudice to any other rights, Microsoft may terminate this EULA if you fail to comply with the terms and conditions of this EULA. In such event, you must destroy all copies of the SOFTWARE PRODUCT and all of its component parts.

3. **COPYRIGHT.** All title and copyrights in and to the SOFTWARE PRODUCT (including but not limited to any images, photographs, animations, video, audio, music, text, SAMPLE CODE, REDISTRIBUTABLES, and "applets" incorporated into the SOFTWARE PRODUCT) and any copies of the SOFTWARE PRODUCT are owned by Microsoft or its suppliers. The SOFT-WARE PRODUCT is protected by copyright laws and international treaty provisions. Therefore, you must treat the SOFTWARE PRODUCT like any other copyrighted material **except** that you may install the SOFTWARE PRODUCT on a single computer provided you keep the original solely for backup or archival purposes. You may not copy the printed materials accompanying the SOFTWARE PRODUCT.

4. **U.S. GOVERNMENT RESTRICTED RIGHTS.** The SOFTWARE PRODUCT and documentation are provided with RESTRICTED RIGHTS. Use, duplication, or disclosure by the Government is subject to restrictions as set forth in subparagraph (c)(1)(ii) of the Rights in Technical Data and Computer Software clause at DFARS 252.227-7013 or subparagraphs (c)(1) and (2) of the Commercial Computer Software—Restricted Rights at 48 CFR 52.227-19, as applicable. Manufacturer is Microsoft Corporation/One Microsoft Way/Redmond, WA 98052-6399.

5. **EXPORT RESTRICTIONS.** You agree that you will not export or re-export the SOFTWARE PRODUCT, any part thereof, or any process or service that is the direct product of the SOFTWARE PRODUCT (the foregoing collectively referred to as the "Restricted Components"), to any country, person, entity, or end user subject to U.S. export restrictions. You specifically agree not to export or re-export any of the Restricted Components (i) to any country to which the U.S. has embargoed or restricted the export of goods or services, which currently include, but are not necessarily limited to, Cuba, Iran, Iraq, Libya, North Korea, Sudan, and Syria, or to any national of any such country, wherever located, who intends to transmit or transport the Restricted Components back to such country; (ii) to any end user who you know or have reason to know will utilize the Restricted Components in the design, development, or production of nuclear, chemical, or biological weapons; or (iii) to any end user who has been prohibited from participating in U.S. export transactions by any federal agency of the U.S. government. You warrant and represent that neither the BXA nor any other U.S. federal agency has suspended, revoked, or denied your export privileges.

---

## DISCLAIMER OF WARRANTY

**NO WARRANTIES OR CONDITIONS.** MICROSOFT EXPRESSLY DISCLAIMS ANY WARRANTY OR CONDITION FOR THE SOFTWARE PRODUCT. THE SOFTWARE PRODUCT AND ANY RELATED DOCUMENTATION ARE PROVIDED "AS IS" WITHOUT WARRANTY OR CONDITION OF ANY KIND, EITHER EXPRESS OR IMPLIED, INCLUDING, WITHOUT LIMITA-TION, THE IMPLIED WARRANTIES OF MERCHANTABILITY, FITNESS FOR A PARTICULAR PURPOSE, OR NONINFRINGEMENT. THE ENTIRE RISK ARISING OUT OF USE OR PERFORMANCE OF THE SOFTWARE PRODUCT REMAINS WITH YOU.

**LIMITATION OF LIABILITY.** TO THE MAXIMUM EXTENT PERMITTED BY APPLICABLE LAW, IN NO EVENT SHALL MICROSOFT OR ITS SUPPLIERS BE LIABLE FOR ANY SPECIAL, INCIDENTAL, INDIRECT, OR CONSEQUENTIAL DAM-AGES WHATSOEVER (INCLUDING, WITHOUT LIMITATION, DAMAGES FOR LOSS OF BUSINESS PROFITS, BUSINESS INTERRUPTION, LOSS OF BUSINESS INFORMATION, OR ANY OTHER PECUNIARY LOSS) ARISING OUT OF THE USE OF OR INABILITY TO USE THE SOFTWARE PRODUCT OR THE PROVISION OF OR FAILURE TO PROVIDE SUPPORT SERVICES, EVEN IF MICROSOFT HAS BEEN ADVISED OF THE POSSIBILITY OF SUCH DAMAGES. IN ANY CASE, MICROSOFT'S ENTIRE LIABILITY UNDER ANY PROVISION OF THIS EULA SHALL BE LIMITED TO THE GREATER OF THE AMOUNT ACTUALLY PAID BY YOU FOR THE SOFTWARE PRODUCT OR US$5.00; PROVIDED, HOWEVER, IF YOU HAVE ENTERED INTO A MICROSOFT SUPPORT SERVICES AGREEMENT, MICROSOFT'S ENTIRE LIABILITY REGARDING SUPPORT SERVICES SHALL BE GOVERNED BY THE TERMS OF THAT AGREEMENT. BECAUSE SOME STATES AND JURISDICTIONS DO NOT ALLOW THE EXCLUSION OR LIMITATION OF LIABILITY, THE ABOVE LIMITATION MAY NOT APPLY TO YOU.

---

## MISCELLANEOUS

This EULA is governed by the laws of the State of Washington USA, except and only to the extent that applicable law mandates govern-ing law of a different jurisdiction.

Should you have any questions concerning this EULA, or if you desire to contact Microsoft for any reason, please contact the Microsoft subsidiary serving your country, or write: Microsoft Sales Information Center/One Microsoft Way/Redmond, WA 98052-6399.

PN 097-0002296

# System Requirements

To get the most out of the *A+ Certification Training Kit*, including the companion CD, you should have a computer equipped with the following minimum configuration:

- Pentium II processor and motherboard

- Microsoft Windows 98 (minimum) or Microsoft Windows 2000 (recommended); access to earlier operating systems (Microsoft Windows 95 and MS-DOS) is a plus

- 32 MB of RAM (64 MB or more recommended)

- 2-GB hard disk drive

- 3.5-inch floppy disk drive

- CD-ROM drive (20x minimum recommended)

- Display system capable of 800 x 600 resolution or better (1024 x 768 recommended for best viewing of demonstration videos)

- Mouse or other pointing device

- A printer

- A modem with Internet connection

To view the electronic version of the book on the companion CD, you will need Microsoft Internet Explorer 4.01 or later. A version of Microsoft Internet Explorer 5.5 is supplied on the companion CD. For more information, see the README.TXT file on the companion CD.

To view the demonstration videos on the companion CD, you will need a machine with standard multimedia support and an HTML browser. A version of Microsoft Windows Media Player 7 is supplied on the companion CD.